HITLER'S GENERALS

HITLER'S GENERALS

EDITED BY

Correlli Barnett

GROVE PRESS
New York

Printed in the United States of America

Library of Congress Cataloging-in-Publication Data

Hitler's generals.
Includes index.
1. World War, 1939–1945—Germany. 2. Generals—
Germany—Biography. 3. Marshals—Germany—Biography.
4. World War, 1939–1945—Biography. 5. Germany. Heer—
Biography. 6. Hitler, Adolf, 1889–1945. I. Barnett, Correlli.
D757.H546 1989   940.53'43   88-37875
ISBN-13: 978- 0-8021-3994-8

Grove Press
an imprint of Grove/Atlantic, Inc.
841 Broadway
New York, NY 10003

Distributed by Publishers Group West

www.groveatlantic.com

10 11 12 13 14   10 9 8 7 6 5 4 3 2

CONTENTS

CONTENTS

CONTENTS

PART V
The Innovators

ILLUSTRATIONS

MAPS
(in chronological order)

CONTRIBUTORS

CORRELLI BARNETT is the author of many distinguished books, among them *The Desert Generals, The Sword Bearers, Britain and Her Army, The Collapse of British Power, Marlborough, Bonaparte* and *The Audit of War*. He has also acted as an historical consultant and scriptwriter for BBC Television. Since 1977 he has been Keeper of the Churchill Archives Centre and a Fellow of Churchill College, Cambridge. From 1973 to 1985 he was also a member of Council of the Royal United Services Institute for Defence Studies. He lives in Norfolk and is Vice-President of the Eastern Arts Association. He is a Fellow of the Royal Society for Literature and of the Royal Historical Society.

SHELFORD BIDWELL was educated at Wellington School, Somerset and the Royal Military Academy, Woolwich. In the Second World War he served in the Royal Artillery in Tunisia, as a staff officer in Italy, and later as an instructor at the Staff College. After retiring as a brigadier he worked as editor and deputy director in the Royal United Services Institute for Defence Studies in London, of which he is now vice-president. His published works in military history include *Tug of War: The Battle for Italy 1943–1945* (1986).

MARTIN BLUMENSON served in Europe during World War II and in Korea during the Korean War and is a retired lieutenant-colonel, US Army Reserve. Educated at Bucknell and Harvard Universities, he has held the King Chair at the Naval War College, the Johnson Chair at the Army War College, the Mark Clark Chair at the Citadel; he was Visiting Professor of Military and Strategic Studies at Acadia University, Visiting Professor at Bucknell University, Professor at the National War College, and Professorial Lecturer in International Affairs at the George Washington University. He is the author of fifteen books, including *Mark Clark*, the two volumes of *The Patton Papers* and *Patton: The Man Behind the Legend*.

BRIAN BOND was educated at Worcester College, Oxford and lectured in history at Exeter and Liverpool Universities (1961–66). Since then he has taught in the Department of War Studies at King's College, London and is now Professor of Military History. His books include *The Victorian Army and the Staff College* (1972), *Liddell Hart* (1977), *British Military Policy Between the Two World Wars* (1980) and *War and Society in Europe 1870–1970* (1984). He is currently a Council Member of the Army Records Society and the Society for Army Historical Research, and is President of the British Commission for Military History. He lives at Medmenham in Buckinghamshire.

FIELD-MARSHAL LORD CARVER started his military career in 1935 in the Royal Tank Corps. In the Second World War he commanded a tank battalion and an armoured brigade while still in his twenties. After the war he commanded an infantry brigade and division, and held many important posts on the staff before becoming Commander-in-Chief Far East in 1967, Chief of the General Staff in 1971, and Chief of the Defence Staff between 1973 and 1976. His most recent books are *The Seven Ages of the British Army*, *Dilemmas of the Desert War* and *Twentieth Century Warriors*.

CARLO D'ESTE holds a Master's degree from the University of Richmond (Virginia) and has been writing military history since retiring as a lieutenant-colonel from the United States Army in 1978. He is the author of *Decision in Normandy* (1983) and the recently published *Bitter Victory* (1988). He lives in Massachusetts and is currently researching a work on Anzio.

WALTER GÖRLITZ is a professional writer and the author of many books on nineteenth- and twentieth-century German military history, including *The German General Staff* (1953), *The Kaiser and his Court: The Diaries of Admiral G. A. von Müller, Chief of the Naval Cabinet* (1961), *Paulus and Stalingrad* (1963), *Le Maréchal Keitel* (1963). He lives in Hamburg.

GENERAL SIR JOHN HACKETT, born in Australia of an Irish father, read Greats and Modern History at New College before joining his great-grandfather's regiment, the 8th Kings Royal Irish Hussars, and serving in World War II in the Middle East (wounded in both Syria and the Western Desert), Italy and then (with another wound) commanding a parachute brigade at Arnhem. He was later to be GOC-in-C Northern Ireland, Deputy Chief of the General Staff and Commander-in-Chief British Army of the Rhine as well as Commander Northern Army Group in NATO, before leaving the service in 1968 to spend seven years as Principal of King's College in the University of London. He is still a Visiting Professor in Classics there. He has been President of both the UK Classical and English Associations. He has written

I Was a Stranger, The Third World War and *The Untold Story*, and many articles and reviews.

FRANZ KUROWSKI is an historian and journalist and the author of books in contemporary and military history. His studies of the Saxons, Friesans and the city-states of Venice and Genoa have gone into several editions. He is the author of numerous works on military history and has collaborated with Admiral Dönitz, Field-Marshal von Manstein and Generals Student and von Manteuffel. Many of his books have been translated into several languages.

RICHARD LAMB, a journalist, broadcaster and historian, was educated at Merton College, Oxford. He is the author of *Montgomery in Europe* (winner Yorkshire Post prize for best first work, 1983); *The Ghosts of Peace 1935–1945* (1987); and *The Failure of the Eden Government* (1987). He is currently writing a book on the drift to war between 1922 and 1939, to be published in 1989 on the 50th anniversary of the outbreak of the Second World War. A Territorial officer before the war, he served in the North African and Italian campaigns. He was Editor of *Military History Monthly* (formerly *War Monthly*).

BARRY A. LEACH was educated at the Trinity School of John Whitgift and Sandhurst, and served in the British Army on the Rhine in the 1950s. While attached to the *Bundeswehr* he developed his interest in German military history that led to a doctorate at the University of British Columbia. He is the author of *German Strategy against Russia, 1939–41* (1973) and *German General Staff* (1973). He is also an active conservationist and has written *Waterfowl on a Pacific Estuary* (1982) and numerous articles on wetland management in Canada and on rural development in the Himalayas. He lives at White Rock, British Columbia, Canada.

KENNETH MACKSEY, MC, RTR, served in the Royal Armoured Corps and Royal Tank Regiment from 1944 until retirement in 1948 when he became a full-time military historian and author. Educated at Goudhurst School, at Sandhurst and at the Staff College, Camberley, he saw military service in northwest Europe and various parts of the Far East. Since 1980 he has been a consultant to the Canadian Army in the writing of interactive military scenarios, of which *First Clash* is the first of a series. He is the author of thirty-five books, including *Guderian: Panzer General*; *Kesselring, Maker of the Luftwaffe* and *Rommel, Campaigns and Battles*; besides histories of the Royal Tank Regiment and Royal Armoured Corps.

MARTIN MIDDLEBROOK is a former poultry farmer who turned to writing military history after a visit to the First World War battlefields. His twelve published books range from *The First Day on the Somme* to *Operation*

Corporate (the 1982 Falklands War) and on to *The Fight for the 'Malvinas'*, the first book by a British author about the Argentine forces in the Falklands War. Each summer he takes parties of visitors to the First World War battlefields. His home is in Boston, Lincolnshire.

SAMUEL W. MITCHAM, JR holds a PhD degree from the University of Tennessee and is Associate Professor of Geography and Military History at Henderson State University in Arkadelphia, Arkansas. He has written several books on the German Army in World War II, including *Rommel's Last Battle*, *Hitler's Legions*, and *Hitler's Field Marshals and Their Battles*. He lives in Nashville, Arkansas.

KLAUS-JÜRGEN MÜLLER is Professor of Modern and Contemporary History at the University of the *Bundeswehr* at Hamburg and Professor at the University of Hamburg. For several years he was the President of the Committee of the Federal Republic of Germany for the History of the Second World War. In 1967–70 he was Director of Studies at the Staff Academy of the *Bundeswehr*. He has written numerous articles and books on the history of the Second World War, on international politics, the Third Reich and on French contemporary history, including *The Army, Politics and Society in Germany 1933–1945* (1987).

ROBERT O'NEILL is the Chichele Professor of the History of War and a Fellow of All Souls College, Oxford. He has worked in the fields of military history, international relations and strategic studies. His books include *The German Army and the Nazi Party 1933–1939*; *Vietnam Task*; *General Giap, Politician and Strategist*, and *Australia in the Korean War* (2 vols.). He served with the Australian Army in the Vietnam War, was head of the Strategic and Defence Studies Centre at the Australian National University, Canberra, 1971–82 and Director of the International Institute for Strategic Studies, London, 1982–87.

GENERAL FERDINAND VON SENGER UND ETTERLIN was the son of the subject of Chapter 16. He served in Cavalry and Panzer Grenadier units on the Italian and Russian fronts in the Second World War, losing his right arm in 1944. He studied law at Göttingen University before returning to the German Army on the formation of the *Bundeswehr*. He retired in 1984 as Commander-in-Chief of the Central Region of NATO. General von Senger was the author of numerous books on armoured warfare and equipment. He died in 1987 while this essay was in draft. It has been completed by his son, Stefan von Senger und Etterlin.

EARL F. ZIEMKE served with the United States Marine Corps in the Pacific during World War II. He holds a PhD in history from the University of Wisconsin. Formerly a supervisory historian in the Department of the Army, he is currently a research professor of history at the University of Georgia. His books include *The U.S. Army in the Occupation of Germany*, *The German Northern Theater of Operations*, *Moscow to Stalingrad: Decision in the East*, and *Stalingrad to Berlin: The German Defeat in the East*.

The editor and the publishers would like to acknowledge the help provided by Mrs Rosemarie Baines, who translated Chapters 2, 5, 6, 8 and 18.

GLOSSARY

Abwehr	German Military Intelligence
Blitzkrieg	'Lightning attack'
Freikorps	Volunteer Corps
Gestapo	*Geheimestaatspolizei* (State Secret Police)
Luftwaffe	German Air Force
OKH	*Oberkommando des Heeres* (Army General Staff)
OKW	*Oberkommando der Wehrmacht* (Armed Forces General Staff)
Panzer	Armoured
Reichswehr	German Army
Reichsheer	The abbreviated 100,000-man army left to Germany after the Treaty of Versailles (1921–1935)
SA	*Sturmabteilung*, Storm Troops, the 'brownshirts', a paramilitary organization banned in 1932
SD	*Sicherheitsdienst*, Security Service of Party and SS
SS	*Schutzstaffeln*, Protection Squads of Shock Troops, originally in parallel with SA, but increasingly separate and powerful
Truppenamt	'Troop Office', disguised Army General Staff after Versailles Treaty restrictions
Waffen SS	Armed SS: military formations of the SS
Wehrkreis	German military district centred on an important city
Wehrmacht	The Armed Forces, including Army, Navy, Air Force, and Waffen SS
Wehrmachtamt	Armed Forces Office at War Ministry

INTRODUCTION

CORRELLI BARNETT

A study of Hitler's generals must start with Hitler himself, for without him there would have been no victories, no defeats, no marshal's batons, no bomb plots, no trials by 'people's courts' or international military tribunals, no hangings; no war at all. Adolf Hitler was, like Bonaparte, a titanic failure as supreme warlord, but, unlike Bonaparte, he has so far not been glorified by a posthumous myth explaining away all his political and military errors, and attributing to him nobly constructive aims which he never had. Except for a few crypto-fascist historians, no one has yet sought to argue that Hitler would have avoided particular disasters and achieved ultimate victory had it not been for the blunders of his generals. Yet the parallels between Hitler and Bonaparte are obvious. While loudly prating of their patriotism both were foreigners in the countries they led into catastrophe. Both were social upstarts with chips rather than epaulettes on their shoulders. Both were romantics cherishing soaring fantasies of imperial conquest. Both failed to invade England and chose instead to invade Russia, thereby meeting their doom. Both began their wars with a run of flashy quick victories, and ended them by losing a series of grim attrition campaigns. Both men were in a hurry, compelled to be so for economic and political reasons; and both were therefore colossal gamblers.

And there is another parallel: the wars that both initiated and conducted left in their wake Europes profoundly different politically and socially from those existing beforehand; and yet neither warlord had *intended* these new Europes, each planning something totally different. While Bonaparte had set out to create a Europe dominated by a French empire stretching from the Baltic to the Adriatic, Portugal to East Prussia, Hitler had intended his war to leave behind a 'Thousand Year' Germanic Reich and a German-dominated European 'New Order' extending from the North Sea and the Atlantic to the Urals. Yet while the age of romanticism and liberalism credited Bonaparte with creating the nineteenth-century European political order, with its middle-class nation-states, something far from his mind – rather like crediting a bulldozer with the building eventually erected on the site it had cleared – few

I

have credited Hitler with the creation of the post-1945 European order. Yet the division and permanent weakening of Germany, the evolution of the European Community and the spread of democracy to all European states west of the Iron Curtain all ultimately resulted from the *dénouement* of Hitler's catastrophic failure as a warlord.

In other words, although Bonaparte and Hitler are much on a par in terms of ultimate bankruptcy as empire-builders by force of arms, Bonaparte has got away with it in terms of reputation, receiving from posterity a press ranging (with few exceptions) from admiration to hero-worship. For the Napoleonic legend provided exactly the right package for the intellectuals of the 'romantic' nineteenth century. His record, suitably edited and distorted, was transformed into that of a standard-bearer of liberal progress, a liberator of nations, and even a military genius (despite the small matter of his finishing up a prisoner on St Helena). But Hitler has enjoyed none of these advantages. He stands for the past, not for the future, of twentieth-century European ideas – super-race rather than supermarket. By the time the last shot was fired in Hitler's war in 1945, fascism was already *démodé*. As an ideology it belonged to the distant pre-1914 era of romantic nationalism and glorification of military might; as a system it was totally and finally discredited by the discovery of the full horror of the extermination camps.

As a warlord Hitler, in contrast to Bonaparte the professional soldier, exemplifies the amateur, devoid of understanding of the fundamental principles of grand strategy or operations; ignorant of – contemptuous of – logistics; unwilling, perhaps unable, to confront the realities of the battlefield, such as that the bravest soldiers can only prevail for so long against fatigue, casualties and superior numbers, or that a lost battle is a battle lost, and must be broken off. Yet Bonaparte the professional can also be accused of ignoring logistics and the limits of his soldiers' powers of endurance, and of defying the reality of lost battles, lost campaigns, lost wars. Nevertheless, he retained his extraordinary personal spell over his marshals right up to the final disasters of the 1814 campaign which brought the armies of his enemies into Paris. Hitler too possessed until the end a similar hypnotic power of personality which enabled him to brain-wash sceptical and disillusioned generals into renewed faith in the possibility of victory; to intimidate even the bravest and toughest.

It is therefore in Hitler's personality that there lies the key to the central mystery of why a generation of able commanders and staff officers from the most deeply professional officer corps in the world became subservient to his purposes, why the best of them failed to deflect him from his disastrous decisions, why most of them continued to serve him with zeal, or at least with a resigned sense of duty, until sacked or until the Third Reich's final wreck. It is in Hitler's personality that there lies the key to how, where, when and under what handicaps his generals would practise their professional skills.

Thanks to newsreel film Hitler can be conjured up alive on the screen at Nazi party rallies in full flight of passion. The impact of his personality on his audiences can be gauged from the expressions on their faces: those of men and women as high on his oratory as if injected. Let an early adherent, Putzi Hanfstängl, himself an educated and cultured man, explain how Hitler cast his spell on a beer-cellar audience in the 1920s:

> I looked round at the audience. Where was the nondescript crowd I had seen only an hour before? What was suddenly holding these people ...? The hubbub and the mug-clattering had stopped, and they were drinking in every word. Only a few yards away was a young woman, her eyes fastened on the speaker. Transfixed as though in some devotional ecstasy she had ceased to be herself, and was completely under the spell of Hitler's despotic faith in Germany's future greatness.

Once Hitler had attained power, with all the self-confidence bred by this, he exerted the same spell over individuals at close quarters. Albert Speer, a highly able technocrat and a forceful enough character, testifies to this. In judging the conduct of Hitler's generals his ability to charm, to con and to bully should never be forgotten. In 1935 the British Foreign Secretary, Sir John Simon, and League of Nations Secretary, Anthony Eden, were taken in; in 1937 Lord Halifax, then Foreign Secretary, was taken in; in 1938 Neville Chamberlain, the British Prime Minister, was taken in. Meanwhile a procession of distinguished private British visitors, including Lloyd George, was also taken in. If non-Germans, politicians with good reason to be suspicious of him, could fail to perceive Hitler's inherent evil, that is, his moral void – if they could be so manipulated by him – how should German soldiers, with their narrow professional understanding, do better? After all, in Hitler's proclaimed values and purposes from coming to power in 1933 up to the triumph of 1940 the generals encountered a coarsened but nevertheless still sympathetic version of their own aspirations – Germany re-armed and raised from defeat and world slump to her traditional standing in Europe; the nation restored to discipline, patriotic solidarity and soldierly duty; a Germany and a Europe rid of the menace of Bolshevism. Even Nazi anti-semitism, in its pre-war manifestations, offered a crude and brutal caricature of the polite but ingrained anti-semitism widely prevalent in the officer corps. Hitler therefore resembled a virus which takes over the body's cells by so closely resembling the body's own biochemistry as to deceive the body into accepting it.

The insidious process is well described in *Hitler's Generals* by Professor Robert O'Neill's studies of Colonel-General Baron von Fritsch and General Beck, respectively Commander-in-Chief of the German Army in 1934–8 and Chief of Staff in 1935–8; in Professor Brian Bond's portrait of Field-Marshal von Brauchitsch, Commander-in-Chief from 1938 to 1941; and Walter Görlitz's account of Field-Marshal von Blomberg, Minister of Defence in

1933–8. Yet almost all the portraits in *Hitler's Generals* give insight into how decent men, honest professionals, came to be seduced step by step by Hitler's false patriotism and cunning manipulation, starting with the swearing of the oath of personal allegiance to Hitler (so binding themselves to him by their own rigid code of soldierly honour and duty derived from centuries of service to legitimate monarchs); continuing with acceptance of such acts of outright gangsterism as the mass murder of SA leaders (and one of their own number, General von Schleicher, and his wife) in 1934; and ultimately leading to connivance in, or passive acceptance of, or failure openly to oppose to the point of resignation, Hitler's criminal directives for the conduct of the war in Russia.

As the nature of Hitler's régime became more evident in the course of the war, the generals confronted a moral conundrum which they were singularly ill-equipped by their a-political training and tradition to solve – where lay a soldier's duty to the Fatherland if not in simple obedience to his oath to Hitler? Each found his own answer, ranging from Keitel's dog-like devotion and Reichenau's outright radicalism (portrayed here by Walter Görlitz) through the ambiguity of Rundstedt's stance (described here by Professor Earl Ziemke) to the eventual active opposition of the 1944 bomb plot conspirators Witzleben, Speidel and Stülpnagel (whose characters, outlook and motivation are the subject of studies in this book by Professor Hans-Jürgen Müller) on the grounds that soldierly loyalty to the Fatherland demanded the breaking of their oath, and Hitler's betrayal and assassination. But most of the generals sought an answer to the dilemma in fulfilling their professional task while seeking as best they might within their own sphere of responsibility to prevent or mitigate the implementation of Nazi policies towards Jews, partisans and Slavic '*Untermensch*'. In this regard the late General von Senger und Etterlin has contributed to this book a thoughtful and moving portrait of his distinguished father General Frido von Senger, a humanist, a devout Christian, a man with the truest sense of soldierly honour.

Yet if Hitler's more and more evident criminality on a monstrous scale presented his generals with a fundamental moral challenge, his conduct of grand strategy and military operations presented them with no less of a professional problem. How best to manage an amateur warlord with a mystical faith in his own genius that no facts from the real world outside could shake? How to conduct campaigns foredoomed by grand-strategic misjudgment, such as Hitler's 'no retreat' policy in Russia from Stalingrad to Berlin, and again in North Africa and Normandy? Field-Marshal Lord Carver's appraisal of Field-Marshal von Manstein's generalship on the Eastern Front brilliantly illuminates this issue; so too do Carlo D'Este's and Richard Lamb's studies of Field-Marshals Model and von Kluge during their periods of command on both the Eastern and Western Fronts. Yet the moral and the professional dilemmas fused together. Professor O'Neill shows how Fritsch and Beck were simultaneously trying to combat Nazi influence over the Army and slow down Hitler's breakneck pace of military expansion. Martin Blumenson's re-assessment of Field-Marshal Rommel brings out afresh that Rommel's disenchantment with the Führer from 1942 onwards stemmed from his realization that Germany had lost the war, and that Hitler was uncaringly leading her to total destruction.

From the very moment that Hitler first came to power in January 1933, therefore, the fortunes of the German officer corps, collectively and individually, became bound up with his personal adventure in pursuit of fantasies of continental domination. It may be, as Professor A.J.P. Taylor has argued, that Hitler never had a blue-print of expansion and conquest, complete with dates, but instead often responded opportunistically to crises brought about by the drift of events or the actions of others, as in the case of the occupation of Austria in 1938. Yet there is such a broad consistency about his expressed aims and dreams from the early 1920s onwards as to leave little doubt which direction he meant to travel when time and occasion should serve, or that he meant armed force to provide the key instrument in realizing these dreams. His testament *Mein Kampf*, published in 1925–6, envisaged a German colonial empire carved out of Soviet Russia. He told the army leaders just after becoming Chancellor in 1933 that Germany must solve her economic problems by conquering markets, that this required her rearmament, and that there must be expansion towards the East (i.e., Russia) and 'ruthless Germanization of it'. He told Göring in 1936 that Germany must defeat Soviet Russia. In November 1937 he informed his generals that 'for the solution of the German question, all that remains is the way of force.' His political objectives were, then, first to restore Germany as a great power, free of the trammels of the Versailles Treaty, then to create a Greater Germany, embracing Austria, Czechoslovakia and Poland, and adding their German-speaking populations to the 'Master Race'. From this vast base in Central and Eastern Europe would then be launched the climactic conquest of Russia, followed by the colonization of its 'Lebensraum' by the Master Race.

The next question is: How well adapted to the fulfilment of such grandiose aims was Hitler's state-policy-cum-grand-strategy or 'total strategy'? Ronald Lewin was surely right in his marvellous study *Hitler's Mistakes* (London, Heinemann, 1984) in saying that the fundamental weakness of Hitler's 'total strategy', that which rendered ultimate failure inevitable, lay exactly in its amorality and nihilism, springing from Hitler's own nature as an egotist driven by unappeasable resentments and hatreds. This was what determined that his empire could never rest on the consent or even the acquiescence of its subject peoples, but only on naked force. In turn, such naked force – coupled with cruel oppression – served to raise up and cement the coalition of states which finally destroyed him, the German Army and Germany. But, given this fundamental weakness, how well adapted to Hitler's total strategy, considered

5

on its own terms was his political and military conduct of affairs?

From 1933 to 1939 his total strategy was carried out by means of psychologically brilliant bluff, enabling him to enjoy all the gains of conquest without the pains of a huge defence budget or a war costly in lives and money. In 1933-6 he spent just enough on armaments to give a fillip to the economy along with a programme of public works. By 1936 Germany had climbed out of the Depression, and a golden age appeared to have dawned for the German people. The new armaments, coupled with rapid expansion of the Army and the new Luftwaffe, and displays of military pageantry, served to make Germans feel that they were a great nation again, while at the same time enabling Hitler to con the British and French into believing that he had embarked on a war economy in peacetime, which was far from the case. From 1935 onwards Hitler succeeded in frightening the British and French – especially the British – into seeking a deal with him before he became too strong altogether. In 1937 Chamberlain's government gave Hitler a clear signal that it would connive at German expansion in central and eastern Europe if only it were done in a seemly way, by international agreement, and not just by obvious smash-and-grab. Thus Hitler was operating the strongest of all ploys, in diplomacy as well as war: the strategic offensive coupled with the tactical defensive. He stirred the pot, twanged the nerves of pacifistic democratic statesmen with propaganda about the strength of his armed forces and his willingness to use them, and waited successfully for the democracies to come creeping to him. Clausewitz wrote that war was a continuation of policy by other means; in the late 1930s Hitler made policy a continuation of war by other means.

By means of his 'shop-window' rearmament and his well tuned rantings about the terrors that would ensue if Germany were not accorded her just deserts, Hitler achieved his greatest diplomatic triumph at Munich in 1938, when Chamberlain persuaded France to abandon her ally Czechoslovakia, and the two democracies handed him the Sudetenland, which happened to contain the powerful Czech frontier defences. The Munich Agreement radically altered the strategic balance of Europe in Hitler's favour, opening the way to his final occupation of Czechoslovakia in March 1939, which in turn uncovered the southern flank of his next victim, Poland. But Munich marked not only Hitler's triumph over Chamberlain and Daladier, but also over the leadership of the German Army.

That leadership certainly saw war as a legitimate instrument of policy, as it always had been in European affairs, but war waged at the right time and with a strong and thoroughly well prepared army, as in 1866 and 1871. The foreshortening of the possible date for a conflict from 1940 (dismayingly close as even that was) to 1938, when the German Army remained in the middle stage of expansion, training and equipping, horrified them. For Germany to become embroiled again in a war with France and Britain over Czechoslovakia would, they contended (Beck, the Chief of Staff, in particular), lead to yet another cataclysmic national defeat. There was even half-hearted talk of an anti-Hitler coup d'état. But the generals misunderstood Hitler's game of armed diplomatic bluff as much as did his British opponent, Neville Chamberlain. In the event, Hitler's bloodless victory at Munich discredited, divided and unnerved the military doubters and Beck was replaced by Halder, a lesser and narrower man (vividly portrayed in this book by Professor Barry Leach). With Fritsch already discarded in February 1938 after being framed on a homosexuality charge by the Gestapo, and replaced by Brauchitsch, a good soldier but (as Professor Brian Bond shows in his admirable analysis of his character in this book) weak and vacillating as a head of the Army, Hitler had achieved complete dominance over the generals.

However, by summer 1939 his run of successful conquest without war was coming to an end. His 'shop-window' rearmament had provoked the Allies, and especially Britain, into embarking on their own rearmament, but in depth; preparation for real war, and particularly in the air. His occupation of the rest of Czechoslovakia in March 1939 convinced western opinion that he was indeed following a planned timetable of expansion, and must be stopped. Chamberlain, instead of handing Hitler the keys to Poland as he had the keys to Czechoslovakia in 1938, gave a guarantee to Poland that Britain would support her if she was attacked. When in August 1939 Hitler sought to repeat his ploy of threats coupled with blatant military preparations, the Poles refused to budge. So for the first time he had to choose between backing down in a crisis or turning the threat of force into a reality – and when Germany was still relatively unprepared for a major war. Emboldened by his cynical pact with Soviet Russia in August 1939, which freed him from the menace of a two-front war, and believing that Chamberlain would be no more likely to go to war over Danzig than the Sudetenland, he ordered his generals to launch an attack on Poland. Amoral as he was, Hitler was flabbergasted when this produced a British declaration of war because of fidelity to principle and a promise.

So he had got Germany into that conflict with Britain and France against which Beck had warned in vain, and which Beck had argued that Germany must lose in the end. Here was Hitler's first outright mistake as director of Germany's total strategy; indeed the crucial mistake from which ultimate catastrophe was to flow. That the mistake *was* catastrophic did not become immediately apparent. The generals led the 'shop-window' Wehrmacht of 1939 with high professional skill in a classic campaign which crushed Poland in three weeks, while the French Army which they had so much feared hardly stirred from its lines in support of the Poles.

What next? After the Polish campaign Hitler and Chamberlain alike believed that the war would now peter out; Hitler because he could see no reason for the Allies to carry it on now that Poland, their *casus belli*, had been swallowed up; Chamberlain because he simply could not believe that the belligerent powers would really allow the present 'phoney war' to blaze out into another great European conflict fought to the death. The sticking point lay in Hitler's trophies of Czechoslovakia and Poland, which Chamberlain insisted must be returned to their rightful owners as a condition of peace; not one Hitler was likely to accept. When therefore the British government rejected Hitler's 'peace' offer in October 1939, Hitler had to re-think his total strategy. Having stumbled into a general war with armed forces good only for *Blitzkrieg* campaigns each lasting a few weeks, he faced the self-inflicted problem that within a year or so France and Britain could be militarily more powerful than he, thanks to their rearmament in depth – unless he embarked on the maximum mobilization of Germany's still largely peacetime economy. But such a switch to a war economy would damage his credit with the German people for having so far given them butter as well as guns.

He therefore again opted for a *Blitzkrieg*, this time against France and the Low Countries; another high-risk gamble. Once again his generals proved lukewarm or positively cool, especially round the feet. They remembered too well the German Army's defeat in 1918 at the hands of Haig and Foch. With Brauchitsch as their mouthpiece they sought to persuade Hitler to abandon the project, as Professor Brian Bond and Professor Barry Leach describe from different angles in their studies of Brauchitsch and Halder in this book. In a repetition of the pattern during the Czech crisis of 1938 professional opposition to Hitler's new venture deepened into a tentative conspiracy to depose him, so further lowering his opinion of his generals. Confronted in a conference in November 1939 by Hitler in a well acted rage, the generals crumbled and tamely got on with the task of planning the coming offensive, *Fall Gelb* ('Case Yellow').

Hitler had given as its objectives the conquest of territory in the Low Countries and northern France, rather as in 1914–18, in order to establish air and submarine bases much closer to England while at the same time pushing Allied air bases further away from the Ruhr industrial region. These were curiously limited prizes for so huge and risky a venture. Like Ludendorff's offensives in spring 1918, *Fall Gelb* lacked an overall political aim, so remaining a purely military project conducted in a policy vacuum. Hitler therefore here stands guilty of breaching Clausewitz's fundamental principle that war is always a political act.

The operational planning for *Fall Gelb* found the military conservatives on the Army General Staff (*Oberkommando des Heeres*: OKH) led by Halder in conflict with the bold strategic innovators – Manstein, Chief of Staff to Rundstedt (Commander-in-Chief Army Group A), Rundstedt himself, and Guderian, Germany's panzer warfare expert and now commander of 39th Panzer Corps. The controversy is clearly illuminated in this book by Field-Marshal Lord Carver's professional appraisal of Manstein, Kenneth Macksey's portrait of Guderian, and Professor Earl Ziemke's study of Rundstedt, as well as by Bond on Brauchitsch and Leach on Halder. Hitler himself, characteristically, backed the innovators and gamblers; in fact, it was he who first conceived of the basic idea for a thrust from the Ardennes through the Allied centre to the Channel coast, instead of the General Staff's plodding concept of a direct advance against the Allied left wing in the Belgian plain, a repetition of the Schlieffen Plan of 1914.

In the event, and despite moments of doubt and loss of nerve on both Hitler's and the generals' part (but not on Guderian's) Operation *Sichelschnitt* (Sickle-cut) proved an unimagined triumph, destroying the whole Allied northern army group and paving the way for the final defeat and fall of France, the great enemy of 1914–18, after only six weeks of battle. Thus the prowess of the panzer divisions in the field under the leadership of such men as Guderian and Rommel had made possible the political prize that had been absent in Hitler's original concept for the offensive in the west.

For Hitler and the German people this amazing and unexpected deliverance seemed to mark Germany's victory in the present war, and they celebrated it as such. The share of munitions production in the German economy was actually to fall in the latter months of 1940.

Historians have been so dazzled by *Sichelschnitt's* brilliance and by its stunning success in bringing France down that they have not questioned whether Hitler's decision to attack France and the Low Countries really constituted sound long-term 'total strategy' in the first place, or instead another decisive error of judgment. In the winter of 1939–40 it had been perfectly plain in Berlin that the British and French were themselves highly reluctant to end the so-called 'phoney war' by launching a grand offensive; evident also that the French Army's morale was gradually rotting as it sat idle in its defences – that the French nation's enthusiasm for the war was waning likewise. Thanks to the Russo-German Pact, Germany's oil and raw material supplies were assured, so nullifying the Allied attempt at maritime blockade. Was it therefore in Germany's interest to open up the war by an offensive in the west? Can it not be argued that the German drive from the Meuse to the Channel and the subsequent fall of France was in fact a *political* blunder though a *military* masterpiece? For what flowed from the victory of May–June 1940 was the lost Battle of Britain; the abortive preparations to invade England (Operation *Sealion*); the ever increasing support of the United States for the British cause; Italy's entry into the war that eventually led to the entanglement of German forces in the Balkans, North Africa and the Mediterranean. It can be further argued that, by fostering in Hitler an overweening self-confidence, the triumph over France coupled with the superb professional performance of the German Army provided key factors in his fatal decision to attack Soviet Russia in 1941. Of course Hitler could not have been expected to foresee such far-reaching consequences when he was contemplating *Fall Gelb*, yet there must always be the risk in opening up quiescent situations that the ramifications

9

may prove harmful as well as unpredictable. Hitler's original aim for the offensive in the west does not seem in any way to justify acceptance of that risk and that unpredictability.

The first consequence of his defeat of France lay in the totally unexpected problem of improvizing a cross-Channel invasion of England. This time it was the admirals who opposed him, successfully arguing that it would be impossible to transport the German Army to Kent and Sussex in the face of the Royal Navy until and unless the Luftwaffe had won complete air superiority over the Channel. In the event the victory of Royal Air Force Fighter Command saved the German generals from having to put their *Sealion* plan to the test. But even before Hitler in October postponed *Sealion* until spring 1941 (in fact, for good), he had decided to invade Soviet Russia, the final directive to prepare for Operation *Barbarossa* being issued on 5 December 1940.

Why did he make this fateful decision? Stalin had scrupulously fulfilled every shipment of supplies specified under the Russo-German Pact; there was no sign at all that he meant to turn off the tap. Since it was Hitler's reckoning that the Soviet armed forces were such poor stuff that they could be defeated in six weeks, he cannot really have believed that Germany stood in danger of a Russian attack. His claim that Russia constituted Britain's last hope, and that once Russia was smashed Britain would make peace was hardly well founded, since Russia was then not even a belligerent, was in no way supporting Britain's fight, while Britain was very evidently looking to America for rescue rather than to Russia. It must be conjectured that Hitler simply believed that as an opponent Britain was as good as defeated, and that it was now time to fulfil his cherished dream of founding a Germanic empire on Russian soil. But whatever the motivation, here was his second decisive mistake of 'total strategy' (the first being to get Germany into a general war at all) and all his own.

For his senior soldiers – Brauchitsch, Halder, Rundstedt – were filled with gloomy foreboding at the prospect of campaigning in Russia, again and again pointing the operational problems (as the relevant portraits in *Hitler's Generals* describe). Hitler believed that his 'shop-window' (as they still were) armed forces could crush the Soviet Union by *Blitzkrieg* as they had Poland and France. His generals too shared Hitler's poor opinion of the Red Army, as for that matter did the British General Staff. Nevertheless Hitler played down, as his generals did not, the Russian factors of space, distance and bad communications; the immense problems of logistics and movement. And just like *Fall Gelb*, *Barbarossa* lacked a clear political aim. Hitler stated its objectives as an advance to the east of Moscow, the destruction of the Red Army's powers of resistance, and the establishment of a kind of permanent military frontier between German-occupied Russia and the remainder. Bismarck would not have recognized this as making sense as a war aim. Nor would the Elder Moltke have recognized the final plan for *Barbarossa*, as it fuzzily emerged from Hitler's arguments with his generals, as offering a coherent strategy for a successful war in fulfilment of national policy. Professor Bond's and Professor Leach's accounts of how the final plan took shape are particularly enlightening, for they show that while Brauchitsch and Halder saw the primary objective as the Red Army itself (and hence wished to hunt it down by driving straight on Moscow), Hitler (backed by alternative advice from Jodl) opted for economic prizes, and so gave priority to advances on the wings, in the Ukraine and the Baltic states.

Despite the initial showy successes – deep advances, vast encirclements (brought alive in this book by Kenneth Macksey's description of Guderian's leadership of his panzer corps) – *Barbarossa* was doomed by this strategic ambiguity. For almost two months Bock's Army Group Centre, on the road to Moscow, lay stalled round Smolensk while Hitler re-deployed its panzer forces to assist Rundstedt's Army Group South in conquering the Ukraine. When the advance on Moscow was resumed at the very end of September, it was too late: sheer attrition of man, beast and machine, coupled with the onset of freezing winter, was to bring the German Army to a halt by the first week of December.

For the first time, then, the *Blitzkrieg* formula for quick, cheap victories had failed; an act of offensive war lacking a clear political objective or coherent strategic design had petered out all too appropriately, and perhaps inevitably, without a decision. For the first time Hitler found himself entangled in a protracted land war, a war of attrition; and for the first time he had to contemplate turning the German economy over to large-scale munitions production. When to *Barbarossa*'s failure is added Hitler's quite needless declaration of war on the United States after the Japanese strike on Pearl Harbor on 7 December, thus ensuring that America's mighty industrial and military weight (once mobilized) would fall on Germany's neck, it can be seen that December 1941 marked the moment when Hitler's conduct of total strategy had rendered inevitable his ultimate defeat at the hands of overwhelming human and industrial resources. All the rest of the campaigning to follow, the transient hopes, the sour disappointments, the ever more bitter quarrels with his generals (except for lackeys like Keitel, Jodl and Warlimont, whose personalities and roles are ably portrayed by Walter Görlitz) were merely incidental to this process.

The failure before Moscow and the opening of the great Russian winter counter-offensive also directly led to the final destruction of the German Army's traditional professional independence, for on 19 December Hitler dismissed Brauchitsch and himself assumed the post of Commander-in-Chief – in function as well as title. Henceforward Hitler dwindled from national leader deciding state policy into an executive supreme commander over Germany's various war fronts and, in the case of the crucial Eastern Front, to a mere amateur commander-in-chief conducting day-to-day operations in the field.

The focus of interest with regard to his relationship with his generals therefore begins to alter from the high command level to that of army-group or even army command. The issues under dispute likewise shrink from the grand questions of total strategy – rearmament, peace, war, and the choice of victims for attack – to those of operational manoeuvre, and even to mere tactics.

Hitler's planning for 1942 displays the constricted new pattern. For the first time since 1938 there were to be no new adventures, no opening of fresh fronts, but instead a resumption of the stalled invasion of Russia. The offensive, *Fall Blau* ('Case Blue'), was limited to the southern half of the front – a recognition of Germany's weakened strength relative to the Soviet Union. And *Fall Blau*, for all its initial breakthrough and its immense gains of territory, was like *Barbarossa* basically flawed by ambiguity of strategic aim. Overriding his generals, Hitler gave the offensive two separate objectives on 90-degree divergent axes – the Caucasus oilfields and the Volga crossing at Stalingrad. His amateur attempts to control the deployment of his forces and his opportunistic changes of mind further compromised the campaign. By September 1942 the drive into the Caucasus, spearheaded by the 1st Panzer Army under Kleist (whose problems are well analysed by Professor Samuel Mitcham), had crawled to a stop, another victim of insurmountable logistical difficulties and of sheer attrition.

Hitler's headquarters at Vinnitsa was now the scene of violent arguments between him and his generals: Hitler at his gutter nastiest. On 24 September Halder was sacked, the last diminished embodiment of the Moltke tradition of the Chief of the General Staff as an independent professional of high intellectual stature. For Hitler Stalingrad had become the main objective of German effort; more than a focus, an obsession, so rendering it the Verdun of the Second World War. The 6th Army, commanded by Paulus (not a Prussian *Junker* but a middle-class pro-Nazi, whose mediocrity is brought out by Martin Middlebrook's essay), slogged on street by street, its flank protection entrusted by Hitler to Romanian troops. Hitler's début as commander-in-chief had now left the *Fall Blau* armies thinly spread round a vast perimeter of useless conquest. It was the high tide of his life's adventure.

When on 19 November 1942 Russian counter-strike forces under Zhukov smashed through the Romanians and on 22 November completed their encirclement of Paulus's 6th Army, a new and last phase opened in Hitler's relations with his generals – that of his utter refusal to face the realities of defeat, of inferior resources, and of the limits to even the German soldier's powers of endurance and fighting skill. Since Hitler saw himself as an infallible military genius, it followed that all the disasters on the bitter road back to Berlin in 1943–5 derived from the incompetence and lack of willpower of his generals; worse, their disloyalty to their Führer.

The catastrophe that finally overtook Paulus at Stalingrad in February 1943 stemmed entirely from Hitler's refusal to sanction an early break-out before the Russian ring could be consolidated. The comparable surrender of all the German–Italian forces in Tunisia in May 1943 likewise stemmed from his refusal to heed Rommel's warnings after Montgomery's victory in the Second Battle of Alamein and the Anglo-American landings (*Torch*) in French North Africa in November 1942 that the campaign in Africa was lost, and that all Axis forces should be withdrawn. Only Manstein's and Kleist's mastery of the art of operational manoeuvre and consummate staff work (as Field-Marshal Lord Carver and Samuel Mitcham describe) saved the armies in the Caucasus from a similar fate, where again Hitler refused to sanction a retreat until perilously late.

Now Hitler had not only lost the political initiative in the war, but also the military initiative. His attempt to regain it in 1943 on the Eastern Front by attacking a single sector, the Kursk Salient, with all available panzer forces, failed with enormous losses that weakened defensive operations for the rest of the year. From now on till the end of the war Hitler cannot be said to have been pursuing any kind of 'total strategy', for he was reduced to *ad hoc* patching of unravelling situations, as Soviet Russia launched one gigantic offensive after another, and the Anglo-Americans invaded Sicily, Italy, and finally France. The years 1943–5 for Hitler are like the years 1812–15 for Bonaparte: refusal to yield up territory in good time, vain and costly counter-offensives, fresh armies raised, only to be swallowed up in turn.

What political objective did he think he was still trying to realize as he sat in his map-room war-gaming? There was the hope that the 'V-weapons' (the V-1 ram-jet flying bomb, and the V-2 rocket) would bring Britain down after all – an absurd hope, given the numbers of such weapons and the limited explosive power of the warheads. But above all, drawing on the example of Frederick the Great, he believed that by holding on, by prolonging the war as long as possible, the enemy coalition would break up in internecine quarrels. He quite rightly perceived – as did Göbbels – that the alliance between Stalin's Communist Russia and the two capitalist democracies was entirely unnatural; that the partners entertained conflicting political aims in Europe; and that they would eventually come to a breach (as they in fact did in 1945–7). But just like Bonaparte in his time, Hitler could not see that it was himself that held the coalition together; and that so long as he was alive and free, it would go on holding together.

For apart from the conviction among the Allied peoples and their leaders that he was a trickster and a criminal who had carefully planned aggressive war, there was the question of his régime's barbaric treatment of the Jews, Poles and Russians. Even though the nature and scale of the 'final solution' were not to be known until Allied armies liberated the extermination camps, enough was already known of Nazi oppression to convince western opinion that Hitler and his regime must be totally eliminated. In Russia his deliberate policy of murdering 'commissars', partisans and any other inconvenient civilians or prisoners had roused the Russian people's abiding hatred of the invader, so permitting even Stalin and the Communist Party successfully to mobilize and direct 'the Great Patriotic War'. Hitler's irrational, and politically and militarily needless, treatment of the '*Untermensch*' must therefore constitute his third decisive blunder, and one springing directly from that nihilistic and hate-driven psychology which Ronald Lewin argues pre-destined him to failure.

A graphic account of Hitler wrestling in the toils of this destiny is provided in this book by Walter Görlitz's portraits of the generals who lived and worked closest to him in the mentally stifling and unreal environment of his headquarters – Keitel, Chief of the Combined Armed Forces and Army Staffs, Jodl, Chief of the Armed Forces Staff (*Oberkommando der Wehrmacht*, OKW: the command organization set up by Hitler in rivalry to the Army General Staff (OKH), now only responsible for the Eastern Front), and Warlimont, his deputy. Kenneth Macksey offers a different perspective in describing Guderian's valiant and soldierly efforts as Chief of the Army General Staff from July 1944 to March 1945 to arouse some awareness in the Führer of the realities beyond the map-table on which he was playing out his fantasies.

Meanwhile the generals in the field sought with high professional distinction to make military sense of Hitler's caprices; to save by operational skill inherently lost campaigns. Field-Marshal Lord Carver, with the insight of an armoured commander himself, analyses Manstein's achievement in 1943–4 in wielding his army group in southern Russia like a rapier against the Russian bludgeon, again and again halting the Red Army by well timed counter-strokes to a flank. Shelford Bidwell describes how Kesselring maintained his brilliant step-by-step defence of the Italian peninsula in 1943–5 in the face of superior numbers and enemy air superiority, while the late General von Senger's portrait of his father, the commander of 14th Panzer Corps at Cassino, reveals the professionalism and fighting spirit that enabled German field formations again and again to outfight their opponents. And Martin Blumenson's study of Rommel, Richard Lamb's of Kluge and Carlo D'Este's of Model describe with what energy, resilience and resourcefulness was conducted the campaign in the west in 1944–5 despite Hitler's calamitous misjudgments with regard to command structure, release of reserves, 'no retreat' orders and the final ill-timed and foredoomed counter-stroke at Mortain at the end of the Normandy battle. Franz Kurowski's account of Manteuffel's and Dietrich's attempts in December 1944 to carry out Hitler's impossible directive for Operation *Herbstnebel* ('Autumn Smoke' – the Ardennes offensive) to reach Antwerp and cut the Allied armies in two fittingly rounds off this theme of professionalism in the service of bad strategy.

If the historian may pronounce a judgment on the German generals of the Hitler era, it is that professionalism is not enough; technical brilliance is not enough; obedience to an oath and to orders is not enough. What their traditions, upbringing and training had failed to give Hitler's generals was a wider sense of political and social responsibility; a belief that to obey their own consciences constituted the highest duty of all. Only the 'bomb plot' conspirators of July 1944, Witzleben, Speidel and Stülpnagel (the subjects of a sympathetic but penetrating study in the present work by Professor Klaus-Jürgen Müller), succeeded in so completely breaking the mental and moral bounds of a narrow professionalism as to embark on positive action to destroy Hitler and his régime.

The selection of individual subjects for this book could only be arbitrary, for the total muster of Hitler's field-marshals and colonel-generals alone amounted to fifty-three; and critics will no doubt regret the omission of this or that commander. The editor has, however, sought to achieve a representative coverage of the main theatres of war and of the different levels and facets of generalship: high command, theatre and army-group command, leadership in the field, life in the *Führerhauptquartier*.

PART I

The Anti-Nazi Generals

FRITSCH

BECK

I

FRITSCH, BECK AND THE FÜHRER

Colonel-General Werner Freiherr von Fritsch
Colonel-General Ludwig Beck
and the Führer

ROBERT O'NEILL

Two stubborn, disapproving generals[1] dared to question Hitler's plans for the subjugation of eastern Europe before they were put into effect. Between 1934 and 1938, they obstructed his path both out of personal disapproval of Nazism, and, more importantly, out of deep anxiety for the future security of Germany. Hitler had to co-exist with them for three reasons: he believed he could not afford to alienate the Army any more than he was doing in other ways; he still had respect for the professional capabilities of his most senior military officers; and they were, after all, the appointees of his own government – the one as Chief of the General Staff of the Army, the other as the Army's Commander-in-Chief.

The former, General Ludwig Beck, was the deeper thinker of the two and the weightier obstructor of Hitler's grand designs. None the less he was the subordinate of the latter, General Freiherr Werner von Fritsch; hence it is appropriate to look first at the senior of the two.

When Hitler seized power in January 1933 he already had in mind, vaguely if not in concrete form, the *Lebensraum* solution to Germany's economic problems. He had cast the Army in the leading role in conquering and securing the necessary new territory in eastern Europe and even before coming to power had given his ideas public utterance. In his first week in office, Hitler called together his senior military commanders and began to let them know a little of the dramatic role he had in store for them. Germany had to conquer new territory in the east. Suddenly the Army had lost its aura of being unwanted and ill nourished and was promised a leading part in creating the new German Reich, a state whose strength Hitler intended to outclass that of Imperial Germany, to which most of the military looked back with considerable nostalgia.

Hitler's reception on that occasion was cool, even critical, according to the notes of several of the participants. Rather than being swept naively off their feet by promises of new weapons, more men under command and promotion, Hitler's generals were, for the most part, sceptical. They did not believe that Hitler's vision was feasible and tended to regard the speech as part of the tactics of Hitler's domestic policy, aimed at winning to his side the old conservative army which had helped to block and frustrate his ambitions in the 1920s. Hitler did not fail to note the generals' scepticism and lack of enthusiasm for his ideas but he did not return to the subject in their hearing for another year. He concentrated on reform of the High Command, working through one of the few uncritical admirers he had in field-grey, General von Blomberg, Defence Minister, and through the less-admiring President, Field-Marshal von Hindenburg. The Army Commander-in-Chief, General Freiherr Kurt von Hammerstein-Equord, was anathema to Blomberg and Hitler, but the Führer left it to his minister to decide when to get rid of this forceful, independent-minded and yet somewhat indolent gentleman who much preferred hunting and shooting to the labours of administration. The fact that Hammerstein had been Blomberg's senior in military terms since 1930, although they were only two weeks apart in age, had done nothing to improve relations between them. By the end of 1933 there had developed a swirling miasma of intrigue, rumour and counter-rumour which led to Hammerstein's resignation.

The choice of his successor fell upon General von Fritsch, not through Hitler's preference – indeed he, like Blomberg, favoured the more politically sympathetic General von Reichenau. Hitler overplayed his hand and provoked a forceful intervention from Hindenburg in one of his last significant acts before his health failed and his power ebbed completely. Hindenburg chose Fritsch essentially for military reasons after discussion with several advisers including former Reichschancellor von Papen, who held Fritsch in very high regard. Hitler and Blomberg accepted the situation.

When Hammerstein's pending fall became known to Fritsch in late 1933, he hesitated before accepting the appointment. He had imagined that his current posting was to have been his last before retirement, and had little desire to inherit the problems of his predecessor. He accepted only after consultation with his mentor and former Army Commander, General Hans von Seeckt. On 3 January 1934, Fritsch began the process of taking over from Hammerstein, and on 1 February he became the new Army Commander-in-Chief, 'against the wishes of the Führer and Blomberg', as he wrote four years later.[2]

The character of Werner Freiherr von Fritsch is one of the great enigmas of the pre-war period. There are almost as many pictures of him as there are authors who have written about him. Perhaps the least confusing way in which to treat his character might be to consider separately the two main aspects of his life – first Fritsch the soldier, pure and simple, and second Fritsch the man (in the sense of 'political animal') in a complicated society.

As far as his capability as a soldier can be estimated without the test of high command in war, he appears to have reached a level of professional skill attained by only a handful of generals in any country. He was one of those rare soldiers who could inspire through his personality, by its combination of stimulating zest and quiet confidence, not only those who came into close and regular contact with him, but also the greater part of his subordinates from Army Headquarters to the combat units. The obvious standard to measure him against is that of Seeckt. There seems no doubt that amongst the members of the German Army of the Fritsch era, his popularity and authority, two qualities which are not always linked, exceeded those of the widely respected Seeckt by a marked degree.

While the essence of Fritsch's ability lay in his personality, it was based also on several other more assessable qualities. His performance at the *Kriegsakademie* in the years 1907–10, where he topped his class with the extraordinary grades of 9 in both tactics and military history, the two dominating subjects, gave him a status in the Army matching that of the double first at Oxford or Cambridge. His first confidential report as a young officer comments: 'An excellent officer, a passionately keen horseman, and an outstanding comrade.' Here again, the combination of professional ability and comradeship is worth noting.

During the First World War he served chiefly as a Staff officer, although the head wound which he received from a grenade in 1917 testified that he was not one of those Staff officers who never went near the Front. While he was serving with the German forces in the Baltic campaign of 1919, as Chief of Staff to the Commander, General von der Goltz, he attracted the attention of the French International Allied Commissioner, General Niessel. Niessel wrote:

> Major von Fritsch is young, arrogant and extremely self-confident. It seems he has no qualms about playing hide and seek with truth or evading uncomfortable issues. He has all the faults of character of the Prussian general staff officer, who frequently considers himself superior – and rightly too – to the ordinary mortal.[3]

This description tells us almost as much about the writer as the subject. It was as if Niessel had expected to find such a man in the uniform of an officer of the Great General Staff. When he did find him, or was allowed to gain the impression that he had, his prejudices ran away with him. It must have given

German military districts in 1933

Fritsch and his colleagues a great deal of amusement to have had such a chaperone. None the less the picture of the young German officer who shows no compunction in deceiving his former enemy by outright lying is also worth noting.

During the years after the First World War, Fritsch served in several postings, alternating between the General Staff and regimental duty. His papers show that he regarded the *Freikorps* as a danger threatening the new republic, and that its members ought to be prevented from returning home in organized bands. He saw the Kapp Putsch as a calamity as it had led only 'to renewed splits amongst the people'.[4] The same memorandum showed that he regarded Bolshevism as the chief danger, not only for Germany, but also for Europe, and that German assistance should have been given to Pilsudski, so that the Red Army forces might have been defeated as close to the Russian border of Poland as possible. His service in the Baltic campaign brought him into contact with Seeckt, and a friendship developed which was to last until Seeckt's death in 1936. In 1924 he was appointed Chief of Staff to the Commander of *Wehrkreis* I (the First Military District) in East Prussia. After two years, he

22

became head of the Operations Department of the General Staff (*I Abteilung,
Truppenamt*), another key position, where he worked directly under Blomberg,
who was at that time Chief of the General Staff (*Chef des Truppenamts*). When
he was appointed to command *Wehrkreis* III (Berlin) in October 1932 he was
in the front rank of the leaders of the *Reichswehr*, modern and progressive in
the outlook on military problems and capable of inspiring the devotion of
those who served under him. He was an outstandingly good choice for handling
the military problems of the German Army.

Unfortunately, the problems which faced the Army in the years after
Fritsch's appointment were more than merely military. The difficulties of re-
expanding the Army were small compared with the political complications
which attended the functions of the Army under the Nazi régime. While
Fritsch may have been well equipped to handle the former, it is to be greatly
regretted that this military proficiency was accompanied by a low order of
political consciousness and dexterity. Fritsch's development was not broadly
based, and this deficiency in 1880 had its origins in his childhood.

Fritsch was born a Rhinelander in 1880, and served in a Hessian regiment.
He was the only son of middle-class parents, and he had a rather isolated
childhood. His father exercised extremely strict control over him, which
inhibited him to such a degree that very few people ever came to know him
on personal terms. In a letter of 4 September 1938 he wrote:

When you write further that I am often difficult to understand, you are doubtless
correct. From my earliest days, I have never spoken with anyone about myself.
I simply cannot do it, and if anyone tries to penetrate me in this direction, he
only achieves the reverse.[5]

This loneliness and isolation, strange though it may seem, are not incompatible with his success in an exclusively male profession, where personal
relations would appear to be of great importance. In many ways this isolation
may have suited him, and could have helped him to become such a devoted
professional soldier. He was able to get along with people quite well, yet they
never saw inside him. He automatically maintained a front of reserve over his
personal life and so it was no difficulty for him to subscribe to the military
code of ethics, which demanded a high degree of self-abnegation. He did not
like talking about himself, so he abhorred social occasions, where his only
activity would be to listen to someone else talking about himself. It is not that
he was anti-social in principle. With company which he liked and respected,
he could be the most charming companion, or interesting host. When this
company was lacking he was much more interested in pursuits such as riding.
He enjoyed his work, so he could usually find much to interest himself, and
as a result, he tended to become more proficient. This process tended to

become cyclical, assisting his progress, and increasing his yield of satisfaction. As military leadership demands a large amount of self-sufficiency on the part of the leader, he found himself well suited to the challenge, and the satisfaction of inspiring their confidence was probably an acceptable substitute for human companionship on the intimate level.

These considerations may also explain his life-long bachelorhood. In his youth he was on occasions a very sociable subaltern, but a woman had to be outstanding to attract his attention. His internal nervous energy, his isolation and his ability may have combined to make him into a perfectionist, and raised a barrier between him and anything which might compromise what he had achieved already. Furthermore, at the age at which a rising young officer was most likely to marry, the mid-thirties, he was away fighting a war. He later admitted his desire to have married and to have had children.

If these were his attitudes towards normal social life, then it would have been difficult for him to avoid a lack of sympathy, or even a feeling of repulsion, towards politicians. Not only did their seemingly self-centred behaviour conflict with his military code of ethics, but they also contradicted his personal reserve, his principles of making as little fuss as possible, and possibly even his strict Protestant Christianity. Above all, he disapproved of political soldiers, of whom General Kurt von Schleicher, former Defence Minister and Hitler's predecessor as Chancellor, seemed to be the perfect model. In 1932, when he was commanding the 1st Cavalry Division at Frankfurt an der Oder, his Chief of Staff, Colonel Freiherr von Weichs, reported back to him after a conference which he had attended at the Defence Ministry, conducted by Schleicher. Weichs was about to report what had happened, when Fritsch broke him off with, 'No! It is all lies!'[6]

He did once turn his thoughts in a political direction when Seeckt was dismissed from office in 1926. As one of his closest advisers, he advised Seeckt to resist his removal by force. This wild counsel shows at least as much political ignorance as loyalty to Seeckt. However, he was not unaware of his limitations in this direction. In 1937, he wrote:

I have made it my guiding rule to limit myself to the military field alone, and to keep myself apart from any political activity. I lack everything necessary for politics. Furthermore, I am convinced that the less I speak in public, the more speedily can I fulfil my military task.[7]

With these views on politics and politicians in general, he was not likely to be a keen supporter of Hitler and his National-Socialists. He became known for making frequent and unguarded critical comments about the Nazis to all and sundry when he felt annoyed by them. One morning, Colonel Gotthard Heinrici entered his office for the usual morning discussion. There was much celebrating and revelry going on in the streets. Fritsch asked Heinrici why they were celebrating. Heinrici replied that it was the Führer's birthday. 'Why celebrate that!' was the loud ironic response.[8] At the parade at Saarbrücken on 1 March 1935, to mark the return of the Saar to Germany, Fritsch stood on the reviewing platform where, according to American journalist William Shirer standing next to him, 'he poured out a running fire of sarcastic remarks about the SS, the Party, and various Nazi leaders from Hitler on down. He did not disguise his contempt for them all.'[9] He was thus an easy target for the secret microphones of the Gestapo in the telephones and offices which he used in the course of his work.

So it was an odd set of relationships within the High Command, once Fritsch had overcome his doubts and had taken office. Hitler and Fritsch had very little to do with each other. Fritsch had no right of direct access, and Blomberg transacted all the usual defence business with the Führer. When Fritsch did see Hitler, it was usually in Blomberg's presence. Their relations were therefore restricted to formal correctness, which was, until 1938, always observed on both sides. Fritsch's presence had a strange effect on Hitler. While Hitler would talk quite freely with Blomberg, and even argue, he always felt inhibited when Fritsch was present, and never let anything slip – either in substance or in form. Fritsch, for his part, never tried to argue things out with Hitler until 5 November 1937, preferring to thrash matters out with Blomberg, or simply to voice a protest to Hitler through Blomberg. Hitler once described Fritsch as 'the incorruptible Englishman'.[10] Fritsch's outlook on Hitler is summed up in his oft-repeated words: 'Hitler is Germany's fate for good and for bad.'[11]

Whether Hitler had studied the nature of his new Army Commander or not is not known, but the words which he chose to greet Fritsch on the latter's assumption of office would have confirmed Fritsch in his conception of his task: 'Create an army of the greatest possible strength, inner resolution and unity, on the best imaginable foundation of training.'[12] He would have been wiser to have given more weight to the prophetic words with which Ludendorff advised him: 'Hitler remains loyal to no one – he will betray even you inside a few years!'[13]

The relationship between Fritsch and Blomberg was always tense. Although Fritsch was able to co-exist with Blomberg, he must have found great difficulty in feeling sympathetic towards a man who was playing a part which Fritsch felt improper for a military officer. Moreover, his past experience of Blomberg had made him aware of the minister's propensities for romanticism, fantasy and novelties, and of his habit of acting from a sudden impulse. However, they were able to co-operate sufficiently well for the discharge of their official duties, and they avoided a major crisis in their relations. Fritsch was usually able to persuade Blomberg to take to Hitler matters about which Fritsch had complained, but he was exasperated by the ease with which Blomberg allowed himself to be beaten down by the Führer.

Two months before Fritsch's assumption of his new office, the German Army had received a new Chief of the General Staff, General Ludwig Beck. Like Fritsch, Beck had been chosen on the basis of his military ability and also, like Fritsch, had very little to speak of by way of private life.

Beck, like Fritsch was born a Rhinelander in 1880, near Wiesbaden, into a quiet, respectable, upper-middle-class family. His father was a highly skilled metallurgical engineer, with a strong academic bent. This bent was present in the young Ludwig, and became one of his most outstanding characteristics. He entered the 15th Prussian Field Artillery Regiment in 1898, and spent most of the period before the First World War in Alsace-Lorraine. This beautiful country aroused in him a deep love of its characteristic villages, its woods and its valleys, and to retire to a house in Alsace always remained one of his pipe-dreams. His service as a junior officer had been sufficiently proficient to enable him to be selected for General Staff training, which he completed between October 1908 and July 1911.

During the First World War, he served as a Staff Officer in divisional and higher headquarters. For the last two years of the war, he served on the Staff of the Army Group *Deutscher Kronprinz* with the then Major Max von Viebahn, who relates how Beck carried heavy responsibilities which sometimes in effect embraced command of the entire Army Group. In this position, Beck acquired the habits of intense industry which were to mould the whole shape of his future life. He became accustomed to working fifteen hours a day, and to going for long periods without any free time. He even gave up one of his few relaxations – playing the violin. He particularly distinguished himself at the end of the war by his planning of the withdrawal of German forces totalling ninety divisions, under difficult and pressing circumstances.

The only romance of his life blossomed briefly in the mid-war period. He married Amalie Pagenstecher, the daughter of a Bremen merchant, on 12 May 1916. They had a brief wartime honeymoon, and he returned to the Front. Their daughter Gertrud was born in 1917. However, the health of Frau Beck deteriorated severely, and she died on 16 November 1917, leaving the upbringing of Gertrud to her father. His reaction to this loss was, similar to that of Montgomery, to immerse himself totally in his profession. He grew more and more apart from the social life that tended to surround rising young officers. He was shy and withdrawn. Few things repelled him more than the artificial bonhomie of officers' messes. Life's burdens increased further when he developed a stomach complaint which robbed eating of pleasure. He ate two simple meals a day, with a warm drink as his only sustenance in the middle of the day. This was not the kind of diet with which to sustain vitality, especially as he used to continue his work to a late hour after dinner. Despite the few opportunities which he had for using it, he never lost his personal charm.

On 1 October 1929 he became Commander of the 5th Artillery Regiment in Fulda. During this time, he began to wonder whether Germany would be better off under Hitler and the Nazis than continuing to endure the frustrations of Weimar politics. His part in the trial of Lieutenants Scheringer, Ludin and Wendt, three young officers charged with spreading Nazism in the Army, is illustrative of his views at the time. He spoke in open court in defence of the character of Scheringer, which, as his Commanding Officer, he was obliged to do. He went beyond the bounds of military duty, however, by showing sympathy with Scheringer's ideas. As soon as Groener, the Defence Minister, heard of this testimony he wanted to have Beck dismissed. Hammerstein, then Chief of the General Staff and an admirer of Beck's qualities, dissuaded Groener, and Beck went on to become a divisional commander. Beck's flirtation with Nazism proved short-lived as he found out more about the people who comprised the movement.

In the years 1931 to 1933, he was busy with the writing of a manual of tactics which was to become one of the most renowned of German military publications – the T.F. or Die Truppenführung. This became his best known work, and gained him a great reputation for the clarity of his ideas and expression. For a military publication the book has one other unusual feature – it is written in prose of some elegance. This, together with the large number of other studies which he wrote during his lifetime, mark him as a thinker in the tradition of Moltke the Elder.

Thus, in October 1933, it was difficult to go beyond Beck in the quest for a new Chief of the General Staff, and despite the episode of the trial of the three lieutenants, he was the man whom Hammerstein chose to be his closest adviser and assistant. In view of the difficulties of that first year of the Nazi rule, Hammerstein must have been aware that his period of office was drawing to a close. Beck would have to serve as the only sort of bridge which he could build between his era and that of his successor.

Moving to Berlin was a mixed blessing for Beck, for he much preferred life in the open country to office work in a city. However, he had scope for his one form of recreation, horsemanship, in the Tiergarten and the Grünewald, and he settled down to a busy routine. He had ridden regularly since he was a youth, and was an expert judge of horses. An equestrian gift was the one sort which gave him great pleasure on birthdays and other anniversaries. He rose every morning at 5.30 and rode from 6 until 8 o'clock. Breakfast followed, and by 8.30 he was being driven to his office in the Bendlerstrasse. Work commenced at 9 o'clock, and continued without a break until nearly 7 p.m. Then he would return home, and dine. After dinner, he would usually go to his desk and do another three hours' work before midnight. On this pattern of rest, nutrition and relaxation he was probably rarely in the good, robust form which he needed in order to take on the Nazis.

He resided in a simple double-fronted, grey stucco house, No. 9 Goethestrasse, Lichterfelde. He deliberately chose a simple house which he could afford entirely on his income without any special allowance. He shunned the more luxurious official residence which could have been his, since he realized the tentacles which favours of that sort could send out to bind a man's honour to his job long after the two had become incompatible. Beck's honour was not to be bought. As he said to his daughter, he did not want to owe anything to anyone, especially Hitler. His friends were chiefly military colleagues, especially Manstein, Hammerstein, Hossbach, Heinrich von Stülpnagel, and above all, Fritsch. This group was to widen later as he turned more to conspiring against Hitler during the war, and included men of distinction from many walks of life, such as the historian Friedrich Meinecke, and the members of the opposition group the *Mittwochgesellschaft* (Wednesday Club).

The main criticism which has been made of Beck is that he was too conservative and incapable of making a decision in an unfamiliar environment. There is no doubt that his basic mould of character was conservative. He was also cautious, and adhered strictly to the dictum of Moltke: 'Erst wägen, dann wagen' ('First consider, then venture'). But both parts of this process must be given weight – he was prepared to take risks, after due consideration. It may be that his idea of consideration was somewhat more thorough than that of his colleagues, but he carried the greater responsibility. His planning of exercises for the General Staff using armoured formations of the size of a division, or even of a corps in 1935, when Germany scarcely had any tanks at all, and no combat models, shows anything but excessive conservatism. His decision-making powers had been proved during World War I under conditions in which he bore unusual responsibility, and where an inability to make up his mind would have resulted in his rapid dismissal, instead of his distinguished record of promotion.

However, he was no match for the fast play of the Nazis. Initially he attacked practical details of their plans in which they might have recognized an error, rather than risk a full confrontation on basic strategy. His resistance was made ineffective by the simple expedient of shutting him out. Beck obtained a face-to-face interview with Hitler twice on official matters during his five years of office as Chief of the General Staff. However, the quantity and scope of the studies which he wrote at this time show what a clear grasp he had of the international strategic issues of his day. He could see the best solutions, but was not able to put them into effect. It is a pity that this insight was not wedded to the dashing, driving personality of a Seeckt rather than that of the similarly conservative and introverted Fritsch.

Fritsch and Beck formed a strong and close partnership within the High Command. They were old friends, and Fritsch had worked with Beck on the committee which had directed the writing of *Die Truppenführung*. However, their relations in early 1934 became clouded, due to Fritsch's suspicion that, in the debates taking place about reorganization, Beck was attempting to restore the General Staff to its former, pre-1918 position, and to render Fritsch as Commander-in-Chief superfluous. It did not take very long for them both to realize that there was grave misunderstanding between them, and all doubts were speedily dissolved in what became a very strong personal friendship.

This was the environment in which Fritsch had to attempt to carry out his task. He was quite clear what this was – on the one hand to see that the re-establishment of German military parity was efficiently conducted and on the other to keep Germany out of a major war, which he knew Germany would lose. He wished the Army to expand gradually, so that its skill and efficiency would not be sacrificed for the sake of mere size. He intended to base this new Army on the old traditions, despite the efforts of the Nazis to stress a complete break with the past. He took office at a critical point when the efforts of the SA (Brown Shirts) to replace the Army were near their height, and he became involved in a struggle with Röhm, the SA leader, from the outset. It is not surprising that he later wrote of the situation which confronted him in early 1934: 'I found before me a heap of rubble, and in particular there was a far-reaching lack of confidence in the highest authority.'[14]

The four senior positions within the German High Command were occupied by two different types of men. Blomberg and Reichenau (whom Blomberg had made head of his own office) represented the spirit of the new political era, while Fritsch and Beck embodied the traditions of the old. Initially, these differences do not appear to have caused disruption. Relations between Fritsch and Blomberg had been sufficiently close in 1933 for Blomberg to have told Fritsch that he wanted him to succeed Hammerstein, and Beck took office in a spirit of confidence that he could work with Blomberg. However, the differences between their objectives swiftly reinforced their differences in outlook and personality. Blomberg and Reichenau were concerned with the adaptation of the *Reichswehr* to the Nazi government, the Nazi Party, and Nazi ideology, so that political-military relations ran as smoothly as possible. Fritsch and Beck saw their task as to rebuild the Army but on the old model, not as an arm of the Nazi Party.

As soon as these two different aims began to conflict with each other, the forces of individual personality set these two pairs on to ever-diverging courses, splitting the potential unity of the Armed Forces which could have served to restrain Hitler. Out of this, Hitler was able to increase his personal power by allowing the two groups to fight each other, while he remained as an onlooker, or sometimes performed the functions of an adjudicator, until he finally broke both groups individually.

One of the major problems that Fritsch and Beck had to contend with was Nazi indoctrination of the Army. Both were opposed to this politicization of their troops but, given the stance of Blomberg and Reichenau, there was little they could do, including resignation, to stem the tide. Men who knew Fritsch well during this period, such as Manstein, Heinrici, Viebahn, Hossbach, Halder, Erfurth and Foertsch have all reported his opposition to the Nazification of the Army, and that he protested frequently to Blomberg about it. How these protests were received is unknown, except in the broadest outlines. We do know that Fritsch was becoming increasingly anxious in 1937, and that his health had begun to deteriorate. There is also evidence of weariness and resignation in his letters to his friend the Baroness von Schutzbar-Milchling. It is possible that, as he was under the direct command of Blomberg and Hitler, he made his protests as a matter of course, but believed himself obliged to carry out the orders of his superiors when the protests met with no response. He may also have been haunted by fears of the consequences of his being replaced by his old rival, Reichenau, and have believed it to have been his duty to carry on, despite everything, in the hope that at least Germany's military security from outside attack would be guaranteed by the reconstruction of the Army under his cautious leadership. It is not difficult to see how Fritsch would have justified his remaining in office, but by 1937 it was essentially military Micawberism, but instead of something turning up, Fritsch's fortunes turned down.

The reactions of the other generals followed on from those of Blomberg and Fritsch. On the one hand, there were those who regarded the dissemination of Nazism within the Army with favour, or equanimity, as did Brauchitsch, Reichenau and Dollmann. On the other, there were those who opposed the political indoctrination of the Army, such as Beck, Weichs and Ulex. They saw that Fritsch was able to achieve little against it, and believed that the only thing to be done was to cut their losses in the political fight, and set about their actual military duty, leaving politics to the politicians. The outlook suited the Party admirably. Its co-ordinated policy of indoctrination was able to gather gradual momentum, assisted by the successes of Hitler's foreign policy. The effectiveness of the indoctrination was to be shown both by the hesitation which was induced in the minds of those generals who considered armed revolt in 1938 and 1939, and by the tenacity with which many soldiers clung to Nazi beliefs throughout the war. The predominant mood was appropriately summed up by the commander of the 17th Division, Lieutenant-General Friderici, in his farewell address to the division before his re-posting, on 30 March 1939, thus: 'The Führer Adolf Hitler gives us the example. We will follow him gladly into the German future – come what will!'[15]

The more time went by, the less chance Fritsch and Beck had of exercising restraint on the military policies of the Third Reich, since the Army was being filled beneath them with the spirit of Nazism, transferred from the Hitler Youth, from the schools, and from the other Party organizations, by the thousands of youths who, from 1935 onwards made up the mass of the striking power of the Army. Thus the process of German rearmament served to tighten the Party's influence both at the top and at the grass roots of the *Wehrmacht*. The Army became increasingly less able to exercise control over its own fortunes.

Rumours abounded in the mid-1930s alleging friction between the Army and the Party. There were many references to hostility between Fritsch and the Party, and between Fritsch and Reichenau. One published report included the so-called *Blue Book of the Reichswehr*, which was supposed to have been submitted to Hindenburg by Army officers after the shooting of the SA leaders on 30 June 1934, calling for a change in the government, with Fritsch as Vice-Chancellor, Hammerstein as *Reichswehr* Minister, and Nadolny as Foreign Minister. It is interesting that such a report should have been published, not only for the Gestapo to read at such a time, but also for the Army as a whole, for it does raise the thought that Fritsch in particular was a most reluctant servant of the Nazi régime. The publicity may have been an attempt to show this idea to be utterly ridiculous. It may also have been an attempt to exercise a constraint on Fritsch.

Himmler even went so far as to designate a day on which he believed Fritsch was to attempt a putsch against the Nazis. Fritsch recorded that he thought that the rumours put the day as 10 January 1935, but other evidence suggests that it was 13 January. Blomberg was informed, although it is not known from which side the warning came. Accordingly, he called a meeting of the senior officers of the Army for the night in question, in Berlin. His motivation for his action would have depended upon the source of his information. Blomberg invited Himmler to address this meeting. Fritsch related in a memorandum of 1 February 1938:

> In this speech I was accused of inviting a Professor, who was also a senior legal adviser to the Government, I think his name was Schmidt, to give an address one Thursday at Army Headquarters. Göring held that it would be shown in this address that a putsch was permissible, according to constitutional law. This, in the presence of the Minister and many officers! The invitation had been issued by the Training Branch of the General Staff. The man was and is totally unknown to me. The address was cancelled.
>
> I bring this episode in, only to demonstrate that nothing is too ridiculous to be used against me.[16]

It is surprising, in view of Fritsch's own words, that he tolerated such treatment in front of his own subordinates, and continued to carry out his functions in loyal obedience to Hitler. However, there are a number of factors which may account for Fritsch's failure to perceive at the beginning of 1935 that he was being exploited for as long as he was co-operative, by a movement which was basically evil. First, Hitler was his Supreme Commander, not Himmler. Hitler had, only a few days previously, reaffirmed his faith in the leaders of the forces, and brought about a relaxation of the tension between the Army and the SS. It was only six months since Hitler had made an example of the leaders of the SA, so Fritsch may have continued to place confidence in Hitler as an effective leader. Second, the process of building up the Army, and thereby of restoring national security, was in full swing, so what did the personal attacks and insults of the onlooking group of lesser Party leaders amount to? Fritsch's first duty, he may have told himself, was to rebuild German security, not to become engrossed by such petty issues and people.

The hatred of the ss for the Army did not abate for long, however, for in summer 1935, the ss units quartered at the exercise range, Altengrabow, insulted the Army in general, and Fritsch in particular in the vilest terms. Fritsch summed up the ensuing trend in relations with the ss thus:

> While it was possible in the following period to achieve a good, in many cases even confidential relationship with all of the officers of the Party, this was not the case with the ss. This may be, when seen from our side, because there was scarcely a single senior officer who did not feel that he was being spied upon by the ss. Also, it became known again and again that, contrary to the expressed orders of the Deputy to the Führer, ss men who were serving in the Army had orders to report on their superiors. Unfortunately, these matters came to my attention only in such a manner that I could not pursue them.[17]

Fritsch's summary is well supported by the available documentary evidence. The story of the relationship between the ss and the Army was a series of clashes, usually of a minor nature, but sufficiently severe to indicate that there was much bitterness beneath the surface on both sides.

While Fritsch remained in office, he kept up a continuous pressure to restrain the growth of the ss *Verfügungstruppe*, the forerunner of the Waffen ss. Fritsch's views on this force were set out in his memorandum of 1 February 1938:

> Finally, it is the ss *Verfügungstruppe*, which, expanded further and further, must create an opposition to the Army, simply through its existence.
>
> Even though the Army does have a certain right of inspection with regard to the training of the ss *Verfügungstruppe*, this ss unit develops itself totally apart, and, it appears to me, in deliberate opposition to the Army. All units report unanimously that the relationship of the ss *Verfügungstruppe* to the Army is very cool, if not hostile. One cannot help forming the impression that the hostile attitude towards the Army is blatantly encouraged within the ss *Verfügungstruppe*. This hostility finds its outward expression in the failure of many ss men to salute officers.[18]

The second major problem confronting Fritsch and Beck was how to prevent Hitler from precipitating a major war which Germany would, they were convinced, be bound to lose. Hitler's address to the generals of 3 February 1933 and a second, made on 28 February 1934, giving greater detail on his long-term strategic planning, were rationalized by many of his audience as domestic manoeuvring. They simply did not believe that Germany could, in the space of several years, achieve the necessary degree of military superiority over putative foes to east and west. Nor did they reckon that the Führer was a gambler on the grand scale, willing to go to war against the advice of his professional military leaders.

The re-militarization of the Rhineland in March 1936 should have taught them a powerful lesson in this regard but it did not. Even Hitler was nervous that the French would retaliate and inflict humiliation on him. After the occupation had been accomplished by the *Wehrmacht* and Hitler's fears had subsided, Blomberg implored him to withdraw before the French marched. Hitler refused, the French failed to march and Blomberg was humiliated. Hitler's confidence in his own judgment soared while that of his military leaders sagged.

On 5 November 1937 another turning point came in relations between Hitler and his generals. At a conference in Berchtesgaden he told Blomberg, Fritsch, Admiral Raeder, General Göring, and Foreign Minister von Neurath that Germany would have to acquire *Lebensraum* in eastern Europe by military force, commencing in 1943 at the latest, exploiting as far as possible the tensions existing between Britain, France and Italy. The reaction of Blomberg and Fritsch was strong. They urged repeatedly that Britain and France could not be permitted to be cast as Germany's enemies, and argued that the French Army would not be so tied down as Hitler alleged by an Italian war and that France could not take the field with superiority against Germany's western defences. Fritsch estimated that the French would need only twenty divisions to secure the Italian frontier in the Alps, while the rest would give them superiority against Germany, enabling them to march into the Rhineland. Special consideration had to be given to the fact that France would have the lead in mobilization, to the limited defensive strength of the German fortifications, which Blomberg stressed particularly, and to the poor condition of the four motorized divisions which were intended for the defence of the west.[19]

Blomberg drew attention to the strength of the Czech defences whose construction corresponded to the Maginot Line. Fritsch added that, as a result of Hitler's remarks, he would cancel the leave which he had intended to start on 10 November 1937. Hitler rejected this by remarking that the possibility of conflict was not so close.

The Foreign Minister, Neurath, held that a conflict between Britain, France and Italy was not as close as Hitler would like to accept. Against this, Hitler said that they would be at war with each other as early as summer 1938. As to the French and British superiority alleged by Blomberg and Fritsch, Hitler repeated that he thought it unlikely that France would attack Germany and that he was convinced that Britain would not participate. Should the Mediterranean conflict lead to general European mobilization, then Germany was to move against Czechoslovakia at once. If the powers not involved in the war declared that they were disinterested, Germany would do likewise. Göring suggested that, in view of Hitler's remarks, operations in Spain ought to be curtailed. Hitler agreed, but reserved the timing of this decision to himself.

The fact that the available evidence gives no indication that Blomberg and Fritsch made protests to Hitler on moral grounds about the implications of his policy has been used to infer that the two generals had no moral objections to Hitler's aims, that their disagreement with Hitler was limited to purely technical issues. This inference ignores other factors, which especially in the case of Fritsch, were likely to have been much more significant. He must have been well aware by late 1937 that Hitler was not a man to be impressed by moral considerations when an important matter of policy was at stake. If he was to be dissuaded at all from this policy of aggression, military objections were likely to have been far more effective than moral ones. Furthermore, the nature of a moral confrontation is so absolute that Fritsch must have known that it would lead to his being ousted and replaced by someone more pliable.

Their subsequent reactions to the meeting illustrate clearly the differences of character between Blomberg and Fritsch. Blomberg swung around to the view that the purpose of the conference was much more closely linked to the question of resource allocation than war planning. He assured Raeder afterwards that the purpose of Hitler's opening remarks had been to urge Fritsch and Neurath to accept a faster rate of rearmament. Fritsch continued to be very concerned about the whole question of war and war-planning. On 7 November Neurath discussed the gravity of the situation with him and Beck. They agreed that Fritsch was to speak personally to Hitler in order to impress the military impossibilities of his plans on him, while Neurath was to seek another time to present the objections they saw from foreign policy considerations.

Fritsch saw Hitler on 9 November, at the Berghof, Berchtesgaden. No record of the conversation has survived, but the force of Fritsch's objections was indicated by Hitler's refusal to see Neurath until mid-January 1938. On the same day as his discussion with Hitler, Fritsch wrote to the Baroness von Schutzbar:

> Again and again new and difficult matters are brought before me which must be attended to before my departure. I am really very tired and exhausted, far more than you can tell from my appearance.[20]

On the following day Fritsch departed for nearly two months' holiday in Egypt. He was back in Berlin on 2 January 1938, and the next day wrote: 'My mistake was to have stayed there much too long.'[21] Fritsch was only too correct in this view, for his enemies in the SS, Himmler and Heydrich, had framed him with a charge of homosexuality. Conveniently for the Nazi hierarchy, who also wished to get rid of Blomberg, the Defence Minister in an excess of late middle-aged *joie de vivre* had married on 12 January 1938 a young lady with a dubious past, including posing for pornographic photographs. Perhaps Heydrich had even planted her in the Minister's office, where she worked as a typist. The scandal quickly shook Blomberg from his perch and the Army had few regrets at his resignation.

The Fritsch case provoked much more controversy because the charges lacked credibility. Fritsch, acting against the advice of his friends (including Beck), resigned, only to be cleared by a special court of inquiry. Of course he was not reinstated: the more pliable Walter von Brauchitsch was put in his place. Fritsch went on to a lonely and troubled retirement which was terminated by the outbreak of war in September 1939. At the front with his old regiment he sought and found the solace of death at the hands of a Polish sniper before Warsaw on 22 September.

To several of Fritsch's colleagues and subordinates, who could now see clearly what the Nazi régime was like, the Fritsch affair represented a call for action. They counselled Fritsch during the crisis to defy Hitler by force, to attempt a putsch. This Fritsch refused steadfastly to do, holding that a personal attack on his honour was no justification for the bloodshed which would follow open resistance to the Nazis. Thus despite leaving a deeply troubled senior echelon amongst the military, the Fritsch affair made no consequential impact on Army–Party relations.

Beck was now more isolated but still, as Chief of the General Staff, he carried responsibility for preparing the operational plans decreed by Hitler's grand design. He oversaw the planning for the annexation of Austria in March 1938 under protest. Once again the lack of reaction by other governments, particularly those of Britain and France, reinforced the view that Hitler knew more about foreign policy than his generals.

When Hitler turned his attention towards Czechoslovakia in April 1938 Beck sent Brauchitsch a closely argued critique. He concluded that Britain and France would not let Germany get away with seizure of Czechoslovakia, even if it meant a long war, whose unfavourable outcome could not be doubted if America provided assistance. The final part of Beck's memorandum summed up his concerns about the basic weakness of Germany's strategic situation and, implicitly, about the folly of Hitler's policy:

1. Germany's military situation is, taken as a whole, not to be compared with the weakness of the past years, but it is not as strong as in 1914, because all the powers which might possibly be arrayed against Germany have rearmed to a considerable degree – in some cases to the strongest possible. Besides this, Germany will have for years into the future, Armed Forces which are not ready for use, as is known. The military-political situation of Germany does not provide the prerequisite conditions of space to enable the nation, lying centrally within the continent, to withstand a major war on land, sea and in the air. Hopes

35

based on the neutral nations showed themselves to be ill-founded in the World War. The very lack of space will make it impossible for Germany to endure a long war successfully.

Germany's defence economy is poor, poorer than in 1917–18. For this reason also Germany is not fit for a long war.... However, a European war would be conceived and conducted by our opponents from the outset as a long war.

2.   The hope to solve the Czechoslovakian problem by military means during this year without the intervention of Britain and France is groundless. The key to the question: war or peace? lies with either Germany or Britain. Agreement over Czechoslovakia is possible, because Britain wants nothing from this danger spot. The prerequisite is that Germany agree to a solution which is still tolerable for Britain. She will never give us a free hand against Czechoslovakia. If we antagonize Britain over Czechoslovakia, other possible benefits which we might receive from a well disposed Britain, even if only partly so, will disappear. From a Britain which is hostile towards us we will receive nothing. Britain is preparing herself to throw her sword into the balance should Germany seek to force a solution to the Czechoslovakian problem which is not suitable to Britain. It has always been her principle to align herself against the strongest Continental power. Even if the attitude of Britain in relation to Germany is different today from 1914, it is still clear that however strong we may be, we are confronted by a coalition which is more powerful than we are. In this case, France and Russia are already on the side of Britain, and America will attach herself to them, perhaps only through supplies of war materials. Britain, with her enormous power, which continues even today, despite the criticisms of personalities who do not know Britain the world power from their own observation, will be able to compel the other small powers who are concerned to go along with her or cut us off economically during the course of a war at the latest.[22]

Beck's counsel was ignored and planning for invasion of Czechoslovakia was accelerated. His further memoranda arguing strongly and clearly against this undertaking led to a widening rift between himself and Brauchitsch and to his repeated offers of resignation, all of which Brauchitsch refused to accept.

In notes prepared for a meeting with Brauchitsch on 16 July 1938 Beck wrote:

History will burden these leaders with blood-guilt if they do not act in accord with their specialized political knowledge and conscience. Their military obedi- ence has a limit where their knowledge, their conscience and their sense of responsibility forbid the execution of a command. If their warnings and counsel receive no hearing in such a situation, then they have the right and the duty to resign from their offices. If they all act with resolution, the execution of a policy of war is impossible. By this they have saved their country from the worst – from ruin. It is a lack of greatness and of recognition of the task if a soldier in the highest position in such times regards his duties and tasks only within the limited framework of his military instructions without being aware of his highest responsibilities towards the nation as a whole. Extraordinary times demand extraordinary measures.[23]

Finally Brauchitsch yielded to Beck's requests to call a meeting of senior generals so that he could put his views before them and obtain their reactions. At the meeting Brauchitsch read a memorandum which he claimed to be his own but almost certainly had been written by Beck, arguing that general war would result from the invasion of Czechoslovakia and Germany would be defeated. The Army's leaders had to exert their influence on Hitler and make him realize the dangers of his policy, Brauchitsch argued. The meeting went well from Beck's point of view. The generals agreed that both the Army and the German people did not want war and that though the *Wehrmacht* could defeat the Czechs, it could not hope to prevail against the array of enemies which Germany would have if it attacked Czechoslovakia. Brauchitsch, evidently animated by the spirit of the meeting, closed the discussion with the observation that such a war would mean the end of German culture.

He saw Hitler soon afterwards but came away worsted by the encounter. The Führer's contempt for his generals mounted, Brauchitsch's personal position was weakened and preparations for attacking Czechoslovakia went ahead busily as before. By way of riposte Hitler confronted his senior generals on 15 August 1938 and told them that their fears were groundless. He knew Chamberlain and Daladier and as long as they remained in power there would be no general European war resulting from a German invasion of Czechoslovakia.

Three days later Beck, in a final stormy meeting with Brauchitsch, simply refused to serve any longer. At least this act of defiance succeeded and Hitler agreed to Beck's departure, but only on condition that it be kept secret. He handed over to his successor, General Franz Halder, on 27 August 1938, having recognized clearly that military obedience had its limits.

Beck went off into obscurity, gravitating into the internal opposition to the Nazis incorporated in the *Mittwochgesellschaft* where he came to play an increasingly important role. Deeply implicated in the plot which foundered when Hitler miraculously survived Colonel von Stauffenberg's attempt to blow him up on 20 July 1944, Beck committed suicide. He was to have been the head of state of the new Germany. He must have been able to see, once news of Hitler's survival came through, that Germany had no salvation other than through defeat and ruin, and he had no future other than death by his own hand or that of the Nazis.

How then are Fritsch and Beck to be judged? Clearly as military men they were of high calibre, admired and respected by their colleagues and subordinates for their professionalism. The power and proficiency of the *Wehrmacht*, developed largely during their period in office, is more than adequate testimony to their military expertise. When it comes to the field of military-political relations, the verdict must be less in their favour. They could see that Hitler was leading Germany along the path to destruction but they had no impact in changing the outcome.

Of course it may be argued in their defence that as military men their duty was simply to obey their political masters, but world opinion has demonstrated through the Nuremberg trials and reactions to other post-1945 conflicts that this line of reasoning has little credence. Indeed Fritsch and especially Beck knew and shared the view that they did carry some responsibility for military affairs and had a wider duty than simply to obey.

Their mistake was essentially one of judgment as to when and how firmly to make this dissent felt. Evidently both had some faith in persuasion as a means of changing Hitler's policies up until the time of their resignations. This was a basic error. Hitler was not to be persuaded – he was the Führer and had set his heart on conquest. To have been effective Fritsch and Beck would have had to have been much sharper and more conspiratorial politically, building within the *Wehrmacht* a concentrated and solid opposition to Hitler's war plans with which he would have had to have compromised. Without the Army his plans could not have been carried through. But the logic of such a compromise for both sides would have been a huge change in power relations between the Nazis and the generals. What that secret, concentrated opposition would have had to have been was, in effect, the foundation of a successful coup d'état. Beck saw this more clearly than Fritsch, but by then it was too late in the day. He did not command any troops, the Army was poised to attack Czechoslovakia and, the ultimate irony, Chamberlain and Daladier fulfilled Hitler's prophecy, not Beck's.

NOTES

1 This chapter is based on the author's *The German Army and the Nazi Party 1933–39*, Cassell, London, 1966. All sources drawn on in this analysis are set forth in the footnotes in that volume.

2 General Werner Freiherr von Fritsch, memorandum of 1 February 1938, to be found in the papers of General Ludwig Beck in the Bundesarchiv, Federal Republic of Germany, File H 08–28/3.

3 John W. Wheeler-Bennett, *The Nemesis of Power*, Macmillan, London, 1961, pp. 301–2.

4 Fritsch memorandum of 28 March 1920, cited in Adolf Graf von Kielmansegg, *Der Fritsch Prozess 1938*, Hoffman und Campe Verlag, Hamburg, 1949, p. 22.

5 Kielmansegg, *op. cit.*, p. 17.

6 Field-Marshal Maximilian Freiherr von Weichs, unpublished memoirs, Bundesarchiv, File H 08–19/5.

7 Kielmansegg, *op. cit.*, p. 27.
8 Conversation with General Heinrici, February 1964.
9 William Shirer, *The Rise and Fall of the Third Reich*, Reprint Society, London, 1962, p. 315.
10 Friedrich Hossbach, *Zwischen Wehrmacht und Hitler*, Wolfenbüttler Verlag, Hanover, 1949, pp. 107–8.
11 *Ibid.*
12 Wolfgang Foerster, *Ein General kämpft gegen den Krieg*, Münchener Dom Verlag, Munich, 1949, p. 21.
13 Hossbach, *op. cit.*, p. 144.
14 Fritsch memorandum of 1 February 1938, *op. cit.*
15 Records of Wehrkreis XIII, Office of Military Historical Research, Freiburg-im-Breisgau, File 184.
16 Fritsch memorandum of 1 February 1938, *op. cit.*
17 *Ibid.*
18 *Ibid.*
19 A full eye-witness account of the conference of 5 November 1937 is given by Hitler's military adjutant, Colonel Friedrich Hossbach. Hossbach, *op. cit.*, pp. 207–20.
20 Kielmansegg, *op. cit.*, p. 34.
21 Kielmansegg, *op. cit.*, p. 36.
22 Foerster, *op. cit.*, pp. 82 *et seq.*
23 Foerster, *op. cit.*, pp. 102 *et seq.*

CHRONOLOGY: WERNER VON FRITSCH

1880, August 4	Born at Benrath, near Düsseldorf
1886–98	Educated at Düsseldorf, Posen and Hanau
1898, September 21	*Fahnenjunker* in the 25th Hessian Artillery Regiment
1900, January 27	*Leutnant*
1907, October 1	*Kriegsakademie*, Berlin
1909, October 18	*Oberleutnant*
1911, April 1	Great General Staff, Berlin
1913	Anti-aircraft observer training
1913, March 22	*Hauptmann* in Great General Staff
1914–18	General Staff Officer to the 4th Army, the 47th Reserve Division, the 1st Guards Division, the 10th Army, the Air Force, the 6th Reserve Corps and Grenzschutz Nord
1917, September 16	*Major*
1919	General Staff Officer to General von der Goltz, Baltic Area, Grenzschutz Nord, and other General Staff appointments
1920	*Reichswehr* Ministry
1922	Commander of the 2nd Battalion of the 5th Artillery Regiment
1923, February 1	*Oberstleutnant*

1924–26	Chief of Staff to the 1st Division, Königsberg
1926, January	Director of Operations, *Truppenamt*
1927, March 1	*Oberst*
1928	Commander of the 2nd Artillery Regiment
1930	*Artillerieführer* II
1930, November 1	*Generalmajor*, Commander of the 1st Cavalry Division, Frankfurt an der Oder
1932, October 1	*Generalleutnant*, Commander of *Wehrkreis* III
1934, February 1	*General der Artillerie* and Commander-in-Chief of the Army
1936, April 20	*Generaloberst*
1938, February 4	Retired
1938, August 12	Honorary Colonel of the 12th Artillery Regiment
1939, September 22	Shot, before Warsaw

Fritsch was a Protestant, and his decorations included the Iron Cross, First Class, and the Hohenzollern House Order.

CHRONOLOGY: LUDWIG BECK

1880, June 29	Born at Biebrich, near Wiesbaden
1886–98	Educated in Biebrich and at the *Humanistisches Gymnasium*, where he completed his Abitur
1898, March 12	Entered the 15th Prussian Field Artillery Regiment
1898–9	Attended the *Kriegsschule Neisse*
1899, August 18	*Leutnant*
1902, October 1	School of Artillery and Engineering, Charlottenburg
1903, September 18	Battalion Adjutant, 15th Field Artillery Regiment
1908, October 1	*Kriegsakademie*
1909, September 17	*Oberleutnant*
1911, July 1	15th Field Artillery Regiment
1912, March	Great General Staff, Berlin
1913, October 1	*Hauptmann*
1914, August 2	General Staff Officer to the 6th Reserve Corps
1915–16	General Staff Officer to the 117th and 13th Reserve Divisions
1916–18	General Staff Officer to the Army Group *Deutscher Kronprinz*
1918, April 18	*Major*
1918–19	Great General Staff, Berlin
1919–22	Special duties assigned by General von Seeckt
1922, October 1	Battalion Commander, 6th Artillery Regiment, Münster
1923, April 15	*Oberstleutnant*
1923, October 1	Director of Staff Officer Training, *Wehrkreis* VI
1925, October 1	Chief of Staff, *Wehrkreis* IV
1929, October 1	Commander of the 5th Artillery Regiment, Fulda
1929, November 1	*Oberst*

1931, February 1	*Generalmajor*
1931–2	Preparation of manual *Die Trüppenführung*
1932, February 1	*Artillerieführer* IV, Dresden
1932, October 1	Commander of the 1st Cavalry Division, Frankfurt an der Oder
1932, December 1	*Generalleutnant*
1933, October 1	*Chef des Truppenamts*
1935, July 1	*Chef des Generalstabs des Heeres*
1935, October 1	*General der Artillerie*
1937, July 16–20	Visit to Paris, talks with Marshal Pétain, General Gamelin and War Minister Daladier
1938, August 27	Hands over his office to *General der Artillerie* Halder
1938, September 1–30	In temporary command of the 1st Army (West Wall)
1938, October 31	Official retirement, promoted *Generaloberst*
1944, July 20	Death

Beck was a Protestant, and he spoke French and English. He married Amalie Pagenstecher on 12 July 1916. His wife died on 16 November 1917. His decorations included the Iron Cross, First Class, and the Hohenzollern House Order.

WITZLEBEN

STÜLPNAGEL

SPEIDEL

2

WITZLEBEN, STÜLPNAGEL AND SPEIDEL

Field-Marshal Erwin von Witzleben
General of Infantry Karl-Heinrich von Stülpnagel
Lieutenant-General Dr Hans Speidel

KLAUS-JÜRGEN MÜLLER

Is it really possible to pay tribute to these three outstanding men in a single essay? At first glance the differences seem too great. Witzleben and Stülpnagel came from old established families ennobled for military service, Witzleben from Thuringia, Stülpnagel from Uckermark, whereas Speidel was the off-spring of a middle-class family of civil servants from Württemberg.

The three differed widely in age, Witzleben being half a decade older than Stülpnagel, and Speidel eleven years younger than Stülpnagel.

Witzleben had been a cadet and throughout his life remained a typical product of this military group in behaviour and attitude. One of his closest confidants in the resistance said of him:

> Witzleben was a man of refreshing simplicity. Political ruses, such as the office general Halder resorted to, were alien to him. Perhaps not too widely read, certainly no connoisseur of the fine arts, he was rooted in the noble traditions of the old Prussian officer corps, dedicated to country life, a passionate huntsman.[1]

Stülpnagel and Speidel, however, both grew up in the comparatively liberal atmosphere of their home towns, the former in Frankfurt am Main, the latter in the Württemberg capital Stuttgart. They both received a classical education at a gymnasium and retained for most of their lives a quest for knowledge and a special interest in historical-political and philosophical topics; already at school Stülpnagel showed an above-average mathematical talent, while Speidel

43

displayed literary skills and interests. Both pursued academic studies intimately. As a young officer Speidel studied at the universities of Stuttgart and Tübingen and in 1925 even got his PhD with a historiographical thesis; Stülpnagel studied for a short while in Geneva prior to embarking on a military career.

All three men were in the infantry but spent their military youth in regiments of very different character: in 1901 Witzleben entered the West Prussian 7th Life-Grenadier Regiment König Wilhelm I in Liegnitz, Silesia, a regiment rich in tradition; in 1904 Stülpnagel became a cadet officer in the 115th Grand-Ducal Hessian Life-Guard Infantry Regiment in Darmstadt, and Speidel joined the Württemberg Guard-Grenadier Regiment König Karl in Ulm, whose colonel was the King of Württemberg.

Men like Witzleben and Stülpnagel were still moulded by the pre-First World War peacetime Army; they lived through more than a decade of the fame and glory of the Wilhelmine military monarchy, whereas Speidel only joined the Army as a volunteer in November 1914, after the outbreak of the First World War.

Stülpnagel was the only one of the three who had attended the Prussian War Academy prior to 1914, and went to war as a General Staff officer of the classical mould; Witzleben started as a regimental officer, fought as company and battalion commander near Verdun and Arras, and only after being badly wounded was he sent on one of the intensive wartime General Staff courses. Speidel, as the youngest of the three, received the (disguised) General Staff training specially geared to the post-war *Reichswehr* and only became a General Staff officer in 1930, by which time Witzleben was already Chief of Staff of a division and military district. Despite all these differences, the factors were already beginning to emerge which influenced the lives and professional careers of these dissimilar personalities in so similar a way: i.e. participation in the First World War and attachment to the General Staff.

They had participated in the *Materialschlachten* (battles of matériel) of the first modern war between highly industrialized nations. At the end of the war Witzleben and Stülpnagel had reached the rank of Captain, Speidel was a Second Lieutenant and, as a company commander and adjutant to the regiment, experienced in active service. All three were taken into the *Reichswehr*. During the years that followed, Witzleben and Stülpnagel both alternately served either in regimental posts or on the General Staff. By 1933 both had reached the rank of Colonel. Witzleben, the elder, had become commander of a regiment and served in more senior positions on the General Staff, namely as Chief of Staff of the 6th Division in Münster, where he was the superior of one of the most active plotters in the anti-Hitler resistance, the later General Oster. In 1931–2 Stülpnagel, without doubt the intellectually more brilliant of the two, was delegated to compile the regulations for 'troop leadership', together with Ludwig Beck who had just been promoted to Major-General and who later became Chief of the General Staff and the most central personality in the resistance against Hitler. These regulations formed the theoretical basis for the training of German troop leaders and also strongly influenced the corresponding regulations of the American, Russian and Turkish armies. Stülpnagel owed this assignment to his reputation of being an officer with outstanding military technical knowledge, significant operational skill and broad military education.

However, the collaboration with Beck was to prove fateful for him. When in October 1933 Beck became Chief of the General Staff of the German Army he called Stülpnagel to Berlin and entrusted him with the running of 'Foreign Armies' branch of the staff, tasked with gathering information about the armies of other nations and the analysis and development of military policy. Beck shared Stülpnagel's concepts and respected his sober, realistic approach. Beck belonged to that group of senior officers which favoured swift and comprehensive German rearmament, disregarding the League of Nations Disarmament Conference at Geneva. He saw a possibility for this in an alliance with the National Socialists. Beck therefore called Hitler's takeover of power in 1933 the 'first major ray of light since 1918'.

Although it was not yet manifest in 1933, the personal relationships that developed within the small officer corps between men like Beck and Stülpnagel or Witzleben and Oster were to have fateful consequences for each of these men in the wartime German resistance.

However, for the time being matters seemed to progress differently. Between 1933 and 1939 Stülpnagel, Witzleben and the much younger Speidel all made outstanding careers – due not only to their military capabilities, but to a large extent also as a result of the general situation having become favourable to a military career. The German Army's expansion, from the 7 divisions of 1933 to the more than 100 divisions with which Germany went to war in 1939, offered opportunities for promotion and success. During this time Witzleben progressed from Colonel to Colonel-General and to command of an army, and finally – nine months later – in 1940 to Field-Marshal. Stülpnagel, who had also been a Colonel in 1933, became a divisional commander in 1937 and finally in 1939, General of Infantry and Deputy to the Chief of the General Staff of the *Wehrmacht* (OKW). The young Speidel, just starting service in the General Staff in 1930, became six years later chief of the 'Foreign Armies West' branch of the Army General Staff, and then first General Staff officer to a division and Lieutenant-Colonel.

Paradoxically the period of rapid and brilliant promotion was at the same time also the period of progressive disillusionment for the two older men. During those five years from 1934 to 1938 the bases for their later uncompromising resistance to Hitler developed. However, this process of development from initial co-operation with the Nazi regime to opposition and lastly resistance did not run smoothly; moreover it varied from individual to individual.

As far as we can see from unreliable sources this progression was relatively straightforward in Witzleben's case. Unburdened by intellectual scepticism, uncomplicated and blessed with a perception for the essential, he reacted to what was happening around him as soon as his political ideal, i.e. the autonomy of the Army as guarantee for a powerful authoritarian national state, seemed to be adversely affected. When at the beginning of February 1934 his Chief of Staff, Colonel von Manstein – later Field-Marshal – issued a memorandum protesting against the introduction of racist doctrines – the so called 'Aryan paragraph' – into the Army he supported this action with all his authority. Such a measure was tantamount to a party-political ideological control over the Army. It therefore contradicted his concept of autonomy of the Army in the state; it also contradicted the doctrine of the 'two pillars', Army and Party, supporting the state – a doctrine decreed by the Defence Ministry and accepted by Hitler (a clever tactical move made with inner reservations). When in the summer of 1934 some conservative Young Turks from the group surrounding Vice-Chancellor von Papen contacted Witzleben in order to persuade him to join in the internal power struggle between the radicals within Hitler's party and Hitler's conservative political allies, he immediately indicated his willingness.

After Hitler's murderous act of violence against the SA leadership of Ernst Röhm in 1934, in which not only many conservative personalities but also the former Chancellor, General von Schleicher, and another former General, Bredow, fell victim, Witzleben (together with the Generals von Leeb and von Reichenau) hesitated no longer in asking the Commander-in-Chief of the Army for an inquiry by court-martial into these murders. He, however, could not see through the fine web of political intrigues in this inner political power struggle in Germany; a web woven not least by leading men in the Defence Ministry. It was therefore easy for those responsible in the Ministry to let this inquiry fizzle out. Political intrigues were alien to General von Witzleben.

The death of Hindenburg a few days later is said to have hit him very hard. Had not the old Field-Marshal had his roots in the same concept of values from the long-past world of Prussian-German monarchy?

The second grave crisis of the National-Socialist régime after the Röhm affair lay in the Blomberg-Fritsch affair at the beginning of 1938. This was to become a decisive factor for Witzleben and many others in their development towards uncompromising resistance to the régime. The shameful intrigue against the widely revered Commander-in-Chief of the army, Colonel-General Baron von Fritsch, enraged him deeply. The negative experience he had had as commander of the Berlin *Wehrkreis* (military district) in his essential contact with representatives of the Nazi Party now became politically significant.

At the height of the Fritsch affair Witzleben himself was not in Berlin. He had gone into a sanatorium in Dresden for convalescence. He only returned to Berlin in the middle of February 1938 after vital decisions had been made. But he recognized with clear perception that a power struggle between the army and radical elements within the NS movement (SS, Gestapo) lay at the bottom of this affair. Decisively, as was his habit, he none the less contacted the National-Socialist (but critic of the Party) Deputy Police President of Berlin, Count von der Schulenburg. Together with him and the commander of the 50th Infantry Regiment, Colonel von Hase – both incidentally victims of the wrath of the régime after 20 July 1944 – he discussed the possiblity of taking measures against those Nazi factions hostile to the Army. When two young officers of the Potsdam Infantry Regiment, Henning von Tresckow – later one of the most outspoken opponents of Hitler – and Count Baudissin, both deeply outraged by the intrigue against Fritsch, told him that they wanted to resign from the Army, he encouraged them to stay on, saying that the day of reckoning would come for the instigators of the plot against Fritsch and officers would be needed then.[2]

Witzleben's attitude during the Röhm affair and the Fritsch crisis showed, on the one hand, his manly and resolute response when the honour and interest of the Army were involved and values were at stake to which he felt committed. It showed on the other hand that he was increasingly determined to preserve the position of the Army in the face of attacks from the ranks of the Nazi movement, if necessary using force. Because of the lack of clear-cut sources it is difficult to say whether at that time he had already rejected the Third Reich and Hitler. But it is certain that he, as the Berlin military commander who had to arrange the annual military ceremonies on Hitler's birthday, never succumbed to the fascination the dictator exercised over others. According to the President of the Reichsbank, Schacht, Witzleben once remarked: 'I never liked the fellow.'[3] In the summer of 1938 during the Sudeten crisis Witzleben took the decisive step from involvement in the internal political power-struggle to resistance to the régime and finally to staging a coup.

Stülpnagel's development in comparison was considerably more complicated, although not less consistent. As chief of the 'Foreign Armies' branch he was not only the adviser responsible to the Chief of General Staff on military-political matters and thus foreign policy, but he also very soon became one of Beck's closest confidants. He totally approved of Beck's military views in the early 1930s: swift unilateral rearmament without restriction by international agreement. The Army was to be tripled and equipped with heavy weapons as quickly as possible; any conceivable intervention on the part of the guarantor powers of the Versailles and Locarno Treaties would thus entail an unpredictable risk: the so-called 'risk army' being a deterrent and the basis for a future army of initially 36 and ultimately 65 divisions.

The German Foreign Office advocated international control of rearmament by an armament convention as a guarantee for the country's safety. However, Beck, supported by Stülpnagel, insisted on massive unilateral rearmament. Although condemning provocative foreign policy moves, they did not appreciate that it was their very military policies which were seen abroad as the actual provocation. The State Secretary of the Foreign Office, von Bülow, feared that unilateral German rearmament would isolate the Reich and result in a foreign alliance against it. 'All powers of any significance are against us,' he told the Chief of General Staff in the summer of 1934.[4] 'If', he wrote in a memorandum to the Foreign Minister,[5] 'we were to continue to rearm without restraint or co-ordination we are heading for grave danger.' France and Great Britain would not tolerate such a rearmament.

However, the Chief of General Staff persisted in his concept. Already in 1934 he demanded the introduction of general conscription and militarization of the Rhineland zone. In a very curious mixture of farsightedness and armament-obsessed stubbornness Stülpnagel himself wrote in autumn 1934 in a military-political report that Great Britain was concerned about the German air rearmament and if one could defuse this concern somehow, Germany's military-political position would be greatly improved. However, he argued that this would not be achieved by making concessions in the rearmament programme but by influencing public opinion in Great Britain: 'Abandoning air rearmament is totally out of the question and would only be interpreted as a sign of weakness in England.'[6] In this he was completely supported by the Chief of General Staff, who responded to any deterioration in foreign relations with an even more emphatic adherence to unilateral rearmament, in fact even by another turn of the rearmament screw! Between 1934 and 1936 Stülpnagel, in contrast to Beck, seemed to adopt a more realistic view of the situation to which unilateral rearmament of the Reich had led. He began to send urgent warnings to the Chief of General Staff; and in the middle of April 1935 his analysis of the military-political situation opened with the sentence: 'In case of an armed conflict Germany would find herself in a position which is far more unfavourable than in 1914.' His conclusion was unambiguous: 'If at all possible, avoid confrontation ... guard against encirclement, even if you have to make sacrifices.'[7]

While Beck as late as 1936–7 was still initiating a massive rearmament boost and tackling the formation of an 'offensive army' comprising a nucleus of large panzer and motorized formations, Stülpnagel seemed to become more and more concerned about the international repercussions this kind of rearmament would entail. Obviously he had foreseen sooner than the Chief of the General

Staff into what dilemmas foreign and military policies aiming solely for military power would lead the Reich.

Could his move away from the centre, the General Staff, to taking a troop command have been a sign of resignation or even an indication of the fact that he no longer wished to be co-responsible for these policies? We do not know. In a private letter to the Chief of the General Staff of December 1936 in which Stülpnagel forcefully points out the consequences of such policies we may find a clue: he criticizes the 'nervous haste and rashness . . . of our foreign policies'. He regrets that 'so many significant successes . . . are jeopardized by the degree of mistrust, fear and hate which we arouse', and at the end he warns with near-prophetic words: 'We may keep the world in a state of unrest for a little while but there will come a time when it rebels and calls us to order.'[8] These are different words from those he used in the military report of 1934 quoted above. It is clear that Stülpnagel recognized the disastrous effects of Germany's military and foreign policies sooner than Beck, policies which he himself in a responsible position had helped to devise but from which he distanced himself now. This seems to be the origin of his later fundamental opposition to the Hitler régime. And as he met his 'Road to Damascus' in military and foreign policies earlier and more vigorously than his Chief of Staff, so in 1938 he recognized earlier than Beck that Hitler himself and not the alleged 'radical Nazi circles' constituted the actual war-monger.

So it is not surprising that, in view of the different but basically converging developments of Stülpnagel and Witzleben, both officers played leading roles in the first serious conspiracy of late summer 1938 which was to have led to a coup.

In February 1938 Witzleben and Stülpnagel met again in Berlin. Stülpnagel had just been appointed by his old friend Beck as Staff Officer responsible for military training. In April Hitler unleashed the international Sudeten crisis which culminated in the famous weekend in May when the Czechs mobilized and the danger of war loomed over Europe. Beck said later that after May he only had the one thought: 'how peace can be maintained in Europe'.[9] In conferences and in memoranda he tried to stem the policies that exacerbated the risk of pan-European wars, arguing that a war against Czechoslovakia could not be isolated; that the Army was ill prepared to fight the western powers with any hope of success. But Beck still believed that 'the war-mongers' were to be found among the 'radicals' of the Nazi movement, in the ss, the sd and in the circles around Ribbentrop and Göring. Stülpnagel, however, tried to convince the Chief of General Staff that Hitler himself was the originator of these doomed policies. Probably due to his sober realism and the insight into Hitler's foreign policies he had enjoyed as former chief of the military-political branch of the General Staff, he assessed the situation sooner

THE ANTI-NAZI GENERALS

than Beck. It is certain that he then made contact with Lieutenant (later General) Oster and the determined opposition group within the German Secret Service, and that Witzleben probably arranged this.

At that time Beck's thoughts were far removed from a coup. He had in mind rather to impede Hitler's war-mongering policies through a 'strike by the generals', a collective resignation by all commanding generals. At the same time, this blow against the supposed war-mongers and opponents of the Army in the SS and SD would initiate a process of purging the internal political scene. On the other hand, at the height of the Sudeten crisis, Stülpnagel, Oster and their like-minded colleagues intended to go one step further. However, sources for this assumption are not clear.

Meanwhile Beck's plan to render the SS powerless and to eliminate prominent representatives of the regime would have hit the Nazi rule hard, modifying it fundamentally. It is difficult to ascertain where exactly the dividing line runs between preparations for a blow against fractions of the ruling mechanism and a genuine coup. None the less Stülpnagel had more radical aims than Beck. But Beck's plan did not work out: the Commander-in-Chief of the Army, Brauchitsch, and leading generals did not follow him. The Chief of the General Staff resigned and his deputy, General Halder, succeeded him.

With Halder's appointment, new avenues opened up for Stülpnagel. Disenchanted by Beck's limited perception and lack of conspiratorial determination, Stülpnagel put all his money on Halder who, unlike Beck, belonged to his generation (being only one and a half years older), and whose military career, although advanced by a year, had developed parallel to his own. Halder respected his intimate friend Stülpnagel especially: he 'was a nobly thinking, honest officer of the best old tradition ... an intellectual person of high political interests and tact and we understood each other excellently. He was one of those people who were convinced that Hitler was an enemy of the Fatherland, who were in constant inner conflict and spurred others into action.' He was not a rash hothead '... but always maintained a calm and reflective attitude towards the question of resistance without losing the overall view of the situation.'[10]

Stülpnagel had Halder's complete confidence; for a long time therefore he had considerable influence on the resistance activities of the new Chief of the General Staff, who he suspected quite rightly would react more resolutely against Hitler and his policies than Beck. Halder and Stülpnagel neither shared Beck's illusion about which were the originators of irresponsible policies risking war, nor did they have his optimism in assuming that they could persuade the dictator by means of memos or an outright resignation.

Like Stülpnagel, Halder had urged Beck to more energetic action. We have evidence of Halder's original hatred of the Nazi régime. So Stülpnagel did not only find a close friend in the new Chief of the General Staff but also a determined opponent of Hitler. Halder appointed Stülpnagel immediately as his deputy.

The opposition in the General Staff clearly received a new impetus with these two men at the top: they would not refrain from staging a coup if war could be averted; they were now aiming at Hitler's removal by an overthrow in order to avert a war, but not, however, at any price as the radical plotters around Oster intended.

Halder empowered Stülpnagel to prepare for the eventuality of a coup, in case Hitler's policies should unleash a war against the western powers. Stülpnagel made contact with Witzleben who – in contrast to the Chief of the General Staff – was in direct command over troop units in the Berlin *Wehrkreis*. Witzleben, never acting out of the blue but only after thorough investigation, let Stülpnagel brief him about the political situation and he also consulted the President of the Reichsbank, Schacht, who for some time had critically watched the direction of Hitler's foreign policy and the development of the domestic political situation. Schacht was greatly impressed by Witzleben's determination. For him Witzleben was always 'the first and ... most determined general to recognize the necessity for Hitler's removal and to tackle this task wholeheartedly.'[11] Like a dynamic leader of troops who, once having made a decision based upon a detailed assessment, acts without hesitation, Witzleben acquainted a few junior but reliable commanders with the situation, among them the commander of the Potsdam Division, General Count Brockdorff-Ahlefeldt. He ordered Oster to gather an assault party of young officers who were to storm the Chancellery and arrest or, if necessary, shoot Hitler. Witzleben even employed a civilian conspirator in his *Wehrkreis* to act as an intermediary to the Oster group, while pretending that this person was sorting family papers for him.

Among the conspirators considerable differences existed as to the final aim. For the General Staff officers a coup represented the last desperate attempt to prevent a war. For Witzleben and the Oster group the real objective was the coup and an imminent war provided a good reason. Halder's potential plan was thus overshadowed by the plans for a coup on the part of a radical faction among the plotters. Stülpnagel, empowered by Halder to co-ordinate the coup preparations, was obviously the middleman between these two power groups.

But the coup did not take place at this time. The appeasements of Hitler by Britain and France culminating in the Munich conference removed the justification for an overthrow. The newly formed conspiracy collapsed. The radical group around Witzleben and Oster was appalled. Their reaction was: 'Chamberlain saved Hitler.' Halder and Stülpnagel on the other hand were relieved that a war had been averted without violence. As patriots they welcomed the growing power of the Reich, but as members of the opposition they recognized very well that Hitler's prestige had also grown. Therefore, between Munich and the outbreak of war in 1939 the opposition remained paralysed and in a state of collapse.

Whereas the opposition in Berlin was incapable of action, Witzleben, transferred to Frankfurt am Main as Commander-in-Chief of Army Group 2, realistically and with determination began to devise a long-term conspiratorial strategy within his new sphere of activity. Although for the time being he saw little chance of an overthrow, this farsighted and resolute general, now removed from the centre in Berlin and without up-to-date information, was unwilling to give up. Together with his Chief of Staff, General von Sodenstern, and his first general-staff officer, Vincenz Müller, both of them extremely sceptical about National-Socialism, he searched for reliable troop commanders who could influence their juniors towards an anti-Hitler opposition. Fundamentally this plan was aimed at the creation of conspiratorial cadres in certain circles of the Officer Corps. It was an enterprise which, planned within the framework of any opposition was tremendously bold and unusual in the context of the German military tradition. Witzleben and his confidants acted on the assumption that in view of inadequate rearmament and the incomplete fortification of the West Wall (Siegfried Line) they would have two to three years before their next confrontation with Hitler's policies. This was a misjudgment, for on 1 September 1939 Hitler attacked Poland and unleashed a European war. Witzleben became commander of the 1st Army on the Western Front, which was part of Army Group C under Colonel-General Ritter von Leeb. During the 'Phoney War' in the autumn and winter of 1939–40 Witzleben waged several battles against the Nazi Party and the SS within his sphere of command. When the occasion arose, for example, he ordered his army to prevent, if necessary by armed intervention, violence against the Jews by Party units.

A new cause for staging a coup arose when, in the middle of September 1939, it became known that Hitler was planning an attack against the western powers, including the violating of Belgium's and Holland's neutrality. The General Staff received this news with horror. They wanted to preserve the fruits of victory over Poland. Instead of risking an offensive in the west with uncertain results they strove to prevent an expansion of the war; indeed if possible to end it. Facing this situation there gathered a group of activists and critical younger officers of the régime, men like Lieutenant-Colonel Oster in the *Abwehr* and Colonel Wagner in the General Staff who were both in contact with civilians in the opposition such as Goerdeler, Schacht and the retired Colonel-General Beck. Contact was also established with the opposition group in the Foreign Office, around the brothers Kordt who had a friendly relationship with Secretary of State von Weizsäcker.[12]

This group of activists was convinced that the spread of war could only be prevented by a coup d'état and that equally this was an opportune time to get rid of the loathed régime. The information they received about criminal oppression and genocide in occupied Poland presented them additionally with strong moral motivation. At the same time senior military personnel were quite clear in their minds that any offensive against the western powers would prove fatal in a military and political sense. Stülpnagel acted. At the end of September he presented Halder with a memorandum, proving that the German forces were not capable of breaking through the Maginot Line and that for years to come, a war could only be conducted on a defensive basis. Other commanders like Leeb and Bock warned emphatically against an expansion of the war. Even at OKW men like Warlimont did not hide their disapproval of an offensive in the west. The Chief of the General Staff as well as the Commander-in-Chief of the Army, Colonel-General von Brauchitsch, protested against Hitler's plan but found the dictator uncompromising in his desire to beat the western powers at any cost. At the beginning of October Hitler issued directives for the assault in the west. From the middle of that month onwards Halder, under severe strain due to these developments, toyed again with the idea, albeit hesitantly, of averting an expansion of the war by an act of force. Stülpnagel forcefully encouraged him in developing this idea.

So Karl-Heinrich von Stülpnagel once more became a central figure in the conspiratorial power-game. He found himself between the two groups, the younger activists on the one hand and the Chief of the General Staff and the senior commanders on the other. Being the realist he was, he had to dampen the overzealousness of the dynamic activists and their impatient insistence on an immediate coup without discouraging them too much. But as a determined and convinced opponent of Hitler he, at the same time, sought to pressure the still hesitant General Staff into action. How much he was the driving force at this moment is shown in his reaction to Halder's argument that the C -in- C of the Army, Brauchitsch, must participate in a coup d'état despite the fact that he had not yet been won over. Stülpnagel's determination and his dynamism as an opponent of the régime were reflected in his reply: 'You depend unnecessarily on this Brauchitsch! ... If he doesn't co-operate you just arrest him!'[13] Halder, in a state of agitation, rejected such a proposal. But towards the end of October he too clearly accepted that Hitler was stubbornly bent on expanding the war. The chief of the General Staff now seriously considered the idea of overthrowing Hitler. He sent Stülpnagel to the Western Front to talk to the Commanders-in-Chief of the three Army groups, Leeb, Rundstedt and Bock. Only Leeb, who had previously protested in a memorandum against the planned offensive in the west, co-operated. After Stülpnagel's visit he wrote a letter to Brauchitsch, the Commander-in-Chief of the Army, reminding him of his responsibility to the German people and signalling undisguisedly his willingness to participate in any action: 'Perhaps the fate of the entire German people will depend on you within the next few days ... I am

53

prepared to support you fully in the days to come and accept any consequence necessary.'[14] This success was due to Stülpnagel's efforts.

At the beginning of November Halder empowered Stülpnagel to start preparations to meet the eventuality of a coup becoming necessary. With this a second short but intensive phase of conspiracy against Hitler began, in which Stülpnagel was the central figure. He co-ordinated the activities of the various conspiratorial power groups – the activists in the *Wehrmacht*, the opposition in the Foreign Office and the group at OKH where the 'special branch' was converted into a conspiratorial working group. He maintained contact between Beck and the civilian conspirators, as well as with the senior troop commanders on the Western Front, with Witzleben, Leeb and Hoeppner.

Never before had there been such an intensive and extensive planning for a coup d'état. But on 5 November 1939 the enterprise faltered. Halder, after a discussion between the Commander-in-Chief of the Army and Hitler, lost his nerve. He interpreted Hitler's furious threats against the General Staff as an indication that Hitler had received information about the plot. He ordered the immediate destruction of all documents and called off the coup plan. Stülpnagel and several other activists attempted in vain to make Halder change his mind. In the middle of November Stülpnagel made one last attempt. He travelled to the Western Front to see Leeb and Witzleben. The latter, as determined as ever, supported Stülpnagel in all his actions. He established contact with all the panzer generals critical of the régime, men like Hoeppner and Geyr von Schweppenburg. Above all he despatched his first General Staff officer, Colonel Vincenz Müller, to see Halder and to urge him into action. But all these efforts were in vain. A discussion arranged by Stülpnagel in January 1940 between Beck and Halder ended in discord. Obviously Halder had lost interest. Believing more and more in the success of the offensive in the west he proceeded brilliantly to plan and lead Hitler's lightning campaigns. But he was no longer part of the conspiracy. He even removed the active conspirators from about him on the General Staff.

It is not known whether this led to a cooling off in the relationship of trust between him and Stülpnagel. It is quite possible that the severe illness Stülpnagel suffered at the beginning of 1940 and from which he never fully recovered may have had psychosomatic causes. The disappointment of this convinced opponent of Hitler must in any case have been immense.

After his temporary recovery Stülpnagel counted his losses and asked for a troop command. He became Commander of the 2nd Army Corps which, in the second phase of the French campaign, was deployed on the right wing of Kluge's 6th Army. He led this corps successfully during the breakthrough of the Weygand line, advancing across the Somme and Seine to the Loire estuary. At the same time Witzleben with his 1st Army attacked the northern section of the Maginot line from the Saar region. In only three days his troops broke through this supposedly impregnable fortified line. For this achievement

Witzleben was appointed Field-Marshal on 19 July 1940.

After France's capitulation in June 1940 Witzleben, Stülpnagel and the younger Speidel took up important posts which, however, distanced them all from the centre where decisions were taken, and which offered no opportunities for a coup d'état.

Witzleben became Commander-in-Chief of the newly formed Army Group D, which occupied the region south of the Seine. As Commander-in-Chief West from June 1941 to the middle of March 1942 he was responsible for all the occupied territories in France and Belgium. He gathered around him a group of opposition officers, the nucleus of the later 'Paris Fronde'. When, on 23 March 1941, on the occasion of his 40th anniversary as a serving officer, Hitler sent him a telegram and a signed photograph, the Field-Marshal's answer contained the ambiguous phrase 'he would continue to do his best in whatever position he was placed'.[15] He never faltered in his rejection of the régime. But what action could he take from France? When Beck and Goerdeler toyed with the idea of initiating an overthrow by a formal proclamation by the Army in the west, Witzleben had to convince them that this was a utopian idea. He had only a few troops available in France which were ready for battle, while he assumed that the Luftwaffe and the Navy stationed in the west were loyal to the régime, an assumption which was to prove correct on 20 July 1944.

When the retired Ambassador von Hassell visited Witzleben in Paris in 1942 he found him 'more aged than he needed to be'. Apart from that, Hassell reported the Marshal as being in good shape, 'of clear motivation and sound judgment'. Von Hassell's statement that Witzleben 'was not very informed about the situation on the Eastern Front as well as anywhere else' was indicative of the isolation of Witzleben's position in Paris, for this was the time of the catastrophe of Stalingrad.[16]

Stülpnagel had been seconded to being chairman of the commission, based in Wiesbaden, which supervised the implementation of the Franco-German armistice. Prior to that he met in Fontainebleau Halder and some of the former conspirators of OKH at Zossen. He was still determined to carry on as a member of the resistance. But Hitler was at the peak of his triumph. The moment was not auspicious and the necessary means were not available. None the less men like Stülpnagel, Oster and a few others kept alive the idea of resistance until, at the beginning of 1942, a new start could be made.

During the eight months of his acting as chairman of the armistice commission in Wiesbaden Stülpnagel made every effort to reach agreement with France in a rational way so as to spare the defeated enemy any humiliation. He opposed, as far as he was able, any attempts at exploitation such as the payment of unnecessarily high occupation costs. However, this policy earned him a severe reprimand from Berlin. Much as he tried in his official position to let rationality and chivalry prevail, he realized that no scope for action existed in Wiesbaden in relation to an anti-Hitler conspiracy.

At the same time Dr Speidel, now Lieutenant-Colonel in the General Staff, returned to France, becoming Chief of Staff to the Military Governor of France, an office which was held first by General Streccius and then by Joachim von Stülpnagel, a cousin of Karl-Heinrich Stülpnagel.

In this post he soon had to deal with Nazi measures to exploit and loot French resources, and with the chaotic interference by Nazi-Party agencies in the responsibilities of the military commander. Speidel soon recognized the dictator's 'divide and rule' tactics and his unwillingness to reach a reasonable settlement with defeated France. In his struggle against the proliferation of Nazi-Party rule he appointed the famous author Ernst Jünger who worked on his staff 'to investigate the underground infighting between Army and Party'.[17] His task was to uncover the disastrous political repercussions caused by Party interference. At this time the 'George circle' began to gather around Speidel and Jünger, so called because they met in the Hotel George V in Paris – a group of opponents of the régime on the staff of the Military Governor who were also sensitive lovers of literature and art. Ernst Jünger later wrote that 'Under Speidel's aegis, in the centre of the military machine, we formed a kind of ... intellectual order of chivalry; we met in the belly of the leviathan and searched for the chance to save our hearts for the weak and unprotected.'[18] And it was through this group that Speidel and his like-minded colleagues succeeded eventually in helping distressed French people and easing their plight. But when in late summer 1941 the French resistance became increasingly active and even made attempts on the lives of German occupation personnel, he was unable to prevent the policies of massive repression, mainly the execution of hostages, directly ordered by Hitler and the OKW. It was the responsibility of Speidel and the staff of the Military Governor of France to implement such policies. He was able by clever manipulation to scale down the killing of hostages but unable to prevent entirely such inhuman retaliatory practices. Could it be that this experience provided the first impetus for the inner development which eventually led him to embrace uncompromising resistance to Hitler? However, initially all he could do was to emphasize the long-term consequences resulting from such policies.

In the spring of 1942 Speidel was transferred to the Eastern Front as Chief of Staff of an Army Corps and later became Chief of Staff at an Army headquarters. At this time he had already taken a deep aversion to the manifestations of the Hitler régime – the corruption, violence, politically irresponsible exploitation and inhuman terror. But he had not yet taken the final step towards active resistance. Although a visit to General Beck in Berlin on his way to the Eastern Front brought them together in their criticism of the régime, they did not yet engage in conspiratorial discussions. The experience of Hitler's disastrous interference in military operations and Speidel's co-operation with Germany's allies (he was temporarily Chief of Staff to the German general commanding the German Liaison Mission with the Italian 8th Army in Russia) provided the final proof that the war situation was in military and political terms a near catastrophe. And in the Stalingrad winter of 1942–3 he gradually became convinced that the war could not be won and that Hitler's leadership would eventually destroy the Reich.

To begin with, the catastrophic situation caused not least by Hitler's war leadership undermined the confidence of the clearsighted General Staff officers at Army Headquarters. In addition decisive talks with colleagues who had already been briefed about a potential plot gathered momentum. So in April 1942 Speidel met colleagues and friends in senior positions such as Stieff, Wagner and Heusinger and discussed with them the necessity of 'fundamental changes'. In October 1943 Henning von Tresckow, who had meanwhile become the driving force in the conspiracy, made contact with him and obviously convinced him that the dictator had to be ousted. Speidel himself summarized his views at the end of 1943 with the words:

> The year 1943 started with the catastrophe of Stalingrad and ended with the collapse of the Italian front and the Russian counter-offensive. Therefore the only solution left was to remove Hitler. As things stood, only the Army could attempt this. The salvation of the Fatherland depended on it. Such thoughts stirred us on this last day of the old year [1943].[19]

Speidel had undergone the typical conversion from a critic of the régime to a man of determined resistance: it was this combination of specialized military insight and ethical resentment which lead him ultimately in to the ranks of the resistance.

Two years earlier Karl-Heinrich von Stülpnagel had succeeded his cousin Otto von Stülpnagel as Military Governor of France in Paris. Prior to that he had been on the Eastern Front for more than seven months, until the end of November 1941, in command of the 17th Army. He was forced to relinquish this senior position for health reasons. He had had the same experience in Russia as Speidel had had in France: although an imperturbable opponent of the régime he could not avoid getting involved in the racial-ideological war of extermination Hitler was waging in the east. His position there was certainly more difficult than that of Speidel in Paris. In Russia a different, much more brutal, war was fought than that in western Europe. Besides, Speidel as Chief of Staff held only a secondary position while Stülpnagel as an Army commander directly exercised responsibility.

A document from his Army Headquarters dated 21 August 1941 calling for an 'intensified campaign against the Jews' bore his signature.[20] Had he only routinely signed a document drafted by an officer of his Staff? Had he not been able to alter it or prevent its issue without exposing himself to ideological suspicion? Or could 'conformity to and affinity with National-Socialist ideology' or even 'ideological activities' have swayed Stülpnagel as in the case of other senior officers? Hardly! Or was it a matter of 'a common image of the enemy'?[21], for instance primary anti-communism and traditional anti-semitism. We do not know, but it cannot be ruled out.

Stülpnagel's attempt to modify an instruction issued by OKW calling for indiscriminate repression demonstrates how a higher commander on the Eastern Front can become entangled. Contrary to such instructions Stülpnagel ordered that 'collective measures were not to be taken indiscriminately', so as not to alienate the Ukrainian population. But then he continues to say that in cases 'where swift action is required ... especially against Jewish Komsomols ... as saboteurs and gangleaders', action should be taken.[22]

Later, as Military Governor of France, Stülpnagel no longer had direct influence over the kind and extent of repression, especially the killing of hostages, that he had had on the Eastern Front. From March 1942 the responsibility for this had been transferred to the newly installed Senior SS and Police Commander, the SS General Oberg, though not before Stülpnagel had tried to calm the tense situation in France by various means.

He managed to establish a reasonably good relationship with Oberg, a 'relatively moderate representative of Himmler'.[23] Both men had formerly served in the same regiment. Oberg regularly consulted the Military Governor on current affairs. A certain complicity due to common knowledge was therefore unavoidable. Moreover, the number of hostages killed was considerably reduced by this collaboration since Oberg likewise detested it. Stülpnagel, however, was not able to prevent other repressive measures, for example arrest on racial grounds, deportations and the infamous 'Night and Fog' decrees.

So it was not surprising that the Military Governor was under mental stress. Ernst Jünger who met him at this time wrote: 'His noble character inclines towards the intellectual assessment of man ... as statesman ... he never lost sight of our situation ... he is tired though ... his face betrays sorrow.'[24] Speidel, who visited him briefly at the beginning of December 1942, noticed how he, as a person, was in conflict with his position as representative of the occupying power and of Nazi rule in France. 'The amorality of the régime plunged him, a person of highly ethical principles, into a continuous mental torment.'[25] This was the harder to bear since he clearly recognized the situation. Speidel reported: 'He saw the futility of continuing the war and discussed quite candidly the necessity for ending the war and bringing about a change ... in the régime.'[26] He therefore tried several times during the summer of 1943 to re-establish contact with his former co-conspirators in Germany. He travelled to Brussels to see his colleague, the Military Governor of Belgium, General von Falkenhausen, who was also in contact with the opposition group around Beck. Von Falkenhausen personally dispatched a trusted officer to

Beck in Berlin. In this way the network for a conspiracy was rewoven after some time of stagnation.

The war situation and his increasingly unbearable moral position drove Stülpnagel into action. Ulrich von Hassell, a member of the Berlin 'Fronde' formed the impression that 'it had become a burning issue' for Stülpnagel 'to avoid the abyss';[27] without doubt, the abyss into which Hitler's policies and war strategy would plunge the Reich but also the abyss into which the Military Governor felt himself thrown politically as well as morally.

Stülpnagel's attitude reveals a problem which has led writers of history to controversial assessments: how can the fluctuating intensity in the activities of some members of the German resistance be explained? How do we interpret the fact that some of the very first resistance fighters seemed temporarily to suspend all their activities against the Nazi régime, only to emerge again during the period prior to 20 July 1944? And how is one to comprehend that they were, to a certain extent, implicated directly or indirectly in Hitler's policies of conquest and repression? With respect to Stülpnagel, the opinion has been expressed that the effect of the victory in France created a kind of elation which overshadowed all existing motivation of resistance. It is thought that finally in the war against the Soviet Union imperialistic and ideological principles replaced the previously existing and effective Christian and humanitarian ones.[28]

It is debatable whether one can define such precise phases in motivation. Without doubt there was a stagnant phase in the anti-Hitler conspiracy between the victory in the west and the changing fortunes of war in the east and in the Mediterranean theatre. This became apparent from the end of 1942 onwards, and during this phase many of the former resistance activists remained passive. But one ought to discriminate more accurately. It cannot be denied that quite a few men of the 1938–9 opposition changed their critical attitude between 1940 and 1942–3 as a result of the success of German weapons. In addition, those opposing the Hitler régime had from time to time doubted whether it would be auspicious to topple a dictator at the height of his success, power and prestige. Would the people, under such circumstances, understand or even support a coup? On the other hand it is doubtful whether men like Witzleben and Stülpnagel ever relented in their opposition to the régime even during this phase. It has to be borne in mind that at that time they had been transferred to positions which initially did not offer them opportunities to plan a conspiracy effectively. And it is furthermore doubtful whether, with their confirmed opposition to the régime, these men ever showed anti-communist and national-imperialistic tendencies, such as was the Wilhelmine heritage of this generation.

One can therefore not speak of clearly defined phases of motivation; it must be seen as a very complex process during which, along with external circumstances, frequently changing factors of motivation influenced the way the resistance manifested itself. So during this process of development of the resistance we see attitudes such as Halder's, who since the beginning of 1940 had rejected any action of this kind, and those of Stülpnagel and Witzleben who, limited to displaying exterior passivity whilst suffering under the yoke of a repressive system, privately maintained their opposition. This was important when from 1942 onwards younger men emerged from the ranks of the resistance, bringing with them new determination and dynamism and giving new vigour to the conspiracy. These men had been promoted during the war to leading military positions in which serious opportunities for a conspiracy opened up.

Speidel belonged to the new generation of the resistance. After nearly two years on the Eastern Front he had been promoted to Lieutenant-General and Chief of Staff to an Army. In April 1944 he was transferred to France and became Chief of Staff of Army Group B, whose headquarters were at La Roche-Guyon, west of Paris. Commander-in-Chief of the Army Group was Field-Marshal Rommel. Hitler had given Rommel an assignment which was to decide the war, that is, to fend off the anticipated invasion by the Anglo-American forces. It was Rommel himself who had selected his Swabian compatriot Speidel as his Chief of Staff. This new position offered Speidel a historic chance: to win over the most popular Marshal of the Third Reich for the anti-Hitler conspiracy. And this was the problem that the German resistance movement faced at the beginning of 1944.

In Paris Speidel met an already firmly established group of activists which had been consolidating around his old boss in the 'Foreign Armies' branch, Stülpnagel, now Military Governor. Beside Stülpnagel, Lieutenant-Colonel Hofacker was another central figure of this 'Fronde'. He was a cousin of Stauffenberg and the son of a former general from Württemberg under whose command Rommel had fought in the First World War. Hofacker enjoyed Stülpnagel's unreserved personal and political confidence. He was the go-between for the Berlin and the Paris circles of conspirators. During the latter half of 1943 Count von Schulenburg emerged from the Berlin group to co-ordinate the Berlin plans with those of Paris. Stülpnagel personally went to the capital for this purpose. It was vital to co-ordinate plans since several discrepancies still existed between the Paris and Berlin concepts of resistance, such as the question of Hitler's assassination. Hofacker led the group relentlessly demanding the dictator's death; Stülpnagel and several others rejected the idea of assassination for political as well as ethical reasons. They had no intention of making a martyr out of Hitler but instead wanted to arrest him and put him on trial before a German court. There was also the problem of safeguarding foreign relations in the course of a coup d'état. Stülpnagel despatched a confidant to Madrid and Lisbon to make contact with the Allied powers. He believed in the possibility of negotiating a cease-fire with the western powers after a successful coup d'état. When this proved impossible,

Stülpnagel even got in touch with the French resistance via a middleman.

The critical factor, though, was to win over Field-Marshal Rommel to the conspiracy. Stülpnagel had only a few troops available whereas Rommel, apart from enjoying enormous prestige, had an entire Army Group at his disposal. If, at an appropriate moment, he were to lead the Army in the west in a revolt against Hitler, then success was guaranteed.

One of the Paris conspirators wrote in retrospect: 'in this difficult situation there was a glimpse of hope, when Speidel was appointed Chief of Staff to Army Group Rommel. Speidel, an unusually capable officer, politically far-sighted, was not unknown to us.'[29] Immediately after his arrival Speidel went into action. Already on 15 April 1944 he had submitted a report to the Field-Marshal assessing the war situation, especially on the Eastern Front, in which he also informed Rommel about Hitler's genocide policies in eastern Europe. All this seemed to make a great impact on Rommel. Speidel lastly established a rapport between Stülpnagel and Rommel, both known to each other from the time they were instructors at the Dresden War Academy. On 15 May the two men had a detailed discussion. It is doubtful, though, whether during this talk they already came to an agreement about a proper schedule to pursue the so-called 'Rommel-Stülpnagel plan for the western solution'. According to this plan Hitler was to be arrested during a visit to the Western Front, at home the Nazi régime was to be toppled, and the occupied western territories were to be evacuated in agreement with the Allies. In the east the war was to be continued but with a shortened front.

Several of these points were discussed frequently by the conspirators but at this moment Rommel was not quite ready to take the initiative. The Field-Marshal needed time to think before he could take the final decision to act against Hitler's war strategy and the prolonging of the war. In this process Speidel played a vital role. It is obviously to his credit that Rommel assessed the war situation as hopeless and that he viewed Hitler's strategic decisions with grave concern. Two months earlier Rommel, if not uncritical, was still regarded as 'the Führer's loyal paladin'. Had he not, at the end of February, brusquely rejected an indirect approach by Goerdeler?

Speidel's reports and assessment of the situation led the Field-Marshal to make contact with other men in opposition. At the end of May he sent Speidel to Germany to have discussions concerning the conspiracy with the Foreign Minister von Neurath and a senior local politician from Württemberg. Under Speidel's influence the Field-Marshal – basically an apolitical soldier – gradually began to reflect upon the political consequences of the situation. Speidel accelerated this process by every means available. So, little by little, important opposition personalities arrived at the Château of La Roche-Guyon for more or less detailed discussions with Rommel.

The extent to which the Field-Marshal was finally won over to the conspiracy cannot be established due to the poor documentary evidence. This question has therefore become a matter of controversy.[30] The various accounts which Speidel, as the only survivor of the inner circle of the conspirators, published after the war are not clear. When reading them one has to allow for the fact that immediately after the war Speidel was determined 'to elevate Rommel to the status of national hero of the German people',[31] as he is supposed to have told General von Schweppenburg. From Speidel's version one may gain the impression that Rommel appeared as a man totally committed to the resistance. But after careful evaluation of the sources one must assume that Speidel failed precisely in this, namely in winning over the Field-Marshal totally to the conspiracy; that is, to the assassination of Hitler, and the overthrow of the régime. The opinion that Rommel formed for himself between mid-May and mid-July, particularly his increasingly critical attitude towards Hitler's war, may undoubtedly be attributed to Speidel's influence. But the Field-Marshal was unwilling either to condone a coup or an assassination. In this respect he was not in agreement with the Berlin group nor with the Paris 'Fronde' members. This may not have been manifest to the Berlin group or to the circle around Stülpnagel. Did Speidel not brief the Field-Marshal accurately enough about the plans of the Berlin group or was he himself badly informed? These questions may have to be left unanswered for ever.

The Field-Marshal on the other hand – not least under the influence of his Chief of Staff – may have realized that, particularly after the Allied landing in Normandy, a 'political solution' for ending this futile war had to be found. He was equally determined – should Hitler refuse – that he himself would have to take the initiative for ending the war by ordering the cessation of the fighting in the west. Rommel seemed to have gone no further than this, nor did the suggestions of Speidel and the other conspirators seem to have persuaded him. In mid-June he had already written to his wife that in view of the Allied superiority one had now to 'resort to politics'.[32]

At the same time he mentioned to Admiral Ruge, his naval deputy, the possibility of a unilateral cease-fire. On 16 July he told an officer who had been serving in his staff in Africa that, if Hitler did not draw the consequences, he would open up the Western Front; the only thing that then still mattered was that the Anglo-Americans should reach Berlin before the Russians.[33]

But Speidel's intensive efforts to induce the Field-Marshal were in vain. On 17 July 1944 Rommel was seriously injured by a British air attack. During the critical hours of 20 July he was not available.

By 13 July Stülpnagel and his co-conspirators in Paris had completed their preparations for a coup. After a consultation with Rommel, Hofacker, Stülpnagel's confidant in the conspiracy, travelled to Berlin on 11 July in order to brief the group around Count von Stauffenberg on the situation in the west. The decision taken by the Berlin group on 16 July to strike on 20 July was to a considerable extent due to Hofacker's efforts. One day later, on 17 July 1944, the conspirators in Paris faced a totally changed situation. Because of Rommel's hospitalization, the key role in developments in the west was given to Field-Marshal von Kluge (since the beginning of July the Commander-in-Chief West) who was going to take over command of Army Group B from 19 July onwards. Would he play the part allocated to Rommel? Indeed, Tresckow had already informed him about the plans of the newly formed conspiracy back on the Eastern Front in 1943, but one could never be quite sure of him: he was not called 'Der Kluge Hans' ('clever Hans') for nothing, a nickname pointing not only to his undeniable intellectual prowess but also to his chameleon-like character. Success on 20 July 1944 therefore depended solely on whether von Kluge could be won over to the cause of an overthrow and be prevailed upon to take the initiative on the Western Front. When, a little after 4 p.m., Stülpnagel received the news in Paris that the Berlin conspirators had begun the coup he acted swiftly and decisively: first, he issued the order to arrest the leadership of the SS and SD in Paris. Troops of the Military Governor of Paris executed this order speedily and successfully, thus also setting the coup in motion in the west. Second, Stülpnagel went to La Roche-Guyon to spur Kluge on to further action. However, the Field-Marshal was not immediately available. He had gone to the Normandy Front for discussions with Army and Corps commanders.

At the headquarters of Army Group B Speidel was taken totally by surprise at the news that the coup had been set in motion in Berlin. Hofacker had not informed the Paris conspirators of the decision taken on 16 July, because he realized that differences of opinion prevailed in this matter. And without Kluge's instructions Stülpnagel was unable to proceed. Moreover, soon contradictory reports arrived from Berlin and from the Führer's headquarters in East Prussia. It was at the Château of La Roche-Guyon, headquarters of Army Group B, that the final decision in the west concerning the coup was made. Stülpnagel and Hofacker arrived there towards evening. Kluge, returning from the front a little earlier and bewildered by the news of the coup, was initially undecided, the more so as contradictory reports of the events and the development of the situation came in from the Reich. Should he – as Rommel had intended – terminate the fighting in the west? The news that Hitler had survived the attempt on his life was obviously crucial. Stülpnagel and Hofacker in a dramatic scene implored him to join the conspiracy and bring about a *fait accompli* in the west. But the Field-Marshal refused: 'Yes, if the swine had died,' he is supposed to have answered. Even Stülpnagel's disclosure that he had more or less initiated the coup in Paris with the order to arrest SS and SD members could not prompt him into action. 'Well, gentlemen, an abortive coup then,' was his reply. The SS were released at his request. During the same night he sacked Stülpnagel and advised him to don civilian clothes and 'disappear somewhere'.[34]

Stülpnagel's courageous initiative in Paris and his striving to persuade Kluge into a decision remain the only determined act performed by a German General outside Berlin on 20 July. He paid for it with his life. Next day he was summoned to OKW to report. On the journey to Germany he tried to shoot himself near Verdun where he had fought in the First World War. Although his suicide attempt failed, he was blinded. Arrested by the Gestapo he was ruthlessly interrogated, and hanged on 30 August. On the same day two of the other Paris conspirators were also executed, namely Colonel von Linstow, his Chief of Staff, and the First Quartermaster (Senior Staff Officer) West, Colonel Finckh. After prolonged interrogation Hofacker died on the gallows on 20 December. Field-Marshal Kluge, deposed by Hitler on 17 August and summoned to headquarters to report, poisoned himself. His indecision and his denunciation of Stülpnagel could not save him. He feared that an exhaustive inquiry would bring to light his conspiratorial contacts of 1943.

Beside Rommel and Kluge, Field-Marshal von Witzleben was the third Field-Marshal to lose his life in the aftermath of the overthrow attempt. Since being transferred to the Führer-reserve Witzleben, after the death of his wife, seemed to live a retired life in the country, resentful, unwell (he had to undergo a stomach operation), and alone. In reality, however, he had never severed his connections with the conspiracy. After Stalingrad he declared his renewed willingness to participate. He was designated to take over command of the entire *Wehrmacht* after Hitler had been ousted. In the course of the preparations for the coup he signed the order which on 20 July the conspirators sent to all military offices. It began with the words 'The Führer Adolf Hitler is dead', and then went on to declare a state of emergency and the forces' assumption of executive power under Witzleben's command.[35]

On 20 July 1944 Witzleben was his usual self: clear in mind, realistic, unpretentious and honest, undeterred, determined and consistent. Having been informed that the coup had begun with Stauffenberg's action in East Prussia, Witzleben in the afternoon of that day first went to Zossen, the headquarters of the OKH, where the Quartermaster General, General Wagner (who had been acquainted with the conspiracy), was unable to give him accurate information on the state of events. Irritated by the obvious lack of co-ordination in sending information through, the Field-Marshal went to the Bendlerstrasse in Berlin, the headquarters of the Ministry of War and of the Commander of the Home Army. He arrived towards 7.30 p.m. and immediately announced his arrival in correct military protocol to Colonel-General Beck, his junior in military rank, who was to become head of state. But then, under the impression that the enterprise lacked resolute action, he began to criticize relentlessly. It was he who, prior to the coup, had again and again pressed for careful planning and decisive action. This seemed to be absent now. During his interrogation later he repeated that it had been an unforgiveable mistake not to have made sure that there were reliable troop units in Berlin. When Stauffenberg reported to him in the Bendlerstrasse Witzleben grumbled at him: 'Nice mess, that!' After a short discussion with Beck and Stauffenberg he obviously gained the impression that the coup had been abortive. He turned away and drove to the estate of his friend, Count Lynar, to await the henchmen of the Gestapo in dignity.[36] Even when facing the Nazi Public Prosecutor and though exhausted by brutal interrogation he tried hard to maintain an upright and valiant composure. And this was the way he died on 8 August 1944.

The only survivor of the central circle of the conspiracy was General Speidel. On 20 July the members of the Army Group Staff loyal to the régime and Field-Marshal von Kluge did not suspect him to have been one of the conspirators. This was partially due to the fact that Speidel on this day was totally occupied with his duties as Chief of Staff of the Army Group, for crucial battles were being fought near Caen and St Lô. Partially it was attributable to his circumspection and caution. He practically left it to Stülp-nagel and Hofacker to deal with Kluge. In front of the uninitiated he acted the role of the passive observer. Fundamentally he had fulfilled his function within the conspiracy during the planning of the coup, namely attempting to persuade Rommel and making contacts for the conspiracy in the west. His caution, though, did not save him from arrest and interrogation by the Gestapo after his name had been mentioned by some conspirators already detained. Hitler himself ordered his arrest. However, the Army Court of Honour refused to expel him from the Army, although Keitel stressed that the Führer was convinced of Speidel's guilt. Thus he was spared public prosecution. But until the end of the war he was dragged from prison to confinement in a fortress. Ultimately, before the ss were able to liquidate him and other prominent detainees, he was freed by Allied troops in Bavaria.

After the war, when Speidel had become one of the highest ranking generals of the new *Bundeswehr* and a NATO commander, the question arose – certainly not without an ulterior motive – how it was that Speidel as one of the chief conspirators managed to save himself? Insinuations were made that he achieved this by incriminating Rommel during interrogation. Rommel's and Speidel's documents, as well as those of the Gestapo interrogation, had obviously become lost or had been destroyed. Subsequent evidence by a former Gestapo official contradicts the fact that, during deliberations by the Court of Honour, several generals voiced their suspicion that incriminating statements made by the Chief of the ss Reich Security Head Office, Kaltenbrunner, could possibly be Gestapo forgeries. Moreover Colonel-General Guderian, amongst others, vehemently pleaded in Speidel's favour. In a letter to Hitler from military hospital Rommel emphatically insisted on Speidel's innocence and reminded the Führer that he personally had awarded him the Knight's Cross at his headquarters.

Speidel himself assured his critics that he had a clear conscience. In the absence of reliable source material his statements must be accepted as being as valid as those of his critics.[37] But it cannot be denied that from 1943 at the latest he was working against the régime and later in France played a decisive role during the preparations for the coup.

Witzleben, Stülpnagel and Speidel embodied three generations of officers of the old Army. Their lives were shaped by radical political and social changes, especially by grave political and moral challenges. They were 'soldiers of the downfall', their destinies inevitably linked to the end of an era of Prussian-German military history. Witzleben's and Stülpnagel's tragic deaths on the gallows symbolize this ultra-personal fate in a moving way. They were also 'soldiers in opposition' and as such they reacted to the challenge of a detestable system in an impressively humane manner, a system which they served, and their links with which they ultimately severed, only to pay a high price for so doing.

NOTES

1 Hans Bernd Gisevius, *Bis zum bitteren Ende* ('To the Bitter End') Zürich, 1946, 2 vols, vol. II, p. 143.

2 Reiner Pommerin, 'Erwin von Witzleben', in Rudolf Lill and H. Oberreuther (eds), *20.Juli – Portraits des Widerstandes* ('20 July – Portraits of the Resistance'), Düsseldorf and Vienna, 1984, p. 355.

3 *Ibid.*

4 Notes of 30.7.1934, printed in Klaus-Jürgen Müller, *General Ludwig Beck, Studien und Dokumente zur politisch-militärischen Vorstellungswelt und Tätigkeit des Generall stabschefs des deutschen Heeres 1933–1938* ('General Ludwig Beck, Studies and documents of the political-military conception and activities of the Chief of General Staff of the German Army 1933–1938'), Boppard, 1980 (= Papers of the Federal Archives, vol. 30), p. 358.

5 Letter from Secretary of State von Bülow to Foreign Minister von Neurath of 16 August 1934, *Akten zur Deutschen Auswartigen Politik (ADAP)* ('Documents German Foreign Policy'), Series C, vol. III/1, Document 162.

6 Notes Colonel i.G von Stülpnagel (Commander T3) of September 1934, printed in Müller, *General Beck*, p. 371.

7 Notes Colonel i.G. von Stülpnagel (Commander T3) on the military-political situation of 11.4.1935, printed in Müller, *General Beck*, p. 434–6.

8 Letter from Major-General von Stülpnagel to General of Artillery Beck of 30.12.1936: literary bequest Beck, Federal Archives–Military Archives NL 08-28/2, extracts quoted in Klaus-Jürgen Müller, *Das Heer und Hitler. Armee und National-sozialistisches Regime 1933–1940* ('The Army and Hitler. Army and the National-Socialist Regime 1933–1940'), Stuttgart, 1968, 2nd ed. 1989, p. 232.

9 Notes Major (retd) Holtzmann of 17.11.1938, printed in Müller, *General Beck*, pp. 579–82.

10 Notes Colonel General (retd) Halder (Interview) of 22.3.1968 printed in

Heidemarie Countess Schall-Riaucour, *Aufstand und Gehorsam. Leben und Wirken von Generaloberst Franz Halder, Generalstabschef 1938–1942* ('Rebellion and Loyalty. The Life and Work of Colonel General Franz Halder, Chief of General Staff 1938–1942'), Wiesbaden, 1927, p. 230.

11 Hjalmar Schacht, *75 Jahre meines Lebens* ('Hjalmar Schacht, 75 Years of my Life'), Munich, 1953, p. 491.

12 Ulrich von Hassel, *Vom andern Deutschland. Aus den nachgelassenen Tagebüchern 1938–1944* ('The other Germany. From his diaries 1938–1944'), 2nd edn, Zürich and Freiburg, 1946, p. 18, and Gerhard Ritter, *Carl Goerdeler und die deutsche Widerstandsbewegung* ('Carl Goerdeler and the German Resistance Movement'), Stuttgart, 1955, p. 198 (Letter of 11.10.1938).

13 Quoted from Schall-Riaucour, *Halder*, p. 266 and Müller, *Heer und Hitler*, p. 494 (Letter from Halder of 10.11.1965 and interview of 14.4.1967).

14 Letter from Colonel General von Leeb to Commander in Chief of the Army of 31.10.1939, printed in *Generalfeldmarschall Wilhelm Ritter von Leeb. Tagebuchaufzeichnungen und Lagebeurteilungen aus zwei Weltkriegen, aus dem Nachlass Herausgegeben und mit einem Lebensabriss versehen von Georg Meyer* ('Field-Marshal Wilhelm Ritter von Leeb. Diary notes and strategic assessments from two world wars, published posthumously together with a brief outline of his life by Georg Meyer'), Stuttgart, 1976, p. 472.

15 Quoted in Pommerin, *Witzleben*, p. 395.

16 Hassell, *Diaries*, p. 220.

17 Hans Speidel, *Aus unserer Zeit. Erinnerungen* ('Our generations. Reminiscences'), Berlin, Frankfurt-am-Maine, Vienna, 1977, p. 110.

18 Ernst Jünger, *Strahlungen, Das Erste Pariser Tagebuch* ('Vibrations, The First Paris Diary'), Munich, 1964, p. 72 (entry of 13.11.41).

19 Speidel, *Erinnerungen*, p. 153.

20 Helmut Krausnick and H. H. Wilhelm, *Die Truppe des Weltanschauungskrieges. Die Einsatzgruppen der Sicherheitspolizei und des SD 1938–1942* ('The army of the war of ideologies. Special Units of the security police and the SD 1938–1942'), Stuttgart, 1981, p. 220.

21 See the assessment in Manfred Messerschmidt, *Motivationen der national-konservativen Opposition und des militärischen Widerstandes seit dem Frankreich-Feldzug* ('Motivations of the national-conservative opposition and the military resistance since the campaign against France') in Klaus-Jürgen Müller (ed.), *Der deutsche Widerstand 1933–1945* ('The German resistance 1933–1945'), Paderborn, 1986, pp. 70–1, as well as in Krausnick-Wilhelm, *Truppe des Weltanschauungskrieges*, p. 218. Krausnick, *op. cit.*, p. 220, in this context points out a memo by Stülpnagel from the year 1935 in which he discovered anti-semitic formulae and the equation of Jews and Bolsheviks (as promulgated by the National-Socialists).

22 Order from AOK 17 of 30.7.1941: extracts printed in: Krausnick-Wilhelm, *Truppe des Weltanschauungskrieges*, pp. 218–19.

23 See the formulation by Hans Umbreit, *Der Militärbefehlshaber in Frankreich 1940–1944* ('The Military Governor of France 1940–1944'), Boppard, 1968 (= Militärgeschichtliche Studien, vol. 7) (= Studies on military history, vol. 7), p. 114.

24 Ernst Jünger, *Strahlungen II, Das Zweite Pariser Tagebuch* ('Vibrations II, The

Second Paris Diary'), Munich, 1965 (dtv [Deutscher Taschenbuchverlag]) 282, p. 268 (entry of 31.5.1944).

25 Hans Speidel, *Invasion 1944. Ein Beitrag zu Rommels und des Reiches Schicksal* ('Invasion 1944. A contribution to the fate of Rommel and that of the Reich'), Frankfurt am Main, Berlin, Vienna, 1979 (Ullsteinbuch 33006), p. 57. Speidel characterizes Stülpnagel as 'a chivalric person of highly operative and tactical skills ... outstanding military ability and sound judgment are harmoniously complemented by a refined sense for moderation. He was educated in the humanities and had diplomatic skill.'

26 Lecture by Joachim von Stülpnagel on 5 November 1985 to the Regimental Reunion of Infantry Regiment 67 (manuscript in possession of the author). Compare also the passage from a letter the former army adjutant of the 17th Army, Count von Pilati, wrote to Stülpnagel's widow in 1946, in which he says: 'Already from January 1941 onwards when working in close collaboration with your husband (at army headquarters in Zakopana) my eyes were opened and the logic of all NS crimes committed during peacetime and, to an increasing degree, during the first years of the war was explained to me.'

27 Hassell, *Tagebücher*, p. 287.

28 See Messerschmidt, *Motivationen*, p. 67.

29 Wilhelm Ritter von Schramm, *Der 20. Juli in Paris* ('The 20th July in Paris'), Bad Wörishofen, 1953, p. 35 (Zitat des einstigen Kriegsverwaltungstrates beim Militärbefehlshaber Freiherr von Teuchert) (Quotation by the former war administration adviser to the Military Commander Baron von Teuchert).

30 *Die kontroversen Positionen* ('The controversial positions'); W. Ose, 'Rommel', in Lill and Oberreuther, *Portraits des Widerstandes*; David Irving, *The Trail of the Fox. The Life of Fieldmarshal Erwin Rommel*, London, 1977; c.f. also the different versions of Speidel in *Invasion 1944* and *Erinnerungen*.

31 Statement by General Geyr von Schweppenburg to the author and in an unpublished essay for the Research Institute of Military History in Freiburg i.Br. Cf. Irving, *Trail of the Fox*, p. 407.

32 Quoted after Irving, *Trail of the Fox*, p. 348.

33 *Ibid.*, p. 377.

34 A detailed representation of the events in Paris by Ritter von Schramm, *Der 20. Juli in Paris, Teil II*; Speidel, *Erinnerungen*, Ch. 8.

35 Printed in *Spiegelbild einer Verschwörung. Geheime Dokumente aus dem ehemaligen Reichssicherheitshauptamt* ('Reflected image of a conspiracy. Confidential documents from the former Security Headquarters of the Reich'), edited by Hans Adolf Jacobsen, Stuttgart, 1984, vol. I, pp. 14–15.

36 Detailed report of the events at Bendlerstrasse/Berlin by a surviving chief protagonist: H. B. Gisevius, *Bis zum bitteren Ende*, vol. II, pp. 308–58; cf. also the investigation reports in *Spiegelbild einer Vershwörung*, passim. Good synthesis in Peter Hoffmann, *Widerstand-Staatsstreich-Attentat. Der Kampf der Opposition gegen Hitler* ('Resistance-Coup-Assassination. The Fight by the Opposition against Hitler'), 3rd edn, Munich, 1979, Chs XI and XII.

37 Speidel's version: *Erinnerungen*, Ch. 9; massive criticism in Irving, *Trail of the Fox*, pp. 387–411. P. Hoffmann, *Widerstand*, p. 785, footnote 140 replies to Irving's

criticism that he 'contradicts himself . . . in the vital points' by his source material quoted.

CHRONOLOGY: ERWIN VON WITZLEBEN

1881, December 4	Born in Breslau
1891	Joined cadet corps
1901, March 22	Second Lieutenant in 7th Grenadier Regiment König Wilhelm I (2nd West Prussian) in Liegnitz
1914	Company leader in 6th Reserve Infantry Regiment
1916	Commander 2nd Battalion of 6th Reserve Infantry Regiment
1917	Ia, 108th Infantry Division
1918	Ia, 121th Infantry Division
1919	Company commander in 8th Infantry Regiment in Frankfurt an der Oder
1919	Captain
1923, April 1	Major, General Staff 4th Division, Dresden
1927	Staff of Infantry Leader III in Potsdam
1929, January 1	Lieutenant-Colonel
1928-9	Commander 2nd Battalion 6th Infantry Regiment
1930	Chief of Staff of *Wehrkreis* VI (6th division) in Münster
1931, April 1	Colonel and Commander of 8th Infantry Regiment in Frankfurt an der Oder
1933, March 1	Infantry Leader VI in Hanover
1934, February 1	Major-General and Commander of 3rd Division and Commander at *Wehrkreis* III, Berlin
1934, October 1	Lieutenant-General
1936, October 1	General of Infantry
1938, November 10	Commander-in-Chief of 2nd Army Group in Frankfurt am Main
1939, September 1	Commander of 1st Army on the Western Front
1939, November 1	Colonel-General
1940, July 19	Field-Marshal
1940 October 26	Commander-in-Chief of Army Group D in France
1941, May 1	Commander-in-Chief West, in Paris
1942, March 15	Transfer to Führer-reserve
1944, August 4	Expelled from the Army by the so-called 'Court of Honour'
1944, August 8	Executed

CHRONOLOGY: CARL-HEINRICH VON STÜLPNAGEL

1886, January 2	Born in Berlin. Grew up in Frankfurt am Main, passed his Abitur at Lessing gymnasium

1904	Summer term reading law at University of Geneva
1904, October 1	Joined 115th Regiment 1st Grand-Ducal Hessian infantry (Life Guards) in Darmstadt
1906, January 27	Second Lieutenant (commissioned from 21 July 1904)
First World War	Captain in General Staff
1924, March 1	Captain and company commander in 3rd Infantry Regiment in Deutsch-Eylau
1925, January 1	Major
1928, June 1	Commander of 2nd battalion 5th Infantry Regiment in Neuruppin
1930, February 1	Lieutenant-Colonel
1932, December 1	Colonel
1931–2	Delegated to revise Army regulations for troop command
1933, March 1– October 1937	Head of 'Foreign Armies' branch of the *Truppenamt*/General Staff of the Army
1935, October 1	Major-General
1936, October 6	Commander of the 30th Infantry Division in Lübeck
1937, October 1	Lieutenant-General
1938, February 5	Senior Quartermaster II (Training) in the General Staff of the Army
1938, August 27	Senior Quartermaster I and Deputy Chief of General Staff of the Army
1939, April 20	General of Infantry
1940, May 30–June 20	General Commanding 2nd Army Corps. Participation in breakthrough of Weygand line under 4th Army (von Kluge)
1940, June 21–1941, February 15	Chairman of German armistice commission in Wiesbaden
1941, February 15– November 25	Commander of 17th Army on the Eastern Front (Army Group South) (fell ill on 9 October 1941)
1942, February 13– 1944, July 20	Military Governor of France
1944, August 30	Executed

CHRONOLOGY: HANS SPEIDEL

1897, October 28	Born in Metzingen/Württemberg
1914, November 30	After emergency (war), Abitur in Stuttgart, joined 123rd Guard Grenadier Regiment König Karl von Württemberg
1915, November 19	Second Lieutenant, platoon commander, Battle of the Argonnes
1916	Company commander, Battle of the Somme
end of 1916	Adjutant to 2nd battalion, 123rd Guard Grenadier Regiment
1918	Regimental adjutant, Guard Grenadier Regiment

1919	ADC to Infantry Leader 13 in Stuttgart
1919	Started course at Technical University, Stuttgart (subjects: History, Germanic studies, Aesthetics)
1920–22	Training as 'leader assistant' (camouflaged General Staff training course)
1922–9	Platoon Commander 13th Infantry Regiment in Ludwigsburg
1929–30	Continuation of 'leader assistant' training (3rd year), Berlin
1930	Delegated to France on linguistics course
1930, October 1	General Staff officer and collaborator in section 'Western Europe' of 'Foreign Armies' branch of *Truppenamt*/General Staff of the Army
1933, October 1–1935, October 1	Assistant to military attaché in Paris
1936, October 1	Company Commander of 8th (machine-gun) company in 56th Infantry Regiment in Ulm
1937, October 1	Ia of 33rd Infantry Division in Mannheim and Major in the General Staff
1939, January 1	Lieutenant-Colonel in the General Staff
1939, October 1	Ia in the headquarters staff of 9th Army Corps on the West Wall
1940, May 10	Campaign in France under 6th Army (von Reichenau)
1940, May 31	Delegated to Staff of Army Group B (von Bock) with special assignment of planning attack on, and occupation of, Paris
1940, June 15	Chief of Staff to military governor of Paris
1940, August 1	Chief of General Staff to military governor of France in Paris
1941, February 1	Colonel in General Staff
1942, March 25	Chief of Staff of 5th Army Corps on the Eastern Front
1943, January 1	Major-General
1943, January 5	Chief of Staff to German general at the headquarters of the Italian 8th Army
1943, February 5	Chief of Staff at army-unit Lanz/Kempf on the Eastern Front (Army Group South)
1943, August 15	Chief of Staff at headquarters of 8th (German) Army on the Eastern Front
1944, January 1	Lieutenant-General
1944, April 15	Chief of Staff of Army Group B (Field-Marshal Rommel) in France
1944, September 7–1945, April 29	Gestapo detention in fortress (freed by French troops of Corps Béthouart)
1946–7	Studies of history of war for History Division of US Army
mid-1948	Adviser for defence policies to Bavarian Premier

end 1948	Adviser for defence policies to Federal Chancellor and Federal Minister Wildermuth
February 1949 onwards	Lecturer at University of Tübingen (modern history in the 'Studium Generale' syllabus at Leibniz College)
1951, January 1	Military expert (in collaboration with General Heusinger) at administrative office Blank (forerunner of Federal Ministry of Defence)
1951, October 1	Military leader of German EVG (European Defence Community) Delegation in Paris
1954, October 22	German military negotiator for German entry into NATO
1955, November 10	Lieutenant-General of *Bundeswehr*
1955, November 22	Chief of Department for Combined Forces at Federal Ministry of Defence in Bonn
1957, April 2	Commander-in-Chief of NATO Land Forces in Central Europe (ComLandCent) at Fontainebleau
1957, April 5	General (four stars) of *Bundeswehr*
1963, September 30	Resignation as ComLandCent upon pressure from General de Gaulle
1963	Special adviser to Federal Government in matters of Atlantic defence
1987	Died

PART II

The Desk Generals

BRAUCHITSCH

3

BRAUCHITSCH

Field-Marshal Walter von Brauchitsch

BRIAN BOND

As Commander-in-Chief of the German Army during the period of its most spectacular victories between 1939 and 1941, Brauchitsch – though less important than Halder – made a substantial contribution to the direction of operations for which he was awarded a field-marshal's baton. This aspect of his career has received a few plaudits from historians, but the great majority of references criticize him for his vacillating and ineffectual opposition to Hitler both on purely professional matters and on wider political and moral issues. This critical verdict is unlikely to be overturned because Brauchitsch, though a more interesting and attractive personality than most of his peers, lacked the strength of character and moral commitment even to be considered for the role of tragic hero.

Walter von Brauchitsch was born in Berlin in 1881 into an upper-class family with a long tradition of unquestioning service to the Prussian state. In 1900 he was commissioned into the élite 3rd Guards Infantry Regiment and had already shown professional promise before 1914 by gaining entry to the War Academy and serving on the General Staff in Berlin. In the First World War he distinguished himself as a staff officer and won the high decoration of the Hohenzollern House Order, as well as the Iron Cross, first class.

Although the General Staff was abolished under the terms of the Treaty of Versailles, Brauchitsch continued to serve in its substitute, the *Truppenamt*, where as head of the Training Department from 1922 to 1925 he proved himself to be in the vanguard of military progress by organizing manoeuvres to test the possibilities of using motorized troops in conjunction with aircraft.

Thereafter he made steady progress towards the highest positions in the Army, through such appointments as Chief of Staff to *Wehrkreis* VI (1927), Inspector of Artillery (1932), Commander of *Wehrkreis* I in East Prussia in 1933, Commander of the 1st Army Corps in 1935, and of Army Group 4, Leipzig, in 1937.

Brauchitsch was not a politically oriented officer, but rather a strict professional soldier in the Schlieffen mould. He admired Hitler personally, but detested many aspects of Nazism, including the Party's interference with the role of the established churches in the Army. Unfortunately for Brauchitsch his was not a forceful, dominating personality; indeed he was somewhat reserved, inhibited and sensitive. These traits, and the circumstances in which he accepted the post of Commander-in-Chief, proved to be fatal handicaps in his relationship with the Führer.

Brauchitsch was a man of elegant appearance and always dignified in his bearing. In Manstein's words:

> He was correct, courteous and even charming; although this charm did not leave one with an impression of inner warmth. Just as he lacked the aggressiveness that commands an opponent's respect ... so did he fail to impress one as a forceful productive personality. The general effect was one of coolness and reserve.[1]

Manstein also noted that Brauchitsch 'preferred to have decisions suggested to him rather than to take and impose them on his own initiative'. Like his first Chief of Staff, Beck, Brauchitsch was widely read in fields outside his profession, and allegedly shocked his fellow generals by including among his hobbies 'Study of the economic and political questions of the day'! In the light of his performance as Commander-in-Chief this has an ironic ring. Before his promotion to the highest office he had not been noted for pro–Nazi sympathies; indeed he was apt to sneer at Party enthusiasts, saying of young officers who greeted him with the Nazi salute that he did not want to run the risk of having his eyes poked out.[2]

Brauchitsch's unhappy private life undoubtedly played an important part in his otherwise puzzling conduct over the Fritsch affair when in January 1938 Fritsch was suspended from duty and summoned to be interrogated by the Gestapo on a trumped-up charge of homosexual conduct; namely his willingness to enter into negotiations with Hitler as a possible successor before Fritsch was tried, and without prior consultation with senior colleagues such as Beck. Brauchitsch had been separated from his wife for five years and had to support her and four children without private financial resources. He wished to secure a divorce in order to marry a lady of dubious background, Charlotte Schmidt, who was described as a '200 per cent Nazi', but his wife insisted on a financial settlement well beyond his means. Thus he had sought refuge in his work and was to be found in his office at all hours 'working like an ox'.[3]

In a detailed analysis of the negotiations with Hitler fittingly headed 'The Servitude of Brauchitsch', Harold C. Deutsch proves that Brauchitsch accepted at least 80,000 Reichmarks directly and in person from Hitler's personal Chancellery. This placed him in a treble bind: he had received what amounted to a bribe from Hitler; his second wife's reputation could be publicized to his disadvantage as had happened to Blomberg over his marriage to a prostitute (as it turned out) with a police record; and henceforth Brauchitsch's second wife never scrupled to undermine his opposition to Hitler by reminding him 'how much we owe to the Führer'.[4]

The political concessions to Nazi Party ideology which Brauchitsch had to make were also significant. Hitler's first choice as Fritsch's successor was probably the openly pro-Nazi Reichenau, but he was unacceptable to the senior generals. Rundstedt had been suggested by Beck but was rejected by Hitler. Göring had already proposed Brauchitsch as a dignified figure without strong political views, and Rundstedt acquiesced. In negotiations lasting several days Brauchitsch agreed to Hitler's conditions that he must be prepared 'to lead the Army closer towards the State and its philosophy' and that, if necessary, he would choose a more suitable Chief of Staff than Beck. On a third condition, that he be prepared to recognize a reorganization of the High Command structure, Brauchitsch asked for time to study the implications.

In effect by accepting the post of Commander-in-Chief before Fritsch had been tried, and without consulting his senior colleagues, Brauchitsch had compromised his position in both personal and professional terms. In acting as he did, Brauchitsch made it virtually impossible for the Army to present a united front to stop Hitler from usurping personal control. Deep personal obligation, combined with a growing sense of vulnerability to pressure and blackmail, go far to explain why this distinguished soldier was henceforth so often to stand before Hitler (in Halder's expression), 'like a little cadet before his commandant'.[5]

Immediately after the confirmation of his appointment as Commander-in-Chief on 4 February 1938, Brauchitsch was confronted with his first important challenge: the impending trial of Fritsch. He was placed in an extremely awkward dilemma. On the one hand his fellow generals (the *Generalität*) expected him to uphold the Army's interest against political interference; and Beck and Canaris kept him fully informed of the opposition's discoveries that Fritsch had been framed by the Gestapo backed by Himmler's ss. On the other hand Hitler made clear his hostility to Fritsch, and Brauchitsch was well aware that months of negotiations lay ahead before his own divorce proceedings were completed and the promised money paid over.

Brauchitsch temporized, promising those who were pressing him to take drastic action against Himmler and the ss that he would do so once the trial had revealed the full iniquities of the Gestapo. However, his position was effectively undermined by Hitler when on 12 March – less than a week before the Fritsch trial was due to conclude – he insisted on the immediate invasion of Austria in order forcibly to bring about the *Anschluss*. Beck and Brauchitsch had opposed this improvised military operation purely on professional grounds of the risk of a wider conflict. In the event much incompetence was revealed, but Hitler achieved a bloodless victory and a further humiliation of OKH (the Army General Staff).

Fritsch could not be found guilty on the ludicrous evidence presented, and Brauchitsch was a member of the court which acquitted him on 17 March. Nevertheless he was effectively ruined, Göring in particular making clear that he was opposed to any form of rehabilitation that might lead to Fritsch's re-employment. Brauchitsch temporized, but refused to undertake any positive action such as confronting Hitler with the blatant injustice his predecessor had suffered. Instead he salved his conscience by doing what he could to ameliorate Fritsch's enforced retirement, for example by placing horses, staff officers and a car at his disposal. The Fritsch crisis revealed Brauchitsch to be lacking in both finesse and determination; he had allowed himself to be deflected by Hitler's henchman, Keitel, and he had failed to act vigorously against the enemy he had derisively called 'this pigsty Himmler'.[6]

Hitler skilfully stilled the last rumblings of the *Generalität*'s disquiet over the Fritsch affair when, in May 1938, he informed Brauchitsch of his intention 'to proceed militarily against Czechoslovakia in the near future'. Shortly afterwards Brauchitsch addressed the Army's senior commanders and, in the absence of Beck, told them that an unavoidable clash with Czechoslovakia was imminent, and in these circumstances he could not contemplate resignation over the treatment of Fritsch. He could only beg those who had thought of resigning to reconsider their decision. Had Beck been present he would surely have disputed the certainty of war over the Sudeten issue, but Brauchitsch's 'bolt from the blue' left the generals in a quandary.[7]

The generals' opposition to war over Czechoslovakia has been summarized in Robert O'Neill's chapter on Beck, for whom it became a life-or-death issue over which he was prepared to resign and to organize a coup against Hitler. Though less committed than his Chief of Staff, Brauchitsch too feared that military intervention in Czechoslovakia would lead to general war. Under pressure from Beck he accordingly called a meeting of the Army's leaders on 4 August, at which he intended to read a speech prepared by Beck, calling for unconditional support for opposition to the Führer's plans. Brauchitsch, however, conducted the conference circumspectly and did not force the issue of unconditional support for a *démarche* to Hitler. He expressed anger at the way OKW (principally Keitel and Jodl) had dropped their plans on his desk without prior consultation, and he read out a dissenting memorandum from Beck without revealing its author. When Brauchitsch solicited the generals' opinions General Adam, responsible for the as yet inadequate defences in the west, strongly supported Beck's line and declared that he (Adam) *was* prepared to confront Hitler – a tacit rebuke to the Commander-in-Chief. Only two generals, Busch and Reichenau, spoke out in favour of unconditional obedience to the Führer, and the latter shortly afterwards undermined the Commander-in-Chief's position by reporting the meeting to Hitler, who demanded Beck's resignation as the ringleader of the opposition to his plans. Brauchitsch defended his Chief of Staff, but was ordered to tell him to stop presenting critical memoranda. By early August Beck had concluded that Brauchitsch would neither force the issue of mass resignation by the generals, nor reorganize the High Command so as to re-assert the Army's autonomy as against OKW acting as a mouthpiece for Hitler. Resentment grew between Beck and Brauchitsch to the extent that weeks before the former's resignation Halder, his deputy, had already replaced him as the real representative of the General Staff.[8]

The Commander-in-Chief remained doubtful about the Führer's political and military judgment, but his power base was extremely weak, particularly as Hitler had been informed of his attempt to rally the generals to oppose his plans against Czechoslovakia. On 3 September 1938, when Brauchitsch made a further representation to Hitler at the Berghof, he was treated to a tirade of personal abuse. Brauchitsch and Halder again discussed with Hitler the dangers facing Germany on 9 September during the Party Rally at Nuremberg, the argument continuing till 4.00 a.m. the following morning. Keitel and Jodl expressed their growing disillusionment with Brauchitsch for repeatedly questioning Hitler's judgment. Still, to his credit, as late as 28 September the Commander-in-Chief begged Keitel to do everything possible to avoid an invasion of Czechoslovakia. The bloodless occupation of the Sudetenland on 1 October thanks to Chamberlain's surrender at the Munich conference seemed to prove Beck and his fellow conspirators wrong, and served to deepen Hitler's contempt for the pusillanimous Army leaders. Brauchitsch almost certainly remained unaware of the fact that, had war broken out and a coup been attempted, he had been selected by the anti-Hitler conspirators to be the nominal interim supreme authority of government until a civilian caretaker administration had been formed. Brauchitsch was shortly to emphasize the gulf between himself and the conspirators, by issuing a general order on 18 December praising the Führer's great gifts and urging the officer corps to be second to none in the purity and strength of its National-Socialist thought.[9]

Brauchitsch emerges with little credit from the Munich crisis. He was a sound judge of the Army's relative unpreparedness, but his political insight was scarcely more acute than Beck's. He has understandably received a bad press from the voluminous publications of the conspirators and their sympathizers. Ulrich von Hassell, for example, repeatedly expresses his exasperation with Brauchitsch, remarking that (he) 'hitches his collar a notch higher and says "I am a soldier; it is my duty to obey"'. But, as Manstein counters, civilians like Hassell

> forget the essential difference between plotting from behind a desk when one is no longer in a position of responsibility ... and committing oneself, as leader of the army, to a *coup d'état* which can imply civil war in peacetime and lead to the victory of one's external enemies in time of war.[10]

Towards the end of March 1939, Hitler hinted to Brauchitsch that he had decided to use force against Poland, and in the following months OKH played the dominant role in drawing up the plans for *Fall Weiss* (an attack on Poland). Few serving officers were opposed to war with the traditional enemy, Poland, and the Commander-in-Chief was not among them – though his attitude was ambivalent. Indeed the *Generalität* was deflated after its disastrous miscalculation over Czechoslovakia, and its leaders realized that they had little or no influence with Hitler. Beck made a desperate appeal to Brauchitsch to join in the planning for a military putsch to stop Hitler going to war, but the Commander-in-Chief simply ignored his letter. Even Halder rejected a personal appeal from Beck, arguing that the Führer must be supported in his campaign for Danzig, and that Britain would not go to war for such a cause. There would be time to consider deposing Hitler *after* the Polish question had been solved.[11]

During the short, victorious campaign in Poland, Hitler made virtually no attempt to interfere with the conduct of operations, leaving Brauchitsch and Halder free to get on with their own business. Keitel noted at Nuremberg that Hitler had only occasional meetings with Brauchitsch during this campaign, at which he made suggestions but 'never committed himself so far as to give an order'. Halder effectively ran the campaign with virtually no interference or guidance from Hitler, and he never once spoke on the telephone to Hitler, Keitel or Jodl.[12]

In view of the controversy over the 'Commissar Order' and the other directives which deeply involved the Army in the war of barbarity on the Eastern Front in 1941, it is important to establish that Brauchitsch and OKH were all well aware of the SS's criminal activities in Poland from September 1939 onwards.[13] Indeed the Quartermaster-General had drawn up an agreement with Heydrich *before* the campaign, and Brauchitsch was fully aware of the fact. On 7 September 1939 Hitler met Brauchitsch in his private railway coach for two hours' discussion on the political future of Poland. He instructed the Army not to interfere with SS operations. A subsequent discussion between Canaris and Keitel made it clear that Brauchitsch had been briefed on the planned executions of Polish clergy and nobility and was only concerned to safeguard the *Wehrmacht*'s reputation. On 20 September Hitler told Brauchitsch at Zoppot that he favoured the deportation but not the elimination of the Polish Jews. Two days later when he met Heydrich, Brauchitsch stipulated only that the expulsion operation must not interfere with the Army's movements. Brauchitsch issued the instruction to his field commanders: 'The police task forces have been commanded and directed by the Führer to perform certain ethnographical tasks in the occupied territory.' Military commanders were not to interfere and could not be held responsible. Furthermore Brauchitsch was made well aware of General Blaskowitz's courageous protests against the activities of SS murder gangs, but so far from backing him and other field commanders who made objections, the Commander-in-Chief actually helped to downplay and stifle their grievances. As Colonel Seaton concludes:

> It was in Poland that the generals and the officers and other ranks of the German Army were brought face to face with the stark reality of Hitler's racial policies, for the brutalities of the round-ups were there for all to see.... Germany's path to national and moral degeneration and destruction began in Poland.[14]

Although the eclipse of OKH as the authority responsible for military policy on land was not finally complete until Hitler retired Brauchitsch in December 1941 and took over direct command of the Army, it had already lost control of grand strategic matters before the Polish campaign but at least retained its authority in the operational sphere.

After its brilliant success in Poland, OKH assumed that Hitler would terminate the war in the west by a negotiated settlement like that at Munich. Brauchitsch and his chief staff officers were planning for an indefinite defensive on the Western Front and, like the majority of the field commanders, had no confidence that the Army could achieve a decisive victory against France and Britain.

Yet on 27 September 1939 Hitler dumbfounded and dismayed his senior commanders when, without previously consulting Brauchitsch, he informed the three service Commanders-in-Chief of his decision to take the offensive in the west that autumn, and in so doing to violate the neutrality of Holland, Belgium and Luxemburg. This decision was embodied in Hitler's memorandum of 9 October 1939, which was issued as a directive through OKW.

This constituted a remarkable infringement of OKH's professional responsibilities especially, as General Walter Warlimont later admitted, as OKW's staff was simply incapable of planning in detail a major land campaign at this time. In other words, Hitler, working through OKW, had decided not only what operations the Army should undertake, but also when and how they should be conducted. Originally Hitler fixed 15 October as the deadline, and also laid down *how* the offensive was to be conducted; namely by by-passing the Maginot Line by way of the Low Countries. The Commander-in-Chief of the Army had suffered a humiliating demotion in status from being – at least notionally – a senior military adviser to the head of state to a subordinate bureaucrat obliged to draw up a plan of campaign in which he had no confidence.[15]

Why did Brauchitsch bow to this *fait accompli*? Probably he realized the futility of immediate opposition but hoped, after a show of good will, to talk Hitler out of his plan. Moreover, in view of the need to withdraw and re-equip formations still in Poland, the timetable set by Hitler was optimistic and even reckless, so Brauchitsch may have counted on bad weather – a more effective argument than reasoning with Hitler as even the pro-Nazi but militarily realistic Reichenau soon discovered – to delay the offensive until the following spring. Such a delay would provide further opportunities to end the war by a political compromise.

Halder's immediate reaction as Chief of the General Staff to Hitler's shock announcement on 27 September was that he must resign. Brauchitsch, allegedly with tears in his eyes, successfully pleaded with him to stay, saying: 'I cannot do without you. How am I to contend with this man without your help?' Henceforth, Brauchitsch promised, Halder would be in complete charge of operations and the two would stay or resign together. Brauchitsch kept his word and when he was dismissed in 1941 he released Halder from his pledge and entreated him to stay on.[16]

On 19 October OKH issued its first hasty directive for the western offensive, *Fall Gelb* (Plan Yellow). This envisaged the main thrust being driven through Belgium by seventy-five divisions under Army Group B, with the aim of destroying the bulk of the British and French forces in Belgium and north-eastern France. Army Group A would play a subsidiary supporting role to the south. This was a not very imaginative variant of the Schlieffen Plan executed in 1914, and it is hard to see how it could have produced the decisive results actually achieved by the drastically revised 'Manstein Plan' (*Sichelschnitt*) of May 1940. One can only speculate that Brauchitsch and Halder had not applied themselves wholeheartedly to an operation in which they lacked confidence: certainly they conveyed their distaste for the task by leaving it to Keitel to read out the details to Hitler.

While Halder was implicated in the conspiracies against Hitler during the autumn of 1939, Brauchitsch remained non-committal, although he was to some extent aware of what was going on. If Hitler knew of this plotting, as seems possible, it would have added to the contempt he felt for the Army's leaders' pessimism and defeatism. Hitler's scorn is epitomized by the remarks he made to a group of Luftwaffe officers before the start of a conference that autumn: 'Here comes my Coward Number One,' he said as Brauchitsch entered the room, and added, 'Number Two!' when Halder joined him.[17]

With a new deadline for the western offensive set for 12 November 1939, Brauchitsch secured an audience with Hitler at noon on 5 November to impress on the Führer the Army's unreadiness and unwillingness to undertake this risky operation. In this mission Brauchitsch had the unanimous support of the senior commanders on the Western Front. Irving describes this as 'one of the strangest encounters in the history of their uncomfortable partnership'. With incredible ineptitude Brauchitsch chose to stress the Army's poor discipline and lack of fighting spirit. In Poland, he said, the infantry had shown little verve in attack and at times the NCOs and officers had lost control. He even spoke of 'mutinies' in some units, and referred to acts of drunkenness and indiscipline reminiscent of the ugly scenes towards the end of World War I. This touched a raw nerve and Hitler exploded into one of his characteristic rages. Hitler snatched Brauchitsch's memorandum and tossed it into his safe before submitting the unhappy general to a harangue for condemning his entire army on the strength of a few incidents. Later that day Hitler referred to the memorandum as a pack of lies, and dictated a note for Brauchitsch's dismissal, only to be talked out of this drastic step by Keitel on the grounds that there was no suitable successor for the compliant Commander-in-Chief, whose long family tradition of state service would make it impossible for him to rebel.[18] But for the time being the western offensive was postponed, ostensibly due to unfavourable weather.

On 23 November, Hitler addressed the principal *Wehrmacht* leaders at the Reich Chancellery and used the occasion for a devastating denunciation of the Army generals who doubted his determination and ability to launch a decisive offensive in the west. Speaking with 'unexcelled vehemence, brutality and cynicism', the gist of his harangue was that the German soldier was the best in the world and must not be let down by pusillanimous leaders. Hitler made it clear he would destroy anyone who opposed him. To rub in the Army's humiliation he called back Brauchitsch and Halder for another lecture denouncing 'the Spirit of Zossen' (the location of OKH headquarters). The generals were reduced to a state of 'appalled intimidation'. Brauchitsch offered his resignation but it was contemptuously brushed aside.[19] Henceforth Halder never seriously committed himself to the anti-Hitler conspiracy. Open resistance to Hitler's plans for a western offensive collapsed that day, and though the opposition continued to conspire in secret for a takeover, their prospects of success had been severely shaken by the demoralization of the Army leaders.

What the generals' open resistance had failed to achieve was none the less accomplished by an unusually severe winter, which caused the execution of Plan Yellow to be postponed at least a dozen times. From the early months of 1940 the Army's leaders became increasingly enthusiastic about the prospects of success in the west as training, equipment and, above all, the operational plans were improved. Brauchitsch in particular immersed himself in the detailed work of preparing the Army for war as an escape from the wider issues over which he had failed to make any impression on Hitler, or salvage any genuine independence for OKH against the usurpation of its functions by OKW. But Halder had some non-committal contacts with civilian and military opposition groups, and early in April 1940 conveyed to Brauchitsch a version of the 'X' report, that is, the brief and mysterious document obtained from the Vatican which outlined the terms on which Britain would negotiate peace with a post-Hitler government. Halder himself was sceptical about the authenticity of the document, but felt it his duty to show it to Brauchitsch. The latter studied the document overnight and next morning told his Chief of Staff:

> You should not have shown this to me. What we face here is pure national treason.... We are at war. That one in time of peace establishes contact with a foreign power may be considered. In war this is impossible for a soldier.[20]

He added that since this was a clash between different philosophies of life, the removal of Hitler would be useless. Brauchitsch wanted to have the man who had handed over the document arrested, but Halder deflected him by saying, 'If there is anyone to be arrested then please arrest me.' Brauchitsch never betrayed the conspirators, but nor did he give them any help or encouragement.[21]

As the season for the spring offensive drew near, Brauchitsch remained doubtful about the chances of success. On 8 March 1940 Ulrich von Hassell, one of the leading civilian conspirators, was told by Brauchitsch's cousin that 'At heart he was uncertain and very troubled; if he could be relieved of the responsibility for taking action he would "tolerate" it.' A few days later von Hassell noted in his diary that the Commander-in-Chief 'is being treated more and more badly and pushed into the background'. He gave the conspirators who tried to enlist his intervention against the 'black pirates' (the ss) the impression of an inwardly broken man.[22]

Nevertheless when Admiral Raeder proposed the invasion of Denmark and Norway, Brauchitsch and Halder were appalled at the risks involved, and adamantly refused to allow OKH to develop the plans. Quite possibly they hoped Hitler would attempt this venture and meet with disaster, thus opening the way for the conspirators to carry out a coup. In the event OKH was completely by-passed, Hitler for the first time taking direct responsibility for a campaign, assisted by the OKW Operations Staff and a small improvised Corps Headquarters under General von Falkenhorst. This unorthodox method of organizing a campaign caused Halder to note in exasperation: 'Not a single word passed between the Führer and the Commander-in-Chief of the Army on this subject. Get that on the record for the war historians.'[23]

Hitler's first serious intervention in the conduct of operations might well have resulted in the catastrophe needed by the conspirators, since he wanted to evacuate Narvik only a few days after it had been captured. Warlimont, who observed the Führer closely in the critical phase of operations, commented on his 'truly terrifying weakness of character'. Hitler sat hunched on a chair in a corner of the Reich Chancellery, 'unnoticed and staring in front of him, a picture of brooding gloom'. Unfortunately Jodl remained cool and decisive at OKW, and the combination of competent commanders and troops in the field brought off a remarkable victory.[24] Henceforth Hitler was encouraged to interfere in operational matters even down to the tactical level.

Unlike some of the field commanders such as Reichenau and Fromm (commander of the Replacement Army), Brauchitsch and Halder remained sceptical of victory in the west up to the very moment the offensive was launched.[25] Opinions differ as to how long and how vehemently OKH resisted the adoption of the 'Manstein Plan' in February 1940, but this was certainly one of Hitler's more inspired interventions in the professional military sphere. In other aspects, such as securing the Maas and Albert Canal bridges, Hitler's obsessional interventions in favour of the SS and the Luftwaffe against the General Staff only served to increase friction and confusion.

During the brilliant six-week campaign in the west, Brauchitsch was constantly on the move by air or road, doing his utmost to maintain personal contact with the leading troops. Halder was left in charge of operations and did a superb job, taking the right direction on several occasions when Hitler's nerve failed. On the approach to the Channel coast, for example, Halder felt that Hitler and OKW grossly exaggerated the danger of the panzer forces' open southern flank, and he and Brauchitsch vainly opposed the pause ordered on 17 May. In the case of the more critical halt before the Dunkirk perimeter on 25 May, Hitler, with the support of Rundstedt, interfered directly with OKH's direction of the campaign.[26] Brauchitsch and Halder lacked the prestige and determination to restrain Hitler, but they did not offer their resignations. Brauchitsch was included among the twelve field-marshals created on 19 July 1940 and, in Manstein's opinion, he had fully earned his baton.[27]

In contrast to their reactions to the projected campaigns in Scandinavia and France, Brauchitsch and Halder showed unusual optimism and enthusiasm for the invasion of southern England (Operation *Sealion*), which Hitler ordered them to prepare on 13 July. It was the failure of the Luftwaffe to win command of the air over south-eastern England, and Raeder's pessimism over invasion projects, that caused Hitler to postpone, and in reality to abandon, the enterprise. Meanwhile Brauchitsch and Halder discussed a possible Mediterranean strategy in support of their Italian ally for the capture of Gibraltar, Egypt and Palestine but did not express any strong opinions about it. In any case, Hitler displayed no real interest in any strategic objectives in the Mediterranean.[28]

As early as 13 July 1940 Halder noted after a conference with Hitler that the Führer was inclined to coerce Britain into capitulation by depriving her of her only hope of support in Europe – the Soviet Union – by knocking out the latter that autumn. This wildly optimistic scheme was encouraged by the erroneous intelligence that Russia had only between 50 and 75 good divisions, though more realistic estimates were soon substituted.

Since this was the momentous decision which, retrospectively, was seen to have cost Germany the war, there has understandably been considerable interest as to who originated this impetuous project.[29] In his excellent study *German Strategy Against Russia 1939–1941*, and in his essay in *Hitler's Generals* (see p. 101) on Halder, Barry Leach* points out that the Chief of Staff himself initiated preliminary operational plans against Russia in June 1940 on the basis of his own estimate of the political situation, namely that in the long term Soviet intentions towards Germany were bound to be aggressive and should therefore be pre-empted by a decisive German offensive in 1940. More surprising than Halder's initiative, it seems clear that Brauchitsch also anticipated Hitler's thinking by advocating a preventive war against Russia that summer.[30] This remarkable optimism on the part of Halder and Brauchitsch, that Russia could be defeated in a swift autumn campaign, was based on grossly inaccurate estimates of Russian strengths and capabilities. By the end of July 1940 Hitler had decided that the invasion of Russia should not be launched until May 1941. Halder and Brauchitsch acquiesced. When they discussed the project on 30 July 1940 Halder noted 'we should do better to keep friendship with Russia. . . . We could hit the English decisively in the Mediterranean, drive them out of Asia.' The following day Hitler accepted the arguments of Keitel and Jodl that there was no time to defeat Russia in 1940 because five months' campaigning would be necessary and 'a stand-still in winter would be serious'. He concluded that Russia must be dealt with in spring 1941. Warlimont is surely correct in deducing that in July 1940 Hitler himself reached the unalterable decision to attack Russia due to his 'permanent, deep-rooted and deadly hatred of Bolshevism'.[31]

From the inception of the project to invade Russia (Operation *Barbarossa*) until December 1940, the working out of the entire plan of campaign, including the assembling of forces and the initial objectives, was left completely in the hands of OKH. OKW, and Jodl, the OKW Chief of Operations Staff, in particular, took no part in this OKH planning, nor was Jodl invited to attend any of the war-games held by the Army general staff in the autumn of 1940.[32]

This enormous operation at last fully exposed the fact that the German higher command organization had not been designed for war, and although improvisation had sufficed for the previous lightning campaigns, it was patently inadequate for war against Russia. As we have seen, political and grand-strategic aspects had been increasingly dealt with by OKW, so that OKH had to formulate military plans in a vacuum. To make matters worse, OKH had its own internal weaknesses; for example at the outbreak of war the main headquarters had moved to Zossen, leaving behind a considerable staff in

---

*Professor Leach kindly sent me a copy of his essay on Halder while my own contribution was in preparation.

Berlin. Brauchitsch also found he lacked specialist arms advisers, and so new sections had to be created. Another weakness was that the 'Foreign Armies East' branch within OKH was poorly informed on conditions in the Soviet Union or indeed on the Red Army beyond the Russian border areas.[33] In this matter OKH shared the general ignorance of Soviet military strength common to all the European general staffs.

By the end of October, Halder's chief planning officer, Paulus, had completed his draft invasion arrangements. Two Army Groups (von Leeb and von Bock) were to be employed north of the Pripet Marshes, one moving towards Leningrad and the other towards Moscow, while a third Army Group (von Rundstedt) was to penetrate the Ukraine in the south. In the first phase little emphasis was placed on the Soviet forces in the Baltic States or on economic advantages; rather the classic objective of destroying the enemy's forces was highlighted. In consequence of separate Army Group war-games, the three groups all expressed concern about the immense problems posed by space and manpower. The widening-funnel shape of the invasion route into the Russian heartland meant that an initial front of 1,300 miles would rapidly expand to 2,500 miles. Other drawbacks were discussed, giving the lie to the notion that the German generals were all complacent about the prospects for *Barbarossa*. For example, it was going to be extremely difficult to maintain some $3\frac{1}{2}$ million troops and $\frac{1}{2}$ million horses in a vast country in which there were few roads and a different railway gauge. The Replacement Army had only half a million men – just sufficient to replace losses in a summer campaign. There was an acute shortage of motor vehicles and fuel, and tank production in 1941 never exceeded 250 vehicles per month.

For all these reasons, and because they doubted the Führer's strategic judgment, Brauchitsch and Halder concluded that the destruction of the Red Army must be the overriding aim and that economic considerations must have a low priority. The main thrust must be pushed all the way to Moscow on the central front. This, they argued, would draw in the bulk of the enemy forces, and the seizure of Moscow would not only achieve a major disruption of control and communications, but would also make it difficult for the Red Army to re-establish a continuous front. Soviet sources subsequently confirmed the wisdom of this operational analysis.[34]

At the fateful conference on 5 December 1940, Hitler presented an alternative plan secretly drawn up by Jodl's staff at OKW, which placed more emphasis on exploiting advances on the flanks and less on the need to take Moscow.[35] Against Halder's advocacy of the OKH plan, Hitler reasserted the prime importance of the Baltic and Ukrainian flanks and of economic objectives. Moscow, in his view, was not so very important. When Brauchitsch came to Halder's support he was crushed by insults and abuse. The Army's leaders had to give way and the conference concluded that initial planning for Army Group Centre should only go as far as Smolensk, some 200 miles short

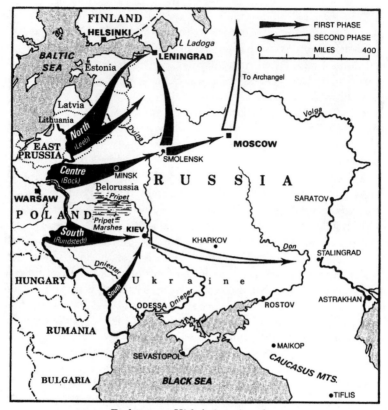

Barbarossa: *Hitler's invasion plan*

of Moscow. The Führer would decide the issue when Smolensk fell. As
Colonel Seaton points out, 'In this lacuna lay one of the causes of German
failure in 1941.' The resulting Directive (No. 21) of 18 December was long,
rambling and indecisive in its aims. Several disconnected objectives were
mentioned but none was given priority. Indeed, in Colonel Seaton's words,
'Hitler was about to send the German Army into the Soviet Union on a four
year will-o'-the-wisp chase after seaports, cities, oil, corn, coal, manganese
and iron ore'.[36]

Halder and Brauchitsch may have perceived the inherent contradictions
and dangers in *Barbarossa*, but they did not argue against Hitler's alternative.
In the following months there was little OKH could do to prepare forces
adequate to take on this gigantic task: manpower, equipment and training
facilities were all limited and several minor campaigns in the Balkans and
Mediterranean had to be planned (and some carried out) before *Barbarossa*
was eventually launched.

88

There is some evidence that Brauchitsch was affected by the prevailing euphoria resulting from Germany's further military successes in conquering Yugoslavia and Greece in the early months of 1941. At the end of April he summed up the prospects of *Barbarossa* as follows: 'Massive frontier battles to be expected; duration up to four weeks. But in further development only minor resistance is then still to be reckoned with.'[37] Moreover, after Hitler's final pep-talk to senior commanders in the Reich Chancellery on 11 June 1941, Warlimont recorded that as far as he could judge all those present were in confident mood.[38]

Before discussing the German Army's catastrophic failure in Russia which culminated, for Brauchitsch, in dismissal and the end of his active career, it is necessary to examine his and OKH's involvement in the issue of orders which played a large part in making the war on the Eastern Front one of ideological fanaticism and barbarity. In his evidence at the Nuremberg Trials Brauchitsch lied about his knowledge of, and responsibility for, the issue of illegal orders and the appalling conduct that resulted; and other senior officers who survived to write their memoirs or give interviews to sympathetic historians, naturally attempted to place all the blame on Hitler, Himmler, Heydrich and the SS. Historians have long been aware that a clear division cannot be drawn between a professional army respecting the laws of war in the combat zone and the criminal SS units perpetrating all manner of atrocities in the rear areas.[39] As long ago as 1960, in *The House Built on Sand*, Gerald Reitlinger showed that OKH could not escape indictment for approving the Commissar Order and other ideological decrees, while more recently Dr Jürgen Förster, after thorough research for volume four of the German Official History, has concluded:

Barbarossa was a carefully planned war of extermination.... Although it was Hitler who wanted to transform *Barbarossa* into a war of extermination against Bolshevism and Jewry, it was the *Wehrmacht* senior officers and their legal advisers who cast his ideological intentions into legally valid form.[40]

In his notorious address to the *Wehrmacht* leaders, including Brauchitsch, in the Reich Chancellery on 30 March 1941, Hitler made it clear that this was to be an ideological crusade in which every commander must be involved. The elimination of the communist leaders and officials would be in their hands as much as in those of Himmler and the police. The troops would be expected to strike towards the rear with the same ruthless methods they used at the front: commissars and GPU officials were criminals and must be treated as such. This did not mean that the troops would be allowed to get out of hand, but they would have to forget the concept of soldierly comradeship between enemies because it was inapplicable to communists. At this time Hitler assumed that Russian resistance would speedily collapse, so he was contemplating a purge of communist officials on a horrendous scale in which the High Command was to be fully implicated.

When Brauchitsch gave evidence at Nuremberg on 9 August 1946 he was sixty-five years old, in poor health and going blind. He told a good deal less than the whole truth about his involvement with the Commissar Order, and on other critical matters, but was treated remarkably leniently by his cross-examiners. He said that the three Army Group commanders had protested to him after Hitler's speech on 30 March that such an ideological way of waging war was intolerable to them. Brauchitsch allegedly told them that it was no use his speaking to Hitler, but he would see to it that the orders actually issued would secure the maintenance of discipline 'along the lines and regulations that applied in the past'.[41]

At Nuremberg, Brauchitsch protested that he knew nothing of the murders of commissars and had received no reports that Hitler's decrees had been implemented. Brauchitsch died in 1948 before he could be tried by a British tribunal in Germany, but the documents presented there showed that he had been lying; his own decrees implementing Hitler's instructions had been widely circulated, and he *had* received reports from all three Army Group commanders detailing the execution of commissars. In his evidence, Halder claimed that he had suggested to Brauchitsch that they should both demand dismissal rather than to be a party to the Commissar Order, but the Commander-in-Chief had persuaded him to stay on because of their responsibilities to the troops.[42]

However, as Dr Jürgen Förster has shown conclusively,[43] OKH was deeply involved in the two decrees concerning the 'Exercise of Military Jurisdiction' and 'The guidelines for the treatment of Political Commissars' issued respectively on 13 May and 6 June 1941.

The origin of these orders is rather complex. The first draft for the abandonment of courts-martial came from OKW on 28 April, but then OKH drafted its own orders on 6 May and added measures to be taken against the commissars. Within OKH it was Halder, rather than Brauchitsch or the 'general officer on special duties', Eugen Müller, who was responsible for this draft order of 6 May. Indeed Müller was subject to Halder's authority in this matter, and Halder made clear in his diary his belief that German soldiers would also have to wage an ideological war. Halder's draft was used by OKW in the orders issued on 13 May and 6 June. Together these two decrees went well beyond minimal compliance with Hitler's intentions. They not only instructed the troops to shoot suspected guerillas 'while fighting or escaping', but also took the initiative against the 'bearers of the Jewish-Bolshevik world view', and provided for the execution of commissars. The two decrees were justified as necessary to ensure absolute security for the German troops.

Brauchitsch subsequently signed and circulated amendments to the OKW directives. His amendment to the Commissar Order (8 June 1941) was tantamount to a justification for killing commissars. This latter amendment assumed in advance that the Bolsheviks by definition would ignore the principles of humanity and international law: 'In particular it must be expected that the treatment of our prisoners by the political Commissars of all types ... will be cruel, inhuman and dictated by hate.'[44] This decree begged the crucial question of how commissars could be identified before being shot on sight. As Reitlinger acidly comments, with the protection of the Jurisdiction Order the German soldier could 'shoot everything down to a postman or refuse-collector'. Furthermore courts-martial were not to be wasted on Russian civilians or guerillas whose fate could be determined by any German battalion commander or officer of higher rank.[45]

In effect the Commissar Order became an excuse for the wholesale murder of prisoners of war, while the Jurisdiction Order justfied or condoned the extermination of civilians on a vast scale. Brauchitsch's claim in self-defence that he took action to nullify Hitler's instructions rests on his annex to the Jurisdiction Order which he issued on 24 May. This order for the maintenance of discipline was issued to no less than 340 commands. It purported to be a commentary on the Führer's wishes designed to avoid wasting combat troops in mopping-up operations, and was concerned with serious cases of rebellion. The individual soldier must not act as he thought fit towards the civilian population, he must be bound by the orders of his officers. But since the officers had virtually been given *carte blanche* to shoot whom they pleased it is difficult to see how Brauchitsch's insistence on unit discipline could modify Hitler's orders in the slightest degree.

Brauchitsch's annex to the Jurisdiction Order was never reissued but he was responsible for several orders to adapt the order to operational circumstances. The Commander-in-Chief's acquiescence in the ideological war of extermination is also evident in the activities of the General for Special Assignments, Eugen Müller, who, though operating directly under Halder, was ultimately responsible to Brauchitsch. For example, in a speech to intelligence officers and judge-advocates from each of the army commands in Warsaw on 11 June 1941, Müller endorsed the Commissar Order by stating: 'Of two enemies one must die. Do not spare the bearer of enemy ideology but kill him.' In practice some field commanders and their liaison officers turned a blind eye to the atrocities perpetrated by the ss *Einsatzgruppen* so long as they caused no disturbance in the combat areas, whereas others actually helped them. Several commanders objected to the Commissar Order in 1941 including Ritter von Leeb, who persuaded Brauchitsch and Keitel to protest against the order on practical grounds; namely that the certainty of execution if captured was actually enhancing the power of the political commissars in the Red Army. Hitler brusquely rejected this memorandum and compelled Brauchitsch to issue further instructions confirming the rules for screening prisoners. The only modification the protest achieved was that executions of prisoners were to be carried out inconspicuously and as far from camps as possible. For the remainder of 1941 utter chaos reigned in the prison camps, with thousands of victims dragged off to execution under the vague description of 'racially inferior elements', which included the sick and disabled. The vital consideration to bear in mind is that until the end of 1941 Hitler assumed he would achieve total victory over Russia, and there was little danger of reprisal since he held over a million prisoners whereas only a few thousand Germans were then in enemy hands. When indiscriminate slaughter of prisoners and civilians was drastically reduced soon after Brauchitsch's dismissal, the reasons were purely pragmatic; namely the urgent need for slave labour in Germany and the *Wehrmacht*'s need for field auxiliaries.[46]

The best that could be said in mitigation of Brauchitsch's part in the barbarization of the war on the Eastern Front would be that he was narrowly concerned throughout with the security of German troops and the pacification of the areas they had overrun. But, as suggested above, Brauchitsch was too thoroughly implicated in the ideological and illegal aspects of the campaign for this plea to be convincing. It is clear that Brauchitsch accepted that this was an ideological war in which the customary rules would not apply.

Ulrich von Hassell foresaw and castigated this excuse in his diary entry for 16 June 1941:

> The Army must assume the onus of the murders and burnings which up to now have been confined to the SS. They have assumed the responsibility, and delude themselves and others by reasoning that does not alter the essence of the problem – the necessity for maintaining discipline, et cetera. Hopeless sergeant majors![47]

In the opening weeks of the Russian campaign there is, as one would expect, little evidence of friction between OKH and Hitler. In the first week of July, Hitler and Halder spoke as though the war was virtually won, and on 8 July Hitler instructed Brauchitsch not to send any new tanks to the Eastern Front. There were also to be drastic reductions in the number of infantry divisions. On the same day, 8 July, Hitler told Brauchitsch and Halder that Moscow must be devastated to drive out its population, but this would be achieved only by terror bombing. Unlike OKH, who regarded the capital as a vital strategic target, Hitler saw it only as the seat of Bolshevism, and had intended from the outset to give priority to Leningrad and the Ukraine. Air raids on Moscow accordingly were carried out on 21 and 22 July, but they achieved little. In mid-July, after a period of wavering, Hitler was reaching the momentous decision to give top priority to the capture of Leningrad. To achieve this he proposed to detach General Hoth's panzer forces from Army Group Centre and send them 400 miles north-east, while at the same time diverting Guderian's panzer group 400 miles southward from the Moscow front to

Army Group South. This would leave von Bock with only infantry forces for the advance on Moscow to which Hitler now assigned a low priority.[48]

Halder saw this as a potentially disastrous error because he regarded the destruction of the Russian forces before Moscow as far more important than deep advances on the northern and southern flanks. Von Bock, von Rundstedt and even Jodl agreed with him. But, according to Halder, Brauchitsch was already cracking up:

> If I didn't have my faith in God and my own inner buoyancy, I'd go under like Brauchitsch, who's at the end of his tether and hides behind an iron mask of manliness so as not to betray his complete helplessness.[49]

Hitler's decision to give priority to the northern and southern thrusts at the expense of Moscow was implemented in Directive No. 33 issued on 19 July. A supplement to this Directive on 23 July minuted:

> After mopping up operations around Smolensk and on the southern flank, Army Group Centre, whose infantry formations ... are strong enough for the purpose, will defeat such forces as remain between Smolensk and Moscow.... It will then capture Moscow.[50]

By 30 July, however, Hitler was forced to accept that without his armoured forces, von Bock's Army Group could not make progress towards Moscow against General Timoshenko's forces. Directive No. 34 issued that day accordingly stated that 'Army Group Centre will go over to the defensive, taking advantage of suitable terrain'. This was to be repeated in a supplement on 12 August which stated that the advance on Moscow could not be resumed until Leningrad had been taken and the flanks secured. But the enemy must still be deprived of his government, armament and traffic centre around Moscow 'before the coming of winter'.[51] Time was already running out for Hitler, and the advance on Moscow on the central front was not in fact to be resumed until the beginning of October. Meanwhile, on 18 August, Brauchitsch made one of his last attempts to assert his authority as the professional head of the Army by protesting in writing about the low priority given to the capture of Moscow. Hitler dismissed his memorandum, replying that seizing the Crimea and the Donets basin and cutting off the Russian oil supply from the Caucasus, in the south, and cutting off Leningrad and joining up with the Finns in the north were all more important objectives to achieve before the onset of winter.[52]

Whether or not the adoption of the strategy favoured by OKH would have brought victory in 1941 must remain uncertain; but what is clear is that by the summer, as things began to go seriously wrong for the *Wehrmacht*, Hitler's increasing and haphazard interference in OKH's sphere of responsibility was making life intolerable for Brauchitsch and Halder. Brauchitsch considered resignation but believed, probably correctly, that Hitler would not allow it.

When the general German offensive towards Moscow was resumed in October, all went well for about two weeks with substantial advances made and enormous bags of prisoners. But the manpower shortage was now so acute that General Fromm, in command of the Replacement Army, hinted to Brauchitsch that the time had come to make peace proposals to Moscow. With the onset of winter weather, the advance on the central front became a desperate attempt to reach Moscow and find shelter. By November it was evident to most front-line commanders (though Halder remained surprisingly optimistic) that the Army was simply inadequately equipped for its task and would have to go onto the defensive or risk annihilation. Hitler tried to transmit his fanatical faith in will-power to the unfortunate Brauchitsch. On 28 November he was summoned to the Führer and given impossible orders together with insults heaped on his head. A few days later the Russian counter-offensive began to drive back Army Group Centre nearly 200 miles and thereby forced even Hitler to accept that victory was unattainable in 1941.[53]

It is not difficult to imagine what these interviews, coupled with the desperate military situation, did for Brauchitsch's already failing health. He suffered a heart attack early in November and was shortly afterwards described as 'a broken man'. His experiences with the Führer became ever more humiliating. On 29 November, for example, Rundstedt was summarily dismissed from command of Army Group South without Brauchitsch even being informed. On 6 December Brauchitsch and Halder completely failed to get Hitler to accept the reality of the exhausted state of the troops and the dreadful conditions of the front; but they themselves were partly to blame because they had suppressed commanders' reports about the declining morale of the troops. Halder noted in his diary: 'The experiences of today have been shattering and humiliating. The C-in-C is little more than a post box.'[54] The Führer was now dealing directly with the commanders of Army Groups over Brauchitsch's head.

Brauchitsch had been considering asking permission to retire on the grounds of ill-health, but on 19 December 1941 Hitler relieved him of his duties and took over himself the responsibilities of Commander-in-Chief of the Army. Hitler allowed this most senior officer, who had been associated with some of his greatest victories, to retire without any decoration and only a modest financial award. Evidently he was to be made a scapegoat for the failure in Russia. Göbbels's diary entry for 20 March 1942 encapsulates the view which the Führer wished to circulate:

The Führer spoke of him only in terms of contempt. A vain, cowardly wretch who could not even appraise the situation, much less master it. By his constant interference and consistent disobedience he completely spoiled the plan for the eastern campaign as it was designed with crystal clarity by the Führer.[55]

Even Halder seems to have been relieved at Brauchitsch's dismissal, and even thought for a few days that he would be able to recover authority over the Army via Hitler, only to find that he had to channel all his communications through Keitel.[56]

Brauchitsch did not meet Hitler again after his dismissal. He was kept informed of the conspiracies to depose Hitler but played no active part in them. Indeed after the failure of the plot of 20 July 1944 he published an article in the *Völkischer Beobachter* condemning the attempted putsch and welcoming the appointment of Himmler as Commander-in-Chief of the Home Army. Worse still, he denounced several former comrades. At Nuremberg Brauchitsch tried to justify himself to Halder by claiming that he had published the article in the hope of saving a condemned relative. Whether this was true, or he was simply trying to save his own skin by currying favour with Hitler, it was, to use Harold C. Deutsch's term, a dastardly action.[57]

In August 1946 Brauchitsch gave perjured evidence at the Nuremberg Trial as a witness in the case of the High Command. He denied, falsely in each case, that he had received payment from Hitler to facilitate his divorce; that he had any foreknowledge of the plans to wage aggressive war between 1938 and 1941; and that he had received any information about the implementation of the Commissar Order in Russia in 1941. He was then sent to the prisoner of war camp for senior officers at Bridgend in South Wales, whence he was brought back to Münsterlager to stand trial before a British tribunal; but various delays occurred and he died before the end of the year (1948).[58]

Robert O'Neill summed up Brauchitsch as 'a man with an outstanding military record but ... crippled by an infirmity of purpose which made him ineffective when dealing with unfamiliar problems.'[59] Brauchitsch in his four years as Commander-in-Chief was a tortured but less than heroic character. If, on the one hand, he lacked the courage and political commitment of Beck, who chose to resign and risk his life and reputation in conspiracy against Hitler; on the other he was not a completely subservient time-server like Keitel and Jodl. At the outset, in 1939, he impressed his colleagues as one of the best half-dozen generals in the Army; a man of culture, charm and professional integrity, albeit with limited political insight. But his driving ambition to become Commander-in-Chief, fuelled in part by the laudable desire to keep out Reichenau, but probably even more as a means of obtaining his divorce and reviving his flagging career, caused him to become fatally dependent on the continuing goodwill of those who had promoted him, such as Keitel and, behind him, Hitler. The way in which he achieved the command-in-chief could not have endeared him to many of the senior generals, and his reputation declined further when he issued Nazi decrees, failed to save Fritsch from disgrace, and was humiliated by Hitler when he protested at the Army's unreadiness for war in the west. After his warnings had been proved premature by the series of astonishing victories in 1940 and early 1941, it is not too difficult to imagine how Brauchitsch could have subdued his misgivings about Hitler's judgment and decided to soldier on loyally whatever the consequences.

The consequences were to be disastrous for Brauchitsch, the Army and the state. He and Halder failed to preserve the independence and integrity of OKH as a centre of strategic advice against the encroachments of OKW and Hitler. Though ambivalent about the invasion of Russia, they drew up outline plans which Hitler then drastically altered. Neither Halder nor Brauchitsch resigned, and it seems probable that they shared in the general euphoria during the opening phase of *Barbarossa*. When the operation began to go badly wrong through inadequate forces and excessive dispersion, they protested repeatedly but failed to change Hitler's mind. Much worse for his reputation, Brauchitsch became inextricably entangled in the issuing and execution of criminal Nazi decrees which played a significant part in causing the peculiarly horrific nature of the war in the east. Characteristically Brauchitsch was eventually relieved of his command because of ill-health and despondency, and not from any noble gesture on behalf of the troops or of professional honour. His, then, is not a particularly edifying personal story, and perhaps the best that can be said of him is that in a less ideological era and under a less demonic overlord than Hitler, Brauchitsch might have exemplified the more honourable tradditions of the German officers corps.

NOTES

Acknowledgments: I am most grateful to Dr Jürgen Förster and Professor Klaus-Jürgen Müller for their expert comments on the draft of this essay. I have adopted most of their suggestions and am alone responsible for any imperfections which remain.

1 Erich von Manstein, *Lost Victories*, London, 1958, pp. 75–6.
2 Albert Seaton, *The German Army 1933–45*, London, 1982, pp. 104–5.
3 *Ibid.*, p. 105.
4 Robert J. O'Neill, *The German Army and the Nazi Party 1933–1939* (Corgi paperback edn), London, 1968, pp. 205–7. Harold C. Deutsch, *Hitler and His Generals*, Minneapolis, 1974, pp. 216–30.
5 Deutsch, p. 230.
6 Deutsch, pp. 280–2, 331–6; O'Neill, pp. 211–12, John W. Wheeler-Bennett, *The Nemesis of Power*, London, 1961, pp. 376–8.
7 Deutsch, pp. 401–2.
8 Nicholas Reynolds, *Treason Was No Crime: Ludwig Beck*, London, 1976, pp. 161–5.
9 O'Neill, pp. 227–31; Seaton, pp. 109–10. Walter Warlimont, *Inside Hitler's Headquarters*, London, 1964, pp. 16–17, 21.
10 Ulrich von Hassell, *The Von Hassell Diaries 1938–1944*, pp. 13, 36, 38. Manstein, p. 75.

11 O'Neill, pp. 233–9; Reynolds, pp. 182–3.

12 Warlimont, p. 32; Seaton, pp. 118–19.

13 Helmut Krausnick and Hans-Heinrich Wilhelm, *Die Truppe des Weltanschauungskrieges*, Stuttgart, 1981. See also the chapters by Christian Streit and Jürgen Förster in Gerhard Hirschfeld (ed.), *The Politics of Genocide: Jews and Soviet Prisoners of War in Nazi Germany*, London, 1986.

14 Seaton, p. 119. Gerald Reitlinger, *The House Built on Sand: the Conflicts of German Policy in Russia 1939–1945*, London, 1960, pp. 70–1. David Irving, *Hitler's War*, London, 1977, pp. 192–5.

15 Manstein, pp. 71–4, 84–5; Warlimont, pp. 36–7, 51; Seaton, pp. 120–3.

16 Harold C. Deutsch, *The Conspiracy against Hitler in the Twilight War*, Minneapolis, 1968, pp. 192–5.

17 Irving, p. 43.

18 *Ibid.*, pp. 47–8; Deutsch *The Conspiracy against Hitler*, pp. 226–30, 235, 240, 258–9.

19 Deutsch, *The Conspiracy against Hitler*, pp. 261–3; Warlimont, pp. 58–9.

20 Deutsch, *The Conspiracy against Hitler*, pp. 289–312.

21 See the *Von Hassell Diaries*, op. cit., pp. 96–7, 106–7, 122–3 for the conspirators' vain attempts to involve Brauchitsch.

22 *Ibid.*, pp. 114, 116.

23 Warlimont, p. 73; Wheeler-Bennett, p. 494.

24 Warlimont, pp. 76–81; Seaton, pp. 132–3.

25 Wheeler-Bennett, pp. 496–7, 500.

26 Seaton, pp. 141–43n; Warlimont, pp. 90, 95–7; Irving, pp. 120–1.

27 Manstein, p. 150.

28 Gerhard Schreiber 'The Mediterranean in Hitler's Strategy in 1940' in Wilhelm Deist (ed.), *The German Military in the Age of Total War*, Berg Publishers Limited, Leamington Spa, 1985.

29 See especially the contributions of Jürgen Förster and Ernst Klink (pp. 9–11, 204–11) in *Das Deutsche Reich und der Zweite Weltkrieg*, Band 4, Stuttgart, 1983.

30 'On July 21, 1940, Brauchitsch was able to submit to the *Führer* an outline plan which contained aims, concentration, and comparative strengths for a military blow at Russia in fall 1940.... New German historical research has shown that this "proposal of extraordinary optimism" was based upon a contingency plan for the 18th Army which had already been issued', Jürgen Förster, 'The Dynamics of Volksgemeinschaft: the Effectiveness of the German Military Establishment in the Second World War' (awaiting publication). See also Barry A. Leach, *German Strategy against Russia 1939–1941*, Oxford, 1973, pp. 58–60.

31 Warlimont, pp. 113–14.

32 For Jodl's role in the planning of *Barbarossa* see *Das Deutsche Reich und der Zweite Weltkrieg*, Band 4, p. 230.

33 Seaton, pp. 161–4.

34 *Ibid.*, pp. 164–5.

35 H. R. Trevor-Roper (ed.), *Hitler's War Directives*, London, 1964, pp. 48–52.,

36 Seaton, pp. 165–6.

37 Robert Cecil, *Hitler's Decision to Invade Russia, 1941*, London, 1975, p. 129.

38 Warlimont, p. 147.
39 See especially Jürgen Förster's chapter (vii) in *Das Deutsche Reich und der Zweite Weltkrieg*, Band 4 and his and Christian Steit's essays in G. Hirschfeld (ed.), *The Politics of Genocide*, op cit.
40 J. Förster, 'New Wine in Old Skins? The Wehrmacht and the War of Weltanschauungen, 1941' in W. Deist (ed.), *The German Military in the Age of Total War*, pp. 304, 308–9. For an even more severe verdict on the Army's responsibility for the barbarous war on the Eastern Front, see the study by Krausnick and Wilhelm referred to in note 13.
41 Reitlinger, pp. 70–1.
42 Reitlinger, pp. 71 ff.
43 Förster's chapter in Deist (ed.), pp. 309–14 and his essay 'The German Army and the Ideological War against the Soviet Union' in Hirschfeld (ed.) *passim*.
44 Reitlinger, p. 79.
45 Reitlinger, pp. 80–1.
46 Reitlinger, pp. 83–94, and the essays by Steit and Förster in Hirschfeld cited in note 39 above.
47 *Von Hassell Diaries*, p. 181.
48 Warlimont, pp. 179–80; Irving, p. 284; Trevor-Roper (ed.), pp. 82–4.
49 Irving, pp. 287–8.
50 Trevor-Roper (ed.), pp. 85–90.
51 *Ibid.*, pp. 91–5.
52 *Ibid.*, pp. 95–6; Seaton, p. 177.
53 Seaton, pp. 180–2.
54 Warlimont, pp. 195, 205–6, 613 note 11; Irving, p. 342.
55 Warlimont, pp. 212–13.
56 *Das Deutsche Reich und der Zweite Weltkrieg*, Band 4, p. 614.
57 Wheeler-Bennett, p. 696; Deutsch, *Hitler and His Generals*, p. 227n.
58 Reitlinger, p. 70. For Brauchitsch's interrogation at Nuremberg see *The Trial of Major War Criminals*, part 21, London, 1949, 9 August 1946, pp. 23–40.
59 O'Neill, p. 205.

CHRONOLOGY: WALTER VON BRAUCHITSCH

1881 4 October	Born in Berlin
1900	Commissioned *leutnant*, 3rd Guards Regiment of Foot
1901	3rd Guards Field Artillery Regiment
1906	Battalion Adjutant
1909	Regimental Adjutant and *Oberleutnant*
1910–12	Student at the War Academy and on the General Staff in Berlin
1913	*Hauptmann*
1914	On the Army General Staff and, on outbreak of war, General Staff Officer 16th Corps
1915	General Staff Officer, 34th Division
1918	Major and General Staff Officer, 1st Guard Reserve Division and

	First General Staff Officer, Guard Reserve Corps. Awarded the Iron Cross First Class
1919	Staff Officer to *Wehrkreis* II
1921	Commander, Second Battery of the 2nd Field Artillery Regiment
1922	Staff Officer in the *Truppenamt* where he organized manoeuvres to test the possibilities of using motorized troops in conjunction with aircraft
1925	*Oberstleutnant* and Commander Second Battalion of the 6th Artillery Regiment
1927	Chief of Staff to *Wehrkreis* VI
1928	*Oberst*
1930	Major General and Departmental Head in the *Truppenamt*
1932	Inspector of Artillery
1933	Lieutenant-General, and succeeded Blomberg as Commander of *Wehrkreis* I (in East Prussia) and the 1st Division
1935	Commander of the 1st Army Corps
1936	Promoted General of Artillery
1937	Commander of *Heeresgruppe* 4, Leipzig
1938	(4 February) Colonel-General and Commander-in-Chief of the Army
1939	Awarded the Party Gold Badge (March) and the Ritterkreuz (September)
1940	(19 July) Field-Marshal
1941	(19 December) Retired
1948	Died

Brauchitsch married Elizabeth von Karstedt on 29 December 1910 and was divorced in February 1938. In September 1938 he married Charlotte Schmidt.

HALDER

4

HALDER

Colonel-General Franz Halder

BARRY A. LEACH

In retrospect Colonel-General Franz Halder seems to be the most controversial, even paradoxical, of the generals in Hitler's service. He took office as Chief of the General Staff in 1938 declaring himself fundamentally opposed to the Nazi régime and yet he helped to win its most spectacular military victories. In the daily performance of his duties he tried to exemplify Moltke's dictum, 'Genius is diligence', but produced plans for operations against Czechoslovakia in 1938 and France in 1939 that provoked scorn from Hitler and embarrassment from his subordinates. He appeared to support plots for Hitler's removal but could never quite bring himself to the final act. He headed an organization devoted to the perfection of military leadership but was bitterly critical of successful field commanders like Guderian and Rommel, who showed tactical flair and operational initiative. Even his personal behaviour was paradoxical; in spite of his stiff bearing, cropped hair, clipped moustache, and pince-nez spectacles, his attempt to maintain the appearance of a cold, controlled, bureaucratic disciplinarian was undermined by a tendency to become emotional to the point of tears under stress. Here, perhaps, lies the clue to the paradox, for Halder, more than any of his colleagues, was under stress from the day he took office as Chief of the General Staff in the midst of the Czech crisis, till the day of his dismissal with disaster looming at Stalingrad. Ultimately events forced all Halder's colleagues to face the fact that adherence to traditional standards of honour and decency had become treason, and loyalty to the head of state a crime. The dilemma split the General

Staff and finally, on 20 July 1944, tore it apart.

The General Staff was already divided and weakened when Halder was called to fill the place vacated by the isolated and disillusioned Ludwig Beck. Its status had been reduced by defeat in 1918 and by the terms of the Treaty of Versailles that forced upon it a clandestine existence (as the *Truppenamt*) within an army the size of a police force, serving a republic it could not respect. Even when the General Staff emerged from concealment in 1935, the creation of an independent *Luftwaffe* with its own General Staff and the controversy over the creation of a tri-service *Reich* General Staff prevented the restoration of the status and influence enjoyed by the General Staff of Moltke and Schlieffen. The creation of the High Command of the Armed Forces (*Ober-kommando der Wehrmacht*, OKW) was somewhat offset by Hitler's readiness, demonstrated in the preparations for invading Austria in 1938, to treat the new staff merely as his military secretariat and to depend directly upon the General Staff of the Army for operational planning to meet his immediate needs. Nevertheless, the General Staff was further subordinated to the High Command of the Army (*Oberkommando des Heeres*, OKH) which included also the Office of the Chief of the Replacement Army, the Army Ordnance Office and Arms Inspectorates, the Army Administration Office and the Army Personnel Office. Although the Chief of the General Staff was regarded as *primus inter pares* among the heads of these offices, this did not give him immediate access to the Head of State; this right was reserved for the Commander-in-Chief. However, Hitler permitted von Brauchitsch to bring his senior subordinates to audiences and conferences if the topic under discussion warranted their presence. But he made it clear that the Chief of the General Staff should confine himself to the operational level of planning, and to organizational and administrative matters associated with it. Beck's refusal to be excluded from grand-strategic planning and his insistence on submitting memoranda warning Hitler of the long-term consequences of his policy of expansion doomed his own career and demonstrated the limits of the General Staff's competence. Hitler regarded Beck's actions as 'sabotage' and was incensed that the General Staff 'instead of being grateful that it is able to work in its true area of expertise ... rejects the very idea of war.'[1] Beck further weakened his position by refusing to attend Führer conferences. Instead he sent Halder, who as *Oberquartiermeister* I (OQuI) was his deputy. Halder had already come to Hitler's attention as a 'modern' general. Now he seemed, in contrast to Beck, to be a soldier 'who presents his ideas openly'.[2]

Brauchitsch, who had replaced Fritsch as Army Commander-in-Chief, also respected Halder as an efficient and reliable subordinate who had served him well in the Training Branch in 1930 and had returned to head that branch in 1936. It was von Brauchitsch who had selected Halder to replace the brilliant but difficult Erich von Manstein as OQuI in February. When Beck resigned on 26 August 1938 Halder seemed to be his natural successor. There were, however, problems. Halder was seen by many senior officers, including Beck himself, as a diligent but dull mediocrity, 'a very good soldier but hardly a man of great calibre'.[3] According to Halder's own post-war account, he told von Brauchitsch that, in view of his well known anti-Nazi attitude, it would be better if someone else, perhaps Manstein, was selected. But von Brauchitsch, who had been offended by von Manstein's high-handedness when he was OQu I, appealed to Halder not to let him down. Halder requested time to consider the matter and went off to consult Beck. The relationship between Halder and Beck had been strained since February when von Brauchitsch had selected his former subordinates from the Training Branch, Halder, von Stülpnagel and von Greiffenberg, for service in place of Beck's protégés, von Manstein and his associates. Although Beck had created the situation that put Halder in his place at Hitler's councils, he had come to resent him, especially when Halder was tactless enough to criticize his memoranda as an ineffectual means of influencing Hitler. Halder's readiness to perform Beck's role had added to the Chief of Staff's isolation. Nevertheless, Beck conceded that if anyone could continue the struggle against Hitler, Halder was the man. So Halder claims that he went back to von Brauchitsch the next day and warned him that he would accept the office of Chief of the General Staff, 'only to make use of every opportunity that ... [it] offered to fight against Hitler and his system.'[4] In view of the attempt that von Brauchitsch was making at this time to remain loyal to Hitler, it is very doubtful that Halder was quite so frank. Nevertheless, the Commander-in-Chief knew that as a monarchist nurturing his past ties with the Crown Prince of Bavaria and as a practising Christian his candidate was no admirer of Hitler and his régime.

Accounts based on Halder's post-war statements describe his antipathy towards Hitler as dating back to the 1920s. However, a letter written on 6 April 1934 revealed a more ambivalent attitude that differentiated between 'the Chancellor's sincere intentions' and the influence of his 'really second-rate' satellites.[5] Nevertheless, the unscrupulous way in which Hitler used the Army's acquiescence in the Röhm purge to murder General von Schleicher, his wife and his former chief assistant, forced Halder and his colleagues to recognize that the evil of the Nazi movement stemmed from the Führer himself. By the end of 1934 he was sending his superiors frank reports describing the attitudes and actions of the SA, SS, and Gestapo and the strained situation in *Wehrkreis* VII resulting from the increasing pressure of the régime on the churches. However, Halder was certainly exaggerating when he later claimed that his critical reports caused the War Minister, General von Blomberg, to demand his dismissal, but that he was protected by General von Fritsch. Four years later, when von Fritsch himself was forced to resign from his post as Commander-in-Chief by the sordid plot devised by the SS, Halder, according to his own account, urged Beck to march troops on the Gestapo headquarters in Berlin.[6] Whatever the truth, Himmler was certainly aware of

Halder's hostility towards the Party and ss and warned Hitler that Halder had no frontline experience and was known in the Army as 'the mother of God's general'.[7] This nickname, based upon the erroneous assumption that all Bavarians were Catholics, may have aroused some concern in Hitler's mind. Unlike the Evangelical Churches, the Church of Rome had shown a reserved attitude towards the Nazi movement, and its members were still seen as Germans with loyalties divided between Berlin and Rome. So, when Hitler heard that von Brauchitsch had selected this Bavarian and actively Christian general to be Beck's successor, he immediately asked, 'Is he a Catholic?'

In fact, he was a Protestant, born in 1884 to a Würzburg family that had sent its sons to the Bavarian officer corps for 300 years. He had won academic distinction as a cadet and was commissioned in the Royal Bavarian Field Artillery in 1904. His capabilities as a staff officer were quickly recognized and, in spite of his efforts to be posted to the front, he was, as Himmler asserted, employed throughout the First World War on various staffs including that of Crown Prince Rupprecht's Army Group. His observations at Verdun and on the Somme gave him a deep aversion to positional warfare and fostered his conviction that 'operations demand movement'. In the *Reichswehr* he developed a reputation as an expert on training and manoeuvres, and it was his direction of the *Wehrmacht* manoeuvres in 1937 that first won him favour with Hitler.[8]

These manoeuvres were important to Hitler as a means of displaying the growing power of the *Wehrmacht* to potential friends and foes. But Halder was more concerned with testing the new panzer division as a means of conducting deep and decisive operations against the flank and rear of an enemy. Thus it was remarkable that Halder's first major task as Chief of the General Staff, his presentation of the Army's plan for the invasion of Czechoslovakia to Hitler on 9 September 1938, was an 'appalling disaster' because he failed to deploy the panzer and motorized forces to Hitler's satisfaction. Hitler responded with a devastating critique accusing von Brauchitsch and Halder of employing motorized divisions against objectives that did not enable them to make full use of their mobility, and of tying the panzer divisions to infantry advancing on foot.[9]

Hitler's ADC, Major Gerhard Engel, who described these painful scenes in his diary, had already observed that the new Chief of Staff appeared to be 'highly nervous' and 'at the end of his self-control'. At their first meeting Halder had astonished the young officer by placing a pistol on his desk with the remark that he knew that he was being followed and 'would not allow himself to be shot down without defending himself'.[10] Halder's extraordinary behaviour was due to the fact that even while planning the invasion of Czechoslovakia, he had kept his word to Beck and had become involved in a plot against Hitler. Through Colonel Hans Oster, Deputy Chief of the *Abwehr* (Armed Forces Intelligence Office), he had established contact with Hjalmar

Schacht, Minister without Portfolio, and Dr Hans Gisevius, a counsellor in the Ministry of the Interior. At their first meeting early in September Halder struck Gisevius as an 'obedient functionary' resembling 'a colourless, bespectacled schoolmaster with somewhat taut features in an inexpressive face'. However, he began to speak of 'this madman' Hitler with such acerbity that Gisevius could not recall having heard 'so eloquent an outburst of stored-up hatred'.[11] Nevertheless, his first impressions were revived when Halder revealed deep qualms about leading the Army into civil war and involving the officer corps in open revolt. He preferred to stage a 'fatal accident' or, in the event of war, an anonymous bombing of Hitler's train. Later he warned the plotters that he had no executive authority and could only advise the Commander-in-Chief of the Army. Since von Brauchitsch had given no sign of support, hopes turned to General Erwin von Witzleben, Commander of the Berlin Military District, and several of his trusted subordinates who declared their readiness to take over the capital and arrest or shoot Hitler if he insisted on pushing Germany into a war. Although Halder gave the impression that 'he was willing to take the first step without daring to take the second',[12] he evidently remained mentally committed to the plot, for when the Munich conference cut the ground out from under it, Halder, far from being relieved, was 'in a state of complete collapse, weeping and asserting that all was lost'.[13] Even in retrospect this event stirred an emotional response from Halder. In an interview with the present writer on 23 June 1969, he became agitated at the memory of the 1938 plot and rose from his chair, shaking an accusing finger with the words, 'it was your Prime Minister, your Prime Minister [Chamberlain] who ruined our hopes by giving in to Hitler!'

In the weeks that followed Halder returned to his characteristic routine and immersed himself in the details of military administration. He rose at 5.00 and went riding until 7.30. After breakfast he received the morning reports from his branch heads, then conferred with the officers of the OKH and liaison officers until noon when the rest of his staff went to lunch. He remained in his office and read through the mass of paper that was delivered daily to his desk. Then the flow of visitors resumed until dinner, between 8 and 9 p.m., after which he refreshed himself with a short nap. He next worked on his correspondence and on his notebook into the night until about 1 a.m. or later.[14]

Halder began to keep shorthand notes as a lieutenant-colonel and continued the habit throughout the rest of his career. The pre-war volumes were lost, but the wartime notebooks were recovered from their hiding place and became known as Halder's *Kriegstagebücher* or war diaries. The daily entries summarized each day's work as an *aide-mémoire*. As a result, matters of secondary importance that might more easily be forgotten often received more space than major topics. Furthermore, many notes were brief, even cryptic, for the sake of secrecy. Nevertheless, they reflect the vast array of routine detail tackled by Halder as well as the discussions at planning meetings and Führer conferences that shaped German operations in the first three years of the Second World War.[15]

In the months before the war, Halder's main concern was to form within the General Staff strong planning teams that could, by their virtuosity, challenge the rival influence of Wilhelm Keitel and Alfred Jodl in the OKW. So to plan the invasion of Poland he formed a 'working staff' under the respected Colonel-General von Rundstedt, consisting of three outstanding General Staff officers, Lieutenant-General von Manstein, Colonel Günther Blumentritt, and Major Reinhard Gehlen. It was obvious that by advancing from East Prussia, Silesia, and Slovakia, German armies, spear-headed by mechanized formations and supported by a strong tactical air force, could quickly envelop the Polish forces in a swift operation of the type that came to be styled *Blitzkrieg*. Halder's biggest worry was that Britain and France might declare war and move against the weak German forces in the west. However, after studying the problem, he concluded that nothing serious could occur before the bulk of German forces had completed the conquest of Poland and moved to defensive positions facing France and the Low Countries.[16] The agreements with Russia and the quick, decisive victory over Poland might even convince the western powers that they should come to terms with Germany. Thus it came as a shock when after the Polish campaign the OKH learned that Hitler had decided to launch a major winter offensive in the west.[17]

This news came on top of a crisis in the relationship between Halder and von Brauchitsch, who had spent much of his time during the Polish campaign visiting the front, leaving Halder to direct operations from the field HQ of the OKH at Zossen, outside Berlin. During his travels von Brauchitsch had sent confusing and sometimes contradictory instructions. Hitler also began to interfere in operational decisions, and, to make matters worse, failed to keep the military staffs informed on current political and diplomatic agreements. On 10 September Halder had noted that 'the Army Command must not be pushed around by the vagaries of politics; otherwise it will suffer a breakdown in confidence.'[18] By the end of the Polish campaign Halder had reached that point, so he persuaded von Brauchitsch to leave him, as Chief of the General Staff, in unequivocal control of operations. Halder accordingly found himself charged with the task of planning an attack in the west that he and most field commanders believed had doubtful prospects at any time, but could only lead to disaster in the winter.

After the war Halder claimed that he and the General Staff attempted to counter Hitler's 'unimaginative replica of the Schlieffen Plan' with a proposal for remaining on the defensive until the Allies advanced into the Low Countries and then countering their move with a thrust from the Ardennes.[19] There is no historical evidence to support this version. In fact Halder complied with

Hitler's demands but made repeated criticisms and protests at the idea of a winter offensive, to which Hitler responded with a series of directives and memoranda.[20] As in the Czech crisis, Halder now found himself trapped between the demands for decisive military action from an impatient and critical Führer, and the appeals of the opposition for his support in a coup. Again the refusal of von Brauchitsch to participate in any action against Hitler placed Halder under such stress that he ceased to function effectively. On 16 October, after a meeting at Zossen, a shocked Admiral Canaris told Lieutenant-Colonel Groscurth that Halder had suffered 'a complete nervous collapse'. The Colonel, equally disappointed, noted in his diary that 'a Chief of the General Staff has no business breaking down. Just like 1914.'[21] Groscurth's comparison was fully justified. The Kaiser's arbitrary demand for a complete change of plan on the eve of World War I had reduced the Chief of the General Staff, the younger Count von Moltke, to 'a mood of almost complete despair' in which 'faith and confidence were shattered'. Later, when his armies faltered and fell back from the Marne, Moltke was described as having 'broken down completely'. Furthermore, in the final months of the war another crisis on the Marne led to a similar collapse in the First Quartermaster General, Erich Ludendorff, who was described by one of his staff colonels as 'quite broken'. Evidently only a leader of unusually phlegmatic temperament, like von Hindenburg, could maintain the iron discipline, rigid self-control and high professional performance demanded of the men at the top of the General Staff without giving way under conditions of extreme stress to a loss of confidence or even to the hysteria that often lies beneath the surface of the authoritarian personality.[22]

Helmuth Groscurth was in fact a major source of Halder's stress. Both he and Legation Counsellor Hasso von Etzdorf had been attached to the General Staff by their respective chiefs, Admiral Canaris, head of the *Abwehr*, and Ernst von Weizsäcker, State Secretary of the Foreign Office, to bolster Halder's determination to act against Hitler.[23] The plotters based their persuasion on three main topics: Nazi policy in Poland, the rivalry between the ss and the Army, and Hitler's apparently irrational demand for a winter offensive. Further concerns and recommendations for action were expressed in the 'Etzdorf-Kordt memorandum' presented to Halder in the third week of October 1939. In response to these pressures Halder's mood ranged between 'exhilaration and darkest depression'.[24] But he seemed prepared to act and, in late-October, gave Groscurth permission to prepare a plan similar to the one worked out in 1938. This task was supervised by the OQuI, General Karl-Heinrich von Stülpnagel. With tears in his eyes Halder admitted to Groscurth that 'he had been going to Emil [Hitler] for weeks with a pistol in his pocket finally to shoot him down.' While Halder went off to visit the field commanders in the west, von Stülpnagel allocated the troops needed for the coup and conducted other 'stirring matters' that convinced Groscurth that at last 'there will be action' if, on 5 November, Hitler confirmed his decision to attack.[25]

On that fateful day von Brauchitsch entered the Reich Chancellery armed with all available arguments against the offensive. When, twenty minutes later, he staggered 'chalk white ... with a twisted countenance' out of the meeting, Halder, waiting in an ante-room, knew that confirmation of the attack order must be expected.[26] Yet on arriving back at Zossen the Chief of the General Staff, instead of ordering the *Attentat* to proceed, excitedly instructed von Stülpnagel and Groscurth to cancel their plans and burn all incriminating documents. The reason for Halder's loss of nerve was apparently a remark of Hitler's quoted by von Brauchitsch in the account of the disastrous meeting that he gave during their drive back to the field HQ. In his outburst of anger Hitler had stated that he was well aware of the 'spirit of Zossen' and was determined to stamp it out. Halder, assuming that the conspiracy had been betrayed and that Himmler's security forces might arrive at any moment, evidently panicked.[27]

While the plotters were busy destroying the evidence of their guilt von Brauchitsch's state of shock was giving way to a mood of resentment at the treatment to which he had been subjected. He now told Halder that although he would do nothing, he would 'also do nothing if someone else did something'.[28] This was not enough to encourage Halder to order the *Attentat* after all; instead he sent Groscurth to persuade Wilhelm Canaris to act, a suggestion that was angrily rejected by the astonished and resentful admiral. In the weeks that followed the plotters at the OKH and the *Abwehr* tried to improvise alternative schemes, but they had little encouragement from Halder who emerged from the traumatic experiences of 5 November determined to concentrate on his professional duties.

Meanwhile, bad weather had caused a postponement of the offensive long enough to give Hitler the opportunity for further dickering with the Army's plan by suggesting that a force of panzer and motorized divisions should be formed in Army Group A to attack Sedan via Arlon south of the Ardennes forest.[29] Shortly before Colonel-General von Rundstedt took command of Army Group A on 25 October, his Chief of Staff, Lieutenant General von Manstein, had called at Zossen to collect his copy of the plan for *Fall Gelb* (Plan Yellow). Like Hitler, he was disappointed to find that it was an unimaginative repetition of 'an old recipe', and he proceeded to draft an alternative plan designed to achieve a decisive victory by placing the main weight of the offensive with Army Group A for a surprise attack through the Ardennes. This would enable the attackers not merely to push the enemy forces out of Belgium, but also 'to cut them off from the Somme'.[30] By January 1940 the staff of Army Group A had submitted seven major memoranda and numerous letters urging the change of plan, but to no avail.

Halder's initial failure to respond positively to von Manstein's proposed change of plan is understandable. Until the long postponement in January the offensive was 'never more than two weeks away'.[31] There was simply no time for a major redeployment. Even the limited adjustments demanded by Hitler apparently resulted in a reckless dispersal of the crucial mobile forces. As for von Manstein's plan, it appeared to be a risky operation, dependent on good weather for effective air support and for unimpaired mobility through the difficult terrain of the Ardennes. Furthermore, just as the initial surprise of its location wore off, the main thrust would arrive on a major river obstacle, the Meuse. To a man sceptical about the possibility of any success, this plan seemed to offer no advantages over the more cautious one already in hand. Nor was Halder alone in his scepticism. Colonel-General Fedor von Bock, a haughty Prussian who usually referred to Halder as 'the Bavarian', complained bitterly about the reduction of the mobile forces in his Army Group B on the grounds that 'in attempting to be strong everywhere, we are really not strong anywhere'.[32] Heinz Guderian, whose 19th Panzer Corps had been sent on Hitler's insistence to Army Group A, at first complained that his forces were not strong enough to achieve decisive results there.[33] Nevertheless von Brauchitsch and Halder clung to the view that the main effort could be shifted to whichever army group achieved the greater success in its initial attack. This evoked from von Manstein the reminder that 'according to [a dictum of] Moltke, errors in the initial deployment cannot be corrected in the course of the operation'.[34] Such comments can hardly have improved von Manstein's reputation with Halder, who had probably been offended at the fact that Beck had by-passed him and recalled von Manstein to plan the invasion of Austria in 1938. He had also had disagreements with von Manstein over his handling of operations in Poland. Now the feelings of both von Brauchitsch and Halder flared into resentment when this subordinate staff officer presumed to question the validity of their entire operational plan. Paradoxically, their own doubts about the prospects of their plan served only to sharpen their hostility towards their outspoken critic.

Even before the controversy over Case Yellow, Halder had been nursing the idea of posting von Manstein away from the General Staff by promoting him to the command of a corps. Manstein's third memorandum, dated 30 November, confirmed the decision. At the same time Halder decided to rid the General Staff of several other officers, notably Lieutenant-Colonel Groscurth, whose presence had contributed to the stresses and storms of the past months, and von Stülpnagel, on whom he was now pushing the blame for the *Attentat* plans. In fact, illness spared von Stülpnagel the humiliation of a posting, but von Manstein was shocked by Halder's unscrupulous action. Subsequent attempts to question the wisdom of von Manstein's removal or to put him in command of the panzer group formed as the spearhead for his plan came to nothing.[35]

Groscurth was also upset by his treatment at Halder's hands. On 13 January he had been summoned to hear a long lecture on the political situation from the Chief of the General Staff, who was 'very noble and sincere in manner, sometimes very loud and excited, and once almost in tears.' Halder's main aim was to justify his failure to strike at Hitler, and since Groscurth's response did not appear to be positive, the decision to post him to the command of an infantry battalion ('a degradation') followed ten days later.[36]

Halder's meetings with Groscurth in January and, a month later, with Canaris, reveal his attitude early in 1940. He saw no real basis for a putsch against the régime 'because the troops still believe in the Führer'. Furthermore, Halder was convinced that he had 'a great, unified officer corps' behind him. As in 1914, it was only 'the old officers who were pessimistic'. Obsessed by the fear that failure to go through with the offensive might be attributed to a loss of nerve, like that of his predecessor the younger von Moltke in 1914, Halder preferred to compare his situation with that of Ludendorff, who 'had also made a last desperate effort in 1918, and had not thereby damaged his historical reputation'. He had evidently forgotten that the failure of the German offensive and the success of the Allied counter-offensives had led to a collapse of Ludendorff's confidence. Halder's preoccupation with his own historical reputation appalled the plotters, but he now regarded them as 'reactionaries' who wanted 'to turn back the wheel of history'. As for the actions of the Nazi régime in Poland, they were 'really not so bad' and 'would be forgotten later'. To Groscurth's indignation, Halder even protested to Canaris his ignorance of the plans made to kill Hitler in November and pushed the blame on von Stülpnagel. The ss, Halder claimed, was not a serious threat; like other internal problems, it could be dealt with when the Army was strengthened by its future success in the unavoidable struggle with Britain.[37]

Halder's show of confidence in the coming offensive was not simply the result of desperation. Even as he was engineering von Manstein's removal, he began to perceive the possibility of achieving a decisive success by adopting his rival's ideas. The shift of Hitler's interest to the invasion of Norway, breaches of security in the west, and an unusually harsh winter all combined to bring an indefinite postponement of the offensive and gave Halder the opportunity to attend Army Group and Army war-games in the first half of February. These confirmed the validity of placing the main weight behind operations culminating in a deep thrust to the Channel coast. Meanwhile, Hitler, still hankering after a great concentration of armour on the Ardennes sector, had his ideas confirmed by von Manstein at a luncheon meeting at the Reich Chancellery. Afterwards Hitler applauded von Manstein's proposals and condemned von Brauchitsch and Halder for 'thinking like cadets'.[38] But at the Führer conference the next day Hitler found that the two generals had anticipated his demands and were ready to transfer three panzer divisions and the entire 4th Army to Army Group A. The completeness of Halder's conversion to the new plan was later demonstrated when he curtly rejected the doubts expressed by von Rundstedt and his Staff about pushing the tanks forward across the Meuse, and when he calmly and firmly countered von Bock's fears about the risks entailed in the location and the character of the new main thrust with the argument that it was these very elements that gave it the advantage of surprise.[39] Nevertheless, Halder's post-war attempts to claim the *Sichelschnitt* plan as his own are not supported by the contemporary evidence.[40]

In spite of the irritation and anger aroused by Hitler's interference, especially his well-known confirmation of von Rundstedt's 'halt-order' before Dunkirk on 24 May, Halder was delighted that the offensive in the west developed in a 'positively classic manner'. Once the panzer spearheads were across the Meuse, the success of the campaign depended on the complex flow of men, material, and supplies into the narrow corridor from Sedan to the sea. The co-ordination and the control of these massive movements must stand as one of the great achievements of the German General Staff. Halder's letters to his wife reflected his sense of personal satisfaction and pride. 'My operations are rolling like a well edited film,' he wrote. 'I ... push pieces across the chess board in accordance with my conception of how they should come into play ... [and] after two or three days ... there they stand, all ready for action in the right place.' Colonel Eduard Wagner, Quartermaster General, reported that, 'It is fantastic how the entire machine is functioning,' and described Halder as the 'high priest of the General Staff, [with his] unprecedented technique and great operational skill.' Yet at the moment of victory Halder told his wife that he 'trembled inwardly at the scale of events'.[41]

With the defeat of France Halder had to face hard realities. Far from the Army strengthening its own position as he had hoped, it had made Hitler master not only of Germany but of central and western Europe. It was the Führer who emerged from the struggle triumphant in the eyes of the German people. But the triumph was flawed. Britain refused to recognize the hopelessness of her situation, and, in the east, the Soviet Union had made gains from Hitler's policies and now stood face to face with the Reich, its very existence a threat and challenge to the 'New Order' in Europe. When Halder visited Berlin a week after the fall of France, von Weizsäcker, at the Foreign Office, told him that, 'We can maintain the successes of this campaign only with the means by which they were won, namely, with military force.'[42] Weizsäcker was lamenting the fact that even after such a victory Hitler's régime could never expect to establish viable peacetime relationships with other powers. But for Halder this implied a confirmation of Hitler's continued dependence on the Army that was not unwelcome to the Chief of the General Staff. Though Hitler took the credit for the *Blitzkreig* victories, Halder was now personally confident that he and his General Staff had been the real architects of Germany's military triumphs. With a meddling amateur as Chancellor and an ineffectual Field-Marshal as Commander-in-Chief of the Army, Halder saw his own position as similar to that of Ludendorff in World

War I, except that his Army had achieved the victory in the west that had eluded the old First Quartermaster General. To Halder and the Army leaders it now seemed more logical to ensure their position in the new order by meeting the remaining military challenges than by reviving the moral doubts that had so reduced their stature in the eyes of the Führer during the grim months of the past winter.

Halder's daily notes make it clear that Russian action in the Baltic states and in Bessarabia and Bukhovina had drawn his attention eastward even before the fall of France. On 18 June he instructed Major Gehlen, head of the Fortifications Group of the Operations Branch, to review measures for a vigorous defence of the eastern borders of the Reich, and a week later he reinforced the 'striking force' in the east with panzer and motorized divisions under Guderian's Panzer Group HQ. During his birthday visit to Berlin on 30 June Halder learned from von Weizsäcker that Hitler's eyes too were turned eastward, but on the next day a visit to the Chief of the Naval Staff, Admiral Schniewind, confirmed that the first priority was the British problem still to be resolved in the west. On arriving at HQ OKH, now located at Fontainebleau, and without waiting for confirmation from the OKW of Hitler's future intentions, Halder told Colonel von Greiffenberg to form within Operations Branch, two special groups to enable the General Staff to tackle simultaneously both the problems in the west and the east: how to achieve the swift defeat of Great Britain and 'how to deliver a military blow at Russia that will force her to recognize Germany's dominant role in Europe.'[43]

The solutions to these rival yet interrelated problems remained for Halder the two main aims of the General Staff's planning for the rest of his career. Furthermore, the initial planning for operations against Russia was initiated by Halder on the basis of his own estimate of the political situation. Hitler's pact with communist Russia and the subsequent surrender of Lithuania and the Polish territory won with German blood were an anathema to him.[44] His assumption that in the long term Soviet intentions towards Germany were bound to be aggressive justified planning a redeployment that would avert the threat of Soviet intervention during *Sealion* and, later in 1940, enable Germany to achieve the 'political aims' in the east described by von Brauchitsch at the conference with Hitler on 21 July 1940. These were designed to revive the conditions imposed on Russia by the Treaty of Brest-Litovsk in 1918 which created a chain of buffer states under German domination from the Baltic to the Black Sea.[45] In spite of later suggestions that this concept was a 'preventive war', it differed from Hitler's only in the area of territory to be seized and in the degree of inhumanity in the treatment to be meted out to the Russian people.

The initial belief in the OKH that the Soviet Union could be defeated, like Poland, in a swift autumn campaign was evidently based on the study hastily conducted by the Feyerabend-Gehlen 'eastern group' and on the inaccurate estimates of Russian strengths and capabilities produced by the 'Foreign Armies East' branch under Colonel Eberhardt Kinzel. Optimism may also have been fostered by the readiness of the Soviet Union to make peace at Brest-Litovsk in 1918 and at Riga in 1921 even at the expense of giving up vast tracts of its western territories. However, Hitler was understandably doubtful about the feasibility of defeating Russia before the end of 1940 and on 31 July he confirmed his decision to prepare for an invasion of Russia to take place in May 1941. For him 'the winning of a certain area would not be enough', the aim of the campaign must be 'the destruction of Russia's vital power'.[46]

Hitler's decision not to strike until the spring of 1941 was welcome because, by the end of July, von Brauchitsch and Halder had been forced to recognize the difficulties involved in achieving the defeat of Britain. Halder had long regarded this as essential to put a final end to the Germans' position as a 'Helotenvolk' of the British. 'England's fight', he had told the Head of the War Economy and Armament Office, General Thomas, 'is not directed only against the [Nazi] régime, but against the entire German nation.'[47] At first the Army leaders had viewed the prospect of a cross-Channel invasion with optimism, but on 17 July Admiral Raeder warned von Brauchitsch that 'the risk was great enough to involve the loss of all the invasion armies.'[48] Only at the end of July did the Navy admit that the losses and damage sustained in the Norwegian campaign had reduced its available surface strength to 1 cruiser, 4 destroyers, and 3 torpedo boats. This, in Halder's view, meant that all previous statements by the Navy were 'rubbish' and that a landing was now 'completely impossible'.[49] As a result, on the evening of 30 July he and von Brauchitsch conducted a complete reappraisal of German strategy and examined alternative aims in the Mediterranean and the Middle East. They concluded that it would be preferable to maintain 'friendship with Russia' and to encourage Soviet aspirations towards the Straits and the Persian Gulf. Hitler, however, was not yet ready for such changes and, next day, when he announced his decision to attack Russia in 1941, he also informed his service Chiefs that the Luftwaffe should try the effects of an all-out air offensive against England in the hope of achieving a collapse of the British will to resist.[50]

As in the Polish campaign, Halder delegated the planning for the attack on Russia to several subordinates. For this he was later criticized by von Manstein.[51] But, in fact, Halder's action was probably motivated, not by a lack of confidence resulting from his earlier difficulties in planning the campaigns in Czechoslovakia and the west, nor, as he later claimed, by his 'inner rejection' of the idea of attacking Russia,[52] but rather by the multiplicity of tasks confronting him. As his notebooks reveal, Halder always tried to exercise personal supervision over all aspects of the General Staff's work, and by the summer of 1940 these had become so diverse that both he and the OKH as a whole were severely overstrained. Nevertheless, when Colonel von Greif-fenberg and Lieutenant-Colonel Feyerabend proposed a major thrust across the Ukraine, Halder, uncertain about the use of Romanian territory, intervened to suggest that the main effort should be directed along the Baltic coast then, swinging towards Moscow, sweep southward to take the Russian forces in the Ukraine in the rear.[53] He also interfered with the planning conducted by General Erich Marcks, Chief of Staff of the 18th Army, by again stressing the importance of Moscow and by down-playing the thrust towards Kiev that Marcks, and also Hitler, had stressed in their original concepts of the campaign.[54]

In September 1940 the new OQuI, General Friedrich Paulus, was given the task of developing the plans for the operation against Russia. Paulus was selected because, having served under Guderian and von Reichenau, both associated with panzer operations, he would give the General Staff a more 'modern' outlook. He was, however, a reserved man who could methodically present both sides of an argument but had difficulty in reaching a decision. He ordered the Chiefs of Staff of the three Army Groups allocated to the east to conduct their own operational studies.[55] But even when Georg von Sodenstern of Army Group South echoed his own misgivings about the relationship between the forces available, the distances to be covered and the time available, Paulus failed to formulate these doubts into an effective case for a complete reconsideration of the Army plan.

Similar doubts about the feasibility of defeating Russia by means of a single, short *Blitzkreig* campaign were expressed by the German Military Attaché in Moscow, General Ernst Köstring, and in a military geographical study of European Russia produced by the War Mapping and Survey Branch of the General Staff. The latter stressed the significance of the Caucasus and the size and economic strength of Asian Russia, and pointed out that both of these regions lay beyond the range of a single campaign.[56] Hitler had from the start included the Caucasus in the objectives to be won in 1941, but Halder did not consider the problem during the planning and turned to it only after the campaign had commenced.[57] Furthermore, General Marcks, having completed his operational study, focused his attention on the broader strategic implications of the invasion of Russia and, a month later, handed to the OQuIV, von Tippelskirch, a memorandum outlining his deep concerns at the prospect of fighting the Anglo-American-Russian coalition that would probably result unless the Russian campaign was completed in 1941. This, in turn, seemed unlikely for logistical reasons. Tippelskirch and Kinzel did nothing to dispel Marcks' concerns, yet there is no evidence that he or the OQuIV made any attempt to bring them to Halder's notice.[58] The 'team spirit' fostered by Halder in the General Staff was evidently having a stifling effect on the free expression of ideas.

As a result it was in a mood of optimism that von Brauchitsch and Halder presented the Army plan for the invasion of Russia to Hitler on 5 December 1940. However, the Führer, perhaps under the influence of the study conducted by Colonel Lossberg, a member of Jodl's OKW Operations Staff, rejected the importance of the thrust towards Moscow and suggested that part of Army Group Centre should turn northward instead to assist in cutting off the withdrawal of the enemy from the Baltic States (see map on page 88). This new concept was written into Directive No. 21 for Operation *Barbarossa* and into the Army's Deployment Directive, but was neither truly accepted nor openly rejected by Halder. This evasion laid the foundation for serious conflict in the course of the campaign.[59]

A further deception occurred a few weeks later when Hitler requested a study of the Pripet Marshes that the planners had so far assumed would be unsuitable for military operations. The study concluded that, in spite of the bad roads, the light railways in the area would indeed allow the Russians to move forces in all directions, and so 'a threat from the Polesie [Pripet] to the flanks and rear of the armies advancing on Moscow or on Kiev could very well lie within the realm of possibility'. However, this sentence was omitted from the final version of the study, dated 21 February 1941, that was presented to Hitler.[60]

Also at this time very real logistical and economic concerns were coming to light. In January 1941 Halder was informed that the delay to be expected while converting the Russian railways to the German gauge would make the flow of supplies dependent on motor transport for 600 miles. But the lack of surfaced roads and Germany's 50 per cent deficiency in tyres made it very doubtful that the truck columns, many of which were to be improvised from the civil economy, could meet the demands of the campaign. Worse still, General Thomas revealed that supplies of fuel oil and petrol were sufficient only for the concentration of forces and two months of combat. Yet Halder made no attempt to bring this shattering information to Hitler's notice, and Thomas's attempt to do so was blocked by Keitel. At the Führer conference on 3 February Halder clung doggedly to the conviction that 'everything must be achieved by the trucks'.[61]

Halder's strategic priorities in the winter of 1940–1 can be seen in his notes for the conference of senior General Staff officers held on 13 and 14 December 1940. Although Hitler's improvised 'strategy on the periphery' and Mussolini's opportunism had made it necessary to plan operations against Gibraltar, Vichy France and Greece, Halder still saw a direct attack on Britain as preferable to a sprawling Mediterranean strategy dependent on the Italian and German navies for the protection of its vital supply lines. But he also shared Hitler's view that, if an invasion of England was not feasible, 'the decision over the hegemony in Europe would be achieved in a struggle with Russia'. 'We do not seek a conflict with Russia,' Halder said, 'but from the spring of 1941 we must be ready for this task also.' Most of the discussions on the second day of the conference were devoted to preparations for the east.

Halder also took the opportunity to counter the concern that staff officers were falling behind the field commanders in promotion and recognition. He affirmed his ideas on the principles and practices of the General Staff, based upon the tradition of 'Achieve much, appear little.' He told his audience that it had been his good fortune to work with 'the great names of our profession ... Gallwitz, Kuhl, Ludendorff, and Hindenburg'. It was clear that Halder felt that the mantle of their greatness now rested on his shoulders, and, he continued,

> As long as I am the 'Guardian of the Grail' we shall not depart by one hair's breadth from this spirit of the German General Staff. I expect you to educate the German General Staff in this manner.[62]

Yet something was lacking in the education and the performance of the German General Staff under Halder. The flame which had burned brightly under the elder Moltke had been rekindled under von Seeckt in spite of the restrictions of Versailles. Beck, too, in his remote, aloof way, had managed almost instinctively to keep it burning. Manstein had revealed the difference under Halder when, wounded by the pettiness of his banishment, he had told Colonel Schmundt that 'Halder cannot abide any contradictions; with Beck things were rather different'.[63] Beck, like Halder, had been a tireless worker who devoted himself to his duties and demanded from others the same high standards that he set for himself, but he was not mean-spirited. Halder, lacking the touch of genius himself, resented originality and demanded loyalty before all else. One of the most gifted staff officers in the OKH, Henning von Tresckow, told Halder's secretary that, 'We are trained to be machines and must adapt our opinions. Little value is placed on our development as individuals.'[64]

To the General Staff the individual mattered less than the system that was developed to provide a military methodology with standardized approaches to problem-solving, planning, and the formulation and issue of orders. It had its own style of communication and jargon. It found strength in clarity and consistency. But the resulting uniformity also limited independent thought and reduced perspective. This danger could be averted only if men of unusually broad vision rose to the top. Halder was not such a man. His intellect and temperament were not strong enough to carry him beyond his training and experiences as a staff officer and as an instructor of staff officers. His ideas were still based on eighteenth- and nineteenth-century concepts of war. *Blitzkreig* had provided an armoured spearhead, supported by the 'aerial artillery' of the *Luftwaffe*, that well served the operational and tactical needs of the limited campaigns in Poland and the west. It was here that Halder and his selected subordinates showed their 'virtuosity of operational technique'.[65] But after the fall of France the war took on a continental dimension for which they were both mentally and materially ill equipped. Their responses to both the dangers and the possibilities in the Mediterranean were isolated and uncoordinated. Their nagging doubts about attacking Russia before finishing the war with Britain were not fully expressed within the General Staff, let alone with their opposite numbers in the Navy and Air Force. The importance of economic objectives in Russia, and, even more, of winning the support of the Soviet people against Stalin's régime, were not perceived as important compared with the challenge of trying to win with *Blitzkrieg* operations and battles the decisive victory that had eluded Charles XII and Napoleon. But even if Halder and his branch heads had possessed a higher level of strategic vision, the régime of Adolf Hitler would have given them little encouragement to exercise it.

Officers like von Tresckow, who retained their independence of thought and judgment, had already become increasingly indignant at the inability or unwillingness of their superiors to act against the crimes of the SS in Poland. Now that the plans for the occupation of the eastern territories in Russia and the so-called 'Commissar Order' made it clear that such crimes were to be extended on an even vaster scale, many members of the General Staff were aroused to shame and anger. Halder himself was glad to leave most of the burden of liaison with the SS in the hands of Field-Marshal von Brauchitsch and his General for Special Duties, Eugen Müller. Nevertheless, Müller's Legal Affairs Group lay directly under Halder's authority, so his post-war denial of responsibility for the Army's involvement in the ideological warfare in the east was quite unjustified.

Meanwhile, the Chief of the General Staff turned in the spring of 1941 to the tasks of propping up the Italian front in North Africa and safeguarding the flank of *Barbarossa* by invading Greece and so preventing the creation of a British-backed Balkan front. Erwin Rommel was Hitler's choice for the command of the *Afrika Korps*. Halder would have preferred a man more suited to defensive warfare and was soon giving vent to his irritation at the way Rommel was 'rushing about' and 'frittering away his forces'. At first he considered flying to Libya himself to bring 'this soldier gone raving mad' to heel, but he decided instead to send Paulus who had once served in the same regiment as Rommel.[66] It was fortunate for the British in the months that followed that Halder lacked the strategic imagination to recognize the opportunities opened up by Rommel's tactical and operational flair.

The Balkan campaign also presented difficulties. The terrain, the weather, and, above all, uncertainties about the timing of Bulgarian co-operation and about the attitude of Yugoslavia led to repeated changes of plan. But the most drastic of all such changes, resulting from General Simovic's coup d'état in Belgrade on 27 March, did not find Halder as totally unprepared as he later claimed when he asserted that the outline plan for the invasion of Yugoslavia had to be improvised during the drive from Zossen to the Reich Chancellery.

In fact, Halder and Colonel Adolf Heusinger, head of the Operations Branch, had worked on such a plan in October 1940 and had even conducted secret negotiations in November and December for the participation of a Hungarian force.[67] Hitler's angry decision to attack Yugoslavia certainly made the attack on Greece easier and quicker than Halder had expected, but it also added to the burdens of occupation and confronted the *Wehrmacht* with a long and costly partisan war. Nevertheless, the fact that only 17 of the 30 formations allocated to the Balkan campaign were actually used suggests that other factors, notably weather conditions and delays in equipping the motorized forces and supply columns, contributed to the need to delay *Barbarossa* from May 1941 till 22 June.[68]

Since 1940, when planning for the invasion of Russia began, Halder had made a set of assumptions that ultimately had disastrous effects on the outcome of the campaign. The first was the belief that the initial *Blitzkrieg* attack, spearheaded by four panzer groups, would achieve a decisive victory by completely destroying the bulk of the ponderous and poorly led Soviet forces in the frontier battles. Second, Halder believed that the need to defend the western industrial regions would force the Russian High Command to push its reserves as far forward as possible, at least to the Dvina-Dnieper line which would be quickly breached by the panzer groups thrusting towards Leningrad, Kiev and, above all, Moscow. Halder's third assumption was that the battle for the capital would be decisive because the last Russian reserves would surely be committed to it.

The events that followed the German attack soon forced Halder to modify his assumptions about the Russians' strength, combat capabilities, dispositions and intentions. The Soviet forces offered brave and determined resistance and mounted counter-attacks that were often suicidal. Large numbers of Soviet troops slipped out of the huge pockets that proved difficult to keep closed, especially when the panzer commanders were eager to push on eastwards. Furthermore, the Russians repeatedly created new defensive lines on the path and flanks of the German advance. The memoirs of Soviet military leaders give the impression that there was no overall plan and that the defensive battles were improvised, using reserves of men and material as they moved westward from the interior. Thus it is arguable that the Russian forces were saved in part by their dispersion resulting, not from astute planning, but from uncertainty and confusion in the weeks immediately preceding the German attack and during the initial battles.[69]

In spite of the German failure to achieve the aims of the first phase of Operation *Barbarossa*, Halder clung with increasing desperation to the belief that the final issue could be decided at the gates of Moscow. This he did in spite of, perhaps because of, the mounting conflict that it caused between Hitler and himself. For since November 1939 Halder had directed his opposition to Hitler, not towards plotting and assassination, but towards the assertion of his own will in the direction of operations for the achievement of a victory that would assure the place of the General Staff in the Third Reich and its history.

Once it was clear that the great battles on the frontiers were not going to be decisive, Hitler revived all his earlier demands for the conquest of the Baltic coast and Leningrad in the north and of the economic wealth of the Ukraine, Donetz Basin, and the Caucasus in the south. By now Halder was also willing to recognize the importance of the economic objectives in the south but he coupled these, not with Leningrad, but with Moscow. Dropping all earlier evasions, he presented his case for a thrust towards the Soviet capital at the Führer conference on 23 July. When Hitler rejected his proposal he was reduced almost to despair. He wrote to his wife:

> I can predict ... exactly where this nonsense will lead. Without my trust in God and my self-confidence, I would be like Brauchitsch who has completely lost all energy and hides behind a steely hauteur so that his inner helplessness is concealed from view.[70]

On 23 August, the day on which Hitler instructed Guderian to turn his panzer group south to Kiev, Halder admitted that the goal of finishing off the Russians in 1941 would not be achieved. In spite of the great encirclement battles that followed at Kiev in September, and at Viasma and Briansk in October, the decisive victory again eluded the German Army.

Hitler himself, embittered by the evasion, delays and failures that he blamed on the OKH, now left Halder to summon the Chiefs of Staff of the Army Groups and armies to Orsha to discuss the operational objectives for the resumption of the offensive when the ground froze. With the convening letter the Chief of Staff distributed a map marked with two proposed lines to be reached. The 'minimum line' extended from the eastern shore of Lake Ladoga, southeast through Kovroff (halfway between Moscow and Gorki), southward to the Don at Pavlovsk, thence around the Don bend to Rostov. The 'extreme line to be attempted' stretched from Lake Onega southward beyond Vologda to Gorki, thence along the Oka River line south to the Don and then east even to Stalingrad and thence southwest across the open steppes to Voroshilovsk, Maikop and Tuapse. Halder admitted that the attempt to reach such far-flung objectives before the full onset of the Russian winter involved risks, especially in view of the exhausted state of the troops and the difficulties of supplying them. Nevertheless, he argued, failure to press on when the enemy was weak and disorganized would be regretted next spring.[71] On 12 November Halder arrived at Orsha with leading members of 'his team' on the General Staff. The discussion next day was dominated by two forces: Halder's desperate will to press on, doubtless inspired by the cautionary memories of the younger Moltke's collapse of will on the Marne in 1914, and Ludendorff's personal breakdown in July and August 1918 after the failure of his offensives and in the face of successful French and British counter-strokes; and, on the other hand, the realities faced by the troops, exhausted and exposed without winter clothes or shelter, and at the end of failing supply lines. As Guderian's Chief of Staff, Lieutenant-Colonel von Liebenstein, bluntly reminded Halder, 'This was not the month of May and we were not fighting in France!'[72] The result was a compromise; limited offensives to reach the Don bend in the south, the east side of Lake Ladoga in the north and, above all, Moscow in the centre. For Halder still clung to the hope that the capture of the capital would bring a collapse of the Soviet Union. The effort to fulfil that hope cost the lives of thousands of soldiers fighting under appalling conditions. It exposed the extended German armies to the counter-offensive launched by Marshal Zhukov on 6 December.

Brauchitsch had suffered a heart attack on 10 November. Later, when he was dismissed as the scapegoat for the failure at Moscow, Halder, long embarrassed by the Commander-in-Chief's reduction to the role of letter-carrier between Hitler and the OKH, did not regret his departure. Even though Hitler decided to fill the post of Commander-in-Chief himself, Halder remained as Chief of the General Staff. He did so to maintain continuity in the direction of the operations and to foster continued loyalty in the General Staff. His sense of duty to the troops in the field also kept him at his post, especially as the crisis they faced in the Russian snows was partly of his own making. Ambition may also have played a role; with von Brauchitsch gone and no one to come between him and the Head of State, Halder may have felt that the General Staff had at last been restored to something like its old status. If so, it was a delusion, for many of the traditional responsibilities of the OKH had now to be shared with the OKW. Hitler, interested only in exercising control over operations and the Personnel Branch, had loosely delegated the rest of the Army Commander-in-Chief's responsibilities to Keitel. Further the OKW was now given operational direction over all theatres of war except the Russian Front. This alone was left to the General Staff. Worse still, the division of the direction of operations in different theatres between the two staffs meant a further deterioration in the overall grand strategic direction of the war, especially as Hitler immersed himself in the details of the deployment of each and every division. According to Heusinger, Halder did examine the question of going over to the defensive in the east. But it was 'impossible in 1942 even to mention this to Hitler' because he dreaded surrendering the initiative to the Russians and Americans.[73]

Nevertheless, Halder made a real effort to make the new command structure work. He wrote to the field commanders welcoming Hitler's new role in terms so obsequious that this letter must be regarded as a further step in the writer's suppression of his honour and dignity.[74] Hitler's Army ADC described how, although Halder came to the Führer conferences with the same group of 'wailing Willies' that had attended with von Brauchitsch, things went unexpectedly well at first because 'the Chief of the General Staff made a visible effort to foster a good atmosphere'. Nevertheless, several staff officers were soon offended when Halder took every opportunity to criticize von Brauchitsch and to blame him for earlier decisions that were 'in conflict with the Führer's views'.[75]

Since September 1939 Halder had participated in fifty-four Führer conferences, an average of fewer than two a month. Now he was required to attend daily, spend much time in preparation, two hours on the road between Angerburg and Rastenburg, and long periods in indecisive argument over the map-table. Nevertheless, he managed to avoid major quarrels with Hitler during the winter of 1941–2, and supported him in his order to stand fast on the Eastern Front during the Russian winter offensive. If this prevented a débâcle, much of the credit for the improvisations of operations, organization and supply that helped the German armies survive the winter must go to Halder and his team of department heads, especially Heusinger and Wagner. However, it must be noted that when Hitler sent several senior generals into retirement, dismissal or even imprisonment for disobedience, Halder made no move to defend them. More understandable was his decision to replace Colonel Kinzel, whose serious underestimations of Russian capabilities had contributed to the failure of *Barbarossa*. His successor as head of the Foreign Armies East Branch was the remorseless, industrious and ambitious Colonel Reinhard Gehlen. But when Halder carried the results of Gehlen's work to Hitler, with revelations about Russian tank production and other disagreeable information, they provoked only outbursts of angry disbelief.

Halder knew from the start that the German offensives towards Stalingrad and the Caucasus in 1942 were no less a gamble than *Barbarossa* in 1941. His fears about the strength of the Russian reserves, and the weakness of the diverging German thrusts, dependent as they were for flank protection on the ill-equipped armies of Hungary, Italy and Romania, were shared by the front commanders.[76] A serious breach of security and von Bock's insistence on diverting his armour into the battle for Voronezh created an atmosphere of acrimony and distrust at Hitler's HQ. In spite of warnings from Halder, Hitler's interference resulted first in 'a useless concentration of armour in Rostov', then in a premature and weakened southward advance towards the Caucasus, while part of von Manstein's army was transferred from the Crimea to Leningrad. Only a month after the start of the offensive Halder noted that Hitler's 'chronic tendency' to underestimate the Russians was becoming 'grotesque' and dangerous. His leadership had deteriorated onto a 'pathological reaction to impressions of the moment, and a total lack of any understanding of the command machinery and its function.'[77] As the 6th Army was pushed into its fatal battle in the ruins of Stalingrad and List's Army Group became over-extended in the difficult terrain of the Caucasus, Halder was numbered among the scapegoats by the angry, sulking, and resentful Hitler.

When Halder's dismissal finally came on 24 September he described it in his notebook in cool, subdued terms. But it was an unpleasant scene, and Halder left the map-room alone, shunned by the officers of Hitler's entourage. Engel was ordered by an embarrassed Schmundt to attend the former Chief of the General Staff, who, with tears in his eyes, thanked him saying, 'If you had experienced what just happened to me you would understand how I appreciate that you are with me.'[78] Perhaps Engel remembered his first meeting with Halder back in 1938. Then, too, he had found the General isolated and threatened. Since then he had trodden a long and hard path. Deluded by hopes of greatness both for himself and for the General Staff, Halder had abandoned his promise to oppose Hitler and had followed a course of service without loyalty and duty without honour that had resulted in the defeat of Germany's armies and the division and humiliation of the General Staff.

After the attempt on Hitler's life on 20 July 1944 Halder was arrested and spent the remainder of the war as a prisoner of the Gestapo. Compared with many of his comrades on the General Staff, he was fortunate. His earlier association with the opposition was not sufficiently proven to justify his execution. Yet after the war it was enough to exonerate him from responsibility for his later deeds. He served fourteen years with the US Army Historical Division and was rewarded in 1961 with the Meritorious Civilian Service Award, the highest American civilian award for services to the state.

NOTES

1 Hildegard von Kotze (ed.), *Heeresadjutant bei Hitler, 1938–1943. Aufzeichnungen des Majors Engel*, Stuttgart, 1974 (hereafter cited as Engel), p. 33.
2 *Ibid.*
3 Ulrich von Hassell, *The Von Hassell Diaries, 1938–1944*, London, 1948, p. 19.
4 Heidemarie Grafin Schall-Riaucour, *Aufstand und Gehorsam, Offizierstum und Generalstab im Umbruch. Leben und Wirken von Generaloberst Franz Halder, Generalstabchef 1938–1942*, Wiesbaden, 1972, p. 97 n. 9.
5 Klaus-Jürgen Müller, *Das Heer und Hitler, Armee und nationalsocialistisches Regime, 1933–1940*, Stuttgart, 1969, p. 348.
6 *Ibid.*, pp. 348–9, 609ff.
7 Engel, p. 26.
8 Hauptmann Martin, 'Wehrmachtmanöver 1937' *Jahrbuch des deutschen Heeres*, 1938, Leipzig, 1937, pp. 169–73; R. J. O'Neill, 'Doctrine and Training in the German Army, 1919–1939', in M. Howard (ed.), *Theory and Practice of War*, Indiana University Press, 1975, pp. 160–1.
9 Engel, p. 36; see also *International Military Tribunal*, XXV, 338-PS, pp. 429–32, 441–5, 463–4, 466–9; Telford Taylor, *Sword and Swastika, Generals and Nazis in the Third Reich*, Chicago, 1969, pp. 210–14.
10 Engel, p. 35.

11 Hans Bernd Gisevius, *To the Bitter End*, trans. by Richard and Clara Winston, Boston, 1947, pp. 288ff.
12 *Ibid.*, p. 287.
13 Engel, p. 39.
14 Conversation with Halder's former adjutant, Burkhard Mueler-Hillebrand; July 1965; see also Luise Jodl, *Jenseits des Endes. Leben und Sterben des Generaloberst Alfred Jodl*, Vienna, 1976, p. 30.
15 Hans-Adolf Jacobsen, 'Das Halder-Tagebuch als historische Quelle', *Festschrift Percy Ernst Schramm zu seinem siebzigsten Geburtstag von Schülern und Freunden zugeeignet*, Band II, Wiesbaden, 1964, pp. 251–68; Hans-Adolf Jacobsen (ed.), *Generaloberst Halder, Kriegstagebuch*, Band I, Stuttgart, 1962 (hereafter cited as Halder, *KTB*), pp. vii ff.
16 Halder, *KTB*, I, pp. 3–8.
17 *Ibid.*, pp. 84, 86ff.
18 *Ibid.*, p. 70; see also Helmut Krausnick and Harold C. Deutsch (eds), *Helmuth Groscurth, Tagebücher eines Abwehroffiziers, 1938–40*, Stuttgart, 1970 (hereafter cited as Groscurth), p. 209.
19 Franz Halder, *Hitler as Warlord*, London, 1950, pp. 27–8; Schall-Riaucour, pp. 145–6; Hans-Adolf Jacobsen, *Fall Gelb: der Kampf um den deutschen Operationsplan zur Westoffensive, 1940*, Wiesbaden, 1957, p. 273 n. 14.
20 Matthew Cooper, *The German Army, 1933–1945, Its Political and Military Failure*, London, 1978, pp. 178ff., 195ff.
21 Groscurth, p. 218.
22 Correlli Barnett, *The Swordbearers*, Harmondsworth, 1966, pp. 22ff., 115, 372ff., 384ff.; Barbara Tuchman, *The Guns of August*, New York, 1962, p. 78ff.
23 Groscurth, pp. 15ff., 42ff.; see also Harold C. Deutsch, *The Conspiracy Against Hitler in the Twilight War*, Minnesota, 1968, pp. 82–3, 85–7.
24 Deutsch, p. 204.
25 Groscurth, pp. 222–4.
26 Halder, *KTB*, I, p. 120; Engel, pp. 66–7; Groscurth, pp. 224–5.
27 Groscurth, pp. 224–5; Deutsch, pp. 230ff.
28 Gisevius, p. 420.
29 Fedor von Bock, *Generalfeldmarschall von Bock, Kriegstagebuch: Mai 1939–Mai 1945*, Microfilm no. T-84, US National Archives, Washington, DC, n.d., entry 25 October 1939; Walter Hubatsch (ed.), 'Quellen zur neuesten Geschichte III (Tagebuch des Generalmajors Jodl)', *Die Welt als Geschichte*, 1952, pp. 274–87 (hereafter cited as Jodl), p. 282.
30 Erich von Manstein, *Lost Victories*, trans. A. G. Powell, London, 1958, pp. 94ff.; Jacobsen, 1957, p. 70.
31 Cooper, p. 200.
32 Bock, 11 November 1939.
33 Halder, *KTB*, I, p. 128.
34 Jacobsen (1957), p. 81.
35 Halder, *KTB*, I, pp. 206, 208, 219.
36 Groscurth, p. 245; Halder, *KTB*, I, p. 171.
37 Groscurth, pp. 241, 246–7; Hassell, p. 88.

38 Engel, p. 75.
39 Jacobsen (1957), pp. 33ff.; Halder, *KTB*, I, p. 208.
40 Halder (1950), pp. 28–9; Schall-Riaucour, pp. 149–50.
41 Schall-Riaucour, p. 152; Halder, *KTB*, I, p. 291; Elizabeth Wagner (ed.), *Der Generalquartiermeister. Briefe und Tagebuchaufzeichnungen des Generalquartiermeisters des Heeres, General der Artillerie Eduard Wagner*, Munich, Vienna, 1963, pp. 167ff.
42 Halder, *KTB*, I, p. 347.
43 *Ibid.*, II, p. 6; see also Ernst Klink, 'Die militärische Konzeption des Krieges gegen die Sowjetunion', *Das deutsche Reich und der zweite Weltkrieg*, Band IV, *Der Angriff auf die Sowjetunion*, Stuttgart, 1983, pp. 206–7, 212–13.
44 Halder, *KTB*, I, p. 80; Klink, p. 191.
45 Halder, *KTB*, II, pp. 32–3; Klink, pp. 213–14; see also Barry A. Leach, *German Strategy Against Russia, 1939–1941*, Oxford, 1973, pp. 58–60; cf. Robert Cecil, *Hitler's Decision to Invade Russia*, London, 1975, pp. 73–5.
46 Halder, *KTB*, II, pp. 49–50.
47 Georg Thomas, 'Gedanken und Ereignisse', *Schweizerische Monatshefte*, Falkenstein, December 1945, quoted in Deutsch, p. 267.
48 Ronald Wheatley, *Operation Sea Lion*, Oxford, 1958, p. 41.
49 Halder, *KTB*, II, pp. 40, 43–4.
50 *Ibid.*, pp. 45, 48.
51 Manstein, p. 79.
52 Schall-Riaucour, pp. 156–9; see also Halder, 1950, pp. 38ff.
53 Halder, *KTB*, II, pp. 37, 39.
54 *Ibid.*, pp. 50, 51; see also Bryan I. Fugate, *Operation Barbarossa, Strategy and Tactics on the Eastern Front, 1941*, Novato, Ca., 1984, pp. 64–8.
55 Walter Görlitz, *Paulus and Stalingrad*, trans. R. H. Stevens, New York, 1963, pp. 109ff.
56 Klink, pp. 195–7.
57 Leach, pp. 146–50.
58 Klink, pp. 226–7.
59 Klink, pp. 235ff.; Fugate pp. 76ff.; Leach, pp. 107ff.
60 Klink, p. 244.
61 Halder, *KTB*, II, pp. 240, 256ff.; Georg Thomas, *Geschichte der deutschen Wehr- und Rüstungswirtschaft, 1918–1943/45*, ed. Wolfgang Birkenfeld, Boppard am Rhein, 1966, pp. 17–18; Hans-Adolf Jacobsen, *Kriegstagebuch des Oberkommando der Wehrmacht*, Band I, Stuttgart, 1965, pp. 316–17.
62 Halder, *KTB*, II, pp. 229–30.
63 Engel, p. 75.
64 L. Jodl, p. 48.
65 Herbert Rosinski, *The German Army*, New York, 1966, p. 113; see also L. H. Addington, *The Blitzkrieg Era and the German General Staff, 1865–1941*, New Jersey, 1971, pp. xv, 53–4, 216.
66 Halder, *KTB*, II, p. 377.
67 *Ibid.*, pp. 131, 134, 140, 143; see also Martin van Crefeld, *Hitler's Strategy 1940–1941, The Balkan Clue*, Cambridge, 1976, p. 145.

68 Crefeld, pp. 166, 170ff.; Leach, p. 165ff.; Department of the Army, *The German Campaign in the Balkans*, Washington, DC, 1953, pp. 148ff.

69 See John Erickson, *The Road to Stalingrad*, New York/London, 1975, pp. 46, 50ff., 90ff., 101ff.; see also the memoirs of Marshals Vasilevsky, Eremenko, Rokossovsky and Zhukov and of General Shtemenko. In contrast to these accounts Fugate asserts that the Russians' defence was based on a secret plan dividing their forces into 'tactical, operational and strategic echelons'. However, he admits that this is 'based largely on conjecture' (p. xix).

70 Schall-Riaucour, p. 166.

71 *Bundesarchiv-Militärarchiv*, RH 21–2/879 with map, Freiburg i.B.

72 Heinz Guderian, *Panzer Leader*, trans. Constantine Fitzgibbon, London, 1952, p. 247.

73 Walter Warlimont, *Inside Hitler's Headquarters, 1939–45*, translated by R. H. Barry, London, 1964, pp. 215–19, 227; see also Adolf Heusinger, *Befehl im Widerstreit*, Tübingen and Stuttgart, 1950, pp. 154ff.

74 *Bundesarchiv-Militärarchiv*, RH2/v 156.

75 Engel, p. 119.

76 *Ibid.*, p. 123.

77 Halder, *KTB*, III, p. 489.

78 Engel, p. 128.

CHRONOLOGY: FRANZ HALDER

1884, June 30	Born at Würzburg, son of Maximilian Halder (later Major-General) and Mathilde, née Steinheil
1902, June 30	Passed Abitur, Theresien Gymnasium, Munich
1902, July 14	Entered 3rd Royal Bavarian Field Artillery Regiment in Munich
1904, March 9	Promoted *Leutnant* on completion of course at military school
1906–7	Attended the Artillery School, Munich
1907, September 23	Married Gertrud Erl
1911–14	Attended Bavarian Staff College, Munich
1912, March 7	Promoted to *Oberleutnant*; passed Interpreter's Examination in French
1914, August 2	Ordnance Officer, HQ 3rd (Bavarian) Army Corps
1915, January 6	2nd General Staff officer, 6th (Bavarian) Infantry Division
1915, August 9	Promoted to *Hauptmann*
1917, March 26	HQ, 2nd Army
1917, June 14	General Staff officer, 4th Army
1917, July 12	General Staff officer, Bavarian Cavalry Division (Eastern Front); General Staff Officer, Supreme Commander, East
1917, 30 October	HQ, 15th Reserve Corps; HQ, Army Group Crown Prince Rupprecht, West
1918, December 20	Adjutant, Bavarian General Staff
1919, October 1	Training Branch, Reichswehr Ministry
1920, August 17	*Kommandatur*, Munich

1921, October 1	Tactics Instructor, Staff Courses. *Wehrkreis* VII, Munich
1923, October 1	OC 4th Mountain Battery, 7th Artillery Regiment, Landsberg am Lech
1924, March 1	Promoted *Major* with seniority from 1 April 1923
1925, December 1	Director of General Staff Training, *Wehrkreis* VII, Munich
1927–9	General Staff Officer Ia of *Wehrkreis* VII, Munich
1929, February 1	Promoted *Oberstleutnant*
1929, April 1	Leader of Group II, later I, Branch T4 (Training), Reichswehr Ministry
1931, October 1	Chief of Staff, *Wehrkreis* VI, Münster, Westphalia
1931, December 1	Promoted *Oberst*
1934, October 1	Promoted *Generalmajor*, Artillery Commander 7, Munich
1935, October 15	Commander, 7th Division, Munich
1936, August 1	Promoted *Generalleutnant*, in charge of Manoeuvres Staff, Army manoeuvres, 1936
1936, November 12	Head, Training Branch, General Staff of the Army, Berlin. Director, Manoeuvres Staff, *Wehrmacht* Manoeuvres, 1937
1937, October 12	*Oberquartiermeister* II (OQu II) Training, General Staff of the Army
1938, February 1	Promoted *General der Artillerie*
1938, February 10	*Oberquartiermeister* I (OQu I) Operations, General Staff of the Army
1938, September 1	Chief of the General Staff of the Army
1939, October 29	Awarded Knights Cross of the Iron Cross
1940, July 19	Promoted *Generaloberst*
1942, September 24	Removed from office and transferred to the Reserve
1944, July 21	Arrested by the Gestapo
1945, January 31	Dismissed from the Army
1945, February 7	Imprisoned in Flossenburg concentration camp
1945, April 7	Transferred to Dachau concentration camp
1945, April 30	Released
1945, May 5	Prisoner of war
1947, June 30	Released
1948–61	Head, Historical Liaison Group, Historical Division, US Army
1961, November	Awarded the Meritorious Civilian Service Award of the USA
1972, April 2	Died

BLOMBERG

5

BLOMBERG

Field-Marshal Werner von Blomberg

WALTER GÖRLITZ

Towards the end of the nineteenth century, General of Infantry Herman von Blomberg (1836–1924), commanding General of the 2nd Army Corps in Stettin (Pomerania), was considered to be one of the most outstanding soldiers of the Prussian Army. His family was not of the old-established nobility. During the Seven Years' War a certain Captain von Blomberg had sought employment in the army of Frederick the Great. He claimed to have served in the small army of the Duke of Kurland and to be of aristocratic descent (which could neither be proved nor disproved). He also intimated that he was related to the Barons von Blomberg in the Lippe Dukedoms (which was not at all true). However, he proved to be a valiant officer, on account of which the Royal Heraldic Office in Berlin raised no objection to him using an aristocratic name. The family did not possess material wealth and had only the honour of wearing the King's coat and carrying the King's sword, as did many smaller Prussian families of poor 'military nobility'.

His nephew, Werner von Blomberg, born on 2 September 1878 in Stargard, Pomerania, as son of a Captain and Emma von Tschepe und Weidenbach (of the Silesian nobility), was to rise even higher than his uncle, namely to the rank of Field-Marshal and War Minister of the Reich, and thereafter to gamble away and lose his heritage and high office.

Like his uncle and his father, Werner von Blomberg was educated in the cadet corps, which was then a tough course. He joined the infantry, became an officer like all his ancestors, and was in 1911 transferred to the General

Staff on account of his outstanding intelligence. He, indeed, surpassed all his comrades as far as intellectual interests and a yearning for knowledge were concerned. It was precisely because of these qualities that later many generals considered him to be an outsider. In the First World War he made a career as General Staff officer, became First General Staff Officer (Ia) with the 7th Army on the Western Front and, after the revolution of 1918 which ended the Hohenzollern monarchy and led to the Armistice, was accepted with very high commendations into the *Reichswehr*, the small professional army of 100,000 men allowed the new German republic under the Versailles Treaty. Here he served from 1927 to 1929 as chief of the troop office (*Truppenamt*), the disguised small General Staff. In this capacity he undertook the obligatory trip to Soviet Russia, the fruit of the (secret) good relations between the *Reichswehr* and the Red Army.

With his intellectual agility, Blomberg was very susceptible to new impressions and ideas. He was extremely impressed by the image the Red Army presented, that of a very strong professional army equipped for modern times. He also formed the impression that the Soviet communist régime was based on two pillars, the Party and the Armed Forces. But the fact that almost all commanders were members of the Communist Party of the Soviet Union, and that therefore Party and forces were closely linked, escaped the German visitors. Neither could they foretell from these sporadic visits that the Party Secretary-General, Joseph Stalin, was in 1929–30 engaged in a quiet purge of the Commander Corps, especially of old Tsarist officers who had sworn allegiance to the red flag.

At any rate, Blomberg was enthused by his visit to the Soviet Union. Unlike most of the higher-ranking officers of the Army command, who still nourished sentimental memories of the monarchy which disappeared in 1918 in so deplorable a manner, Blomberg displayed democratic tendencies, since the state which the Army served was now a republic. A decisive factor for Blomberg's future career was the fact that he did not get on very well with the powerful chief of the ministerial office at the Defence Ministry, Major General Kurt von Schleicher. Schleicher, together with the aged President of the Republic, Field-Marshal von Hindenburg, and his son, Colonel Oskar von Hindenburg, had all progressed through the ranks of the 3rd Regiment of the Guards. Schleicher was at that time still *persona grata* at the presidential palace in the Wilhelmstrasse. We do not know to this day the reason for this mutual antipathy between Schleicher and Blomberg. It may be that Schleicher, who still nourished ideas of a possible restoration of the monarchy, considered Blomberg too 'democratic a general'.

However, Blomberg disappeared from the Berlin scene and became commander of the military district (*Wehrkreis*) I in east Prussia and commander of the 1st Infantry Division stationed there. East Prussia had been geographically separated from the Reich since the peace settlement of 1919, when part of west Prussia was annexed to Poland in order to give Poland access to the Baltic. The Chief of Army Command there was Schleicher's old crony General Baron von Hammerstein-Equord, presumably not a friend of Blomberg's either. In 1932 Blomberg suffered a severe personal blow. His wife Charlotte, née Hellmich, died aged only 43. She had also been an officer's daughter, but contrary to the marriage traditions of the Blombergs, her family was not an aristocratic one. In addition, Blomberg's 'friends' in Berlin burdened him with another most uncongenial mission. He was ordered to the League of Nations Headquarters at Geneva, where he was to conduct the sluggish disarmament negotiations as the leader of the German military delegation – for which he undeniably possessed just the right degree of diplomatic skill and suavity. According to the Treaty of Versailles and the Covenant of the League of Nations, all the signatories had committed themselves to disarm. Germany, as the defeated power, had already largely done so under compulsion. Since other powers, headed by France, had no intention of following suit, the question arose for Germany as to whether such conduct might warrant a modest increase of her own forces.

While Blomberg was based in Geneva, a tug of war began in Germany, and especially in Berlin, as to whether political power should be transferred to Hitler or, indeed, whether power *had* to be transferred to him. Schleicher, Chancellor and Defence Minister since 2 December 1932, failed in his attempt to outmanoeuvre Hitler politically. On 29 January 1933 Blomberg received a telegram in Geneva asking him to report to President von Hindenburg in Berlin as soon as possible on the morning of 30 January. To speed matters up, Colonel Oskar von Hindenburg himself met Blomberg at the station. Plans were afoot to pair the National-Socialist Hitler as Chancellor with the Catholic conservative ex-Chancellor von Papen as Vice-Chancellor, in replacement of General von Schleicher, the Chancellor and Defence Minister. Blomberg was to become Defence Minister, precisely for the reason that he was an enemy of Schleicher. Legally this appointment was tantamount to a breach of the constitution, for according to the Weimar Republic constitution still in force, only a civilian could become Defence Minister. In May 1932 Schleicher had therefore formally handed in his resignation from the Army prior to joining the cabinet of Papen as Defence Minister. And now? The President of the Republic, who often took advantage of the oath he had sworn on the constitution, wanted to see an active-service general as Defence Minister in order to provide a counter-balance to Hitler. Moreover, according to the old Prussian tradition, the office of Defence Minister was barred to civilians. So, the legally very doubtful appointment of Blomberg was sanctioned by special decree.

No record of Blomberg's response to this sudden appointment exists, but none the less it was a triumph for him. The existing *Ministeramt* was converted to a *Wehrmachtamt* (Armed Forces) Office. Blomberg ordered his confidant, Chief of Staff Colonel Walther von Reichenau, from Königsberg to Berlin and entrusted him with the running of this office. Reichenau, however, athletic, wiry, energetic, and willing to take responsibility, a gleaming monocle in his eye, was no friend of desk work. But in a time of crisis such a bold Chief of Staff and a slightly more cautious Defence Minister complemented each other admirably. Moreover, during an election tour Hitler made in East Prussia in early summer 1932, Reichenau had been introduced to the Führer personally; and Hitler had assured him that Germany would rearm if he became Chancellor. Could there have been a German officer who did not like to hear that? At the time Reichenau was occupying himself with the question of reform of the army structure. The relationship between officer and private had to be restructured in a technological age. From now on Reichenau put his money on Hitler whom he thought approachable. However, Reichenau, who was fond of a feudal way of life, was less keen on the Nazi Party itself and its bigwigs.

After their respective appointments Blomberg and Reichenau immediately faced critical issues. When Hitler came to power, he controlled his own paramilitary Nazi Party army, i.e. the SA (*Sturmabteilung*) which in January 1933 consisted of about 400,000 men. He had personally been its 'Highest SA Führer' since 1931 while Captain Ernst Röhm, a Bavarian ex-officer, was its executive Chief of Staff. After the failed Hitler coup of 1923 Röhm had gone to Bolivia where, employed in a German military consultancy, he had worked his way up to the rank of Lieutenant Colonel. He had undoubtedly hoped that, should Hitler get into power, his SA would combine with the small German professional army and form the nucleus of a new 'people's army' from which the 'reactionary' generals would be barred. Many of the leaders of SA units in the Reich were former front officers who saw themselves as future generals. Others, of the mercenary type, like the former page-boy and waiter, Karl Ernst, SA *Gruppenführer* (group leader) of Berlin-Brandenburg, and the former front-line lieutenants Hans-Peter von Heydebreck and Edmund Heines in Stettin and Breslau began to lead a very wild existence, suiting themselves and presuming they could do as they liked. After the union of the SA with the 'Stahlhelm League of Front Soldiers' (the private army of the Nationalist Party) was completed in the autumn of 1933, Hitler's party army of Brownshirts had increased to about 2 million men. However, apart from being equipped with machine guns for house-to-house and street fighting against political opponents before 30 January 1933, this army was largely unarmed. Röhm organized the formation of standing armed 'staff guards' in each SA equivalent of an Army Corps area. He also created for himself a personal 'staff guard'. However, the great change anticipated by the SA leaders did not materialize. There was now confused talk of a 'second revolution'. Röhm, notoriously homosexual, and usually drinking more than he could carry, very often fortified by strong French champagne and cognac, went about bragging that he, a Captain and General Staff officer, could 'manage' a former corporal (i.e. Hitler). He finally lost his head in the process!

At the Defence Ministry, Generals Blomberg and von Reichenau now faced a tricky task. On the one hand, tension was increasing between the SA and the *Reichswehr*, which led not only to unpleasant clashes but sometimes to actual attacks by unruly SA men on Army officers – an undoubtedly untenable situation. On the other hand it was, from the generals' point of view, inadvisable to deploy the Army against the SA. After all, here was a reserve of 2 million volunteers who would play a vital role when, as was anticipated, Hitler reintroduced general conscription. The third and most worrying point was that Blomberg and Reichenau for a long time did not know what Hitler's stance in this conflict between SA and Army was. According to the Weimar Constitution, the most significant article of which had become invalid already, the President of the Republic, the aged von Hindenburg, was still Commander-in-Chief of the Army. Only he, and under no circumstances the Chancellor, Hitler, could *de jure* order deployment of the Army. But Hindenburg, now aged 78, had gone to his estate in East Prussia because of illness, and so events were to develop outside his sphere of influence.

Blomberg consequently acted with caution. When the Leader of Infantry, *Wehrkreis* III, Major-General Keitel, reported to him the unusual request from the Berlin SA leader Ernst to take over 'supervision' of the secret ordnance stores for the eastern frontier defence for which Keitel was responsible, Blomberg assured him that relations with the SA gave no reason for concern. The commander of *Wehrkreis* II, Stettin, Lieutenant General von Bock, announced to the young officers who had been attacked by the SA that such attacks were most unacceptable and would have to be reported to the Minister, who would not be pleased with such news. Yet the opportunity also existed to use the SA groups for pre-military training of young officers. Blomberg had one great advantage: he very quickly won Hitler's confidence. Mentally volatile and easily enthused, he considered the new Chancellor simply wonderful, and Hitler, for his part, possessed an inimitable feeling for recognizing those who respected him and were willing to follow him unconditionally. Very soon he confided more in Blomberg than in his SA Chief of Staff, Röhm, who, besides, had openly called him a 'crank' on many occasions.

Röhm had two mortal enemies in the party leadership. One was the present Reich Minister for Aviation Herman Göring, who, as a former Air Force officer, hated any lack of discipline. The other was the SS leader Heinrich Himmler who was aiming to transform the SS (*Schutzstaffen*), Hitler's black-uniformed bodyguard, into the only significant National Socialist armed force in the Reich. In the spring of 1934 the chief of the *Wehrmachtamt*, Reichenau, must have learnt that the SS was preparing for open conflict with the SA. And in June Blomberg finally succeeded in persuading Hitler to conclude an alliance between army and party to forestall any machinations by the SA. Blomberg was permitted to publish an article in the *Völkischer Beobachter* specifying how party and army were to constitute the two pillars of the Third Reich –

an unmistakable warning to the SA, and for Blomberg perhaps a reminder of the false impression he had formed of the Red Army's role in the Soviet Union.

So much is certain: at the Defence Ministry they firmly believed in a Röhm coup. Röhm, however, suffering badly from rheumatism, had no intention of staging a coup for which, in any case, his million-strong para-military force was not equipped. Instead he attempted to postpone any decision by ordering his SA to take a four-week holiday from 1 July 1934. Prior to that he convened a meeting for 30 June 1934 of all higher SA officers at Bad Wiessee to inform them about his strategy – he also underwent a cure for his rheumatism there. Himmler, Heydrich (Himmler's chief of the SS security service), and Göring used this opportunity to massacre the entire SA leadership, having won over the ever-irresolute Hitler by means of false reports that Röhm and his confrères were planning a coup d'état.

In June 1934 Blomberg showed Keitel a list of 78 names – he did not specify whose names – of persons to be arrested. As a precautionary measure he advised the entire *Reichswehr* to come to a state of readiness from 28 June onwards. Now Blomberg and Reichenau, who had not informed the Army leadership of the details, only had to await the outcome of the Bad Wiessee, Munich and Berlin meetings with their arms folded. Was this not a strategico-political master-stroke? The Army stood ready for action. But the SS relieved them of the bloody task. The blood bath among SA leaders and among conservatives, to which the ex-Generals von Schleicher and von Bredow also fell victim, being an act outside the law, the Chancellor Hitler immediately proclaimed himself 'Highest Judge of the People' on the fictitious justification of a plot. Blomberg and Reichenau refrained from making any comments about the whole affair. The important thing was not to dirty one's hands. The SA had now been reduced to insignificance.

Other problems, other conflicts and immense new tasks arose in 1935. In March 1935 Hitler announced the re-introduction of general conscription, with the formation of an Army of 36 Divisions and 12 Army Corps. The Defence Ministry became a War Ministry, the *Truppenamt* again openly a General Staff of the old style. On Hitler's birthday, on 22 April 1936, Blomberg was promoted to Field-Marshal. He needed a new man to head the *Wehrmachtsamt* (Armed Forces Office), a new body under him set up against the opposition of the Army Commander-in-Chief and Chief of Staff. For this task he secured General Keitel, whom he knew from the First World War to be an organizational genius and with whom he had worked closely in the *Truppenamt*.

As War Minister, Blomberg was now overall Commander-in-Chief of the *Wehrmacht*, comprising all the forces of the new Third Reich. Göring, promoted to Colonel-General, was in charge of the newly, but independently, formed Air Force. As Colonel-General he was subordinate to a Field-Marshal.

At the same time Göring was Aviation Minister and as such equal to his cabinet colleague Blomberg. Such overlaps were common in this officially strictly departmentalized Hitlerite state, in this autocracy consisting of several sub-autocrats.

In spite of this irrevocable muddle, Blomberg set to work on a theoretical solution of his main and favourite task: the reorganization of the Armed Forces top command structure to meet a potential defence situation. At the *Wehrmachtamt* a small 'National Defence' section existed, a nucleus for a future *Oberkommando der Wehrmacht* (Armed Forces General Staff). Blomberg was firmly convinced that, in an emergency, there should be such a tripartite leadership for all three forces, i.e. Army, Navy and Air Force, and that the age of unilateral ground warfare was over. But Göring, Luftwaffe Commander-in-Chief, was equally convinced that he would never submit to such leadership, the more so as 'his' Air Force represented a power tool in the inner political rivalry of the Third Reich. And third, the Army Command – now known as the *Oberkommando des Heeres* (Army General Staff), with Colonel General Baron von Fritsch as C-in-C and General Beck as Chief of the General Staff – insisted that, in an emergency, the Army High Command alone was competent to lead, and that a conflict could be decided only on land. Blomberg found ardent supporters for his idea in his chief of the *Wehrmachtamt*, General Keitel, and in the head of the *Wehrmachtamt*'s 'national defence section', Lieutenant-Colonel Jodl. When finally, in June 1937, he dared to issue his first general directive on command organization in war, a cry of indignation broke out from the Army General Staff. A memoranda battle ensued between the various departments but, significantly, Hitler kept well out of it all. At this time he hardly ever worried about such problems, not least because he believed that, with Blomberg in charge, all was well. And indeed it was. In an emergency, so Blomberg argued, a 'Generalissimo' with a small OKW staff could be employed. But, in 1937, the filling of such posts was not discussed further, as far as is known.

Field-Marshal von Blomberg's public image grew. He was chosen to represent Hitler in June 1937 in London for the coronation ceremony of King George VI. He gave the memorial address in Munich for General Ludendorff, First Quartermaster-General and Hindenburg's influential adviser in the First World War, who died on 20 December 1937. Hitler's Luftwaffe adjutant, Captain Nikolaus von Below, a friend of Blomberg's children from his first marriage, confirms that Hitler had complete trust in Blomberg.

General Keitel and his wife, actively engaged in social activities as was customary among officers' families, could not understand why Blomberg did not care for these. But Blomberg was leading a secret life. Since about 1934 – according to his daughter Dorothea, who kept house for him – he would don civilian clothes in the evening, order his chauffeur to drive him to a prearranged but alternating location, give instructions to pick him up again after a few hours, and disappear into the night. The widower was seeking amorous adventures – a strange pastime for a War Minister. During these escapades, presumably at the beginning of 1937, or even earlier, he must have met an attractive young 'lady' by the name of Margarethe Gruhn who, likewise, sought an 'acquaintance'. The widower, now almost 60, fell for this creature 'experienced in love'. He became almost her slave, called her 'Eva' and decided to marry her. Presumably 'Eva' had also fallen in love with the tall, handsome aristocratic gentleman.

In December 1937 Blomberg informed General Keitel that he intended to remarry, that his future wife was from a humble background but that this was no shame in the Third Reich. Later he described 'Eva's' mother as an ironer and presser. In fact she was a laundress in New Cologne. In the same month, Blomberg (although aware that Göring was vying to take over his post) confided in Göring that he wanted to remarry but that there was another suitor. Could Göring remove him? Göring, most co-operative in such situations, ensured that this man was paid off and sent abroad. Had 'honour' still been meaningful and had the world of the officer corps and of the aristocracy still been intact, then Blomberg would have had to hand in his resignation for the sake of this woman. Misalliances, after all, happened in the best of families. But Blomberg wanted everything: both 'Eva's' sexual experience and his office, reputation and uniform. To secure these Blomberg asked Hitler and Göring to be wedding witnesses, convinced that they would protect him completely should there be any difficulties. On 12 January 1938 the civil wedding ceremony took place in the great hall of the War Ministry, in the absence of Blomberg's children from his first marriage. Two weeks later, this macabre farce collapsed. Margarethe Gruhn, now Frau von Blomberg, was known to the vice squad and had previously been convicted of dealing with pornographic photographs (something she had obviously hidden from her high-ranking husband).

Initially, Hitler was speechless and horrified because he felt he had been conned by a nobleman. On 27 January 1938 Blomberg had to go, as was announced officially, for 'reasons of health'. However, on leaving, he advised Hitler to take over command of the *Wehrmacht* himself, having learnt that General von Fritsch, the Army Commander-in-Chief, had been accused of homosexual practices. Hitler took this advice – to his own, the forces' and the Reich's detriment, and appointed no successor to Blomberg as Defence Minister. Blomberg became *persona non grata* in the Führer state. Nobody was allowed to mention his name. To get him out of the limelight, Hitler personally paid for him to go on a world tour as a present. Blomberg completed only half of it and then settled in Bad Wiessee.

At the beginning of 1939 he contacted Keitel in great secrecy: he was prepared to dissolve his second marriage if Hitler would reinstate him in office – a naive approach. Naturally, Hitler rejected such a request and mentioned to Keitel that he himself had initially offered Blomberg this solution. Blomberg had then declined. In order to cover up his second wife's background, Blomberg took an unusual step: in the *Almanach de Gotha* (equivalent to Burke's Peerage) he gave 'Eva's' name as 'Elsbeth Grunow', a rather dubious proceeding considering that notices of this nature have documentary validity. At the collapse of the Third Reich in 1945 the former War Minister was arrested. He died in internment in Nuremberg on 14 March 1946, from a heart attack. His two officer sons died on the battlefield for 'Führer, folk and fatherland', as the charming phrase went.

BIBLIOGRAPHY

See combined bibliography on Blomberg, Keitel, Jodl, Warlimont and Reichenau on page 219.

CHRONOLOGY: WERNER VON BLOMBERG

1878, September 2	Born in Stargard (Pomerania) as son of a captain. Cadet corps, infantry officer
From 1911	General Staff officer (Ia) at 7th Army headquarters on the Western Front. Transfer to *Reichswehr*
1927–9	Chief of *Truppenamt* (troop office)
1929–33	Lieutenant-General and commander of *Wehrkreis* (military district) I, East Prussia
1932–3	Despatched to disarmament conference in Geneva as leader of German military delegation
1933 January 30–March 1935	Defence Minister
1935 March–1938 January	(from 1936 onwards in the rank of Field-Marshal) War Minister. Dismissed from the forces because of marriage scandal. Not reinstated.
1945	Interned by Allies
1946, March 14	Death in Nuremberg prison

KEITEL

JODL

WARLIMONT

6

KEITEL, JODL AND WARLIMONT

Field-Marshal Wilhelm Keitel
General of Artillery Alfred Jodl
General of Artillery Walter Warlimont

WALTER GÖRLITZ

Wilhelm Keitel was born on 22 September 1883 on his family estate at Helmscherode, near the present spa of Gandersheim in the lower Harz mountains
and in the western part of the Dukedom of Brunswick. The estate, covering
about 650 acres, was not easily managed on account of the soil conditions and
divisions of the estate into the family manor and two separate farms. It had
been the property of the Keitels since 1871. Originally the family had leased
land, first from the Prince Elector and later from the King of Hanover. The
grandfather of the later Field-Marshal had acquired land in the Welf dukedom
of Brunswick because he had no desire to live under Prussian rule after the
last Hanovarian King, George v, had been deposed by Bismarck. The first
maxim at Helmscherode was loyalty to the old dynasty, even in, and because
of, its misfortune. This concept of loyalty sucked in, as it were, with the
mothers' milk seems to have grown within the Field-Marshal perhaps sub-
consciously and under different circumstances. However, American interrogation officers and psychologists, ignorant of his family background, likened
him to the prototype of a 'Preussischer Junker'.

His mother came also from an old established family of tenant farmers. She
died when he was five years old, after giving birth to his brother Bodewin.
There had been no military tradition in the family. Their interests were limited
to agriculture, horses and hunting. Politics for them, restricted by their hatred
of Prussia, only mattered as far as protective tariffs or free trade in the new
German Reich might affect agriculture. The young Keitel had a private tutor,

as was the fashion among estate owners; though quite intelligent he was only an average pupil. At the Gymnasium in Göttingen he just scraped through his Abitur. Initially, only agriculture, horses and hunting attracted him as a vocation. In the last two decades of the nineteenth century, however, the enthusiasm of the young middle-class generation for the new Reich and its powerful Army excited him too. He, like many of his school friends, considered the only modern career to be a military one. So the young Keitel made a decision which took him to the highest rank in the Army; and to a shameful death at the gallows.

In 1901 he joined the 46th Prussian Field Artillery Regiment in Wolfenbüttel near Brunswick – and the only Brunswicker battery. So strict was the rule in the Keitel household, that the heir to Helmscherode could not possibly commence his career under the 'Prussians'. Second Lieutenant Keitel soon proved to be an efficient, intelligent and extremely industrious officer. Another Second Lieutenant, Günter Kluge, son of a general who was later ennobled, served in the same regiment. Although the two lieutenants' paths were to cross many times later on, they did not easily tolerate each other. Kluge thought Keitel a swot and a dull bore, and Keitel saw Kluge as a typical product of the Prussian cadet corps: too dashing, arrogant and presumptuous.

His superiors soon recognized that Second Lieutenant Keitel possessed an outstanding talent for organizational and tactical duties. He was appointed Staff Captain to the regiment, a post in which he was responsible for all matters of mobilization. In 1909 he married Lisa Fontaine, a daughter of a wealthy farm owner at Wülfel near Hanover. The Fontaines were possibly even more intractable Welfs than the Keitels. The young woman was intellectually much more aware than her husband and very fond of good literature and music. Perhaps they complemented each other the better with their contrasting interests. It is not reported anywhere that Wilhelm Keitel ever read a book other than military or war history and related writings. He might possibly have commented that his 'duty' did not allow him time to do so; and he was inclined to be on duty all the time.

In the First World War he went into action with the 46th Artillery. In September 1914 Lieutenant Keitel received a shrapnel wound in his right lower arm. Being physically robust, the Lieutenant soon recovered. In March 1915 the great turning point came: the first leap towards the top. He was called into the General Staff. Reason: his organizational abilities, sound judgment in tactical matters and an unflagging dedication to duty. He did not have to go through the classical schooling for the Prussian general staff, the principle of which was the co-responsibility of its officers for the decisions of High Command. This no longer mattered. However, if the adage coined by the legendary Chief of the General Staff, Count Schlieffen – 'The day has 24 hours and if these are not enough, then the "Herr" should take the night as well' – has ever been incarnated, then the new General Staff Captain was a prime example.

Two factors are of significance: one, that Keitel became an officer in the General Staff at all, and two, that he came from the artillery. After the war on the Western Front degenerated into an unimaginative positional struggle which consumed men and materials to an unexpected extent, the General Staff officer of lower units, Divisions, Army Corps and Armies had the task of organizing and administrating the battle. For this mode of warfare the artillery became the decisive heavy weapon – no longer the cavalry, the pride of the aristocracy and pet of monarchs, which had ridden its last charges in 1914 on all fronts and had bled to death in the rapid fire of rifles and machine-guns. Looking at the careers of the leading officers of the German Army in the Second World War, one sees that many of these generals – Keitel, Jodl, Beck, Halder, Fritsch, Warlimont, Brauchitsch – came from the artillery. In an era when full motorization was still a mere dream, this weapon had a certain static character. It explains why these gentlemen, after the First World War, protested so vehemently against the rising panzer arm with its dynamic movement, a new fire-spitting battle cavalry of enormous breakthrough power.

Keitel became First General Staff Officer (Ia) of a reserve infantry division and in 1917–18, during the last phase of the war, Ia of the Marine Corps deployed in Flanders, consisting of superfluous crews of the Imperial Navy and generally considered to be élite troops. While in the reserve division Keitel made the acquaintance of Major von Blomberg, Ia of the 7th Army, with whom his later career was to be closely connected. Keitel was very impressed by Blomberg, a widely educated officer of the traditional General Staff calibre who was interested in a thousand things outside duty, but he never managed to be close to him personally. Obviously, Blomberg had a way of remaining unapproachable despite a charming manner in a social context.

The Ia of the Marine Corps had never been interested in politics. One thing though must already have been obvious to him, that the High Command of the Army, responsible for the Army and the then subordinate Air Force, and the High Command of the Navy each aspired to conduct their own war. The German Kaiser and King of Prussia, Wilhelm II, in the role of 'First War Lord' should have been the co-ordinator but, unfortunately, he totally lacked this ability. One can only guess how many of the Welf dreams instilled into the young Keitel had faded together with the image of the Kaiser. Into his place now stepped the forceful image of the 71-year-old Field-Marshal von Hindenburg. None the less, the news of the Navy mutiny at home in November 1918, the dissolution of the reserve units, and the flight of the Kaiser into neutral Holland must have hit Keitel like an earthquake. In letters to her mother, his wife poured out her scorn and contempt for 'Willy', as she had always called the 'Prussian Monarch', and his shameful exit from the stage after so many bombastic speeches.

Keitel never criticized the conduct of the Kaiser; it would have been unworthy of an officer, and, moreover, the sovereign was a taboo subject. And yet, for a long time, a personally signed picture of Crown Prince Wilhelm was to grace his desk even at the War Ministry of the Weimar Republic. One day it disappeared and nobody seems to know why! Keitel, the ex-Guelph, still displayed a strange attachment to the House of Hohenzollern (which Hitler later hated). Keitel could be very sentimental at times.

Much to his annoyance, however, the Ia of the Marine Corps in Brussels was obliged to fly the red flag of revolution on his official car, in order to arrange the details of the retreat of his corps at the end of the war. Keitel felt he no longer understood the world. Should he now take his leave and assist his father with managing Helmscherode? This would have corresponded with his instincts. His duty as a soldier, however, commanded that he stay serving a new, alien republic. When forming the new 100,000-man professional army permitted by the Versailles Treaty, General von Seeckt, the C-in-C, did not overlook this tiger of an organizer, Wilhelm Keitel. According to the terms of the Treaty of Versailles of 1919, neither a General Staff nor staff training was allowed. The new army was not to possess heavy weapons, artillery of more than 10.5 calibre, tanks or aeroplanes. So men had to improvise. Under the surface everything remained the same. At High Command, the General Staff was disguised by the formation of a troop office (*Truppenamt*). So-called 'leader assistants' replaced the General Staff officers.

Apart from some tours in command of troops, as was obligatory for a 'leader assistant' career, Keitel served finally, until 1933, in the rank of Colonel and branch chief in the *Truppenamt* as leader of the 2nd Branch (T2) 'Organization'. This was an indication of how his talent was appreciated.

General von Seeckt reorganized the Army in such a way that the seven infantry divisions permitted under the Versailles Treaty could be trebled in an emergency. Three generals (one divisional commander, one infantry and one artillery 'leader') were allocated to each division. The latter two were each supported by a 'leader assistant', thus forging small nuclei for future divisional staffs. The chief of Branch T2 was not only responsible for day-to-day organizational matters, but also for the supervision of the secret, but voluntary 'eastern frontier defence' (*Grenzschutz Ost*) against any Polish encroachment on the Reich. Here Keitel's passion for horses was an advantage. The frontier defence, especially in Pomerania, consisted mainly of members of the land-owning aristocracy who worked in conjunction with the Stahlhelm League of Front-Soldiers (*Stahlhelm Bund der Frontsoldaten*). Keitel found in these genuine Prussian *junkers* men of kindred spirit.

In the *Truppenamt* he met old acquaintances and made new friends, all of which were to play a role in his later life. Head of the Branch T1 from 1927 to 1929 was Keitel's old acquaintance, Major-General Werner von Blomberg. But not even now did they enter into a closer social contact. Keitel, however, worked in close collaboration with another acquaintance, Colonel Hermann Geyer, on plans for reorganizing the Higher Command echelons of the forces, similar to those which Blomberg then had in mind. Both forces, the Army and the Navy, should be brought into better co-operation under a single *Wehrmacht* Operations Staff. Keitel, with remarkable insight, unselfishly insisted, however, that he himself was not suitable for leadership of such a staff, since he lacked the necessary thorough grounding and leadership qualities.

In this era of the 1920s, these were only theories, intellectual sand-table games. Practical matters at that time comprised an obligatory journey to Russia, since the government of the Reich maintained secret but sanctioned relations with the Red Army of the Soviet Union. *Vice versa*, Soviet Commanders (officers with traditional titles of rank were not known in the Red Army) were directed to Berlin for training. In 1931 Keitel and Major-General von Brauchitsch (of Branch T4 of the *Truppenamt* training) travelled to Moscow, in civilian clothes for reasons of confidentiality. The Soviet Union then possessed a very strong, well equipped professional army, together with some voluntary territorial reservists who were less well provided for. The German guests were naturally shown only what they were supposed to see. Keitel was much impressed first by the size of this vast empire, and second by the professional Army which existed alongside the ruling party, the Communist Party of the Soviet Union. The German officers were not aware that the military and political leaderships in Russia were closely linked by membership of the same Party; but instead they formed the impression of a two-pillar structure of Party and Army, each with equal rights.

Keitel's time in the *Truppenamt*, regulated by the ever-precise clock but allowing the opportunity for a refreshing morning ride in the Tiergarten, was probably the last normal phase of his life. However, it was overshadowed by the agricultural crisis of 1932 and the political turmoil of the same year, the replacement as Chancellor first of Brüning by Papen and then by the War Minister, Lieutenant-General (retd) von Schleicher, and last the rise of Hitler's NSDAP.

If Keitel was in any way politically oriented, he opted for the authoritarian policy of Franz von Papen as Chancellor. Neither he nor his wife trusted the Nazis. He never even mentioned Schleicher, former head of the ministerial office of the War Ministry and now War Minister. Perhaps, in his diary started in the Nuremberg prison, he had wanted to banish the memory of von Schleicher's murder by the SS on 30 June 1934. Moreover, he had had no official contact with that eternal political intriguer and meddler. The majority of the officer corps, without doubt, did not consider Schleicher to be a real soldier any more.

Illness forced Keitel to be absent from the last politically decisive phase between December 1932 and January 1933, when the Weimar Republic was on its death-bed. He had to take an involuntary rest following a neglected vein inflammation in his leg which developed into a thrombosis. He and his equally ailing wife went to the High Tatra in Czechoslovakia to recuperate. It was here that he learned that on 30 January 1933 the aged President of the Republic, Field-Marshal von Hindenburg, had appointed Adolf Hitler to be Chancellor of the Reich. The President was at the same time Commander-in-Chief of Army and Navy. Soldiers had to obey, according to Keitel's credo. But, at that moment, Wilhelm and Lisa Keitel were less than happy with Hindenburg's decision. They had no knowledge of the background of this so-called 'power seizure'. Nor did they anticipate what Hitler had in store for them and what their fate would ultimately be. Illness and convalescence were the only two elements in Keitel's life that ever caused him to be absent from his duty.

General von Blomberg became the new War Minister of the Reich, precisely because the failed Chancellor von Schleicher had never liked him. The ministerial office in the War Ministry was changed to a *Wehrmachtamt* (Armed Forces Office), an administrative staff for the new office holder. Attached to this was a small department (L = *Land*) for national defence. Schleicher's old and intimate personal friend, General Baron von Hammerstein-Equord, a gentleman of grand-seigneurial mannerisms, remained C-in-C of the Army despite his dislike of desk work, particularly at a time when more administration was called for with plans to enlarge the Army. A time of unrest began for Keitel. On 1 October 1933 he became Major-General and Infantry Leader *Wehrkreis* III in Potsdam; then from October 1934, under the disguise of 'Artillery Leader 6' (i.e. of the 6th Division – the Treaty of Versailles was still in force), he was entrusted with the formation of the future 22nd Infantry Division in Bremen. As Commander in Potsdam he experienced directly the conflict between the Army and the SA, Hitler's Party army which had grown by now to 2 million men.

Like almost all higher officers, Keitel then believed that a coup was being planned by the Chief of Staff of the SA, Captain Ernst Röhm, who behaved towards Hitler in an arrogant manner. Keitel welcomed Hitler's bloody stroke against the SA leadership on 30 June 1934. However, he reacted in silence to the simultaneous murder by the SS of two retired generals, Schleicher and his former right-hand man von Bredow.

Keitel's personal opinion of Hitler had changed suddenly after he had met this man, who was capable of holding the masses in thrall, at a conference of high-ranking SA leaders and Army officers in Bad Reichenhall in 1933, where he and the Austrian had exchanged a few words with each other. Keitel was no 'homo politicus'; he did not possess any sound conservative conviction and totally lacked inner sovereignty of character. Keitel was deeply impressed by the Führer, as the former painter was now officially known. Hitler's ability to draw even those prejudiced against him under his spell cannot be explained;

it must be accepted as a historic fact. For the time being, Hitler forgot about Keitel; but Keitel did not forget Hitler. The Führer had marvellously impressed him.

Back as troop commander, occupied with organization, training and tactical leadership of his units during manoeuvres, Keitel was newly stimulated. But then came the thunderbolt from Berlin. He was to be tied to the desk once more, precisely because he was considered to be the desk worker *par excellence*. The new War Minister, von Blomberg, formerly commander in the *Wehrkreis* I in East Prussia, had appointed his Chief of Staff from Königsberg, Colonel Walther von Reichenau (who had met Hitler there) to be Head of the *Wehrmachtamt* (Armed Forces Office). Reichenau, although talented, ambitious, a good tennis player and all-round sportsman, was anything but a desk worker. Blomberg required a reliable *chef du bureau*. So General von Fritsch, since February 1934 the Commander-in-Chief of the Army, and the head of the Army personnel office, General von Schwedler, both recommended Keitel, who was equally known to Blomberg. Keitel was not at all pleased. He hesitated. Should he not take over the management of Helmscherode which, after his father's death, he had carried on part-time? The estate needed a new landlord. His stepmother, second wife of his father, lived there too, but she and Lisa Keitel were not on very friendly terms. Besides, Lisa would prefer to have, as she assumed she was going to have, a more interesting social life in Berlin as wife of the senior military bureaucrat at the War Ministry. Thus, Keitel took the last decisive step in his life and, on 1 October 1935, he became head of the *Wehrmachtamt*.

During 1935 many changes were taking place. Hitler had unilaterally abolished the Versailles Treaty restrictions on Germany's Armed Forces: an army of 36 Divisions (12 Army Corps) was to be created. A new German Air Force under the command of the former airman, Colonel-General Göring, would be formed, adding a third armed force to the existing two. Blomberg had become War Minister of the Reich and on the Führer's birthday he was appointed Field-Marshal and Commander-in-Chief of the *Wehrmacht* (comprising all three services). Easily influenced, sensitive and readily impressionable, Blomberg was an ardent admirer of Hitler. Obviously, Blomberg himself had won the confidence of the Austrian demagogue who, after the death of old Hindenburg on 2 August 1934, had become absolute ruler of the German Reich as Führer and Chancellor.

Keitel had expected the transfer of responsibility to him at the beginning of October 1935 to be a solemn occasion. Instead, Major-General von Reichenau, the inevitable monocle firmly lodged in his eye, appeared in tennis gear and murmuring something about a tournament at 'Blue-white' (one of the fashionable tennis clubs in Berlin) handed his successor the most important secret documents before disappearing again, relieved to be rid of the inconvenient paper work. Keitel was shocked. What concept of duty was this? The

Wehrmachtamt was a complex organization consisting of various branches for home and overseas defence, war industry, law and finance. The organizer Keitel (who was not, as often believed, a stupid man, whatever his limitations) formed new, strictly defined, areas of responsibility. Industry was a weak point. This department, run by officers under General Thomas without experience in industrial management, lacked clear direction from Hitler as to his political objectives. But as far as could be seen, a war was not imminent, and so rearmament was framed merely for the traditional task of defending the Reich.

As Chief of the *Wehrmachtamt*, Lieutenant-General Keitel believed that the fulfilment of his favourite concept was near: that is, to have a single overall command of all three services, should the necessity arise. His idea found a favourable reception from the War Minister. Blomberg had contemplated creating a *Wehrmacht* Operations staff to unite the direction of Army, Navy and Air Force. In case of war, one 'Generalissimo' should preside over all the forces. We do not know whether he imagined himself in this role. Keitel found a true collaborator in the Head of Branch 'L' (National Defence), Lieutenant-Colonel Alfred Jodl. From the beginning, however, these plans were flawed. The Commander-in-Chief of the Air Force was Colonel-General Göring, old Party comrade of, and second in the Nazi Party to, Hitler. As Colonel-General he was subordinate to Blomberg; as Minister for Aviation of the Reich he was equal. In the covert struggle amongst Hitler's satraps he considered 'his' Air Force not least as a political lever. Later Keitel described this situation as 'impossible'. There was nothing to be done, however, since Hitler rather enjoyed this confusion over spheres of authority.

None the less, a memoranda feud developed between the War Ministry and High Command of the Army – Colonel-General Baron von Fritsch and the Chief of the General Staff, General Ludwig Beck – particularly after Blomberg, in June 1937, had issued his first directive concerning a combined military command. Fritsch and Beck saw this as an outrageous act of audacity. It had always been customary in Germany for the High Command of the Army, together with the Army General Staff, to be in sole charge of the conduct of national defence. The Navy and the Air Force were seen as only auxiliary forces, an indication that the Army High Command's thinking was behind the times. This feud was still continuing when the Blomberg marriage scandal broke in 1938. The most extraordinary point in these internal rivalries was that all participants, Keitel, Jodl, Fritsch and Beck (or Beck's deputy, Lieutenant-General von Manstein) never gave a thought to the opinion of the autocrat at the top, Hitler. In their view, this was not his business.

The personal relationship between Keitel and Blomberg remained distant. The slightly stale and conventional social intercourse between officers' families did not occur. Blomberg's wife had died in 1932 at the age of 43 and Keitel believed Blomberg to lead a retired life as a widower. Their children became friendly, however. Keitel's oldest son, Karl Heinz, fell in love with Blomberg's daughter, Dorle (Dorothea von Blomberg); a pretty and charming girl who ran the home for her father.

In December 1937 Blomberg informed Keitel that he was most definitely going to remarry, that his future wife came from a humble background but that in a National-Socialist Germany it was no shame to take as one's wife a child of the people. Somewhat surprised, Keitel took note of this information. At Christmas 1937 Dorle and her sister were guests in the Keitel house in Kielgenstrasse, whilst their father was staying in Oberhof, a skiing resort in Thuringia, presumably with his future wife. At the beginning of 1938 Dorle von Blomberg and Karl Heinz Keitel, Second Lieutenant in the cavalry, became engaged. On 12 January 1938 – exactly on Göring's birthday, which was usually celebrated with great pomposity – the civil wedding between Blomberg and a young, very attractive 'lady' took place in utmost secrecy with only Göring and Hitler as witnesses and in the absense of Blomberg's sons and daughters by his first marriage. Keitel, who was naturally not invited either, only learned that the lady was a 'Fräulein Gruhn'.

The couple disappeared on their honeymoon, which was interrupted by the sudden death, in Eberswalde near Berlin, of Blomberg's aged mother. During the funeral service, Keitel saw the new Frau von Blomberg but she was veiled. On 23 January 1938 the Berlin chief of police, Count Helldorf, asked to see Keitel urgently. He showed him documents and a police photograph of Blomberg's second wife, which had come to light when the young woman had registered her change of address to the Tirpitzufer, Blomberg's private apartment at the Ministry. According to these papers, she was a certain Margarethe Gruhn, born 1913, and known to the vice squad. Keitel was unable to identify the woman in the photograph, since he had only seen her in veils, but he referred Helldorf to Göring who after all had been a witness at their wedding and should know the new Frau von Blomberg. The Minister himself was not available, since he was settling his mother's estate in Eberswalde. Keitel was rather embarrassed, the more so because of his son's engagement to Blomberg's daughter. Since he was not aware of Göring's secret ambition to seize power over the War Ministry, it seemed to him the simplest way, at that time, to hush up the whole affair.

But the scandal spread to the highest circles after Göring had identified the Margarethe Gruhn in the police photograph as the new Frau von Blomberg and had so informed Hitler. Initially, Hitler was at a loss, shocked and outraged because Blomberg had used him as a marriage witness. In any case, Blomberg was finished. No sooner had this scandal blown over when the Gestapo or SD (*Sicherheitsdienst*) of the SS opened up another one with even greater repercussions: a clumsily compiled dossier against the Commander-in-Chief of the Army, Colonel-General Baron von Fritsch. Hated by the SS as a conservative and Christian, he was alleged to have transgressed the homosexuality law. A carefully briefed male prostitute, previously convicted of blackmail, was to appear as witness.

Hitler, who had never thought it possible for an aristocrat to marry a 'whore', now believed anything. Fritsch, however popular, was finished too. As always in times of crises, Hitler acted rashly and imprudently. He saw 'General *von* Keitel' (as Hitler then called him) as his military sheet-anchor. He had obviously forgotten that they had met before. He now implored Keitel to remain by his side and support him, when he (Hitler) personally took over supreme command of the *Wehrmacht*. Temporary successor to Fritsch as Army Commander-in-Chief – until the case was investigated by a court martial – was to be General von Brauchitsch, a proposal Blomberg may have made previously after Hitler's own candidate, General von Reichenau, had been unanimously rejected by the generals.

For a short while Keitel became involved in the design of a unified command structure for the *Wehrmacht*. Hitler, a former corporal, became Commander-in-Chief. The War Ministry was abolished. In its place, the *Oberkommando der Wehrmacht* (High Command of the Forces, or OKW) was formed, serving also as a military administration under the General of Artillery Keitel as its 'chief' – but without any executive power. Keitel was quick, though, to appoint his brother, Major-General Bodewin Keitel, to the Army personnel office to ensure at least some influence. He advised Hitler to appoint Major Rudolf Schmundt, whom he had met earlier, as his *Wehrmacht* ADC. He also pleaded successfully for the appointment of the former commander of Army Group 4 (Leipzig), Colonel-General von Brauchitsch, to be the new Commander-in-Chief of the Army. Brauchitsch, of old Silesian nobility (which had supplied Prussia with many generals), was a product of the Guards Field Artillery and of the old General Staff. He was, moreover, a fine soldier of first-class manners, if less critical of National-Socialism than Fritsch. He was, in Keitel's opinion, a gentleman of the old school with sound judgment in military matters and possessing the talent necessary for conducting strategy along classical lines. Hitler liked him too. As had previously happened in the 'memoranda feud', however, both Keitel and Brauchitsch reckoned without their chief, the 'Oberösterreicher', as the old General von Rundstedt, doyen of the Officer Corps, used to call Hitler when in an angry mood. Neither gentleman had worked closely with Hitler before. Both were thereby to meet their fate.

A tremendous workload now rested upon Keitel. Many officers expected more from him than he was able to give. None of them, not a single general, ever vied for his post or sought to displace him. Already, during his time at the Ministry, his wife, in her letters to her mother, had worried about 'Wilhelm's anxiety', about his constant fear of failing people's expectations of him or of not coping with the workload. His anxiety became even more intense now. He was always 'on the trot', something not immediately associated with this tall, well-built man. One of his wartime Air Force ADC's, Captain von Szymonski, coined the phrase: 'There a German Field-Marshal hurries along, while his ADC follows at a solemn pace.' During the remaining period of peace, from 4 February 1938 to 1 September 1939, he, as Chief of the *Oberkommando der Wehrmacht* (OKW), and his wife had to fulfil frequent social engagements. Even these he considered a 'duty'. In his last notes of September 1946, when facing death, he very much regrets not having been a free man then, able to dispose of his time at his own discretion. Even at night he was not safe from telephone calls from his new warlord, who habitually turned night into day and half the day into night. Besides, Keitel loved a good meal and treasured a good night's sleep despite all the work. He finally philosophized that a soldier's vocation was 'unfree' and did not require too much of a critical intellect.

On 4 February 1938, after wild rumours about the military leadership crisis in Berlin had been circulating abroad, Hitler announced great changes. This was also the day on which the last chapter of Keitel's life story began: the time of 'entanglement'. In the Nuremberg Trials against the principal war criminals, an international military tribunal comprising representatives of the four victorious powers brought the following laboriously compiled charges (new to international law) against Field-Marshal Keitel: drawing up plans for, and carrying out, an aggressive war; offending against peace; committing war crimes and crimes against humanity. Although in no case the originator of the acts of which he stood accused, Keitel had none the less been an obedient lackey. He had signed orders he had not given, orders against which his conscience rebelled, as he notes at the end of his life, but which none the less had been set in motion through his signature. Why? General von Seeckt, Commander-in-Chief of the Army from 1920 to 1926 and creator of the small 100,000-man army of the Weimar Republic, had declared obedience to constitute the honour of the new officer corps. This meant obedience to Seeckt himself in the first instance and only then to the republican state which Seeckt, as a theoretical monarchist, did not respect. The old Field-Marshal von Hindenburg, President of the Reich from 1925 to 1934, once grumbled that that man (Seeckt) would ruin the character of the entire officer corps. In addition, there was Keitel's legacy from his forefathers, the legacy of generations of princely tenants in the Guelph state of Hanover. The will of the most gracious ruler and landlord was supreme law. The will of the monocrat in a '*Führerstaat*' of Hitler's creation was, by public law, also supreme law. In a material sense the estate-owner of Helmscherode was an independent man. Keitel, however, did not possess this old-style sense of independence.

Hitler soon grew accustomed to having this ever-conscientious and exceedingly hard-working administrator in charge and used him as his 'maid of all work', although he never completely trusted him, seeing Keitel as a general in the old Prussian mould. All Hitler's generals remained somewhat alien to him. Keitel too had the impression that the Austrian-born Führer felt somewhat shy and insecure amongst these mostly aristocratic Prussian gentlemen. Would they really obey him – who had only achieved the rank of corporal – unconditionally? Consequently Hitler often overreacted in tone of voice and mannerism, became aggressive and rude, or made demands which were practically impossible to carry out. As much as Keitel initially admired this sinister man as a seemingly ever-successful statesman, and later on, after the surprise victory over France in 1940, as a 'general', he never felt quite at ease with him. Nor did Keitel ever understand how Hitler, after having emphasized that responsibility for all actions rested solely upon himself, could simply put a bullet through his head to escape earthly justice. In his view, this was dishonourable. It reminded him of a gambler who, having lost his last penny in roulette, simply took his leave of life.

The year 1938 proved a troubled one. In March, by a chain of unfortunate events, Hitler annexed Austria. The *Wehrmacht* Operations Office under Keitel's authority witnessed an embarrassing event. The Chief of the Army General Staff, General Beck, whom Hitler had wanted to replace without delay, had remained in office upon the insistence of Keitel and Brauchitsch. Beck succeeded in placing Major-General von Viebahn, highly respected by him as a confidant, at OKW as Chief of the Operations Office (*Führungsamt*). When on 10 March 1938, in order to pre-empt the plebiscite for a German Christian and free Austria called for by the last Austrian Chancellor von Schuschnigg, Hitler ordered the invasion of Austria, Keitel found to his utter consternation that the *Oberkommando der Wehrmacht* had made no contingency plans whatsoever. So everything had to be improvised. While Keitel accompanied the Führer on his entry into Austria, back at OKW in Berlin, General von Viebahn suffered a nervous breakdown, believing the Second World War was about to break out. Not very impressive. So Viebahn disappeared, and control was transferred once more to Keitel's confidant, Jodl.

Austria became Hitler's 'Ostmark' and Hitler began his second move, the break-up of Czechoslovakia, already deeply outflanked from Austria and Silesia. Hitler's pretext was to enforce the right of self-determination for the minority Sudeten German population of the country. Code name for this enterprise was 'Plan Green'. Here Keitel experienced for the first time what baseness lay hidden in Hitler when the latter elaborated upon the developments in German-Czech relations for which one had to be prepared. Keitel heard Hitler remark in an undertone that it might, for instance, happen that the German ambassador in Prague was murdered. Keitel did not immediately grasp what the Führer meant. Slowly it dawned on him that Hitler was contemplating setting up such an assassination as a pretext for invasion. Hitler continued to say that the First World War was, after all, caused by an assassination. Keitel began to wonder what kind of human being this was.

In the summer of 1938 the Chief of the General Staff, Beck, tried to wage a memoranda campaign against the taking of military action against Czechoslovakia that could lead to a new world war; when he failed in this and offered his resignation, it was immediately accepted. Keitel opined that he would not shed a tear over Beck's departure. He did not then expect Beck's successor, General Halder, to hold similar views. In the course of planning the deployment against Czechoslovakia, Hitler and the new heavenly twins of the OKH, Brauchitsch and Halder, clashed very severely over Hitler's intention to launch a concentrated panzer offensive on Prague via Pilsen. Brauchitsch and Halder opposed Hitler stubbornly, but naturally lost their battle on the map. Keitel admonished Brauchitsch for becoming so vehement. Did they (Brauchitsch and Halder) really believe a war would break out over the Sudeten-German problem? Much worse could happen, and then his position as Commander-in-Chief of the Army would be lacking authority. Worse was to happen than either of them ever anticipated.

In March 1939 Keitel, along with Hitler's entourage, moved into Prague Castle. Success, he mused, always impressed a soldier favourably. Keitel had no fundamental objection to the campaigns against Poland, Denmark-Norway (the first and last campaign where the *Oberkommando der Wehrmacht* was in direct control), Belgium, the Netherlands and France. The victory over France, grandiose in a military sense, had an overwhelming effect on all the generals, including Keitel, though he himself would never have admitted it. None the less, it may have been possible that he really did utter the phrase, widely mocked, that Hitler was 'the greatest general of all times'. As mentioned before, Keitel could be very sentimental.

In July 1940 Hitler arranged a ceremony for paying tribute to the victorious generals. On this occasion Keitel was promoted to Field-Marshal and received an endowment of 100,000 Reichsmarks. Befitting his character, he felt very embarrassed. One became a Field-Marshal on the battlefield but not at a desk! He never touched the money. He deposited it in a blocked account, despite the fact that Helmscherode could have benefited from such a cash injection. In the summer of 1940 he allowed his wife and himself his first and only leave in this war. After that it was back to mountains of paperwork and the management of the OKW administration. But there had been casualties. Keitel, against his reason, felt rather hurt when Hitler, in March 1940, had created a new Ministry of Armament and Munitions under the command of his chief road construction engineer, Dr Fritz Todt. Management of war industry, which had never been designed to cope with a big war, had not run smoothly. In September 1939 an ammunition crisis had occurred, but was carefully hushed up. And General Professor Dr Becker, Chief of the Army Ordnance Department, had not committed suicide over nothing in late autumn 1939.

Keitel was totally alarmed though when, in late summer 1940, he learned of Hitler's plan to attack the Soviet Union, his official ally. This was the 'war' Hitler had often predicted for the years 1942–5 when German armament would have reached its peak. Eradicating Bolshevism and gaining *Lebensraum* in the east for the German people were Hitler's original wishful ideas. This was to be the crusade of the Greater German Reich, the renaissance of the old collapsed Reich which had once included Austria, Bohemia and Moravia, and which was to be resurrected in a de-Christianized form. The campaign was codenamed *Barbarossa* in memory of that powerful Emperor Friedrich I Barbarossa who had perished in a crusade to the Orient in 1190. To Hitler, victorious in the whole of western and northern Europe, everything now seemed achievable. There was, though, without doubt, another motive, namely the hidden fear that his health could fail him soon.

Keitel, *Reichsmarschall* Göring and the Commander-in-Chief of the Navy, Grand Admiral Raeder, all protested against the Russian offensive. Keitel even wrote a memorandum to Hitler which was lost in the files and probably did not survive the war. All the leading soldiers were unanimous in believing that such a war would exceed Germany's strength, especially as the war against England had not finished yet. Hitler tried to persuade Keitel and the others that the campaign against the Soviet Union would only last the summer of 1941 and that Stalin's empire would be destroyed before the onset of the Russian winter.

At the end of March 1941 Hitler announced to his generals and admirals a new kind of war, one based on opposing world views and in which the question of 'to be or not to be' was to be decided.

Every traditional restraint on warfare, all chivalry towards the opponent, had to be abandoned. Out of this inhuman principle then emanated those orders which Keitel signed and for which he was made answerable to the military tribunal after the main culprit had made his exit. These included the 'Commissar' Order, whereby communist political officers with combatant status serving with the Red Army were to be liquidated; the jurisdiction decree which forbade court-martial procedures against those Germans who had committed offences against the civilian population; the so-called 'Night and Fog' decree which permitted detention in the Reich of resistance fighters without informing their next of kin of their whereabouts; the order not to recognize members of enemy commandos (even when wearing uniform and undoubtedly being soldiers) as prisoners of war, but to hand them over to the security service for 'treatment'.

In his notes Keitel confessed how unhappy he had felt in his post. On three occasions at least, after arguments, he begged Hitler to relieve him of his duties, to transfer him. But Hitler had no intention of letting him go. As his chief of military administration and as his military representative in dealing with the Reich's allies against the Soviet Union in Budapest, Bucharest and Helsinki, Keitel had in many ways become indispensable to Hitler. In September 1941 when, during another argument, Hitler had accused him of false information and had said that he basically felt surrounded by 'numbskulls', Keitel was ready to hand in his resignation and then shoot himself. By chance Jodl intervened, took the pistol from his desk and said rather naively that in a war every soldier had to endure to the end. Was there a way out of this vicious circle? Hardly for a man of Keitel's temperament. For this he lacked the necessary pride and feeling of spiritual superiority over this plebeian who had seized power and was now leading the Reich to ruin.

When at noon on 20 July 1944 a bomb placed by Colonel Count Stauffenberg exploded in a hut at the Führer's headquarters in east Prussia, Keitel reacted characteristically. Deeply outraged, he led the lightly injured Führer into the open, whereupon Hitler apparently said that Field-Marshal Keitel, for one, was to be relied upon. While Stauffenberg on his return to Berlin during the afternoon and evening of that day tried hard by telephone to organize a coup with the help of the reserve army, Keitel likewise tried hard by telephone to prevent the district and military commanders from obeying orders from Berlin. He won this telephone battle, a macabre triumph. In Keitel's view, all this was shameful perfidy. One had to stand by one's master, especially in his misfortune; honour, as he knew it, demanded this.

The imminent end of the Third Reich released him in a strangely sad way from a burden which had become almost unbearable. The Chief of OKW, together with the OKW Operations Staff, had already left Berlin and was in continuous 'retreat', not to say flight, from the Red Army via Mecklenburg to Holstein when, on 30 April 1945, Hitler took his own life. Now the Field-Marshal was a free man, the highest ranking officer of the *Wehrmacht* which was in a state of collapse. Most of the Reich had already been occupied by the enemy. The price of this kind of freedom was too high.

Keitel and the OKW Operations Staff joined Grand Admiral Dönitz, who had taken control over the remaining Reich after Hitler in his last will had ironically named him President. Dönitz wanted to replace Keitel by Field-Marshal von Manstein. But nobody was aware then that Manstein had already given himself up into British captivity on the estate of Count Waldersee in Waterneverstorf in Holstein. Thirteen days of so-called 'freedom' followed at the residence of the Grand Admiral in Flensburg-Mürvik. On 13 May 1945 British military police arrested Keitel, later to be put on trial before the international military tribunal as a principal war criminal.

It proved difficult to find a German defence counsel for the accused man, the more so because the power of a German lawyer in the Nuremberg Trials was very limited. During the trial Keitel, soldier through and through, accepted the responsibility for having carried out the orders issued by another person who was no longer answerable to earthly justice. His defence counsel, Dr Otto Nelte, a business lawyer acquainted with the Fontaine family, found it extremely difficult to follow his client's way of thinking. As to the charges brought against him, he pleaded 'not guilty'. There was only one last wish the Field-Marshal expressed, and that was execution by firing squad, befitting his rank. The military tribunal granted him no clemency. The sentence of 1 October 1946 pronounced 'death by hanging'. The similarly accused and condemned *Reichsmarschall* Göring evaded death on the gallows at the last minute by taking poison late at night on 15 October. At dawn on 16 October 1946, Field-Marshal Keitel was hanged.

On 25 August 1939 three people were standing in front of the former War Ministry in the Bendlerstrasse: Major-General Alfred Jodl, Chief of the *Wehrmacht* Operations Office, his first wife Irma, née Countess von Bullion, and their friend of long standing, Luise von Benda, receptionist to General of Artillery Halder, Chief of the General Staff of the Army. The attack on Poland had been planned for 26 August, but only Jodl knew of this. However, the suspense and fear of war had dominated the mood at OKW and in the General Staff for days. Luise von Benda asked whether this was just another 'bluff' as in the previous year in the Sudeten crisis? Jodl replied that he very much feared it would be serious this time. Then he used the words: 'If we board this boat, then there will be no getting off.' Irma Jodl could not hold back her tears.... In 1914, twenty-five years before, army and people together had greeted the First World War in a mood of elation, an emotion which could no longer be rationally understood or indeed sympathized with now in 1939. After 30 January 1933, the day of Hitler's seizure of power and his appointment as Chancellor of the Reich, Major Jodl, then in the Operations branch of the *Truppenamt* (the camouflaged General Staff) had said that he very much feared that this would bring another war.

Alfred Jodl was born on 10 May 1890 in Würzburg, son of a retired Bavarian artillery captain. His father, although a soldier with all his heart, had had to quit active service because of his intended marriage to a girl of a simple Franconian farming and milling family. In the first place, because of her farming background his future wife did not fulfil the social requirements then customary for a lady of the officer corps, and secondly, the financial basis for a suitable life style, assets of at least 20,000 gold marks, were neither available nor could be raised. There were five children from this marriage: three daughters who all died young and two sons, Alfred, who was to play a historic role and be hanged, and Ferdinand, who at the end of the Second World War in 1945 was General commanding the Mountain Corps in northern Norway. Hostile though the Norwegians felt towards the German occupiers, the Norwegian government never brought charges of war crimes against him.

Alfred Jodl went to grammar school and after joining the cadet corps he entered the 4th Bavarian Field Artillery Regiment as an officer cadet. Under the German empire, in times of peace, the Royal Bavarian Army remained an independent body. Its ideal of an officer differed from that of the Prussian Army in so far as a good general education was a prerequisite. None the less, we do not know of any special intellectual interest Jodl might have had. He became Second Lieutenant in 1912. Very soon afterwards he married the 'woman from a different world' (in Jodl's words), Irma, Countess von Bullion, five years his senior and, also in his own words, far more intelligent than he. She came from an old established Swabian family of princes with no male heir. Her father Colonel (retd) Count Bullion had tried in vain to dissuade his daughter from this alliance, because of the differences of age and class.

Jodl served in the First World War as an artillery officer. He earned a good reputation and, after qualifying for service on the General Staff, was accepted after the war into the 100,000-man *Reichswehr*. From 1920 onwards he trained as a 'leader assistant', a euphemism for Staff Officer because the maintenance of a General Staff had been banned under the Versailles Treaty. Later on he praised two people in particular as good masters; one was General Wilhelm Adam, a native Bavarian like himself, and the other Colonel Hierl. Hierl was removed from the Army by General von Seeckt, the Commander-in-Chief of the *Reichswehr*, because he did not agree with Hierl's idea of introducing a general compulsory labour service in place of the now prohibited general military conscription. Hierl in his rugged Bavarian manner was a typical National-Socialist from the beginning. But many colleagues also dubbed Jodl a 'revolutionary' because of his very personal views of the future relations between working people and soldiers, and of the restructuring of the relationship between officers and subordinates in a technological age. These were ideas of reform, which Jodl in the end did not pursue further since his military employment did not offer him any possibilities to do so. However, not unlike the rest of the officer corps, he kept a sceptical distance from National-Socialism as then preached by Hitler.

Jodl's appointment in the last days of the Weimar Republic as a Major in the Operations branch of the *Truppenamt* in the Army High Command was significant. The chief here was his old instructor General Adam who in October 1933 had to vacate the post in favour of Lieutenant-General Beck. Adam was no friend of National-Socialism whereas Beck, it must be noted, welcomed at that time this 'national elevation', in the justified hope that Hitler would reintroduce freedom to rearm. Ludwig Beck, as much a soldier as a philosopher of war of the Clausewitz type, must have been an extremely impressive personality. The Polish military attaché said of him: 'C'est Moltke lui-même.' Jodl was full of admiration for him and, although he disapproved of coup d'états, none the less mourned Beck's death when, after two unsuccessful suicide attempts following the failure of the 1944 bomb plot against Hitler, Beck met a horrible death from a sergeant's pistol on the evening of 20 July that year. General Beck, for his part, as he wrote in a reference, had recognized in Jodl 'a man with a future'.

On Beck's recommendation, Jodl, in 1935, joined the *Wehrmachtamt* (Armed Forces Office) under the War Minister von Blomberg. His appointment was as leader of the National Defence branch, charged with working out a tripartite command of the Armed Forces. Blomberg, Keitel and also Jodl (much to Beck's disappointment) were strong advocates of this concept. General Beck, since 1935 Chief of the Army General Staff, and the Commander-in-Chief of the Army, Colonel General Baron von Fritsch, adhered to their conviction that in matters of defence, the High Command of the Army and the General Staff alone should have control of all operations. During this bureaucratic wrangle, in which Hitler was not involved, Keitel developed a personal dislike for Beck. Jodl, however, continued to admire Beck secretly, despite all differences of opinion. But Jodl's duties within the 'national defence' and his close contact with Keitel and Blomberg led to further unforeseen complications.

On 5 November 1937, in a speech lasting several hours, Hitler described his future plans to Blomberg, and to the three Commanders-in-Chief of the forces, i.e. Army, Navy and Air Force, Fritsch, Raeder and Göring, and to the Minister of Foreign Affairs, Baron von Neurath. Although the full text of this speech has not survived, we do know that Hitler announced that the annexation of Austria and the crushing of Czechoslovakia were his 'unalterable' objectives. Keitel and Jodl did not take this announcement seriously, but the extremely frightened Fritsch did. Fritsch knew that no risks could be taken with an incomplete and hastily constructed new Army. Blomberg, on the other hand, had already got accustomed to his Führer's endless tirades. Moreover, Hitler immediately assured them that a war would not occur before 1942 or 1945. Jodl, along with many other officers, had been enthralled by Hitler's non-violent successes – the introduction of general conscription in 1935 and the occupation of the demilitarized zone of the Rhineland in 1936. And the victors of 1918? They had acquiesced in all of it.

Jodl had no personal dealings with Hitler at this stage. Then Blomberg's marriage scandal with 'Fräulein Eva Gruhn' blew up. Jodl, as he noted in his diary, was totally surprised by this. Then followed Fritsch's fall because of alleged homosexuality. Jodl did not believe a word of this lie. It was characteristic that the officers then employed at the War Ministry who were in favour of Hitler's leadership were nevertheless concerned that as a result of these actual or fictitious scandals, the Nazi Party chiefs and Himmler's ss could gain influence over the Armed Forces. It was essential for the forces to remain united, not against, but alongside the Party. This once more confirmed Blomberg's two-pillar theory of 1934, prior to the Röhm coup d'état, of the Army and the Party as the twin supports of the state.

After Blomberg had disappeared with his dubious spouse, Fritsch had retired, and the War Ministry had been converted into the *Oberkommando der Wehrmacht* (High Command of the Armed Forces) with Keitel as its chief under Hitler's personal command, Colonel Jodl remained in the National Defence branch. Beck was about to install General Max von Viebahn, whom he personally respected very much, into the new OKW as Chief of the Operations Office. Jodl, in a peculiar way, experienced with von Viebahn's appointment the first of a series of 'leadership crises' which were to face him in the course of his career. When Hitler on 10 March 1938 unexpectedly ordered the invasion of Austria to forestall a plebiscite in favour of a German, Christian and free Austria called for by the last Austrian Chancellor, von Schuschnigg, OKW had nothing to do, for the conduct of the invasion fell to OKH (the Army General Staff). General Keitel, chief of the OKW, accompanied Hitler on his triumphal entry into his former fatherland. Colonel Jodl was facing a more difficult task. His superior, General von Viebahn, suffered a severe nervous breakdown because he believed that Hitler's act of violence would unleash the Second World War. After all, in 1919, by the Treaties of Versailles and Saint Germain the victorious Allies had quite emphatically ruled out any union between Germany and Austria. Viebahn suffered weeping fits, locked himself into his office and Jodl had quite a job calming him. He was replaced and admitted to an asylum. The victorious powers of 1919 did not fire a single shot in the cause of a 'free Austria'. Keitel, relieved to be rid of Viebahn in this incredible way, transferred control back to Jodl.

However, his office was not consulted when Hitler risked his second coup in 1938, 'Plan Green', a contingency plan to annex the Sudetenland to the Reich by force and crush Czechoslovakia. During the Czechoslovakian crisis which culminated in Chamberlain's and Daladier's surrender of the Sudetenland at the Munich conference, Hitler acted in collaboration with only the High Command of the Army (OKH), Colonel-General von Brauchitsch, the Commander-in-Chief, and Chief of the General Staff, General Ludwig Beck (who had resigned at his own request in August) and his successor, General of Artillery Franz Halder.

At last, a way out of this dilemma was in sight for Jodl. He was promoted to Major-General and, after six years of desk work, was entrusted with a troop command. He became 'Artillery Leader 44', based temporarily in Vienna, which was one of the bases for the formation of the later 44th Infantry Division with Austrian, or as they were now called, 'Ostmark', reserves. The 'great K', as Jodl sometimes called Keitel in his letters, hinted that Jodl might be appointed commander to the 2nd Mountain Division from 1 October 1939. Jodl's favourite pastime was mountaineering and this prospect filled him with delight. Keitel arranged for Staff Colonel Warlimont to replace Jodl.

Jodl's dream of becoming a divisional commander came to an abrupt end when the 'great K' cabled him on 23 August 1939 to report back to Berlin. 'Plan White', the contingency plan for the invasion of Poland, was nearing its final stage. Poland, in total misapprehension of her real situation and relying on her brave but inadequately equipped army (together with Britain's 'guarantee'), opposed Hitler's demand that the Free City of Danzig administered by the League of Nations and the 'Polish corridor' between West and East

Prussia should be returned to Germany. Hitler, on the other hand, was totally convinced that neither Britain nor France would intervene for Poland's sake.

In planning the invasion of Poland, the *Wehrmacht* Operations Office was once again not consulted, the task being left entirely to the Army General Staff (OKH). It did not require much strategic skill since Poland could now be attacked on her southern flank from Moravia and Slovakia, and from the north from East Prussia.

But Jodl, as Chief of the OKW Operations Office, and General Keitel now accompanied the Führer and the Chief Commander of the Armed Forces to the front as soon as war began. On 3 September 1939 Major-General Jodl was introduced to Hitler for the first time. Alfred Jodl was fourth-generation Bavarian farming stock. The tall officer with his angular features and open candid gaze must have impressed Hitler differently from those aristocratic gentlemen groomed in the Prussian mould and sometimes wearing a monocle (which Hitler disliked intensely). They had always made him feel somewhat uneasy. However, he liked Jodl immediately.

For Jodl, his last six-year period of service, as Chief of the OKW Operations Office, now began. In August 1940 his office was renamed 'OKW Operations'. It remained, however, a staff without any command power, without clearly outlined duties, existing alongside the OKW as an administrative office for the receipt and the processing of news and reports from the front, and the execution of orders on behalf of the all-powerful and omniscient autocrat, Adolf Hitler, who was always right. The only major exception when Jodl acted truly as a Chief of Staff and was able to demonstrate his leadership qualities occurred in Operation *Weserübung* (Weser Exercise) in April 1940, namely the swift occupation of Denmark and Norway, forestalling an English invasion of Norway which was aimed at throttling the iron-ore supply from Sweden into the Reich via Narvik. Jodl successfully carried out this mission on 9 April 1940 in a head-on race with an English-French expeditionary force.

In planning Operation *Weserübung* against time a tripartite control of land, sea and air forces under OKW, outside the authority of the Army General Staff (OKH), went effectively into operation, proving for the first and only time, and thanks to Jodl's skill, that the old Blomberg-Keitel concept of a tri-service command structure under OKW really worked.

During the Norwegian campaign, Hitler interfered only when *Blitzkrieg* operations, like most military operations, had their moments of crisis. In the iron-ore port of Narvik mountain troops under General Dietl were trapped by British, French, Polish and Norwegian troops, after superior British naval forces had totally demolished the German destroyer flotilla just outside Narvik. The German propaganda media had often praised Hitler's steely decisiveness. Now it became obvious to those close to him that this Commander-in-Chief of the Armed Forces had bad nerves after all. Narvik, he demanded, should be evacuated. Dietl's forces should retreat to the nearby Swedish territory and be interned there. Hitler's order was issued. Both Jodl and the General Staff officer of the Army allocated to him, Colonel von Lossberg, considered this to be nonsense. Within a few weeks the Allies were to be attacked on the Western Front in France and the Low Countries, and then they would be forced to withdraw their expeditionary force from Norway. In the meantime, Dietl just had to hold out. Hitler's order was successfully thwarted. This was to have unexpected consequences. The autodidact had learned a new lesson: in any subsequent crisis the order was to read: 'Hold at any cost.'

During Hitler's breathtaking victories in France and the Low Countries in the summer of 1940 Jodl once again only played the role of head of Hitler's military office. The soldiers were not unimpressed by Hitler's successes. Was he not a genius after all? Jodl himself believed so, as did the 'great K'.

In the wave of promotions after the victory on 19 July 1940, Jodl became General of Artillery by skipping the rank of Lieutenant-General. Even within the ranks closest to Hitler it was now assumed that England would make peace. But the British Prime Minister Churchill held firm. General Jodl was the first soldier to be apprised of Hitler's intention to attack Russia because he feared that Russia might one day stab Germany in the back. Hitler had no scruples whatsoever about the fact that since August 1939 a friendship pact with Stalin had existed. The 'crusade' to the east and the elimination of 'Jewish Bolshevism' had always been two of Hitler's fundamental ideas. This was what he meant when he intimated darkly again and again in the 1930s that a war would not break out before 1942 or 1945. Now in 1940, the man who had conquered western and northern Europe was convinced he could achieve anything with the 'best army in the world' to support him. Also the question as to how long his health would stand the strain of his Führer's existence seemed to occupy him more and more. Jodl viewed Hitler's plans with scepticism. Others like Keitel openly objected. But like a sleep-walker Hitler went his way. In a massive summer campaign in 1941 the German Army would demolish Stalin's gigantic empire. By the onset of the Russian winter it would all be over.

In the winter crisis of 1941–2 after the German failure to take Moscow, and the massive Russian counter-offensive, when the German Army seemed near defeat, General Jodl had the opportunity to admire the iron will with which Hitler ordered the front-line formations to stand fast, often by taking ruthless measures against reluctant generals. The consequences of the winter crisis affected Jodl. The Commander-in-Chief of the Army, Field-Marshal von Brauchitsch, resigned on account of a heart condition. Hitler personally took over command of the Army and divided up staff responsibilities. The Army General Staff (OKH) was solely responsible for all matters at the Eastern Front. The *Wehrmacht* Staff (OKW) continued to deal with all other theatres of war. At this time there was effectively only one active front other than Russia – in North Africa, where Rommel was given the assignment in 1942 to thrust forward to the Egyptian frontier with his German and Italian *Panzerarmee Afrika*. On paper Hitler now had two Chiefs of General Staff, Halder (OKH) and Jodl (OKW), but the latter enjoyed less responsibility than the former.

For Jodl, life in the Führer's headquarters *Wolfschanze* (Wolf's Lair) in East Prussia and later during the stifling summer of 1942 at the advanced headquarters *Werwolf* in the western Ukraine near Winniza was sheer agony. Later, before the Nuremberg Tribunal, he described Hitler's command post as a mixture of cloisters and concentration camp. It began with trivial everyday matters. Like Keitel, who appreciated a good cigar, Jodl enjoyed his cigarettes, whereas Hitler was a fanatical non-smoker. Nobody was allowed to smoke in his presence. Keitel appreciated a good wine or a cool beer, so did Jodl; Hitler was a fanatic teetotaller. Women were strictly taboo. Strategic discussions, usually chaired by the intellectually totally inept Führer, were frequently long and tiring. Hitler was in the habit of deviating into irrelevant monologues, whereas the General Staff officers were accustomed to discussing factual problems in a clear and concise manner and dealing with the necessary, often urgent, decisions. Consequently tension arose.

In Hitler's view the summer offensive of 1942 should bring about a final decision in the Russian campaign with the capture of Stalingrad on the Volga and Astrakhan on the Caspian Sea, and by occupying the oilfields in the Caucasus. The outskirts of Stalingrad were reached in August 1942, with the German forces already weakened, but the battle stuck in street and house-to-house fighting. Army Group A under Field-Marshal List had reached the edge of the Caucasus equally exhausted and without reserves. The 49th Mountain Corps under General Konrad was supposed to push forward to the Black Sea ports. However, the fighting strength of the troops was waning, and there arose problems with lack of reserves. List felt inclined to abandon his mission, now seemingly impossible. A discussion with Hitler at the end of August 1942 resolved this disagreement. When none the less the offensive made no significant progress, Hitler despatched Jodl to visit Field-Marshal List and General Konrad instead of, more appropriately, the Chief of the General Staff, Colonel-General Halder, whom Hitler no longer trusted. On 7 September 1942 Jodl returned, only to corroborate List's and Konrad's reports that the troops were at their last gasp. Hitler suggested the dropping of parachute troops in the Tuapse region, but this was not feasible due to difficult terrain in the landing area. The ensuing discussion was private, and different versions exist as to its outcome. In any case, Jodl, who was accustomed to Hitler's vile temper, witnessed the most extraordinary outburst of rage from him and he, as a true Bavarian, gave as good as he got. It can be said with great certainty that 7 September 1942 was the day when Hitler realized that he could not possibly win the war in Russia. He had put everything on one card, and it had not come up trumps. Jodl, for his part, made it quite clear to

Hitler that he considered it beneath his dignity eternally to pass on impossible orders and that he (Hitler) could find somebody else for that. He then slammed the door and left.

Hitler was outraged. What now? Of course, it was all the generals' fault, not his – or was it because he had left incapable generals in their posts? He henceforth refused to shake hands with his Staff officers and declined to join the communal luncheon table. He ordered Reichstag stenographers to his headquarters to take down any strategic discussions verbatim so that, he insisted, the generals could not twist his words.

From the day of the Polish campaign Hitler had donned field-grey uniform. Now he loathed field grey because all the officers were wearing it. He also planned a major reshuffle: Jodl was to go, Keitel was to go and the Chief of the General Staff, Colonel-General Halder, whom he had found increasingly unsympathetic, was to go too. But in the end Hitler dismissed only Colonel-General Halder, on 24 September 1942, in a most undignified outburst of temper. It soon became apparent that Hitler was not keen to see new faces around him. It may even be that the icy manner with which Jodl continued to discharge his duties impressed him; he was finally to promote him to the rank of Colonel-General on 30 January 1944.

In the winter of 1942–3, renewed discussions took place about the appointment of a Chief of the General Staff of the *Wehrmacht* with comprehensive authority. This would have lent new weight to the OKW Operations Staff. Field-Marshal von Manstein was the preferred candidate for this post. Jodl thought it unlikely that Hitler would tolerate a man of such strong personality near him. Moreover, could an autocrat of Hitler's makeup ever delegate power? This would be tantamount almost to a partial abdication. The vicious circle closed in around them all, not least around Jodl. He adopted a stoical attitude, telling Luise von Benda that they all had to believe in victory; whoever was not capable of such a belief might as well put a bullet through his head....

In spring 1943 Jodl's wife died in tragic circumstances. She had to have major spinal surgery and had gone to Königsberg in East Prussia, as this was still a place safe from air raids. However, during the first major bombing attack she had been obliged to stay in a cold, damp air-raid shelter and had contracted pneumonia with fatal consequences. In November Jodl married Luise von Benda, who had long been a secret admirer of his. Eight months later, in the assassination attempt on Hitler at noon on 20 July 1944, Jodl was thrown to the ground by the blast of the bomb placed by Colonel Count Stauffenberg. He lost consciousness for a short while and his hair was singed off so that, instead of a general's cap, he had to wear a white bandage for a while. He did not at all understand the motives of the plotters, among whom were many young General Staff officers. Neither did he approve of the behaviour of the retired Colonel-General Beck, intended by the conspirators to be the new head of state. At this time he confessed with great bitterness and hopelessness that for him the officer corps no longer existed. His mistrust, even of his closer comrades, grew. But Jodl persevered. As he had once said to Keitel – in war a soldier had to last out in the post to which he was allocated.

So, trapped by an overbred, functionalized concept of obedience, he walked straight into catastrophe, into the collapse of the third German Reich created and wrecked by Hitler. And as a loyal soldier he undertook his last task which Grand Admiral Dönitz, fictitiously named President of the Reich in Hitler's will, imposed upon him. This was to sign the unconditional capitulation of the German forces on 7/8 May 1945 at the Allied headquarters at Rheims on French soil. This signing of the capitulation had to be repeated on 9 May by Field-Marshal Keitel in front of Marshal Zhukov, the Soviet Commander-in-Chief, at Karlshorst near Berlin. At midnight, on 8/9 May 1945, a cease-fire was declared in Europe. For the victorious Allies the unconditional surrender of the Third Reich had now been accomplished, and they did not acknowledge the Dönitz interim government. On 23 May 1945 Colonel-General Jodl, along with the Grand Admiral and his government, was arrested by the English.

Like Keitel, Jodl was charged as a 'principal war criminal' by the International Military Tribunal at Nuremberg, and like Keitel he never had any real power of command but had merely administered instructions and orders issued by the one who held the real power. The Nuremberg Court convicted him of his war crimes and crimes against humanity, and pronounced a sentence of death by hanging. An appeal was turned down. The sentence was carried out on 16 October 1946 at 2 a.m.

In September 1938 Colonel Walter Warlimont, acting commander of the 26th Artillery Regiment in Dusseldorf, was appointed acting head of the National Defence branch of the new High Command of the Forces (OKW). The chief of OKW, General Keitel, who had known Warlimont from the days of the *Reichswehr*, seemed to think that he had made a good choice. Theoretically he was not so far off the mark, although Colonel Warlimont did not share Keitel's ideas of creating a regular OKW operations staff. Warlimont, born on 3 October 1894 in Osnabrück, son of a publisher, was then almost forty-four years old, an officer of above-average education and immaculate manners, cautious in company, always keeping a slight distance and blessed with a trenchant and critical intellect.

After attending the humanistic gymnasium in his Westphalian home town of Osnabrück, Warlimont, like so many sons of the educated and affluent middle class of that era, joined the foot artillery in Strasbourg in Alsace as a Prussian officer. In the First World War he saw active service at the front, first as a gunner and later as an adjutant, a position which very often served as a springboard for a higher career. No evidence exists as to his reaction to the 1918 revolution and the flight of the German Kaiser and King of Prussia to Holland. But in view of the fact that the young officer joined one of the newly emerging *Freikorps* (volunteer corps), the *Land* (county) rifle corps under General Maercker, in order to re-establish peace and order at home and to fend off any Bolshevik attempts to overthrow the government and the new German republic, one must conclude that he not only chose to pursue a military career but also felt politically involved. To him, being a soldier obviously meant serving the future constitution, for in 1919 units of the *Land* rifle corps were protecting the Constitutional National Assembly in Weimar from agitators.

Warlimont, qualified for the General Staff, was accepted into the small officer corps of the *Reichswehr*, passed through the 'leader assistant' training (the camouflaged General Staff training) and in 1926 joined the Army High Command at the Defence Ministry. He became the 2nd ADC to the chief of the *Truppenamt* (troop office), General von Blomberg, who assessed him very highly. Warlimont had a manifest talent for foreign languages. He was awarded a three months' language sabbatical in England to learn English. In 1929–30 he was sent to the USA to study American methods of industrial mobilization. Thereafter service in the artillery alternated with a secondment to the Military Economics branch of the new *Wehrmachtamt* (armed forces office). After the outbreak of the Spanish Civil War in 1936, War Minister von Blomberg despatched him as military attaché to General Franco with a semi-diplomatic role. The German Reich, that is, Hitler – under the mantle of strictest secrecy – supported General Franco with a Luftwaffe squadron, the Condor Legion, consisting of volunteers. This unit was naturally not under the command of the War Minister. A small mission of Army advisors and instructors and a training section were also provided.

Because of his service in the USA and in Spain, Colonel Warlimont gained a very special position in the officer corps. He was one of the very few officers with practical overseas experience and a realistic world view. He was therefore well suited to run the Operations branch at OKW, the more so as he possessed industrial experience. But were widely travelled officers with a sober sense of realism still needed at OKW, or had the original euphemism 'leader assistant' taken on a new meaning? The ideal of Prussian General Staff dogma and tradition since the days of Scharnhorst and Gneisenau had been co-responsibility of the General Staff officer and the commander for the decisions of leadership. And what was left of it now?

Warlimont quite liked his new boss in the Operations branch at the *Wehrmachtamt*, Colonel Alfred Jodl, an ardent campaigner for a tripartite command structure with a small central staff. But he did not approve of Jodl's authoritarian manner of dealing with his staff, and his way of taking decisions on his own without discussions. Moreover, Jodl was totally under the spell of the Commander-in-Chief of the Forces, Adolf Hitler. On the other hand, Warlimont himself had now become part of Hitler's 'maison militaire' as he called it in his old-fashioned French. And indeed it was just this, a military royal court without defined responsibilities of command authority. Jodl, so Warlimont was told, knew how to run Hitler's 'work staff'. However Jodl, in the rank of Major-General, was transferred to a command appointment in October 1938, whereupon Warlimont became acting head of the *Wehrmachtamt* and of the Operations branch, working directly under General Keitel. Theoretically under, but in practice alongside the OKW, stood like a gigantic block the *Oberkommando des Heeres* (OKH) under Colonel-General von Brauchitsch, the Commander-in-Chief, and the Chief of Staff General Halder. Here Warlimont found friends. He was convinced that, as things stood, OKH would assume the leadership role in an emergency – provided the new Commander-in-Chief of the *Wehrmacht*, Hitler, did not personally interfere. Warlimont meanwhile had no close contact with the gentlemen of the 'maison militaire'. This dark-haired General Staff colonel of medium height, with a reserved and inscrutable manner and keen expression, never betraying servile admiration, unfavourably impressed Hitler, who never trusted this sort of officer.

Following the deterioration of the Poland crisis in the last third of August 1939 General Keitel called General Jodl back to Berlin, and Warlimont was demoted to deputy. In August 1940 the office was given the more martial-sounding name of '*Wehrmacht* Operations Staff', but without extension of its duties or responsibilities or – fantastic to imagine – gaining a superior position over the General Staffs of the three services. Hitler considered a simultaneous co-existence of staffs, command centres and spheres of responsibility an ideal situation. It allowed him to play one office against another. He almost expected one to outdo the other out of obsessive rivalry. Then the final decision would rest with him, the Führer, who was always right and never mistaken.

Later, before the Nuremberg court, General Warlimont stated that never before had a German Army entered into a war more inadequately equipped than that of 1939. The ammunition stock was insufficient, heavy tanks not yet operational, even the stock of bombs inadequate. General Keitel was terrified when he heard Hitler declare on 11 September 1939 in his first war speech that 90 million Reichsmarks had been spent on armament. How could anybody tell such a lie? As it happened, Keitel knew approximately the amount spent on armaments: it was between 35 and 40 million marks. All this resulted from Hitler's strange mentality. He had never had clear objectives requiring suitable sound forward planning. Instead he nurtured wishful ideas, fantasies of what would happen some day, indeed must happen, no matter when and how. How should military personnel, used to precise directives, respond to this?

On the evening of 1 September 1939, the day the German Armies invaded Poland from three sides, Warlimont officially witnessed a scene where not only leading officers crowded around Hitler in the Winter Garden of the old Chancellery but also a number of 'dignitaries' (as he called them), or, in plain language, Nazi Party bosses. To quote Warlimont further, he was 'deeply shocked'. This was not how he expected a general headquarters to look on the first evening of a conflict which inevitably, in his view, would lead to a new world war. Although there was not very much for him to do at the *Wehrmachtamt*, Warlimont was nevertheless relieved that there was no place for him in the Führer's train, when the entire caravan on rails started moving towards Poland on the evening of 3 September, notwithstanding the fact that England and France had declared war.

If Jodl (who was on the Führer's train) saw himself as head of Hitler's military work-staff, a position without power, so Warlimont, banished to a desk and, in the course of the war even rising to the rank of General of Artillery, considered himself pushed into the ungrateful role of deputy or 'second-hand' man. Yet he was able to observe, very much more clearly and quietly critical, the mostly unpleasant developments around him in the ever growing Führer-headquarters with their romantic-sounding names like 'Felsennest' and 'Wolfschanze' ('Falcon's Nest' and 'Wolf's Lair'). In an extensive volume about the German headquarters between 1939 and 1945 – a war-historical analysis – he was to capture his experience of five years' active service and twelve years' imprisonment as an alleged war criminal. He thought it useless to publish personal memoirs, since he himself had experienced little that was exciting and never had to take decisions, right or wrong. In this historical analysis he preferred personally to keep in the background. Very rarely, in a moment of excitement, do we hear his personal viewpoint or, indeed, read his own contemporary words. This highly valuable work often betrays the slightly ponderous style of military correspondence, but it also beguiles through its sober factualness, the fairness with which Warlimont avoids any superfluous derision of Hitler, but only describes his method and faults of leadership. They speak for themselves. As to the author himself, his book is devoid of any complaint or self-accusation, any protestation against often irksome and almost always ungrateful tasks (by comparison, for instance, with Keitel). In photographs Warlimont displays a cool, impenetrable air, and such is the style of his analysis: to write that that is how it was and that is what one had to put up with. Rebellion against the Führer whose faults of leadership grew visibly? Inconceivable for his generation of officers. That would have encroached on politics, and politics was not a matter for soldiers. Post-catastrophe moral sermons to these soldiers are of no use now. One has to take them as they were....

In his analysis General Warlimont writes about the process of Hitler's seizure of military power, for which the Blomberg scandal in January 1938 gave him the means. By 4 February 1938 he had personally taken command of the forces, replaced the War Ministry by the *Oberkommando der Wehrmacht* (OKW) and procured for himself the tool necessary for the administration and supply of the Armed Forces. During the Poland campaign he had basically given a free hand to the OKH, and Commander-in-Chief of the Army and the

Chief of the General Staff. Yet during the *Blitzkrieg* invasion of Denmark and Norway, masterminded by the *Wehrmacht* Operations office, Warlimont experienced Hitler's fatal order in the Narvik crisis in April 1940, which could only just be intercepted and countermanded at the last minute. The *Blitzkrieg* against Russia which started on 22 June 1941 and which was intended to end with the crushing of the Soviet régime at first yielded brilliant successes for Hitler's leadership and his interference in operations. Then came the failure before Moscow, the Russian winter counter-offensive, and crisis for the German Army on the ground and in the High Command. On 19 December 1941, in mid-crisis, the Commander-in-Chief of the Army, Field-Marshal Brauchitsch, resigned. In the ensuing speculation about a potential successor, Warlimont himself apparently introduced the newly appointed Commander-in-Chief of Army Group South, Field-Marshal von Reichenau, into the game. But Hitler rejected him: 'He is too political for my liking. The cat can't stop catching mice.' Finally, in view of the unstable situation at the front, Hitler resolved to take over direct command of the Army himself – the final act of his 'seizure of military power' (according to Warlimont). Fundamentally, this last step corresponded to the inexorable law of autocracy, such as Hitler had assumed – namely the accumulation of all offices and functions on one hand. By this, as we shall learn later, the Führer over-estimated his mental and physical resources.

The functions of the *Wehrmacht* Operations Staff were now separated formally from those of the General Staff of the Army. The General Staff (OKH) remained responsible for the Eastern Front alone. The OKW Operations Staff was charged with the administration of all other theatres of war, without being allocated any clear objectives or, indeed, authority of command.

Therefore the 1942 summer offensive on the Eastern Front was not a matter for the OKW Operations Staff under Jodl and Warlimont. They had to concentrate their attention on Field-Marshal Rommel's North African offensive towards Alexandria and the Suez Canal. However, they unexpectedly became involved in the crisis of August/September 1942 on the Eastern Front, because Hitler had irrevocably fallen out with the Chief of the General Staff, Colonel-General Halder. At the end of August 1942 the offensive of Army Group A, under Field-Marshal List, came to a halt at the northern edge of the Caucasus. Attempts to break through to the Black Sea ports in the western Caucasus failed. The troops needed a rest; the supply problems grew daily. Field-Marshal List was called to Hitler's advanced headquarters, 'Werwolf', near Winnitza in the western Ukraine. Keitel advised him to hand in his resignation straight away. List reputedly replied that this was the first reasonable word he had ever heard Keitel say. List was a Swabian, a very experienced and imperturbable soldier. His report of the situation initially calmed the slightly agitated Führer. Hitler was even prepared to postpone the battle for Baku with its rich oilfields until the following year.

Then List departed again for his headquarters at Stalino in the Caucasus. But, apart from some minor successes, nothing significant was achieved thereafter, and Hitler grew impatient once more. On 7 September he despatched Jodl, whom he now trusted most – and, contrary to all the rules, by aeroplane – to see List. Jodl discussed the serious situation with him and with General Konrad, the general commanding the Mountain Corps in the northwestern Caucasus. They were all agreed that the situation was untenable. When, on his return, Jodl most dutifully conveyed the result of his talk to Hitler he witnessed an outburst of Hitler's rage such as he had never heard before or thought possible (see above, page 160). Field-Marshal List was dismissed on 9 September. Despite being physically far removed from the battlefield, Hitler personally took over the command of Army Group A. The atmosphere at briefings became frosty. General Jodl, obviously aware that Hitler was not keen on seeing General Warlimont, advised Warlimont to absent himself temporarily from such 'briefings'. Moreover, he enquired from Warlimont whether he, Jodl, could square it with his self-esteem to remain in office? Warlimont replied coolly that he could not advise him on this. Whereupon Jodl, depressed, suddenly thought that he had perhaps reacted wrongly himself; that he should not have pointed his faults out to the dictator because that could have undermined his self-confidence; that Hitler would never find better 'National-Socialists' than him and General Scherff (commissioned to write a war history). But what did these officers actually understand by National-Socialism? German National-Socialism, unlike Marxism-Leninism, was not based upon a quasi-scientific doctrine. 'National-Socialism', as defined by an officer like Jodl, simply meant a blind faith in Hitler's genius and strength, without which the Fatherland would be lost.

When General Warlimont, some time after the Jodl crisis, reappeared at 'briefings' he noticed Hitler looking at him with eyes full of hatred. Warlimont wrote: 'This man has lost face, he has realized that his deadly game is up.' There is no doubt that, during the Jodl crisis, Hitler came to the conclusion that he could not win the war against Soviet Russia and that he had got himself into a cul-de-sac. When, about half a year later, Field-Marshal Rommel, recalled from Tunisia, advised him to call for an armistice, Hitler replied that he was aware that the war was lost, but he would fight till the end.

General Warlimont, too, continued with his duties. Or was he seeking a way out of the trap of this 'maison militaire'? We can only speculate. Quite a few officers in the Führer headquarters called him 'fox' because of his cautious reserve in expressing any views. The 4 June 1944 at the Führer headquarters in Berchtesgaden presented a typical situation in which he had to discharge his duties without ever being able to issue correct and reasonable orders. Hitler had gone there to relax. The German command posts in the area of Army Group B in Normandy and the Pas de Calais were convinced that the enemy would not launch an invasion because of a spell of bad weather. The Army Group Commander, Field-Marshal Rommel, had flown to his family at Herrlingen for a short vacation. In Rennes the staff of the 7th Army was engaged in a conference about defence planning for the invasion. When the corps and division commanders were returning from the conference they found themselves in some cases already under attack from American parachute troops who had landed in Normandy in the early hours of 6 June. It was D-Day, the beginning of the decisive invasion in the west, and nobody was in command on the German side. The OKW Operations Staff at the Strub barracks in Berchtesgaden, where General Warlimont was also staying, had been put on high alert since 5 a.m. Warlimont and General Blumentritt, the Chief of Staff to the Commander-in-Chief West, were both convinced that the great invasion had begun. Both wanted to deploy the nearest available panzer and panzergrenadier divisions, the so-called OKW reserve. Warlimont telephoned Jodl who was staying at the 'little' Reich Chancellery in Berchtesgaden. Jodl did not want to make any decisions. He, as well as Hitler, expected the invasion to be launched against the Pas de Calais; the parachute assault in Normandy could possibly be a 'decoy manoeuvre'. He therefore did not think that the moment was ripe to release the reserves. And Hitler? After a long evening tea party, heavily dosed with sleeping drugs, he was in a heavy sleep and could only be roused late in the morning. Rommel had predicted that the first day would decide the success or the failure of an invasion. But, as mentioned, the legendary Field-Marshal was at home on a short family holiday. Much of the day at Berchtesgaden was also taken up by a state visit of the Hungarian government. Next day Warlimont went off to Italy with Hitler's sanction on a long planned tour of the German defences there.

The thunder of the bomb explosion at noon at the headquarters on 20 July 1944 finally severed an existence that Warlimont had found more and more intolerable. Apart from the shock effects of the plot itself, he initially appeared to be unharmed by the bomb and continued to perform his duties despite a deterioration in his general state of health. It was not until September that his disturbed balance and movement led his doctors to diagnose serious concussion. This meant the end of the military career of the Deputy Chief of the OKW Operations Staff. He was transferred to the Führer reserve at OKW but, even after his recovery, not re-employed.

He awaited the end of the Third Reich in a period of inactivity. No sooner was this over when a new and altogether unexpected test occurred. Warlimont, as a former General at OKW, was arrested by the Americans and in the twelfth and last Nuremberg Trial of war criminals in 1948 was sentenced to life imprisonment. The charge, hardly comprehensible, read: war crimes and crimes against humanity. In 1951 the sentence was reduced to 18 years' imprisonment. In 1957 he was released. The trials against leading German soldiers had not remained undisputed in the USA. The General, having had one of the most unusual careers the old Army had known, died on 9 October 1976 in Kreuth, Upper Bavaria, aged 82.

BIBLIOGRAPHY

See combined bibliography on Blomberg, Keitel, Jodl, Warlimont and Reichenau on page 219.

SOURCES

This essay on Keitel is based on the author's book: *Keitel, Verbrecher oder Offizier. Erinnerungen, Briefe und Dokumente des Chefs* OKW ('Keitel, Criminal or General. Memoirs, Letters and Documents of the Chief of OKW'), Gottingen, 1961, from which the cited quotations derive. For further sources see the combined bibliography on Blomberg, Keitel, Jodl, Warlimont and Reichenau on page 219.

CHRONOLOGY: WILHELM KEITEL

1883, September	Born at Helmscherode near Gandersheim, Dukedom of Brunswick. Joined the Army in 46th Field Artillery Regiment. Artillery officer at the Western Front
1917–18	First General Staff Officer (Ia) Marine Corps in Flanders
1926–33	Head of organization branch (T2) at *Truppenamt* (disguised General Staff)
1933–4	Major-General and Infantry Leader 2 in Potsdam
1934–5	Artillery Leader 6 (new organization of 22nd Infantry Division) in Bremen
1935, October 10– 1938, February 4	Chief of *Wehrmachtamt* at War Ministry
1938, February 4–1945, May 13	Chief of the *Oberkommando der Wehrmacht* (OKW)
1940	Field-Marshal
1945–6	Tried by the International Military Tribunal in Nuremberg
1946, October 15	Executed

CHRONOLOGY: ALFRED JODL

1890, May 10	Born in Würzburg as son of a Captain (retd) of the Royal Bavarian Artillery
1910	Joined the 4th Bavarian Field Artillery Regiment

1911	Second Lieutenant, active service in the First World Wa 1914–18
	Transferred to *Reichswehr* (German Army 1921–35)
1932	Major at troop office (General Staff)
1935	Head of Department L (National Defence) at forces offic
1938, October–1939, August 23	Major-General, Artillery Leader 44 in Brunn, temporary base at Vienna
1939, August 23–1945, 23 May	Chief of OKW Operations Office/OKW Operations Staff
1940	General of Artillery
1944	Colonel-General
1946	Death sentence at Nuremberg trial against main war criminals
1946, October 16	Executed
1976	His second wife, Luise Jodl, née von Benda, published th book, *Jenseits des Endes – Leben und Sterben des Generaloberst Alfred Jodl* ('Beyond the End – Life and Death of Colonel-General Alfred Jodl'), very personal memoirs

CHRONOLOGY: WALTER WARLIMONT

1894, October 3	Born in Osnabrück, the son of a publisher. Educated at Humanistisches Gymnasium in Osnabrück
1914	Second Lieutenant in the 10th Prussian Foot Artillery Regiment in Strasbourg, Alsace
1914–18	Front-line service in the First World War. Served in the Freikorps *Land Jäger* corps of General Maercker. Transfer into *Reichswehr*, General Staff training
1927	Second adjutant to Chief of *Truppenamt*, General von Blomberg
1929–30	Sent to USA to study industrial mobilization
1936–7	Military attaché of the War Minister to General Franco in Spain
1938	Commanding Officer, 26th Artillery Regiment in Düsseldorf
1938, September	Head of Home Defence branch and acting chief of *Wehrmacht* Operations Office
1939, August 24 onwards	Deputy chief of *Wehrmacht* Operations Staff
1944	General of Artillery
1944, September	Sick leave due to severe concussion after the bomb plot of 20 July 1944. Transferred to Führer-reserve at OKW, not re-employed

1945	Arrested by the Allies. In 'OKW trial' of October 1948 sentenced to life imprisonment by the military tribunal in Nuremberg
1951	Reduction of sentence to 18 years' imprisonment
1957	Amnesty, released. War-historical studies
1962	Published his major work, *Im Hauptquartier der deutschen Wehrmacht 1939–1945*, published in Britain in 1964 with the title *Inside Hitler's Headquarters*
1976, October 9	Died in Kreuth, Wiesbach, Upper Bavaria

PART III

The Feldherren

RUNDSTEDT

7

RUNDSTEDT

Field-Marshal Gerd von Rundstedt

EARL F. ZIEMKE

A Rundstedt was recorded as grand steward of the Bishop of Halberstadt in the early twelfth century. Subsequently other family members took part in the German eastward expansion into the Mark of Brandenburg and entered into the emerging *junker* class of landed gentry who lived off the labour of their peasants and by the sword. The land was a reliable source of social status but not of money, and younger sons generally had to take military service where they could find it. In the early modern period Rundstedts served in nearly all the western European armies. During the eighteenth and nineteenth centuries, the *junker* predominance in the Prussian officer corps gave them steady employment at home. Karl Rudolf Gerd von Rundstedt was born on 12 December 1875, at Aschersleben in the Harz near Halberstadt. The first son of a hussar officer, he apparently never considered any vocation but that of a Prussian soldier even though he was said to have shown some early talent in drawing, music and acting, especially the last.

After four years as a cadet and graduation from the Gross Lichterfelde senior cadet school, Gerd von Rundstedt (as he preferred to be known) began his active military service on 22 March 1892, eight months before his seventeenth birthday. The month, day and year were important: they gave him a permanent place on the ladder of advancement relative to all other career officers. Having completed an obligatory half-year's service in the ranks and a term as an officer candidate, he became a lieutenant in the 83rd Royal Prussian Infantry Regiment on 17 June 1893. He would have greatly preferred the cavalry, but the family means, which had to provide for four sons, did not permit enrolment in that branch – or in one of the almost as expensive Guards infantry regiments.

Childhood in an officer's household and military schooling from age twelve on had aroused in him an exceptionally strong sense of duty and had as well confined his outlook to military matters. Although he had learned English as a child from an English nurse and mastered French well enough to pass the army interpreters' examination, his principal non-military intellectual pursuit was reading adventure and detective stories, an interest acquired as a youth and retained throughout his life. Admiral Friedrich Ruge recalled discussing Karl May, the German Joseph Conrad or Jack London, with him in May 1944 on the eve of the Normandy invasion.[1] More significantly, he did not adopt the parade-ground mannerisms prevalent among Prussian officers. Possibly owing to his mother's influence and her Huguenot descent, perhaps as deliberate role-playing on his part, he cultivated a courtly demeanour that in later years would enable him to charm Adolf Hitler and impress B. H. Liddell Hart as 'a gentleman to the core'.[2]

After ten years' service, mostly as a battalion and regimental adjutant, Rundstedt reached his next major career milestone in 1902 when he passed the qualifying examination for the War Academy in Berlin. In the same year, he was promoted to senior lieutenant and made an eminently proper marriage to Louise von Goetz, the daughter of a retired major. The War Academy accepted only 160 new students annually, and the examination regularly eliminated all but one in every six or eight applicants. Four out of five of even those who were admitted failed the three-year course. The 35 or so who passed then went on to 18 months' probation in the Great General Staff under the direct scrutiny of the Chief of the General Staff and his deputies, the *Oberquartiermeister*, before becoming entitled to wear the silver collar tabs and carmine trouser stripes of an officer in the General Staff. Having the preposition *von* before one's name could help somewhat at every stage. Rundstedt completed his term in the Great General Staff in early 1909 and then went into the second division of the General Staff, the Troop General Staff, as a captain in a corps headquarters.

The General Staff's rigorous selection and training were employed to perpetuate a body of dedicated, extremely able officers who could function harmoniously as the corporate brain of the Army. A General Staff officer was expected to be a highly competent military technician – and only that – working silently in the background, shunning the limelight and subordinating himself unquestioningly to the common interest. With iron, at times purblind, consistency, Rundstedt exemplified those characteristics throughout his career. He was from first to last the model General Staff officer in the Moltke-Schlieffen tradition, the master technician, reserved in speech to the point of taciturnity and studiously disdainful of personal acclaim.

The outbreak of war in August 1914 terminated a prescribed tour of troop duty as an infantry company commander and brought him back to the Troop General Staff as operations officer in the 22nd Reserve Infantry Division. The division, one of three in the 4th Reserve Corps, followed General Alexander von Kluck's 1st Army across Belgium and into northern France, on the way dropping off detachments to secure the rear area. In depleted condition, the division accomplished the one clear German success in the Battle of the Marne. On 5 September, west of the Ourcq River, it attacked the vanguard of the French 6th Army, which was coming out of Paris behind Kluck's open right flank, and drove it back, thereby becoming the German division that approached closest to Paris. The 22nd Reserve Infantry Division's performance, in which Rundstedt figured significantly, appeared afterward to confirm that the 'Miracle of the Marne' was not predominantly owing to a feat of Allied arms, but to German errors. He himself, in later years, subscribed to the theory that ascribed the defeat to malfunctions in the general staff system, which resulted in the Army High Command's losing touch with the front, and Kluck and his Chief of Staff's allowing their right flank to become exposed and at the same time a gap to open on their left.[3]

After the fighting on the Western Front settled into the trenches in November 1914, Rundstedt, promoted to major, was posted to the military government headquarters in Belgium. In the following spring, he went to the Eastern Front as a divisional chief of staff. There he served with General Max von Gallwitz's 12th Army in the breakthrough on the Narew River line that in July and August 1915 completed the northern half of the German summer offensive in Poland against the Russians. The mobile war in the east (12th Army advanced more than 250 miles between 13 July and 28 November) enabled General Staff officers to exercise their skills – and build reputations.

After the Eastern Front stabilized, Rundstedt was assigned to the military government in Poland until the summer of 1916, when he was transferred to Hungary to be a corps Chief of Staff in the Army Group Grand Duke Karl, which put him nominally in the Austro-Hungarian Army. The Army Group's mission was to defend the line of the Carpathian Mountains and that of the German Chiefs of Staff was to restore the effectiveness the Austro-Hungarian commands had almost completely lost during the successful Russian offensive in 1916 masterminded by General Brusilov. General Hans von Seeckt, whose role in the planning for the 1915 Austro-German summer offensive had won him an early promotion and the order *Pour le Mérite* (both rarely given to Staff officers) was the Army Group's Chief of Staff and Rundstedt's superior.

Keeping dispirited and resentful allies under tutelage required at least as much diplomatic skill as military proficiency. Rundstedt managed the task with the tact and finesse that he would demonstrate again later in a variety of circumstances. In the late autumn of 1917, after the Bolshevik revolution had totally destroyed the Russian offensive capability, he was reassigned: first as

Chief of Staff 53rd Corps, which advanced toward Petrograd (Leningrad) in early 1918 to force Bolshevik acceptance of the German peace terms, and then, after the Treaty of Brest-Litovsk went into effect in March 1918, as Chief of Staff, 15th Corps, in 1st Army (under General Bruno von Mudra) on the Western Front.

In July 1918, 15th Corps took part in the fifth and last German offensive of the series intended by Ludendorff to force the Allies to make peace: an attempt to eliminate the Allied salient round Reims which ended in a crushing repulse. Thereafter 1st Army took part in the month-by-month German retirement in the face of Allied offensives which ended in the Armistice of November 1918.

Germany's defeat and the clauses in the Treaty of Versailles that restricted her to a 100,000-man professional Army and prohibited the Great General Staff cast many career officers adrift. Major Gerd von Rundstedt was not among them. The *Reichswehr* could not offer places to more than one in six of the regular officers in the old Army, but that Rundstedt would be among the chosen was apparently never in doubt. General von Seeckt, the first chief of the *Truppenamt*, the disguised General Staff, enunciated the principle: 'The form changes, but the old spirit remains.'⁴ To him, middle-level officers who, like Rundstedt, had completed the full pre-war apprenticeship, had proved themselves in the war, and who still had a number of years to serve, were the most effective means by which the old spirit could be sustained in the new Army.

The treaty prohibition of a General Staff did not apply as well to the Troop General Staff, which continued to function – although no longer so designated – in 2 group commands (corps headquarters), 7 military districts, and 10 division headquarters. On becoming the *Reichswehr* Commander-in-Chief in June 1920, Seeckt allotted as many of the Great General Staff's former responsibilities to the *Truppenamt* as he could without attracting outside attention and farmed the rest out to the Troop General Staff. Later in the year, he advanced five staff majors to lieutenant-colonelcies. All held their ranks from the same day, 1 October, and were assigned as Chiefs of Staff to troop commands. They were Werner von Blomberg, Fedor von Bock, Kurt von Hammerstein-Equord, Wilhelm von Leeb, and Gerd von Rundstedt. They henceforth enjoyed brilliant careers under the Republic. Rundstedt, who was the senior in length of service, went initially to the 3rd Cavalry Division as Chief of Staff. Over the next eight years, he progressed to Colonel and commanding officer, 18th Infantry Regiment (the first troop command he had held since August 1914), Major-General and Chief of Staff, *Wehrkreis* II, and Lieutenant-General and General commanding 2nd Cavalry Division.

The three years after 1929 were bad for the German Republic but relatively good for the Army, and they began Rundstedt's emergence as a figure of consequence in history. The Great Depression and the rise of the National-

Socialist Party paralysed the *Reichstag* (parliament), and the power to govern passed by default to President Paul von Hindenburg and his personal appointees, among whom General Kurt von Schleicher for a time played a leading part. The Army regarded itself as above party politics and firmly expected its officers as individuals to do the same, but it had political concerns, and Schleicher had been its agent with respect to those throughout the 1920s. In the early 1930s, the crisis in the government and a close friendship with Hindenburg's son enabled Schleicher to promote the Army's interests and simultaneously manoeuvre himself into political prominence. His influence advanced Rundstedt's somewhat junior and more politically venturesome colleagues Hammerstein-Equord and Blomberg, the former to Commander-in-Chief of the Army, the latter to command of *Wehrkreis* I.

Rundstedt, now in his late fifties and approaching forty years' service, appeared to be heading for retirement; but Schleicher also very much appreciated – for both practical and cosmetic reasons – the non-political soldier of which Rundstedt was a sterling example. In January 1932, Rundstedt received the command of *Wehrkreis* III, which, having its headquarters in Berlin, was the premier military district. When Franz von Papen, the Chancellor, and Schleicher, by then Minister of Defence, engineered the destruction of the Social-Democratic government in the state of Prussia in July 1932, Rundstedt's restrained handling of the troops employed lent a tinge of decency to the most disgraceful political act perpetrated before Hitler's accession to power. Two months later, Rundstedt moved up to command of the 1st Army Group with a promotion to General of Infantry.

Next to the Army High Command, the 1st Army Group was the most important German command. From Berlin it controlled four *Wehrkreise* and six divisions, more than half of the Army, and it was responsible for defence of the entire eastern border. Senior to the Army C-in-C, in length of service, his equal in rank and entitled, like him, to the appellation '*Oberbefehlshaber*' (Commander-in-Chief), Rundstedt had become the symbolic first soldier of the Reich. From then on, he appears to have regarded himself as above all the guardian and exemplar of military virtues – as he understood them.

The January 1933 Cabinet crisis that ended in Hitler's appointment to the Chancellorship also terminated Schleicher's foray into politics and brought Blomberg to the fore as Minister of Defence. Hindenburg chose him on the assumption that because he had recently represented the German military interest very effectively at the Geneva Disarmament Conference he would deal equally well with the Nazis. Rundstedt, who said after the war that he had never agreed with Blomberg about anything, thought differently. He and the other senior generals knew Blomberg to be easily influenced and given to political and religious enthusiasms. In the 1920s he had talked democracy. More recently, he had seemed to be becoming drawn to Nazism.[5] Their concern grew when Blomberg brought Colonel Walther von Reichenau, his

Chief of Staff at *Wehrkreis* I, with him to be the chief deputy in the Defence Ministry, and redoubled a year later when he named Reichenau, just promoted to major-general, to succeed Hammerstein-Equord as Army Commander-in-Chief. Reichenau was brilliant, energetic and a radical nonconformist who was believed to be so close to being a Nazi that whether he was an actual Party member or not was immaterial. Manifest ability, boundless ambition, and a direct personal relationship with Hitler made him, in Rundstedt's estimation, the single greatest threat to the Army's traditional place in the German state. Rundstedt and Leeb, who commanded 2nd Army Group, told Hindenburg they could not serve under Reichenau, whom Hindenburg thereupon refused to accept.[6] After the appointment went to General Werner von Fritsch, Rundstedt's former subordinate at *Wehrkreis* III and his junior by five years but an officer of the old school, Rundstedt submitted a request for retirement which Hindenburg declined, saying he needed him then more than ever; and Rundstedt, as he would again and again thereafter, responded to the call of duty.

Early 1934 was indeed a perilous time. The Nazi storm troops, the SA, under ex-captain Ernst Röhm, were threatening to elbow aside the professional army, which they greatly outnumbered, and put themselves in its place as the national army. On 30 June, however, Hitler, whose military plans called for something more than a Party militia, resolved the issue in the Army's favour by murdering the whole top leadership of the SA – and some who were not SA members, among them Schleicher. The Army returned the favour a month later, when Hindenburg died, by recognizing Hitler as supreme Commander-in-Chief of the Armed Forces and taking a personal oath to Hitler (which Reichenau had written) undertaking to serve him loyally 'to the death'. Rundstedt administered the oath in person to the divisions in 1st Army Group; and he appeared along with Blomberg, Fritsch and other senior generals and admirals as a guest of honour at the annual Nazi Party rally in Nuremberg in September 1934. Earlier in the year Eugen Ott, a lieutenant-colonel on the Defence Ministry, had heard Rundstedt and Schleicher 'revile Hitler in a dreadful way'.[7] In his testimony at the Nuremberg war crimes trials, Rundstedt, who had often disparaged Hitler and the Nazis in private, maintained that he had always opposed Nazism but could not do so overtly because 'a soldier cannot participate in political activities'.[8]

The next three years saw a honeymoon between Hitler and the Armed Forces. The Army was growing, even somewhat more rapidly than Rundstedt and his colleagues would have liked. Fritsch kept it aloof from politics, and the SA stayed in its place. The Navy also expanded; an air force appeared almost overnight; and the *Truppenamt* again became the General Staff. Fritsch, as a bachelor completely devoted to his work, delegated a large part of his increasing ceremonial and social duties to Rundstedt, who although by no means gregarious himself carried them off with masterful aplomb. In 1936 he represented the German Army at King George V's funeral.

Even though a third Army Group command had now been activated, the 1st Army Group by late 1935 comprised ten divisions, as many as had existed in the whole Army three years earlier. War could again be thought about in more than suppositional terms. New ideas were in the air. The first panzer divisions were being formed. Yet Rundstedt was not an innovator; his first concern was to carry the professional army's standards over into the expanding conscript army. To him the infantry remained the main and decisive branch, and he looked on armour in anything but an infantry support role with at least some scepticism. But he could tolerate the new ideas – except in one outstanding instance, the new *Wehrmachtamt* which Blomberg and Reichenau proposed should supersede the Army General Staff in wartime as the supreme arbiter of strategy and operations. That the Army General Staff should not, particularly in wartime, remain paramount in the German Armed Forces was sheer anathema to Rundstedt.

On 30 January 1938 Rundstedt was observing a war-game in East Prussia when he received a message from the Chief of the General Staff, General Beck, asking him to return to Berlin at once. Upon his arrival the next day, Beck told him that Blomberg's bride of a few weeks (his second wife and much younger than he) had proved to have a police record and he had been asked to resign, and that Fritsch was being dismissed because he had been accused of homosexuality. That Blomberg should have married a woman with a doubtful past surprised but hardly amazed Rundstedt, who considered Blomberg fully capable of such a vagary. The charge against Fritsch, whom he held in far higher regard, he absolutely refused to believe. That night in an interview with Hitler, who had summoned him to the Reich Chancellery – and instructed him to come in civilian clothes and enter by a rear door – he demanded in the name of the Army and as its senior-active-service officer a court of inquiry for Fritsch.

On the other hand, to demand as well that Fritsch retain his post pending a judicial finding appears not to have occurred to him. When Hitler mentioned Reichenau and General Walther von Brauchitsch as Fritsch's possible successors, Rundstedt rejected Reichenau out of hand 'in the name of the Army', and hastened to throw his support behind Brauchitsch, who 'would be entirely acceptable to the Army as Fritsch's successor'. (Others, notably Hermann Göring and Heinrich Himmler, whose opinions weighed more heavily with Hitler than Rundstedt's did, had already opposed Reichenau.) Even more remarkably, he seems to have imagined that although Hitler was willing to dismiss Fritsch as Army Commander-in-Chief on an unproved charge, he would later consider appointing Fritsch as a generalissimo of all the Armed Forces. During the discussion, Hitler also disclosed that he proposed to abolish the Defence Ministry and create an Armed Forces High Command (*Oberkommando der Wehrmacht*, OKW) with himself as supreme commander.

Rundstedt agreed but insisted, when Hitler mentioned General Wilhelm Keitel, Reichenau's successor in the Armed Forces Office, as the OKW Chief of Staff, that Keitel 'never' be given any command authority because 'we [the Army] do not want that'. Hitler said he did not want it either (and Keitel's subsequent appointment as Chief of OKW made him only a highly-placed supernumerary in the chain of command).[9]

During the Blomberg-Fritsch affair, partly to cover up the scandals, partly to bring more amenable officers into key positions, Hitler ordered a spate of reassignments and retirements. Leeb was retired, Rundstedt, Leeb's senior by about a year, stayed on at 1st Army Group with promotion to Colonel-General.

After the court of inquiry had dismissed the charge against Fritsch as false, and he was sent into retirement nevertheless, he asked Rundstedt to deliver a letter containing a challenge to a duel to Himmler, whose secret police had trumped up the charge. Rundstedt carried the letter in his pocket for several days before returning it with advice to drop the idea because it would only stir up a useless fuss, since Hitler would not allow one of his chief subordinates to accept a challenge and Himmler would not fight if he did.[10]

The Czech crisis in the summer of 1938 brought Rundstedt (briefly) his first major field command, 2nd Army. It also brought him into his first confrontation with Hitler's war programme. On 4 August, when Brauchitsch assembled senior commanders to consider the memorandum, which the Chief of the General Staff, Beck, had prepared advising Hitler not to risk starting a general war over the Sudetenland, Rundstedt supported the consensus view that neither the army nor the country was ready for war. But he was overheard afterward advising Brauchitsch to avoid putting the case so forcefully to Hitler as to jeopardize his position as Commander-in-Chief – and thus revive the Reichenau candidacy.[11] In September 1938, when war seemed imminent and the opposition to Hitler was seeking to organize a coup to overthrow Hitler, Rundstedt responded coldly to the one tentative approach made to him. His attitude on that score remained rigidly the same thereafter. When asked about it at the Nuremberg war crimes trials, he replied, 'I would never have thought of such a thing; that would have been base, bare-faced treachery....'[12]

After leading the 2nd Army in the post-Munich *Blumenkrieg* occupation of the Sudetenland, Rundstedt retired with an honorary appointment as Colonel-in-Chief of the 18th Infantry Regiment, a distinction he seems to have valued more than any other. As a Field-Marshal, he always wore his marshal's insignia on the uniform of a colonel in the 18th Infantry Regiment.

His retirement was brief. In April 1939 he was appointed to head the Working Staff Rundstedt (*Arbeitsstab* Rundstedt), consisting of himself, a Chief of Staff (General Erich von Manstein) and an Operations Officer (Colonel Günther Blumentritt). Hitler had ordered planning begun on *Fall Weiss*, the operation 'to destroy the Polish armed forces ... if Poland adopts a threatening attitude toward the Reich.'[13] The Working Staff Rundstedt was a headquarters in embryo for a southern army group. To preserve secrecy but also because Hitler did not appear to be in any hurry, Rundstedt worked mostly at his home in Kassel while Manstein continued his duties as a divisional commander and Blumentritt his as chief of the training branch in the General Staff.

Hitler appeared a good deal less willing to risk a general war than he had been in the previous summer, and the successful outcome of the Sudeten crisis had persuaded those who had doubted him then that he was not merely a reckless gambler. When Rundstedt brought his enlarged working staff together in the second week of August, the feeling was that they were about to become bit players in an international political drama with a familiar plot and predictable peaceful outcome.[14] The final troop deployment began on 19 August and four days later, in a monastery near Neisse, 60 miles from the Polish border, the Working Staff Rundstedt became operational as Head-quarters, Army Group South.

On the afternoon of the 25th, the troops began closing up to the border, the next day having been designated as the day on which the attack was to begin. That evening Hitler ordered the movements stopped. (Rundstedt had been through a similar experience once before: Hitler had ordered the assault troops into their jump-off positions along the Czechoslovakian border on 26 September 1938, three days before the Munich Agreement was signed.) On the night of 31 August, after being ordered to open the attack the next morning, Rundstedt, who never kept late hours, stayed up after midnight awaiting the second stop order. It did not come.

Although the troop strengths (1.5 million German and 1.3 million Polish) were not vastly disproportionate, overwhelming German superiorities in air-craft, tanks and motor vehicles guaranteed Poland's defeat. To hasten it, Army Groups North and South launched thrusts southward out of East Prussia and northeastward out of Silesia toward Warsaw that would trap the Polish main forces west of the Vistula River. Bock (commanding Army Group North) had 3rd and 4th Armies, Rundstedt 8th, 10th and 14th Armies. Tenth Army, under Reichenau, was the most powerful. Its mission was to smash the Polish 'Krakow' Army, and with panzer and motorized divisions make a 180-mile drive to Warsaw. The 8th Army and 14th Army, the former on the left, the latter on the right, would cover 10th Army's flanks, each also having to contend initially with one Polish Army. Speed was essential to prevent the Polish forces from escaping east across the Vistula and making another stand behind it. For nine days the advance went better than had been expected, and the Army Group staff had little to do other than to report successes. On the afternoon of 8 September, a panzer division had entered the Warsaw suburbs. Finding the city strongly defended, it had withdrawn but remained blocking the roads on the west.

On 10 September, 8th Army reported its left flank under heavy attack. In the rush for Warsaw, the staffs, including the General Staff, had failed to keep

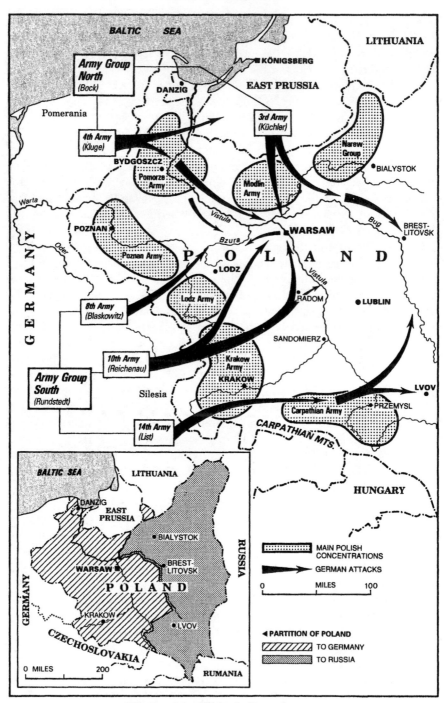

The invasion of Poland, September 1939

had bypassed; and they were trying to break out to the east. Rundstedt left General Johannes Blaskowitz, the 8th Army Commander, to resolve the problem on his flank by himself and, diverting two corps from the advance on Warsaw, began building a front facing north and west along the Bzura River. He and his staff in the next week manoeuvred elements of 8th, 10th and 14th Armies to accomplish the first large-scale encirclement of the Second World War. Although the 120,000 prisoners taken would later appear to be a modest number, nothing comparable had been seen in warfare since the Battle of Tannenberg in September 1914.

While the battle on the Bzura was drawing to its end 30 miles to the west, Rundstedt was bringing all of the Army Group's heavy artillery up to Warsaw. He and Manstein had thought they would have time enough to starve the city into submission, but after the Soviet Army crossed the border in the east on 17 September, Hitler insisted on a faster solution. A three-day artillery and aerial bombardment brought the Warsaw garrison's surrender on the 28th and that of the nearby Modlin fortress the following morning. Since the Polish government had already gone into exile, these surrenders in the field terminated the war.

Rundstedt received the Knight's Cross of the Iron Cross on 30 September. For the next three weeks, as Commander-in-Chief, East, he was military governor of Poland, and then he and his staff were ordered to Koblenz to become Headquarters, Army Group A, one of three Army Groups being deployed on the Western Front. The former Working Staff Rundstedt had become a seasoned team. Rundstedt, through long experience, was thoroughly at home in high-level command. Three officers who knew him well, his successive Chiefs of Staff Manstein, Blumentritt, and Siegfried Westphal, have commented on his command style. They portray him as a Commander-in-Chief of the old (pre-First World War) school; a disciple of the last great Chief of the General Staff, Count Alfred von Schlieffen; a *grand seigneur*; and a master of the operational art with an unerring instinct for correctly assessing military situations. He also observed the First World War principle that the commanding general could direct the battle best from his headquarters, not from the front (as others, most notably Generals Heinz Guderian and Erwin Rommel, were to do in the current war); and he refused to concern himself with details, preferring to work from 1:1,000,000 maps (the scale, incidentally, which was also used at Hitler's headquarters) from which he could take in the entire situation at a glance.[15] His disdain for details led him to depend heavily on his Chief of Staff, which he could do with confidence since Manstein, who had been Beck's operations chief and closest collaborator in the General Staff, was generally regarded as the best military mind in the Army. In his testimony at the Nuremberg Trials, Rundstedt gave his view of his relationship with higher headquarters as having been to propose, if necessary, how an assigned mission could be more effectively executed but 'never' to tell a superior. 'What you are doing is wrong. . . .'[16]

The 'Phoney War' had begun on the Western Front but all was far from quiet in the upper reaches of the German command. Hitler had issued a directive for an offensive against France and the Low Countries that he proposed to have start in mid-November. The senior generals, for their part, were more uneasy over the British and French declarations of war than emboldened by the success of *Blitzkrieg* in Poland. When Brauchitsch canvassed the army-group and army commanders, he found them in unanimous agreement with a conclusion already reached by himself and the Chief of the General Staff, Halder, namely, that an offensive in the west could not secure any decisive result. Hitler rejected Brauchitsch's report and thereafter ignored him. When Leeb, who had been recalled from retirement to command Army Group C, believing Brauchitsch was about to resign, suggested to Rundstedt and Bock (who commanded Army Group B) that he and they do likewise, they said they considered themselves duty-bound to carry out the attack if the order were given.[17]

The General Staff's plan for the offensive was based on an assumption that the most the Army could do would be to push through Belgium, Luxembourg and a part of northwestern France to the line of the Aisne and Somme Rivers where the Allied armies – if they had not done so sooner – would dig in. It assigned the main effort to Army Group B, which with about two-thirds of the panzer and motorized divisions would make a broad sweep through Belgium to the Channel coast and the mouth of the Somme. Army Group A's mission was to cover Bock's left flank by advancing through Luxembourg and the Ardennes Forest toward the Aisne River.

At widely separated points in the command structure, Hitler and Rundstedt's Chief of Staff, Manstein, doubted the necessity of conducting the offensive in a manner that was bound to end in a stalemate. Hitler then still deferred to the senior professionals in purely military matters. Manstein bombarded Brauchitsch and Halder with communications proposing a shift of the main effort to the Army Group A sector and a powerful armoured thrust through Luxembourg and the Ardennes that would cross the Meuse River north of Sedan and thereafter run parallel to the Aisne and the Somme to the Channel. The whole Allied left wing, he predicted, could be enveloped and destroyed, and the anticipated Allied front on the Somme and the Aisne would become instead a 150-mile-wide gap through which the army groups could then plunge south and east behind the Maginot Line. For various reasons, the most valid of which related to von Schlieffen's maxim that the difficulty in executing an encircling manoeuvre was exceeded only by the ease with which one could be frustrated, Brauchitsch and Halder did not welcome Manstein's importunities and took particular care to keep his ideas from coming to Hitler's notice.

However, Rundstedt had approved Manstein's plan 'with that one swift glance that was characteristic of him'; and subsequently, by giving his endorsement, he enabled Manstein to send proposals to Brauchitsch through the command channel, which Manstein otherwise could not have done.[18] Manstein, Blumentritt, and Blumentritt's deputy, Lieutenant-Colonel Henning von Tresckow, carried through the development of the 'New Plan', as Manstein referred to it, while Guderian, the originator of the panzer division and the most successful panzer corps commander in the Polish campaign, provided assurance that the armour could cope with the terrain and cover the required distances.

Rundstedt had an audience with Hitler in late November 1939, at which he did not bring the 'New Plan' to the Führer's attention – although he could have done – according to Manstein, because he feared that to do so would further jeopardize Brauchitsch's already severely impaired position. Rundstedt was on anything but good personal terms with Brauchitsch, but Reichenau had been promoted to Colonel-General after the victory in Poland, and his possible succession to Brauchitsch as Army C-in-C had again become an acute concern to Rundstedt. And again this concern appeared to have been immaterial. Hitler had told Guderian that Reichenau was unacceptable as Brauchitsch's replacement.

On 12 January 1940, Rundstedt counter-signed what was to be Manstein's last and most   forcefully written memorandum about his suggested plan. In it Manstein brought the argument down to a choice between totally defeating the Allies or merely prolonging the war, and he requested that if, as Brauchitsch had maintained, Hitler reserved decisions on changing the plan to himself, then the memorandum be forwarded to Hitler. Two weeks later, Rundstedt, on Brauchitsch's advice, approved Manstein's appointment to command a corps that was to be formed at Stettin, well away from the Western Front. Apparently Rundstedt had reached the conclusion that the time had come for him to part company with Manstein and the 'New Plan', for Brauchitsch had responded sharply to the 12 January memorandum, particularly to the request that he forward it to Hitler over his own head, so to speak; and Rundstedt's support of Manstein had brought him perilously close to breaking his rule against telling a superior he was wrong.[19]

Manstein and his co-workers were not as punctilious as Rundstedt, and they had tentatively established a back-door channel to Hitler through his chief adjutant, Lieutenant-Colonel Rudolf Schmundt. They had kept Schmundt (who came to the Army group periodically to check weather and ground conditions for Hitler) abreast of the general direction their thinking was taking; and once he knew he was being sidetracked, Manstein briefed Schmundt thoroughly. On his return to Berlin Schmundt, struck by the precision with which Manstein had given form to ideas which he had also heard Hitler express, urged Hitler to call in Manstein. On 17 February, after a luncheon for newly appointed corps commanders arranged to conceal the actual reason for Manstein's presence in the Reich Chancellery, in a rare meeting during which the Führer listened and said little, Manstein described the 'New Plan' to Hitler and his military advisor General Alfred Jodl, the Chief of the *Wehrmacht* (OKW) Operations Staff. Hitler summoned Brauchitsch and Halder a day later and told them he had decided to shift the main effort south to Army Group A. In the following week, the 'New Plan' became the *Sichelschnitt* (Sickle-Cut) Plan.

Guderian claimed later that only three persons, he, Manstein and Hitler, really believed in the plan.[20] Whether or not anyone believed unreservedly was less significant than how the doubts were handled. With Manstein off the scene training an infantry corps and Hitler engrossed in preparing and executing the invasion of Norway and Denmark, the chief participants in the final *Sichelschnitt* planning were Halder, Brauchitsch, Rundstedt and his new Chief of Staff, General Georg von Sodenstern. Once the plan had become Hitler's and the Army High Command's property, Halder and Brauchitsch warmed to it rapidly, putting a third more panzer divisions into the armoured spearhead than Manstein had projected, enough, together with Guderian's corps and a motorized corps, to constitute a panzer group (actually a panzer army, although not yet so designated). Halder also asserted that because the mission was exceedingly difficult, it was necessary to take risks and essential to avoid overestimating the obstacles.[21]

Rundstedt, on the other hand, held the Allied Commander-in-Chief, General Maurice Gamelin, whom he had met at the funeral of George V in 1936, in high esteem and believed that he and the French General Staff would know how to interpose obstacles that would be hard to overestimate.[22] Sodenstern, perhaps echoing his superior's opinion, reminded Halder that they were now planning an offensive against the French Army, not the Polish Army; and Rundstedt, far from ready to take risks, worried about his left flank's becoming exposed and about crossing the Meuse, which he expected to be strongly defended.[23] Guderian was dismayed to discover that Rundstedt believed panzer and motorized divisions could not cross rivers without infantry assistance.[24] Given a choice in the appointment of a general to command the panzer group, Rundstedt chose General Ewald von Kleist, an old-school cavalryman, in preference to the tank expert Guderian. As always, circumspection was his watchword, and he was content to leave innovations to others.

The *Sichelschnitt* offensive began at dawn on 10 May 1940 (see map on page 469). During the day, while German tanks streamed southwestward through Luxembourg and into the Ardennes, two British and two French armies wheeled to the north and west in accordance with Gamelin's plan to meet and check the German attack coming through Belgium on the Dyle River line. The two panzer corps of the Panzer Group Kleist, Guderian's 19th and

General Hans Reinhardt's 41st, were on the Meuse on the 13th, two days ahead of schedule, and crossed the river the next day, Guderian at Sedan and Reinhardt 20 miles to the north at Monthermé (see map on page 399). On the 14th Rundstedt was at Kleist's and Guderian's command posts congratulating the troops and encouraging the generals to carry the advance westward from the Meuse at full speed. But later in the day, back at his own headquarters in Bastogne, he learned that French forces were reportedly on the move toward the bridgehead from the vicinity of Paris. No doubt remembering the 'Miracle of the Marne' and his own experiences on the Ourcq River in 1914, he began to have second thoughts about letting the armour run loose, and subordinated the Panzer Group Kleist to General Wilhelm List's 12th Army (infantry).

He then charged List with getting the infantry and armour to work 'in unison' at building a strong bridgehead on the Meuse without 'holding too tight a rein' on the armour.[25] After Guderian's armour made a 40-mile leap westwards in one day on the 16th, getting to within 15 miles of the River Oise, the approximate half-way point between the Meuse and the Channel coast, Rundstedt concluded that the risk to his southern flank was becoming too great, and he reserved the decision on crossing the Oise to himself.[26] To Halder at OKH, however, the breakthrough appeared to be developing 'in downright classical style', and he did not believe the French would gamble their remaining available reserves on a counter-stroke. The next morning, Halder told Sodenstern, Rundstedt's Chief of Staff, that the Army Group ought to continue straight on across the Oise without stopping. At the same time in the morning situation conference at the Führer Headquarters, Hitler was admonishing Brauchitsch to see to the security of the south flank.[27]

At the Army Group A headquarters on the afternoon of the 17th, Hitler gave his full concurrence to an appreciation in which Rundstedt 'emphasized the sensitivity of the south flank', and added, after Rundstedt had finished, that nothing was more important to the entire operation than an absolutely dependable defensive readiness on the Aisne and the Somme.[28] Meanwhile, Panzer Group Kleist was at a standstill. When Kleist had transmitted Rundstedt's stop order to Guderian and Reinhardt early in the morning, Guderian had asked to be relieved of his command. While Hitler was in Bastogne with Rundstedt, List was at Guderian's command post working out a compromise that would allow Guderian to conduct a 'reconnaissance in force' west of the Oise.

General Jodl put down 18 May in his diary as 'a day of strong tension'.[29] At the Führer Headquarters, Hitler, 'raging and yelling', berated Halder and Brauchitsch, accusing them of having spoiled the whole operation and set the stage for a defeat.[30] Keitel, acting for Hitler, visited Rundstedt and received assurances that the south flank was getting the fullest attention – and a suggestion that perhaps the danger was not quite as great as it had seemed since the French had destroyed practically all the bridges on the Aisne, which they would not have done if they were contemplating a counter-attack.[31] Guderian stretched his licence to conduct 'reconnaissance in force' sufficiently to cover taking St Quentin, 10 miles beyond the Oise, but regarded the day as another one mostly wasted. Finally, late in the day, after having confronted Hitler with evidence that elements of the Allied Northern Army Group were retreating out of Belgium towards and across the Somme, Halder secured permission to get the armour back on the move.

Guderian's tanks reached Abbeville at the mouth of the Somme after dark on 20 May (see map on page 399). Turning north, they isolated Boulogne and Calais and closed to the Aa Canal between Gravelines and St Omer, about 15 miles west of Dunkirk in three more days. Halder and Brauchitsch then expected the armour to continue northward past Dunkirk along the Flanders coast to Ostende, in order to bar the Allies' retreat to the sea. The armour did so until late in the day on the 24th, after Hitler and Jodl returned from a flight to Rundstedt's headquarters, which had been moved forward to Charleville on the River Meuse. Rundstedt had suggested that the panzer divisions be held on the Aa Canal where they could 'intercept' the enemy while Army Group B's infantry divisions drove him back from the north; and Hitler had agreed at once, adding that the armour would have to be conserved for coming operations and a further reduction in the encircled area would impair air action.[32]

On the flight back, Hitler told Jodl that he was 'very pleased' with Rundstedt's troop dispositions; it conformed to his own thinking entirely.[33] Later, Brauchitsch, in Halder's words, 'returned from another highly disagreeable discussion with the Führer' bearing an order to halt the armour's advance and leave it to the *Luftwaffe* to finish off the enemy.[34] A few hours later Brauchitsch asked to have the order rescinded, whereupon Hitler then left the answer entirely to Rundstedt, who himself decided the next morning that because they needed to be rested and regrouped for the next phase of the French campaign, he would not send the panzer divisions forward again 'for the time being'.[35]

After twenty-four more hours, the front having been at a standstill for more than two full days, nerves were becoming frayed. Bock complained to Brauchitsch that if Dunkirk were not captured, the British could 'take out anything they want right from under our noses'.[36] Halder and Brauchitsch had premonitions of a great loss of prestige and several weeks' delay in getting the second phase of the campaign started. They conveyed these concerns to Rundstedt; and in the early afternoon Rundstedt, after having gone to consult with Kleist, requested the panzer divisions' release, which Hitler granted on condition that the tanks go no closer to Dunkirk than was necessary to bring the port under artillery fire.

After dark on 26 May, the British transport *Mona's Isle* docked at Dunkirk and began loading troops. A Royal Navy shore party under Captain W. G.

Tennant arrived the next morning to organize a mass evacuation from the beaches. Against the Allied defensive perimeter neither Rundstedt's tanks nor Bock's infantry could regain their former momentum. A military miracle, the second such in which Rundstedt participated, had begun.

At a conference in Charleville on the 29th, when the Dunkirk evacuation was in full swing, Rundstedt told Bock he had held the panzer divisions back because he was afraid the British would throw their entire weight against them and overrun them. Bock believed nothing of the sort could have happened because his own armies 'had the English so tightly by the throat that they would be lucky to get away alive.'[37] After the war, Rundstedt gave a different explanation to a Canadian intelligence officer, Major Milton Shulman, whom he told: 'If I had had my way the English would not have got off so lightly at Dunkirk. But my hands were tied by direct orders from Hitler himself.'[38]

Army Group A's involvement at the Dunkirk beachhead terminated late in the day on 30 May. Its units had by then all been redeployed east of the Oise to a line facing south on the River Aisne. With the 2nd, 12th and 16th Armies and a newly formed Panzer Group Guderian, Rundstedt was to strike south against the remaining part of the French Army, crossing the River Marne east of Paris and continuing on behind the Maginot Line to the Swiss border and the upper reaches of the rivers Loire and Rhône. To protect Rundstedt's right flank, Bock attacked across the Somme between the River Oise and the coast on 5 June, the day after the fighting at Dunkirk ended. Army Group A jumped off on the 9th, crossing the Marne near Château Thierry on the 11th, and taking Verdun, the famous First World War fortress, on the 15th. The French position, dismal from the outset, became hopeless when the German army groups passed Paris. On the 17th, two hours after being appointed to form a government, Marshal Philippe Pétain transmitted a request for an armistice through the Spanish Embassy.

Hitler gave his victory speech to the *Reichstag* – and the world – on 19 July. The generals, in order of rank, were present in the hall as guests of honour. As the emotional climax of his rambling discourse on 'the historically unique events we have experienced', Hitler announced twelve promotions to field-marshal, naming Brauchitsch first, then Rundstedt, Bock and Leeb and farther down the list Keitel and Reichenau.[39] Rundstedt and the others received their personal hand-crafted marshal's batons at a ceremony in the Reich Chancellery four weeks later.

Meanwhile, Führer Directive No. 16, issued on 16 July under the code-name *Sealion*, had given the armed forces another mission: to plan an invasion of England. Anticipating that the war might have to be continued against England, the General Staff had moved to Fontainebleau, 30 miles southeast of Paris. In early July, eight armies remained stationed in France. Rundstedt lodged his staff in the Hotel Henri IV in St Germain on the Seine a few miles downstream from Paris. Had *Sealion* been executed, Army Group A would have been responsible initially for seizing a 100-mile-wide beachhead southeast of London; but although some serious effort was put into planning it, *Sealion* never had Hitler's confidence. At lunch with the Field-Marshals on 14 August, after he had given them their batons, he said he would wait to see what the Luftwaffe could accomplish against the Royal Air Force before making a decision, and he told Rundstedt privately that he regarded the invasion preparations as a 'deception'.[40]

Sealion's postponement on 12 October 1940 to spring 1941 (in fact, forever) and the emergence of new operational possibilities, particularly in the east, occasioned a general redeployment. Bock, named Commander-in-Chief, East, took the Army Group B staff and two armies to occupied Poland. Leeb, with the Army Group C staff and another army, returned to Germany, as also did the General Staff. On 26 October, Rundstedt became Commander-in-Chief, West, and took command of all Army field formations in Holland, Belgium and France. His forces consisted of his own Army Group A (two armies on standby for *Sealion*) and a newly activated Army Group D (three armies on occupation duty in France). He achieved therewith for a time the unique distinction of having two Field-Marshals under his command, Erwin von Witzleben, who commanded Army Group D, and Reichenau, who as commander of the 6th Army was subordinate to Witzleben.

On 31 January 1941, Brauchitsch conferred with Rundstedt, Leeb and Bock at his quarters in Berlin. He told them they were the designated Army-Group commanders for Operation *Barbarossa*, the invasion of the Soviet Union, and could expect to receive an operation order within a few days. The information was no great surprise. Bock had seen a copy of the strategic directive for *Barbarossa* earlier in the month, and the others very likely also knew about it. Rundstedt's Chief of Staff, Sodenstern, had done an operational study for the General Staff in early December. The tone of the meeting was subdued, but no one raised the kind of objections that they had all voiced before the campaign in the west.

The operation order came out on 3 February, and two days later, in St Germain, Halder reviewed it with Sodenstern and subordinate Army Chiefs of Staff. The order gave Army Group A – to be redesignated Army Group South – Reichenau's 6th Army, List's 12th Army, General Karl Heinrich von Stülpnagel's 17th Army, and Kleist's 1st Panzer Group; and assigned to it the sector between the southern edge of the Pripet Marshes and the Black Sea coast (see map on page 194). The overall strategic objective was the same for all three Army Groups, South, Centre (Bock) and North (Leeb) in *Barbarossa*: to trap the Soviet main forces in encirclements close to the Russian border and destroy them there. Army Group South's mission was to destroy the Soviet forces in Galicia, Moldavia and the western Ukraine west of the River Dnieper; and the operation order initially called for one large double envelopment that would close on the Dnieper downstream from Kiev: 6th

Army and 1st Panzer Group were to form the northern arm, 12th Army the southern. But in March 1941, Hitler diverted 12th Army to the invasion of Yugoslavia and Greece, which he began on 6 April, and substituted for it an unwieldy aggregation of 14 Romanian and 7 German divisions under General Eugen von Schobert's 11th Army Headquarters, a doubtful instrument for such an encircling manoeuvre. Rundstedt and Sodenstern then devised a single envelopment that would employ 6th and 17th Armies and 1st Panzer Group in a thrust skirting the southern edge of the Pripet Marshes to the Dnieper at Kiev, where it would turn and run south to the Black Sea coast.

Rundstedt transferred his headquarters to Breslau on 1 April. Because security considerations ruled out advance deployment on Hungarian and Romanian territory, he had to assemble the Army Group initially in occupied Poland along the northern 100 miles of its 500-mile-wide sector. For the first time in the war he did not command the principal offensive forces; the General Staff's plan assigned the main effort to Army Group Centre, which would be operating north of the Pripet Marshes toward Moscow. However, Hitler had not accepted the General Staff's contention that Moscow was a strategically more important objective than the Ukraine, whose agricultural and industrial resources he regarded as the greatest prize to be gained in the campaign.

On 30 March, to inaugurate the final deployment for *Barbarossa*, Hitler assembled the Army-Group, Army and Corps commanders and their Chiefs of Staff at the Reich Chancellery; here he charged them with a role that would permanently becloud many of their reputations, including Rundstedt's. The officers, he demanded, would have to conduct a different kind of war against the Soviet Union, one of extermination in which the Geneva Convention and ideas of chivalry did not apply. Later Rundstedt obediently transmitted to his subordinate commands Hitler's 'Commissar Order' and the order on military justice, the first denying captured commissars prisoner-of-war status and requiring their summary execution forward of regimental command posts; the second subjecting Soviet civilians to execution without trial for acts against the German forces, encouraging collective reprisals, and granting German soldiers virtual blanket immunity from prosecution for acts committed against the civilian population.

On Saturday, 21 June 1941, Rundstedt received and passed on the code-word 'Dortmund', signalling the start of *Barbarossa* at 0310 the next morning. Army Group South faced two Soviet Army Groups: General M. P. Kirponos's Southwest Front, which had four armies deployed south of the Pripet Marshes on the approaches to Kiev, and General I.V. Tiulenev's South Front, two armies covering the Romanian border. Together, the Soviet *fronts* had 89 divisions, against which Army Group South deployed 43 German plus 14 Romanian divisions. Josef Stalin, whose strategic thinking closely paralleled Hitler's in some respects, had expected the lure of the Ukrainian resources to bring the strongest German attack there. Still believing when the invasion began that this would be the case, Stalin sent General Georgi Zhukov, the chief of the Soviet General Staff, to the Southwest Front headquarters in Ternopol on June 22. Zhukov had formerly commanded the Kiev Special Military District, which became the Southwest Front once the war broke out. Although he and Kirponos did not succeed in executing the pre-war plan to stop the enemy on the border and throw him back, they did manage (before Zhukov returned to Moscow on the 27th) to organize a more effective resistance than was being achieved anywhere else along the Eastern Front – so effective that Rundstedt and Sodenstern on the 26th began to think of trying for a relatively modest encirclement well short of the Dnieper River.

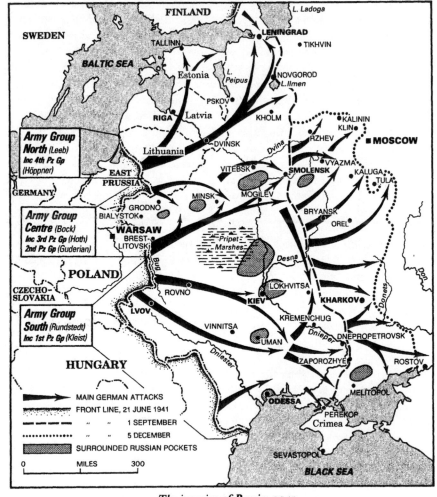

The invasion of Russia, 1941

Heavy rain in the first week of July, complaints from Reichenau that the Soviet 5th Army, which had retreated into the Pripet Marshes, was endangering his left flank, and the prospect of a hard fight on the Stalin Line, the pre-1939 Soviet border fortifications, led to Hitler also taking up the idea of a smaller encirclement. The ensuing decisions revived echoes of the hesitations before Dunkirk. On 9 July, 1st Panzer Group was working its way through a gap in the Stalin Line, and Rundstedt proposed next to send one of Kleist's corps on a fast thrust toward Kiev in order to seize the city and a bridgehead there, and to turn Kleist's other two corps south along the Bug River in an attempt at an encirclement. A bridgehead at Kiev would, he believed, provide an ideal springboard for a subsequent envelopment of the Dnieper, and thus a hedge against the Bug encirclement failing. Hitler approved the swing south and the advance toward Kiev but expressed 'gravest concern' that panzer divisions would be 'uselessly sacrificed' if an attempt to take the city were made.[41] Rundstedt, although he had believed the prize was worth some risk, thereupon ordered that an attack into Kiev was only to be attempted if it could be done without endangering the panzer divisions.

The fastest two-day advance yet achieved in the campaign carried the 13th Panzer Division through Kiev's outer defence ring on 11 July, but there it turned south toward the Dnieper below the city. The encircling drive along the Bug progressed slowly. After the pocket closed in the first week of August, around Uman, 150 miles west of the Dnieper, it netted 103,000 prisoners, but the Soviet Southwest and South Fronts' main forces survived to build a defence on the left bank of the Dnieper and hold a bridgehead at Kiev.

Hitler, Brauchitsch and Halder had meanwhile become locked in the debate over how to put the finishing touches to the war all three believed was virtually won – whether, as Brauchitsch and Halder were convinced, the Soviet Command would sacrifice its last remaining strength to defend Moscow, or whether, as Hitler argued, it was more important to ensure possession of Soviet economic assets in the Ukraine. On 6 August, Hitler flew to Army Group South headquarters at Berdichev to award the Romanian Head of State and Commander-in-Chief, General Ion Antonescu, the Knight's Cross of the Iron Cross, and to show appreciation to Rundstedt, who had developed very cordial relations with the Romanian dictator. After the ceremony, Hitler listened approvingly to Rundstedt's report on his Uman victory; but his demeanour changed when Rundstedt 'stressed the strategic importance of Moscow', as he had promised Halder he would. General Friedrich Paulus, Halder's deputy, who was present at the meeting, reported – to Halder's marked dismay – that Hitler 'again emphatically rejected this line of thinking'.[42]

On 25 August 1941, Hitler having previously resolved the debate over strategy to suit himself, Guderian's 2nd Panzer Group wheeled south away from the Army Group Centre's right flank east of Smolensk and headed on an almost straight-line course toward Romny, 120 miles east of Kiev. On 10 September, after Guderian had crossed the Desna River, the last obstacle in his path, Kleist's Panzer Group (of Army Group South) struck north out of a bridgehead on the Dnieper at Kremenchug, 160 miles downstream from Kiev. Stalin helped the German encirclement by refusing to allow the Russian armies inside the developing pocket to retreat, and in another six days the panzer spearheads met at Lokhvitsa, 25 miles south of Romny. In the mopping up, Army Group South took 665,000 prisoners. In the Babi Yar Ravine, outside Kiev, an SS special detachment killed 34,000 Jewish civilians on 29 September.

After the victory at Kiev, Guderian turned northeast to rejoin Army Group Centre for Operation *Typhoon*, the final drive on Moscow, while Kleist headed southeast toward the Donets industrial basin. Their panzer groups had now been elevated to 'panzer armies'. Fine autumn weather prevailed through early October, and as Army Group Centre completed massive twin encirclements at Vyazma and Bryansk, the armies of Army Group South kept the upper hand over the stunned Russian Southwest and South Fronts. The 11th Army struck into the Crimea. By 24 October, 6th Army had captured Kharkov, the second city of the Ukraine; 17th Army had reached the Donets River below Kharkov; and 1st Panzer Army had taken Stalino, the most important industrial centre in the Donets Basin. But the pursuit was ending; the autumn rains had set in; and the strain of four months' campaigning was showing on the troops, equipment and commands. Reichenau insisted that 6th Army was exhausted and could go no farther. Kleist reported that 1st Panzer Army's tanks were in need of major overhauls that could only be accomplished in Germany.

Meanwhile at OKH Brauchitsch and Halder talked about their 'ideal terminal objective' for the year's campaign: a line, still 300 miles away, reaching from Stalingrad on the Volga River to Maikop in the North Caucasus. When Brauchitsch visited the Army Group South headquarters on 3 November to get Rundstedt's concurrence, Rundstedt told him that the most his army group could possibly do was to advance 75 or so miles to Rostov on the lower Don.[43] A week later, Rundstedt submitted a proposal that Army Group South's operations be stopped 'in order to preserve the troops' striking power' for the next spring.[44]

When Hitler, Brauchitsch and Halder insisted on having the advance continue at least to Rostov, 1st Panzer Army, in rain and mud, pushed a thin wedge eastward along the shore of the Gulf of Taganrog. The SS division *Leibstandarte Adolf Hitler* took Rostov on 21 November. The next day the *Leibstandarte* came under furious counter-attacks from three sides, and Kleist ordered it and 3rd Panzer Corps, of which it was a part, to evacuate Rostov and withdraw 45 miles to the Mius River. But after Brauchitsch demanded that Rostov, which was the gateway to the Caucasus oilfields, be held because giving it up would have grave military and political consequences, Rundstedt obediently rescinded Kleist's order.

On the morning of 29 November, Hitler returned to his headquarters in East Prussia from Berlin, where he had been for the past week participating in a publicity spectacle associated with the renewal of the 1936 Anti-Comintern Pact, the cornerstone of the Rome-Berlin-Tokyo Axis. The worst kind of news awaited him: for the first time in the war, German troops were retreating; the *Leibstandarte*, his own Praetorians, had been driven out of Rostov the day before.

On the 30th, after Kleist again ordered a retreat to the Mius, Hitler, 'casting accusations and aspersions', browbeat Brauchitsch into sending Rundstedt another demand that he intervene with Kleist. Rundstedt was to tell his British War-Office interrogators in July 1945 that he had replied: 'It is madness to attempt to hold. I request that this order be rescinded or that you find someone else.'[45] As Halder recorded it, Rundstedt's reply went to Brauchitsch, not to Hitler; did not contain the 'madness' reference; and did not put the choice between rescindment and his relief quite so sharply.[46] Rundstedt apparently also gave impaired health (the result of a heart attack in early November) as a reason for his relief.[47] Early on 1 December, having concluded, nevertheless, from Brauchitsch's oral report that Rundstedt had wilfully refused a direct order, Hitler dispatched a telegram ordering him to turn the Army Group command over to Reichenau.

Within weeks, Brauchitsch and Bock would also be relieved – and later Leeb as well. Of the four, only Rundstedt went home on a special train with a guard of honour. After Reichenau and Hitler's Nazi Party crony SS General Josef Dietrich, who commanded the *Leibstandarte*, convinced him that the only real choices had been a retreat to the Mius line or losing four divisions, Hitler apologized to Rundstedt for the 'misunderstanding', wished him a swift recuperation and sent him off with full honours.

On 17 January 1942, following Reichenau's sudden death from a stroke, Hitler called on Rundstedt to stand in for him at the state funeral. On 10 March, Hitler summoned Rundstedt, who was then just twelve days away from completing his fiftieth year in military service, to the Führer Headquarters and appointed him to replace the ailing Witzleben as Commander-in-Chief, West.

The theatre headquarters was still in St Germain, but it had, in June 1941, become an OKW command, which brought it directly under the OKW. Consequently, Rundstedt, as theatre and Army Group D commander, henceforth dealt on operational matters with Jodl's OKW Operations Staff, not with the Army General Staff – a somewhat ironic circumstance in the light of his earlier efforts to preserve the General Staff's primacy. On the other hand, since Hitler had not given Keitel (the titular Chief of OKW) any actual command authority and had made himself Commander-in-Chief of the Army after Brauchitsch's dismissal, the command channel was little different from what it would have been had Rundstedt stayed on the Eastern Front.

In the west, 1942 was a year of 'alarums and excursions'. The United States' entry into the war and Soviet appeals for a 'second front' impelled Hitler to begin building the so-called 'Atlantic Wall' and to order a high state of readiness and constant alert on the coast from the Netherlands to the Spanish border. British commando raids at St Nazaire in March and Dieppe in August intensified his anxiety, although they were swiftly and sharply repelled. On 10 November, two days after the Allied landing in North Africa, Hitler ordered Rundstedt to execute Operation *Anton*, the occupation of Vichy France. *Anton* added some 350 miles of coastline along the Mediterranean to Rundstedt's responsibilities, along with the mission of maintaining smooth relations with Marshal Pétain, a task at which Rundstedt's command of French and his ability to play both the *grand seigneur* and the bluff soldier made him outstandingly effective.

The Soviet winter and summer offensives in 1943 also took a heavy toll in the west, which became a manpower reservoir for the Eastern Front. In the first 10 months of 1943, 38 divisions (mostly three regiments strong) and nearly half a million troops in mass drafts went east. Rundstedt had not begrudged the Eastern Front the help, but finally, on 25 October 1943, he sent Hitler a comprehensive situation estimate coldly and precisely setting down his own and the western Allies' capabilities. The Allies, he concluded, had sufficient forces assembled in Britain to strike whenever they chose and would not let very much more time pass without doing so. His forces, on the other hand, had undergone a year-long decline in quantity and in quality. His 29 infantry divisions, many with only two regiments, were having to use limited-service men and 'Turkic' elements (Soviet minorities), and of his six panzer and motorized divisions, none was fully trained and all were short on personnel and equipment. Hitler responded a week later with a directive giving the west absolute priority over the Eastern Front in troops and war material until after the 'decisive battle' against an Allied invasion had been fought.[48]

Hitler's concern was genuine, and in late November 1943 he brought Field-Marshal Erwin Rommel and the Army Group B staff (not the same as in 1939–41) from Italy to inspect the defences on the Atlantic coast. No doubt in considerable part to avoid having so powerful and ambitious a figure ranging at will throughout the theatre, Rundstedt, in mid-January 1944, placed Rommel in command of Army Group B, responsible for defending the coast from the mouth of the River Loire north up to the Dutch-German border.[49]

Rommel's personality and style contrasted with Rundstedt's in almost all respects. Just turned 51, he was the youngest Field-Marshal, and he had no ties to the old Prussian military tradition or to the General Staff system. He had been a junior front line officer in the First World War and always in troop or training commands thereafter. He was constantly on the move, leading from the front. He had a more open relationship with Hitler than any other top officer, but he was also close enough to the growing anti-Hitler conspiracy to be regarded among its members as Hitler's interim successor. Rundstedt, now 69 and suffering from heart trouble and rheumatism, kept more than before to his headquarters. His contacts with Hitler were few and formal. From their first meeting in December on, Rundstedt and Rommel also differed in their thinking with regard to a strategy for meeting the anticipated Allied landing.

Rommel's presence in the theatre command structure engendered a strategic controversy in some respects reminiscent of that over the *Sichelschnitt* Plan in 1939–40. In his October 1943 appreciation, Rundstedt had proposed to defeat an invasion on the beaches, but he had also taken into account the possibility that the enemy might, after all, secure a lodgment. To deal with such an eventuality, he had projected a central theatre reserve of panzer divisions. Rommel contended that the decision could only be secured at the water's edge and that all of the forces, including the panzer divisions, would have to be there from the first because Allied air superiority would prevent subsequent movements. The advantages of each approach were the disadvantages of the other. Rundstedt's strategy held the panzer divisions together and afforded a chance at defeating the enemy in a panzer battle after he had landed – provided the reserve could be deployed. Rommel's strategy guaranteed getting the armour into action immediately but would disperse the panzer divisions. Rundstedt had the stronger basis in orthodox military doctrine and, as theatre commander, the greater authority; but he stayed aloof from the argument, leaving his side of it mainly to his chief of Panzer Troops, General Leo Geyr von Schweppenburg. However, Geyr was two grades lower in rank and infinitely less influential than Rommel, who had direct access to Hitler and did not hesitate to use it.

In late April 1944, having by then stationed ten panzer divisions in the west, Hitler imposed a compromise in which he supported Rundstedt in form and Rommel in substance. He gave Rommel's Army Group B three panzer divisions, constituted the forces south of the Loire as Army Group G, giving it three panzer divisions, and left the remaining four divisions as the theatre reserve. Thereafter the question was not only whether the reserve could be brought into action but also whether it could mount a decisive panzer battle in that event. As a further result of Hitler's compromise, Rundstedt no longer exercised direct command anywhere. Hitler gave himself control over the theatre panzer reserve, and the remaining 54 divisions were placed under Rommel (35 divisions) and the Army Group G commander, General Johannes Blaskowitz. In practical terms, the Commander-in-Chief, West, had therewith become virtually superfluous except as a conduit between Hitler and the Army Groups. As Rundstedt later said, 'My sole prerogative was to change the guard at my gate.'[50]

The Allied landings in Normandy on D-Day, 6 June 1944, created a situation in which neither Rundstedt's and Rommel's experience nor Hitler's intuition served Germany well. All three expected another, stronger and more dangerous, landing north of the River Seine in the Pas de Calais on the shortest and easiest route to the German heartland. Fostered by Allied deceptions, that miscalculation persisted into July, beclouding decisions and probably doing more than the Allied air forces to prevent reinforcements reaching the front in Normandy from other sectors. In three weeks the Allies had consolidated the beachhead and expanded it to the west across the Cotentin Peninsula and on the east toward Caen. On 27 June, the United States 1st Army took Cherbourg. This solid beachhead and possession of a port guaranteed a permanent Allied presence on the Continent whether or not another landing might still be to come. By all earlier German calculations, including Hitler's own, the war was lost.

When Hitler called Rundstedt and Rommel to a conference at his Bavarian retreat near Berchtesgaden on 30 June, Rundstedt meant to tell Hitler that it was time to end the war but did not get a chance.[51] Whether he really wanted a chance is open to doubt. Reportedly, in the preliminary discussions either to that meeting or one two weeks earlier, in both of which they had agreed Hitler would have to be told, he had said to Rommel, 'You know and love the people. You do it.'[52] In any event, Hitler delivered a lecture on the necessity of holding the beachhead line exactly where it was at all costs and did not let either Field-Marshal express an opinion. (Rundstedt's frequently quoted subsequent remark on the telephone to Keitel, 'Make peace, you idiots!' stems from an account by his Chief of Staff, Blumentritt, and is probably apocryphal.)[53]

Rundstedt did, however, endorse and forward to Hitler a situation estimate in which Rommel and SS General Paul Hausser, who was commanding the 7th Army in Normandy, had concurred. Written by Geyr, who was commanding the reserve armour at the front, it dismissed a continuation of the present static defence as 'futile tactical patchwork', and recommended a withdrawal around Caen, where Geyr's four panzer divisions were tied down, in order to free the divisions for a subsequent counter-attack.[54] On 1 July, Hitler decided to relieve Geyr and Rundstedt. He told Geyr over the telephone and accused him of defeatism. With his Field-Marshals, three of whom he had dismissed so far that year, he had lately adopted a less direct approach, and Rundstedt had himself provided a pretext. In talking to Keitel at Berchtesgaden, he had expressed doubt as to how much longer he could 'meet the demands' of his position.[55] On the 2nd, an adjutant brought Rundstedt an Oak Leaf Cluster to his Knight's Cross and a personal letter from Hitler granting 'with regret' his 'wish to be relieved', and telling him that Field-Marshal Günther von Kluge would be his replacement.[56] At his farewell meeting with Rommel, Rundstedt said he was thankful he would not be in command during 'the coming catastrophe' and would 'never again' accept a command.[57]

The news release about the change implied that 'impaired health' would keep Rundstedt out of active command, but that the Führer expected to employ him on 'special assignments' in the future.[58] A very special assignment was not long in coming. After the abortive July 1944 attempt to assassinate Hitler, Rundstedt was appointed to preside over a 'court of honour' the purpose of which was to expel from the Armed Services the officers who were implicated in the assassination plot and thereby deny them the right to a court martial and a soldier's death by firing squad. The court of honour was not allowed to question the accused or hear witnesses, and was required to make its decisions solely on the basis of evidence which the Gestapo presented to it. In four one-day sittings during August and September, the court found against 55 officers, including 1 Field-Marshal (Witzleben), 11 other general officers, and 17 General-Staff Officers. Except for 9 who were already dead, these then became eligible to be hanged or beheaded after humiliating trials in a Nazi 'People's Court'. Guderian said that he and several other members of the court of honour, with Rundstedt's 'constant support', did their best to save any man they could, but only succeeded in a few instances.[59] Rundstedt kept silent on that as on many other matters.

The court of honour would very likely have had to consider the cases of another two Field-Marshals, Rommel and Kluge, had they not committed suicide. As it was, Rommel's death by self-administered poison after the choice Hitler had given him between suicide and a state funeral or a trial for high treason, brought Rundstedt another 'special assignment' – to deliver the eulogy at Rommel's state funeral as the Führer's representative. Rundstedt testified at Nuremberg that he had not heard any 'rumours' about the cause of Rommel's death and, if he had, he would have refused to represent Hitler because 'that would have been an infamy beyond words'.[60]

While the court of honour was in session, events elsewhere were once again drawing Rundstedt into active participation in the war. In mid-July, after Rommel was badly injured during an air attack, Hitler had added direct command of Army Group B to Kluge's responsibilities as Commander-in-Chief, West. When Field-Marshal Walter Model replaced Kluge in mid-August, Model also had assumed the combined posts; but by the end of the month the Allies were rapidly advancing toward the Low Countries and the German border and had landed in southern France. Model then reported that he could no longer manage both the theatre and the Army-Group commands, and Keitel recommended reinstalling Rundstedt as Commander-in-Chief, West. Several days later, Hitler summoned Rundstedt to the Führer Headquarters. According to Keitel, when the two met, Hitler said, 'Field-Marshal, I would like to place the Western Front in your hands again,' and Rundstedt replied, 'My Führer, whatever you order, I shall do to my last breath.'[61] On

5 September, his staff welcomed him back to the theatre headquarters, which was by then in Germany at Arenberg, near Koblenz.

What Hitler expected to accomplish by recalling Rundstedt was, and remains, unclear. He certainly did not propose literally to entrust Rundstedt with the Western Front, or, since Model (who was easily as self-willed a personality as Rommel) stayed on in command of Army Group B, to give him even as much authority as Kluge and Model had for a time held. He spoke glowingly to Keitel about the 'great respect' Rundstedt enjoyed throughout the Armed Forces, and that may have been the determinant.[62] With the front in shambles and the command structure severely shaken, he needed a symbol of stability and a link to the brighter past, which Rundstedt, the seemingly indefatigable 'first soldier of the Reich', could provide.

And a near-miracle did ensue. United States 1st Army troops crossed the German border on 11 September, but the pursuit which the Allies had launched across the River Seine in the last week of August was coming to an end. Late in the month, Army Group B heavily defeated Operation *Market Garden*, an Allied airborne attempt to seize bridges across the Maas, Waal and Lower Rhine Rivers in Holland. In October 1944, the Allied advance stopped everywhere from the North Sea to the Alps. The Allies' predominant problem – except in the case of *Market Garden* in which Model showed why he had been known on the Eastern Front as 'the lion of the defense' – was that they had outrun their supplies.

The German recovery had the aspect of an earned victory – particularly since the Allied commands could not disclose that they had simply run out of logistical steam – and Rundstedt's return was taken on both sides to have been the key element in it. Under the headline, 'Gerd von Rundstedt, the *Wehrmacht's* best general, takes over western defense of Germany', the most widely read American magazine, *Life*, pronounced him 'by far the greatest of the Prussian masters who almost won the war for Hitler, Germany's last hope [and] a far deadlier foe than Rommel or any Nazi general could have been.'[63] Model, who was indeed a Nazi general, was in fact by far the deadlier foe. He, like Manstein, possessed a virtuosity in the field that Rundstedt could not have matched and self-confidence in dealing with Hitler that Rundstedt did not have, but from the Allied side he appeared to be an upstart Hitler favourite with nothing like Rundstedt's solid attainments. Consequently, in General Dwight D. Eisenhower's headquarters, it was Rundstedt 'whom we always considered the ablest of the German generals.'[64]

The Ardennes offensive in late December 1944 at once became 'the Rundstedt offensive'. The total surprise and the initial 50-mile-deep plunge through the United States 1st Army's front seemed unmistakably to bear the Rundstedt hallmark. In a widely published interview, Field-Marshal Sir Bernard Montgomery said, 'I used to think that Rommel was good, but my opinion is that Rundstedt would have hit him for six. Rundstedt is the best German general I have come up against.'[65] Actually, the plan for the 'Rundstedt offensive' was Hitler's and had been completely worked out in OKW before Rundstedt and Model saw it. Both had believed the given objective, Antwerp, was unattainable, but Rundstedt, as he had with subordinates before, had left the arguing mostly to Model. In the event, it was American complacency and a week of bad weather which kept the Allied Air Forces grounded, not German proficiency, that gave the offensive the limited measure of temporary success it achieved.

Model's subsequent skillful defence of the Rhineland set the Allies' schedule back by almost two months, but swift defeat became inescapable on 7 March 1945 when the American 9th Armoured Division captured a bridge over the Rhine at Remagen. The next day Keitel alerted Rundstedt to a probable change in command; and on the 11th Hitler told the Propaganda Minister, Joseph Göbbels, that Rundstedt had not been up to commanding the battle in the west because he was too old and too old-fashioned in his outlook on warfare. Nevertheless, he and Göbbels agreed that Rundstedt was 'a highly respectable officer' who had done the Nazi cause 'great service, particularly in the liquidation of the 20 July plot.'[66] That night Hitler received the Field-Marshal in the Reich Chancellery, awarded him the Swords to his Knight's Cross, took the responsibility for the failure in the Ardennes on himself, and told him that Field-Marshal Albert Kesselring had been appointed Commander-in-Chief, West.[67] Once again the parting was not necessarily irrevocable, but events soon made it final.

American troops took Rundstedt prisoner at Bad Tölz, in Bavaria, on 1 May and, after allowing newspaper correspondents to question him, sent him to 'Ashcan', the collection centre for highest-level war crimes suspects located in Spa, Belgium, where he was one of the earlier arrivals. To the war correspondents, he appeared frail and sounded somewhat warlike, assuring them that had he not been in a hospital recovering from a heart attack, he would not have surrendered without a fight because doing so would have been 'despicable and shameful'. He also declared that he would have defeated the invasion on the beaches had the Allies not possessed overwhelming air superiority and had he not been desperately short of motor fuel.[68]

After he succeeded in proving – easily, though with some diminishment of his professional stature – that he had not been at the centre of German war planning and command or, as had been suspected, the guiding spirit of the General Staff or the power behind Hitler, Rundstedt was omitted from the roster of major war criminals to be tried before the Nuremberg International Military Tribunal. However, lesser war crimes charges, but equally serious in their potential personal consequences kept him under arrest and eligible for trial for four years. His reactions to Hitler's orders on the treatment of Soviet commissars and civilians and to the killing of Jews were seen to have been at best faint-hearted; and his old *bête-noire* and former subordinate at Army

Group South, Reichenau, had issued embellishments on the Hitler orders, at least one of which the Army Group had circulated as a model for its other commands to adopt.

After his release in May 1949 from a detention that had on the whole not been onerous, Rundstedt settled at Celle, in the British Zone of occupied Germany, where he died on 24 February, 1953. A small group of former officers in frock coats and top hats and some First World War veterans carrying a cavalry standard followed the hearse to the graveside. The officiating clergyman spoke of the deceased's 'simple demeanour and noble character' and told the mourners they were witnessing 'the burial of the last great Prussian'.[69]

The military convention that ascribes credit for a force's achievements to its commander will keep Rundstedt's name prominent in the history of the Second World War, but he will not assume a place among the truly great Prussians. A Yorck von Wartenburg he certainly was not, nor even a Mackensen to Manstein's Seeckt. He also was not a credibly tragic figure, overwhelmed, as has been claimed, in a struggle between duty and conscience and by an implacably evil system. Duty and service to the nation were for him too frequently a means of evading moral and professional responsibility, and as the 'first soldier' of the Reich and the guardian of the old-school Prussian General Staff's principles, his performance approached caricature. The Elder von Moltke admonished General Staff officers to 'be more than you seem'. Gerd von Rundstedt seemed to be more than he was.

NOTES

1 Friedrich Ruge, *Rommel in Normandy* (San Rafael, CA, 1979), pp. 164–5.
2 B. H. Liddell Hart, *The German Generals Talk* (New York, 1948), p. 71.
3 Günther Blumentritt, *Von Rundstedt the Soldier and the Man* (London, 1952), p. 22.
4 Friedrich von Rabenau, *Seeckt: Aus seinem Leben* (Leipzig, 1940), p. 193.
5 International Military Tribunal, *Trial of the Major War Criminals* (Nuremberg, 1948) (hereafter IMT), v. 21, pp. 38, 50.
6 Walter Görlitz, *Kleine Geschichte des deutschen Generalstabes* (Berlin, 1967), pp. 284–6, 292–5.
7 Friedrich-Karl von Plehwe, *Reichskanzler Kurt von Schleicher* (Esslingen, 1983), p. 190.
8 IMT, v. 21, p. 40.
9 Rundstedt's account of the 30 January 1938, interview, summarized here, is printed in Hermann Förtsch, *Schuld und Verhängnis* (Stuttgart, 1951), pp. 102–3.
10 Erich von Manstein, *Aus einem Soldatenleben* (Bonn, 1958), p. 311.
11 Klaus-Jürgen Müller, *Das Heer und Hitler* (Stuttgart, 1969), p. 336.
12 IMT, v. 21, p. 30.

13 Walther Hubatsch, *Hitler's Weisungen für die Kriegführung* (Koblenz, 1983), p. 17.

14 Erich von Manstein, *Verlorene Siege* (Bonn, 1955), p. 23.

15 *Ibid.*, p. 23; Blumentritt, p. 41 and *passim*; Siegfried Westphal, *Heer in Fesseln* (Bonn, 1952), p. 57.

16 IMT, v. 21, p. 48.

17 Wilhelm von Leeb, *Tagebuch aufzeichnungen und Lagebeurteilungen aus zwei Weltkriegen* (Stuttgart, 1976), p. 199.

18 Blumentritt, p. 59; Manstein, *Siege*, p. 93.

19 Manstein, *Siege*, pp. 114–18; Hans-Adolf Jacobsen, *Fall Gelb* (Wiesbaden, 1971), pp. 80–2.

20 Heinz Guderian, *Panzer Leader* (New York, 1952), p. 91.

21 Jacobsen, *Gelb*, p. 133.

22 Blumentritt, p. 64.

23 Jacobsen, *Gelb*, p. 132; Blumentritt, p. 65.

24 Guderian, p. 91.

25 Hans-Adolf Jacobsen, *Dokumente zum Westfeldzug 1940* (Göttingen, 1960), pp. 27–9, 32–4.

26 *Ibid.*, p. 38.

27 Franz Halder, *Kriegstagebuch* (Stuttgart, 1962), v. 1, pp. 297, 300.

28 Jacobsen, *Dokumente*, p. 42; Militärgeschichtliches Forschungsamt (hereafter MGFA), *Das Deutsche Reiche und der Zweite Weltkrieg* (Stuttgart, 1979), v. 2, pp. 290–1.

29 Jacobsen, *Dokumente*, p. 44.

30 Halder, v. 1, p. 302.

31 Jacobsen, *Dokumente*, p. 46.

32 MGFA, v. 2, p. 294.

33 Jacobsen, *Dokumente*, p. 73.

34 Halder, v. 1, p. 318.

35 Jacobsen, *Dokumente*, pp. 77, 79.

36 *Ibid.*, p. 85.

37 *Ibid.*, p. 95.

38 Milton Schulman, *Defeat in the West* (New York, 1948), p. 43.

39 Max Domarus, *Hitler Reden und Proklamationen 1932–1945* (Munich, 1963), v. 2, p. 1540.

40 Leeb, p. 251; Andreas Hillgruber, *Hitler's Strategie Politik und Kriegführung, 1940–1941* (Frankfurt am Main, 1965), p. 170.

41 Halder, v. 3, p. 60.

42 *Ibid.*, v. 3, p. 150.

43 MGFA, v. 4, pp. 528–30.

44 Halder, v. 3, p. 285.

45 Shulman, p. 68.

46 Halder, v. 3, p. 319.

47 Andreas Hillgruber, *Deutsche Grossmacht und Weltpolitik* (Düsseldorf, 1982), p. 324.

48 Dieter Ose, *Entscheidung im Westen 1944* (Stuttgart, 1982), pp. 28–32.

49 *Ibid.*, pp. 42–4.

50 Chester Wilmot, *The Struggle for Europe* (New York, 1952), p. 189.
51 Blumentritt, p. 234.
52 Hans Speidel, *Invasion 1944* (Chicago, 1950), p. 71.
53 The 'idiots' (or 'fools') epithet appeared first in Shulman (p. 120) and Wilmot (p. 347), both of whom attributed it to interviews with Blumentritt, whose Rundstedt biography (p. 238) merely states, 'You should end the war.' Since the exchange could only have occurred on or after 1 July and Keitel by then knew Rundstedt was being dismissed and another Commander-in-Chief, West was appointed, that it took place at all appears doubtful.
54 Ose, p. 152.
55 Dermot Bradley and Richard Schulze-Kossens, *Tätigkeitsbericht des Chefs des Heerespersonalamts* (Osnabrück, 1984), p. 149.
56 Blumentritt, pp. 238–9.
57 Speidel, pp. 72, 108.
58 Domarus, p. 2113.
59 Guderian, p. 346.
60 IMT, v. 21, p. 47.
61 Office of the US Chief Counsel for Prosecution of Axis Criminality, *Nazi Conspiracy and Aggression* (Washington, DC, 1948), Supplement B, p. 1285.
62 *Ibid.*, p. 1285.
63 David Cort, 'The Last Prussian', in *Life*, 25 December, 1944, pp. 58–63.
64 Dwight D. Eisenhower, *Crusade in Europe* (New York, 1949), p. 386. See also Wilmot, pp. 434–6.
65 *New York Times*, 8 January 1945, p. 6. This portion does not appear in the interview notes reprinted in Bernard Law, Viscount Montgomery of Alamein, *Memoirs* (New York, 1958), pp. 278–81.
66 Hugh Trevor-Roper (ed.), *The Goebbels Diaries, The Last Days* (London, 1978), pp. 104–5.
67 Blumentritt, p. 279.
68 *New York Times*, 5 May, 1945, p. 5.
69 *Time*, March 1, 1953, p. 27; Hillgruber, *Grossmacht*, p. 331.

CHRONOLOGY: GERD VON RUNDSTEDT

1875, December 12	Born
1892, March 22	Entered active service
1893, June 17	Lieutenant
1896, October 1	Battalion adjutant, 83rd Royal Prussian Infantry Regiment
1900, March 22	Regimental adjutant, 83rd Royal Prussian Infantry Regiment
1902, September 12	Senior lieutenant
1902, October 1	Accepted in War Academy
1907, April 1	Attached to Great General Staff
1907, March 24	Captain
1910, October 1	Staff officer, 11th Corps
1912, September 13	Company commander, 171st Infantry Regiment
1914, August 1	Operations officer, 22nd Reserve Division

1914, November 28	Major
1914–15	Government General, Brussels
1915	Division Chief of Staff, 12th Army
1915–16	Government General, Warsaw
1916–17	Corps Chief of Staff, Army Group Grand Duke Karl
1917–18	Chief of Staff, 53rd Corps
1918	Chief of Staff, 15th Corps
1920, October 1	Lieutenant-Colonel
1920, October 1	Chief of Staff, 3rd Cavalry Division
1923, February 1	Colonel
1923, October 1	Chief of Staff, 2nd Infantry Division
1925, March 1	Commander, 18th Infantry Regiment
1926, October 1	Chief of Staff, Group Command II
1927, November 1	Major-General
1928, November 1	Commander, 2nd Cavalry Division
1929, March 1	Lieutenant-General
1932, January 1	Commander *Wehrkreis* III and 3rd Infantry Division
1932, October 1	Commander-in-Chief, Group Command I
1932, October 1	General of Infantry
1938, March 1	Colonel-General
1938, September 26	Commander-in-Chief, 2nd Army (and Group Command I)
1938, October 1	Retired
1938, November I	Colonel-in-Chief, 18th Infantry Regiment
1939, August 23	Commander-in-Chief, Army Group South
1939, October 1	Commander-in-Chief, East
1939, October 30	Commander-in-Chief, Army Group A
1940, July 19	Field-Marshal
1940, October 26	Commander-in-Chief, West
1941, April 1	Commander-in-Chief, Army Group South
1941, December 1	Transferred to command reserve
1942, March 10	Commander-in-Chief, West and Army Group D
1944, July 3	Transferred to command reserve
1944, September 4	Commander-in-Chief, West
1945, March 11	Transferred to command reserve
1945, May 1	Prisoner of war
1949, May	Released from prisoner-of-war status
1953, February 24	Died

REICHENAU

8

REICHENAU

Field-Marshal Walther von Reichenau

WALTER GÖRLITZ

In 1914, the year of the outbreak of the First World War, a German satirical magazine published a caricature featuring a Prussian officer hurdling in shorts and vest, with spurs on his plimsolls, and armed with a gigantic monocle. This was aimed at Lieutenant von Reichenau of the 1st Guards Field Artillery. Accompanied by Carl Diem, the founder of German athletics, and two other experts he had visited the USA in the previous year in preparation for the Olympic Games planned for 1916. The Americans called them the 'German Olympic Committee'. The Prussian lieutenant, who had long been a member of the officers' team in the Berlin Sports Club, was very impressed by the Americans whom he found to possess a practical mind, faith in the future and a sense of realism. Their small officer corps treated sports as a matter of fact. But for a Prussian Guards Officer modern sports such as football and athletics were quite another matter. The 'chic' in-things were equestrian sports and tennis, the latter a particular favourite of Lieutenant von Reichenau. A good officer had to be skilled in riding and fencing and had to be a good pistol shot. Everything else was in bad taste. Hunting, which von Reichenau equally appreciated, was acceptable but horses as such did not interest him. It was not much consolation to von Reichenau that the young princes Friedrich Sigismund and Friedrich Carl of Prussia, of royal descent, also shared his enthusiasm for sport and that Crown Prince Wilhelm played football. The Prussian orthodox aristocracy was in any case of the opinion that the Hohenzollerns were flirting too openly with modern times.

These were all pointers to an unusual career full of U-turns, and which was to come to an abrupt and premature end.

Walther von Reichenau was born on 8 October 1884 in Karlsruhe, son of a Lieutenant-General and the daughter of a middle-class family from Münster. His family had been ennobled for their military service by the Dukes of Nassau, who had been deposed by Bismarck in 1866. The von Reichenaus were therefore without property and without specifically Prussian tradition. None the less, an officer's career was traditional in the family. In 1903 Walther von Reichenau joined the 1st Guards Artillery Regiment as a cadet officer. In 1904 he became a Second Lieutenant.

His father resigned from the service and, as a ballistics expert, joined the board of Erhardt, the then well known weapons factory in Düsseldorf, a competitor of Messrs Krupp in Essen. In 1908 Reichenau was granted leave of absence to accompany his father on a business trip to South America. The Argentinian government in Buenos Aires was especially interested in modern German weaponry. This trip was an unusual experience for a young Prussian officer. Later Reichenau emphasized again and again how vital it was for an aspiring officer to possess overseas knowledge and to have a command of foreign languages. He himself spoke excellent English, which stood him in good stead during his 1913 trip to the USA. As a result of these trips and his passion for sports he remained an outsider in the Army. Some remarkable 'bon mots' of his have been passed on from his time as Second Lieutenant before the First World War. During an argument with a colleague, the latter said: 'Everything you say, Reichenau, is totally unmilitaristic.' Reichenau replied: 'That may be, but it is the essence of what a soldier should be like.' With this remark, he drew the dividing line between the 'militarism' of the Wilhelmine era, in which military behaviour encroached upon civilian social life, and true soldierly spirit. When inducting new conscripts the old, silly army joke was told them: 'You come as civilians, you will leave as human beings!' Reichenau argued differently: one should never tell these young people 'you don't know anything, you can't do anything'; instead one must encourage them, tell them that they know a lot already, that they are capable, but that they will learn more and become good soldiers. He always maintained his love for the troops, even as a Field-Marshal.

The First World War put an end to sporting contests and plans for the Olympics. Reichenau had been seconded to the War Academy at the outbreak of war in August 1914. As regimental adjutant, he went to the front with the 1st Guards Reserve Field Artillery Regiment, was transferred to the General Staff on account of his extraordinarily varied talents, and served on all fronts, west and east. His dedication to an officer's career was not shaken by the 1918 revolution. He joined the frontier defence in Upper Silesia as 1st General Staff Officer of the 7th Cavalry Rifle Division, a voluntary formation of the new

provisional Army. The re-created Polish Republic had shown signs of appro-
priating this vital industrial area with its considerable Polish minority population. Here at the turn of 1918–19, in Milisch Castle, he met twenty-four-
year-old Countess Alexandrine von Maltzen, daughter of Count Andreas von
Maltzen, lord of the manor of Milisch and three adjoining estates – a Silesian
landed magnate. On 3 April 1919 they were married. For the present Staff
Captain von Reichenau, an officer of the minor aristocracy, this marriage into
the Silesian nobility was almost tantamount to being raised to a higher class.
Reichenau was a 'ladies' man' as the saying goes. Later, in 1940, in Paris, the
famous *chanson* singer Lucienne Boyer called him 'le plus charmant des
maréchaux allemands'. But there is no reason to believe that his marriage was
anything but happy.

Despite some adverse criticism it was a foregone conclusion that this highly
talented General Staff officer with widely varying interests would be accepted
into the new *Reichswehr*. In 1920 Reichenau, now a colonel, had been promoted
to Chief of Staff in *Wehrkreis* I in East Prussia, along with General von
Blomberg as the new commander of the 1st Division. Blomberg was then
considered to be 'very able', whilst Reichenau remained a very colourful
'outsider'. It was no secret that the Chief of the *Ministeramt* (the minister's
office of the War Ministry), General von Schleicher, did not like Blomberg.
If Blomberg were disposed of to distant East Prussia, which was geographically
and politically separate from the rest of the Reich, and Reichenau seconded
to be his Chief of Staff, then one would get rid of two unpopular birds. It is
known that Reichenau himself did not think highly of Schleicher.

The turning point in his life and in his career occurred in 1932, after
Blomberg had been despatched to Geneva as military head of the German
disarmament delegation, and Reichenau had to deputize for him in the *Wehrkreis*. When, in autumn 1932, Hitler arrived by plane from Danzig to make
an election speech in the exhibition hall in Königsberg, Reichenau asked his
wife to go and listen to this man who was moving more and more into the
limelight, active service officers like himself being barred from such political
meetings because the *Reichswehr* was apolitical. Frau von Reichenau listened
to Hitler and was, in her own words, 'impressed'. The same afternoon the
Reichenaus, together with Hitler, were invited for tea by the *Wehrkreis* pastor.
The pastor (later 'Reich Bishop' of the Evangelical Church loyal to the Nazi
régime) was an enthusiastic National-Socialist. Over tea he arranged for Hitler
and Reichenau to be left alone. It was the first time that Hitler had met a
Reichswehr officer of a higher rank. He gave one of his habitual monologues
about rearmament which he, as Chancellor, would initiate. Reichenau asked:
'Whom would you appoint for this?' Hitler replied quickly: 'Schleicher!'
(Schleicher was now Defence Minister in the Papen Cabinet.) Hitler was even
speaking the truth at this moment, for Schleicher (whom the young Frau von
Hindenburg, daughter-in-law of the aged President of the Republic and Field-

Marshal, called 'Fouché') was secretly maintaining contact with the NSDAP, although he for his part in no way welcomed the possibility of Hitler becoming Chancellor.

Hitler thought that he had 'convinced' Reichenau, as he used to put it, that he was 'the man'. And Reichenau himself? He really did form the conviction that Hitler could be the man to lead Germany out of its calamities. It took him seven years to change his mind. But none the less he was so much a master of his situation that he was able to correct his own views mercilessly.

Various versions of the following story exist: Reichenau, during the days immediately prior to Hitler's coming to power, is supposed to have been at the Defence Ministry or even in the outer office of the President himself, after the President had rigorously forbidden the generals to voice their objections to a Hitler Cabinet or indeed to an opposition Cabinet under Papen. According to Frau von Reichenau's testimony, however, he never was in Berlin at this time but at his post in Königsberg. Visits to Berlin were very difficult to arrange due to the workload. Colonel von Reichenau apparently told the generals who protested against a Hitler Cabinet as well as an anti-Hitler/Papen Cabinet: 'Actually the generals should now arrest the Field-Marshal [Hindenburg]!' Whatever the truth, this remains a 'story'. Such sarcastic, cynical behaviour was very untypical of Reichenau. But similar 'stories' were to be fabricated around him throughout his career, starting from the rumour that he was a 'Nazi' continuing with piquant stories about his extra-marital affairs, and ending with biting references from fellow generals about him being a 'sports general'.

On 30 January 1933, the day that Hitler became Chancellor, the commander of Reichenau's *Wehrkreis*, Blomberg, became Defence Minister by request of the President. Blomberg immediately named his Chief of Staff as Chief of the *Ministeramt* (Ministerial Office), now however re-named the *Wehrmachtamt*. The former chief, Colonel von Bredow, a personal friend of Schleicher's, was honourably retired in the rank of Major-General. The Chief of the *Wehrmachtamt*, now also promoted to the rank of Major-General, was soon to rise to a higher post. On 1 February 1934 the Chief of the Army High Command, General Baron von Hammerstein-Equord, the last associate of the ex-Chancellor and Defence Minister von Schleicher, retired. Hitler immediately suggested Reichenau, who had impressed him at their talk in Königsberg, as his successor. President von Hindenburg, still Commander-in-Chief of the Army, opposed this vehemently on the grounds that Reichenau was too young, too superficial, too 'fickle'. It remains uncertain to what the latter refers: was it to Reichenau's sports activities or to rumours of his amorous affairs?

At the time of their appointments Reichenau and his minister were confronted immediately with the problem of Hitler's private Nazi Party Army, the SA, and some of its vile group leaders in Berlin-Brandenburg, Pomerania and Silesia – Karl Ernst, Hans Peter von Heydebreck and Edmund Heines.

The saying that, first of all, the 'brownshirts' must be disciplined, is attributed to Reichenau. The Chief of Staff of the SA, Captain Röhm, and his colleagues nursed some muddled ideas about the SA 'swallowing up' the *Reichswehr* and the 'reactionary' generals being removed. For a long time though, as far as Blomberg and Reichenau could judge, it remained uncertain what action Hitler would take. They both dreaded the thought of a bloody confrontation between the *Reichswehr* and the SA. After all, the SA had now grown to 2 million men and so represented a potential of volunteers which should not be ignored when, as one hoped, general conscription was to be reintroduced.

In spring 1934, after dithering for a long time, Hitler decided in favour of the *Reichswehr* against the SA leadership. Reichenau did not comment on this long-drawn-out indecision, during which he may have used his personal influence over Hitler. Neither do we know whether he approved or disapproved of the decisions taken, the bloody murders which the SS were empowered to carry out and which were committed on 30 June and 1 July 1934 under the pretext that Röhm was planning a coup d'état. Nor indeed do we know whether Reichenau was at all aware of any of these hushed-up crimes other than the murder of Schleicher and von Bredow.

In an interview given to Stanislas de la Rochefoucauld, correspondent of the Paris *Petit Journal* in August 1934, Reichenau quoted Hitler: 'The *Reichswehr* can rely upon me as much as I rely on the *Reichswehr*.' His comments on the 'Röhm coup' were: it had become obvious that the SA was no longer a military but a political body. Then followed a forced remark about the murder of Schleicher and Bredow: their deaths had been very distressing to the generals, but for some time Schleicher had given the impression that he was really no longer a soldier. And Bredow? Reichenau remained silent. Then the interview turned to the inevitable topic of disarmament. Reichenau replied diplomatically that, of course, they – the Germans – were in favour of it but only on the basis of equal rights. He himself was surprised that Paris could not comprehend that a Germany armed on this basis represented the optimum guarantee of France's safety and would free Paris of its nightmare of '*sécurité*'. The general, skilled in international sports negotiations, proved a well-versed diplomat. Stanislas de la Rochefoucauld did not trust him!

The events of 30 June 1934 had a long-lasting effect on Reichenau; they left him with a distinct aversion against the SS leader, Heinrich Himmler, his Chief of the SS Security Service (SD), Heydrich, and the others of those responsible for the shooting. When he was commanding general in Munich he overtly avoided contact with the SS leader who often stayed there. Once he had no choice but to accept an invitation to stay at Himmler's estate on the Tegersee. However no SS units were attached to the 6th Army led by Reichenau in Belgium, France and Russia.

When, in March 1935, Hitler unilaterally abolished the armament restrictions of the Versailles Treaty, Reichenau's career began to rise steeply. He became General commanding the new 7th Army Corps in Munich and, following the Blomberg-Fritsch crisis on 4 February 1938, Commander-in-Chief of Army Group 4 in Leipzig. During this crisis Hitler had proposed him as the new Commander-in-Chief of the Army in succession to Fritsch. But Hitler's latest confidant in the *Oberkommando der Wehrmacht* (OKW), General Keitel, as well as the rest of the generals, protested indignantly. They unanimously rejected the 'sports general', whom they also secretly suspected of planning a re-structuring of the forces. This was a case of misplaced courage, and of objections against the right man; one who was indeed occupied with plans for an Army reform, precisely because of his experience in team events.

Reichenau's passion for sports brought him other triumphs. He was naturally engaged in the preparations for the 1936 Berlin Olympic Games. He was the originator of the 'Olympic village' at Jüterbog near Berlin. He himself was unable to participate in the Games themselves because in May 1936 he was sent for several months to China, the purpose of this trip remaining unexplained. Since the 1920s the Küomintang Chief, Chiang Kai-shek, had been supported by a team of German advisers, excellently qualified officers, much to the silent anger of Berlin where every trained officer was now needed for the expansion of the German Army, and much to Tokyo's undisguised anger, since Japan had conquered Manchuria and could well do without the Chinese national army being advised by German soldiers. Presumably Reichenau was sent to deal with these problems. As we know, he was not successful. Instead, at the beginning of February 1938, the highest accolade a sportsman can wish for was awarded to him. Upon the suggestion of the President of the International Olympic Committee, Count Baillet-Latour, he became the German member of the Committee.

In the Polish campaign, which Hitler began on 1 September 1939 without officially declaring war, General of Artillery von Reichenau was entrusted with the command of the 10th Army. This Army now incorporated a number of panzer and motorized divisions, and it was hoped that he possessed sufficient skill to command the panzer groups on the battlefield by radio communication. The 10th Army was subordinate to Army Group South under Colonel General von Rundstedt. The 'sports general' chose a selection of the most beautiful German poetry, a small volume by the Insel publishing house, to sustain him spiritually on the battlefield. Few people knew that he was fond of German literature and classical music, but, alas, his hectic lifestyle allowed little time for this.

In the lightning campaign against Poland, Reichenau's army succeeded in making the planned thrust against Warsaw across the Vistula. The Army Commander performed a bravura act which, in military terms, was unnecessary. In order to make contact with an advanced unit he himself swam across the river, after which he suffered a first slight fainting attack. He was now almost 55 years old. His athletic appearance was praised in NS propaganda whenever reports about him were published. Did his prowess begin to fail him? His father had died relatively young from a cerebral haemorrhage when taking a walk in a Düsseldorf street.

Worse still: Reichenau experienced the dark side of Hitlerite warfare which, on the German side, gave the war a Janus mask. The SS *Leibstandarte* Adolf Hitler, a motorized regiment, staged a wild slaughter of Jews at Radom under the leadership, of all things, of its director of music. Hundreds of men, women and children were massacred. Reichenau was outraged, ordered a military enquiry into these crimes, and wrote to Hitler that he no longer wished to see such a unit incorporated in his army. Other generals in Poland equally tried to stop the Jewish pogroms. Himmler responded by persuading Hitler to impose independent jurisdiction on the entire SS. The generals lost their fight against these murders.

Promoted to Colonel-General, Reichenau and his army, re-numbered as the 6th Army, were despatched to the Western Front. After the surprisingly swift victory over Poland and her partition between him and Stalin, Hitler wanted to 'resolve' the situation in the west with one mighty blow against France and England, also involving neutral Belgium and Holland. He wanted this offensive to be launched during the autumn of 1939. The High Command of the Army – Colonel General von Brauchitsch and the Chief of the General Staff, General Halder – which had set up its field headquarters in Zossen near Berlin, tried to delay the offensive in the west, not least because of the weather, with eventual success. This resulted in November 1939 in tension between Hitler and the generals lasting several weeks, during which Hitler spoke spitefully of the 'spirit of Zossen'.

As far as he was able, Reichenau maintained personal contact with Hitler, while avoiding contact with Brauchitsch and Halder in Zossen. He purposely acted on his own and attempted, in November 1939 in a private meeting with Hitler, to dissuade him from launching the western offensive. Reichenau still hoped that there could be a negotiated peace with the western democracies. His own 6th Army was scheduled for deployment into neutral Belgium under the *Fall Gelb* (Plan Yellow) plan. Reichenau called this 'downright criminal', for he had enough international contacts to realize how the world would respond to such action. The 'great war' in the west had not yet opened up. In any case, the enemy must be left to make the first move with regard to such a major offensive. One had to contain oneself and wait. It seemed perfectly clear that the enemy would advance through Belgium in order to launch an offensive into the Ruhr industrial area.

Hitler came to major decisions only with great difficulty and after endless wavering, but once he had made a decision, it became his 'unalterable will', as he himself would call it. He therefore did not pay attention to Reichenau's protestation that Germany would lose the Second World War as she had lost the First; Hitler opined that the First World War had been lost only because of the 'stab in the back' by the 'November criminals', mainly the Jews, and not because of military weakness. In short, Reichenau, who for years had believed Hitler to be a great statesman, now realized that he in fact was a man obsessed and that a reasonable discussion with him was impossible, the more so as he was unwilling to tolerate any other viewpoint. If, however, it was any consolation for Reichenau, he had done everything in his limited power.

Then, to his utter amazement, came the surprisingly swift and total victory in the west over the Netherlands, Belgium and France in May and June 1940. Crowning his military career, he personally accepted on 28 May the capitulation of King Leopold III of Belgium and his army. But when peace did not follow the victory, Reichenau with his superior intelligence must have asked himself again whether he might not have been mistaken in his judgment of Hitler.

In July 1940, together with other army leaders, Reichenau was promoted to Field-Marshal and received an endowment. With this he acquired a farm in the Saxon district of Torgau (which, of course, was to be lost again in 1945). Soon his justified scepticism about Hitler's leadership returned, when Hitler announced his plan to invade the Soviet Union, then Germany's official ally. Reichenau considered this was not only unnecessary but also an enormous risk. However, he was no longer a healthy man, something he neither admitted to himself nor to others. In winter 1941, while on holiday in Berlin, during a dinner at 'Horcher' at which his only son, 2nd Lieutenant Friedrich Karl von Reichenau, was also present, he suffered a slight stroke. However, he recovered fairly rapidly.

Reichenau, as commander of the 6th Army, participated in the planning of the Soviet campaign within Army Group South under Field-Marshal von Rundstedt. His attitude was characteristic. In front of a vast map of the Soviet empire he instructed briefly and precisely, as was his custom, his corps and divisional commanders about their deployment. Then pointing to the map, he said: 'The Führer believes that this campaign will be over by autumn'; pause, a cold glance through his monocle: 'I hope the Führer is right.' Another pause: 'Thank you, gentlemen.'

Before the invasion of the USSR, he fell ill again from phlebitis and severe thrombosis. But during the advance into the Ukraine he seemed once more to be the 'sports-hardened man' of propaganda. To the despair of his Chief of Staff, General Helm, and his Staff officers, he personally went into combat in difficult situations, such as the first battle for Kharkov, in order to inspire the hesitant infantry. In the middle of this bitter fighting the dark side of the war caught up with him once more. On Hitler's order, SD (*Sicherheitsdienst* = SS Security Service) task forces were allocated to the armies. They were directly responsible to the SS leader, Heinrich Himmler, and their main task was the extermination of the Jews in the east. The armies, although not permitted to impede their 'actions', were expected to provide food and lodging for them.

On 20 August 1941 the SD Task Force IVa, allocated to the 6th Army, murdered 90 Jews at Belaya Tserkov, among them women and children. This, naturally, happened without the knowledge of the Field-Marshal so that, after the crime had been committed, he could do no more than summon the task-force leader and curtly tell him that he did not wish such acts to be committed behind his or the Army's back. The task-force leader took this reprimand coolly: the Field-Marshal could not give him orders, and anyway was only an 'aristocratic reactionary'.

In the second half of September 1941 Reichenau's 6th Army took Kiev, the capital of the Ukraine. He appointed a city commandant who, while in the process of installing himself at the former KGB headquarters, was blown up with the whole building. The Russians had the habit of placing time bombs in vital buildings before their own troops abandoned a town. Reichenau was particularly embittered about this underhand act and about the fact that the Russians in 1941–2 killed the wounded and prisoners immediately after they had been captured. Consequently he was one of the advocates of the controversial 'harsh' order which was issued in October 1941 demanding that the troops keep their distance from the Russian civilian population.

Army Group South was not only to conquer the Donetz industrial area but also the Caucasian oilfields. At the end of November 1941 it became obvious that its leading troops had come to a halt. Field-Marshal von Rundstedt was replaced. Reichenau, while retaining direct command of the 6th Army, became Commander-in-Chief South in December 1941. He immediately took the only logical and necessary action by ordering a withdrawal to the line of the River Mius. He then picked up the telephone and asked to be connected to the Führer's headquarters in far away East Prussia. He reported to the Führer, without embellishment, that he had just given an order on his own initiative: the withdrawal of the Army Group to the Mius River. Hitler had never been used to being so taken by surprise. Who would risk it? This, however, was Reichenau's last, but successful, *coup de main*.

Shortly afterwards the Russians outside Moscow launched their winter counter-offensive against the totally over-stretched units of Army Group Centre. On 19 December 1941 the Commander-in-Chief of the Army, Field-Marshal von Brauchitsch, resigned because of acute heart trouble, and during discussions about his successor, Reichenau was once again mentioned. Hitler rejected him immediately. He knew now that this man, whom he had thought to be absolutely 'loyal' for so long, was really a totally independent, politically astute soldier. He now mistrusted Reichenau, as Reichenau mistrusted him. A future conflict was, so to speak, on the cards. But this game was never played.

The 15 January 1942 seemed to be a normal day at the headquarters of Army Group South in Poltava. Despite a sharp frost, the Field-Marshal went on his usual morning jog. At lunch he suddenly felt unwell. He went out to the entrance of the mess, presumably to get some fresh air. His Chief of Staff, General Helm, followed him and saw him leaning against the wall. He was heard murmuring: 'Damn it, damn it,' before collapsing from a cerebral haemorrhage, just as his father had done. Hitler ordered the transfer of the unconscious Reichenau into the clinic of the famous sports doctor, Professor Hochrein, in Leipzig. On 17 January 1942, during this flight, which was interrupted owing to fog by an emergency landing in a newly ploughed field near Cracow, Field-Marshal von Reichenau died from heart failure. He left a memorandum for Hitler outlining a total reorganization of warfare on the Eastern Front. Hitler ordered a state funeral for Reichenau, from which he, naturally, absented himself.

CHRONOLOGY: WALTHER VON REICHENAU

1884, October 8	Born in Karlsruhe, son of a later general
1903	Cadet officer in the Guards 1st Field Artillery Regiment
1904	Second Lieutenant
1908	Trip to South America with his father
1913	Trip to USA with Carl Diem and others (German Olympic Committee)
1914	First World War, adjutant to the 1st Guards Reserve Field Artillery Regiment. Transfer to General Staff
1918–19	First General Staff officer of the 7th Cavalry Rifle Division/Frontier Defence Upper Silesia. Joined *Reichswehr* as General Staff officer
1929–33	Colonel and Chief of Staff in *Wehrkreis* I, East Prussia
1933–5	Major-General, Chief of *Wehrmachtamt*
1935–8	General commanding 7th Army Corps in Munich
1935–6	Planning for 1936 Olympic Games in Berlin (Olympic village)
1936, May–October	Trip to China
1938	Member of the International Olympic Committee
1938–9	General of Artillery, Commander-in-Chief of 4th Army Group in Leipzig
1939, September	Commander of 10th Army in Poland
1939–42	Commander of 6th Army. Campaigns in Belgium, France and Russia
1940, July 19 onwards	Field-Marshal
1941, December 1/2 onwards	Also Commander-in-Chief of Army Group South on the Eastern Front
1942, January 17	Died from heart failure on a flight from Poltava to Leipzig

BIBLIOGRAPHY

Combined bibliography for the essays on Blomberg, Keitel, Jodl, Warlimont and Reichenau.

Nikolaus von Below, *Als Hitlers Adjutant 1937–1945*, Mainz, 1981.
Karl Demeter, *Das deutsche Offizierkorps in Gesellschaft und Staat*, Frankfurt, 1962.
Gerhard Engel, *Heeresadjutant bei Hitler 1938–1943. Aufzeichnungen des Majors Engel*, Stuttgart, 1974.
Waldemar Erfurth, *Geschichte des deutschen Generalstabs 1918–1945*, Göttingen, 1968.
Hermann Foertsch, *Schuld und Verhängnis. Die Fritsch-Krise*, Stuttgart, 1951.
Walter Görlitz, *The German General Staff*, London, 1953.
Walter Görlitz, *Keitel Verbrecher oder Offizier. Erinnerungen, Briefe, Dokumente des Chefs OKW*, Göttingen, 1961.
Walter Görlitz, Privatsammlung Generalfeldmarschall von Reichenau (unpublished material for a projected biography).
Helmuth Greiner, *Die Oberste Wehrmachtführung 1939–1943*, Wiesbaden, 1951.
Helmut Grosscurth, *Aus dem Tagebuch eines Abwehroffiziers 1938–1940*, Stuttgart, 1970.
Friedrich Hossbach, *Zwischen Wehrmacht und Hitler 1934–1938*, Wolfenbuttel/Hannover, 1949.
IMT-Prozess Nürnberg Band I-XXXXII, Nürnberg 1947/49, vgl. v.a. Bd. XXVIII Tagebuch Jodl.
David Irving, *Goering*, London/New York, 1986.
Hans Adolf Jacobsen, *1939–1945 Der Zweite Weltkrieg in Chronik und Dokumenten*, Darmstadt, 1961.
Alfred Jodl, Das dienstliche Tagebuch des Chefs des Wehrmachtführungsamtes v.13 Oktober 1939 bis 30 Januar 1940 (herausgegeben von W. Hubatsch 'Die Welt als Geschichte' 12 [1956]).
Luise Jodl, *Jenseits des Endes. Leben und Sterben des Generaloberst Alfred Jodl*, Vienna, 1976.
Bernhard von Lossberg, *Im Wehrmachtführungsstab*, Hamburg, 1949.
Klaus Jürgen Müller, *Das Heer und Hitler. Armee und nationalsozialistisches Regime 1933–1940*, Stuttgart, 1959.
Percy Ernst Schramm, *Kriegstagebuch des Oberkommandos der Wehrmacht*, Frankfurt, 1961 f.
Fritz Freiherr von Siegler, *Die höheren Dienststellen der deutschen Wehrmacht 1933–1945*, Munich, 1949.
Walter Warlimont, *Im Hauptquartier der deutschen Wehrmacht 1939–1945*, Frankfurt, 1962.

MANSTEIN

9

MANSTEIN

Field-Marshal Erich von Manstein

FIELD-MARSHAL LORD CARVER

In his book *The Other Side of the Hill*, based on conversations and correspondence with the German generals held as prisoners of war after 1945, Liddell Hart wrote:

> The ablest of all the German generals was probably Field-Marshal Erich von Manstein. That was the verdict of most of those with whom I discussed the war, from Rundstedt downwards. He had a superb strategic sense, combined with a greater understanding of mechanized weapons than any of the generals who did not belong to the tank school itself.[1]

General Keitel, no friend of Manstein's, corroborated this view when he wrote in the memoirs he composed while awaiting trial at Nuremberg:

> I myself advised Hitler three times to replace me [as Chief of Staff of the Armed Forces] with von Manstein. . . . But despite his frequently expressed admiration for Manstein's outstanding talents, Hitler obviously feared to take such a step, and each time turned it down. Was it sheer indolence on his part or some other unvoiced objection he had to him? I have no idea.[2]

And Andreas Hillgrüber, one of Germany's most distinguished military historians, has described him as 'undoubtedly Germany's most significant personality in the Second World War'.[3]

The future Field-Marshal, born in Berlin in 1887, came of impeccable military stock, his father and mother and his adopted parents being all of the military families of the Prussian nobility. The tenth child of Eduard von Lewinski, a general of artillery, he was adopted by his mother's childless sister, Hedwig, née von Sperling, married to Georg von Manstein, who became a general of infantry.* Although not a landowner, General von Manstein was well off, as both his and his wife's family had received a *dotation* for their services in the Franco-Prussian War, in which the general's father had commanded a corps. After five years at the Strasbourg Lycée, the thirteen-year-old Erich entered the *Kadettenkorps*, and, when in Berlin, did duty in the Corps of Pages at the court of Kaiser Wilhelm II. At the age of twenty, he was commissioned into the prestigious 3rd Regiment of Foot Guards, in which Hindenburg served. Contemporaries in the regiment included von Brauchitsch, Commander-in-Chief of the Army from 1938 to 1941, and others, notably Hindenburg's son Oskar and Generals Schleicher and von Hammerstein-Equord, who were to be leading figures in the military intrigues of the 1930s.

Both at home and in the army, therefore, he was brought up in the traditions and general ethos of the old Prussian military caste, reinforced by that of his Lutheran puritanism: what he described as the army's 'traditional notions of simplicity and chivalry and its soldierly conception of honour'.[4] In his extreme correctness and insistence on the strictest standards of behaviour, discipline and etiquette, he was a typical product of his milieu; but he was not at all the loud-mouthed, unimaginative, jack-booted boor represented by British caricaturists of his type. One might gain that impression from one of the best known photographs of him, a full-faced portrait, showing him with all his decorations, one eye slightly closed and his features set in a grim expression, which savours of arrogance. But other pictures, showing him side-faced, with his long hooked nose and a lively, intelligent expression in his eyes and the set of his mouth, portray him in a different light. Both contain the truth. He was arrogant and intolerant at times, and something of a martinet; but he was highly intelligent, with a clear, quick brain. Behind a cold, reserved exterior, he was an emotional man, who kept his feelings under strict control. Above all, he had great strength of character, standing up to his superiors, including Hitler, if he thought they were wrong, and coping with one critical situation after another with fearless determination and resolution, based on a clear perception of the situation. As a result he gained the respect and affection of those who served him, inspired by the example he set.[5]

Like Montgomery, he was respected for the speed and sharpness with which he analysed the essentials of a problem, for the brevity and clarity of his orders, and for the calm, cool calculation by which he arrived at his decisions. His outlook on life is revealed in the description in his memoirs of his son Gero,

---

*Another sister was married to the future Field-Marshal and President Hindenburg.

at whose burial in the field in Russia he was present:

> The officer's calling was his mission in life, and he fulfilled it with a maturity
> rare in one so young. If one can speak of a young aristocrat in this sense, then
> he was one indeed. Not merely in outward appearance – he was tall, slim and
> fine-limbed, with long, noble features – but most of all in character and outlook.
> There was not a single flaw in the boy's make-up. Modest, kind, ever eager to
> help others, at once serious minded and cheerful, he had no thought for himself,
> but knew only comradeship and charity. His mind and spirit were perpetually
> open to all that is fine and good. It was his heritage to come of a long line of
> soldiers; but by the very fact of being an ardent German soldier, he was at once
> a gentleman in the truest sense of the word – a gentleman and a Christian.[6]

In that tribute to his son, we hear echoes of the military monastic order of the
Teutonic Knights, of which von Manstein and his like felt themselves the
direct descendants. *Chevaliers sans peur et sans reproche* was what they aspired
to be. No wonder that they looked down with arrogant disdain on the *parvenus*
politicians and industrialists who tried to push them aside, and even more so
on the boorish rabble who came to power in 1933 under the banner of the
National-Socialist Party's swastika. Their disdain was nevertheless tempered
by their relief that some order was being imposed on the chaotic political and
economic situation which had prevailed in the last years of the Weimar
Republic. They had regarded that as a process of self-destruction that could
end in the same way as it had in Russia. Manstein and his contemporaries saw
their task as preserving the Army as a guarantee of the maintenance of the
nation itself and its eventual resuscitation as a great power. He approved the
decision of his superiors to oppose the Kapp putsch in 1920, writing that 'the
use of force against the authorities (however distasteful the existing form of
authority might be) is not only totally contrary to the German military tradition
but ... very seriously jeopardizes the position of the army vis-à-vis the people',[7]
an attitude he was to take when approached by those who plotted a coup
against Hitler. He supported von Seeckt in believing that the fiasco of the
Kapp putsch, which had been supported by Ludendorff and General von
Lüttwitz, demonstrated that the officer corps must keep itself strictly apart
from politics, 'averting its eyes' from contemporary political developments
and working for a future in which the external security of the nation would
be entrusted to a new German Army. The year of the putsch saw his marriage
to Jutta Sybille, daughter of Artur von Loesch, a landowner near Namslau in
Silesia. The loss of the family's principal estate to Poland in the revision of
the frontier by the Treaty of Versailles influenced von Manstein's attitude to
'The Eastern Question'.[8]

Manstein's career gives the lie to the theory, popular with the British, that
officers can be classified into two categories: those who make good commanders
and those who make good staff officers; and that to be qualified to exercise

higher command successfully, one must have had experience of command at lower levels. Lack of that experience was cited by Alanbrooke and Montgomery as a criticism of Eisenhower. After seven years at regimental duty, von Manstein entered the *Kriegsakademie* as a student in 1913; but the imminence of war in 1914 brought this avenue to the élite General Staff to an abrupt end. On mobilization, he was posted as adjutant of the 2nd Guards Reserve Regiment, equivalent, in British Army terms, to brigade-major of a reserve infantry brigade. When he recovered from wounds received on the Eastern Front in November 1914, he served on the operations staff of two different Army headquarters first on the Eastern and then on the Western Front. That was followed by postings as Chief Operations Staff Officer first of a cavalry division on the Eastern and then of an infantry division on the Western Front. He did not command any body of troops during that war.

Between the wars also he served almost continuously on the Staff, his only spells of command being as a company commander for two years with the 5th Infantry Regiment at Angermunde in Pomerania from 1921 to 1923, one year in command of the Jäger battalion of the 4th Infantry Regiment at Kolberg (modern Kolobrzeg in Poland) in 1933, and in command of the 18th Infantry Division at his wife's home town of Liegnitz for a few months in 1938. None of them involved any active operations. Command of 38th Corps in the invasion of France in 1940, at the age of fifty-three, was therefore his first operational command. His lack of experience does not appear to have been any handicap to him in that command, which involved only three weeks of active operations for his corps, little resistance being encountered after its initial fight to cross the Somme. His real test was command of 56th Panzer Corps in the invasion of Russia, where he demonstrated all the best qualities of an operational commander in the field, recognized by his subsequent appointments as commander of 11th Army and of Army Group Don, later renamed Army Group South.

Von Manstein was a fervent admirer of the elder Moltke and modelled his strategy, the organization of his staff, and his exercise of higher command on the principles which that great soldier evolved from the teachings of Clausewitz and Scharnhorst. The most important principle was that the strategy must be right: if that were wrong, no amount of tactical brilliance, dogged determination or superiority of morale or material could compensate for it. Having formulated a plan to meet that strategy, and assembled the forces and deployed them to conform to it, subordinate commanders must be given the greatest possible freedom to conduct operations thereafter: only if co-ordination of their plans or actions with neighbouring formations was involved, should the higher command intervene. It must monitor, not direct, the action of its subordinates. If too tight a control were exercised, opportunities would not be exploited. For such a system to succeed, organizations, procedures and tactical methods must be standardized, and specialization of staffs and units should be discouraged. Both the general plan and its execution must retain the highest possible degree of flexibility. To achieve that, the commander must always have a reserve and must not tie down large forces to static defensive positions. The strength of the German army, von Manstein believed, lay in its superior ability to conduct mobile operations. The aim must therefore be to create the conditions for such operations, in which offensive action and surprise could be exploited. He was a firm disciple of Clausewitz in his belief that the destruction of the enemy's armed forces was the only sound strategic aim, and that it should be reflected at the lower level of operations and tactics. With his First World War experience, he avoided frontal attacks if he possibly could.

These principles, which von Manstein put into practice as a Chief of Staff, and as a Corps, Army and Army Group Commander, were not unique to him, but were believed in and generally practised by most senior German commanders in the Second World War, contrary to the misleading picture painted to the officers of the British Army of the time. They had been taught that German officers were rigid automatons, blindly obeying the unimaginative dictates handed down from on high. Nothing could have been further from the truth, as von Manstein's own exercise of command demonstrated. They were masters of flexibility and improvisation, and generally allowed their subordinates a greater freedom of action than did most British commanders. They did however expect their orders, when given, to be obeyed.

These sound principles contrasted with both the principle and the practice by which contemporary British army officers were trained. They were greatly influenced by the small-scale operations overseas which were their stock in trade. Strong emphasis was placed on the need for reconnaissance – finding out where the enemy was and in what strength – before deciding what grouping of forces was needed and how they should be deployed. The separate lives led by the different arms in peacetime militated against standard and well practised procedures for co-operation on the battlefield, and encouraged that specialization which the heirs of the elder Moltke deplored. When the British came face to face with the Germans in mobile warfare in North Africa in 1941, the superiority of the latter's methods became painfully apparent.

In spite of not being a member of the élite German General Staff, von Manstein held some of the most important Staff appointments, notably head of the Operations Branch of the General Staff (*Operations Abteilung* I) in 1935 and, a year later, *Oberquartiermeister* I, deputy to Beck, who, as Chief of the General Staff, was subordinate to the Commander-in-Chief of the Army, then von Fritsch. In the former post, Manstein made a major contribution in proposing the concept of 'assault artillery', the *Sturmgeschutz*, a tracked armoured vehicle which carried a short-range, direct-fire gun firing high-explosive shells, to work in close direct support of infantry. This was the task which most French tanks were designed to perform, as was the British infantry support tank of the time, although its armament was hopelessly unsuitable for the task, being limited to a machine-gun and an anti-tank gun of limited penetrative power. Manstein had to fight both the panzer arm and the artillery, who regarded it both as a rival on the battlefield and a competitor for resources, from the production line to the front itself, as indeed it was. It can be argued that the German army would have been better served if the effort devoted to this *Sturmartillerie* had been devoted to tanks with turrets which could traverse 360 degrees. Whether or not that is a valid argument, there is no doubt that these vehicles, equipped later with more powerful guns, including anti-tank weapons on a large scale, were popular with the infantry and treated with respect by their enemies. The Soviet army also adopted them.

In those high Staff appointments von Manstein was involved in drawing up the plans for the reoccupation and remilitarization of the Rhineland in 1936, and for the possibility of war with France and Czechoslovakia thereafter. Although officially removed from the post of *Oberquartiermeister* I when von Fritsch was dismissed in February 1938, he assisted Beck, whom he greatly admired, in drawing up the plans for the invasion of Austria in the following month. His close association with Fritsch and Beck made him suspect to Hitler, and he was relegated to command of 18th Infantry Division in Silesia. His ability and experience as a staff officer, however, made him a natural choice as Chief of Staff, first, to von Leeb's army for the invasion of Czechoslovakia in 1938 and then to Rundstedt's Army Group South for the invasion of Poland in 1939. Manstein did not pretend that that task posed any great difficulty, the German army being able to invade Poland from three different directions, East Prussia, Silesia and Slovakia. The only problem was what risks to take in leaving the west lightly defended against France, and that was not his concern. But it was a valuable experience of active operations for the German Army and for von Manstein himself in working with von Rundstedt. They complemented each other well, von Manstein being a master of detail and von Rundstedt refusing to get involved in it, restricting himself to the broad brush, lending his weight when necessary when his Chief of Staff ran up against opposition, as he often did, never being one to suffer fools gladly.

The test of this was to come when von Rundstedt and his staff were transferred to the west as Army Group A in the centre. The transfer was largely due to pressure from Manstein. It had originally been intended that von Rundstedt would remain in Poland as Commander-in-Chief East. Manstein blamed the Commander-in-Chief of the Army, von Brauchitsch, and his Chief of the General Staff, Halder, for not proposing, after the campaign in Poland, a clear strategic plan for the future, based either on seeking peace with France or Britain, or on defeating their forces. If the latter, it would have to be carefully thought out and prepared. In its place, they found themselves having to react to a decision, announced by Hitler on 27 September 1939 without any previous consultation, to take the offensive in the autumn, violating the neutrality of Holland, Belgium and Luxemburg. The only aim given was 'to defeat the largest possible elements of the French and Allied Armies and simultaneously to gain as much territory as possible in Holland, Belgium and Northern France as a basis for successful air and sea operations against Britain and as a broad protective zone for the Ruhr.' Von Manstein rejected that as muddled strategy without a clear aim, to achieve which forces could be concentrated.[9] A possible strategy would have been to remain on the defensive and force Britain and France to attack and face the problem of breaching the neutrality of the Low Countries. However, that would hand the initiative to them, and time would eventually be on their side. He therefore sought a strategy which would inflict a decisive defeat on the French forces and any which Britain deployed on the Continent.

The plan proposed by von Brauchitsch from OKH (*Oberkommando des Heeres* – High Command of the Army) was a mere repetition of Schlieffen's 1914 plan, the main effort to be made on the right through Belgium by von Bocks Army Group B, which, with three armies, was allotted the bulk of the force's, including almost all the panzer and mobile infantry divisions, leaving von Rundstedt with two armies, totalling twenty-two non-mechanized infantry divisions, with the subsidiary task of protecting von Bock's southern flank. Apart from resentment at being restricted to this minor rôle, von Manstein regarded the plan as strategically unsound, leading to a head-on clash between von Bock's Army Group and the combined Belgian, British and French Armies. He proposed a more daring and ambitious one, designed to destroy the British and French forces in two scythe-like sweeps. Having consulted Guderian, the tank expert, as to the feasibility of a major thrust by panzer forces through the Ardennes and across the Meuse, and obtained his agreement, he proposed that the main effort should be made by Army Group A in that direction. One army, crossing the Meuse north of Mézières, would head due west for the Channel ports, north of the Somme, cutting off the British and French Armies, which it was assumed would have moved into Belgium. A second, crossing north and south of Sedan, would turn southeast and pre-empt a French counter-attack from that direction while a third would guard the flank along the Meuse from Sedan to the Maginot Line near Longwy.

Von Rundstedt forwarded the plan to OKH, where it was ill received. Continued pressure by him and Manstein led to Hitler's agreement to a modification which would create an OKH reserve to be switched to whichever Army Group made best progress. Manstein rejected this as a recipe for failure, but his plan had not been accepted when he was promoted to command 38th Corps, after a conference to consider it at Rundstedt's headquarters at Koblenz on 7 February 1940. However, when he reported to Hitler on taking up his new appointment on 17 February, he took the opportunity to explain his proposal in detail and succeeded in persuading the Führer, who issued an order on 20 February that it should be adopted. Manstein denied that the change of plan, as others asserted, had been caused by the capture in Belgium in January of a staff officer of the 7th Airborne Division, who had crash-landed there with the operational plan of *Luftflotte* I.

The final plan did not follow von Manstein's proposal entirely, the pre-emptive counter-attack to the southeast being replaced by a less offensive flank-protection rôle; but it was the essentials of it which undoubtedly gave Germany its startling *Blitzkrieg* victory in May and June 1940, although the full fruits were withheld by the hesitations of the higher command in imposing restraint on Guderian.

Manstein's persistence in pressing for his plan made him unpopular with OKH. He had no high opinion of von Brauchitsch, whom he accused, in his memoirs, of 'a somewhat negative inflexibility rather than creative resolve' and of having 'preferred to have decisions suggested to him rather than to take and impose them on his own initiative'; and he wrote that 'he frequently evaded decisions in the hope of being spared a struggle to which he did not feel equal'.[10] Of Halder, who had started his career on the Bavarian, not the Prussian, General Staff, he wrote that 'he had a remarkable grasp of every aspect of staff duties and was a tireless worker.... "Genius is diligence" might well have been his motto. Yet the man hardly glowed with the sacred fire that is said to inspire really great soldiers.'[11] Manstein believed that his appointment at that juncture to command a corps, and one that was not destined for a leading part in *Fall Gelb*, was 'due to a desire on the part of OKH to be rid of an importunate nuisance who had ventured to put up an operational plan at variance with its own'.[12]

Manstein's chance to show that he had some of that sacred fire came at the end of May 1940, when 38th Corps was ordered to take over from 14th Panzer Corps bridgeheads over the Somme near Amiens. Typically, instead of remaining on the defensive, as he had been told, while the Panzer Corps continued operations towards the Channel ports, von Manstein proposed an attack to pre-empt one by the British and French; but he was not allowed to launch it until the whole of von Kluge's 4th Army was ready to launch a major attack across the river on 5 June. The 38th Corps's attack was opposed by a French-African division and an Alsatian one. Once his divisions were over the river, von Manstein led from the front. 'The field commander whose reaction [here] is to wait for unimpeachable intelligence reports to clarify the situation has little hope of being smiled upon by the Goddess of War,'[13] he wrote, and, disregarding his principle of leaving his subordinates freedom of action and restricting interference by higher headquarters, he dashed here and there in his *Kübelwagen*, spurring on everybody from division to company commander. His corps was the first to get troops across the Seine at Vernon on 10 June. He requested permission to thrust on, but Kluge refused until the corps on his right had crossed three days later. His next targets were Le Mans, which he reached on 19 June, and Angers on the Loire. Later that day, he found his reconnaissance battalion held up on the Mayenne 14 miles from Angers.

> On going down to the most forward position by the river, some distance from
> the bridge [he wrote] I discovered that, away from the bridge itself, the enemy
> was obviously not present in any great strength – if indeed he were there at all.
> Spotting a squadron commander who was apparently waiting on the bank to see
> whether the enemy would give up the bridge voluntarily, I advised him to swim
> across further downstream. If he wished, I added, I should be glad to go with
> him. The offer worked. Shortly afterwards the squadron – naked as God made
> them – plunged into the river and reached the far bank unscathed.[14]

He then sent his aide-de-camp, Lieutenant Graf, to order the battalion
commander to cross the Loire that night instead of dossing down to sleep,
which they did, Graf crossing in the leading rubber dinghy. By 22 June, when
the armistice was signed at Compiègne, he had two divisions across.

He was to exercise command in the same way with 56th Panzer Corps in
the invasion of Russia in June 1941 from near Tilsit in East Prussia, but was
to experience a high degree of frustration in the process. All went well at first
up to and including the crossing of the Dvina at Dvinsk, where his leading
division, 8th Panzer, captured the important bridges intact, by that time 60
to a 100 miles in advance of the other corps of 4th Panzer Group and of the
16th Army. Manstein's reaction was to continue his thrust.

> It goes without saying [he wrote] that the further a single panzer corps – or
> indeed the entire panzer group – ventured into the depths of the Russian
> hinterland, the greater the hazards became. Against this it may be said that the
> safety of a tank formation operating in the enemy's rear largely depends on its
> ability to keep moving. Once it comes to a halt, it will immediately be assailed
> from all sides by the enemy's reserves.[15]

That principle is easier to propound than to put into practice. Tanks, and the
crews who man them, cannot keep moving continuously. Tanks have to
be refuelled, maintained and repaired, and their guns supplied with more
ammunition. Crews have to sleep and eat. The same applies to other arms –
artillery, infantry and engineers – who must accompany and support the tanks,
and a continuous advance could outstrip air support in those days of aircraft
with limited range. A pencil-like thrust by a single armoured formation could
become very vulnerable, if it did not, as it had in France, throw the enemy
into confusion. These considerations no doubt influenced General Hoeppner,
commander of 4th Panzer Group, in holding Manstein at Dvinsk until 41st
Panzer Corps on his left had reached and crossed the river.

Thereafter von Manstein was continually frustrated as the main route
towards Leningrad was allotted to 41st Corps and he was diverted to the
right through marshy, forested country, where roads were non-existent. His
frustration was intensified when, the two corps of the Panzer Group having

become widely separated in mid-July, his was encircled. It was the first occasion on which he had had to face an adverse operational situation, and he showed the combination of calm resolution, clear-headedness and swift decisiveness which were to be the hallmark of his exercise of command of Army Group Don in later years. Disappointed in his hopes of a swift capture of Leningrad, von Manstein favoured abandonment of the attempt to reach it and a swift redeployment to concentrate effort towards Moscow. Having not been involved in any way in the strategic direction of the campaign, his critical attitude towards OKH was revived, blaming von Brauchitsch and Halder for not insisting that a clear strategy, based on military objectives, was followed, instead of giving way to Hitler's directives, based on the acquisition of territory for political or economic purposes.

Before he could become involved in this controversy, von Manstein was moved to the other end of the huge front. On 12 September 1941 he was ordered to leave immediately to take command of 11th Army in von Rundstedt's Army Group South to replace General von Schobert, who had been killed when his light aircraft landed in a Russian minefield. The Army on the extreme right of Army Group South had recently forced a crossing of the Dnieper and had under its command not only two German corps but also the Third Romanian Army, consisting of a mountain corps and a cavalry corps. Manstein found himself faced with two divergent tasks: to drive on eastwards to seize Rostov, the vital crossing-point near the mouth of the Don, and to occupy the Crimea. The aim of the latter was to deprive the Russians of the use of its airfields, from which they could bomb the Romanian oilfields, and to remove the threat to the right flank of his eastward advance. His first task was to attack the Perekop isthmus, one of the only two land approaches to the Crimea. As it was less than 5 miles wide and was flanked by sea which was too shallow for assault boats, there was no possibility of manoeuvre. Nevertheless 54th Corps cleared the 10-mile deep defences in five days, the determined infantry assault by two infantry divisions with massive artillery support inflicting heavy losses on the Soviet garrison. So fierce was the fighting that one German divisional commander appealed for the battle to be broken off, but Manstein insisted that a supreme effort must be made to break through.

Thereafter von Kleist took over the drive to Rostov, while the Romanians assumed responsibility for coast defence, and von Manstein, with his own 11th Army, concentrated on clearing the Crimea. There was little opportunity for him to exercise his strategic and operational flair; but his expert knowledge of all arms, of organization and of staff work, when added to his sound judgment and determination, ensured that the task was effectively accomplished. Until March 1942 he had no tanks to help him. Having defeated the counter-attack launched by the Soviet Army from the Kuban into the Kerch peninsula in May, he was able to concentrate his forces on the final phase, the capture of

Sevastopol itself. It was a major siege operation, involving a massive concentration of artillery, finally completed on 4 July, von Manstein being
rewarded by promotion to Field-Marshal.

His period of command in the Crimea was marked by two controversial
issues. The first was the affair of General Graf von Sponeck, commander of
33rd Corps. On 29 December 1941 a strong Soviet force landed at Feodosia,
behind the German division in the Kerch peninsula. Fearing its encirclement,
von Sponeck ordered an immediate withdrawal, the division abandoning its
guns. Manstein dismissed him, Sponeck demanding a court-martial, which,
presided over by Göring, condemned him to death. Hitler commuted the
sentence to fortress imprisonment, but later had him shot after the 20 July
1944 plot. Manstein is blamed by some for his hasty dismissal of Sponeck,
which eventually led to his death. Any other commander would have dismissed
him in such circumstances. If Sponeck had not asked for a court-martial, he
might not have suffered the fate he did.

The other issue formed the subject of the charges brought against him at
his trial by a British military court for war crimes in 1949. It centred on
the treatment of Russian prisoners of war and on the activities of the SS
Einsatzgruppen, acting on Hitler's orders to eliminate Jews in captured territory. Their activities were usually carried out in the rear areas behind the
operational boundaries of Armies, but the whole of the Crimea was an operational area, and in November 1941 Manstein signed an order, reflecting one
sent to him from Army Group South, which included the words 'the Jewish-
Bolshevist system ... must be exterminated once and for all' and should
'never again be allowed to invade our European *Lebensraum*'. In his favour it
must be said that the order concluded with the words: 'Severe steps will be
taken against arbitrary action and self-interest, against savagery and indiscipline, against any violation of the honour of the soldier.'[16] At his trial, he
was acquitted of any direct complicity in breaches of the Geneva Convention
or of the accepted Laws and Usages of War, but was found guilty of using
Russian prisoners of war for construction work and clearance of minefields,
of allowing civilians to be deported for work in Germany, and on seven charges
of not having taken sufficient steps to prevent 'irregularities' taking place in
his area of command.

Victory in the Crimea was followed in August 1942 by a switch back to the
area of Leningrad, von Manstein taking his headquarters and most of the
heavy artillery used at Sevastopol to participate in a renewed attempt to
capture the city, which was unsuccessful. The short time he spent in that area
was marred by the death in action of his elder son, serving in the neighbouring
16th Army.

On 20 November von Manstein returned to the south to form, with his
11th Army Headquarters, Army Group Don (see map on page 256). This
was in response to the critical situation caused by the Soviet encirclement of

von Paulus's 6th Army and part of Hoth's 4th Panzer Army in the bend of the Don immediately west of Stalingrad. Manstein's appointment was to pose him with a challenge as a commander far more severe than any he had hitherto faced. Henceforward he was continuously faced with odds stacked against him. Unsound strategy lay at the heart of the crisis. List's Army Group A had penetrated to the Caucasus, leaving a wide gap between his rear and the forces of von Weichs's Army Group B, which was strung out all along the Don, dangerously reliant on allied Armies, Hungarian, Italian and Romanian. The strongest elements, 6th Army and 4th Panzer, were stuck out in the salient at Stalingrad, the capture of which obsessed Hitler, himself now being not only Commander-in-Chief of the *Wehrmacht*, but, since the dismissal of von Brauchitsch in December 1941, directly of the Army also, Halder remaining as Chief of Staff of the latter. Manstein therefore found himself immediately under Hitler's command, Halder at OKH being the intermediary. Hitherto his relations with the Führer had been good, although von Manstein had never been inclined to favour the Nazi Party and his association with von Fritsch and Beck told against him. His background, outlook and temperament were far removed from those of the Nazi leaders, and he certainly regarded Göring and Himmler with a distaste that bordered on hatred. He respected Hitler's quickness of mind, retentive memory, energy and appreciation of the possibility of exploiting opportunities, but condemned him for his arrogant belief in his own superiority of knowledge, judgment, intuition and will-power. In respect of the conduct of military affairs, his criticism centred on Hitler's lack of understanding of what could or could not be achieved with the resources available, due to his lack of appropriate military experience; on Hitler's failure to understand that the strategic aim must be the destruction of the enemy's armed forces, and that this necessitated concentration of the maximum force at the crucial spot, not a dissipation of force in pursuit of several different objectives at once; on his unwillingness to take risks, a symptom of which was his reluctance to take difficult decisions; on his predilection for hanging on to places more for their symbolic than for their military value; and, above all, for his refusal to organize the chain of command properly. On several occasions von Manstein told him to his face that he should not attempt to carry the burden himself of being Head of State, Supreme Commander of the *Wehrmacht*, Commander-in-Chief of the Army and overall commander of the Eastern Front, and that he should have a Chief of Staff of the *Wehrmacht* as his principal military adviser, through whom orders to all fronts should be issued, and that the Eastern Front should have its own Supreme Headquarters, separate from OKH. His arguments fell on deaf ears, and, as he became increasingly frustrated at the consequences of the faults in the system, he vented his anger on Zeitzler, who had taken over from Halder as Chief of the General Staff in September 1942.[17]

On 5 January 1943, feeling particularly exasperated at the rejection of his

demand for operational freedom and request for reinforcements, he signalled
to Zeitzler:

> Should these proposals not be approved and this headquarters continue to be
> tied down to the same extent as hitherto, I cannot see that any useful purpose
> will be served by my continuing as commander of Don Army Group. In the
> circumstances it would appear more appropriate to replace me by a 'sub-
> directorate' of the kind maintained by the Quartermaster-General.

He explained that the Quartermaster-General's 'sub-directorates' at Army
Groups were headed by older Staff officers who ran their formation's supply
and transport services in accordance with direct instructions from the central
directorate.[18]

Army Group Don's first priority was to attempt to re-establish contact with
the cut-off 6th Army, but von Manstein and Hitler were soon at loggerheads
over the purpose for which this was necessary. Hitler saw it as a means of
retaining and extending 6th Army's hold on Stalingrad, primarily for political,
but also for economic and military reasons. He believed that it would serve
the same purpose as von Falkenhayn had intended that the attack on Verdun
should serve in the First World War. Manstein took the opposite view. He
feared that the whole southern front was endangered as long as its effort was
concentrated in the Don bend and unless 6th Army could be extracted and
employed elsewhere. His first demand therefore was for Paulus to attempt to
break out to the southwest to meet his relieving force, which he could only do
if 6th Army were withdrawn from Stalingrad. The combination of the refusal
of Hitler to agree to that and the failure of Göring to live up to his promise
to keep 6th Army supplied by air undermined the possibility of von Manstein's
plan succeeding. The longer it was delayed, the less the chance of success and
the greater the danger that the Soviet forces might cut off all the forces of
both Army Groups A and Don, as well as the Crimea, by a major thrust
through the weakly held front on the Don west of Stalingrad. In spite of
Hitler's orders, von Manstein did, on 19 December, order Paulus to attempt
a breakout, but the latter, relying on Hitler's order and his refusal to allow
6th Army to redeploy, insisted that he was unable to do so. Some historians
blame Manstein for acquiescing and not giving Paulus an unequivocal order,
flouting that of Hitler.

He cannot be judged by the standards which would have applied to, say, a
British commander in similar circumstances. By assuming direct command of
the forces in Russia himself, Hitler had ensured that any challenge to or
disobedience of his orders was a direct challenge to the state. If Manstein and
Paulus had agreed between them to disregard his orders, they would be directly
challenging his authority as Head of State. In effect, they would be instigating
a civil war in the middle of a foreign one. If they were to do that, they would

have needed the support of the other senior generals and of the German people. They could certainly not assume that, no preparation of any kind having been made to obtain it. In any case, for a newly-appointed army-group commander to take that momentous step was foreign to Manstein's nature and upbringing. However bad the situation, he had the soldier's ingrained belief that somehow or other the situation could be, and must be, saved. If Manstein is to be criticized, it is on the grounds that he never flew to see Paulus and discuss these matters with him.

As the situation reached crisis in January 1943, the chances of saving 6th Army becoming remote and the threat further west increasing as the rivers froze up and the ground became hard, von Manstein saw that the only hope of averting a worse situation was to withdraw Army Group A from the Caucasus. He had already on several occasions suggested that it should transfer forces to reinforce Hoth's hard-pressed 4th Panzer Army south of Stalingrad. The latter was trying at one and the same time to establish contact with Paulus and to ward off Russian attacks, which, if successful, could penetrate to Rostov, leaving the route through the Crimea to the Kuban, across the Kerch strait, as the only supply line to Army Group A. Time and time again Manstein represented that, unless he were reinforced from elsewhere, disaster might ensue. At the same time, by adroit juggling with his forces and improvisation, he warded off Soviet attempts to sever his links with Army Groups A and B. As long as there was still some hope of at least part of 6th Army breaking out, von Manstein supported Hitler in insisting that Paulus must continue to resist. The time could be used to readjust the deployment of Army Group A to make possible a strengthening of the position on the Don. But Hitler's refusal to allow Paulus to withdraw from Stalingrad, or Army Group A from the Caucasus, meant that the opportunity was lost, and by 22 January the Russians had captured 6th Army's only remaining airfield. Manstein then supported Paulus's request for permission to surrender, which Hitler refused. Manstein contemplated resignation, and explains in his memoirs why, on that occasion and on others, he refrained from doing so, in spite of the wish 'to be released from responsibilities rendered almost unbearable by the interminable nerve-racking battles that had to be fought with one's own Supreme Command before it would accept the need for any urgent military action':

> The first point is that a senior commander is no more able to pack up and go home than any other soldier. Hitler was not compelled to accept a resignation, and would hardly have been likely to do so in this case. The soldier in the field is not in the pleasant position of a politician, who is always at liberty to climb off the band-wagon when things go wrong or the line taken by the Government does not suit him. The soldier has to fight where and when he is ordered. There are admittedly cases where a senior commander cannot reconcile it with his responsibilities to carry out an order he had been given. Then, like Seydlitz at the Battle of Zorndorf, he has to say: 'After the battle the King may dispose of

my head as he will, but during the battle he will kindly allow me to make use of it.' No general can vindicate the loss of a battle by claiming that he was compelled – against his better judgement – to execute an order that led to defeat. In this case the only course open to him is disobedience, for which he is answerable with his head. Success will usually decide whether he was right or not.

To which he added that responsibility towards the soldiers under one's command must always weigh heavily in the matter, as must the effect of any disobedience on neighbouring formations.[19] All professional soldiers would echo these sentiments.

Von Manstein's reputation rests on, and must be judged by, his performance as an army-group commander in the intense struggle which ensued between the Don and the Dniester from January 1943 to March 1944, when he handed over the merged Army Groups Don and B, renamed South, to Model, under whom it acquired the new title of Army Group North Ukraine. The argument between Manstein and Hitler about strategy continued throughout the period, Hitler's judgment being continuously proved wrong by events, and disaster only being averted by Manstein's resolution and skill in handling his forces. True to his belief in the need to pursue a mobile strategy, aimed at the destruction of the enemy's forces – described by the nineteenth-century German strategist, Delbrück, as *Niederwerfungstrategie* – von Manstein wished to pull back the over-extended German forces in the south, drastically shortening the line and reducing the forces needed for its defence, so that a reserve could be formed for offensive use. He wished to see the situation in the south reversed, with Soviet forces extended, offering a vulnerable right flank, instead of the Germans being extended with a very vulnerable left one. He proposed enticing the Russians in the direction of Romania and Hungary, when a major counter-offensive should be launched from the area of Kharkov, which would cut them off with their backs to the Black Sea. This offensive should be launched in the summer of 1943, before the Anglo-Americans, at that time bogged down in North Africa, could intervene on the Continent. If his plan were to be put into effect, a major redeployment, including the withdrawal of Army Group A from the Caucasus – perhaps also from the Crimea – would have to be put in hand immediately.

Hitler would have no truck with such a concept. His arguments were that possession of the Caucasus area and the Donetz Basin denied vital oil and mineral supplies to the Soviet Union, which could be decisive in limiting its war effort, while these supplies, and the oil of Romania, were of great importance to that of Germany. Abandonment of the Caucasus area and the Crimea could influence Turkey to join the Anglo-Americans, and of the Crimea would put Romanian oil at risk. As long as the Russians were forced to attack strongly held defences, he argued, their losses would exceed those of Germany and her allies and could not be sustained for long. To effect the withdrawal proposed by Manstein would call into question the whole object of Operation *Barbarossa*, indeed of the war itself. His strategy, if it can be called that, was in effect what Delbrück called *Ermattungstrategie*, the strategy of exhaustion or attrition. The result of this basic difference in strategies was that the Germans pursued neither, nor could von Manstein ever persuade Hitler or Zeitzler to engage in a serious consideration of long – or even medium – term strategy. He found himself continuously forced to adopt short-term measures to avert disaster, reacting to the initiative which was left in Soviet hands. His skill in warding off the succession of blows, postponing the dangers which he foresaw, and of which he gave repeated warnings, merely encouraged Hitler in his distrust of prophets of doom.

There is no doubt that Manstein was right in recognizing that Operation *Barbarossa* had failed in its original aims, which were too ambitious. There was no longer any hope of a military victory over the Soviet forces which would make it possible for the Germans to dictate terms, as they had at Brest-Litovsk in 1918. Manstein's demand for the creation of a reserve, which could only be done by withdrawal to a shorter line further west, was the only strategy which held out a realistic hope of stabilizing the military situation in Russia, and perhaps bringing about an end to the war, before the Anglo-American forces landed on the Continent. Whether or not his ambitious plan for a major counter-offensive southeast from Kharkov would have succeeded, is more difficult to judge. Hitler's refusal to authorize withdrawal from the Kuban, the Crimea and the Donetz Basin inevitably proved fatal.

In essence, von Manstein's problem throughout the period was how to readjust his front facing east, so that he could transfer forces from that direction in time to hold or to counter-attack Soviet forces aiming to cut off his lines of communication in the rear, which also served von Kleist's Army Group A. Obvious targets of a Soviet offensive were the vital crossings of the Dnieper at Dnepropetrovsk and Zaporozhe. To insure against the danger of a Soviet offensive, exploiting the weakness of the fronts held by Allied Armies on the right of Army Group B, penetrating to that area, von Manstein proposed withdrawal not only from the salient in the Don bend, but also from the Donetz Basin. At the end of January 1943 First Panzer Army, the northernmost element of Army Group A, was placed under von Manstein's command, and by 7 February it had moved through Rostov and was west of the Don, von Kleist withdrawing the rest of his forces from the Caucasus into the Kuban area, east of the Strait of Kerch. Army Group Don was no longer burdened with the task of protecting his rear.

On 6 February von Manstein flew to see Hitler and proposed to him the plan already described, as well as that for a properly organized Supreme Command, failing to persuade him of either. When Hitler insisted that he continue to hold the whole industrial area of the Donetz Basin, Manstein argued for withdrawal at least from the part east of the River Mius, maintaining that, if Hitler insisted on trying to hold on to it, he would probably lose both Army Group Don and the whole of the basin. In the end he received Hitler's reluctant permission to withdraw to the Mius. One result of this conference was that von Weichs's Army Group B was disbanded, von Manstein taking over his forces and the Army Group being renamed Army Group South. It extended his area of responsibility to include Kharkov.

At this time Soviet forces had been thrusting through Army Group B's extended line, pushing forward from the Don to the Donetz between Voroshilovgrad and Kharkov and penetrating beyond it, cutting the railway east of Dnepropetrovsk, so that only the Dnieper crossing at Zaporozhe could be used. Meanwhile Kharkov was attacked and, to Hitler's fury, evacuated by the SS Panzer Corps under Army Detachment Lanz, before Manstein had been able to establish command over it. General Lanz had received a direct order from Hitler to hold the city at all costs and was promptly replaced by General Kempff. Hitler contemplated sacking Manstein also and flew to his headquarters at Zaporozhe on 17 February with that in mind, staying there for two days. Von Kleist was also summoned there. Manstein impressed on the Führer the gravity of the situation and the need to employ all mobile forces in counter-attacks, not in holding ground. While his infantry Army (Army Detachment Hollidt) had withdrawn its two corps to the Mius under constant Soviet attack, Manstein had redeployed 1st and 4th Panzer Armies, withdrawn from the Don, to counter-attack these penetrations on his northern flank. Assisted by a counter-attack delivered by the SS Panzer Corps south of Kharkov, the Soviet threat to the Dnieper crossings was defeated, heavy casualties being inflicted on the Soviet First Guards Army. The initiative having temporarily passed to the Germans, Manstein exploited it to recapture Kharkov, which the SS Panzer Corps took on 14 March, while further north Kempff also regained Belgorod. By this time frost was giving way to mud and von Manstein was unable to persuade Busch at Army Group Centre to co-operate in eliminating the salient (further north again) west of Kursk.

Delay in dealing with that salient was to prove fatal. Its elimination was to be the aim of the German 1943 summer offensive, Operation *Citadel*, Army Group South pinching off its neck from the south at Belgorod, using 4th Panzer Army and Army Detachment Kempff, with 11 panzer or panzer grenadier and 5 infantry divisions, while Army Group Centre attacked its northern flank with 6 panzer and 5 infantry divisions. It was planned to start as soon as the ground would be dry enough in May; but, against the advice of both army-group commanders, Hitler decided to postpone it until June, in order to strengthen the panzer divisions with more of the new Tiger and Panther tanks. Manstein warned him that delay might mean that it could coincide with an Anglo-American landing on the Continent, the North African campaign having just ended with the fall of Tunis. Guderian, who was present

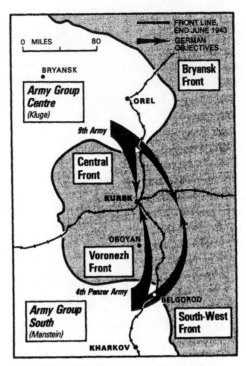

Operation Citadel *and the Kursk salient*

at the conference and opposed the plan, arguing that tank losses would be crippling and that priority should be given to the west, wrote that 'Manstein, as often when face to face with Hitler, was not at his best.'[20] In the event, owing to delays in the delivery of the tanks, the operation was not launched until 5 July and ended in failure after eight days of fierce fighting – the biggest tank battle ever – in which heavy losses were suffered by both sides.

Manstein now realized that the last chance of a successful strategic offensive in the east, before the Anglo–American landings, or the threat of them, drew off forces to the west, had passed. It was no longer possible, as Soviet forces increased in numbers every month, to pursue a strategy of 'annihilation': the best that could be expected was an operational stalemate. For that, a secure strategic position must be established, the basis of which must be an adequate reserve. In those circumstances it was pointless to hang on to the Crimea, let alone the Kuban bridgehead. The Donetz Basin must be abandoned and the line of the Dnieper held, until at least the Crimea had been evacuated. The situation that had prevailed the previous winter was now being repeated, as the Soviet forces, driving west from Kursk, threatened Kiev in mid-September, while Hitler attended another crucial conference at von Manstein's headquarters at Zaporozhe. Persuaded by the latter's arguments, he agreed to von

Manstein's withdrawal to the Dnieper and von Kleist's from the Kuban, Kleist maintaining that he could not complete the transfer of his forces to the Crimea until 15 October.

Manstein's withdrawal was made under constant pressure from Soviet land and air forces. In his memoirs he described the problem he faced:

> From a front of 440 miles, we had to withdraw three armies over only five crossings, and, having crossed the river, they had to redeploy to form another defensive front as wide as their previous one and be fully deployed again before the enemy could gain a foothold on the southern bank. It was this very process of concentrating the entire forces of each army at one or at most two crossing points that gave the enemy his big chance.[21]

The successful execution of the withdrawal by the end of September, under constant pressure, was a feat of military skill and resolution at all levels, from Army-Group Headquarters down to the troops in the front line, which it is doubtful if any other Army could have equalled. The speed and efficiency with which, in a country of poor communications, the German forces, some of them still dependent on horsed transport, could carry out complicated moves in the face of the enemy was a remarkable tribute to the training and military competence at all levels. Von Manstein was an inspiring example of these qualities.

But withdrawal to the Dnieper did not remove the threat which had been von Manstein's principal concern since he first took over command of the Army Group Don: that his northern flank could be turned to threaten his rear. Soviet forces were soon across the river between Dnepropetrovsk and Kremenchug, and a counter-attack by 1st Panzer and 8th Armies failed to dislodge them. At the beginning of November 1943 the Soviet 1st Ukrainian Army Group also crossed the river just north of Kiev. Once more von Manstein found himself having to take troops from his eastern flank on the lower Dnieper in order to try and restore the situation on his northern flank in its upper reaches. Abandonment of the Dnieper bend, from Zaporozhe south to Melitopol, would mean that the Russians could cut off the Crimea. Manstein blamed himself for committing 40th Panzer Corps to that area instead of to restoring the critical situation further north, but excused his decision on the grounds that Hitler, having provided him with additional panzer divisions for the express purpose of holding the Dnieper bend, would not have permitted any other course.

At the beginning of November Kiev became the crisis point, and von Manstein was again involved in an argument with Hitler over priorities. The Führer insisted that he must not abandon Nikopol, on the Dnieper below Zaporozhe, because of its vital manganese deposits, while von Manstein trotted out the same argument he had used over the Donetz Basin: that for the sake of hanging on to it, he might lose the whole of the Army Groups

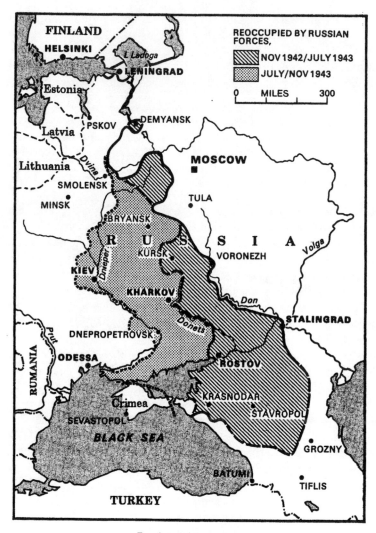

Russian gains, 1942–3

South and A, as the position of 4th Panzer Army round Kiev became ever
more precarious. Kiev was in fact lost on 6 November, the Russian thrust to
the southwest from there being brought to a halt by a counter-attack by 48th
Panzer Corps ten days later, to the relief of von Manstein, whose headquarters
at Vinnitsa would have been threatened if it had been allowed to proceed any
further. Nevertheless the situation in that area remained critical, as the ground
hardened and the river froze over, as did that in the Dnieper bend, where the
Soviet 3rd and 4th Ukrainian Fronts were clearly planning a renewed offensive.

On 4 January 1944 Manstein went to see Hitler and argued for a withdrawal from the Dnieper bend and the Crimea, and the formation of a new army in reserve in the area of Rovno, 200 miles west of Kiev. Only if he were given substantial reinforcements, which could only come from the other Army groups on the Eastern Front or from those deployed in Italy or in France in anticipation of an Anglo-American landing, could abandonment of those areas or a disaster in the Ukraine be avoided. When Hitler refused, citing the effect of such a withdrawal in southern Russia on Turkey, Romania and Bulgaria, or of one in northern Russia (to provide him with reinforcements) on Finland and the Baltic states, von Manstein, alone with him and Zeitzler, reverted to his proposal for a sound organization of the higher command. Hitler, who suspected that von Manstein saw himself as either the Supreme Chief of Staff, or else the Commander-in-Chief of the whole Eastern Front, rejected it on the grounds that only he had the necessary authority. 'Even I cannot get the Field-Marshals to obey me,' he said. 'Do you imagine that, for example, they would obey you any more readily? If it comes to the worst, I can dismiss them. No one else would have the authority to do that.'[22]

Von Manstein's prognostications were soon borne out by events. A major westward thrust on the boundary between Army Groups Centre and South brought Soviet forces to Rovno, while another, south of Kiev, encircled 11th and 42nd Corps. At the same time 6th Army, in Army Group A, on his right was forced back to the Dnieper, so that the Crimea was cut off, and 8th Army was forced out of Nikopol, von Manstein switching 1st Panzer Army northeastwards to restore the situation east of Vinnitsa and relieve the encircled corps. By mid-February 1944 Army Group South had been pushed well away from the Dnieper, except in its lowest reaches, and forced most of the way back towards the Bug. Manstein now became concerned at the open gap between his left flank and the Pripet marshes. Once more he wished to withdraw his over-extended right wing, which could no longer cover the approach to the Crimea, in order to reinforce his left, so that he would not be outflanked and forced southward into the Carpathian Mountains.

At the beginning of March the Soviet forces renewed a general offensive by all the four Ukrainian Fronts, which prevented von Manstein from conducting an orderly withdrawal to, and standing on, the line of the River Bug. By the middle of the month the Russians were across it in some places and heading for the crossings of the Dniester. It was at this stage that von Manstein was summoned with other Field-Marshals to Berchtesgaden to witness the handing over to Hitler of a declaration of loyalty to the Führer which each of them had been persuaded to sign in order to counteract propaganda based on a statement by General von Seydlitz, who had been captured at Stalingrad. Manstein took the opportunity to propose a redeployment from the Bug of von Kleist's 6th Army and his own 8th to cover the area between the Dniester and the Pruth, leaving Army Group A, with the Romanians, to cover the approaches to Romania. At the same time he asked for reinforcements to strengthen his left wing to prevent his army group from being forced into the Carpathians or back behind Lvov.

Hitler refused to agree, insisting that 6th Army should remain on the Bug. He pinned his faith henceforward on providing garrisons for key centres of communications and ordering them to hold out indefinitely, a course which von Manstein firmly opposed, running counter, as it did, to his principle of retaining operational flexibility. Troops in defensive positions, which had been stocked with supplies to last a siege if need be, could not be rapidly deployed to meet a changing situation. On the day following this meeting, two Soviet tank armies broke through towards the Dniester crossings at Czernowitz and Kamenets Podolsky, threatening to cut Army Group South's communications back to Poland, and to separate 8th Army and 1st Panzer Army from the SS and 4th Panzer Armies. After argument about what 1st Panzer Army should do, both between von Manstein (who wished it to attack westward to join the other panzer armies) and Hitler (who wished it to hold its existing position while also clearing its communications to the west) and between Manstein and its commander, General Hube (who wished to move south and join von Kleist), von Manstein prevailed. Soviet forces then drove a wedge between the Army Groups South and A, von Manstein's 8th Army, south of the wedge, passing to von Kleist's command.'[23]

By this time Hitler had lost confidence in Manstein. On 30 March he was summoned again to Berchtesgaden, having only been there three days before. After the evening conference, Hitler handed him the Swords to his Knight's Cross, and then told him that he was to hand over his Army Group, to be renamed Army Group North Ukraine, to Colonel-General Model, at the same time assuring him that it was not because he had lost confidence in him. He pretended that because the days of 'grand-style operations' had passed, and what was needed in future was a stubborn defence, Model was better suited to the tasks which lay ahead. Manstein suspected that the reason for his dismissal was that at a conference at Berchtesgaden on 25 March Hitler had had to give way to him over the issue of 1st Panzer Army in front of other senior officers. Hitler assured him that he would be given another appointment 'before long'. After von Manstein had shaken hands with the words, 'I trust, *mein Führer*, that the step you have taken today will not have any untoward effects,' von Kleist received the same treatment, Army Group A, as Army Group South Ukraine, being handed over to General Schörner, who, with Model, was waiting outside. Throughout the interview, Hitler's attitude had been correct and courteous, almost friendly. He did not want to count Manstein among his enemies.[24]

The relations between Manstein and Hitler were determined by their conflicting politico-strategic views. As the situation in Russia, and in the war generally, turned progressively against him, and the prospect of achieving his original aims faded away, Hitler combined a trust in technical miracles with fatalism. Fighting to the bitter end was the only fate worthy of the Germans, if they could not achieve the aims he had set for them. Where that last fight took place was of no great importance. Manstein took an entirely different view. The object of fighting was to obtain the best possible compromise end to the war, so that the Slavonic hordes could be kept away from Germany, which must be given another chance to restore the strong place in Europe and the world which Bismarck and his hero, the elder Moltke, had established. Had he understood Hitler's basic point of view, he might have been persuaded to associate himself with those who planned a coup, among whom was his respected old chief, Beck. But Manstein pinned his hopes on persuading Hitler to adopt his proposals for both strategy and the organization of higher command, and, in retrospect, he explained his reasons for adopting an equivocal attitude towards the resistance in these words:

> As one responsible for an army group in the field I did not feel that I had the right to contemplate a *coup d'état* in wartime because in my view it would have led to an immediate collapse of the front and probably to chaos inside Germany. Apart from this, there was always the question of the military oath and the admissibility of murder for political motives. As I said at my trial: 'No senior military commander can for years on end expect his soldiers to lay down their lives for victory and then precipitate defeat by his own hand.[25]

Officers of the armed forces of every country are accustomed to the conflict of loyalty between that to their subordinates and that to their superiors, and are sometimes faced with a conflict of loyalty between different superiors. Earlier in the British Army's history, senior officers were sometimes faced with a conflict between loyalty to their democratically elected political masters and the Crown, or the interests of the nation as they perceived them; but none has faced the severe test which Manstein and his fellow senior commanders had to grapple with in the middle of a struggle for survival against powerful and remorseless enemies. That both his own countrymen and his captors believed that he had acted honourably was demonstrated by their attitudes towards him during and after his trial at Nuremberg in 1948. One must bear in mind that Hitler, who was undoubtedly democratically elected, retained popular support, certainly until the Anglo-American landings in France had achieved victory.

Manstein's defence at Nuremberg of the General Staff and OKW (*Oberkommando der Wehrmacht* – High Command of the Armed Forces), in which he did not yield to the temptation to accuse individuals, was influential in securing their acquittal as criminal organizations, but it did not save him from a subsequent trial by a special British military court on charges of war crimes brought against him by the Russians, to which allusion has already been made. He himself and many of his captors, military and legal, found it distasteful that, having surrendered personally to Field-Marshal Montgomery in Schleswig-Holstein in May 1945, and thereafter been accepted as a prisoner of war, he should have been treated like a common criminal and brought to trial; but it was certainly preferable to handing him over to the Russians, as they demanded. It was ironic that, having been released in 1953, after he had served four of the eighteen years' imprisonment to which he had been sentenced, he should have been called upon in 1956 by Adenauer's West German Government (faced by appeals from Germany's former enemies to join them in forming a military alliance against the Soviet Union) to advise on the formation of a resuscitated German Army.

NOTES

1 B. H. Liddell-Hart, *The Other Side of the Hill*, London, Cassell, 1948, p. 94.
2 Walter Görlitz (ed.), *The Memoirs of Field Marshal Keitel*, London, William Kimber, 1965, p. 53.
3 Ursula von Gersdorff (ed.), *Geschichte und Militärgeschichte. Wege der Forschung*, Frankfurt, Bernard and Graefe Verlag, 1974. Andreas Hillgrüber, *Generalfeldmarschall Erich von Manstein in der Sicht des kritischen Historikers*, p. 349.
4 E. von Manstein (translated by Anthony Powell) *Lost Victories*, London, Methuen, 1958 and 1982, p. 77.
5 Hillgrüber, p. 351.
6 Manstein, p. 271.
7 Hillgrüber, p. 353.
8 *Ibid.*, p. 351.
9 Manstein, pp. 98–102.
10 *Ibid.*, p. 75.
11 *Ibid.*, pp. 79–80.
12 *Ibid.*, p. 120.
13 *Ibid.*, p. 137.
14 *Ibid.*, p. 137.
15 *Ibid.*, p. 185.
16 Hillgrüber, p. 357.
17 Manstein, pp. 273–86.
18 *Ibid.*, p. 386.
19 *Ibid.*, p. 361.
20 Heinz Guderian (translated by Constantine Fitzgibbon), *Panzer Leader*, London, Michael Joseph, 1952, p. 307.
21 Manstein, p. 469.
22 *Ibid.*, p. 505.
23 *Ibid.*, pp. 540–3.
24 *Ibid.*, pp. 544–6.
25 *Ibid.*, pp. 287–8.

CHRONOLOGY: ERICH VON MANSTEIN

1885, November 24	Born in Berlin, tenth child of Eduard von Lewinski, an artillery officer who rose to rank of general. Adopted by his mother's sister, Hedwig von Sperling (married to Georg von Manstein, an infantryman who also rose to general), who had no children of her own
1893–5	From age 8 to 10, educated at the Lycée in Strasbourg, then joined the Cadet Corps at Plön and Berlin, where he also served in the Corps of Pages
1906, April 6	Ensign in the 3rd Foot Guards
1907, January 27	*Leutnant*
1911, July 1	Battalion Adjutant
1914, June 19	*Oberleutnant*
1914, August 2	Adjutant to 2nd Guards Reserve Regiment; served in Marne campaign
1914, November	Severely wounded on the Eastern Front
1915, June 17	Staff Officer with Army Group Gallwitz in Poland and Serbia
1915, July 24	*Hauptmann*
1915, August 19	Adjutant, HQ 12th Army
1916, January 22	Staff Officer, HQ 11th Army on Verdun Front
1916, July	Staff Officer, HQ 1st Army on the Somme
1917	Senior Operations Officer to 4th Cavalry Division in Courland (Estonia)
1918, May	Similar post with 213th Assault Infantry Division on Western Front
1919	General Staff Officer, *Grenzschutz Ost* (Frontier Defence East), Breslau. Staff Officer to General von Lossberg in Berlin and Kassel, drawing plans for 100,000 Versailles Treaty Army
1920	Married Jutta Sybille von Loesch, by whom he had two sons and a daughter; the elder son being killed in action in Russia in 1942
1920, October 1	Company commander with 5th Infantry Regiment at Angermunde in Pomerania
1923–7	General Staff Officer to *Wehrkreis* I, II and IV
1927, February 1	*Major*
1927, October 1	General Staff Officer to Infantry Leader IV
1929, September 1	Operations Branch of the *Truppenamt*
1932, April 1	*Oberstleutnant* (lieutenant-colonel)
1932, October 1	Commander of Jäger Battalion of the 4th Infantry Regiment, Kolber
1933, December 1	*Oberst* (Colonel)
1934, February 1	Chief of Staff to General von Witzleben at *Wehrkreis* III, Berlin
1935, July 1	Head of Operations Branch (*Op Abt I*) of the Army General Staff
1936, October 1	*Generalmajor*

1936, October 6	*Oberquartiermeister* I (Deputy Chief of Staff) under General Beck
1938, February 4	Commander of 18th Infantry Division, Liegnitz. Later recalled to staff as Chief of Staff to General von Leeb during Munich crisis
1939, April 1	*Generalleutnant*
1939, August 18	Chief of Staff, Commander-in-Chief, East, later Army Group South (under Rundstedt), serving through the Polish campaign
1939, October 23	Chief of Staff to Army Group A (Rundstedt) in West
1940, February 15	Commander 38th (Infantry) Corps. Served in conquest of France, May-June 1940
1940, June 1	*General der Infanterie*
1941, May	Commander 56th Panzer Corps in East Prussia, in Hoeppner's 4th Panzer Group in Field-Marshal von Leeb's Army Group North. Took part in advance on Leningrad
1941, September 13	Commander 11th Army in Rundstedt's Army Group South, with task of securing Crimea
1942, July 1	Field-Marshal (after completion of conquest of Crimea)
1942, November	Commander of Army Group Don, renamed Army Group South in February 1943
1944, March	Dismissed by Hitler
1944, April 2	Transferred to Führer-reserve
1945, May	Surrendered to the British
1949, August	Tried by British military court on war crimes charges; acquitted on most of them; sentenced to 18 years' imprisonment, later reduced to 12
1953	Released
1973, June 10	Died

KLEIST

10

KLEIST

Field–Marshal Ewald von Kleist

SAMUEL W. MITCHAM JR

Paul Ludwig Ewald von Kleist was an aristocratic Prussian cavalry officer of the old school. The descendant of a long line of Prussian generals and aristocrats, he was very much the product of his background and ancestry. Three members of his family had been field-marshals, and no less than thirty-one held the *Pour le Mérite*.[1] In many ways he was the prototype of the old-time Prussian General Staff officer, and this tradition governed his career and actions throughout his life. He was a Royalist and openly favoured the restoration of the House of Hohenzollern, even after the rise of Adolf Hitler. He further alienated the generally anti-religious Nazis by holding to his Christian convictions. Kleist was a Knight of Honour of the Order of St John Hospitaller of Jerusalem, a famous religious order. In 1935 Prince Oscar of Prussia, the Order's Grand Master, made him a Knight of Justice of the Order.[2] Throughout his life, Kleist looked upon the Nazi Party with a distaste he did not bother to hide. He was, however, a non-Nazi, as opposed to being an anti-Nazi. He was not the stuff of which conspiracies are made. Kleist swore an oath of allegiance to Hitler in 1934 (along with the rest of the Army), and he would never go back on that oath. On the other hand he was not blindly obedient either, which is why Hitler twice forced him into retirement and finally ended his military career.

He was born in Braunfels an der Lahn, in the province of Hesse, on 8 August 1881. He joined the Army in March 1900 (before his nineteenth birthday) as a *Fahnenjunker* in the 3rd Royal Field Artillery Regiment, and was patented *Leutnant* (second Lieutenant) on 18 August 1901. His early career was typical for a young aristocratic officer of his day. He did his gunnery training, became a battalion adjutant in 1904, and was named regimental adjutant in 1907. The next year he transferred to the mounted branch. After attending the cavalry school at Hanover (1908–9), he was promoted to first lieutenant in 1910 and was sent to the War Academy in Berlin, to undergo General Staff training. Later that year he married Gisela Wachtel, a young lady he apparently met while he was stationed in Hanover. His marriage was a happy one, and he remained devoted to his wife for the rest of his life.

Kleist graduated from the prestigious War Academy in late 1911 and was assigned to the 14th Hussar Regiment at Kassel as a General Staff officer. He was promoted to *Rittmeister* (captain of cavalry) in March 1914, and was transferred to the Staff of the 1st Prince's own Hussar Regiment shortly before the outbreak of the First World War.

Captain von Kleist spent most of the war on the Eastern Front. In October 1914 he was given command of a cavalry squadron, which he led in the Battle of Tannenberg, where Hindenburg and Ludendorff turned back the Russian invasion of East Prussia. In October 1915 he returned to General Staff duty and was assigned to the 85th Infantry Division, a Landwehr (reserve) unit on the Russian Front. He successively served as a brigade adjutant, a deputy divisional adjutant, and as Ordnance Officer of the 17th Corps. He became Chief of Staff of the Guards Cavalry Division in 1917. The Guards were transferred to the Western Front after the Russians signed the armistice of Brest-Litovsk in early 1918, and Kleist fought in the Reims battles and in the Champagne and Meuse sectors. He was assigned to the Staff of the 225th Infantry Division shortly before the end of the war.

After the armistice Kleist returned to his family in Hanover, unembittered by his experiences. He joined the *Reichswehr* and held a variety of staff and training appointments. His service record is vague about the years 1919 to 1923, but apparently he served on the Staff of Infantry Command 6 (part of the 6th Infantry Division) at Münster and with the 13th Cavalry Regiment.[3] After twenty-two years in the Army, he was promoted to major on 1 February 1922. He had served his apprenticeship. In the following fourteen years he was promoted rapidly, advancing to lieutenant-colonel in 1926, then colonel (1929), major-general (1932), lieutenant-general (1933) and general of cavalry (1936).[4] His assignments also increased in importance and responsibility. He was Instructor of Tactics at the Cavalry School at Hanover (1923–6), Chief of Staff of the 2nd Cavalry Division at Breslau (1928–9), Chief of Staff of the 3rd Infantry Division and later of *Wehrkreis* III (III Military District), both in Berlin (1929–31). In early 1931 he became commander of the élite 9th Infantry Regiment at Potsdam, and on 1 February 1932 he assumed command of the 2nd Cavalry Division at Breslau, replacing Gerd von Rundstedt, who moved up to the command of *Wehrkreis* III. Kleist moved his family to that Silesian city, bought an estate near there, and made it his permanent home. Photographs show that it was quite beautiful.

Meanwhile, Gisela von Kleist gave him two children, both sons. Johannes Jürgen Christoph Ewald von Kleist had been born in Hanover in 1917, while his father was still at war. Hugo Edmund Christoph Heinrich was born in 1921, also in Hanover. Both were raised in the same tradition as their father, who was a devoted family man. The oldest son, also called Ewald, followed his father into the Army and served as a captain of cavalry on the Eastern Front during the Second World War. Heinrich had a severe asthmatic condition which made him medically unfit for military duty. He nevertheless served in Russia also, as an agricultural specialist.[5]

In 1936 the 2nd Cavalry Division was dissolved, and the divisional head-quarters was upgraded to a corps HQ and was redesignated *Wehrkreis* VIII. Kleist became commander of the new *Wehrkreis*, responsible for Army expansion in Silesia. His new command included three infantry divisions, several HQ formations and administrative staffs, as well as the 3rd and 4th Frontier Zone Commands, para-military units which guarded the Czecho-German and Polish-German borders.

Kleist performed his duties at Breslau with his usual steady dependability. However, after the compliant Colonel General Walter von Brauchitsch became Commander-in-Chief of the Army in February 1938 in place of the framed von Fritsch, numerous high-ranking but anti-Nazi officers were transferred or retired. Among those sent into the wilderness was the openly pro-Royalist cavalryman, Ewald von Kleist, who distinctly disliked the upstart Nazis.

Despite the forced nature of his retirement, Kleist received a significant departing honour when he was authorized to wear the uniform of the 8th Cavalry Regiment. He was so touched by this honour that he continued to wear the yellow cavalry epaulettes with the number '8' on them – instead of the normal carmine epaulettes of a general officer – until he was promoted to Field-Marshal. Kleist was also carried on the rank list as if he were still on active duty and was presented with an autographed portrait photograph of Adolf Hitler: sure signs that the Führer thought he might need Kleist in the future.

For the next year and a half, Kleist lived the comfortable life of a retired country gentleman at Weidebrück, his country estate near Breslau. He was an avid hunter and owned several fine hunting rifles and shotguns, which were found by the Allies when they captured him in 1945. He also watched his eldest son follow in his footsteps when he was commissioned *Leutnant* of cavalry and posted to the 9th Cavalry Regiment at Fürstenwald in the autumn of 1938.[6]

Despite Kleist's anti-Nazi views, Hitler and his cronies never doubted his intelligence or his professional ability. With war clouds gathering over Poland, they recalled him to active duty in August 1939. He was given command of the newly-created 22nd Corps, which was part of General von List's 14th Army, on the southern flank of Rundstedt's Army Group South. Kleist's corps, which included one panzer, one light and one mountain division, performed well in Poland. It captured the Polish oilfields near Lvov and, on 17 September, linked up with General Heinz Guderian's 19th Panzer Corps near the River Bug, thus cutting Poland in two.[7]

Following the surrender of Poland, Kleist was sent to the Western Front and, on 29 February 1940, given perhaps the most significant appointment of his career: command of the principal panzer forces in *Sichelschnitt*, the plan for the western offensive of 1940 (see map on page 469). His HQ was temporarily designated 'Panzer Group Kleist', and he was placed in control of three panzer corps: Reinhardt's 41st (6th and 8th Panzer Divisions), Guderians's 19th (1st, 2nd and 10th Panzer Divisions), and von Wietersheim's 14th (three motorized divisions). Five out of the ten German panzer divisions were under his direct command. Ewald von Kleist was thus the first man to direct a panzer Army, although the term would not be officially used for another year and a half.

Why was a cavalryman named to such an important command? He had not led panzer troops until the Polish campaign of 1939. Although he had done well in Poland, his accomplishments certainly did not equal those of Guderian, who had been one of the founders of the panzer arm. In fact, Kleist had never been particularly well disposed toward the armoured branch, which was replacing his beloved horses with smelly engines. The answer to this extremely important question was fundamental: it was that the senior generals of the German Army had not yet fully accepted the panzer troops or the concept of the *Blitzkrieg*. They distrusted Guderian himself due to his abrasive personality and his apparent closeness to Hitler. They felt the respected and tough Kleist could keep a tight rein on the brilliant but impetuous Guderian, who might endanger the entire operation by taking precipitate actions. In other words, Kleist's steady and conservative mentality was seen as a necessary balance to the potential rashness of the daring Guderian.

Panzer Group Kleist was given the most critical task of the entire campaign – to break through the center of the Allied front and penetrate to the English Channel, so trapping the Allied Northern Army Group (the British Expeditionary Force and the 1st and 7th French Armies) against the sea.

Kleist made perhaps the most critical decision of his military career on 12 May, the second day of the campaign, when his panzer group was making its tricky approach march through the Ardennes. That day Hitler sent Colonel Rudolf Schmundt, his chief adjutant, to Kleist's command post. Through him, Hitler asked Kleist the critical question: did he intend to cross the Meuse the next day, or should he wait for the arrival of the foot soldiers of List's 12th Army? Even Guderian, with uncharacteristic caution, favoured delay. Kleist replied that he intended to attack 'at once, without wasting time'. Hitler approved the decision and ordered the attacks be supported by the Stuka dive-bombers of the 8th Air Corps.[8] The next day Guderian's men crossed the Meuse near Sedan, and by nightfall on 14 May the defenders of Sedan had been routed. By the end of 16 May the gap in the French front was 62 miles wide and the French had virtually no reserves with which to plug it.

However, Kleist was advancing too rapidly for Adolf Hitler, who was frightened by his own success, but too slowly to suit Guderian, with whom he had a number of heated arguments. On 16 May, Guderian, on being ordered to halt his advance in order that the infantry divisions could catch up, demanded to be relieved of his command. Kleist was 'momentarily taken aback' by the demand,[9] but he was not given to backing down from his subordinates. He sacked Guderian on the spot.

Some historians have been critical of Kleist for relieving Guderian, but this author is not among them. Kleist had intended to reprimand Guderian for disobeying orders, but had not intended to relieve him. It is highly unlikely that Kleist would have sacked him had he not literally asked for it. Unlike some other generals, notably Rommel, Schörner, and von Kluge, Kleist demonstrated a reluctance to relieve his senior commanders throughout his career. He merely wanted his orders obeyed – insisted upon it, in fact – as any commander worth his salt must. If Guderian did not want to be relieved, he should not have (literally) asked for it.

Later that day, on instructions from Rundstedt, Colonel-General List (commanding 12th Army) imposed a compromise by which Guderian would be restored to command and permitted to conduct a reconnaissance in force beyond the Oise – a compromise accepted by Kleist, who had not sacked Guderian out of personal animosity, being not that type of man.[10]

On 19 July 1940, after France surrendered, Kleist was promoted to colonel-general. After a brief period of occupation duty he was sent to the Eastern Front, where Hitler had new enemies to face. Except for brief periods of leave, he would remain on the Eastern Front for the rest of his active career.

Kleist's 22nd Panzer Corps was redesignated 1st Panzer Group and sent to Bulgaria in early 1941. It was earmarked to spearhead the invasion of Greece; however, during the night of 26/27 March, the Cvetkovic's pro-Axis government in Yugoslavia was overthrown by a coup. It was replaced by a *junta* under General Simovic, the former commander of the Yugoslavia Air Force. Hitler quickly decided to invade Yugoslavia as well. He assigned the task to Colonel-General von Weichs' 2nd Army. Kleist's 1st Panzer Group formed the major attack force of this army. The invasion was set for April 8.

Considering the short preparation time, the poor state of Yugoslavia's road system, and the difficult nature of the mountainous terrain through which he attacked, Kleist performed brilliantly in Yugoslavia. He quickly smashed the Yugoslav 5th and 6th Armies and entered Belgrade at the head of the 11th Panzer Division at 0630 (German time) on 13 April. Kleist is sometimes given credit for capturing the city; actually, however, elements of the 2nd SS Motorized Division *Das Reich* under SS Obersturmführer (SS Lieutenant) Klingenberg had entered the city from the north and had accepted Belgrade's surrender at 1900 the previous evening.[11] Klingenberg's daring feat does not detract from Kleist's own accomplishments, which were not forgotten by the vanquished. He had little time to rest on his laurels, however. First Panzer Group quickly deployed to southern Poland, to assemble for Operation *Barbarossa*, the invasion of the Soviet Union (see map on page 194).

Kleist did not distinguish himself in Russia in 1941 to the extent that other panzer commanders did. One reason was that the terrain of Galicia and the western Ukraine (through which he attacked) was heavily wooded and traversed by few roads. He was also badly outnumbered in tanks. Stalin had deployed his best formations and much of his armour on the southern sector, probably with an eye to a future invasion of Romania. The 600 tanks of the 1st Panzer Group were opposed by 2,400 Soviet tanks, many of which were qualitatively superior to Kleist's PzKw IIIs and IVs. 'Apart from surprise, we depended for success simply on the superior training and skill of the troops,' the Colonel-General said later.[12] Taking advantage of Russian inexperience, he nevertheless managed to break the Stalin Line on 6 July and closed the Uman pocket on 8 August. Here 103,000 Soviet soldiers, including two army commanders, were captured, and 317 tanks and 1,100 guns were captured or destroyed.[13] Later, on 14 September, he and Guderian (now commander of the 2nd Panzer Group) closed the Kiev pocket, where 667,000 Russians were captured, and 3,718 guns and 884 armoured vehicles were captured or destroyed.[14]

After Kiev, Kleist's group was upgraded to 1st Panzer Army (on 6 October 1941) and headed south, to begin his thrust on Rostov, the final objective of Rundstedt's Army Group South for 1941. He advanced east and then south, cutting behind Soviet forces delaying Manstein's 11th Army near Melitopol. Together they destroyed the Soviet 18th Army at Chernigovka, capturing more than 100,000 men, 212 tanks and 672 guns.[15]

Kleist did not want to take Rostov because he knew he could not hold it. The heavy fighting, long supply lines and poor terrain had taken its toll on his panzer army. Only 30 per cent of the trucks that had crossed into Russia were still running. Also, the Russian winter was setting in and his left flank was dangerously exposed. Nevertheless, Hitler insisted that Rostov be taken. Kleist began his final advance on 17 November and took the city on 20 November. But he was thrown out again on 28 November. It was the first major reverse German ground forces suffered in the Second World War: a dubious distinction for Kleist, who had nevertheless handled his forces as well as could be expected under the circumstances. Hitler relieved Rundstedt of his army-group command for this defeat and even went to Russia with the intention of sacking Kleist and his Chief of Staff, Zeitzler. However, when he discussed the matter with ss General 'Sepp' Dietrich, the commander of the 1st ss Panzer Division, the long-time Nazi had nothing but praise for Kleist. Realizing he had been wrong, Hitler retained the one-time cavalryman in his command and later re-employed Rundstedt.

Kleist played the major role in the Battle of Kharkov in May 1942 when, as commander of Army Group Kleist (*Armeegruppe Kleist*) (1st Panzer and 17th Armies), he led the major counter-attack against Timoshenko's spring offensive. Kleist probably saved Paulus's 6th Army from destruction. About 239,000 Soviet troops were captured and 1,250 tanks and 2,026 guns were captured or destroyed. Kleist then returned to command of 1st Panzer Army, now part of Field-Marshal List's newly-formed Army Group A, and in the 1942 German summer offensive spearheaded the south-eastwards thrust toward the Caucasus and the Baku oil region. When the advance stalled, Hitler sacked List on 9 September and assumed command of Army Group A himself: a new peak in military interference by the Führer. Meanwhile, Paulus's 6th Army was driving on Stalingrad on the eastward axis of Hitler's divergent offensive.

Colonel-General von Kleist warned Hitler against using the Hungarians, Italians and Romanians as flank protectors for the 6th Army during its struggle for Stalingrad, but the Führer would not listen.[16] On 21 November 1942, two days after the Russians launched their successful counter-stroke against the Romanians north and south of Stalingrad, Hitler was finally persuaded to shed the responsibility of directly commanding Army Group A in the Caucasus. He was succeeded by Kleist. Next day the Russians closed the ring round Paulus's 6th Army at Stalingrad.

Kleist's new command consisted of 1st Panzer Army (General von Mackensen) and 17th Army (Colonel-General Ruoff). Kleist now proved to be an extremely capable army-group commander in a precarious and dangerous situation. Despite Hitler's 'no retreat' interference and heavy Russian attacks (and thanks also to Manstein's valiant battles at the head of Army Group Don to keep Kleist's communications open), Kleist managed to withdraw 1st Panzer Army through Rostov in January 1943 before the enemy could cut it off in the Kuban. It was then transferred to Manstein, who so desperately needed

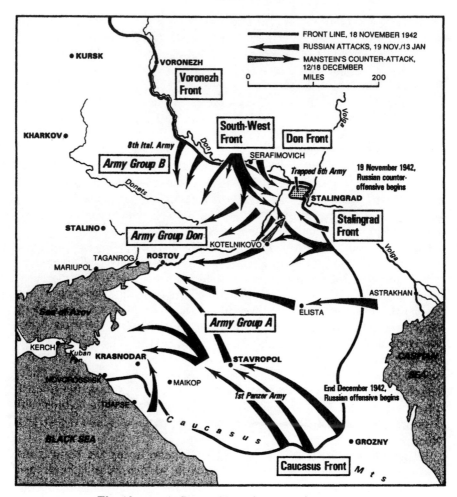

The tide turns in Russia, November 1942–January 1943

panzer reinforcements for his manoeuvres outside the Russian ring round the
6th Army in Stalingrad. But 17th Army was now cut off in the Kuban and
Kleist was in a critical position. The Soviet command had the opportunity of
destroying Army Group A and bagging another 400,000 men – a haul larger
than Stalingrad! It threw everything it could into the effort, committing eight
armies in concentric attacks against Army Group A, but was thwarted by
Kleist. Completely isolated, he conducted a brilliant winter retreat to the
Kuban Line, which he held against all attempts to break it. For this defensive
success, he was promoted to field-marshal on 1 February 1943.

Ironically, some of the successes to which Kleist owed his promotion were
due to his ignoring Hitler's instructions concerning the treatment of the

peoples who previously had lived under communist domination. In September 1942, Kleist had remarked: 'These vast spaces depress me. And these vast hordes of people! We're lost if we don't win them over.'[17] And win them over he did – by the thousands. With great foresight, he appointed two former military attachés to Moscow to his staff: Lieutenant-General Ritter Oskar von Niedermayer and Major-General Ernst Koestring. Niedermayer, who had retired from the Army in 1935, had been a professor of geopolitics at the University of Berlin before he was recalled to active duty. He had organized and briefly commanded the 162nd Infantry Division, which included men from the Russian territories of Georgia, Armenia, Azerbaijan, Kazakstan and Turkestan, as well as volunteers from Iran, Afghanistan, and other eastern territories who joined the German Army to fight the Russians and communism. Like Kleist, Niedermayer was an outspoken critic of the Nazi policy of treating the non-German peoples of the Soviet Union as subhumans (*Untermenschen*).

Niedermayer and Koestring provided Kleist with truly expert advice on the treatment of the occupied territories and their ethnic (non-Russian) peoples. As a result of these policies, 825,000 men were recruited to fight Stalin's régime. These men included Karachoevs, Kabardines, Ossets, Ingushts, Azerbaijanis, Kalmucks, Uzbeks, and especially Cossacks. In September 1944 Hitler allowed some of these men to be incorporated into the Army of National Liberation under the former Soviet General Vlassov, but by then Germany had lost almost all of its captured territory in the Soviet Union and the war was as good as lost. Kleist, however, was allowed to employ his recruits as auxiliaries and in specially formed Cossack cavalry regiments under German command. An entire Cossack cavalry corps was later formed from these recruits.

Fritz Sauckel, Plenipotentiary for Labour Allocation (i.e., head of slave labour importation for Nazi Germany), and Gauleiter Erich Koch, the infamous Reichscommissioner of the Ukraine, among others, protested against Kleist's humane policies. Kleist had even gone so far as to order his subordinates to make sure that 'voluntary' labour recruitment programme in his area were actually voluntary! Koch and Sauckel were furious, of course, but their protests cut no ice with the Prussian cavalryman. Kleist went so far as to summon SS, Gestapo and 'Police' officials to his headquarters and categorically told them to their faces that he would tolerate no excesses in his zone of command.[18]

Kleist's humane policy was so successful that it even elicited half-hearted praise from Joseph Göbbels, the Nazi minister of propaganda.[19] Had Kleist's ideas been implemented throughout the east, they very conceivably could have changed the course of the war.

Field-Marshal von Kleist held the Kuban until September 1943, when he was finally allowed to evacuate it. Over a period of 34 days he and his naval commander, Vice-Admiral Scheurlen, ferried 227,484 German and Romanian soldiers, 28,486 Russian auxiliaries, 72,899 horses, 21,230 motor vehicles, 27,741 horse-drawn vehicles and 1,815 guns across the Straits of Kerch to the Crimea. The Soviets launched several heavy attacks against him, but they were repulsed with severe losses. All that the 17th Army lost was the fodder for its horses.[20] Most of the evacuated units were hurried through the Crimea to join Colonel-General Karl Hollidt's reconstituted 6th Army, guarding the northern approaches to the Perekop Isthmus. Hitler assigned this new army to Kleist's Army Group A after the Kuban evacuation, 17th Army being assigned the task of defending the Crimea.

Kleist's last campaigns were characterized by increasing friction with Hitler over the Führer's mishandling of the war. Kleist called for the abandonment of the Crimea from the time the Kuban evacuation was completed. He went so far as to issue the order to evacuate the peninsula on his own authority on 26 October, but Hitler countermanded it the same day. Even after the Soviets finally reached the Perekop Isthmus on 1 November and cut off the 17th Army in the Crimea, Kleist continued to agitate for its evacuation by sea.

On numerous occasions, Kleist called for timely retreats which Hitler refused to authorize until they were absolutely forced on him, with much greater casualties as the result. Finally pushed behind the River Bug at the beginning of 1944, a line he could not hold with his depleted divisions, Kleist conspired with Hollidt and General Otto Woehler, the commander of the 8th Army on the southern wing of Manstein's Army-Group South, to ensure that the retreat to the Dniester would be made in time. On 26 March 1944 he informed Zeitzler (now a Colonel-General and Chief of the General Staff of the Army) that he had taken over command of 8th Army from Army-Group South (from which it was now separated by a Russian thrust) and would issue the order to withdraw to the Dniester that afternoon, with or without OKH's permission. Shaken, Zeitzler asked him to see Hitler first. The Field-Marshal agreed to see the Führer the next day, but only after he was sure that the withdrawal was ready to begin immediately. 'Someone must lay his head on the block,' he told Zeitzler.[21]

Presented with a virtual *fait accompli*, Hitler authorized the withdrawal of the 6th and 8th Armies on 27 March. Permission was conditional only on Kleist's holding the bridgehead from Tiraspol to Odessa, the main supply port for the Crimea. The next day the two armies were in full retreat from the Bug, pursued by the Russians.

This incident quite likely cost both Ewald von Kleist and Erich von Manstein their commands and ended their military careers. Hitler had wanted to replace Manstein as early as the first part of 1943. Kleist had also annoyed the Führer by his constant calls for the evacuation of the Crimea; by his humane attitude toward 'subhumans'; by advising him in November 1943 to appoint a First Quartermaster General (Commander-in-Chief) of the *Wehrmacht* to direct operations on the Eastern Front; by his pro-Monarchist views; by his high-handed treatment of Nazi officials and the SS; and by his threat to take matters into his own hands if Hitler did not give him permission to retreat from the Bug. Hitler had said of the two Field-Marshals as early as July 1943: 'I can't trust Kleist or Manstein. They're intelligent, but they're not National Socialists.'[22]

On 30 March the Führer's personal aircraft landed at Kleist's airstrip at Tiraspol to pick up the Commander-in-Chief of Army Group A. It then flew on to Lvov, where it collected Erich von Manstein. That evening on the Obersalzburg, Hitler presented them with the Knights' Cross with Oak Leaves and Swords, and relieved them of their commands. Hitler told both Manstein and Kleist that he approved of all that they had done, but the days of the master tacticians were over on the Eastern Front; what he needed now were commanders who could summon the last ounce of resistance from their troops. Even now, Kleist took the opportunity of his last meeting with Hitler to recommend that he make peace with Stalin and end the war while Germany could still hope for acceptable terms. Hitler assured him that there was no need to do so, because the Soviet Army was almost exhausted.

General Zeitzler tended his resignation when Hitler announced that he was relieving Kleist and Manstein. Hitler curtly rejected the resignation, but the attitude of the Chief of the General Staff probably explains why Hitler dealt with Kleist and Manstein in such a civilized manner.

Kleist went into retirement at Wiedebrück, where was he arrested by the Gestapo in 1944 in connection with the 20 July assassination attempt on Hitler, in which one of his cousins (also named Ewald) was deeply involved. Field-Marshal Kleist himself knew of the resistance movement but had not reported it; therefore he was guilty of a crime under Nazi law, although he had not been actively involved in the unsuccessful coup attempt. The Nazis, however, did not want to put such a respected Field-Marshal on trial before the People's Court, especially after the execution of Field-Marshal von Witzleben, and so they released Kleist and let the matter drop.

Except for this brief interlude, Ewald von Kleist lived quietly in retirement at Weidebrück from April 1944 until early 1945, when the Russians invaded Silesia and neared Breslau. The Field-Marshal and his wife emigrated to the tiny village of Mitterfels in lower Bavaria, while his oldest son, still a captain on active duty, blew up the family home to prevent it from falling into the hands of the Russians.[23]

The elder von Kleist was variously reported as being captured by the British in Yugoslavia and as having surrendered to the Americans at the end of the year.[24] C. R. Davis, who interviewed members of the Kleist family, said that Kleist was taken into custody by a patrol from the US 26th Infantry Division on 25 April 1945. In any event, Kleist was to be held in a total of twenty-seven different prisons in the next nine years. He was handed over to the Yugoslavs in 1946, was tried as a war criminal, and sentenced to fifteen years' imprisonment. Two years later he was extradited to Russia, where he was charged with having 'alienated through mildness and kindness the population' of the Soviet Union.[25] He remained in Soviet captivity for the rest of his life.

In March 1954 the former army-group commander was transferred to the Vladimir Prison Camp (a prison for German generals, located about 110 miles east of Moscow). Here the Russians allowed him to write and receive one postcard-size letter per month to his family – his first contact with them in eight and a half years.

Ewald von Kleist died of 'general arteriosclerosis and hypertension' at Vladimir on 15 October 1954 – the only one of Hitler's marshals to die in Soviet captivity. Two years later his eldest son, Ewald, was released from prison after spending 10 years in Siberia. He died in 1976. Frau Gisela von Kleist died in West Germany in May 1958, and Kleist's youngest son passed away in 1973. The Field-Marshal is buried in an unknown grave somewhere in the Soviet Union.

As a military commander, Field-Marshal von Kleist was no genius – although he showed flashes of genius. Although space precludes an account of tactical details, his retreat to and evacuation of the Kuban in 1943 were masterpieces of military leadership. His men knew that they were being led by a highly competent general and they liked him and had confidence in him, for he had earned their trust and respect. He was so solid and dependable that he inspired confidence, both from subordinates and from his senior officers. Perhaps a little too conservative, he is not to be ranked in the same category as Manstein and Rommel, arguably the best of Hitler's generals. He must, in this writer's view, be placed just behind them, in the second rank of military greatness.

But as a human being he stands even taller. He was warm-hearted and caring, although he could be just as tough when the situation demanded. Ewald von Kleist was an officer and a gentleman in an era when such characteristics were liabilities. He had a moral code reminiscent of an earlier time. No matter what the circumstances he never yielded or compromised when it came to this code – consequences be damned. In the end he paid the full price for this attitude. He deserved a better fate.

NOTES

1 Hermann Plocher, 'The German Air Force Versus Russia, 1943', *United States Air Force Historical Studies*, No. 155 (Maxwell Air Force Base, Alabama: United States Air Force Historical Division, Air University, 1965) (hereafter cited as

'Plocher MS 1943'). Plocher, an astute observer, was a lieutenant-general in the Luftwaffe. In the east he served as Chief of Staff to General Ritter Robert von Greim (1941–3) and as Commander of the 4th Air Division (1943).

2 C. R. Davis, *Von Kleist: From Hussar to Panzer Marshal* (Houston, Texas: Lancer Militaria, 1979), p. 26 (hereafter cited as 'Davis').

3 See Davis, pp. 9–10. An abbreviated copy of Kleist's personnel record is found in the Air University Archives, Maxwell Air Force Base, Alabama.

4 Wolf Keilig, *Die Generale des Heeres* (Friedberg: Podzum-Pallas-Verlag, 1983), p. 172.

5 Davis, pp. 9, 105–6.

6 *Ibid.*, pp. 10–11.

7 For the details of this campaign, and 22nd Corps' part in it, see Robert M. Kennedy, *The German Campaign in Poland (1939)*, United States Department of the Army Pamphlet 20–255 (Washington, DC: United States Department of the Army, 1956).

8 A. Goutard, *The Battle of France, 1940* (New York: Ives Washburn, 1959), p. 122; Heinz Guderian, *Panzer Leader* (New York: Ballantine Books, 1957), p. 78 (hereafter cited as 'Guderian').

9 Guderian, p. 87.

10 For the details of Kleist's operations in France and the Low Countries, including his relation with Guderian, see Samuel W. Mitcham, Jr, *Hitler's Marshals and their Battles* (Briarcliff Manor, New York: Stein & Day, 1987).

11 United States Department of the Army, *The German Campaign in the Balkans (Spring, 1941)*, United States Department of the Army Pamphlet 20–260 (Washington, DC: United States Department of the Army, 1953), pp. 50–2.

12 B. H. Liddell Hart, *The German Generals Talk* (New York: Quill, 1979), p. 175.

13 Hermann Plocher, 'The German Air Force Versus Russia, 1941', United States Air Force Historical Studies *Number 153* (Maxwell Air Force Base, Alabama: United States Air Force Historical Division, Air University, 1965); also see James Lucas, *Alpine Elite: German Mountain Troops of World War II* (London: Jane's, 1980), pp. 86–126, for an excellent and detailed description of the Battle of Uman.

14 Paul Carell, *Hitler Moves East* (Boston: Little, Brown, 1965; reprint edn, New York: Bantam Books, 1966), pp. 123–9 (hereafter cited as 'Carell, 1966').

15 Carell, 1966, pp. 300, 324–7; Plocher MS, 1941.

16 Richard Brett-Smith, *Hitler's Generals* (San Rafael, California: Presidio Press, 1976), p. 167.

17 Juergen Thorwald, *The Illusion* (New York: Harcourt Brace Jovanovich, 1975), p. 65.

18 Alan Clark, *Barbarossa: The Russian-German Conflict, 1941–45* (New York: William Morrow, 1965), p. 135; Davis, p. 16.

19 Paul Joseph Goebbels, *The Goebbels Diaries*, Louis P. Lochner, ed. and trans. (Garden City, New York: Doubleday, 1948; reprint edn, New York: Universal-Award House, 1974), pp. 389, 532.

20 Paul Carell, *Scorched Earth: The Russian-German War, 1943–44* (Boston: Little, Brown, 1966; reprint edn, New York: Ballantine Books, 1971), pp. 154–68.

21 Earl F. Ziemke, *Stalingrad to Berlin: The German Defeat in the East*, United States

Department of the Army, Office of the Chief of Military History (Washington, DC: United States Government Printing Office, 1966), p. 285.
22 David Irving, *Hitler's War* (New York: Viking, 1977), p. 618.
23 Davis, p. 17.
24 Plocher MS 1943; Louis L. Snyder, *Encyclopedia of the Third Reich* (New York: McGraw-Hill, 1976), p. 196.
25 Davis, p. 17.

CHRONOLOGY: EWALD VON KLEIST

1881, August 8	Born in Braunfels an der Lahn, Hesse
1900, March 13	*Fahnenjunker*, 3rd Royal Field Artillery Regiment
1901, August 18	*Leutnant*
1904, January 3	Battalion adjutant
1907	Regimental adjutant
1908–9	Cavalry School, Hanover
1910, January 27	*Oberleutnant*
1910, October 1	Graduated from War Academy
1911, December 19	General Staff Officer, 14th Cavalry Regiment
1914, March 22	*Rittmeister* (Captain of Cavalry)
1914, October 19	Transferred to 1st Prince's Own Hussar Regiment
1915, October 17	GSO, 85th Infantry Division
1916, January 1	Brigade Adjutant
1916, June 1	Deputy Divisional Adjutant
1916, October 29	Ordnance Officer, 17th Corps
1917, June 1	Artillery School, Wahn
1917	Chief of Staff, Guards Cavalry Division (date unclear)
1918, July 19	General Staff, 225th Infantry Division
1919–23	Staff, Infantry Leader VI; later with 13th Cavalry Regiment
1922, February 1	Major
1923, October 1	Instructor of Tactics, Hanover Cavalry School
1926, December 1	Lieutenant-Colonel
1927, March 1	Staff, 2nd Cavalry Division
1928, April 1	Chief of Staff, 2nd Cavalry Division
1929, July 1	Chief of Staff, 3rd Infantry Division
1929, October 1	Colonel
1931, February 1	Commander, 9th Infantry Regiment
1932, February 1	Commander, 2nd Cavalry Division
1932, October 1	Major-General
1933, October 1	Lieutenant-General
1936, August 1	General of Cavalry; Commander, *Wehrkreis* VIII
1938, February 28	Retired
1939, August	Recalled as Commander, 22nd Corps
1940, February 29	Commander, Panzer-Group Kleist
1940, July 19	Colonel-General
1941, early	Commander, 1st Panzer Group

1941, October 5	Commander, 1st Panzer Army
1942, November 21	Commander-in-Chief, Army Group A
1943, February 1	Field-Marshal
1944, March 30	Retired
1945, April 25	Captured
1954, October 15	Died in Vladimir Prison Camp, Russia

KESSELRING

I I

KESSELRING

Field-Marshal Albert Kesselring

SHELFORD BIDWELL

Albert Kesselring has been neglected by military historians. His career as an Air Force commander in the great days of the *Blitzkrieg* was overshadowed by the victories of the dashing panzer generals. When he was appointed Commander-in-Chief in the Mediterranean all eyes were on Rommel. After that it was his fate to direct long and losing battles in Italy, and the last months of his career were spent defending his homeland, when the Third Reich was foundering in Hitler's self-created Ragnarok. In fact, Kesselring had three careers, all of them memorable. The Germans can today legitimately admire the General Staff officer who played so important a part in rebuilding the German Army after the First World War or, to be precise, building the new unified *Reichsheer* which took the place of the separate armies of the Kaiser's Empire. He then went on to become one of the founder members of the Luftwaffe, airman and Field-Marshal. The British, who have a long experience of defensive battles and retreats, have good reason to respect the German who against heavy odds held the Allies in check in Italy during a fighting withdrawal of 800 miles lasting twenty months from the toe of Italy to the banks of the River Po.

Kesselring was born in Bavaria, of good bourgeois stock, in 1885. His father was a schoolmaster and town councillor in Bayreuth, where young Albert attended the Classical Grammar School, matriculating in 1904, determined to follow the profession of arms. Not being the son of an officer, he was unable to enter the Military Academy as a cadet without a probationary period, but that was no penance. 'I was always a soldier, heart and soul,' he declares on the first page of his *Memoirs*,[1] and he seems to have greatly enjoyed his attachment as an officer-aspirant – a *Fahnenjunker*, roughly equivalent to the old rank of 'ensign' in the British infantry – to the 2nd Regiment of the Foot Artillery in the Bavarian Army, stationed at Metz, in Lorraine, then part of the German Empire. There he received the long and thorough training given to all German regular officers, including the handling of every kind of artillery equipment, courses at the Military Academy and, later, the Artillery School, where he acquired the elements of what we would now call weapon technology. Tactical instruction, in which he showed a keen interest, was taught not only in the classroom but on instructional visits to the neighbouring battlefields of the Franco-Prussian War of 1870, where he began the study of the 'operational art' he was to demonstrate in masterly fashion forty years later.

The 'foot', or marching artillery, as opposed to the fashionable horse and field artillery, had the unglamorous role of siege warfare and manning the fixed armaments of the great fortress systems like Metz, which hitherto had played an important part in strategy, but in the German armies this was being altered. The 'garrison' artillery – the British term – was undergoing conversion to a mobile heavy artillery branch able to accompany the armies in the field, with the happy consequence for Kesselring that when war broke out in 1914 he was to gain valuable experience of manoeuvre and operations in the field, instead of supervising the polishing and oiling of a battery of heavy cannon housed in gloomy casemates while waiting for an enemy to arrive. It was not long before he was moved from his guns to the headquarters of a regiment as adjutant, a post corresponding to the staff captain in a British brigade. (The German 'regiment' consisted of three battalions.) In the winter of 1917 he was transferred to the General Staff, a sure sign of outstanding ability. He served in the headquarters of a division and then with the 2nd Bavarian Army Corps until the Armistice, when he returned to his native Bavaria and regimental duty. To his alarm and dismay he found Bavaria in a state of revolutionary upheaval. The 'bolsheviks', as he calls them, had overthrown the monarchy and set up a Marxist state, assisted by many of the returned soldiers, disillusioned by the war, some infected by the ideas of those who had served on the Eastern Front and seen the Russian Revolution at first hand. The mutineers had rejected the authority of their officers and set up their own committees. Kesselring was, for a time, under arrest on suspicion of plotting a counter-revolutionary putsch. That, in fact, was not long delayed. The 'bolshevik' prime minister was assassinated, and in the ensuing civil war, which was by no means confined to Bavaria, the right-wing factions prevailed, but for Kesselring, an authoritarian by temperament, disorder of any kind was repellent. He decided to resign his commission, but his commanding officer appealed to him as a regular and a trained staff officer to remain for at least as long as it took to organize a peaceful demobilization. Throughout his life Kesselring regarded a call to duty as imperative. He obeyed, and eventually decided to continue his military career.

When Kesselring had been serving on the Eastern Front while assisting with truce arrangements he had had a close view of the disintegration of the Russian Army under Bolshevism, believing at the time that German troops could never behave in such a fashion. The revolution in Bavaria made a profound impression on him. Kesselring was never a Nazi and during the inter-war years resolutely avoided political entanglements, but of the two evils he preferred fascism to communism. As a result, in due course he followed the example of his comrades in the German officer corps who swore the fatal oath of loyalty to Hitler in person, instead of to the German state. This, as we shall see, was to have disastrous consequences for him at the end of the war after, as he believed with good reason, forty years of honourable service.

The turning point of Kesselring's military career came in 1922, when he was summoned to Berlin to join the headquarters set up to organize the new German state Army (*Reichsheer*) under the constraints laid down in the provision of the Versailles peace treaty. They were strict and, for every German officer, humiliating. The unique and élite German General Staff was to be abolished, on the grounds that it had been the driving force behind German aggression, together with the War Ministry. The *Reichsheer* was to be reduced from its demobilization strength of 200,000 to an internal security force of no more than 100,000, without heavy artillery, tanks, aircraft and chemical weapons. An Allied Military Control Commission, staffed by the victors, was created to supervise the work of reduction and ensure that there was no cheating.

The new Commander-in-Chief of the *Reichsheer* (disguised as the '*Chef der Heeresleitung*') ('Head of Army Direction'), the astute, elderly Prussian general and former General Staff officer, Hans von Seeckt, decided to play not merely a double but a triple game of deception. He had to assure the new republican government of Germany that the Army would be loyal and politically neutral (which was perfectly true) while concealing the true nature of the organization he was creating. He had also to throw dust in the eyes of the Allied Control Commission, which seems to have been fairly easy. The physical possession of certain types of weapon may have been banned, but there was nothing to prevent study of modern developments and how they could be procured and employed. The army strength would be no more than specified, but the Control Commission was not allowed to discover that its structure was designed as a basis for expansion and rearmament when the time was ripe. Von Seeckt was not an innovator: that was the work of men who came after him. His aim was simply to recreate a small but excellent army on the model of 1914, with the difference that the whole rank and file was to be a cadre of future under-officers and NCOs.

Clearly, the Head of Army Direction (*Heeresleitung*) had to have some sort of staff, and it seemed only reasonable to recruit it from the best of the mass of officers about to be demobilized and anxious for a post. Von Seeckt naturally chose former members of the General Staff, with a preference for those with technical knowledge, like the artillery officer Kesselring. In this way, and undetected behind the disguise of the *Truppenamt*, the General Staff was reborn, an illegitimate infant but full of vigour, to function once more as the mainstay and brain of the German army, although later the jealous Hitler did his best to limit its traditional freedom to use its initiative. Kesselring was one of those officers with a natural gift for the organizational and administrative side of Staff work. In due course he became, in effect if not in name, Chief of Staff to von Seeckt in his covert role of Commander-in-Chief. In later life Kesselring looked back on his service under von Seeckt as the formative period of his whole career: 'What a model General Staff officer and leader of men!' he exclaims in his memoirs.[2] Von Seeckt had the happy knack of demanding hard work of the highest standard from his subordinates, while at the same time, having given them a mission, he left them to get on with it, with no other supervision than occasionally dropping into their conferences to listen to their arguments; always open to suggestions or fresh ideas, and occasionally making a shrewd comment from the depth of his vast experience. Under him Kesselring learnt the knack of combining this friendly, approachable style without in the least surrendering his authority.

The other lesson that Kesselring learnt from von Seeckt was to refrain absolutely from political meddling, or intrigues to further his own advancement. For him, an officer had only one aim, to do his duty, and his highest virtues were loyalty and obedience. Kesselring served under von Schleicher after von Seeckt's departure, and while he tells us that he profited by Schleicher's political insights, often expressed in amusing or cynical terms, it was not lost on him that Schleicher did meddle too much (paying for it by assassination by the SS in the Röhm purge, 1934).

Kesselring's most important achievement during his service in the *Truppenamt* was to set up a proper staff structure for the procurement of modern weapons for the future army, based on a logical system of beginning with the general-staff requirement, followed by research, the design of pilot models, field trials, acceptance, and finally the drawing up of contracts for full production and issue to the troops. He then turned his attention to the economical use of the Army's limited man-power, adding to his duties the deceptively entitled post 'Commissioner for Retrenchment' (*Sparkommissar*). The administrative levels of the new Army were lumbered with an elaborate bureaucracy in which the simplest matters were referred to a multitude of authorities, wasting not only time and paper but man-hours at all levels from clerks upwards. The answer was simple enough, but it required a forceful personality to carry it out. The establishments were severely cut, freeing officers and NCOs for the combat units, and officials were taught to show initiative and take decisions without consulting everybody who might have a remote interest. Kesselring's memoirs are largely a chronological account of his service. It is a pity that he never set down his views on leadership, tactics and administration at greater length, since many of his brief asides could be included with profit in staff manuals today; for instance, that staff officers in the weapon procurement branch should possess technical knowledge 'head and shoulders' above the scientists and engineers in industry with whom they have to deal, or that 'you cannot make war from a desk'.

In the British Army there is, or was, a tendency to regard administrative staff-work as pedestrian, and those occupied in it as drudges, inferior in status to the operational planners, trainers and tacticians. (Indeed, in the British Staff, administrators were not even given the titles of 'General Staff' officers, but retained their old eighteenth- and nineteenth-century ones such as 'Assistant Adjutant-General' or 'Deputy Quarter-Master-General'.) In the German Army there was but one General Staff, and what the British called the 'AQ' side was regarded as of the utmost importance.[3] When, therefore, Kesselring revealed his extraordinary talent for administration he was a made man; not that his activities were confined only to that. Before he left the *Truppenamt* he wrote a paper advocating the formation of a *Werhmacht* staff; that is, a tri-service or joint general staff; advanced thinking for those days.

In 1933 when Hitler had come to power Germany had as yet no Air Force. The Air Ministry was concerned only with civil aviation. Hitler decided that the time was ripe to test the temper of the victors of the earlier war by introducing the forbidden arm, at first covertly and by slow degrees. The first step was to create an air staff, with Göring, a former airman and a devoted Nazi as Commander-in-Chief, and three Army generals as founder members in the posts of Chief of Staff, chief of operations and the principal administrative officer. The Luftwaffe was to be an independent service, on the model of the Royal Air Force. Kesselring had by then left the *Truppenamt* and was happily in command of an artillery regiment with the rank of full colonel, with high hopes of a step up to *Generalmajor*. To his temporary chagrin he was suddenly informed that his Army service was over, that he was to be retired, and would take up forthwith the post of chief administrator in the Air Ministry, as a civilian. When he protested he was told curtly that as a German officer he was expected to obey orders. He soon saw the reason why, and he was not long out of uniform.

His new task was to spend a lavish budget building a strategically placed network of Air-Force stations, barracks, runways and airfields. His labours were rewarded in 1936 when the chief of the new Luftwaffe staff was killed in an air accident. Göring, who was no fool, had noted Kesselring as suitable for appointment to the highest posts, and chose him to fill the vácancy. It was his final escape from tables of organization, budgets, contracts and bricks and mortar. To prepare him for operational responsibility he was later given command of an 'air region', and by 1939, when war broke out and the Luftwaffe was about to go into action for the first time in Poland, Kesselring was in command of the First Air Fleet (*Luftflotte* No. 1), a 'tactical air force', consisting of high-level bombers, dive-bombers for close support of ground troops, fighters and reconnaissance aircraft.

It is reasonable to ask how a former artillery officer whose experience had so far been entirely in the field of administration could have been regarded as suitable for command for what was after all an entirely new arm, requiring technical skills and operational knowledge that could not have been learnt other than in the air. The first consideration was that the Luftwaffe, though an independent service, had been designed by Army officers for the specific purpose of acting in close co-operation with the Army in the field. (The so-called *Blitzkrieg* formula was simply mechanized mobility plus air-power plus radio communications.) The second was that all General-Staff officers were expected to have a thorough grasp of strategy, the operational art and tactics. The third was that Kesselring himself was not only a born leader, but an intelligent one, whose mind was always open to new ideas and able to adjust to new situations. Characteristically he perceived that if he was to exert the authority and earn the respect of the new breed of young fighting men, the combat pilots, he himself would have to learn to fly. He succeeded in qualifying as a pilot; to be sure, not of high-performance combat aircraft, but competent to handle his personal communication aircraft when he went on visits of inspection. It was no mean feat for a man of forty-eight.

In 1939, to the alarm of his generals (and Göring, if we are to believe Kesselring) Hitler brought off the political coup that secured Soviet Russia temporarily as an ally, and confident that neither France nor Great Britain would be able to stop him, declared war on Poland; a daring and brilliant opening to his long-cherished plans for conquest. The First Air Fleet was grouped with the Northern Army Group commanded by Fedor von Bock, whose role was to thrust from West and East Prussia towards Warsaw. The new *Wehrmacht* gained an easy victory, brilliantly executed and brutally exploited, over a brave army, but one poorly equipped and mentally unprepared for the new form of warfare.

It was a great triumph for Hitler, but the more down-to-earth German soldiers and airmen regarded the Polish campaign as an exercise with live ammunition to prove the new and hastily expanded Army. (The reason why the Army chiefs insisted on delaying the invasion of France and the Low Countries until May 1940 was that, judged by their own rigorous standards, the Army, and in particular the infantry, required gingering up and a lot more training.) Kesselring had no such worries. The Luftwaffe was an élite force, and his own Air Fleet had performed perfectly, following its well thought-out strategy of first winning control of the air by a combination of air combat and bombing the Polish airfields, and then providing the Army with ground support using the terrifying dive-bombers. A final stand by the Polish troops in the streets of Warsaw was rapidly suppressed by ruthless bombardment, Kesselring himself flying over the targets to observe his pilots at work. During the campaign Kesselring, for whom the principle of cheerful co-operation was a watchword, formed a close working relationship with his army colleague, von Bock. They were to be a successful combination in two more victorious campaigns, in 1940, and later in the first surge forward of Army Group Centre into Soviet Russia.

In January 1940 Kesselring was removed from the First Air Fleet, which he had trained and made his own, as a result of what he called 'that rotten affair'; one worth recounting because he describes how for the first time he had a glimpse of the hysteria which was never far below the surface of the Führer's mind and which was to loom over their future relationship. The pilot of a communication aircraft of the Second Air Fleet, carrying a staff officer who had with him some important papers concerning the plan of the forthcoming invasion of France and the Low Countries, lost his way and came down in Belgium. Crew and passenger were arrested, and it was assumed by German intelligence that the whole plan had been compromised. Hitler fell into a rage, sent for Göring and gave him a severe dressing down, blaming the event on the lack of discipline, or worse, of the Luftwaffe. Göring replied as hotly and both men then had, literally, according to Kesselring's account, a screaming row. The commander of the Second Air Fleet and his Chief of Staff were summarily dismissed, the wretched wives of the missing officers thrown into gaol, Göring assembled the senior Luftwaffe officers and passed on the Führer's insults with interest and then, rather lamely, told Kesselring to take over the Second Air Fleet at once 'as he had no one else'. For Kesselring the 'rotten affair' was really another stroke of luck, as he found himself once more in air support of von Bock, and given an opportunity to demonstrate his prowess as a commander in the new game of land/air warfare, which he seized brilliantly.

In the plan for the invasion of the west conceived by Manstein, the role of von Bock's Army Group B was to launch an offensive into Belgium and Holland across terrain seamed with natural obstacles for panzer forces, with the double aim of denying the use of the Dutch airfields to the Royal Air Force and drawing the Franco-British left forward, so creating an opportunity for the main force (Army Group A, including two Panzer Groups) to pierce the French left-centre by advancing through the Ardennes and envelop the whole Allied left wing. Kesselring was far more closely involved in the plannning of the land battle than he had been in Poland. Airborne and parachute troops belonged to the Luftwaffe, so he was responsible not only for their transportation but for their operations on the ground and also their protection in the air. He was also responsible for ground-to-air defence, since the anti-aircraft artillery were Luftwaffe troops. (Including the famous 88 mm FLAK, whose gunners were perfectly ready to turn their hands to acting as assault artillery or to engaging enemy tanks.) The composition of the Second Air Fleet was five groups of fighters, dive-bombers and high-level bombers, a fighter wing, a complete corps of anti-aircraft artillery under a lieutenant-general, and an airborne corps under General Student of one parachute division, an air-portable infantry division and all the Ju52 transports and gliders required to carry it into action. Kesselring's task was to plan a large-scale operation of a type never before attempted in war; nor, indeed, even tried out in an exercise.

It is an old military maxim that the best plans are the simplest, but although this may apply to concepts, in modern warfare staff work and execution are extremely complicated, interlocking in such a way that a hitch in any one part may lead to a series of repercussions leading to the dislocation of the whole manoeuvre. The idea was to overrun Belgium and Holland in *Blitzkrieg* fashion, using the airborne forces to seize key points on the routes along which the panzer spearheads of Army Group B were to advance: Fort Eben Emael, the bridges over the Albert canal and the one over the Maas leading to Rotterdam (see map on page 469). The parachutists were also to capture the airfields near Rotterdam, which would allow the second echelon of the airborne forces to be flown in directly, using ordinary transport aircraft.

Co-ordinating these airborne operations with the battle for air control and close air support of the leading divisions was no simple matter. The main burden of the Staff planning fell on the shoulders of Kesselring and the staff of the Second Air Fleet. In addition Kesselring had some missionary and educational work to perform among von Bock's corps commanders, on whom he had to impress the fact that his anti-aircraft guns required to be positioned well forward in their order of march, and that it was essential that they took every risk to ensure that their vanguards joined hands with the airborne detachments as soon as possible, since they were not equipped to hold ground for long in the face of counter-attacks by tanks and heavy artillery. The only hitch in Kesselring's plan was when the Dutch Army held up the parachutists inside Rotterdam and they called for air support. General Student was severely wounded, radio communications failed and an area of the city north of the river was severely bombed. The Dutch government capitulated the following day. (The incident led later to accusations of terror-bombing designed to intimidate, hotly denied by Kesselring, who claims that his actions were in accordance with international law. Characteristically, then and later, he constantly cited international law in support of his conduct of bombing and anti-partisan operations without, apparently, recognizing that the invasion of Holland itself was a gross violation of that law, or that the Italians had any right to resist the alien army that had without their permission turned their beautiful country into a battleground. His was a strongly legalistic mind.)

Militarily speaking, the Second Air Fleet had been brilliantly successful in the air and on the ground, and Kesselring was rewarded with a Field-Marshal's baton. At the same time, ever the perfectionist, for him the spectacular victory in the west was clouded by the first signs of Hitler's tendency to oscillate between audacity and indecision, almost timidity. In Kesselring's opinion, based on the precepts and maxims of warfare impressed on every German officer, Hitler's first mistake was not to send the panzers hell-for-leather to crush the British Army before it could re-embark at Dunkirk. Instead, the task was given to his air fleet, its effective strength already halved by the previous operations in which they had been engaged, and its pilots exhausted; with the result that the Royal Navy and Royal Air Force (introducing the new Spitfire fighters for the first time) enabled the British Army to escape.[4] The second mistake was not to invade England as soon as possible, before her defences could be organized. As is now known, but not by Kesselring when he wrote his memoirs, Hitler, who was half-hearted about the enterprise, left the planning to the Navy and it was never co-ordinated on a *Wehrmacht*, or combined operation basis. Hitler, after much hesitation, took the great gamble of invading Soviet Russia, hoping against hope that bombing might weaken the determination of the British to continue the war. Kesselring, who had the operational responsibility for what we call the *Blitz*, denies that his airmen were defeated by the Royal Air Force in the Battle of Britain, claiming that the air attack à *outrance* was called off when he had to transfer his command to Poland to prepare for the invasion of Soviet Russia. None the less, he explains that a purely air strategy was mistaken, since the Luftwaffe was equipped only for Army support: it was a technical problem requiring a different type of bomber aircraft and different weapons. Two years later he was to object to Hitler's order to try and subdue Malta purely by air action for the same reason. That an air and airborne attack followed up by landings all along the coast of south-eastern England might well have succeeded is an opinion shared by many with first-hand knowledge of the state of British defence in the summer of 1940.*[5]

Kesselring, ever the optimist, had no doubt about either the wisdom or the morality of invading Russia. Indeed, he was slightly disturbed, he tells us, at finding von Bock 'rather dispirited' at the final eve-of-battle conference, as well he might have been.[6] It did not take a soldier of his intelligence long to appreciate the hazards – the very size of Russia, its population, and its industrial potential – or to note the absence of planning for the logistics of an advance of over 600 miles, or any thought of how a successful invasion was to be exploited in terms of grand strategy. To be precise, the task of von Bock's powerful Army Group Centre was 'operational', not strategic: to destroy the Russian forces deployed between the Polish frontier (as re-defined after the Soviet occupation of 1939) and Moscow. At first all went amazingly well.

---

* Armour, artillery, signal equipment, infantry heavy weapons, motor transport were all deficient or obsolete, and the hastily trained Territorial Army fit for little more than static defence.

Kesselring had made good use of the experience gained in the campaign of 1940 to perfect the machinery for co-ordinating his air operations with von Bock's panzer spearheads. He achieved complete surprise in the battle for air control, destroying over 2,500 aircraft on the ground, and his fighters were able to shoot down the lumbering Russian heavy bombers with ease as they flew in from fields out of range of his own. In July the Army Group rounded up 330,000 prisoners together with 2,500 tanks and 1,500 guns in the envelopment of Bialystok and Minsk, another 310,000 with 3,200 tanks and 3,000 guns in August, and at the end of October bagged an astonishing 650,000 prisoners at Vyazma, 140 miles from Moscow. But the era of triumphant *Blitzkrieg* was already over.

Early in September Hitler in one of his fits of vacillation had been unable to decide whether it was best to let von Bock make for Moscow with all speed, or to advance on a broad front with all three Army Groups in a line abreast. He removed the powerful panzer groups from Army Group Centre, and attached them temporarily to North and South; Bock's advance in the centre was halted, Stalin was given time to bring in strong reinforcements from Siberia. When Bock resumed his offensive in October the Russians made a stand in front of Moscow, and the whole pace of operations slowed down. Whether Kesselring, who was a realist and continually analysed the war situation, admitted in September, if only in his secret thoughts, that the war was lost – because it had not been won quickly – is a matter for conjecture. What he says about Hitler's mistakes is correct, but has to be treated as hindsight. What was of immediate concern to him was the state of his own command. The success of *Blitzkrieg* tactics depended on continuous air support, but when operations no longer moved at lightning speed and went on for month after month the air arm was worn out by lack of maintenance and by pilot fatigue, to which was added attrition when the Soviet air arm was able to recover from its initial defeat. The pressure on the Second Air Fleet was not relieved when the Army changed to defensive tactics: if anything, it increased. To all these burdens was added yet another; a costly and strategically pointless bomber offensive against Moscow. Then there was the Russian winter, for which no provision had been made in advance. Already the autumn rains had made the dirt air strips on which many squadrons were based unusable. The slight shadow which had fallen on Kesselring's ebullient nature after the failure to knock Britain out of the war was now very dark.

He was not, however, fated to spend any more time in Russia. Before the year was out he was in Rome, Hitler's choice as the newly appointed Commander-in-Chief of the Axis forces in the Mediterranean. It is ever fascinating to compare the opposing views of the same military situation with the advantage of hindsight. The British position was, to say the least, very worrying. The campaigns of Greece and Crete in spring 1941 had been serious defeats involving the loss of many valuable troops, Malta was under virtual siege, the passage of the Mediterranean hazardous, there had been serious naval losses including two capital ships torpedoed in Alexandria harbour, and there was a general feeling among the British and Commonwealth troops that the Germans were better armed and better led. Rommel's name and reputation dominated the war in the western desert, while too many British generals had been found wanting and, fairly or unfairly, dismissed. The British winter offensive, *Crusader*, had been only partly successful. Tobruk had been relieved, but Rommel had extricated his army with his usual skill, turned on his pursuers and established a firm defensive front. The British Middle East Command did not think it possible to mount another offensive until May 1942 at the earliest. By contrast, from Hitler's point of view the war in the Mediterranean was a wasteful diversion, undertaken to support his fellow dictator Mussolini when he rashly intervened in the war and found himself in trouble in Greece and North Africa. It was a drain on resources Hitler badly needed in Russia, but since it was impossible to withdraw the German forces from Africa, it was essential to obtain a good return for his investment. The Italians, he felt, were lazy, disorganized, insufficiently aggressive and not making full use of their ample military resources, and their Navy seemed to be so much in awe of the British that it was too frightened to go to sea. What was required was a German general to act as supreme commander to co-ordinate and energize all the operations in the Mediterranean.

It is not clear how he came to choose Kesselring. There is no mention of any close contact between the two men in Kesselring's memoirs, but by the autumn of 1941 Hitler was undoubtedly aware of his reputation. One factor may have been Hitler's dislike and distrust of the old gang of supercilious Prussian aristocrats who had grown up in the days of the *Kriegsakademie* and the supremacy of the Great General Staff. Another may have been service loyalties. According to Kesselring's aphorism, in the *Wehrmacht* the Navy was still at heart 'Imperial', the Army 'Republican' and the Luftwaffe 'Nazi'. That, together with the practical reason for choosing an airman which was that the inducement offered to Mussolini to accept a German supreme commander lay in Hitler's promise to reinforce the Luftwaffe contingent in the Mediterranean theatre, may have influenced Hitler's choice. But Hitler had unerringly chosen the right man; one who was to serve him loyally, but by no means unquestioningly, to the bitter end, and also one who was prepared to cope with a position whose scope, responsibilities and powers were only vaguely defined, if at all – which may well have been Hitler's deliberate intention.

If the carefully considered and meticulous arrangements for political and operational control and the creation of a suitable integrated inter-Allied staff which preceded General Eisenhower's appointment as Supreme Commander in 1942 are compared with their almost total absence in the case of Kesselring in 1941, it is remarkable that he was so patient and undeterred by the failure of all his proposals to gain approval between his arrival in Rome in December 1941, and when his situation changed radically after the secession of Italy from the Axis in September 1943. His official title was *Oberbefehlshaber Süd* (Commander-in-Chief, South), but tri-service command of all Italian troops and German Army units was already exercised by the *Commando Supremo*, whose Chief-of-Staff, General Cavallero, took Kesselring's appointment as a personal slight, and who was disposed to be hostile. No inter-allied staff had been organized, and Kesselring had at his disposal only the staff of HQ Second Air Fleet, which he had brought with him.* Rommel, commanding a joint German-Italian panzer army, came under the Italian field army commander in Africa, General Bastico, who in turn came under Cavallero, and could only be approached by that channel, a circumstance that Rommel was not slow to exploit.

If the mark of an outstanding man is that he can cope with novel problems, whether of war, management or politics, without any previous experience or special education, by using sheer intellect, then Kesselring was such a man, although in his case 'common sense' and 'nous' are probably more appropriate. He never displayed these to better advantage than in the unsatisfactory position in which he found himself. He was blessed with the capacity to grasp what was essential and what could be dispensed with or become the subject of compromise; he had a strong sense of the possible, also essential in the task of politics and diplomacy into which he was immediately plunged; and he was fortified by his simple philosophy that if he had done his best without complaint he had done his duty. He was by nature genial. The troops nicknamed him 'Smiling Albert', and he can be seen in his photographs always wearing a cheerful grin. He liked the Italians and understood their sensitivity, realizing that it was due to wounded pride at their inglorious defeats. He found much to admire in their High Command and their troops, though he was critical of Italian regimental officers. He won over his Italian colleagues by his tactfulness, never asserting his rank and position. Cavallero came round so completely that he agreed to show Kesselring all his operation orders before issuing them. The goodwill and co-operation of the Italian Staff was all-important in improving the arrangements for supplying the Axis forces in Africa, which were chaotic, and required the full attention of Kesselring's trained administrative mind. They were unsatisfactory enough even without the hazards of the sea lanes from the Italian ports to Africa and the land communications which contracted and expanded as Rommel recoiled or went dashing off into the desert.

---

* The HQ of a *Luftflotte*, like that of an *Armeeoberkommando*, was designed to command any groups, corps, etc. placed under it. The whole Second Air Fleet, as it was constituted in Russia, did not move to Italy.

Kesselring may have established a rapport with his allies, from Mussolini downwards, but the insurmountable obstacle to the proper exercise of his authority was the attitude of Rommel, and of his master the Führer who, believing he himself was a military genius, yet often shrank from taking critical decisions while only too ready to meddle in trifling matters. Hitler regularly employed the politician's trick of playing one commander off against another, what Kesselring calls his 'double track' attitude to command. To his great annoyance, he found that Rommel was not only Hitler's current favourite, but enjoyed the privilege of a private channel of communication direct to OKW, and was prepared to use it to circumvent his authority. The situation in Africa was that the commander of the Axis armies, General Bastico, who was a cipher, had directly under him an Italian corps, and the *Panzerarmee Afrika*, under Rommel, consisting of the German *Afrika Korps*, and an Italian corps strong in armour. The effective director of operations was Rommel, who made his own decisions without consulting anyone. He insisted that he would accept no orders, even from Kesselring, unless they were transmitted through Bastico, and as he took not the slightest notice of the latter, he retained his freedom of action. Shortly after Kesselring's arrival he had retreated so far and so fast after his defeat by the 8th Army in the *Crusader* offensive that it alarmed the Italians, who were increasingly nervous of the effect that a setback in Africa might have on civilian morale at home. He was equally prone to advance to grasp some fleeting opportunity regardless of the risks involved, and as he was often spectacularly successful it was not easy to restrain him. Altogether, Kesselring was defeated in three key strategic questions by the combination of Hitler and Rommel. Rommel is the only German officer of whom he writes uncharitably in his memoirs.

Kesselring perceived at once that the obvious key to the supply situation was the possession of Malta. It was too well defended to neutralize by air action alone, and in any case the Luftwaffe lacked the heavy bombers required for the task. Kesselring strove to persuade Hitler to allow him to capture it by an airborne and amphibious assault. The argument grew so heated on one occasion that Hitler seized him by the arm, exclaiming 'in his Austrian dialect: "Keep your shirt on, Field-Marshal Kesselring, I'm going to do it!" '[7] But he never did. Possibly he had been influenced by Göring, who had been alarmed by the severe losses sustained by the airborne troops in Crete. His own excuse was that he could not spare the troops for the task; this was belied by his later finding a parachute division to reinforce the Afrika Korps, and the troops he threw into Tunisia to oppose the Anglo-American invasion of French North Africa in November 1942.

With Hitler's backing, Rommel succeeded in frustrating Kesselring's Mediterranean strategy. Kesselring's view was that the aim was to protect the southern flank of the 'Greater German Reich' during the great struggle in Russia, and for that the correct course was to keep the Axis armies in Africa in being and free to manoeuvre; a policy of mobile but aggressive defence, along the lines Rommel had so far and so successfully adopted. When Rommel, euphoric after his defeat of the 8th Army at Gazala in May and June 1942 and undeterred by his check on the Alamein line in July 1942, decided on a further offensive to be launched in August, promising to be in Cairo in nine days, Kesselring objected, arguing strongly and, as events were to prove, correctly that the Army and the Air Force were operating at the end of a long line of communication, that the British 8th Army was being reinforced and, most important, that it was backed by the still powerful and quite unsubdued Royal Air Force. Hitler, having one of his upswings, chose to back Rommel and the bolder course, sending his Commander-in-Chief South an insulting radio signal telling him that the projected offensive was none of his business. The irony of the affair, as recorded by Kesselring, is that Rommel, after his defeats at Alam el Halfa and Alamein, became a complete convert to the primacy of air-power and was talking of the necessity to retreat to the line of the Alps even before he left Africa for good in March 1943.

It is difficult to agree with Kesselring's view that the final débâcle in Africa could have been averted. In his memoirs he argues that Hitler could have checked the Allied advance from the west by an early intervention in French North Africa, and that Rommel could have done more to delay the long and logistically difficult advance of the 8th Army. It should have been possible to keep the 1st and 8th Armies so far apart that they could have been dealt with separately by taking advantage of the interior line. Again this is hindsight. It is doubtful if Kesselring understood the political situation in French North Africa as well as Hitler did. The balance between the opposing factions there was delicate, and a premature move would have been as likely to arouse opposition as to rally the French forces to the German side. Moreover, the French were better disposed to the Americans than they were to either the British or the Germans. As for Rommel, he was undoubtedly wise to fall back on his supply base and not to fight more than delaying actions against an 8th Army in high spirits and whose commander's 'methodical' tactics, as Kesselring disparagingly but not altogether unjustly calls them, were well suited to a stand-up fight. Where Kesselring's criticisms are well founded is over the general muddle caused by Hitler's interventions, leading to his being once more prevented from imposing unity of command, and the final, fatal decision to defend the shrinking Tunisian perimeter to the last man.

Africa was lost, together with 250,000 Axis troops, including General von Arnim, the Commander-in-Chief. It made a deep impression on Kesselring, and he was determined to prevent such a thing happening in Sicily in July 1943 when the Italian forces in the face of the Allied invasion and effective resistance was limited to the German contingent. Kesselring risked his neck to extricate them. Without either consultation or permission from OKW, he flew to Sicily, ordered the German commander to form a strong defensive perimeter around Messina, collect as many troops in it as possible, German and Italian, and prepare to cross the straits into Calabria. He himself collected every FLAK regiment available to line both shores of the straits and ordered all the fighters within range to provide air cover. In six days and seven nights in August 1943 between 60,000 and 80,000 troops successfully crossed to the Italian mainland, including all the Germans and much valuable equipment required for the battles in Italy that lay ahead. That the vainglorious Patton could not even dent the German defence at Messina, that Montgomery's mysterious indolence led to the 8th Army's failure to pursue a beaten opponent, and that the inactivity of the Allied navies and air forces all contributed to Kesselring's success does not detract from his feat in organizing a German Dunkirk. The question of timely withdrawal was again and again to be the subject of repeated and heated arguments in coming years. He may never have convinced Hitler, but Kesselring once, in 1944, accomplished the unusual feat of silencing him by saying bluntly: 'Of course your troops will always stand and fight to the death if you order them to, but consider whether having lost one army in Africa and another in Stalingrad you can afford to lose a third in Italy.'[8]

With Sicily successfully evacuated, Kesselring was then able to turn his attention to the operational problems of defending Italy, whose invasion he expected at any moment. Those, however, were nothing to his political problems. He only gradually became aware that he was enmeshed in a web of conspiracy. As Hitler justly observed, when it came to intrigue the Italians could make rings round Kesselring and his Staff: 'That fellow Kesselring is too honest for those traitors down there!'[9] On 25 July, with the approval of the King of Italy, Marshal Badoglio and a group of conspirators deposed Mussolini. The shocked Kesselring was assured by the new Italian government that it would continue loyally to prosecute the war, whereas in reality it had already sent secret emissaries to the Allies asking for an armistice. Hitler, who as an expert in conspiracy was equipped with a nose to detect one even as far away as Rome, told Kesselring to cease being duped and to prepare for the worst, ordered a parachute division to be flown at once into Rome, and flooded northern Italy with German troops without asking permission from his ally, or even informing his Commander-in-Chief on the spot. Thereafter events moved quickly. Eisenhower had sent two daring American officers to meet Badoglio secretly and discover his true intentions. On 8 September they sent an encoded signal that he was too terrified of the German occupying forces to do anything, let alone bring the Italian armed forces over to the side of the Allies. That evening, when the invading US Fifth Army was already at sea *en route* to Salerno, Eisenhower authorized a news broadcast from Algiers stating that an armistice between the Italian and Allied governments had been arranged, in the hope of forcing Badoglio's hand. Kesselring, who had already laid his plans, sent out the code signal to all German units 'Bring in the harvest', and they sprang into action to disarm the Italian troops, the only casualty being an Italian general, who indignantly refused and was shot out of hand. Early in the morning of the 9th, the 8th Army hopped over the Messina strait into Calabria, and General Mark Clark's army disembarked at Salerno. Kesselring's first great battle as a commander of armies had begun. He had only passed from a political to a military crisis, but at least he was now on firm and familiar ground.

He had correctly deduced the Allied moves. It was highly probable that they would take the shortest route, across the Straits of Messina, and also that they would make the port of Naples their primary objective. If that was correct, then the Bay of Salerno, just within range of fighter cover based in Sicily, was the place they were likely to choose for their main landing. Accordingly he had already placed the 16th Panzer Division there, with orders to hold on while he concentrated the 10th Army behind it to drive the invaders into the sea. The divisions further to the south were not to become involved in heavy fighting with the 8th Army but were ordered to withdraw behind belts of demolitions and cover the airfields near Foggia. Meanwhile he ordered his engineers to prepare a fortified position running across Italy from the mouth of the Sangro on the Adriatic coast along the mountain crests to Cassino and thence to the mouth of the Rapido-Garigliano river, which forms a natural moat in front of what was to become famous as the Gustav Line. If the 10th Army failed to crush the Allied bridgehead at Salerno it was to wheel back left pivoting on its right, form a defensive line and then gradually withdraw to the Gustav position, where Kesselring intended it to fight all the winter, or longer if necessary.

His hopes of driving Clark into the sea at Salerno and holding Montgomery in Apulia were soon dashed. Montgomery, after pausing to build up his logistic base and clear a line of communication through the demolitions, fought his way doggedly over a seemingly endless succession of steep ridges and fast-flowing rivers up the Adriatic coast, departing from his 'methodical' tactics sufficiently to alarm Kesselring when he out-flanked one of the German stop-lines by an amphibious assault at Termoli. (Throughout the campaign Kesselring was to be perpetually anxious about Allied landings in his rear, and he kept substantial reserves in hand to deal with the threat.) The 8th Army was finally halted in December 1943 just north of the Sangro river by floods after much hard fighting.

Salerno in Clark's view was a near-run thing – he was sufficiently alarmed to consider re-embarkation at one stage – but in retrospect it is clear that supported as his army was by powerful artillery backed up by the guns of the fleet and the Allied air forces, he was too strong for the under-strength and incompletely equipped divisions of the 10th Army (or so it appears from simple calculations of strengths). Kesselring, not without good reason, believed until his dying day that it was Hitler's perversity that had robbed him of a great victory. It was his last, unsuccessful clash with Rommel, who had left Africa sick, defeated and deeply pessimistic. Kesselring, ever the optimist, believed that he could keep the Allies far to the south, while Rommel's advice to Hitler (whose favourite he remained) was that in the face of Allied superiority, especially in the air, the only course was to establish a defence line in northern Italy, even on the southern slopes of the Alps. Hitler, following his 'two track' system, formed all units he had sent into northern Italy into Army Group 'B' and placed it under Rommel, but not under Kesselring, though he was still nominally Commander-in-Chief. His responsibilities were limited to Italy south of Rome and command of Army Group 'C'. During the critical days of September 1943 Rommel, or Hitler, or both combined, refused to send a single unit to reinforce the 10th Army.

Kesselring, however, was never a man to indulge in vain regrets. In any case he had no time for such emotions with difficulties thronging on him. Nevertheless, when he analysed his position at the end of the year, he could feel that it was far from discouraging. The 10th Army was safely ensconced in the Gustav Line, naturally very strong and being continually improved and deepened by the German engineers. Admittedly the disadvantages he faced were severe. His divisions were under strength, and greatly outnumbered in terms of artillery and tanks. The heavy casualties suffered by the Luftwaffe at Salerno had not been made good, and it was no longer capable of giving the Army the support it required or protecting the lines of communication from air interdiction. Accurate intelligence was hard to come by. Against these factors, Kesselring had confidence in his subordinates, who were as good as German generals were expected to be – von Senger was the best tactician on either side – and in the autumn fighting the German soldiers had proved that in battle-craft, determination and close combat they were superior to the effete Anglo-Americans. (Although this was an opinion Kesselring had to modify later.) He saw that the one fatal mistake he could make would be to defend a position so obstinately that his armies would eventually succumb to the sheer weight of Allied fire-power. His correct policy would have to be an elastic defence, inflicting as many casualties as possible and then slipping away to his next main line of resistance, still punishing the enemy in the fighting retreat in which his troops were now experts. The greatest danger was to be trapped by a major landing in his rear, a fear proved to be well founded.

Winston Churchill, who took an active interest in the Italian theatre, felt keenly that the snail's-pace advance of the Allied armies required to be accelerated by some bold and imaginative stroke. He was the originator of a plan to land in force behind the Gustav Line, realized, after much debate, as the landing of the us 6th Corps of the 5th Army at Anzio. General Clark, though he had little confidence in it, was not in a position to force its cancellation. Instead, he advised caution, saying to General Lucas, commander of the 6th Corps: 'Don't stick your neck out, Johnny. I did at Salerno, and got into trouble'; the worst possible advice to give a subordinate cautious by nature engaged in an enterprise that demanded the utmost speed and audacity.[10] (Lucas, in fact, was never given a proper directive, either to build up a strong defensive bridgehead, or to attack a clear-cut objective; nor was his corps organized for aggressive, mobile operation, being composed largely of marching infantry. In retrospect he seems to have acted sensibly.) The 5th Army plan depended for its success on breaking through the Gustav Line and joining the bridgehead troops at Anzio without delay, but the plan was basically unsound and muddled in execution.

Clark had at his disposal an American, two British and a French colonial infantry divisions and an American armoured division. The thrust line of his main attack was to be through the narrow Liri Valley, involving an assault crossing over the River Rapido by the American infantry division, which was to establish a bridgehead through which the armoured division was to make a dash to join the 6th Corps and in company with it liberate Rome. The flanks of the thrust line were to be covered by an attack by the French on the Montecassino massif which loomed over the Liri Valley on its north side, and by a British division on the south. The other British division was to cross the Garigliano near its mouth with the aim of attracting the German reserves. The timings were as follows: the first British division would lead off on the extreme left on 17 January 1944; the other was to cross the Rapido on the 19th, followed by the US division on the 20th, and the leading battalions of the 6th Corps would disembark on the beaches of Anzio on the morning of the 22nd. The main attack was a ghastly failure, the armoured division never crossed, and Lucas found himself on his own, his corps, in Churchill's contemptuous words, 'a stranded whale'; an unjust comparison, since it proceeded to fight stoutly, but it was an offensive, not a defensive battle that had been intended.

Kesselring's reaction to the landing at Anzio was prompt. By 1700 on the 22nd units drawn from every division within reach arrived – 'all higgledy-piggledy' is the phrase used by his translator – but with the instinctive feel of German troops for the correct action in an emergency each made contact with his neighbour to form a cordon hemming in Lucas. Soon divisions began to arrive, to be formed into corps, and the corps were brought under the command of General von Mackensen and his 14th Army headquarters. The 6th Corps was soon fighting for its life. Clark, desperate somehow to take the pressure off Lucas, began the series of attacks on the strongest part of the Gustav Line known to history as the First, Second and Third Battles of Cassino, about which whole volumes have been written. All failed. When the fighting died down in mid-March 1944 Kesselring still held the Gustav Line from coast to coast, but Lucas's 6th Corps at Anzio had defeated Mackensen's counter-offensive. The 6th Corps remained either a hostage to Kesselring, demanding

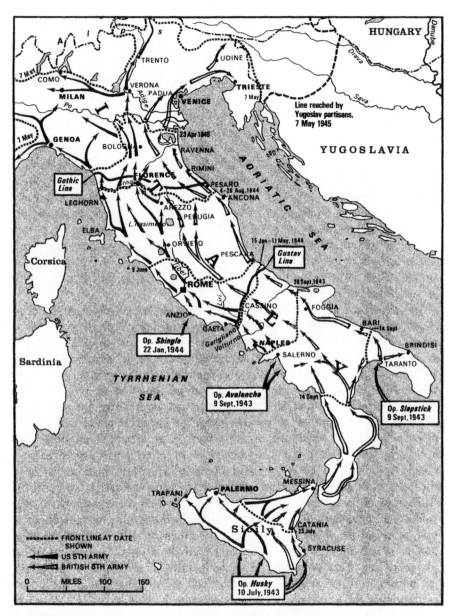

Italy, 1943–45

rescue, or a pistol pointed at the rear of the Gustav Line, depending on the point of view.

By March, therefore, Kesselring had fulfilled his promise to hold the Allies in southern Italy, but the future was bleak. The war in Russia was eating up German infantry replacements, and those that could be spared for Italy were few, very young and poorly trained. His divisions were so reduced that he had to support them by using ex-prisoners of war of Soviet origin – Turkomans, Cossacks and Ukrainians – for administrative duties and as labour in combat units, and he had to order the service and base units to form small battle-groups for use in an emergency. Some of his infantry divisions could do little more than hold the line, so for counter-attacks and the defence of key areas like Cassino he had to rely on élite units like the parachutists and the panzer-grenadiers. A new and ominous development was the aggressiveness of the growing Italian resistance movement, whose bands were harrying his line of communications and ambushing or sniping at German troops in the rear areas, requiring ever more units to be detached to protect them. Had he known the weight of the blow about to fall on the Gustav Line in May it might have removed the smile from even his cheerful face.

In accordance with a plan made by Alexander's new and able Chief of Staff, Major-General John Harding, both the Allied armies in their next effort were to be concentrated on the Cassino-Garigliano front. A British, Canadian and a Polish corps were to break the impasse at Cassino and drive through the Liri Valley, using 1,000 tanks and supported by 1,050 guns. A French corps of three infantry divisions, a mountain division and an irregular corps of 8,000 Moroccan mountaineers was to force a passage through the mountains, and the US 2nd Corps was to advance along the narrow corridor between the mountains and the Mediterranean to Anzio. At an appropriate moment the 6th Corps was to break out of its bridgehead striking north-east, to cut the escape route of the 10th Army. The essence of Harding's plan was to drive the 10th and 14th Armies apart and destroy them separately, and had the Allied and German Groups exchanged commanders that no doubt is what would have happened. As it turned out, no envelopment, no carving-up as was typical of the *Blitzkrieg* took place. A much-quoted saying of the elder Moltke is that no plan survives contact with the enemy. In Italy no Allied plan until 1945 survived exposure to the inability of the Allies to co-operate, the hostility of Clark towards the British and the strong dislike which Leese, commanding the 8th Army, personally entertained for Clark. Clark, who had set his heart on entering Rome before the British, and using only American troops, ordered the 6th Corps to turn its attack north-west away from the north-east across the German line of retreat; he refused to allow any double envelopment since he regarded it as aid to the 'British'. Kesselring, who put the blunder down to Allied incompetence, declared Rome an open city, extricated his forces in masterly fashion, formed a united front with both his armies, and fell back at leisure on his next main line of resistance in the northern Apennines, pausing to give the Allies a bloody nose if they pressed too closely. In the late summer his armies were in the process of manning the outposts of the Gothic Line. (He did not realize that Clark's inactivity after the liberation of Rome on 4 June was due to his having to surrender all his French troops and a US corps for the projected invasion of southern France.)

Both Kesselring and Harding had recognized that the city of Bologna was the key to the battle for northern Italy. Harding's plan was for a concentrated thrust by both armies along the direct route through the mountains. This was discarded in response to the objections of Leese who considered the Adriatic coast offered better prospects to an army strong in tanks, but it is not unfair to add that his previous experience of Clark's ideas of co-operation had disgusted him, and he preferred to act on his own. Alexander weakly allowed each commander to attack on the axis he preferred: Leese towards Rimini, hoping to gain elbow-room for his armour in the plain of Emilia; and Clark on the direct route over the mountains on Bologna, his consent obtained by the transfer to him of one of Leese's corps, with the result that neither army was able to exploit its initial success in breaking into the Gothic defences. Kesselring knew nothing of these bargains, but was thankful to find that the Allies had once more reverted to the policy of dividing their forces. He succeeded in halting both thrusts, but only after some of the bitterest fighting in Italy, even counting Cassino. The 8th Army plugged on in its 'methodical' fashion until it reached Faenza in December, when it halted for the winter. The 5th, after heroic efforts, was halted by Clark on 7 October 1944, having suffered such severe infantry losses that it could not continue the fight, but by then Kesselring had fought his last great battle in Italy. On the 23rd his staff car collided with a heavy gun on tow and he received injuries in the face and head terrible enough to have killed a less robust man. He returned, still only convalescent, to command his Army Group briefly in March 1945. Its situation was dire. Supplies, transport, motor fuel and ammunition were all deficient, some of its best units had been sent to reinforce the battle in the west, but most disturbing, the field reports of the winter fighting showed that the tactics and fighting power of the Allied troops had greatly improved, and the splendid German infantry no longer enjoyed their old superiority. Kesselring perceived that yet another pitched battle would be fatal. He was wondering how best to obtain Hitler's consent to his plan to roll with the punch of the Allies' spring offensive when he was summoned to report to the Führer at OKW. There he learnt that he was to take over as Commander-in-Chief West from von Rundstedt forthwith.

Kesselring's reluctance to speak harshly of anyone (except Rommel) in his memoirs is extended to Hitler, so his reaction to the briefing he was given, 'which lasted hours, was remarkably lucid and showed an astonishing grasp of detail', is of historical interest, quite apart from underlining Kesselring's capacity for accepting any task, however desperate: the Führer, according to himself, was about to win the war. All that Kesselring had to do in the west was to hold on and deny every foot of German soil. A new, fresh Army, the 12th, was in the process of being formed. (It was a phantom.) The Luftwaffe was about to be equipped with a new wonder weapon, the 'People's Fighter'. (Real enough: it was a jet fighter, but never to go into production.) Admiral Dönitz was about to revive the U-Boat war with a new wonder-submarine. Hitler's intention was to stabilize the Russian front, and then he would turn on the Anglo-Americans.[11] Kesselring could not fail to recognize all this as moonshine, but he set about fighting his last battle with the same operational touch and attention to detail as if it were his first.

There is no point in recounting the last desperate manoeuvres of March and April 1945 in defence of Germany against the Western Allies: it is enough to say that eighty-five Allied divisions were pressing on the last German defence west of the Rhine and that the Americans had crossed the river at Remagen. To stop them Kesselring had fifty-one divisions, the majority down to 5,000 all ranks, and very little armour. The Luftwaffe, or what was left of it, was fully engaged in defence against the Allied bombers. Morale was so bad that desertion was rife, and Kesselring had to organize officer patrols and cordons of police to net the men flooding back as soon as a battle started: to such a state had the once proud German Army been reduced.

Kesselring, like his fellow German generals, was kept going by fear of the Russians and what he thought would be the fate of the German armies if they surrendered to them and not to the Allies, and by the Allied leaders' demand for unconditional surrender, but he was too sensible not to realize that the sooner an orderly capitulation took place the better it would be for Germany. As early as the autumn of 1944 he had heard of and approved of the tentative approach made by the ss General Wolff to the United States representative of the oss based in Switzerland. He now fought on with some desperate hope that the German armies on both Western and Italian Fronts would be allowed to surrender to the British or the Americans. In April 1945, when German resistance was about to collapse, his command was extended to include Germany south of the line Hamelin-Brunswick-Brandenburg, Italy, Yugo-slavia and part of the South-East Front against the advancing Russians, and as such he was made the plenipotentiary for surrender in that area. Any hopes of anything other than an abject surrender were dashed when his offer to provide engineer and signals personnel to help restore communications in Germany was ignored. He was thrown into a prison camp and deprived of his Field-Marshal's baton. Worse was in store. He was to be indicted as a war criminal.

In non-legal language the charge against Kesselring was that when in Italy he issued written instructions to those of his commanders engaged in anti-partisan operations which could be interpreted as condoning acts of brutality and he was therefore directly responsible for the frightful massacre of 335 Italians in the Ardeatine caves in March 1944, and also for a total of 1,087 people killed by way of reprisal during the Italian campaign. His team of German lawyers deployed a strong defence under three heads: evidence from some of his own officers and from Italian civil authorities, including a bishop, that he had been scrupulous in avoiding civilian casualties; that the partisans had been completely in breach of those provisions of international law which legitimize the actions of irregulars, franc-tireurs and guerillas, and that in any case Hitler had removed responsibility for security matters in Italy from the Commander-in-Chief and transferred them to the German Security Service (*Sicherheitsdienst*) and the police branch of the ss. Kesselring was not tried at Nuremberg by one of the War Crimes Tribunals presided over by trained lawyers and judges, but as late as May 1947 in Venice by a court-martial composed of British officers advised by a judge-advocate (who takes no part in verdict or sentence); he was there found guilty and sentenced to death. How far this was a miscarriage of justice is too complex a subject to discuss here. It is sufficient to say that the sentence, if not the verdict, aroused enough disquiet in England to lead to Churchill appealing to Attlee (then Prime Minister) to intervene, and Kesselring was reprieved, but condemned to life imprisonment. In 1952 he required skilled medical attention for the after-effects of his head injury, was released and his sentence remitted 'as an act of clemency'.

Throughout his two years as a prisoner of war, his eight weeks awaiting execution and five years in the civil gaol in Werl in the German Federal Republic, Kesselring behaved with courage, dignity and, indeed, the haughtiness appropriate to his rank. He was called as a witness at Nuremberg as to German bombing policy and, nettled by the tone of the cross-examination by the British prosecutor, declared: 'I have given my evidence as a German officer with over forty years' service, and as a German Field-Marshal under oath! If my statements are so little respected I shall make no further depositions,' which drew an apology.[12] He was not grateful for his reprieve. As a German officer he could face a firing-squad with resignation, believing that he was innocent of any crime, but to be locked up with 'professional criminals' and 'the worst felons' was an insult. He did not, however, cease to be cheerful or entirely lose his dry sense of humour. A photograph of him awaiting execution shows him still wearing his famous grin, and carrying a nosegay of wild flowers he had just picked. Asked in Werl how he liked his prison task, he replied, 'In my wildest dreams I never imagined that I would become a paper-bag-gummer....'[13] Fortunately his regime, at first spitefully punitive, was greatly improved, allowing him to study warfare and compose the narrative that was published as his *Memoirs* in England in 1953. Always candid, sometimes unpolished and even artless, they offer a unique insight in to the mind of a German general at grips with the problems of politics and war.

The question remains of the place of Kesselring in the role of generals whose profiles appear in this book. As regards the conduct of operations, the standard of German generals as a class was so good – it is not unfair to say better than their opponents – that any of them could have directed his battles equally well. The German General Staff system produced admirable Corps and Army commanders and their inseparable Chiefs of Staff. Where Kesselring is remarkable is that he had little special training in operations and never graduated through Division, Corps and Army. He had all the requisite qualities, but arrived at them by thinking them out for himself. The principle of mobility – what he calls 'free operations' – the need to keep a reserve, the ability to improvise, and above all the ability to react to a crisis, as he did at Anzio, without a lot of contingency planning – too often so much waste paper – came to him naturally. He was a cool hand. Time and again he choked off Army and Corps commanders begging for permission to give a little ground, yet eventually gave way at the psychological moment. He had immense authority. 'Smiling Albert' he may have been, but no one disobeyed him twice. He sacked Mackensen unhesitatingly for disobeying an order to detach a reserve division to his other army, and also the excellent commander of the 16th Panzer Division, who for four days had held on when under attack by the whole 5th Army at Salerno in 1943, for being slow to respond to an order to counter-attack later that year.

But as said, such behaviour was expected of all German generals. Where Kesselring was unique is that he is the only one who had the difficult task of acting as supreme commander in coalition war, at the interface where politics and grand strategy meet. He is difficult to fault. If he had one, it was the obsessive loyalty and rigid sense of duty that trapped him, and others, in the service of an Adolf Hitler. After forty years we can view his predicament with sympathy.

NOTES

1 *The Memoirs of Field-Marshal Kesselring*, trans. Lynton Hudson, William Kimber, London, 1953 (henceforth *Memoirs*), p. 15.
2 *Ibid.*, p. 20.
3 The German General Staff officer in a formation HQ concerned with supply was the second senior, the '1(b)'. Sometimes at Corps and Army HQ he was referred to by his old designation, the *quartier-* or the *oberquartiermeistergeneral*. Albert Seaton, *The German Army 1939–1945*, Weidenfeld & Nicolson, London, 1982, p. 99.
4 *Memoirs*, p. 59.
5 *Ibid.*, p. 65 and Chapter 11, *passim*.
6 *Ibid.*, p. 88.
7 *Ibid.*, p. 109.

8 *Ibid.*, paraphrased from p. 207.
9 *Ibid.*, p. 171.
10 D. Graham and S. Bidwell, *Tug of War: The Battle for Italy 1943–45*, Hodder & Stoughton, London, 1986, p. 100 and note 4, Diary of General John P. Lucas.
11 *Memoirs*, pp. 237–9.
12 *Ibid.*, p. 295.
13 *Ibid.*, p. 312.

CHRONOLOGY: ALBERT KESSELRING

1885	Born Bayreuth, Bavaria
1904	Accepted as probationer for commission in Bavarian artillery
1914	On active service with his battery on Western Front
1915–17	On artillery Staff in France
1917	Appointed to General Staff, and posted to a division on the Eastern Front
1918	Holds appointments on Staff at Corps and Army level
1919–22	Battery commander
1922	In Defence Ministry as Chief of Staff to General H. von Seeckt, in office of 'army direction'
1929	In charge of manpower reorganization (*Sparkommissar*)
1931–2	Promoted full colonel, commands artillery regiment
1933	Transferred to Air Ministry as civilian director of administration
1936	Appointed Chief of Staff, Luftwaffe
1937	Commander, Third Air Region
1938	Commander, First Air Fleet
1939	Takes part in invasion of Poland
1940	Cross-posted to command of Second Air Fleet, commands land/air operations during invasion of the Low Countries, air operations over Dunkirk and in Battle of Britain
1941	Invasion of Russia. In December appointed Axis Commander-in-Chief in the Mediterranean
1942–August 1943	Involved in air and land operations in North Africa and Sicily, and in Southern Italy
1944	Commander-in-Chief in all Italy and of Army Group C until October, when seriously injured
1945	Returns briefly to Italy, but in March appointed Commander-in-Chief West. Prisoner of war, charged with war crimes
1947	Sentenced to death, reprieved, and began life imprisonment in civilian gaol, Werl, West Germany
1952	Released, as 'act of clemency'
1953	Published memoirs
1960	Died

PART IV

The Battlefront Generals

ROMMEL

12

ROMMEL

Field-Marshal Erwin Rommel

MARTIN BLUMENSON

In the nearly half-century since the Second World War, while the reputations of many major military participants have diminished, Field-Marshal Erwin Rommel's has grown. Highly admired by both sides, not merely for his inspirational leadership and skill but also for his charisma and chivalry, Rommel was a throwback to the medieval knight in his personal traits, a master of modern warfare in his professional attainments.

Although perceived by some observers as no more than a superb tactician and battle commander, deficient in his strategic sense, weak in his logistical appreciation, fitted for nothing higher than divisional direction, Rommel is increasingly regarded as a soldier who had a clear and compelling view of strategy and logistics and a sound and balanced touch for grand operations. That he argued with his superiors demonstrates his opposition to policies now considered inappropriate. That he denounced those who failed to provide him with adequate supplies shows his sensitivity to the support function. That he displayed a pessimism throughout the latter part of the conflict indicates his prescience as to the final result.

Boldness, the use of surprise, a readiness to accept risks, and an intuitive feel of the battlefield distinguished Rommel's exercise of command. Although he often suffered disadvantages, including resources inferior to those of his adversaries, a lack of air superiority, intelligence no match for the Allied Ultra secret intercepts, he was brilliantly successful in attack and remarkably resourceful in defence.

What brought Rommel down ultimately were political, strategic, and logistical matters outside of his responsibilities. Denied the means to achieve victory of a wider scope beyond the individual stage on which he performed, Rommel, like giants before him who met defeat, among them Hannibal, Napoleon, Robert E. Lee, reflects a fame substantially more lustrous than most of his contemporaries.

He had more than his share of luck. Instead of serving as a young officer in the static trench warfare on the Western Front where he might have become ingrained to positional combat, he learned about mobility on other fronts. If attracting Adolf Hitler's favour brought him command of an armoured division in the campaign of 1940 against Britain and France, he had the vision and energy to take his men into the forefront of the *Blitzkrieg*. Instead of fighting on the endless steppes in Russia, where he might have been lost to sight, he operated somewhat independently in the more limited space of North Africa. He had the good fortune to avoid the inconclusive Italian campaign and instead to be at the decisive place where the Allies invaded Normandy.

There was bad luck too. After escaping death on numerous occasions when he led his troops in combat, he became the victim of an Allied pilot who strafed his solitary vehicle on an obscure road between Livarot and Vimoutiers and knocked him out of the war. His serious injury occurred at a critical time, three days before the putsch against Hitler on 20 July 1944, and removed him from the clandestine movement to replace the Führer who had, in Rommel's eyes, lost the war and was senselessly destroying Germany. For a warrior who embodied the best principles and precepts of his profession, it was a stroke of misfortune to serve a detestable master.

Unlike many in the German Army who functioned at high levels of authority and responsibility because of their high-born caste and special education, Rommel was a member neither of the *junker* class of Prussian aristocrats nor of the inner circle of the General Staff, both of which facilitated military advancement. His father and grandfather were solidly bourgeois schoolteachers, instructors in mathematics, in the province of Württemberg, although his mother was of a noble family. Born in Heidenheim, near Ulm, on 15 November 1891, one of five children, Rommel was small for his age and quiet. Despite mediocre grades in his studies, he passed his examinations.

Although his respectable Swabian parents of moderate means lacked influential friends in military society, Rommel entered the Army on 19 July 1910, joining the 124th Infantry Regiment at Weingarten as a cadet. After promotion to corporal in October and to sergeant in December, he gained his commission in March 1911 at the War Academy in Danzig, where he met Lucie Maria Mollin, later his wife.

As a second-lieutenant, Rommel trained with his regiment. Interested in all things military, he was serious in his duties, good at drill. A listener rather than an assertive talker, he established an easy rapport with his men, yet tolerated no slipshod work. He was even-tempered, careful, business-like. Attached to the 49th Field Artillery Regiment in Ulm on 1 March 1914, he returned to the infantry upon the outbreak of the First World War.

Combat revealed at once what became his trademarks. In his first action on 22 August, during the German advance to the Marne, when he reconnoitred with his platoon in a heavy fog near Longwy, he and three men reached the village of Bleid, held by the French. Rounding a farm building, Rommel saw fifteen or twenty soldiers in the road. Without hesitation he opened fire. His platoon came up and, in compliance with his orders, cleared the hamlet, half the men setting houses and barns ablaze with bundles of straw while the others attacked the enemy troops taken by surprise. Rommel's characteristic independence and boldness had paid off.

Near Varennes, he was wounded in the thigh on 24 September when he attacked three French soldiers in a wood even though he had no rounds for his rifle. He received the Iron Cross, 2nd Class. After hospitalization, he led his platoon on 29 January 1915 through barbed wire into a French position, captured four blockhouses, repulsed a battalion counter-attack, then retired with the loss of fewer than a dozen men. Again, bold penetration and independent action had gained results. Rommel received the Iron Cross, 1st Class.

Promoted to *Oberleutnant* (first lieutenant), wounded again in the leg, Rommel was transferred after recuperating on 10 April 1915 to the *Württembergische Gebirgsbattalion*, a mountain unit in the process of forming. The battalion had six rifle companies and six machine-gun platoons, which were combined in various ways as task forces tailored for specific missions. In this assignment, Rommel firmly grasped the nature of combat mobility.

After intensive training on Austrian slopes, the battalion moved to the Vosges Mountains of France, a relatively quiet front. During a leave of absence in November 1916, Rommel married Lucie Mollin in Danzig. Around the end of the year, the battalion travelled to Romania to join the *Alpenkorps*, a corps of mountain warfare troops.

Two conspicuously successful attacks marked Rommel's performance. In January 1917 he and his men infiltrated enemy positions in freezing weather at night, reached the village of Gagesti, opened fire, then collected 400 prisoners. In August, although wounded in the arm, he led four companies in single file through the woods undetected, attacked and captured the strongly fortified position at Mount Cosna.

His greatest feat in the First World War occurred in Italy, after his battalion had been moved, as part of the German 14th Army, to help the Austrians in the autumn offensive on the Isonzo. It was Rommel's exploit, the capture of the key Italian position of Monte Matajur late in October which turned the Battle of Caporetto into an Italian disaster and rout, with a loss of 250,000 prisoners.

What happened was this: When the main attack was held, Rommel took two companies before dawn across the front to the flank, then penetrated the Italian positions by infiltration and captured an Italian artillery battery. Leaving a company at that place, Rommel pushed on. When an Italian battalion counter-attacked his unit behind him, Rommel returned, struck the battalion in the rear, compelled surrender, and captured more than 1,000 prisoners, whom he sent back under guard. The remaining four companies of Rommel's battalion came forward, and he led them all in single file for 2 miles. Cutting a main road, Rommel's men captured a supply column, 50 officers, and 2,000 *Bersaglieri* troops. Rommel then proceeded to the main Italian position, which he entered boldly with several riflemen and called upon the garrison to surrender. Forty-three officers and 1,500 soldiers complied. Continuing, Rommel and his men scaled Monte Matajur from the rear, captured the dominating height and the troops defending it. Although Rommel had been constantly on the move for fifty hours, by his ruthless advance he obtained the surrender of 150 officers, 9,000 soldiers, and 81 guns. For this he received the decoration *Pour le Mérite*, normally reserved for senior generals, and promotion to captain.

Shortly thereafter, with six men, Rommel swam the Piave River during the hours of darkness. After his handful of troops, from widely dispersed positions, fired into the village of Longarone, Rommel boldly walked in, demanded and received the garrison's capitulation.

That was the last of his combat activity. After a leave of absence, he returned to duty to serve in Staff assignments. He had by then made his mark as a leader. By his physical and mental hardiness, his audacity, his ability to create and profit from surprise, he had built his reputation as an outstanding junior officer.

The end of the war hardly interrupted his military career. On 21 December 1918 Rommel rejoined the 124th Infantry Regiment at Weingarten. In mid-1919, he commanded an internal security company in Friedrichshafen, then served a year in a training regiment at Schwabisch Gemund. When he transferred on 1 January 1921 to Stuttgart and took command of a company in the 13th Infantry Regiment, a position he held for almost eight years, he was one of the 4,000 regular officers permitted by the Treaty of Versailles and clearly marked for promotion in a future re-expanded German Army. During Rommel's inter-war years he learned the Army's training and administrative practices thoroughly. He rose in rank, assuming increasing responsibilities and efficiently discharging them. Colleagues remarked his steadfast dedication to, as well as his excellence in all things military and his capacity to inspire the devotion of his troops.

On 1 October 1929 Rommel became an instructor at the Infantry School in Dresden. During his four-year tour, he wrote a book called *Infantry Attacks*, an account of his professional experience and observations. Publication –

400,000 copies were sold in Germany before and during the Second World War – brought him prominence in military circles and attracted the favourable notice of Adolf Hitler.

Promoted to major on 10 October 1933, Rommel took command of the 3rd Battalion, 17th Infantry Regiment, a mountain unit training at Goslar. Two years later, on 15 October 1935, as a lieutenant-colonel, he became an instructor at the War College in Potsdam. He was elevated in 1937 to colonel. His next assignment was director of the War College at Wiener Neustadt from 9 November 1938, but temporary duty took him from time to time to command Hitler's personal security battalion. He was with the Führer in Czechoslovakia's Sudetenland in October 1938 and in Prague on 19 March 1939.

On 23 August 1939, Rommel was promoted to major-general and transferred to Hitler's headquarters with responsibility for the Führer's safety. When Germany invaded Poland, Rommel was in a position to observe the campaign from the top. He was in Warsaw on 5 October, a week after the Polish capitulation.

Returning to Berlin, Rommel formed part of Hitler's extended entourage. Although he was uninterested in politics, Rommel admired the Führer. Hitler's earlier denunciation of the restrictive clauses of the Versailles Treaty had transformed lukewarm approval for him in the Army to a thrill of sympathy. His subsequent restoration of Germany to power and a prominent place in the world sustained and magnified the trust and acclaim. Among those who believed in Hitler himself, Rommel had serious reservations about the Nazis surrounding him.

For his part, Hitler liked Rommel, not only because of his efficiency and attention to duty but also because he was hardly the kind of aristocratic *junker* who made Hitler feel uncomfortable. Aware of Rommel's combat record in the First World War and of his wish to fight again, Hitler asked what job he wanted. Having seen *Blitzkrieg* at work in Poland, Rommel wished for an armoured division. Hitler acceded.

On 15 February 1940, at the age of forty-eight, Rommel assumed command of the 7th Panzer Division stationed at Godesberg on the Rhine. He had less than three months to become familiar with his elements and personnel and to learn how to employ his tools. Always concerned with mobility, he was delighted with the greater speed and range of tanks. When the 'Phoney War' in the west came to a crashing end on 10 May 1940, Rommel's outfit was ready to sow the whirlwind.

Heading a division is the highest echelon where a commander can have intimate contact with the fighting. Instead of directing his troops from a headquarters in the rear, Rommel preferred to lead from the front. As he later wrote,

There are always moments when the commander's place is not back with his staff but up with the troops. It is sheer nonsense to say that maintenance of the men's morale is the job of the battalion commander alone. The higher the rank, the greater the effect of the example. The men tend to feel no kind of contact with a commander who, they know, is sitting somewhere in headquarters. What they want is what might be termed a physical contact with him. In moments of panic, fatigue or disorganization, or when something out of the ordinary has to be demanded from them, the personal example of the commander works wonders, especially if he has had the wit to create some sort of legend around himself.[1]

Rommel was usually with his advanced guard at the cutting edge of combat. In his journal of the campaign of 1940 he forthrightly, although modestly, showed the personal dangers he underwent – almost killed in his tank on at least two occasions – as he pulled his units into a slashing, irresistible attack, pressing always deeply into the enemy rear to provoke amazement, confusion, and eventually paralysis among his adversaries. Had the offensive movement failed, it would be judged reckless. By virtue of its overwhelming success, and particularly Rommel's stupefying swiftness and unexpected appearance on the battlefield time after time, his formation became known as the 'Ghost Division', he himself as the 'Knight of the Apocalypse'. The campaign made him a popular hero in Germany.

The *Sichelschnitt* offensive starting on 10 May debouched through the Ardennes region and rolled towards the sea, eventually cutting off and trapping the bulk of the French and British forces in Belgium. In that advance, Rommel was in the vanguard. He travelled westward across the northern part of Luxemburg without interference, crossed the Belgian border about 30 miles south of Liège, and swept aside slight opposition. Over the Ourthe River on the morning of 11 May, Rommel dispersed French resistance and was on the River Meuse near Dinant on the afternoon of 12 May. He had great difficulty forcing a crossing, but by the morning of 13 May, thanks to his finding a way across a weir himself, his division was the first to be on the far bank. He had a secure bridgehead about 2 miles deep at dawn, 14 May, and he raced southwestward towards Philippeville (see map on page 399). Brushing through a hardly formed French stop-line on 15 May, Rommel penetrated the Maginot Line extension near Sivry and began to drive deep into France. Twelve miles to the west was Avesnes, and Rommel captured the town early on 17 May.

Without pause, he drove westward to Landrecies, where he crossed the Sambre River over a bridge still intact. Continuing for 8 miles, he reached Le Cateau and seized it on 17 May. He had moved nearly 50 miles in two days. Pushing on westwards, Rommel surrounded and captured Cambrai. He reached Arras early on 20 May, then fought for three days to capture it.

On 21 May, however, a small force of British tanks, supported by a few infantry and by some French forces, counter-attacked him by surprise, causing a brief crisis soon overcome by his dynamic leadership, but leading to ripples of alarm all the way up the German chain of command. This was one factor in Hitler's and Rundstedt's decision to halt the Panzer divisions.

When Hitler rescinded the order on the 26th, Rommel advanced northward, curling to the northeast and striking toward Lille. He reached the western outskirts of the city and blocked the roads, thus precipitating its fall. Directed to pause and regroup, Rommel, who had taken more than 10,000 prisoners of war as well as 100 enemy tanks and 27 guns, disengaged his troops for rest, reorganization and resupply. He was ordered to visit the Führer on 2 June and was welcomed by a radiant Hitler who said, 'Rommel, we were very worried about you during the attack.'[2]

The German Army now turned south to finish off the weakened French. Early on 5 June, Rommel and 7th Panzer Division crossed the Somme between Abbeville and Amiens over a bridge still standing and raced ahead. Covering 60 miles in four days, he reached the River Seine at Elbeuf, near Rouen. There on 10 June, he swung 60 miles to the northwest, reaching the coast between Fécamp and St Valéry-en-Caux, and trapping British and French forces seeking to embark for England. On 12 June, about 20,000 troops – the figures vary widely – surrendered. A capitulating French general told him frankly, 'You are too rapid for us.'

Three days later, Rommel returned to the River Seine, crossed it, then resumed the advance to the south and west, the objective this time Cherbourg. Rolling through Evreux, Falaise, and Flers to Coutances before turning north to La Haye du Puits, Rommel approached the port city. He had travelled at speeds of 20 to 30 miles per hour to cover more than 200 miles in two days. His advance of 150 miles in a single day was the longest ever attained in warfare to that time.

Rommel arrived in the outskirts of Cherbourg on 17 June, as Marshal Philippe Pétain was seeking an armistice. Rommel accepted the surrender of about 30,000 men on the morning of 19 June as the government of France was capitulating.

The rest was anticlimax. Rommel drove southward to Rennes, which he reached on 21 June, then continued to the Spanish border to take possession of the Atlantic coast of France. Afterwards, he brought his division back to the Bordeaux area for occupation duties.

In a campaign lasting six weeks, Rommel captured the astonishing total of almost 100,000 prisoners and more than 450 tanks. He lost 682 men killed, 1,646 wounded, 296 missing and 42 tanks knocked out. No one had conducted *Blitzkrieg* with such assurance, balance and speed. Rommel's photograph appeared everywhere in Germany, his name was on everyone's lips.

Despite his remarkable feat, Rommel waited six months, until January 1941, for elevation to lieutenant-general. He then embarked on his North African adventure, with which his name will forever be associated. Despite inhospitable terrain, sandstorms, great variations in temperature, vast distances, an inadequate diet for his troops, shortages of fuel and ammunition, relatively small forces, as well as other difficulties, he showed his power to produce the unexpected. His new assignment enlarged his outlook from a tactical view to one of strategic scope.

The circumstances were these. After the whirlwind campaign in western Europe, the evacuation of Allied troops from the Continent, notably at Dunkirk, and the surrender of France, Hitler unleashed the Battle of Britain in the air to prepare for invasion. As the aerial confrontation was drawing to a close, Benito Mussolini, who had joined Hitler in the attack against France, opened a new theatre of operations. His Army of about half a million men in Libya advanced into Egypt in September 1940, against about 30,000 British troops, the objective apparently the Suez Canal. After initial success and inconclusive gains, the Italians stopped. Late in October, Mussolini further extended his war effort by invading Greece, where he met fierce resistance.

In North Africa, the British counter-attack on 9 December won staggering victories over the Italians, pushing them out of Cyrenaica, the eastern half of Libya. When Mussolini appealed to Hitler for help, Hitler responded by sending Luftwaffe units to Italy in January 1941 to aid the Italian ground forces and to protect Axis convoys in the Mediterranean. In February, Hitler put at Mussolini's disposal the *Afrika Korps*, consisting of two German divisions due to arrive in stages and to be at full strength by the end of May. In command was the newly promoted Rommel, who was to operate under Italian theatre supervision, and to have several Italian armoured divisions under him. Rommel was given essentially a defensive mission, to prevent the expulsion of the Italians from North Africa, but that was hardly his flair.

When Rommel arrived in Tripoli on 12 February 1941, all seemed to be lost. In less than two months, the British had taken Tobruk, Derna, Benghazi, the capital of Cyrenaica, and El Agheila, at the entrance into Tripolitania. They had advanced almost 400 miles westward from their bases and had captured 130,000 Italian troops, 1,300 guns and 400 tanks. Although General Sir Archibald Wavell, the British Commander-in-Chief Middle East, could no doubt have gone on and seized Tripoli, the British government's decision to intervene in Greece deprived him of a corps and compelled him to halt his offensive. This was hardly apparent to the Axis, and the Italians implored Rommel to save Tripoli.

He was thinking of larger things. At his insistence, the first German units coming to Libya unloaded hastily and at night under spotlights. Rommel told his German commanders that they would prevent the English from entering into Tripolitania. But the situation became stable as the British remained in place.

Rommel traveled to the Führer's headquarters on 19 March, received from Hitler the Oakleaves to the Knight's Cross for his actions in France, and learned the conditions of his employment. He could expect no reinforcements. Hitler had no intention of striking a decisive blow in North Africa in the near future. Two days later, Rommel received instructions to prepare a plan to reconquer Cyrenaica. According to all expectations, he could hardly attack until June when his two German divisions would be at hand. Instead, to gain surprise, as he said later in a characteristic statement, 'I took the risk against all orders and instructions because the opportunity seemed favourable.' He foresaw his greatest problem as the continued nourishment of his troops, for the British, abetted by their very secret Ultra intercepts of German signals, of which Rommel was unaware, were destroying many Axis transports in the Mediterranean Sea. With a suitable store of supplies stockpiled for the moment, Rommel launched an immediate offensive.

He struck on 31 March 1941, and what started as a reconnaissance in force developed into a fully-fledged attack. He compelled the British to abandon El Agheila and to lose Benghazi. By April, Rommel was in possession of all Cyrenaica except for Tobruk which held out, although isolated and on the Egyptian border. He could go no farther, for his petrol supplies were depleted. In fairness to Wavell, who under pressure from Churchill counter-attacked to no avail in June, it was to be said that the British were engaged not only in North Africa, but also in Greece, Syria, and elsewhere in Africa.

Rommel, whose operations left the world gasping in astonishment, now commanded *Panzergruppe Afrika*, consisting of his 2 German divisions, 4 Italian infantry divisions, and 2 Italian armoured divisions, all imbued with Rommel's spirit and dash. His reputation was immense. Sir Claude Auchinleck, who replaced Wavell in June 1941, advised his subordinate commanders, 'We speak too much of our friend Rommel.' He wished his troops to think of him as neither magician nor demon but simply as an ordinary German general. Obviously, such was not the case.

Auchinleck attacked on 18 November 1941 (the *'Crusader'* offensive) and by the end of the month forced Rommel, who was still short of supplies, into retreat. Rommel chose to give up ground in order to save his forces. Having the barest essentials of rations and ammunition, he quit Benghazi around Christmas, pulling back a step at a time, and reached the Mersa el Brega defensive line by 12 January 1942. In his final withdrawal, he had suffered no serious harm or loss, but the whole *Crusader* battle had cost him some 340 tanks and some 38,000 killed, wounded and missing.

Hitler despatched Field-Marshal Albert Kesselring and powerful air forces to Italy. As Kesselring gained air superiority over the central Mediterranean, Axis shipments to Rommel increased. On 5 January 1942 a convoy arrived in

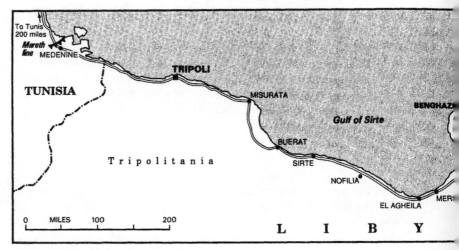

North Africa: the desert battlefield

Tripoli loaded with tanks, guns and supplies. Now in command of *Panzerarmee Afrika*, comprising all the German formations – 15th and 21st Panzer Divisions, and 90th Light – as well as all the Italian, Rommel decided to launch another 'impossible' counter-offensive before the orthodox (British or German) believed he could be ready, issuing his orders only the day before the attack in order to ensure secrecy.

Jumping off during the night of 21 January, Rommel advanced 30 miles to El Agheila and beyond. A week later he was in Benghazi and a few days after that Derna fell. Just as at the beginning of the previous year, a spoiling attack led with great dash caused the progressive disintegration of largely green British formations led by a creakingly clumsy command structure, further enhancing Rommel's moral ascendency over his enemy. By the end of January 1942 the campaign reached equilibrium again in mid-Cyrenaica, with the British 8th Army digging in along the 'Gazala Line', a zone of minefields and defended localities stretching from the Mediterranean to Bir Hacheim.

Both sides now pondered offensive plans. Churchill urged Auchinleck to attack in the desert at shortest possible delay, partly in order to win airfields in western Cyrenaica from which aircraft could cover the sea routes to Britain's hard-pressed island base of Malta. Auchinleck, all too aware of the technical weaknesses and lack of training of his mixed British Commonwealth army, pleaded for delay until overwhelming superiority could be built up. Eventually, and as a result of a direct order from London, the date for a British offensive was fixed for early June. But Rommel struck first, on 26 May. The Axis strategy, agreed between Hitler and Mussolini and their advisers, was that Rommel should defeat the 8th Army and advance to the Egyptian frontier, so neutralizing the British military threat. Here Rommel should halt, and the

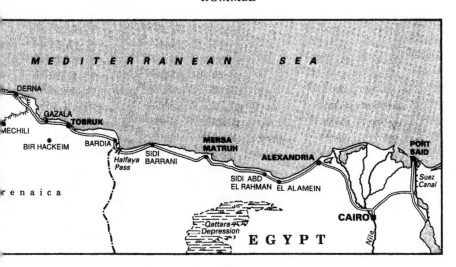

main Axis effort (especially in the air) would be switched to an operation to capture Malta, so putting an end to the Royal Navy's and the Royal Air Force's destruction of Rommel's seaborne supplies across the Mediterranean.

Operation *Venezia*, the offensive against the 8th Army on the Gazala Line, marked the climax of Rommel's performance as a daring battlefield commander against heavy odds, his success entirely due to brilliant quick-thinking opportunism and leadership from the front, in contrast to the slow, ponderous and remote British system of command. When his initial plan to swing south of Bir Hacheim and strike north to the sea, so cutting 8th Army off, failed, he established a 'bridgehead through the British minefields in the centre of the Gazala Line' – from the eastern or British side. Ensconced in this bridgehead behind an anti-tank screen, he smashed ill co-ordinated British counter-strokes, then destroyed the infantry garrisons of the Line piecemeal, including the Free French garrison at Bir Hacheim. On 11–12 June 1942, in a tank battle south of Tobruk at a desert locality dubbed by the British 'Knightsbridge', he inflicted losses of 260 tanks, virtually writing off 8th Army's armoured forces. On 21 June, in a sudden assault, he took the half-derelict fortress of Tobruk (held by Auchinleck at Churchill's urging), with a bag of over 30,000 prisoners. The news was given to Churchill while he was staying with President Roosevelt in the White House; a bleak moment, and one which consummated his obsession with Rommel and the need to beat him. Hitler now made Rommel a Field-Marshal – at forty-nine, the youngest in the German Army.

Rommel and *Panzerarmee Afrika* now stood on the Egyptian frontier. According to agreed general strategy, this was where he should halt so that all resources could be concentrated against Malta. Instead his astonishing victory in the Gazala battles lured him – and Hitler and Mussolini – into an attempt to occupy Egypt and then the rest of the Middle East. Visions opened of linking up with German forces in southern Russia, or driving east to India. Rommel therefore now led his exhausted and greatly diminished army in a chase to Alexandria. But on 1 July 1942, between Alamein (a mere halt on the coastal railway line) and the Quattara Depression, he ran into a freshly reinforced 8th Army under the direct command of General Sir Claude Auchinleck, Commander-in-Chief Middle East. Rommel's attacks foundered under concentrated artillery fire. On 9 July Auchinleck went over to the counter-offensive with a devastating attack by 9th Australian Division along the coast road, which routed the Italian Sabratha Division. Thereafter Auchinleck launched repeated counter-strokes, aiming them exactly at Rommel's Italian formations, thanks to Ultra decrypts of Axis signals. By the middle of July Rommel was having to employ all his German striking forces in trying to hold his own front together. He wrote to his wife: 'it can't go on like it for long, otherwise the front will crack. Militarily, this is the most difficult period I've ever been through.'[3]

He had thus failed to bring his great summer victories to a decisive conclusion. In September (by which time the 8th Army had been heavily reinforced) he tried once more, but was completely defeated in the Battle of Alam Halfa by the new 8th Army commander, Lieutenant-General Sir Bernard Montgomery, who refused to 'mix it' in a fluid armoured battle, but fought a largely static battle with well posted troops under cover of the Royal Air Force's air superiority. Throughout this time Rommel's efforts had been crippled for want of fuel and other necessities. 'The cause of the trouble', he later summarized in great frustration, 'lay in the over-organization and muddle which characterized the Italian supply staffs'.[4]

Having exhausted himself physically, suffering from fainting spells, stomach and intestinal difficulties, an enlarged liver and circulatory problems, beset also by discouragement over the seemingly insoluble difficulty of guaranteeing steady supplies for his troops, and troubled by the beginning of doubt about ultimate Axis victory, he departed from North Africa on 22 September 1942 on convalescent leave. He saw Mussolini in Rome and suggested that unless more supplies were forthcoming, North Africa should be evacuated to save the forces for the defence of Europe. This, Mussolini intimated, was a strategic and political issue beyond Rommel's business. He visited Hitler in East Prussia and tried to make the same point, but had to listen instead to Hitler's discussions of the new Tiger tanks and Nebelwerfer rockets. Then he retired with his wife to Semmering, near Vienna, to clear up his liver condition and erratic blood pressure. As he rested and recuperated, he expressed to his wife his first reservations about Hitler, whose absurd policy and strategy, according to Rommel, were losing the war.

Meanwhile, General Sir Harold Alexander (who had replaced Auchinleck as Commander-in-Chief, Middle East) and Montgomery were planning a huge set-piece offensive at Alamein, thanks to reinforcements of 40,000 men and 300 new Sherman tanks. On 23 October 1942 Montgomery launched the 8th Army into the second Battle of Alamein, with the objective, as Montgomery said, to 'eliminate Rommel'.

On the following afternoon, a member of Hitler's headquarters telephoned Rommel in Semmering to inform him that his successor as Commander of *Panzerarmee Afrika* in North Africa was missing and presumed dead or captured. Was Rommel sufficiently recovered to return if necessary? He was. That evening Hitler himself telephoned. Could Rommel start at once for North Africa if he were needed? Of course. Shortly after midnight, Hitler telephoned again. Would Rommel leave at once? Certainly.

He left on 25 October for Rome, where he learned that the merest trickle of supplies was getting across the Mediterranean, and reached Tripoli that evening. He toured the front early on 26 October and was appalled. The British had command of the air and the sea and were driving the Axis forces, whose reserves were all committed, from the battlefield. He warned Hitler, Mussolini, and Kesselring, the Commander-in-Chief South, to expect a disaster.

His first concern was to re-establish the defensive positions, but the British strength was overwhelming and his counter-attacks were beaten off with heavy losses.

By noon on 3 November, when his Italo-German *Panzerarmee* had lost 50,000 men (half of them captured), 400 tanks and 1,000 guns, when the Italian formations were falling apart, when fuel and ammunition were in very short supply, a message from Hitler directed Rommel to 'stand fast'. Rommel was stunned by Hitler's incomprehension and rigidity. What Hitler demanded was impossible. On the following day, when the British at last broke through his defences, he ordered a general withdrawal. It was the beginning of the end for the Axis in North Africa. Four days later, on 8 November, as his forces were retiring from Egypt, news came of Operation *Torch*, the Anglo-American landings in French Morocco and Algeria, the nearest of these about 1,500 miles to his west.

Continually circumventing 'no retreat' orders from Hitler and Mussolini, Rommel conducted a masterful retrograde movement, conserving the bulk of his remaining troops, delaying Montgomery's pursuit despite continuing shortages of fuel and ammunition. Although Montgomery had superior resources, especially in the air, and advance notice of Rommel's intentions and plans through the Ultra secret intelligence intercepts of Rommel's signals, Montgomery was unable to trap or to overwhelm him. This retreat cements Rommel's reputation as an outstanding leader in the field. Toward the end of November, Rommel was at the Mersa el Brega defensive line, about 600 miles west of El Alamein, 500 miles east of Tunisia. There he paused.

Hitler and Mussolini had as early as 9 November begun to send German and Italian troops into what they called the Tunisian bridgehead, the northeastern corner of Tunisia where Bizerta and Tunis are located, in order to confront the Anglo-Americans. On 20 November, they decided to make their major effort in Tunisia against the Anglo-Americans and French, who had joined the Allies. While the Axis sought to eliminate the Allies in Tunisia and to force Spain to enter the war on the Axis side, Rommel was to defend as much of Libya as he could. But ever since Second Alamein and the *Torch* landings Rommel had recognized that the Axis cause in North Africa was lost.

Rommel departed on 28 November for East Prussia where he conferred with Hitler, arguing that since no improvement in shipping across the Mediterranean could be expected, the long-term policy for North Africa should look ahead to eventual abandonment. Otherwise, the Axis army was sure to be destroyed. A furious Hitler hardly listened. A smouldering Rommel, who resented Hitler's lack of understanding, returned to Rome with Hermann Göring, who promised to look into and improve the supply shipments but who was really interested only in the art treasures of Italy.

Back in North Africa, Rommel decided to move his army out of Libya and into Tunisia. There he would strike westward and disrupt the Allies, perhaps expel them from Tunisia, before turning back eastward and to counter-attack Montgomery. To establish contact between his units and the Italo-German forces in northern Tunisia, Rommel dispatched several thousand Italian troops across the border into southern Tunisia. He was unaware of the difficulties he would encounter with Colonel-General Jürgen von Arnim, who took command of the Tunisian bridgehead on 9 December 1942.

Arnim set about capturing and blocking the passes in the Eastern Dorsale, a mountain range running somewhat parallel with the Tunisian east coast, thereby to create a protected corridor along the seaboard between his army in the north and Rommel's as it entered southern Tunisia. Taking the Pichon and Fondouk passes in the north, Arnim extended his control southward by seizing the Faid Pass on 30 January 1943. This, in effect, was the opening blow of what was to become the Battle of Kasserine Pass.

Meanwhile, on the last day of 1942, Mussolini authorized Rommel to withdraw slowly from Libya into Tunisia. Rommel started his non-motorized troops back across the border on 2 January 1943. He evacuated Tripoli, which the British entered on 23 January after an advance from El Alamein of 1,400 miles. Three days later, Rommel moved his headquarters into Tunisia. He had successfully conducted one of the longest retreats in history. He learned on that day of his eventual relief. No date was set, but after he had established his Italo-German *Panzerarmee* in the Mareth Line defences, he was to turn it over to General Giovanni Messe under the new name of First Italian Army.

Although Rommel suffered from headaches and insomnia, strained nerves and circulatory troubles, he was excited by the prospects in Tunisia. He had held his forces well in hand during a cruel retrograde movement, a great military achievement, and now he looked forward to the chance of going over once again on the offensive. Arnim, with an army of 100,000 men, faced the bulk of the Allies oriented on Bizerta and Tunis in the north, while Rommel, with his army of 70,000, confronted widely dispersed and inexperienced Americans and poorly equipped French forces in the south. It would be some time before Montgomery could assemble his troops for an attack on the Mareth Line. In that interval, Rommel could perhaps demoralize the Americans and French.

Kesselring came to Tunisia on 9 February and arranged with Arnim and Rommel for a strike west of the Eastern Dorsale. Arnim was to advance beyond Faid in the direction of the town of Sbeitla; Rommel, farther south, was to head for Gafsa (see map on page 345). Yet the plan had seriously ambiguous aspects, the most important being the lack of an overall commander. Arnim and Rommel were to operate independently.

Without co-ordinating his effort with Rommel's, Arnim attacked on 14 February and destroyed important French and American formations, driving them back to Sbeitla. Learning by accident on the following day that the Americans and French had abandoned Gafsa, Rommel sent units there to occupy the town, then directed them forward to Feriana and the airfields at Thelepte. They entered these places on 17 February. Rommel, who was settling his rearguards into the Mareth Line, was puzzled by Arnim's failure to press on and take Sbeitla, thereby further demoralizing their opponents.

Rommel pressed for authority to continue his attack. He had his eye on Tebessa, a major Allied supply centre just across the frontier in Algeria, and wished to make a wide envelopment of the Allied forces. On 18 February, he received permission to launch a more limited thrust towards the Sbiba and Kasserine passes in the Western Dorsale. If he penetrated these gaps in the mountains, he would threaten the expulsion of the Allies from Tunisia.

His action started on 19 February. Three days of violent attack produced nothing at Sbiba, where British, French and Americans stood in place. At Kasserine, Axis units entered the pass and seemed about to break through, but a magnificent stand by British, French, and Americans held firmly. Depressed and discouraged, no less by his inability to advance farther than by evidence of the better and more plentiful Allied weapons and equipment, Rommel called off his effort on 22 February and returned to the Mareth Line. He had won a great tactical victory and stunned the Allies in Tunisia, but he had failed to gain a strategic success. Having driven American and French troops 50 miles across the Sbeitla plain from the Eastern to the Western Dorsale, having inflicted on the Americans alone losses of more than 6,000 men (half of them captured), 183 tanks and 200 artillery pieces at a cost to him of fewer than 1,000 men and 20 tanks, Rommel had delivered a stinging and damaging, but less than mortal blow. In large part, his failure to do more resulted from Arnim's refusal to support his offensive. Arnim's rivalry had made it impossible to integrate the two armies into a single directed venture that might have brought disaster to the Allies.

On 23 February, turning over his army to Messe, Rommel moved up to command Army Group Afrika, with authority over both Arnim and Messe. The change came too late. Had Rommel had overall direction earlier, he might have gained an outstanding triumph in Tunisia. On 6 March, Messe attacked Montgomery at Medenine, where he was assembling for an offensive against the Mareth Line, and was crushingly defeated. It was obvious that the Axis could no longer delay Montgomery's assault preparations.

Three days later, Rommel flew to Rome. He saw Mussolini and Kesselring and informed them that further resistance in North Africa was useless. To remain there longer, he said, 'was now plain suicide'. They sent him on to Hitler. Rommel reiterated his wish to evacuate the Axis forces and to concentrate them in defence of Europe, and he pleaded with Hitler to save the troops. Instead Hitler decorated Rommel with the Oakleaves with Swords and Diamonds and ordered him on extended sick leave.

Further disillusioned by Hitler, distressed over the eventual outcome of the war, Rommel watched with dismay as the Tunisian campaign came to its conclusion. As he had predicted, the Allies completed the total destruction of the Axis forces in Tunisia, taking 250,000 prisoners, a total nearly equal to the German losses suffered a few months earlier at Stalingrad. Hitler told Rommel, 'I should have listened to you before.'[5]

With the southern coast of Europe from Spain to Turkey now open to Allied invasion, Rommel could see only dire consequences for the German war effort. 'The moment the first Allied soldier set foot on Italian soil,' he wrote, 'Mussolini was finished.' Worst of all, the German star was also in decline, the High Command hardly up to the trials ahead. Hitler himself, Rommel suspected, no longer expected to win but instead harboured a death wish for himself and for Germany, planning to drag Germany down to ruin with him.

In May 1943 Hitler started to question the stability of the Italo-German alliance. Concerned about a possible Italian withdrawal from the war, he called Rommel to duty at the Führer's headquarters in a vaguely defined staff position. Hitler decided to activate a skeleton Army-Group headquarters at Munich, disguised as a rehabilitation centre. In the event of what Hitler called Italian 'treachery', the supposed 'centre' was to move German troops into Italy, secure the Alpine passes, and occupy the northern part of the country. But nothing was to be done at once in order to avoid precipitating Italian capitulation.

In June or July (probably after the Allied landings in Sicily early in the latter month) Hitler, foreseeing an eventual Allied invasion of the Italian mainland, decided that he would be unable to hold all of the Italian peninsula if Italy surrendered. He determined to establish a defensive line in the northern Apennines in order to protect the agriculturally and industrially rich Po Valley.

False information planted by the British on a body washed up on the Spanish shore convinced Hitler of a forthcoming Allied descent on Greece. He appointed Rommel Commander-in-Chief of the southeastern theatre. Rommel flew to Salonika on 25 July, but late that evening he was recalled to Germany because Mussolini had been deposed from power that very day.

Rommel saw Hitler on 26 July, and the Führer talked of replacing Kesselring, the theatre Commander-in-Chief in Italy, with Rommel. But Hitler made no immediate move to do so, and Rommel went to Munich to take command of Army Group B. In case the Italians surrendered and withdrew from the war, Rommel was to occupy all the important passes, roads and railways in northern Italy while Kesselring withdrew his forces in the south to the north. When Kesselring's troops joined Rommel's in the northern Apennines, Rommel was to assume command over all the German forces in Italy. Enough German units had rolled across the German border into Italy under the pretence of helping the Italians defend against invasion, to enable Rommel to take control of northern Italy on 15 August 1943.

The Allies, after overrunning Sicily in mid-August, invaded the mainland early in September, and Badoglio's post-Mussolini government publicly announced its capitulation. British forces came ashore in the toe and heel of Italy, while American and British units landed at Salerno. In compliance with Hitler's strategy, Kesselring fought at Salerno long enough to extract the German forces farther south, then began a slow and skilful withdrawal up the boot. Rommel consolidated his control over northern Italy, his quick action thereby securing Kesselring's rear. Rommel opened his Army-Group headquarters at Lake Garda on 12 September.

Now ensued a debate between Kesselring and Rommel. Kesselring wished to defend Italy south of Rome, where excellent terrain facilitated positional warfare, in order to keep the Allies far from the Po valley and to prevent them from crossing the Adriatic into the Balkans. Rommel argued for Hitler's original strategy, for he believed that defensive lines in southern Italy would be outflanked too easily by Allied amphibious operations while the long German supply lines would be vulnerable to partisan sabotage and Allied air attack. He recommended an immediate withdrawal to his northern Apennines line.

To Hitler, Rommel seemed pessimistic, even defeatist, while Kesselring appeared optimistic. On 17 September, as the battle at Salerno was ending, Hitler told Kesselring to withdraw slowly to the Gustav Line, just south of Cassino, and there to hold. Hitler conferred with Kesselring and Rommel on

30 September. Rommel questioned the ability to defend in the south. Kesselring was positive in his attitude. Four days later, on 4 October Hitler directed Kesselring to defend the Gustav Line and its advanced positions in strength. He instructed Rommel to build fortifications in the north and to send two of his divisions and some artillery to Kesselring. Later in the month, Hitler telephoned Kesselring, who expressed certainty about keeping the Allies out of Rome. Early in November, Hitler telephoned Rommel, who repeated his doubts.

Making up his mind on 6 November, Hitler named Kesselring as the supreme commander in Italy, and informed Rommel of a special mission he was to undertake. In anticipation of the Allied cross-Channel invasion, expected in the spring or summer of 1944, Rommel was to make tours of inspection of the coastal defences along the North Sea, the Channel and the Atlantic. On 21 November Rommel turned over his command to Kesselring, who formally assumed responsibility for the Italian campaign.

With a small staff, Rommel departed for France. He visited the coastal fortifications in Denmark, the Netherlands, along the Pas de Calais, in Normandy and Brittany. Everywhere he went, he stimulated the morale and *esprit de corps* of the men defending the shore, and improved the defences. On 15 January 1944, Rommel's Army Group B headquarters was strengthened and reconstituted and placed in command of the 7th and 15th Armies in France and the Low Countries. This gave Rommel the responsibility for directing the defence in the west, although the command arrangement remained somewhat ambiguous, for he functioned under the overall theatre Commander-in-Chief, Field-Marshal Gerd von Rundstedt. Nevertheless, from that time on, as the official American historian, Gordon Harrison, has remarked, 'Rommel was the dominant personality in the west with an influence disproportionate to his formal command authority.' A meeting of the senior commanders in the west with Hitler in March 1944 extended Rommel's authority. In May, when a separate Army Group G was formed under General Blaskowitz to defend southern France, Rommel became the commander of the combat troops about to receive the full force of the Normandy invasion.

During the first six months of 1944, Rommel tripled the number of mines in the coastal defence zone to 5 or 6 million. He supervised the construction of strongpoints, resistance nests and troop shelters. He instituted what were called 'Rommel asparagus' to disrupt glider landings, and planted booby traps, tetrahedrons, offshore barriers and assorted obstacles in the logical paths of amphibious forces. Despite his remarkable energy and imagination, as well as his ceaseless tours of inspection, he was unable to complete the fixed defences of the Atlantic Wall to his satisfaction. Shortages of concrete and other materials, as well as lack of time, deprived him of the ability to stop the landings at the water's edge, in the *Rommelbelt*.

For he believed that unless the Germans prevented the Allies from coming ashore in strength, they would be unable to defeat an invasion. The main battle line, he insisted, had to be the beach. This was exactly what Montgomery, the Allied Land Commander, expected and feared. In Rommel's plans to defend the coast, he preferred a linear defence over a defence in depth, static warfare over mobile operations, holding ground over launching a battle of annihilation, fortified positions over striking power. Rundstedt, in contrast, advocated a more orthodox concept, that of holding a strong, mobile force in strategic reserve until the place of the main Allied effort was determined, then launching a classic counter-stroke in depth to overwhelm and destroy the Allied beach-head. Rommel presupposed Allied air supremacy and the inability of the strong strategic reserve to move to the battlefield. Hitler never chose one method over the other, and the resulting strategy was to fall between both notions, with disastrous consequences. Rundstedt assembled an armoured reserve in a central position for immediate commitment against the principal Allied assault when revealed. Rommel placed the bulk of his troops, most of them non-mobile, that is, without transportation, close to the most likely points of Allied descent.

On 5 June 1944, a stormy day that seemed to make Allied landings imposs-ible, Rommel departed for his home in Herrlingen to spend his wife's birthday with her, then to go on to see Hitler at Obersalzburg in order to make plain his deficiencies in manpower and material in the event of an Allied invasion. He wished also to have two more panzer divisions, an anti-aircraft corps and a *nebelwerfer* brigade in Normandy.

Thus he was absent when the first Allied elements came ashore early on 6 June, some from the sky in gliders and parachutes, most from the sea in landing craft. Rommel returned to Normandy that evening. He attempted to seal off and destroy the Allied foothold whilst Rundstedt mustered his theatre reserve, strong in armour, for an attack to the beachhead. But, as Rommel had expected, Allied air forces harassed German movements to the front and knocked out the headquarters of the panzer reserve. Although Rommel's strategy, crippled though it was, confined the Allies to a relatively narrow beachhead, by the middle of June he believed that the Allies had too firm a foothold in France to be dislodged. Although the Germans found it impossible to mount a strong counter-offensive, Rommel was certain that in such an offensive the guns of the Allied navies in the Channel would smash the leading German elements and deny them the ability to regain the beaches. For Rommel, it was already time to think of giving up Normandy and returning to a line of defence to protect the approaches to Germany.

Hitler summoned Rundstedt and Rommel, both of whom held much the same view of the developing campaign, to meet with him near Soissons on 17 June. In the bunker constructed for Hitler four years earlier to enable him to direct the invasion of England, both Field-Marshals asked for more freedom of action in the battlefield, specifically permission to draw on reserves as they wished and also to shorten their lines of defence. Hitler refused. After berating them for their supposed shortcomings and finding fault with their tactical handling of operations, he ordered a rigid defence, the fortress of Cherbourg to be held to the last man, coupled with an overwhelming counter-attack through Bayeux.

Returned to their headquarters, the Field-Marshals tried to follow Hitler's instructions. The Bayeux counter-attack failed on 26 June in the face of a stout British defence. Although the Germans prevented the Allies from enlarging their beachhead, they were unable to stem the haemorrhage of German losses in men and equipment. As German strength wore down, both began to believe that German victory was an illusion, further defence unprofitable.

Called again to meet with Hitler at Berchtesgaden on 29 June, Rommel and Rundstedt listened as Hitler repeated his stand-fast orders. He brushed aside their requests for a flexible defence. They were to continue to confine the Allies to their beachhead. Rommel supposedly asked the Führer how he expected to win the war, a highly daring and dangerous question. When Rundstedt and Rommel were back again in Normandy, their state of discouragement led them immediately to recommend to Hitler a limited withdrawal. On 1 July Hitler responded: all positions were to be held. He relieved Rundstedt as Commander-in-Chief and also the commander of the panzer reserve, Geyr von Schweppenburg, who had criticized what he termed the 'tactical patchwork' of the German operations. When Rommel learned of their removal from command, he said, 'I will be next'.

Instead, Hitler left Rommel in command of Army Group B and replaced Rundstedt with Field-Marshal Hans von Kluge. Although Hitler had apparently warned Kluge of Rommel's pessimism and tendency to disobey orders, Kluge quickly came to share Rommel's views. According to Rommel's estimate in mid-July, the Germans, who had lost 100,000 men in Normandy and had received 6,000 replacements, could hold only a few more weeks at maximum. The German lack of success was rooted in the inability sufficiently to have completed the coastal fortifications, in the less than promised air and naval support, and the positioning of the panzer divisions too far from the coast. Still, Rommel's defensive battle had prevented the Allies from significantly expanding their beachhead. Only after he was gone from the scene would the Allies smash the German left flank, break out of their restricted continental foothold, and institute mobile operations that would virtually destroy the two German armies in Normandy and liberate most of France.

On 17 July Rommel was seriously injured when two Allied aircraft strafed and struck his car. The driver was mortally wounded and lost control. As the vehicle crashed into the ditch, an unconscious Rommel was thrown clear. After a French doctor treated him, he was taken to a Luftwaffe hospital at Bernay, where he regained consciousness and began to recover. He had

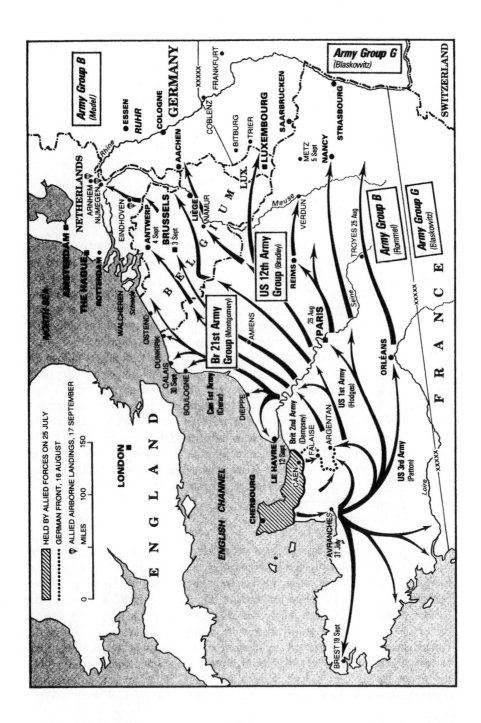

sustained a fracture at the base of the skull, plus three others, as well as splinters in the face.

Three days after Rommel's accident, the putsch against Hitler came to its climax in East Prussia, where a bomb exploded in the Führer's headquarters. Hitler miraculously escaped with his life, although he was slightly hurt. He immediately reasserted his authority and brutally eradicated the conspirators. When one of the principal plotters, von Stülpnagel, mentioned Rommel's name while in delirium, he implicated the Field-Marshal.

Though Rommel had been against assassinating the Führer, he had apparently approved of his removal and imprisonment. After the German failure to defeat the Anglo-American invasion, Rommel felt that to continue the war was senseless and an unnecessary destruction of Germany. He had agreed that if the Führer were deposed from power, he would head a government that would at once seek an armistice with the Western Allies.

On 24 July, Rommel was moved to a military hospital at Le Vesinet, a suburb of Paris. Early in August he was discharged and continued his convalescence at home in Herrlingen. On 7 October he was convoked to a meeting in Berlin but declined to attend on medical grounds. A week later, on 14 October, two generals sent by Hitler arrived at his home. He was given a choice: stand trial and face charges of high treason, or commit suicide. If he chose the latter, no action would be taken against his wife and son.

Rommel thereupon entered the car with the two generals, swallowed a poison capsule, and half an hour later, from a hospital in Ulm, came a telephone call announcing a fatal embolism. Those who saw his body noted the look of contempt on his face. Hitler had eliminated the single personality in Germany who enjoyed sufficient popular and military esteem to try to end the war. The corpse was incinerated to avoid possible incrimination later with regard to the poisoning, and Rommel received a state funeral. Burial was at Herrlingen. On 7 March 1945, as Hitler's Third Reich was crumbling towards dissolution, Frau Rommel received word of Hitler's proposal to erect an elaborate monument at her husband's grave.

Rommel merits the huge acclaim accorded to him. His devotion to the profession of arms was in the best tradition of the gentleman. In a total war fought savagely and brutally, he inspired admiration for his treatment of prisoners. He was not tainted by Nazism. His desire to save his country from further devastation, which led to his involvement in the movement against Hitler and for which he paid with his life, also prompts feelings of sympathy among those who understand the slippery connotations of duty and the need to choose occasionally between the dictates of obedience and morality. With his troops he enjoyed a deep rapport. He cared for them, and although he demanded their best and more, he never squandered them. Without pretension, modest, he tackled all his tasks with clarity, energy and common sense. He utilized surprise, never hesitated to improvise in a developing situation, and was always ready to exploit success.

With his eye constantly on victory, he refused to be deterred from action by obstacles that more reasonable men deemed were too great to overcome. His greatest fault was his tendency to ascribe his own failures to the incompetence of others. Perhaps his greatest achievement, as Correlli Barnett has suggested, was to turn what Hitler and the German High Command saw as a minor defensive action in North Africa into a campaign that became Winston Churchill's obsession and for two years attracted the major land effort of the British Empire.

Rommel has often been compared with General George S. Patton Jr, the foremost American expert in conducting mobile warfare. They never met in battle, Patton coming on the scene in Tunisia after Rommel was gone, and again in Normandy after Rommel's injury. They were much alike in their personal charisma and courage, drive and will-power, technical expertise, willingness to gamble, and impact on the public. Like Patton, who believed in his fate or destiny, Rommel had faith in his star. Both were commanders and executors rather than thinkers or theorists. Rommel had more battle experience, having fought longer in both World Wars. Patton's highest command was of an army, in the role of tactical or operational control. Rommel as an Army-Group commander rose to function on the strategic and political levels. Patton shone in offensive warfare only, while Rommel demonstrated a broad versatility in his combat roles. Both were undoubtedly military geniuses, great captains who epitomized generalship on the field of battle.

NOTES

1 Basil Liddell Hart (ed.), *The Rommel Papers*, London, Hamlyn, 1984, p. 241.
2 *Ibid.*, p. 43.
3 *Ibid.*, p. 257.
4 *Ibid.*, p. 268.
5 *Ibid.*, p. 426.

BIBLIOGRAPHY

Martin Blumenson, *Breakout and Pursuit*, Washington, 1961.
Martin Blumenson, *Rommel's Last Victory: The Battle of Kasserine Pass*, London, 1968.
Martin Blumenson, *Salerno to Cassino*, Washington, 1969.
Charles Douglas-Home, 'Field Marshal Erwin Rommel', in Field Marshal Sir Michael Carver (ed.), *The War Lords*, London, 1976.

Gordon A. Harrison, *Cross-Channel Attack*, Washington, 1951.
B. H. Liddell Hart (ed.), *The Rommel Papers*, New York, 1953.
Jacques Mordal, *Rommel*, 2 vols, Paris, 1973.
Friedrich Ruge, *Rommel in Normandy*, London, 1977.
Desmond Young, *Rommel: The Desert Fox*, New York, 1950.

CHRONOLOGY: FIELD-MARSHAL ERWIN ROMMEL

1891, November 12	Born in Heidenheim, near Ulm
1910, July 19	Joined 124th Infantry Regiment as cadet
1912, January	Received commission at War Academy, Danzig, as second-lieutenant
1914	Awarded Iron Cross, 2nd Class
1915	Awarded Iron Cross, 1st Class
1915, September	First-lieutenant
1916, November	Married Lucie Mollin in Danzig
1917, October	Awarded *Pour le Mérite* and promoted captain
1929–33	Instructor at the Infantry School, Dresden. Wrote *Infantry Attacks*
1933, October	Major
1935–37	Promoted lieutenant-colonel and Instructor at War College, Potsdam
1937	Colonel
1939, August 23	Major-General. During Polish campaign, commander of Hitler's bodyguard
1940, February 15	Assumed command of 7th Panzer Division
1941, January	Lieutenant-General
1941, February 12	Arrived in Tripoli to command *Afrika Korps*
1941, March 19	Awarded Oakleaves to the Knight's Cross
1941, July	General of Panzer Troops, commanding *Panzergruppe Afrika*
1942, January	Colonel-General, commanding *Panzerarmee Afrika*
1942, June 22	Field-Marshal
1943, February	Commanding *Armeegruppe Afrika* in Tunisia
1943, March	Awarded Knight's Cross with Oakleaves, Swords and Diamonds
1943, July	C-in-C of Army Group B, Munich
1943, September	C-in-C of Army Group B in France
1944, July 17	Seriously injured in the head
1944, October 14	Dies after swallowing poison capsule

MODEL

13

MODEL

Field-Marshal Walter Model

CARLO D'ESTE

The mark of a successful commander is the ability to adapt rapidly to constantly changing conditions on the field of battle. Field–Marshal Walter Model was a master of the defence and the commander upon whom Hitler most relied in difficult situations. During more than three grueling years on the Eastern Front, Model earned distinction as 'the Führer's Fireman' for his ingenuity which enabled him to salvage apparently hopeless situations. He was one of the few officers who enjoyed the complete trust of the German leader and at the age of fifty-three became the youngest Field-Marshal in the *Wehrmacht*, fully meriting the plaudits of Guderian who called him 'a bold inexhaustible soldier ... the best possible man to perform the fantastically difficult task of reconstructing a line in the centre of the Eastern Front'.[1]

Model was a paradoxical personality whose rise to High Command in an Army whose upper ranks were dominated by members of the old military aristo-cracy was all the more remarkable because he never belonged to this élite class. Yet contemporary photographs of him (with an ever-present monocle in his right eye) suggested the same stern-faced countenance that typified the Prussian element of the *Wehrmacht*.

There was nothing in Model's middle-class background to suggest he would one day pursue a military career. Born Otto Moritz Walter Model on 24 January 1891 in Gentheim, near Magdeburg, his antecedents were devout Lutheran schoolmasters, not soldiers. His father taught at the local girls' school where he also served as the choir leader. On his mother's side were peasants, horsetraders and innkeepers.

In the waning days of the Second World War, Model ordered his personal papers to be destroyed, and so consequently little is known of his childhood. Although the family moved frequently, young Model seems to have enjoyed a normal upbringing that suggested he would one day continue the family tradition. A good student with a weak constitution, he attended a liberal arts gymnasium in Erfurt where he excelled in Greek, Latin and history and was a member of a literary society.

Model's first exposure to the military occured in 1906 when he attended a church gymnasium in Naumberg an der Saale, where one of the Kaiser's *jäger* battalions was stationed. In February 1908 Model used his uncle's influence as a banker to join the 6th Brandenburgers of the 52nd Infantry Regiment as an officer cadet. The eighteen months he spent attending the *Kriegsschule* in Neisse were the most formative of his life. Although he nearly quit, Model not only survived the harsh training but by the time of his gazetting as a lieutenant of infantry in August 1910 he had become a passionate rider and hunter.

As a lieutenant, Model soon earned a reputation as an ambitious and conscientious officer who was not afraid to speak his mind and who formed no close friendships with his fellow officers, a pattern that was to characterize his entire career.

His first years of service were as the adjutant of the 52nd Regiment's 1st Battalion and later of the Regiment on the Western Front. Near Sedan in May 1915 First Lieutenant Model was severely wounded in the shoulder and hospitalized for a month. His bravery earned him the Iron Cross First Class and the attention of his division commander, Prince Oskar von Preussen (one of the Kaiser's six sons) who, although proposing him for service on the General Staff, thought Model an uncomfortable subordinate.

After sailing through an abbreviated General-Staff officer's course at Sedan in 1916 he returned to the front as a brigade adjutant and then as a company commander where he was again badly wounded. He was awarded the Knight's Cross with Swords and, after recuperating, Model began the first of a series of Staff assignments, including one with the General Staff and a brief mission to Turkey in 1917. He ended the war as a captain in a reserve division.

The Great War earned Model a solid reputation as a capable, hard-working officer of future promise. In 1920 his division commander noted in his final report that Model deserved to serve at the highest levels.[2] Nevertheless, Model considered quitting the Army for a civilian career but changed his mind when his excellent record earned him retention in the 100,000-man *Reichsheer*.

Although many of his former Army comrades were deeply involved in revolutionary activity during the turbulent post-war years, Model stayed aloof. A firm believer in the necessity of the state to maintain order, he never hesitated to suppress rebellion when called upon to do so as a commander of security troops. Throughout his career Model assiduously avoided involving himself in politics, apparently believing it was not the function of the Army to engage in matters of state.

In 1919 Model once again considered leaving the Army but was dissuaded by his uncle. The following year while helping put down a communist general strike in Eberfeld-Barmen (now Wuppertal) in the Ruhr, he met his future wife Herta Huyssen, in whose home he was quartered. They were married the following year and the union produced three children. Typically, Model was known to despise war stories and never discussed politics or the war with his wife.

The formative early years of Model's career exemplified the traits he later brought to High Command in the Second World War. He combined powerful ambition with the traditional German values of religion and country. Even during the intoxicating years of Nazism in the 1930s Model refused to abandon his religion for the fascist version. He was equally comfortable in the company of General Ludwig Beck whom he greatly admired, even though Beck opposed Hitler, and of Pastor Martin Niemöller, the former U-Boat commander and one-time Nazi, who baptized Model's children and later came to represent Christian resistance to National-Socialism.

From another mentor, Lieutenant-General Friedrich von Lossberg, who earned a reputation as a defensive genius in the Great War, he learned the rudiments of strategic defence.

Model's independence of mind and military skills were near perfect examples of von Seeckt's conception of a German officer corps uncorrupted by politics. As the guardian of its traditions and those of the General Staff during the 1920s, von Seeckt could hardly have produced a better example than Model who in 1929 published a monograph on von Gneisenau, praising the Prussian general's intellectual behaviour. In 1930 one of his commanding officers was not alone in believing that Model was the epitome of a Prussian officer.

During the inter-war years he gained notoriety for his ruthless performance of duty. Utterly lacking tact, Model rode roughshod over his subordinates and was outspoken in openly criticizing his superiors. In the highly regimented environment of the German military he not only lacked the social sophistication of the Prussian aristocracy but was equally far removed from the peasant and working-class backgrounds of Hitler and many of the key members of the Nazi régime. Model's attempt to offset his crudeness by behaving like a *junker* was typical of his zeal to attain success.

In the 1930s Model served in a variety of Staff and command assignments. When he was an infantry battalion commander in East Prussia, Model's regimental commander detected pro-Nazi tendencies, and later recalled that his favourite saying was, 'Can't that be done faster?' In 1934 he was promoted to colonel and assumed command of the 2nd Infantry Regiment.

The following year he was appointed head of Section 8 of the General Staff which was responsible for examining technical and doctrinal questions of the future Army. Despite his infantry background and scant understanding of technical matters, Model was an early advocate of motorization and showed an appreciation of the potential of aviation and armoured warfare. Inevitably, this led to his backing of Guderian's ideas for the organization of the German armoured force and its employment of the *Blitzkrieg*.

As usual, Model was a restless and impatient master who drove his subordinates with a heavy hand. In March 1938 he became a general officer and in November was the highly unpopular Chief of Staff of 4th Corps in Dresden. The principal function of a Chief of Staff is to promote unity of effort but under the fiery Model there was disorder and dissension. One officer believed Model's temperament got the better of his intelligence.[3]

The 4th Corps was an active participant in the Polish campaign of 1939 and by the time of the invasion of France in 1940 Model had become a major-general and the driving force of 16th Army. Plainly, Model's unorthodox methods were no impediment to his steady ascent to the highest ranks of the Army.

His Berlin postings brought Model into contact with members of the Nazi Party and it was not surprising that his penchant for order would appeal to the Nationalist-Socialist leadership, especially Göbbels who later introduced him to Hitler. Model never let his relatively junior rank impede his ability to impress Hitler. In 1938, for example, he staged a mock infantry assault against replicas of Czech fortifications that delighted Hitler and thoroughly annoyed Beck, then the Chief of the General Staff.

Like many Germans of his generation, Model seems to have emerged from the First World War with an abhorrence of Bolshevism and a belief that order took precedence over the concept of democracy adopted by the ill-fated Weimar Republic. Although he willingly embraced the Hitler régime, there is reason to believe that Model's support was to some degree a logical extension of his ambition and another of the paradoxes of this complex man. In 1930 he wrote to his mother-in-law that, 'It is important that the state prevent with solid authority any shift to radicalism.'[4] Yet shortly thereafter he unhesitatingly lent his support to a régime whose notorious conduct gave new definition to the term 'radical'.

Within the officer corps opinions were to vary about Model. Those who believed he was an ardent Nazi pointed to his devotion to Hitler, his appointment of a Waffen ss officer as his ADC in 1942 (an act which cost him the confidence of many), and the fact that he was the first senior officer to reaffirm his support for Hitler after the abortive assassination attempt on 20 July 1944.

Others, however, viewed Model as merely a very clever opportunist who used Hitler and Nazism as a convenient means of climbing the Army career ladder.

The very traits that earned Model the enmity of many officers endeared him to his troops and to Hitler: his dogged determination never to accept a situation as hopeless and his reckless disregard for his own safety. Although Hitler preferred Model to the Prussian 'Old Guard' and admired him, even he could be uncomfortable in Model's presence. After one particularly heated exchange in 1942 Hitler remarked, 'Did you see that eye? I trust that man to do it. But I wouldn't want to serve under him.'[5]

In November 1940 Model was given command of 3rd Panzer Division. His superior was the respected armoured commander, General Leo Geyr von Schweppenburg, who considered Model a brilliant if somewhat narrow soldier. Within the division he was regarded with mixed feelings; his troops appreciated his forcefulness, his willingness to share their hardships and his dynamic leadership from the front, while his Staff thought him obnoxious.

These differing allegiances became the norm for a Model command. His troops respected him and his Staffs inevitably requested transfers *en masse*. When he assumed command of 41st Panzer Corps with the rank of General der Panzertruppen in October 1941, the entire Corps Staff asked for relief.

He demanded the impossible from his subordinates regardless of the situation. When he assumed command of Army Group Centre in June 1944 one of Model's first acts was a threat of court-martial for any commander who failed to hold his position. His iron will was reflected in his philosophy of command: 'He who leads troops has no right to think about himself.' Practising what he preached, Model slept little, restlessly roamed the front, often in a Storch reconnaissance plane, bullying his commanders in coarse language, arbitrarily shifting units to plug gaps in the line, and overruling his intermediate commanders, a habit which drove some to contemplate suicide.

During Operation *Barbarossa* in 1941 he demonstrated that he had learnt well from Guderian when his 3rd Panzer Division spearheaded the German drive into the Ukraine and the encirclement of Kiev. When the later German campaign in Russia faltered at Stalingrad in 1942 and then at Kursk in 1943, he was at the forefront of the German effort to stave off the Red Army.

Mere fulfilment of duty in a crisis was not enough to satisfy Model. Much more was required in the form of *'daemonische Geist'* (a 'daemonic spirit'). 'He who has not discovered himself, not organized, not changed things around to suit his own demands, has not known emergencies ... is unjustified in trying to become a leader.'[6]

Inevitably, Hitler saw in the stocky, diminutive Model an officer he not only respected but on more than one occasion rated *'mein bester Feldmarschall'*[7]. Model, in turn, became one of the few German generals with the authority to make decisions and to defy Hitler successfully. In January 1942, when his 9th Army faced encirclement near Rzhev, Model took it upon himself to return to Germany to plead personally with Hitler for reinforcement by a panzer corps. Hitler agreed, but challenged his plan for the corps' employment. During their confrontation Model coldly inquired, 'Who commands the 9th Army, my Führer, you or I?'[8] It was one of the rare occasions when Hitler backed down, and subsequent events validated Model's claim that as the commander at the front he should make tactical decisions. There is little doubt this incident enhanced his standing with the German leader. As von Manteuffel later observed, 'Model stood up to Hitler in a way hardly anyone else dared.'[9]

It was on the Eastern Front that Model earned a reputation as the master of the defensive. His rise from colonel to Field-Marshal was as phenomenal as it was rapid. After commanding 3rd Panzer Division and 41st Panzer Corps during the *Barbarossa* advances, he assumed command of 9th Army at a moment of extreme crisis when the Red Army was beginning to regroup and counter-attack. A rare instance of black humour occured when Model was first briefed on the precarious situation. Someone inquired, 'And what, sir, have you brought us to restore the situation?' Without hesitation an unsmiling Model retorted, 'Myself.'[10] Laughter eased the tension.

It was as a corps commander that Model began to employ his own version of the *kampfgruppen* (informally organized combat and combat support units) to achieve objectives in both defensive and offensive situations. During the Soviet counter-offensives in the winter of 1941–2 he made a powerful impression upon his men through the sheer power of his personality, and his success fostered their conviction that he was a lucky general.

Model's ascent to high command was the antithesis of the fate which befell most of the senior German commanders who fought in Russia. One by one they were dismissed by Hitler: Rundstedt, Leeb, Bock, Guderian and, in March 1944, his most able commander, von Manstein. In 1943 von Paulus surrendered at Stalingrad, an act condemned by Model who in 1945 refused to surrender to the Allies. 'A field-marshal does not become a prisoner,' he said. 'Such a thing is just not possible.'[11] Moreover, the loss of von Brauchitsch due to retirement for ill-health in December 1941 had left Hitler as the Army Commander-in-Chief, a step which ultimately benefited Model.

Model was a key player in Operation *Citadel*, the great Kursk offensive of July 1943. There was considerable dissension over *Citadel* within the German High Command during the planning stage, with von Manstein and Model's superior, von Kluge, anxious to attack the Kursk salient at once before the Russians were able to strengthen their defences. Model urged caution and insisted his 9th Army could not perform its mission unless heavily augmented. As D–Day grew nearer Model voiced his objection to the operation, supported by Guderian who cautioned Hitler that the offensive was 'pointless' and certain to generate heavy losses. What followed was the greatest air/land battle in military history and a crippling defeat for the Germans which is generally considered to have irrevocably altered the course of the war on the Eastern Front in favour of the Russians. Model's army suffered heavy losses and for nearly a month he commanded 2nd Panzer Army in addition to 9th Army, but he emerged from the battle with his reputation intact, if not enhanced.

As the ordeal of the German Army in the East deepened, Model was given additional responsibilities by Hitler. In January 1944 he became Commander-in-Chief, Army Group North, and two months later he became the *Wehr-macht's* youngest Field-Marshal. In the next six months there followed a remarkable series of appointments that included three different army groups, clearly establishing his dominance as the most influential German commander on the Eastern Front. However, by the summer of 1944 the situation there had grown extremely critical. The Red Army firmly took the initiative in June when four Army Groups were unleashed in a mighty offensive to crush the severely undermanned Army Group Centre which was defending the 450-mile Belorussian salient. When the front collapsed during one of the most savage battles of the war the commander, Field-Marshal Busch, was sacked and replaced by Model who could not prevent the destruction of Army Group Centre, which lost 28 divisions and nearly 350,000 men by mid-July. Nevertheless, Model's tactical skills as a 'firefighter' and his ruthless fighting spirit enabled him to patch up the front again. When Hitler bestowed on him the Diamond Clasp to the Knight's Cross on 17 August 1944, he told him: 'Were it not for you, your heroic efforts, and your wise leadership of brave troops, the Russians might have been in East Prussia today or even before the gates of Berlin.'[12] By this time, Hitler had another major crisis on his hands for which he required Model's services.

With Model's Diamond Clasp to the Knight's Cross came that same day an exceptionally difficult new assignment: to assume command of the defence in the West, and restore the desperate situation where the Allies had finally broken out of the Normandy bridgehead and were dismembering the remnants of Army Group B in the Falaise pocket. To make matters worse, the German command structure was equally chaotic. Von Rundstedt had been sacked in July, Rommel was recovering from grave injuries suffered on 18 July and was implicated in the 20 July putsch; and Hitler mistakenly suspected their successor, Field-Marshal von Kluge, of secretly attempting to negotiate a surrender to the Allies. Armed with a hand-written letter of instructions from Hitler, Model arrived (also on the same day) unannounced at von Kluge's headquarters, believing, as had his predecessor, that the situation there was manageable in the hands of the right commander. Instead, he quickly discerned that what von Kluge had reported was true: the German Army in the West was a shambles.

On the surface he appeared to be the same defiant Model, full of fight and determined to carry out Hitler's orders to hold at the River Seine. Encountering the commander of Panzer Lehr Division he was told that the formation was to be pulled from the line for a rest. 'My dear Bayerlein,' Model snapped, 'in the East our divisions take their rest in the front line. And that is how things are going to be done here in the future. You will stay with your formations where you are.'[13]

His loyalty to Hitler notwithstanding, Model was above all a realist, and, as he had demonstrated in the past, he was not above altering his instructions to suit the circumstances. The situation in the West was so bad that he reported that what was left of his panzer and panzer-grenadier divisions were 'five to ten tanks each'.[14] To hold the front required immediate reinforcements of 30 to 35 infantry and 12 panzer divisions. But there were no reserves and in early September 1944 Model felt compelled to provide Hitler with a characteristically blunt assessment: 'The unequal struggle cannot long continue.'[15] When he suspected his unwelcome news was being withheld from Hitler, he endorsed his most important messages 'for submission to the Führer *in the original*'.[16] He had been assured – like so many others Hitler hoodwinked – that new wonder weapons would soon be forthcoming, a claim even Model now began to perceive as empty rhetoric. Privately, he warned Jodl that the Allies had established complete superiority in the West.

There were to be no miracles, and along with his beaten army Model was forced to flee from France. He established his headquarters at Oosterbeek, a suburb of Arnhem, Holland, while he attempted to reconstitute Army Group B. From the time of the débâcle of the German Army in Normandy, Hitler expressed a firm intention to launch a major counter-offensive against the Allies. For this reason, and to remove the heavy burden of dual command from Model, in early September he reappointed von Rundstedt to his former post as Commander-in-Chief West, leaving Model in command of Army Group B. Von Rundstedt was not an admirer of Model, whom he had once disdainfully described as having the makings of a good sergeant-major. Nevertheless, the two managed to tolerate one another successfully.

By the time of Operation *Market Garden*, the great Allied airborne and ground operation to seize a bridgehead across the Rhine at Arnhem, Model had begun to make progress reorganizing and retraining Army Group B. He had a grandstand view of the British airborne and glider landings at Arnhem which forced him hastily to abandon his Sunday dinner and flee to safety. Had the British known of his presence, Model's fate would have been very different.

Certain that the bridges at Arnhem and Nijmegen were the Allied objectives, Model ordered the prompt employment of 9th and 10th ss Panzer Divisions which were refitting nearby. He was later criticized for failing to accept strong representations from subordinates to destroy Nijmegen bridge. It was typical of Model that he argued that the bridge would be needed for a counter-attack. His able corps commander, Lieutenant-General Wilhelm Bittrich, was convinced that Model failed to grasp the appalling strategic consequences of an Allied breakthrough. Nor would Model accept Bittrich's reasons for the German failure to recapture Arnhem bridge. When he told Model that 'In all my years as a soldier, I have never seen men fight so hard', the chilly reply was simply: 'I want that bridge.'[17] Model's decisions escaped criticism when *Market Garden* failed, despite the loss of Nijmegen bridge to the Allies.

Von Rundstedt and Model joined in opposing Hitler's plan for the Ardennes counter-offensive. When he first learned of the scheme in late October, Model noted acidly: 'This plan hasn't got a damned leg to stand on.'[18] Both officers believed the seizure of Antwerp was a hopelessly unrealistic goal and during the preparations for the offensive they attempted to scale down its scope. However, their efforts to reduce Hitler's 'grand slam' to a 'little slam' fell upon deaf ears.

In early December 1944 Model, backed by von Manteuffel and Sepp Dietrich, the designated army commanders in the offensive, spoke forcefully at a conference with Hitler, urging that the plan be reconsidered. Hitler adamantly refused and once again Model was charged with achieving the impossible.

The Ardennes offensive was a desperate gamble that had virtually no chance of success, despite achieving total surprise, because the German resources were just too small. Nevertheless, putting aside his misgivings, Model ruthlessly cracked down on those whom he considered defeatist or who complained about shortages. 'If you need anything, take it from the Americans,' he would reply.[19]

Throughout the battle which raged in the frozen forests of the Ardennes, he was usually to be found at the front exerting his influence to cajole, bully and inspire but ultimately unable to conjure up one more miracle for Hitler. Near St Vith a German lieutenant wrote in his diary: 'Generalfeldmarschall Model himself directs traffic ... a little, undistinguished-looking man with a monocle.'[20]

German losses were enormous and irreplaceable, thus setting the stage for the climatic battle of Model's career. When he was finally permitted to withdraw his battered Army Group, Model pleaded in vain for permission to establish new defences along the Rhine instead of the Siegfried Line behind the German frontier which Hitler insisted be held.

His task was impossible and by March 1945 the Allied armies were threatening the final natural barrier of the Rhine. The situation became desperate when an American armoured force succeeded in capturing the Ludendorff bridge at Remagen. By the end of the month the Rhine had been breached

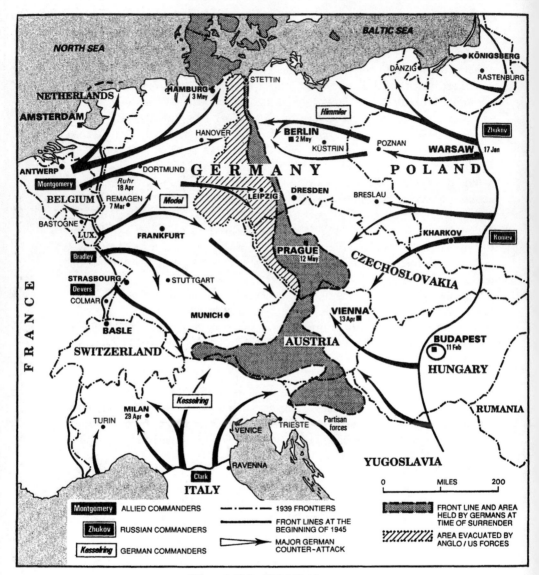

The end of the Third Reich, 1945

along a wide front and the 300,000 troops of Army Group B were trapped in a rapidly closing pocket in the Ruhr.

Von Rundstedt was dismissed by Hitler for the final time and Kesselring summoned from Italy with instructions to restore the situation in the Ruhr. Hitler issued orders there be no further retreat and in attempting to implement them Kesselring ran afoul of Model, whose nerves were clearly stretched to breaking-point. The result was a confrontation between the two Field-Marshals and an outpouring of Model's pent-up frustrations in the form of a scathing denunciation of the folly of OKW, particularly Jodl and Keitel.

Hitler's decree of a 'scorched earth' policy was the last straw. Although several determined attempts were made to break free of the Allied encirclement, Model had evidently grown weary of the Führer's broken promises and the steady stream of futile orders from OKW. At the urging of Reichsminister Albert Speer to spare the Ruhr, Model quietly defied Hitler's order. Although surrender was unthinkable, he fully understood the futility of further resistance and in the final days of the war he refused even to pass on most of the orders received from Berlin.

When the Ruhr pocket was split in two by the Allies in mid-April 1945 Model took it upon himself to order Army Group B dissolved, believing it was his personal responsibility to spare further humiliation. The oldest and youngest soldiers were ordered discharged and the remainder given the choice of surrender or attempting to break out in small groups.

Model's decision to let his troops decide their fate for themselves was a compromise alternative to surrender. Major-General Matthew B. Ridgway, the commander of the 18th US Airborne Corps, sent an emissary with a letter under a white flag for Model urging him to surrender. The emissary returned with one of Model's Staff officers who replied that the Field-Marshal's personal oath to Hitler not only forbade surrender but that even to consider such a proposal violated his sense of honour.

His final days of life were a struggle to determine his fate. On several occasions he recklessly exposed himself in an attempt to be killed during visits to the front. In February he had sent his adjutant, Colonel Theodore Pilling, to Dresden to help his family move west and to supervise the destruction of his papers.

After releasing his Staff, Model, his adjutant, and two other officers evaded the Allied trap and went to ground in a forest near Duisburg while he pondered his fate. His choice of suicide was all but sealed when he learned that the Russians had charged him with war crimes in connection with the death of 577,000 persons in Latvian concentration camps and the deportation of 175,000 others as slave labour. These acts were committed by the SS and there is no evidence he was even aware of them. Early in the Russian campaign he had spurned reprisals as counter-productive. Nevertheless, Model faced certain execution if he fell into Russian hands. About the same time he also learned of an Allied decree that leading German officers would be held responsible for their actions before courts-martial.

For some time he had been continually discussing his options. Of his decision to dissolve Army Group B, he asked his Chief of Staff, 'Have we done everything to justify our actions in the light of history? What is left to a commander in defeat?' Model went on to answer his own question: 'In ancient times they took poison.'[21] General F. W. von Mellenthin, who served as Manteuffel's Chief of Staff, saw a good deal of Model during the final days of his life and later wrote: 'He was visibly seeking a solution to his own inner conflict and clearly perceived that we had lost the war.'[22]

For nearly four days Model brooded about duty, honour and Germany. His torment undoubtedly symbolized the plight of the German officer corps: 'I would never have thought that I would ever be so disappointed. My only aim was to serve Germany.'

In the end, Model could find no acceptable alternative and despite the pleas of his three companions he revealed his decision to end his life. On the afternoon of 21 April 1945, after a farewell handshake for each officer, Model, accompanied by Colonel Pilling, walked out of sight in the forest and killed himself with a single shot from his Walther pistol. His final wish was carried out when his body was secretly buried where he fell. After the war his gravesite was identified by Pilling and his son relocated the Field-Marshal's remains to a military cemetery in the Hürtgen forest, where he is now buried amongst his fellow soldiers.

To the end of his life Walter Model remained a contradictory personality whose code of ethics and Christian beliefs were in sharp contrast to his loyalty to Hitler and National-Socialism. His detractors saw his influential relationship with Hitler, his appointment of a National-Socialist political officer to Army Group B and his refusal to accept the proclamation from the 20 July rebels that the Führer was dead as prime examples of his zealotry. Whether or not Model was an ardent Nazi or merely an opportunist, his behaviour was consistent with that of virtually the entire German officer corps which condoned the excesses of the Hitler régime. In Model's case there was a lifelong refusal to involve himself in political matters even though the German Army had long since become politicized. In fact, the secret of Model's successful relationship with Hitler was that he only challenged the Führer on military issues, never politics.

Although his middle-class background certainly appealed to Hitler, it was Model's professionalism that counted most. Around Hitler he exhibited none of the emotional, erratic behaviour that his troops witnessed at the front. Instead, he conducted himself with confidence, precision and cold calculation that both frightened and impressed Hitler. In short, everything about Model inspired Hitler to entrust him with ever greater responsibility.

Model lacked the charisma of Rommel and the military genius and intellectual depth of von Manstein, operating for the most part on what von Mellenthin calls 'an outstanding talent for improvisation'. He was an outstanding tactician but not a particularly great strategist, yet by mid-1944 Model commanded more than half of the German forces on the Eastern Front. As historian Paul Carell points out, 'Never before in the war had Hitler entrusted so much military responsibility to one man.'[23]

He combined fearlessness and boundless energy with the unparalleled obstinacy which was the source of both his successes and deficiencies as a commander. As the war progressed, Model increasingly distrusted even his closest advisors and tended to rely – to his detriment – upon his own ideas, rarely even bothering to listen to, much less heed, the counsel of others.

In upper echelons of the officer corps he was widely disliked. Von Manstein, for example, praised his achievements in defensive situations but abhorred Model's methods and disdained him as a Nazi. Lieutenant-General Hans Speidel, his Army Group B Chief of Staff, embodied a Staff Officer's view of Model, observing that 'his keen tactical eye was not balanced by an instinct for the possible. He thought too highly of his own ability, was erratic, and lacked a sense of moderation. . . . Although he had been schooled in strategy, he could not rid his mind of the details of tactical leadership.'[24]

Model brought no special defensive techniques to high command despite his tutelage by von Lossberg. Expediency, not originality, was his most dominant trait. A born fighter, Model was the 'fireman' Hitler turned to in dire situations. For all his flaws, he nevertheless achieved extraordinary success for the son of a schoolmaster.

The unusual bond between the feisty Field-Marshal and Adolf Hitler did not end with Model's suicide. Faced with a similar decision, Hitler is said to have remarked that if Model could find the courage to take his own life, so could he.

Of Model's unhappy demise, von Mellenthin has written: 'Following the collapse of the *Wehrmacht*, which to Model was synonymous with the crumbling of all his life's desires, aims and ideals, one can scarcely imagine any other end for him than the suicide he chose. It was his way of remaining true to himself.'[25] It is doubtful that Model's strong sense of honour would ever have permitted the ignominy of a German Field-Marshal facing a Soviet show-trial for the atrocities of the ss.

NOTES

1 General Heinz Guderian, *Panzer Leader*, London (1974 edition), p. 336.
2 Walter Görlitz, *Model*, 1975, pp. 25–6.
3 Lt-Col. Edgar Roehricht, in Görlitz, *Model*, p. 70.
4 Letter of 5 August 1930, *ibid.*, p. 46.
5 *Ibid.*, p. 124.
6 *Ibid.*, p. 128.
7 John S. D. Eisenhower, *The Bitter Woods*, New York, 1969, p. 346.
8 F. W. von Mellenthin, *German Generals of World War II*, Norman, 1977, p. 149.

9 B. H. Liddell Hart, *The Other Side of the Hill*, London (1978 edition), p. 102.
10 Von Mellenthin, *op. cit.*, p. 149.
11 Quoted in Charles B. MacDonald, *A Time For Trumpets*, New York, 1985, p. 34.
12 Von Mellenthin, *op. cit.*, pp. 151–2.
13 Richard Brett-Smith, *Hitler's Generals*, London, 1976, p. 200.
14 Various sources, including: D'Este, *Decision in Normandy*, London, 1983, p. 456; Russell F. Weigley, *Eisenhower's Lieutenants*, Bloomington, 1981, p. 255. Also, Matthew Cooper, *The German Army, 1933–1945*, London, 1978, p. 513.
15 Quoted in Peter Elstob, *Hitler's Last Offensive*, London, 1971, p. 26.
16 Quoted in Chester Wilmot, *The Struggle for Europe*, 1952, p. 486.
17 Cornelius Ryan, *A Bridge Too Far*, London, 1974, p. 327.
18 MacDonald, *op. cit.*, p. 35.
19 Von Mellenthin, *op. cit.*, p. 154.
20 Quote from German lieutenant's diary: quoted in Hanson W. Baldwin, *Battles Lost and Won*, New York, 1966, p. 338.
21 Quoted in MS No. B-593 (German Report Series), in Charles B. MacDonald, *The Last Offensive*, Washington, 1973, pp. 371–2.
22 Von Mellenthin, *op. cit.*, p. 156.
23 Quoted in Smith, *Hitler's Generals*, *op. cit.*, p. 201.
24 Hans Speidel, *We Defended Normandy*, London, 1951, p. 146.
25 Von Mellenthin, *op. cit.*, p. 158.

CHRONOLOGY: WALTER MODEL

1891, January 24	Born, near Magdeburg; arts education
1909, February 27–1910, August 22	Officer cadet training, *Kriegsschule*
1910–14	Service in 52nd Infantry Regiment, including battalion and regimental adjutant.
1914–16	Service on the Western Front
1916, April	(abbreviated) General Staff Officer course
1917–19	Various staff assignments. Retained in 100,000-man *Reichsheer*
1919–25	Various staff and troop assignments, including duty with security forces
1925, October–1928, September	Commanding Officer, 9th Company, 8th Infantry Regiment
1928–30	General Staff Officer, 3rd Division, Berlin
1930–32	Staff Officer, Section 4, Training Directorate, Berlin
1932–3	Chief of Staff, Reich Kuratorium for Youth Fitness
1933–4	Battalion commander, 2nd Infantry Regiment
1934–5	Commander, 2nd Infantry Regiment
1935–8	Head of Section 8, General Staff, Berlin
1938, November–1939, October	Chief of Staff, 4th Corps
1939, October–1940, November	Chief of Staff, 16th Army

1940, November– 1941, October	Commander, 3rd Panzer Division
1941, October– 1942, January	Commander, 41st Panzer Corps
1942, January– 1944, January	Commander, 9th Army
1944, January– March	Commander, Army Group North
1944, March–June	Commander, Army Group North Ukraine
1944, June–August	Commander, Army Group Centre
1944, August 17– September 4	Commander-in-Chief, West (also Commander, Army Groups B and D)
1944, September 5– 1945, April 17	Commander, Army Group B
1945, April 21	Death by suicide, near Duisburg

Promotions

1910, August 22	2nd Lieutenant, Infantry
1915, February 25	1st Lieutenant
1918, March	Captain
1929	Major
1932	Lieutenant-Colonel
1934, October 1	Colonel
1938, March 1	Generalmajor
1940, April 1	Generalleutnant
1941, October 1	General der Panzertruppen
1942, February 28	Generaloberst
1944, March 1	Generalfeldmarschall

Decorations

1915, October	Iron Cross, First Class
1917, February	Knight's Cross with Swords
1942, February	Knight's Cross with Oak Leaves
1944, August	Knight's Cross with Diamonds

ARNIM

14

ARNIM

General of Panzer Troops Hans-Jürgen von Arnim

SAMUEL W. MITCHAM JR

Hans-Jürgen Theodor von Arnim was born at Ernsdorf, Silesia, on 4 April 1889.[1] From the moment of his birth he was destined for a military career. The ancient Prussian house of von Arnim had produced officers for the Fatherland in virtually every generation since its first documented appearance in 1388. Hans-Jürgen's grandfather, Lieutenant-General Theodor von Arnim, had served on the Greater Prussian General Staff from 1850 to 1866, leaving it only to assume command of a division, which he led against the Austrians at the Battle of Sadowa (Königgrätz). More than a dozen members of the various branches of the family served in the Second World War, including four generals.[2]

Young Hans-Jürgen – 'Dieter' to his friends – attended schools at Glogau, near his family's estate, until his father was able to arrange for him to enter the Royal Prussian service as a *Fahnenjunker* on 1 April 1908 – three days before his eighteenth birthday.[3] He successfully completed his officer's training and was commissioned *Leutnant* (second lieutenant) in the élite 4th Prussian Foot Guards Regiment on 19 August 1909, with a date of rank of 17 August 1907. He became a battalion adjutant in the 4th Foot Guards in late 1913.[4]

Second Lieutenant von Arnim went to war with his regiment and served in Belgium and northern France. He was named acting regimental adjutant in late 1914, and received his promotion to *Oberleutnant* (first lieutenant) in January, 1915. On 1 November of that year he was given command of an infantry company, which he led for almost a year. After surviving the trench warfare of Flanders, Dieter von Arnim was sent to the Eastern Front, where he was Ordnance Officer of the 4th Guards Jäger Division. He was promoted to *Hauptmann* (captain) on 27 January 1917.[5]

A few weeks later, with the war going badly for Germany, the young captain finally secured leave and permission to marry Annemarie von Dechend, the 22-year-old daughter of Lieutenant-Colonel Max von Dechend. The couple were wed in Berlin on 26 March 1917. Due to the pressing military situation, there was no time for a honeymoon.[6] Hans-Jürgen returned to the Eastern Front, where he was named divisional adjutant on 4 July. On 20 October 1917 he was given command of an infantry battalion, which he led in the final battles on the Western Front in 1918.[7]

Captain von Arnim emerged from the conflict with a fairly distinguished war record. He had performed credibly on both major fronts, in both Staff and command assignments, and was decorated with the Hohenzollern House Order, the Iron Cross, First and Second Classes, the Wound Badge, and the Hamburg Hanseatic order.[8] He was given a company command in the 29th Infantry Regiment in 1919 and was selected for the new *Reichswehr*, as one of the 4,000 Army officers allowed to Germany under the Treaty of Versailles. The 29th Infantry was stationed at Charlottenburg, a suburb of Berlin, at the time. Arnim's only child, a daughter named Elisabeth, was born here on 21 January 1920.[9]

In the autumn of 1920 von Arnim moved his little family to the inhospitable Baltic seaport of Stettin, where the 2nd Infantry Division was stationed. His service in the *Reichswehr* was typical for a Prussian potential future general. He spent a year as a battalion commander in the 2nd Division (1920–1), and was then divisional adjutant for a year (1921–2). For the next two years he was on the Staff of Army Group 2 at Kassel. This was followed by an assignment to the Reich Defence Ministry on 1 October 1924.[10] This assignment may have been arranged by his father-in-law, who was on the *Truppenamt* (the clandestine General Staff) at the time. In any event it was a fortuitous appointment for Arnim, who enhanced his reputation in *Reichswehr* circles as a capable and energetic commander and staff officer with a genial nature, a capacity for hard work, and an ability to think and act decisively. He also made many valuable contacts that would be useful in the years ahead. He moved his family to Berlin-Charlottenburg and in 1925 was named Senior Adjutant to General von Behrendt, the Commander of Army Group 1, with headquarters in Berlin.[11] After eleven years as a captain he was promoted to major in 1928 – twenty years to the day after he entered the service.[12]

Arnin worked for General von Behrendt until he was replaced by General Otto Haase in September 1929. Arnim was then transferred to *Wehrkreis* VII in Munich, at the request of the district commander, General (later Field-Marshal) von Leeb. Here Arnim served as Chief of Staff to Artillery Leader VII, Major-General Heinrich Curtse.[13] On 1 April 1932 he was promoted to

lieutenant-colonel, and six months later began a two-year tour as commander
of the 1st Battalion, 2nd Infantry Regiment. This was followed by an appointment to the staff of Infantry Leader VI at Münster, where he worked for
Major-General (later Field-Marshal) Günther von Kluge. Arnim became
Chief of Staff of the command a few months later, and on 1 July 1934 was
promoted to colonel.[14]

Dieter von Arnim returned to Berlin in October 1935, and on the 15th of
that month assumed command of the excellent 68th Infantry Regiment, part
of the newly formed 23rd Infantry Division, which had been established in
one of the first phases of Hitler's military expansion. Arnim enjoyed his
assignment in Berlin and remained in command of the 68th Infantry even
after his promotion to major-general (*Generalmajor*). His tour of duty ended
abruptly, however. General of Infantry Erwin von Witzleben, the Commander
of *Wehrkreis* III (the Berlin area) was a prominent member of the secret anti-
Hitler opposition and wanted none but firm anti-Nazis in the key positions in
the district. Although Dieter von Arnim disapproved of the Nazis, Frederician
Prussianism was deeply ingrained in his character and he had sworn an oath
of loyalty to Hitler; thus he was not the stuff of which conspiracies are made.
During the Blomberg-Fritsch crisis of February 1938, the commander of the
23rd Division was retired. Erwin von Witzleben engineered the appointment
of a fellow anti-Nazi, Major-General Count Walter von Brockdorff-Ahlefeldt,
to the vacant post. Brockdorff-Ahlefeldt filled the top divisional slots with
officers whose political views paralleled his own. Arnim was ousted and sent
off to *Heeres Dienstelle 4* at Schweidnitz in Silesia, where he was placed in
charge of the service depot there – a definite demotion.[15] In an undated pre-
war (mid-1930s) report, General Curt Haase (General Commanding 3rd
Corps) wrote that Arnim was 'Very ambitious, advise against his promotion
to divisional commander.' Why Haase opposed Arnim's selection for this post
is unknown, but Arnim was not given such a command until after the outbreak
of the war. On the other hand General Walter Schroth, Commander of 12th
Corps (1938–42), called Arnim 'brave and gallant', and recommended him for
a divisional command. This pre-war report is also undated.

General von Arnim did not complain about his new assignment, but his
friends at OKH felt that he had been done an injustice. On 1 May 1939 he was
recalled to Berlin as a '*Sonstigesoffizier*' (extra officer) and remained there,
cooling his heels, until after the invasion of Poland began. Then, on 12
September 1939, he was ordered to the Saarpfalz to assume command of the
52nd Infantry Division, which was then in the process of forming at Grossborn.

The 52nd Infantry did not participate in the Polish campaign. Elements of
the unit took part in the fighting in France,[16] but the division as a whole was
not engaged.

Despite the fact that he had not yet seen action in the Second World War,
Dieter von Arnim was promoted to lieutenant-general (*Generalleutnant*) on 1

337

December 1939 and, in the autumn of 1940, was ordered to Munich, to take command of the 17th Panzer Division.[17] He had no previous training in or connection with the armoured branch, and his appointment can only be explained in light of his general efficiency and because of his friends in Berlin. The same, of course, could be said of Erwin Rommel, now commanding the 7th Panzer Division, or of Ewald von Kleist, who had directed a panzer group in France. Arnim, however, would prove less successful than these men. General Hermann Geyer (General Commanding 9th Corps) commented on 2 February 1941 that Arnim was a 'well-balanced, calm man. Prudent, judicious organizer and trainer.' Colonel-General (later Field-Marshal) Baron Maximilian von Weichs commented on 25 February 1941 that the 17th Panzer was not yet fully formed, but was still fundamentally good, due to the 'sure, confident hand' of General von Arnim.

The 17th Panzer engaged in training until the early spring of 1941, when it was transported to Poland, where Hitler was preparing his next military adventure. The invasion of the Soviet Union began on 22 June 1941. Arnim's division, which was part of Guderian's 2nd Panzer Group, crossed the Bug above Brest-Litovsk and seized Slonim, its initial objective, on the 24th. It repulsed a sharp Soviet counter-attack the next day, and was engaged in heavy fighting near Schklov on the 26th. The next day, in combat on the outskirts of this town, General von Arnim was seriously wounded and hastily evacuated back to Poland. He left Ritter Karl von Weber in acting command.

Arnim was initially hospitalized at Lvov, but was then sent to Berlin for better treatment. He remained in the military hospital there until early August – except for a brief outing to attend the funeral of General von Weber, who had been mortally wounded on 18 July and died two days later. After being discharged from the hospital, Arnim went on a recuperative leave and continued his convalescence at Charlottenburg until mid-September, when he was officially declared well. On 17 September he resumed command of the 17th Panzer, relieving Major-General Wilhelm von Thoma, the acting commander.[18]

After recovering from his wounds, von Arnim distinguished himself as a panzer commander on the Eastern Front. He led his division in the last stages of the Battle of Kiev, in which 667,000 Russians were captured. Next he took part in the Battle of Vyazma-Bryansk, in which some 663,000 prisoners were taken. During this battle the 17th Panzer Division did what no one thought possible: it seized the bridge over the Desna intact and captured Bryansk, one of the most important railway junctions in European Russia. This victory materially contributed to the speedy collapse of the Soviet resistance in the Vyazma-Bryansk pocket. On 17 October 1941, the last day of the battle, Arnim's men accepted the surrender of 30,000 Russians.[19]

Following the end of this battle, the 17th Panzer was immobilized due to a lack of fuel; then it was resupplied and sent to Orel to join the advance on

Moscow, but was halted by mud beyond the Protva, only about 60 miles from the Russian capital. Here the division waited for the ground to freeze, so the final drive could resume. When it jumped off, however, Arnim was no longer with them. In early November he was promoted to General of Panzer Troops, retroactive to 1 October 1941, and was advised that he would soon be given command of a panzer corps. On 11 November he turned command of the division over to Colonel Licht, and set out for his new command, the 39th Panzer Corps, which was heavily engaged on the northern sector of the Eastern Front.[20]

Due to poor weather and blizzards, Arnim did not reach his new head-quarters until 15 November. He made the last leg of the trip by half-track and sled. Two days later the 39th Panzer Corps came under massive Soviet counter-attacks in the vicinity of Tikhvin. Without support in an inhospitable wilderness, and under heavy attack by dozens of T-34 tanks, Arnim had no choice but to lead a step-by-step retreat to the River Volkhov. He accomplished this mission despite tremendous adversity. The temperature was minus 52 degrees centigrade, and casualties owing to both wounds and frostbite were extremely heavy. By the time the retreat ended on 23 December 1941, the 18th Motorized Division had only 741 men left, while the 12th Panzer Division had 1,144 survivors. The rearguard – two companies of the 51st Infantry Regiment under Lieutenant-Colonel Grosser – had been completely wiped out.[21] General Joachim Lemelsen (General Commanding 47th Panzer Corps and later commander of the 10th and 14th Armies) described Arnim on 31 December 1941 as 'Energetic, prudent [and] enterprising'. He called him a leadership personality and said that 'in a continuous crisis situation he never rested and never lost his nerve.' Lemelsen called Arnim 'an inspiration to his followers' and 'brave and fearless'. He remarked that he was always at the focal point of the battle and was co-operative. General (later Field-Marshal) Walter Model wrote on 13 December 1941 that Arnim was a 'fully proven commanding general. Energetic and willing to accept responsibility.' Colonel-General (later Field-Marshal) Ernst Busch (General Commanding 16th Army) echoed Model's comments on 1 April 1942: 'Energetic and willing to accept responsibility. Influential on the Officers' Corps and [has a] strong relationship with the troops ... in reserve or in the most difficult situations he remains unruffled and strong-nerved.'

The 39th Panzer Corps held its line throughout the harsh Russian winter. In late March 1942, the corps was taken out of the line for a brief rest. The HQ was then given command of the 12th Panzer, 20th Motorized and 122nd Infantry Divisions, plus a few smaller infantry units, and was ordered to rescue the German garrison encircled at Kholm, where 5,000 German soldiers under Lieutenant-General Theodor Scherer were desperately holding on against repeated Soviet attacks.

Arnim organized and planned his attack well. On 1 May, as soon as the weather permitted, he struck. Despite heavy resistance, the spearhead of the 39th Panzer Corps reached the encircled garrison. It did not arrive a moment too soon. Of the original 5,000 men, 1,550 had been killed and another 2,200 had been wounded.[22] Busch praised Arnim's enterprise and management in the Battle of Kholm, while Colonel-General Georg von Küchler (commander, Army Group North) agreed with his otherwise bitter enemy, Busch. He called Arnim an 'energetic, strong-willed personality, as he has proven in the Battle of Kholm.'

After the relief of Kholm, the 39th remained on the line but relatively unengaged, as the focus of the war shifted south, toward Stalingrad and the Caucasus. Not satisfied with this situation, and with time on his hands, von Arnim applied for reassignment with the Army Personnel Office (HPA), where he had many friends. On 30 November 1942, Major-General Schmundt, the Chief of HPA, telephoned Arnim and instructed him to turn his corps over to General of Artillery Robert Martinek. Arnim was summoned to Führer Headquarters at Rastenburg, East Prussia, for an important new assignment.[23]

Accompanied by his ADC, Arnim arrived at the Rastenburg airstrip, where he was met by Schmundt and General Jodl, the Chief of OKW Operations Staff. They informed him that he had been promoted to colonel-general and named commander of the 5th Panzer Army, which was then in the process of forming in Tunisia, even though it was already heavily engaged against the French, British and Americans. Arnim was introduced to his deputy commander, freshly promoted Lieutenant-General Heinz Ziegler, whom he had never met before. The new Army commander was then briefed on the situation in North Africa by Field-Marshal Keitel, the Chief of OKW, and by Hitler himself.

Briefly, the situation was this: Field-Marshal Rommel and his Panzerarmee Afrika had been defeated by Montgomery's British 8th Army at El Alamein on 3–4 November 1942. Then, on 8 November, three Allied task forces under US Lieutenant-General George S. Patton, US Lieutenant-General Lloyd R. Fredendall and US Major-General Charles W. Ryder landed at Casablanca, Oran and Algiers, respectively. They quickly subdued French resistance, which ranged from spotty to nonexistent, and at 0700 on 11 November all French resistance had ended.[24] Meanwhile, Lieutenant-General K. A. N. Anderson's British 1st Army had landed and was soon directing a thrust from Algiers to Tunis – a distance of 500 miles. If Anderson could capture Tunis and the nearby port of Bizerta, Rommel would be hopelessly trapped between two fires. To prevent this, Hitler and Field-Marshal Kesselring, the Commander-in-Chief, South, had rushed all available units to the Tunisian bridgehead.

The 'race for Tunis' was a close thing. Anderson's Anglo-Americans were within 12 miles of the city,[25] supported by 12,000 French troops under General Georges Barre, when they were halted and thrown back by General Walter

Nehring, Commander of the *ad hoc* 90th Corps. The Nazis nevertheless felt a change in command was necessary. Goebbels's agent in North Africa, Alfred-Berndt, called Nehring 'an outspoken pessimist',[26] and Kesselring – a confirmed optimist – complained that Nehring 'drew the blackest conclusions' from an Allied raid on the Djedeida Airfield on 26 November.[27] Kesselring requested that a panzer-army headquarters be established,[28] which of course meant that Nehring would be superseded. Hitler agreed; hence Arnim's promotion and summons to Rastenburg.

The Führer, as usual, was full of promises when he met von Arnim on 3 December 1942. The general asked how many divisions his new Army would have. He was promised three motorized and three panzer divisions, including the élite Hermann-Göring Panzer Division. He asked if the Führer would be able to supply the Army across the central Mediterranean, despite the Anglo-American Navies and Air Forces. Hitler promised that the supplies would be delivered.[29] The Führer confidently informed the colonel-general that he eventually planned to push the enemy out of Algeria and French Morocco.[30]

Von Arnim had spent the last fifteen months on the Eastern Front. Although he disapproved of the Nazi régime, as did most of the Prussian officer aristocracy, he was a professional soldier. When his Supreme Commander gave him his word, Arnim believed him as a general principle. He would be disillusioned in the near future.

When Arnim arrived in Tunisia to assume command of the newly-formed 5th Panzer Army, he had a very mixed bag of units under his command. These included the 10th Panzer division of Lieutenant-General Fischer, two battalions of the 5th Parachute Regiment, the Barenthin Glider Regiment, the 11th Parachute Engineer Battalion, three field replacement battalions, a few miscellaneous units, and the 501st Heavy Panzer Battalion, which was equipped with seventeen of the monstrous PzKw VI 'Tiger' tanks. During the middle two weeks of December he also received much of the inexperienced 334th Infantry Division, which had been formed only a few weeks before.[31] He also had the Italian Superga Division, the 50th Italian Special Brigade, and a few other Italian battalions.[32] Arnim had three principal missions: (1) to prevent the Anglo-Americans from capturing Tunis; (2) to stop the Allies from reaching the sea in southern Tunisia, and prevent them from cutting off Erwin Rommel's Panzerarmee Afrika, now in full retreat following its defeat at El Alamein; and (3) to expand the bridgehead in Tunisia as much as possible, to give it the depth it so badly lacked.

Initially Arnim had to quickly organize his defences to meet the Allied thrusts aimed at eliminating the bridgehead and cutting off Rommel's retreat into Tunisia. He combined most of the miscellaneous German units into the *ad hoc* Division von-Broich (Colonel Baron Friedrich von Broich)[33] and gave it the mission of defending the right (coastal) flank. The 10th Panzer, reinforced with elements of the 334th Infantry Division, defended the centre; while the unreliable Italian Superga Division covered the southern flank.

The first major battle focused on a 900-foot height called Longstop Hill, which barred the Allies' path down the Medjerda Valley, the natural approach path to the Tunisian capital, 25 miles away. Without the hill, no Allied force could advance to Tunis without having its left flank exposed.

The 2nd Battalion, the Coldstream Guards, attacked the hill on 22 December and took it from a battalion of the 754th Infantry Regiment (334th Infantry Division) early the following morning. The Coldstream were relieved by the 1st Battalion, 18th US Infantry Regiment at 0430 that morning. Colonel Rudolf Lang, the German sector commander, launched a counter-attack the same morning with the 1st Battalion of his own 69th Panzer-Grenadier Regiment and – despite heavy rain and deepening mud – retook the hill.[34] The 2nd Coldstream Guards retook the hill a second time at 1700 on Christmas Eve, 24 December.[35]

The Guards were not to hold Longstop Hill for long, because von Arnim also realized the importance of the critical hill. During the morning of 24 December Arnim, accompanied by his Chief of Staff and General Fischer, had inspected the threatened sector. Deeply concerned, Arnim had ordered up his mobile reserves – 2nd Battalion, 7th Panzer Regiment (10th Panzer Division) and additional elements of the 754th Infantry Regiment. As dawn broke on Christmas Day 1942 they were in just the right place to deal the Coldstream a severe blow. By the time that the Coldstream fell back that morning, it had lost one-quarter of its strength, including 3 company commanders, 3 sergeant-majors, and 11 platoon sergeants, after only three days on the Tunisian Front.[36] Meanwhile, the Germans dug in on Longstop Hill. The rain fell in buckets, and all of Tunisia became a quagmire. General Eisenhower, the Allied Commander-in-Chief, was forced to call off the offensive. He called it 'a bitter decision'.[37]

Bitter it no doubt was, for it meant that the Germans had won the 'race for Tunis'. Arnim was now free to secure his exposed southern flank, to prevent the Allies from cutting Rommel's supply line from Tunis, and to enlarge the bridgehead for the arrival of Rommel's Army.

Colonel-General von Arnim was an excellent tactician, as he had proved at Longstop-Hill and on the Russian Front. He proved it again in January and early February 1943, when he retained the initiative against his numerically superior opponents and won a series of important (but not decisive) local victories over them.

In December, Arnim had been forced to entrust his southern flank to the unreliable Italian Superga Division. The French forces under General Juin (about three French divisions plus the British 6th Armoured Division) had pushed the Italians back and seized most of the Eastern Dorsale mountain range, putting them in a position to strike across the coastal plain to the sea, so severing Rommel's supply line. With his right and centre now secure,

Arnim turned his attention to the next threat. On 18 January 1943 he struck the French and British in Operation *Eilbote* (Express Messenger) with elements of the 334th Infantry and 10th Panzer Divisions, plus the 501st Heavy Panzer Battalion. The British generally held their positions, but the French were forced back. Arnim's troops took 4,000 prisoners, and destroyed or captured 24 tanks, 55 guns, 27 anti-tank guns, and 228 vehicles. He broke off the offensive on the night of 23–24 January, due to supply shortages.[38] The Allies counter-attacked on 24 January and continued to do so until the 28th, but they never threatened 5th Panzer Army's grip on the Eastern Dorsale. Meanwhile, Arnim was reinforced with the 21st Panzer Division (Colonel Hans-Georg Hildebrandt), the first formation from Rommel's Army to arrive in Tunisia. On 30 January Arnim threw it forward in a surprise attack on Faid Pass, where it surrounded the poorly equipped French garrison and overwhelmed it before the nearby American armoured units could intervene. The 21st Panzer captured 1,047 men, 25 armoured cars, and 15 anti-tank guns during the operation. Hildebrandt successfully repulsed an effort by elements of the 1st US Armoured Division to retake the pass.[39] Arnim had thus secured his left flank and enlarged the southern sector to an appropriate size just as Rommel was about to arrive with the bulk of his Army.[40]

A few days later, in early February, Arnim attacked the French again. Now designated 19th French Corps under General Louis-Marie Koeltz, they had been reinforced by elements of the American 2nd Corps (Major-General Lloyd R. Fredendall). Arnim scored yet another local victory, destroying a French division and inflicting nearly 1,100 casualties on the 168th Infantry Regiment of the US 34th Infantry Division.[41]

Up until this point, von Arnim had done very well as the German commander in Tunisia. He had, however, been promoted above his ceiling, for, although an excellent tactician, he was too conservative to draw the correct conclusions from the desperate strategic position in which he now found himself.

Rommel's Panzerarmee Afrika was rapidly nearing the Tunisian bridgehead from Libya, pursued by Montgomery's British 8th Army. With him, Rommel had the German 15th Panzer, 90th Light and 164th Light Divisions, plus several miscellaneous German and Italian formations. Rommel's arrival would fundamentally change the situation in North Africa, if only temporarily, for if he and Arnim could combine their forces, they would be in a position to inflict a decisive defeat on the British 1st Army in western Tunisia before Montgomery could intervene with the 8th Army. This Axis opportunity would be all too brief, for Montgomery's arrival in strength would swing the balance back to the Allies, probably for the last time. Rommel recognized this. Unfortunately, Arnim did not.

Arnim did however realize that his long-term prospects were grim. On 8 January 1943, the administrative officers of the two panzer armies reported that between them they would need 150,000 tons of supplies per month to supply all of the troops in Tunisia and Libya. This Arnim duly reported to Kesselring – several times. Four days later Kesselring told Hitler that he could deliver 60,000 tons per month, but he did not compare this figure to the demand, nor did the Führer think to ask.[42]

In January 1943, Arnim received 58,763 tons of supplies, while Rommel received another 6,151 tons in Libya.[43] Rommel abandoned the Libyan ports that month, enabling the Allies to tighten their air and naval grip on the central Mediterranean. The Axis forces were therefore receiving only about 40 per cent of their requirements. It was easy to predict that the Italian *Commando Supremo* would not be able to maintain even current rates in the foreseeable future. Rommel saw only one solution to the dilemma: launch an all-out offensive aimed at decisively defeating the 1st British Army before the 8th Army could arrive to aid them.

It is significant that Arnim had already been in North Africa more than three months and yet neither he nor Rommel had attempted to set up a meeting to discuss co-ordinating their activities. On 9 February 1943, Kesselring arranged the first meeting between his two army commanders at the Luftwaffe base at Rennouch, Tunisia. Arnim and Rommel had last met eighteen years before, when they were both captains, and they had not liked each other then. They were of different classes, this north German aristocrat and this south German schoolteacher's son. Furthermore, Rommel's reputation as a favourite of Hitler's and his outspoken and tactless manner clashed with Arnim's cool professionalism and aloofness.[44] Despite the desperate situation in Tunisia, Arnim could never bring himself to co-operate with his more famous rival. This failure would materially contribute to the Axis defeat in North Africa, and would leave a permanent stain on his military reputation.

Kesselring's plan envisaged nothing less than the total destruction of the Americans in Tunisia. He suggested that Rommel attack the Americans to the south, at the oasis town of Gafsa, while Arnim – with the bulk of the mobile forces – did the same at Sbeitla. Once through the mountains, the German armour would then sweep north, heading for the port of Bône, eliminating the threat to Rommel's right flank and perhaps even cutting off Anderson to the north. Both Rommel and Arnim were enthusiastic about the plan, but Arnim had an important reservation. He did not have enough fuel, he said, for large-scale operations of the type Kesselring envisaged. What mattered, he said, was to inflict large losses on the French and Americans, and to force them to withdraw. He offered to start his offensive on the 12th. Rommel promised to begin his part of the offensive two days later, but, raising his index finger in a characteristic gesture, he added: 'What counts isn't any ground we gain, but the damage we inflict on the enemy.'[45] Arnim said nothing to this – a pregnant silence! – for Arnim's conservative nature was showing itself from the outset; and he, not Rommel, had the bulk of the tanks and the

Tunisia, February 1943

primary mission. Neither Rommel nor Kesselring seemed to appreciate (for the moment, at least) that Arnim's attitude and mental reservations constituted a serious threat to the plan and placed both armies' operations in jeopardy.

Kesselring then sprang his surprise. If the operation obtained the success he thought it would, he would ensure that Rommel would be placed in command of *all* the forces in Tunisia, even though he knew Arnim was anxious for his rival to depart. Later, Kesselring privately told Arnim that he had already consulted with Professor Horster, Rommel's physician, who had recommended that the marshal depart for a rest cure in Europe on 20 February. 'Let's give Rommel this one last chance of glory before he gets out of Africa,' Kesselring said to Arnim.

'Yes,' Arnim replied, smiling. 'One last chance of glory....'[46]

The opponent Arnim faced in mid-February was Major-General Lloyd Fredendall, a loud-mouthed, overbearing and opinionated man who did not

345

have the gift of working well with others. Under his inept command, us 2nd Corps (on the right flank of the British 1st Army) had dug no defensive positions and had laid no minefields. Although his 1st Armoured Division (Major-General Orlando Ward) had more tanks than the three panzer divisions in Tunisia combined, his corps was spread out all over the Dorsale ranges, and he had completely mixed up his armour with the forward elements of the 1st and 34th us Infantry Divisions, so that rapid concentration was impossible. Fredendall had devoted most of his time to making sure his own HQ – located 70 miles to the rear – was secure against Luftwaffe attack. All of his dispositions had been made on the basis of map reconnaissance; he had not visited the front even once.[47]

The German plan called for Arnim to push through Faid to Sidi Bou Zid, to complete his control of the eastern Dorsale. Afterwards he was to drive north to Pichon. Meanwhile, Rommel was to strike at Gafsa, and then was possibly to exploit toward Tebessa, depending on the situation. Arnim was supposed to return the 21st Panzer Division to Rommel after clearing the Faid area.[48] Arnim placed Ziegler in charge of the 10th and 21st Panzer Divisions (about 130 tanks) for the Sidi Bou Zid attack.

Group Ziegler's attack began on 14 February 1943. Spearheaded by the 501st Heavy Panzer Battalion, it roared through Faid pass and struck Combat Command A of the 1st Armoured Division and the 168th Infantry Regiment. The tanks of the 1st Battalion were light Stuart 'Honeys', which were virtually useless against the Tigers, PzKw IIIs, and PzKw IVs of the 5th Panzer Army. The battalion was quickly slaughtered; and the commanding officer captured. The 2nd Battalion fared no better, losing 44 of its 51 Shermans. The 168th Infantry Regiment was also overrun and its commander captured. Two supporting artillery battalions were likewise destroyed and panic set in among some units. By the end of the day, Combat Command A and the 168th were both smashed.[49]

General Ward tried to retrieve the situation the next day by committing his reserve, Combat Command C (Colonel Robert I. Stack), spearheaded by the 54 Shermans of the 2nd Battalion, 1st Armoured Regiment. They ran into an ambush. The 10th Panzer Division (under Broich since Fischer had been killed in action on 5 February) hit them from the north and, at the critical moment, Hildebrandt's 21st Panzer Division struck them from the south. By the end of the day Stack was in full retreat. His infantry was still basically intact, but the commander of the 2nd Battalion had been captured and 50 of his tanks had been knocked out.[50] In two days, Arnim's men had destroyed two tank, two infantry, and two artillery battalions of the us 2nd Corps. Meanwhile, on the southern flank, Rommel moved forward at dusk, only to find Fredendall retreating and Gafsa abandoned.

Rommel now planned to push on to the crossroads village of Feriana, from which he could advance north to Tebessa in Algeria, or northeast through

Thelepte to Kasserine, where he could join up with Arnim's panzers driving from Sbeitla. On the morning of the 16th Arnim refused to release the 21st Panzer Division, on the grounds that Rommel had already taken Gafsa without it and that the division was still engaged in the vicinity of Sidi Bou Zid. He ordered Ziegler to send the 21st Panzer east to take Sbeitla, and he sent the 10th Panzer Division to attack toward Fondouk,[51] far north of Rommel's zone of operations. He was, in effect, dissipating the German effort into the mountains.[52] Rommel at first seemed to have accepted this decision, but soon his nature reasserted itself. He protested to Kesselring and requested that both the 10th Panzer and 21st Panzer Divisions be turned over to him, so he could attack the American supply centre at Tebessa. Kesselring supported Rommel, but felt it necessary to obtain the approval of OKW, Mussolini and *Commando Supremo* for such a change in plan. 'Rommel was forced to kick his heels while von Arnim pressed on with his own operations,' the British General Jackson wrote later.[53] Precious hours were lost while the top Axis commands conferred, sent messages, and deliberated.

Lieutenant-General Ziegler was not a competent handler of armour. He did not even begin his advance until the afternoon of the 16th, and did not attack Sbeitla until noon on the 17th. Meanwhile, the Americans regained their composure and rallied. First Armored Division's Combat Command B (Brigadier-General Paul Robinett) held the town until ordered to retreat as night fell. Robinett conducted as orderly a withdrawal toward Tebessa as was possible with his green troops, and allowed the rest of the 1st Armored Division to escape. Ziegler pursued him in a leisurely fashion; most of Robinett's difficulties were caused by Stuka dive-bombers.[54] By the end of the day, the Allied southern wing was wheeling back to the line of the Western Dorsale mountain ridges. The Germans had already captured nearly 3,000 prisoners and destroyed or captured 169 tanks, but their prey was escaping. Meanwhile, Arnim signaled Rommel that he would send no troops forward of the Eastern Dorsale because of the difficulty in supplying them[55] – in effect ending the operation after a few local victories and doing exactly what the enemy would have wanted him to do.

Commando Supremo took the battle out of Arnim's hands early on the morning of 19 February, when it gave Rommel both the 10th Panzer and 21st Panzer Divisions. Unfortunately, it set Le Kef as the initial objective, meaning Rommel would have to advance to the north, where the Allied reserves were strongest, instead of to the west (via Tebessa), where Rommel might have outflanked them. In addition, without telling either Kesselring or Rommel, Arnim disobeyed orders and withheld much of the 10th Panzer Division, including the Tigers of the 501st Heavy Panzer Battalion.[56] This further sabotaged Rommel's plans. Even after Kesselring summoned him to Tunis on the afternoon of the 20th and severely castigated him for not supporting Rommel properly, Arnim continued to withhold the vital Tigers.[57] Although

Rommel managed to win a last famous victory over the Americans at Kasserine Pass on 20 February, the momentum of the offensive was clearly lost. With Kesselring's approval, Rommel called off the offensive on 22 February. It had been a German victory – but not a decisive one. The last Axis opportunity to avoid defeat in North Africa had been lost.

The next day, 23 February, Army Group Afrika was created. Hitler had already said that he preferred Arnim as its commander, but Kesselring had found Arnim's conduct in the past operation so obstructive that he appointed Rommel to the post instead.[58] At the same time General Vittorio Ambrosio, the Chief of Staff of the Italian Armed Forces, informed Mussolini that Rommel would be replaced by Arnim in the near future.[59] Rommel was, in fact, in ill-health after two years on the Western Desert, and he was suffering from a variety of disorders, including depression. Meanwhile, Panzerarmee Afrika was redesignated 1st Italian Army and placed under the command of General Giovanni Messe, a veteran of the Eastern Front. The German troops in this Army received their orders from Colonel Fritz Bayerlein, Messe's German Chief of Staff.

Colonel-General von Arnim paid little attention to the new command arrangement. On 24 February he flew to Rome without Rommel's knowledge and secured Kesselring's permission to launch his own offensive in northern Tunisia. Appropriately christened Operation *Ochsenkopf* (Oxhead), it was predicated on the assumption that the Allies had greatly weakened their northern flank to contain the Kasserine thrust. The offensive began on 26 February. The German forces included Division 'von Manteuffel' (under Colonel Hasso von Manteuffel, who had replaced Baron von Broich), Weber's 334th Infantry Division, half of the 10th Panzer Division (including the 501st Heavy Panzer Battalion), and newly-arrived elements of the Hermann Göring Panzer Division. The main burden of the defence fell to the British 46th Infantry Division, but also involved the British 78th Infantry Division and the *ad hoc* Division 'Y'.

Oxhead was ill-conceived from the beginning. Manteuffel managed to score a few local successes, but in general the offensive was an overly-dispersed series of ill prepared attacks against an unsurprised enemy in good defensive positions. Arnim's units captured 2,500 prisoners against a loss of about 1,000 casualties, but this success was more than outweighed by the fact that 71 panzers were destroyed, including almost all of the Tigers.[60] By this point, German panzer losses far exceeded supply. In November and December 1942 respectively, 187 and 191 panzers arrived in Africa. In January 1943, the total dropped to 50, rose to 52 in February, and declined to only 20 in March. The total for April would stand at 44, and none were to arrive in May.[61] The British lost fewer than 20 tanks in *Oxhead*, and these were easily replaced.

More serious than the panzer losses was the fact that Arnim's abortive offensive delayed Rommel's own attack against the British 8th Army. On 26

February, Montgomery had only one division at Medenine, facing the 1st Italian Army, so it was definitely vulnerable. When Rommel struck on 6 March, Montgomery had installed the equivalent of four divisions including about 400 tanks, 350 guns, and 470 anti-tank guns.[62] Rommel attacked with all three panzer divisions and was completely defeated. Forty panzers were totally destroyed without the loss of a single British tank. Three days later Rommel left Africa, never to return. He was placed in Führer-reserve and sent on indefinite sick leave. Dieter von Arnim assumed command of Army Group Afrika on 9 March, 1943. He had reached the pinnacle of his military career. General Gustav von Vaerst replaced him at 5th Panzer Army.[63]

Arnim's cause in Tunisia was hopeless from the beginning. When he took over command of the Army Group, he had 350,000 men, of which 120,000 were combat troops. Two-thirds of the fighting troops were German, as were one-third of the support troops.[64] They faced more than half a million Allied soldiers, including more than 250,000 combat troops. He had barely 200 operational tanks to face 1,800 enemy tanks, backed by more than 1,200 guns and 1,500 anti-tank guns.[65] He was defending 387 miles of frontage – far too much for his available forces. The average company sector was 2.5 miles long, and his artillery density was less than one gun per mile. Nevertheless he might have been able to hold at least part of the bridgehead had his superiors been able to supply him. Arnim needed 140,000 tons of supplies per month, but in January only 46,069 tons arrived, and this total fell to 32,967 tons the following month.[66] Two weeks before he assumed command of the Army Group, Arnim sent a situation appreciation to Rommel and Messe, stating that he believed Eisenhower was planning to drive a wedge between the two trapped Armies; however, if he were Eisenhower he would not bother, for 'if no supplies reach us, all will be up in Tunisia by 1st July', even without an Allied offensive.[67]

Arnim conducted the last battles in Tunisia with his usual tactical skill. He has been accused of attempting to hold as much of the original bridgehead as possible – an unrealistic determination that accelerated the Axis collapse in North Africa. This simply is not true. Blame for this decision lies mainly with Kesselring, who, as Rommel said, 'saw everything with rose-colored glasses'.[68] General von Rintelen, German Military Attaché to Italy, was also of the opinion that Kesselring let his excessive optimism cloud his judgment on operations in Tunisia.[69] Arnim, on the other hand, correctly foresaw that the next Allied offensive would be launched on the coastal plain by Montgomery's 8th Army, which had halted before the Mareth Line. A secondary offensive would be launched simultaneously by the US 2nd Corps, now led by the capable Lieutenant-General George S. Patton Jr, with the aim of freezing Arnim's reserves and possibly cutting the Army Group in two. Arnim wanted to shorten his front in the north and withdraw the 1st Italian Army further up the coast, reducing the size of the bridgehead, but permission to do so was denied by Kesselring after a heated argument with Arnim.[70]

Meanwhile, Rommel and Arnim were for once working toward a common goal. On 12 March Rommel wrote to his successor that neither OKW nor *Commando Supremo* would sanction a retreat, but that Hitler would allow the non-motorized Italian units to retreat to the Wadi Akarit positions north of Mareth. Arnim ordered them to withdraw on 14 March, but when General Ambrosio heard of this two days later he angrily forbade it.[71] Meanwhile, US 2nd Corps began its offensive.

Whatever one's opinion of the fractious Patton, he was undoubtedly a leader and a fine motivator of troops in the field. The 2nd Corps that attacked Gafsa on 17 March little resembled the pitiful force that almost collapsed before Arnim and Rommel a month before. Striking with four divisions, Patton smashed the Italian *Centauro* Armoured Division in an operation he characteristically styled Operation *Wop*. He took Gafsa on the 17th and forced Arnim to commit both the 10th Panzer and 21st Panzer Divisions. Although the American advance stalled east of El Guettar (resulting in Patton's sacking of General Ward), Arnim had been forced to commit two-thirds of his mobile reserve on the eve of Montgomery's Mareth offensive.

Montgomery began his offensive on 20 March 1943. His frontal attack initially checked by the 1st Italian Army,[72] he sent the New Zealand Corps around Messe's flank, forcing the complete evacuation of the Mareth position by 28 March. Only the slowness of Montgomery's pursuit allowed Messe to escape, but due to Kesselring's failure to allow Arnim to evacuate the Mareth Line, Messe arrived too late to prepare the Wadi Akarit Line properly for defence.[73]

Meanwhile, Arnim was constantly calling for more supplies. On the 29th he signalled *Commando Supremo* that he had ammunition for only one or two days' fighting and that he had no more stocks for certain weapons, such as medium howitzers. 'Fuel situation similar,' he radioed. 'Large-scale movement no longer possible.'[74]

The same day Field-Marshal Kesselring had a heated argument with General Ambrosio, who wanted to give Arnim permission to retreat to Enfidaville if he felt that the 1st Italian Army was in danger of destruction. Kesselring objected on the grounds that prior approval might make Arnim 'retreat-minded'. Mussolini sided with Ambrosio, who transmitted the order to Army-Group headquarters, so Kesselring sent his Chief of Staff, Major-General Siegfried Westphal, to Tunisia to 'explain' the order to General von Arnim.[75]

The Arnim-Westphal conference yielded no positive results. Arnim refused to consider a series of counter-attacks recommended by Kesselring. Westphal was undiplomatic enough to suggest that the Army Group always seemed to be 'squinting over its shoulder'. Yes, that's right, Arnim replied: they were squinting at the horizon for supply ships that never arrived. He closed the conference with the remark: 'We are without bread and ammunition, as was

Rommel's Army before. The consequences are inevitable.'[76] Later that day he frankly informed General Silvio Rossi (Ambrosio's Chief of Operations) that the enemy, not the 1st Italian Army, would decide how long the Wadi positions would be held. He bluntly recommended that the High Command occupy itself in getting supplies to North Africa, rather than trying to direct operations. The next day he ordered the evacuation of all inessential personnel.[77]

The Battle of Wadi Akarit began on 5 April 1943 and Messe evacuated the position during the night of 6–7 April. During the battle more than 5,000 Italians surrendered and the Pistoia Division virtually ceased to exist. The next day, 7 April, Montgomery linked up with Patton, joining the British 1st and 8th Armies. The ring around Army Group Afrika was closed.[78]

Covered by the remnants of the *Afrika Korps*, Arnim retreated into his final bridgehead.[79] On 13 April, Kesselring transmitted orders from Hitler and Mussolini for Arnim to hold to the last. Kesselring also ordered surplus administrative troops sent to combat or labour units, but stated that absolutely 'useless mouths' could be evacuated. He also promised reinforcements, but did not say how they would be sent, when they would arrive, or how they would be fed.[80] Arnim apparently did not even bother to reply. Supplies were nearly exhausted and 41.5 per cent of the transport sent to Tunisia in March had been sunk. The percentage for April would be the same, and the Army Group would receive less than 30,000 tons.[81] The only reinforcements he had received since February, other than replacements and a few Italian units of marginal value, were part of the Hermann Göring Panzer Division and Major-General Kurt Thomas's 999th Light Afrika Division – a penal unit![82]

On 22 April, General Sir Harold Alexander, the commander of the recently activated 18th Army Group, launched the 'final offensive'. It was not final, for it was halted on the 29th, but Arnim had expended almost all his fuel and ammunition in heavy fighting. By 1 May, he had less than one issue of artillery shells and the supply dumps were empty. During the night Arnim retreated to his final defensive line. The Americans were only 15 miles from Bizerta.[83]

Arnim knew his command was doomed. He had only 76 tanks left and his supply staffs were distilling fuel from low-grade Tunisian wines and liquors.[84] On one pretext or another (mainly illness) he sent off Weber, Manteuffel and his Chief of Staff, Lieutenant-General Gause.[85] Major-General Hildebrandt did not hesitate to accept a new appointment in Europe, as did Lieutenant-General Ziegler, who had proved to be no great asset. On the other hand several officers who were given the chance to leave the diminishing pocket refused to go. Colonels von Quast (Vaerst's Chief of Staff) and Pomtow, the Army-Group Operations officer, elected to remain at their posts, as did General von Vaerst, Major-General von Liebenstein (the commander of the 164th Light Afrika Division), Baron von Broich, Major-General von Sponeck (commander of the 90th Light Division), and Major-General Borowietz, the last commander of the 15th Panzer Division.[86]

One young officer who grudgingly consented to go, but only after he had been given the most stringent orders, was Major Harry von Kathen, Arnim's long-time adjutant and the fiancé of Elisabeth, Arnim's only child. Kathen was instructed to return to Germany to arrange for the care of Arnim's wife and daughter, whom he had resettled at Rietz in the Palatinate in late 1941. In the end, Kathen had to be almost bodily loaded on the aircraft.[87]

On 4 May, Mussolini rejected a plan to withdraw secretly selected commanders and staffs back to Italy, because Kesselring even now assured him that the situation was not desperate. Jodl rejected a similar plan submitted by Schmundt.[88]

On the morning of 6 May the Allies launched their second final offensive. Attacks were launched all along the front, but the main thrust came in a valley south of the Medjerda River, where Arnim had massed almost all his remaining armour – 60 tanks – under the command of the 15th Panzer Division. Arnim had planned to move the 10th Panzer and 21st Panzer Divisions, plus the anti-aircraft battalions of the 19th Flak Division to this sector, even though it would mean denuding the 1st Italian Army's sector, but he lacked the fuel to carry out the move. The main attack was delivered by the 4th British, 4th Indian, 6th Armoured and 7th Armoured Divisions. By the end of the day the British had advanced 12 miles – half the distance to Tunis – and Arnim was signalling that the 15th Panzer Division was destroyed. Only excessive Allied caution prevented the fall of the city.[89]

Arnim continued to try to resist but he had lost control of the battle. Both Tunis and Bizerta fell on the afternoon of 7 May and mass surrenders began. At 0930 General von Vaerst signalled Arnim that his armour and artillery had been destroyed and he was without fuel or ammunition. Fifth Panzer Army surrendered later that day.[90]

On 9 May the last three German aircraft reached Tunisia, deposited a few drums of fuel and some machine-gun ammunition, took on some wounded soldiers and took off again. They left behind an order from Hitler's HQ at Rastenburg – Army Group Afrika was to fight to the last man. Arnim interpreted this order in his own way. The Army Group was to fight to the last bullet – and the last bullet in a tank battle was the last tank or cannon shell.[91]

One by one the units went off the air. Finally, on 12 May, Arnim was captured, along with the Headquarters of the *Afrika korps*. He refused to surrender on behalf of his whole Army Group, on the grounds that he was out of contact with his subordinate units. This refusal made little difference, however. Messe and his German Chief of Staff, Colonel Anton Markert, surrendered the 1st Italian Army on the afternoon of 13 May 1943. An hour later Alexander signalled Churchill that it was all over in Tunisia: 'We are the masters of the North African shores.'

Colonel Pomtow wrote to Paul Carell that Arnim was 'one of the last knights of the Old School'. Carell added that Arnim 'fulfilled his task with a consideration, courage and humanity which neither his own soldiers nor the enemy have forgotten.'[92] Certainly the enemy did not forget one incident. In the first days of May, the RAF attacked the Italian ship *Belluno*, unaware that there were 700 wounded British prisoners on board. Arnim ordered one of his staff officers to send a message to Alexander in the clear, 'Stop the air attack on Tunis harbour. The ship has 700 POWs on board.' Alexander reacted quickly and the aircraft were recalled. Arnim thus saved the lives of 700 British captives. In recognition of this fact, and at Arnim's request, Alexander released 700 wounded Germans after the fall of Tunisia.[93]

Dieter von Arnim was the second-ranking German prisoner in western hands (after Rudolf Hess) at the time of his capture. He initially received considerable publicity, but soon quietly faded from the stage of history. Historians have since been severely critical of him for his undeniable failures in February 1943, especially at Kasserine, when his inflexibly conservative attitude wrecked Rommel's chances of turning the Kasserine attacks into one of the most daring panzer operations of the war. For his decisive failure his overall leadership in Tunisia must also be judged a failure. Historians have, however, generally been too harsh on Arnim, at least in this writer's view. Certainly he was no Rommel – but then a great many generals who lacked Rommel's genius have been dealt with less harshly than Arnim. Although he undoubtedly failed at the strategic level, his record proves he was a gifted tactician. Certainly he did not fail as a human being. He fought his war with a humanity one would expect from one of the last Prussian knights – unlike many of the Nazi generals who subsequently stood trial as war criminals. In recognition of this fact, the British kept him prisoner in a 'beautiful' mansion in Hampshire, England. On 5 October 1943, when his only child married Major von Kathen at the villa of Grosse-Rietz in the Palatinate, they allowed the prisoner to send a radio message of congratulations.[94]

Colonel-General Hans-Jürgen ('Dieter') von Arnim was released from captivity and returned to western Germany in 1947. His lands and investments in East Germany had been confiscated by the communists and he was forced to live on his pension, which was granted in 1949. He died in a nursing home in Bad Wildungen on 1 September 1962, at the age of 73.[95]

NOTES

1 Jürgen von Arnim Personnel Record, United States National Archives, Washington, DC (hereafter cited as 'Arnim Personnel Record').
2 Friedrich von Stauffenberg, 'Hans-Juergen Theodor (Dieter) von Arnim',

unpublished manuscript in the possession of the author (hereafter cited as 'Stauffenberg MS').

3 *Ibid.*

4 Arnim Personnel Record.

5 *Ibid.*

6 Stauffenberg MS.

7 Arnim Personnel Record.

8 *New York Times*, 13 May 1943.

9 Arnim Personnel Record.

10 *Ibid.*

11 Stauffenberg MS.

12 Arnim Personnel Record.

13 Stauffenberg MS. As Artillerieführer VII, Curtse was also one of the two deputy commanders of the 7th Infantry Division, headquartered in Munich.

14 Arnim Personnel Record.

15 *Ibid.*; Stauffenberg MS.

16 United States Military Intelligence Service, 'Order of Battle of the German Army', Washington, DC: United States War Department General Staff, 1942. The 52nd Infantry fought on the Russian Front from 1941 to 1944. It had suffered such heavy losses that it was reorganized as a two-regiment security division in 1943, and was smashed in the Russian summer offensive of 1944. The headquarters was used to form Fortress Command Libau in the Courland pocket in 1945.

17 Arnim replaced Lieutenant-General Friedrich Bergmann, who was given command of the 137th Infantry Division. Bergmann was killed on the Eastern Front on 21 December 1941. Arnim himself was replaced by Major-General (later Colonel-General) Dr Lothar Rendulic, who later distinguished himself as the commander of the 35th Corps on the Eastern Front (1942–3). He later commanded the 2nd Panzer and 20th Mountain Armies and three different Army Groups, but with less success. See Wolf Keilig, *Die Generale des Heeres* (Friedberg: Podzun-Pallas-Verlag, 1983), pp. 30, 273 (hereafter cited as 'Keilig').

18 Stauffenberg MS. Thoma later became commander of the *Afrika Korps* and was captured at El Alamein. He was a prison mate of Arnim's in 1943.

19 Paul Carell, *Hitler Moves East, 1941–43* (Boston: Little, Brown, 1965; reprint edn, New York: Bantam books, 1966), pp. 129, 138–41 (hereafter cited as 'Carell, 1966').

20 Initially Arnim was acting commander only, substituting for General Rudolf Schmidt, who was serving as acting commander of the 2nd Army. Arnim became permanent commander only after Hitler sacked Guderian and named Schmidt commander of the 2nd Panzer Army in late December 1941.

21 Carell, 1966, p. 286.

22 *Ibid.*, pp. 434–7. Kholm had been surrounded since 28 January 1942.

23 Stauffenberg MS.

24 For the story of the Allied invasion of North Africa, see William B. Breuer, *Operation Torch* (New York: St Martin's Press, 1985).

25 Peter Young (ed.), *Illustrated World War II Encyclopedia* (Monaco: Jaspard Polus, 1966; reprint edn, H. S. Stuttman, n.d.), Volume 7, p. 993.

26 Paul Joseph Goebbels, *The Goebbels Diaries* (Garden City, New York: Doubleday, 1948; reprint edn, New York: Universal-Award House, 1971), p. 281.
27 Alfred Kesselring, *A Soldier's Record* (Westport, Connecticut: Greenwood Press, 1970), p. 169.
28 *Ibid.*, p. 170.
29 Paul Carell, *The Foxes of the Desert* (New York: E. P. Dutton, 1960; reprint edn, New York: Bantam Books, 1972), pp. 324–5 (hereafter cited as 'Carell, 1972').
30 David Irving, *Hitler's War* (New York: Viking Press, 1977), p. 459 (hereafter cited as 'Irving').
31 Weber was promoted to major-general on 1 January 1943. He left Africa on 1 May 1943, and later led the 298th and 131st Infantry Divisions on the Eastern Front. Promoted to lieutenant-general on 1 July 1944, his last command was the *ad hoc* Division Warsaw (20 December 1944 to 25 January 1945) (Keilig, p. 363). He apparently shared the blame for the fall of the Polish capital with the 9th Army's commander, General Baron Smilo von Lüttwitz. Weber was not re-employed.
32 I. S. O. Playfair and C. J. C. Molony, *The Mediterranean and Middle East*, Volume IV, *The Destruction of the Axis Forces in Africa* (London: Her Majesty's Stationery Office, 1966), pp. 169–173 (hereafter cited as 'Playfair and Molony, Volume IV').
33 Colonel Baron von Broich had commanded the 6th, 21st and 22nd Cavalry Regiments and the 1st Cavalry and 24th Panzer-Grenadier Brigades earlier in the war. When Lieutenant-General Fischer was killed on 5 February 1943, Broich assumed command of the 10th Panzer Division, which he surrendered on 12 May. He was promoted to lieutenant-general on 1 July 1943, while a POW (Keilig, p. 216). After Broich took charge of the 10th Panzer, Division 'von Broich' was redesignated Division 'von Manteuffel' after its new commander, Colonel Hasso von Manteuffel.
34 George F. Howe, *Northwest Africa: Seizing the Initiative in the West* (Washington, DC: Office of the Chief of Military History, United States Department of the Army, 1957), pp. 339–41 (hereafter cited as 'Howe').
35 Playfair and Molony, Volume IV, p. 188.
36 Howe, pp. 340–1; Charles Whiting, *Kasserine* (Briarcliff Manor, New York: Stein & Day, 1984), p. 143 (hereafter cited as 'Whiting').
37 Dwight D. Eisenhower, *Crusade in Europe* (Garden City, New York: Doubleday, 1949), p. 124.
38 Playfair and Molony, Volume IV, p. 278; Howe, pp. 389–91. This attack was supported by the Italian 50th Special Brigade.
39 Howe, pp. 392–4.
40 B. H. Liddell Hart, *History of the Second World War* (New York: G. P. Putnam's Sons, 1972), Volume II, p. 402 (hereafter cited as 'Hart, Volume II'); Christopher Chant *et al.* (eds), *Hitler's Generals* (New York: Chartwell Books, 1979), p. 134.
41 Whiting, p. 160.
42 Playfair and Molony, Volume IV, p. 274.
43 *Ibid.*, p. 210.
44 Whiting, p. 159.
45 *Ibid.*, p. 162.
46 *Ibid.*, p. 164.

47 *Ibid.*, pp. 163–4; Martin Blumenson, *Kasserine Pass* (New York: PBJ Books, 1983), pp. 83–7.
48 Playfair and Molony, Volume IV, pp. 288–9.
49 Howe, pp. 410–19; Whiting, pp. 173–182; W. G. F. Jackson, *The Battle for North Africa, 1940–43* (New York: Mason Charter, 1975), pp. 339–41 (hereafter cited as 'Jackson').
50 Howe, pp. 419–22; Whiting, pp. 187–91.
51 Playfair and Molony, Volume IV, pp. 293–4; Howe, p. 425.
52 Ronald Lewin, *Rommel as a Military Commander* (New York: Van Nostrand, 1968; reprint edn, New York: Ballantine Books, 1970), p. 255 (hereafter cited as 'Lewin').
53 Jackson, p. 342.
54 Hart, Volume II, p. 405.
55 Playfair and Molony, Volume IV, pp. 294–5.
56 Jackson, p. 342.
57 Lewin, pp. 260–1.
58 Jackson, p. 347.
59 Playfair and Molony, Volume IV, p. 269.
60 Hart, Volume II, p. 411; Playfair and Molony, Volume IV, pp. 326–7.
61 Howe, pp. 682–3.
62 Hart, Volume II, p. 411.
63 Gustav von Vaerst had led the 15th Panzer Division of the *Afrika Korps* from 9 December 1941 until 1 December 1942, except for about two months, when he was recovering from wounds received in the Battle of the Gazala Line. Prior to this he had commanded the 2nd Rifle Brigade. He was promoted to General of Panzer Troops on 1 March 1943 (Keilig, p. 353).
64 Howe, p. 510.
65 Hart, Volume II, p. 412.
66 Howe, pp. 510–13.
67 Playfair and Molony, Volume IV, p. 322.
68 Erwin Rommel, *The Rommel Papers*, B. H. Liddell Hart (ed.) (New York: Harcourt, Brace, 1953), p. 407.
69 Playfair and Molony, Volume IV, p. 395.
70 *Ibid.*, pp. 329–30.
71 *Ibid.*, p. 330.
72 The 1st Italian Army included the Italian Young Fascists, Trieste, Spezia and Pistoia Divisions, plus the German 90th Light, 164th Light Afrika, and 15th Panzer Divisions.
73 Playfair and Molony, Volume IV, pp. 348–59. Arnim had requested the evacuation of the Mareth Line as early as 24 March, but was overruled by Kesselring.
74 *Ibid.*, p. 359.
75 *Ibid.*, p. 360.
76 *Ibid.*
77 *Ibid.*, pp. 360–1.
78 Jackson, p. 375.
79 Howe, pp. 590–1.

80 Playfair and Molony, Volume IV, p. 394.

81 *Ibid.*, p. 417; Howe, pp. 682–3.

82 Despite its origins, the 999th Light fought well. Thomas, the former Commandant of Führer Headquarters (15 February 1940 to 1 September 1942), was killed on 5 May 1943. He was posthumously promoted to lieutenant-general on 1 October 1943 (Keilig, p. 345).

83 Hart, Volume II, p. 427.

84 Irving, p. 514.

85 Manteuffel ended the war as commander of the 3rd Panzer Army on the Eastern Front. Gause would have done better to have remained in Tunisia. After serving as Chief of Staff of Army Group B, 5th Panzer Army and 6th Panzer Army, he was named commander of the II Corps in the Courland Pocket on 1 April, 1945. He surrendered to the Russians in May 1945 and was not released from prison until 10 October 1955 (Keilig, p. 101).

86 Stauffenberg MS. Borowietz committed suicide in an American POW camp in 1945.

87 Stauffenberg MS.

88 Playfair and Molony, Volume IV, pp. 445–6.

89 *Ibid.*; Howe, pp. 646–8; Playfair, p. 451.

90 Hart, Volume II, p. 430.

91 Carell 1972, pp. 353–4; Stauffenberg MS.

92 Carell 1972, pp. 346–7.

93 *Ibid.*

94 Stauffenberg MS; *New York Times*, 1 June 1943.

95 Stauffenberg MS.

CHRONOLOGY: HANS-JÜRGEN 'DIETER' VON ARNIM

1889, April 4	Born at Ernsdorf, Silesia
1908, April 1	*Fahnenjunker*, 4th Prussian Foot Guards Regiment
1909, October 1	Commissioned *Leutnant*
1913, October 1	Battalion Adjutant
1914, November 23	Deputy Regimental Adjutant
1915, January 21	*Oberleutnant*
1915, November 1	Company Commander
1916, October 20	Ordnance Officer, 4th Guards Jäger Division
1917, January 27	*Hauptmann*
1917, March 26	Married Annemarie von Dechend in Berlin
1917, July 4	Divisional Adjutant
1917, October 20	Battalion Commander, 4th Guards Jäger Division
1919, May 1	Company Commander, 29th Infantry Regiment
1920, October 1	Battalion Commander, 5th Infantry Regiment
1921, October 1	Adjutant, 2nd Infantry Division
1922, October 1	General Staff, Army Group 2
1924, October 1	Reich Defence Ministry
1925, October 1	General Staff, Army Group 1
1928, April 1	Major, to date from 1 February 1928

357

1929, October 1	Chief of Staff, Artillery Leader VII
1932, April 1	Lieutenant-Colonel
1932, October 1	Commander, I Battalion, 2nd Infantry Regiment
1934, March 15	Chief of Staff, Infantry Leader VI
1935, October 15	Commander, 68th Infantry Regiment
1938, January 1	Major-General
1938, February 4	Commander, Army Service Depot 4, Schweidnitz
1939, May 1	Extra Officer, OKH Berlin
1939, December 1	Lieutenant-General
1940, October 5	Commander, 17th Panzer Division
1941, June 26	Seriously wounded, Eastern Front
1941, September 17	Resumed command of 17th Panzer
1941, early November	General of Panzer Troops, with date of rank 1 October 1941
1941, November 15	Assumed command of 39th Panzer Corps
1942, December 3	Commander, 5th Panzer Army
1943, March 9	Commander-in-Chief, Army Group Afrika
1943, May 12	Captured
1947	Returned to Germany and released
1949	Granted a pension by the West German government
1962, September 1	Died in Bad Wildungen

PAULUS

15

PAULUS

Field-Marshal Friedrich Paulus

MARTIN MIDDLEBROOK

Paulus and Stalingrad; the names are always linked, the German commander who suffered one of the greatest military defeats in history and the hitherto unknown Russian city where that defeat took place.

Friedrich Paulus was born in 1890, in that narrow window of time which brought him to the First World War as a junior officer and to the Second as a general. His birthplace was Breitenau, a little country town deep in Hesse. His ancestors were of basic country stock but some became minor public servants; Paulus's father was the cashier of an approved school. He inherited good health, a fine physique and a noble bearing from those forebears but he was far from being a 'von', a prefix frequently but mistakenly attributed to him. He soon suffered from his lack of social status. After performing well at school, he applied for a cadetship in the Imperial Navy but was refused. Disappointed, he turned to the study of law at Marburg University but was quickly released from this when the German Army started to expand in 1910 and to widen the social spectrum from which new officers came. He was accepted as an officer cadet by a provincial unit, the 111th Infantry Regiment, a unit which also carried the earlier title of 'Markgraf Ludwig's 3rd Baden Regiment'. Within two years, he was a lieutenant and it was then that he met his future wife, Elena Rosetti-Solescu, a beautiful young woman one year his senior, from a wealthy and aristocratic Romanian family. Her two brothers were serving in Paulus's regiment and it was through them that Paulus met his bride while all were on leave together in the Black Forest.

Their first child, a daughter, was born in 1914, the year in which Paulus went off to war.

The 111th Infantry Regiment was part of the 28th Infantry Division, 14th Corps, 7th Army. The 7th Army was not part of the great drive through Belgium of the Schlieffen Plan but performed the more mundane task of pushing out from the Rhine through the Vosges to confront the right-flank French forces on the frontier and hold them there by steady action to prevent the French high command transferring forces to their threatened left flank. The French, in turn, had their own plan for a violent general offensive ('Plan 17') in Lorraine, and there followed the 'Battles of the Frontier' in which the French attacks were cut to ribbons. Paulus's position at this time was Adjutant of his regiment's 3rd Battalion. In October 1914, after the Battle of the Marne, and the extension of the Western Front towards the coast, the Army found itself north of Arras where the four-year-long trench warfare was beginning. Paulus's regiment may have been in action against British troops on the Vermelles sector in late October but the sources are conflicting and it may be that the French were his only opponents in this hectic opening phase.

Paulus had to leave the front in November because of illness and he never returned to his first regiment. His next posting was as Regimental Staff Officer to a much more prestigious unit, the 2nd Prussian Jäger Regiment. This was part of the *Alpenkorps*, a formation roughly the strength of an enlarged division, which was not normally used for routine trench holding but was reserved for fighting in mountainous country or for use as shock troops. Paulus remained with the *Alpenkorps* for the remainder of the war, moving to the corps headquarters in 1917 and carrying out staff duties throughout. He never commanded any unit of any size at any time in the war.

The *Alpenkorps* served in Romania and Macedonia in 1915 and early 1916 but in June of that year was flung into violent action in the later stages of the Battle of Verdun, making a particularly successful advance against the village of Fleury. The *Alpenkorps* took 2,000 French prisoners but two-thirds of its own strength of 12,000 men became casualties during this period. The corps remained on sectors facing the French until May 1917 until withdrawn for a rest. The next major action was during the series of great German offensives in the spring of 1918. On 9 April, the *Alpenkorps* took part in the attack on the mainly British sector on the Lys. After a further rest in Belgium, the corps was back in action, in defence this time, against the British counter-offensive on the Somme which started on 8 August. The corps had to be withdrawn after a particularly hard fight at Epéhy and spent the final weeks of the war in Serbia.

The Armistice found Paulus holding the rank of captain and with only the routine decorations of the Iron Cross Classes I and II. Little is known of the next few years, except that he managed to stay in the small post-war army which the Allies allowed Germany to retain. He served a two-year spell as a rifle company commander in the 13th Infantry Regiment at Stuttgart (the commander of the Machine-Gun Company was Captain Erwin Rommel) but Paulus spent much more time on Staff duties than with troops.

It was already clear that he lacked the qualities of command. After one exercise in which he did have to command a regiment, the directing staff reported: 'This officer lacks decisiveness.'[1] A personal report from his commanding officer at this period gives an exceptionally clear, and even prophetic, appreciation of Paulus's personality and talents:

A typical Staff officer of the old school. Tall, and in outward appearance painstakingly well groomed. Modest, perhaps too modest, amiable, with extremely courteous manners, and a good comrade, anxious not to offend anyone. Exceptionally talented and interested in military matters, and a meticulous desk worker, with a passion for war-games and formulating plans on the map-board or sand-table. At this he displays considerable talent, considering every decision at length and with careful deliberation before giving the appropriate orders.

His career in the 1930s took him increasingly into the realm of mechanized forces. He commanded one of the earliest motorized battalions in 1934 and in the following year became Chief of Staff at the new Panzer Headquarters in Berlin. He adapted well to the new ideas coming forward about mobile warfare. He was no fervent Nazi and had nothing to do with the formation of the Party or its coming to power. But, coming from the middle class himself, he probably approved of Hitler's 'man-of-the-people' background, his spurning of the old, rigid aristocratic class, and the policies which brought work and prosperity to Germany and new life to the Army.

Paulus's rise continued. He was a major-general in 1939 and held the position of Chief of Staff in the newly formed 10th Army at Leipzig on the eve of the attack on Poland.

Paulus was to spend exactly one year in his new position. His army commander was General Walther von Reichenau, a blunt, forceful, ambitious man and a very able battlefield commander. Culturally, Paulus had little in common with his chief but, professionally, they were a near perfect combination. Reichenau hated routine work, preferring to be out with his forward units. Paulus kept all routine matters running smoothly. The 10th Army was soon renumbered, and as 6th Army built a fine reputation for itself. It swept through Poland without great difficulty and was then transferred to the west for the great 1940 offensive. On 10 May, the three corps under command advanced across the narrow neck of lower Holland ('the Maastricht appendix') and on into Belgium. Little opposition was met until the British Expeditionary Force was encountered on the line of the River Dyle. Thereafter it was harder fighting, pushing the British back all the way to the outskirts of Dunkirk. The high point for Paulus was his presence when Reichenau and King Leopold signed the terms of surrender of the Belgian Army on 28 May.

The 6th Army was not required for further operations before France capitulated three weeks later. It became part of the force earmarked for Operation *Sealion*, the invasion of southern England. The 6th Army's role was to embark at Le Havre and form the left flank of the landing, in the Brighton-Worthing area. Paulus prepared the plans and there was a rehearsal at St Malo in mid-August. But this part of the invasion entailed the longest sea crossing and, as there were insufficient landing craft available, 6th Army's part in the operation was cancelled.

Paulus now received a new posting and became Deputy Chief of Staff and Chief of the Operations Section at *Oberkommando des Heeres* (OKH, the headquarters directing all operations of the German Army); a considerable advancement for Paulus. OKH was at Fountainebleau when Paulus joined on 3 September 1940, but soon moved to Zossen near Berlin when the plans to invade England were abandoned completely.

Paulus was immediately given the task of preparing outline plans for a venture which would lead to his own fate and that of Germany. Hitler ordered plans to be prepared for an invasion of Russia the following spring. Paulus was one of the first to be involved in that mammoth project. He impressed Halder, the Chief of the General Staff, as businesslike and intellectually sharp. The fact that Russia was a nation with which Germany still had a non-aggression pact and with which Germany had shared the conquest of Poland does not seem to have troubled Paulus and there is no record of his advancing any moral or military objection. His wife realized on what project he was working; she had earlier declared her view on the immorality of invading Poland and now expressed the same view about the Russian venture. Paulus told her he had no say in the matter; it was purely a political matter and he, as a soldier, must obey his orders. It was the standard response of the professional officer.

All that winter Paulus and his Staff laboured on the planning for Operation *Barbarossa*. The objective was the swift destruction of the Russian Army which stood between Poland and Moscow. Three Army Groups would carry out the attack. The main thrust would be against Moscow, 600 miles away. The two flanking Army Groups were to capture Leningrad in the north and the Ukraine in the south. Paulus's old 6th Army, still under Reichenau, would be part of von Rundstedt's Army Group South.

Once Hitler had confirmed his decision to invade Russia and active preparations commenced, the planning phase and Paulus's work eased. Paulus was sent to see Rommel in North Africa at the end of April 1941 and remained there for more than two weeks. He observed an attack on the besieged British garrison at Tobruk, which failed, and both studied Rommel's style of command and consulted with him on future plans. Paulus returned to OKH reporting that Rommel was too headstrong and that, unless curbed, would require further reinforcement and thus imperil the coming Russian operation. Paulus toyed with the idea of asking for a field command now that the plans for *Barbarossa* were almost complete. He is believed to have considered advising Rommel's replacement by himself but his wife warned him against it, saying that his career would not prosper in North Africa.

The invasion of Russia began on 22 June 1941, with dramatic advances by the German mobile columns. It was the start of a quieter time for Paulus, for OKH was not planning any further major operations elsewhere. *Barbarossa*, it was hoped, would bring the war to a close. Paulus watched with particular interest the progress of the 6th Army. It took part in the great battle which led to the capture of over half a million Russians at Kiev. He and his old army commander, Reichenau, exchanged letters. Reichenau was obviously in his element, often up with the head of his leading unit. In August, Paulus was sent on a tour of the various headquarters in Russia, to assess on behalf of OKH the competing claims for resources by the commanders.

Paulus's career took an abrupt change of direction early in December. *Barbarossa* had ground to a halt in the conditions of the Russian winter. Moscow and Leningrad held out, and Army Group South had not reached the Caucasus. Its commander, Field-Marshal von Rundstedt, wanted to withdraw to a shorter line from which to see out the winter, but Hitler refused permission. Rundstedt resigned and Reichenau was promoted to fill the vacancy. Reichenau asked that his old colleague, Paulus, should become the new commander of the 6th Army, rather than one of the experienced front-line corps commanders. Hitler and Halder, Chief of the General Staff and Paulus's direct superior, agreed and, on 5 January 1942, the man who had commanded a rifle company for two years in peacetime and then, briefly, a battalion but had never commanded any unit in war, was given the direct responsibility for an army of more than a quarter of a million men. It was a fatefully ill-judged appointment. Even before Paulus reached his headquarters, his old commander and patron, Reichenau, the Commander-in-Chief, Army Group South, suffered a heart attack and was replaced by Field-Marshal von Bock, who took command of the Army Group on the same day that Paulus reached his own new headquarters.

The new commanders found a depressing situation. Their troops, ill-prepared for a Russian winter, were under fierce attack from a reinvigorated

Russian Army. The plans which Paulus had prepared for *Barbarossa* had not envisaged such a situation. Hitler ordered that no further withdrawals should take place. Von Bock passed the orders on to his army commanders. Paulus fought a conventional defensive battle but he made a shaky start. Von Bock judged that he did not handle a Russian attack at Kharkov well, with not enough vigour being displayed. Von Bock persuaded OKH to replace Paulus's Chief of Staff and a new man, Major-General Arthur Schmidt, arrived; he was a staunch Nazi who would be Paulus's Chief of Staff until the end.

But Kharkov was held and it was the Russians who sustained the greater loss when their final attack was beaten off in May. Paulus was awarded the Knight's Cross and received favourable publicity at home. The weather improved and great plans were afoot for the resumption of the German advance in the coming summer. Paulus's son, Ernst, a junior tank officer, was wounded at Kharkov and returned to Germany for hospital treatment; he would thus be absent when the 6th Army marched forward again and would so survive the war. A second son, Friedrich, would be killed in February 1944 at the Anzio beachhead in Italy.

The plans for the summer of 1942 were of the utmost importance and their results represent the watershed between Germany's years of victory and of defeat. This period also marked the removal from influence at the highest level of the 'old guard' of professional German commanders and their replacement by generals more compliant to Hitler, and the advent of Hitler himself to direct command of Army operations. It was a time when the last remnants of common sense gave way to crass over-optimism.

The old *Barbarossa* plan of 1941 was abandoned; there were not enough troops remaining after the winter losses to press ahead on all fronts. The destruction of the Red Army remained the only realistic hope and the South, the least important of the 1941 sectors, was where attention turned. Several variations of plan were considered but *Plan Blue* eventually emerged. After clearing its existing positions to secure a more favourable jumping-off line, Army Group South was to be split into two parts. Army Group A under Field-Marshal List was to push south-eastwards to encircle the Russian forces near Rostov and then thrust on to capture the Caucasus oilfields. Army Group B, whose main component was Paulus's 6th Army, was to push due east *as far as* the River Volga at Stalingrad *but not to capture that city*, in order to prevent Russian reserves moving into the Caucasus. Field-Marshal von Bock objected to the splitting-up of Army Group South and was sacked for his pains; General von Weichs took his place in command of Army Group B. Hitler and his advisers still believed that the hitherto irresistible *Wehrmacht* could destroy all before it; the Russian defence of Moscow during the past winter together with the results of the more recent Battle of Kharkov were believed to have been so costly that the Russian Army was a spent force.

The 6th Army moved forward on 28 June 1942. It was the largest German army on the Eastern Front, with 5 corps (one of them Panzer) containing 14 divisions – 11 infantry, 2 panzer and 1 motorized. It had 350 miles to go to Stalingrad. Initially all went well. The Russian front line was swept away and the panzers sped across the steppe, pausing only to wait for fuel convoys to catch up. The infantry trudged behind. The Russians mostly melted away and avoided a stand; Paulus's attempt to encircle them only succeeded once when, after a three-day battle on the River Don, 40,000 Russians were taken prisoner. It was hot, wearying work. Paulus caught dysentry but performed his duties efficiently. There were constant anxieties about supplies and about the huge, exposed left flank which was opening up with every mile of the advance.

Hitler now changed the plans, strengthening the northern drive towards Stalingrad and enlarging its objectives. The 4th Panzer Army was diverted from the Caucasus drive and sent north towards Stalingrad with orders to join with Paulus's 6th Army, and actually capture the city of Stalingrad, not merely cut the Russian communications by driving to the River Volga. Hitler wished to deprive the Russians of the large tank factory at Stalingrad and also to gain the psychological victory of taking the city which bore the name of the adversary who had denied him the capture of Moscow the previous summer. In this way Paulus and his army were sucked into the Stalingrad graveyard.

Having crossed the River Don on 21 August, Paulus set off on the last 60 miles to Stalingrad. Two days later, his 14th Panzer Corps reached the Volga, north of the city. But the infantry was still straggling behind and the tanks were short of fuel. The Panzer Corps commander believed that he was in danger and sought permission to withdraw; he was isolated at the point of a long corridor far deeper into Russia than any German had ventured, even in 1941. Paulus sacked the Corps commander and ordered the divisional commander who replaced him to stand on the Volga, where support soon reached him. A few days later, the head of General Hoth's Panzer Army, diverted from the Caucasus offensive, came up from the south and reached the Volga south of the city. The two armies met on 3 September and the Russians in Stalingrad were 'encircled', with the Germans on their front and flanks and the wide River Volga behind.

Hitler's determination to take Stalingrad was matched by that of the Russian High Command to hold the city. Stalin ordered that the civilians should not be evacuated; he believed his troops would fight better with the civilians present. Soldiers and civilians alike prepared the city for defence. Marshal Zhukov, the best of Stalin's commanders, and his Staff moved down from the Moscow front. The local party chairman was Nikita Khrushchev, who would one day become the leader of all Russia. The decisive battle of the Second World War was about to take place with Paulus at the centre of the stage. He was the senior of the two Army commanders present and would thus be in overall command on the Stalingrad front from first to last.

He attacked on 21 August, as soon as his army had been concentrated, a straightforward offensive on all sectors. Every German bomber available was sent to raid the city on the night of 23 August, some crews making three sorties. Unopposed, the Luftwaffe bombed Stalingrad from end to end. The Russians would turn many of the ruins into little fortresses. Nine German infantry divisions then attacked in the centre, with 5 panzer and 4 motorized divisions on the flanks. The Russians stood and fought, and the city held. Two days later, Hitler repeated his orders: Stalingrad must be taken.

September was an important month for the whole German Army, with the drain of senior officers who had challenged Hitler's policies continuing. Field-Marshal List, the commander of Army Group A, fighting in the Caucasus far to the south of Stalingrad, was anxious about the failure to capture the summer's objectives and the lateness of the season. He was sacked. On 12 September Paulus flew out of Stalingrad, met up with his own Army Group commander, von Weichs, and the two went to Hitler and pointed out the long, exposed northern flank of Paulus's command, the long lines of communications, and the lack of reserves and reinforcements for Stalingrad. The two generals were not as forceful in expressing their views as List, were apparently satisfied by Hitler's promises of support and his belief that the Russians were nearly finished, and they returned to the front. Later in the month, Halder, Chief of Staff at OKH, also urged Hitler to respond to the seriousness of the situation in southern Russia. But Hitler refused to listen and Halder, too, was sacked. His replacement, General Zeitzler, was never allowed the influence of Halder; Hitler had, in effect, now taken over direct control of operations. He was as determined as ever to press on with the capture of Stalingrad despite all the warnings of the professionals.

Back at Stalingrad, Paulus was finding that the capture of the city was turning out to be a long and costly affair, and winter was approaching. He wished to halt his offensive, and withdraw 14th Panzer Corps to form a reserve. But Hitler insisted that 6th Army must employ all its strength to take Stalingrad. Paulus made no further protest but got on with the task at Stalingrad. Would Hitler have listened if the general had been less courteous, modest and intellectual and more of a Reichenau or Rommel? No one can say. It is certain that there was now no one around Hitler powerful enough to persuade him to call off the offensive.

Paulus's nominal strength was actually increased at this time. Two formations of Romanian troops – the 3rd and 4th Armies – were sent up to hold the static fronts on either side of Stalingrad, releasing German troops to fight in the city. A new 'Romanian-German Army Group' was envisaged to include the Romanian troops and the German 4th Panzer and 6th Armies. Paulus himself was actually being considered for a new Staff position in Berlin at this time but, because of his Romanian wife and relatives, was kept at the front, earmarked to be Deputy Commander of the new grouping which, in the outcome, never came into existence. Another possible release route for Paulus was his own health; he was suffering continuing dysentery and a general run-down in health. He was urged to take sick leave in Germany but refused.

The attacks on Stalingrad continued. A major offensive had started on 13 September, Paulus ordering that the city be cut in two by a drive through the centre to the river bank. This was successful but suffered heavy casualties. Professional historians later judged that it would have been better to attack from either flank and advance up the bank of the Volga, cutting off the Russians in the city from their nightly flow of supplies across the river. Two panzer corps commanders protested at the way their tanks were being used in the city and added their voices to the warnings of the general danger of the situation. Paulus sacked them. The fighting became vicious; it has often been described as an urban version of Verdun. It was close-quarter, room-to-room, cellar-to-cellar, ruin-to-ruin fighting. Paulus's units wasted away at the rate of 20,000 casualties a week. By the end of October, only one tenth of Stalingrad still held out, in the north of the city. But the balance of strength was changing; the earlier German superiority had gone. Stalingrad was the first priority for Russian reserves. Sufficient Russian troops were fed into the city to keep the fight going there, but the remainder were placed as secretly as possible well to the north and south for a planned counter-stroke. Paulus received a mere five battalions of assault pioneers, flown in as street-fighting specialists. At the end of October Paulus warned Army Group B that the Russians were gathering on his flanks, and Hitler was informed. In early November, the winter came. In the middle of the month, Hitler sent Paulus a message urging one last effort to complete the capture of Stalingrad.

On 19 November, the Russians struck (see map on page 256). The attacks fell on weakly held sectors north and south of the city, manned mainly by Romanian forces in the north and by a mixture of further Romanians and units of the 4th Panzer Army in the south. The Russian plan was a simple one, to encircle all of the German forces in the Stalingrad area. They soon broke through the thin defences, particularly in the north. Even the lowest private in the German Army could see that the 6th Army at Stalingrad was in serious danger. It was the vital moment. Decisive action now could have saved the situation. If Paulus had acted boldly, sending some units north and south to hold the Russians while withdrawing the bulk of his force from the ruins of Stalingrad, then much of his army would have been saved. He should have acted quickly by giving his orders and then either sent Hitler a signal,

'In anticipation of your approval, I have ...', or he could have flown out to demand either that his action be sanctioned or that he be allowed to resign. Slow to comprehend the danger, Paulus did nothing. On the third day of the Russian offensive, Zeitzler formally advised Hitler that Paulus should be given orders to withdraw. While Hitler was making up his mind, Göring, through Jeschonnek, his Chief of Staff, promised that the Luftwaffe could keep Paulus supplied. Hitler accepted Göring's assurance, not that of his senior army adviser. He ordered Paulus and his men to remain in Stalingrad as a forward 'fortress' until the following spring. Zeitzler informed Paulus of the decision that day and Hitler followed with a personal order on 22 November, the fourth day of the crisis.

The Russians closed the ring on 23 November and Paulus found himself cut off, with the entire strength of his own 6th Army that had survived the fighting in Stalingrad and also with part of Hoth's 4th Panzer Army and the remnants of some of the Romanian divisions from the flanks. Also present were a mass of supply and rear echelons, a Luftwaffe FLAK division and two airfield organizations, a complete fighter *Gruppe*, part of a Stuka *Gruppe* and other air units. There were between 250,000 and 300,000 men in an area nearly 30 miles long by 20 miles wide, with its front still in Stalingrad but most of its rear out on the open steppe.

Paulus was now prodded by subordinate generals into radioing Hitler for complete freedom of action. Hitler replied on 24 November with a Führer order: 'Create a pocket. Present Volga front and present northern front to be held at all costs. Supplies coming by air.'[3] This was to prove ultimately the death sentence of the 6th Army. The only officer at Stalingrad to show any independence of action was General von Seydlitz-Kurzbach, the most senior of the corps commanders, who urged Paulus, in a memorandum, to withdraw without delay before escape became impossible: 'The complete annihilation of 200,000 fighting men and their entire equipment is at stake. There is no other choice.'[4] But Paulus, ever obedient to superiors, refused to listen to him.

After closing the ring, the Russians almost ignored the Stalingrad pocket, concentrating on pushing the German forces in the Don bend back as far as possible in order to increase the gap between Paulus and any relief force.

The rest was slow descent into catastrophe. The Luftwaffe never achieved a sufficient rate of supply, with the result that Paulus's force steadily declined in its ability to defend itself, let alone break out. Field-Marshal von Manstein was appointed to yet another new Army Group, Army Group Don, with orders from Hitler to link up again with Paulus, but it was nearly a month before this effort could begin, on 12 December 1942. Von Manstein sent an emissary by air to urge Paulus to do all he could to attempt a break-out and meet the relief force. All day the arguments revolved in Paulus's headquarters, with Russian shells landing nearby. It was the last chance for Paulus. In the end, as ever the intellectual Staff officer rather than the ruthless man of action, he refused to move, quoting Hitler's orders that the present positions at Stalingrad should be held. Von Manstein's valiant offensive petered out and all hope was gone by Christmas.

The Russians were ready to deal with Stalingrad by 8 January 1943. They sent Paulus an ultimatum, offering the alternative of honourable surrender or complete annihilation. No guns fired on 9 January while the terms were considered. It is assumed that Paulus consulted Hitler; there was a direct radio link. Paulus refused to surrender, once again following his orders to the letter without any regard to local conditions. The Russians attacked the next day. The final agony of Paulus's troops lasted for three weeks. The Russians advanced from west to east, pressing the Germans back into the city. They captured half of the pocket in the first week and then again paused to demand surrender. Again Paulus refused. By the end of the month, it was nearly all over. Stalingrad was cut into isolated German positions. The defenders, particularly the German troops, fought fiercely despite the appalling privations. The last wounded were evacuated by air on 24 January.

Even Hitler must have realized by now that there was no hope. He awarded Paulus the Oakleaves grade of Knight's Cross on 15 January and then promoted Paulus to Field-Marshal. Knowing that no German soldier of that rank had ever surrendered, he expected Paulus to commit suicide after a last stand. On 31 January, Russian troops reached the building in which Paulus had his headquarters. A young Russian officer entered and demanded, on behalf of his superiors, that the Germans surrender. After much parleying with Paulus's staff, the Russian was finally led to Paulus, who was lying listlessly on a bed. Through an interpreter, the Russian demanded the surrender. Paulus merely nodded. The newsreel film of Paulus signing the surrender shows a haggard, anxious man at the end of his tether.

A few units held out until 3 February but then it was all over. Of the original garrison, 42,000, mostly wounded, had been evacuated by air. The Russians counted 107,800 prisoners – 16,800 in the fighting and 91,000 in the final surrender. There were twenty-four generals among them. The number of Germans quoted as killed varies between 72,000 and 100,000. Two men escaped to reach the German lines. The great mass of prisoners suffered unspeakable misery and privation. Only 6,000 ever returned home, several years after the war.

The unrelenting Russians held Paulus for nearly eleven years. He was kept under what might be termed 'close house arrest' in Moscow and was not harshly treated, although he was subjected to the same pressure as was exerted on all of the captured generals to form a movement renouncing Hitler. Paulus held firm against this until after the July 1944 bomb plot, when he finally gave his support to the movement. Hitler was furious that the most senior German officer in captivity should turn on him in this way. Paulus's wife was urged to renounce his name; she refused. His surviving son was detained but survived the war.

Paulus never saw his wife again; she died in West Germany in 1949. Paulus was released in November 1953, but only to residence in communist East Germany at Dresden. Two years later he contracted amyelstrophic lateral sclerosis (motor neuron disease) and he died in a Dresden clinic on 1 February 1957 at the age of sixty-seven.

History gives a simple and unkind verdict on Friedrich Paulus: gifted Staff officer, uninspired commander, an unquestioning general of the 'orders-are-orders' type. He was a man who enjoyed the intellectual aspects of the profession of war; he never questioned Nazism and was willing to do almost anything ordered by Hitler. Finally, when the fate of a quarter of a million men rested in his hands, he 'froze' and did little but let events take their course to the complete destruction of his army and the miserable deaths of most of his soldiers.

NOTES

The author particularly wishes to acknowledge the use made of *Paulus and Stalingrad* by Walter Görlitz (Methuen, London, and Citadel, New York, both published in 1963); the original work was *Ich Stehe Hier Auf Befehl* (Bernard and Graefe, Frankfurt, 1960).

1 F. W. von Mellenthin, *German Generals of World War II, As I Saw Them*, University of Oklahoma Press, 1977, p. 104.
2 *Ibid.*, p. 114.
3 Paul Carell, *Hitler's War on Russia: The Story of the German Defeat in the East*, London, Harrap, 1964, p. 591.
4 *Ibid.*, p. 596.

CHRONOLOGY: FRIEDRICH PAULUS

1980, September 23	Born at Breitenau in the province of Hesse-Nassau
1910, February	Officer cadet at 111th Infantry Regiment (3rd Baden)
1912, July 4	Married Elena Constance Rosetti-Solenescu; one daughter, twin sons
1914–18	Served, and remained in Army service between the wars
1939–41	Senior Staff positions
1942, January	Commander 6th Army
1942, Spring	Awarded Knight's Cross (Oakleaves, January 1943)

1943, January	Prisoner of war, Stalingrad
1953, November	Released
1957, February 1	Died in Dresden

SENGER

16

SENGER

General Frido von Senger und Etterlin

FERDINAND VON SENGER UND ETTERLIN*

The pinnacles of the Alps glitter pink and white in the afternoon sunlight. The view from my writing table takes in the mountains between Lake Constance and Lac Léman. Warm Mediterranean air currents sometimes leave only the peaks glowing and clear above the mist-enshrouded Swiss northern slopes. Deep below, between me and the Alps, where the Upper Rhine flows in its steep walled valley, lies the small medieval border town of Waldshut. My father was born in the town on 4 September 1891.

The title of the English translation of his memoirs is 'Neither Fear Nor Hope'[1]: fear neither of his enemy nor of the terrors of war, but, in the shadow of despotism in his own country, no hope of a happy outcome. Modern historians have frequently sought to answer the question: when did this hope expire in the minds of the servants of the Third Reich? For most it must have been when the prospect of military defeat dawned on them. Was it any different for him?

His ancestors had come from Bamberg to the country between the Black Forest and Lake Constance where they first flourished in the seventeenth century as lawyers and ministers to lesser princely states in the area; principally to the German Order of Knighthood (*Deutscher Ritterorden*) whose sovereign was the Emperor in Vienna. In the period of reorganization and reconstruction

---

*Completed on the author's death by Stefan von Senger und Etterlin, and translated by Major T. A. Hamilton-Baillie.

following the Napoleonic wars, the family lost their estates and from then on were active exclusively as lawyers or as servants of the state.

His father had had liberal political views but had held Bismarck in high regard. At about the turn of the nineteenth century the sense of separate statehood in Baden had virtually vanished. The circle of friends and acquaintances and contacts in the course of duty had broadened beyond the old frontiers of the lesser states. Men had begun to accept the existence and importance of the German nation-state of the Second Reich, although the new division of the German world ran counter to local traditions of loyalty to Austria and the older German Empire. The German Nation meant more than just the lesser German Empire of the Hohenzollerns.

My father's character was deeply influenced by five factors: ancestral tradition of service to the state, his mother's deep religious convictions, his education in the classics and humanities, his experience of the First World War and lastly the immediate consequences of the defeat of 1918.

The concept of the servant of the state, the essence of loyalty that brooked not the faintest trace of corruption; this was his inheritance from his father. Duty and honour were no distant abstractions: they governed the business of the day, every day. The state servant of the south of Germany, no less than his counterpart in Prussia, held as his talisman that idea of duty defined by Frederick the Great in the foreword to his political memoirs and which drew heavily on Cicero's definition in *De officiis*:

> Le Devoir de tout bon citoyen est de servir sa patrie, de penser qu'il n'est pas uniquement pour lui dans le monde, mais qu'il doit travailler pour le bien de la société dans laquelle la nature l'a placé.

Later, in war, his strictures to his officers[2] to uphold their honour did not imply the kind of lifeless obedience that was the basis of the National-Socialists' understanding of the concept. A soldier's honour and loyalty was for him only thinkable in terms of Christian morality and Christian ethics.

From his mother, who came from a wealthy bourgeois family, he learnt strict observance of the Roman Catholic faith. In 1941 he wrote in a letter:

> It is in just such a family as ours, with no fixed ties to our roots in a particular class of society, that a strong hold to the Church is vital. Without its discipline and rules the character and tone not only of our relationship with God, but also our position in society at large would suffer.[3]

The third factor that influenced the development of his character was his education at Oxford where he arrived as a Rhodes Scholar in 1912 following a year's compulsory military service in a Baden Artillery Regiment. For two years at St John's College he read history and PPE. The experience vastly broadened his world: an enormous step from the rather narrow

376

outlook of the average student of the Wilhelmine years.[4] At the time, the idea
of a career as a professional soldier could not have been further from his mind.
To be at ease in cosmopolitan society, instinctive good manners, a deep love
of the *beaux arts*, and fluency in English and French were the lasting results of
this phase of his life.

It was, by stark and terrible contrast, his experiences in the trenches of the
Western Front in the First World War that provided the fourth major influence
in his life. It was during the tank battle at Cambrai in 1917 that his beloved
younger brother fell in action. He sought and found the mass grave where he
lay in no-man's land:

> We dug for several hours in the mass grave. Then the German counter-attack
> against the British breakthrough passed by us: we dug on. British artillery fire
> against the attack repeatedly forced us to take shelter among the dead.... At last
> we got the body out, which had lain in the lowest of the three levels. I took hold
> of my brother's legs and dragged him thus into my car. On the seat beside me
> sat my lifeless brother.[5]

Hope of a happy outcome lived only in the deepest recesses of his mind. The
battle for survival controlled all other thought.

The fifth important factor influenced him in maturity. As a volunteer, he
took part in the counter-revolution against the Bolsheviks in Saxony. Here
he was confronted for the first time with the fierce mentality of a revolution,
which, on its road to totalitarianism, did not flinch even from the ghastliness
of the genocide of entire sections of society. There seemed at the time some
hope that the new democratic constitution of the Weimar Republic would
somehow triumph over the confrontation politics of extreme right and left.

On 2 December 1919 he married Hilda Margarethe von Kracht, the daughter
of a Prussian general of ancient Brandenburg lineage. It was through her
connections that he made closer contact with the Prussian aristocracy, still in
the inter-war years a significant political force in Germany.

In his outward appearance he had the look of a man who bore distinction
easily. A sharply hooked nose, high forehead, dark and slightly drooping eyes
conveying a vigorous, deep thoughtfulness and independence of mind betrayed
his southern German origins. His tall and slender figure was invariably clothed
in immaculately tailored suits or uniforms; the latter normally with an extra
emphasis on elegance, given by a mild, though for the Prussians rather
shocking, disregard for the dress regulations.

The war had wrecked the prospects of completing his studies and once
again destroyed what family funds there had been. So he gladly accepted the
opportunity of staying on in the *Reichswehr* as a regular officer, which also
meant a transfer to the cavalry from his reserve commission as a gunner. He
shared the general hope that the new nation would gradually be restored to
unity after the polarization of the post-war revolution. For thirteen happy

years he remained a subaltern officer, mostly in regimental service with the 18th Horse (Reiter Regiment 18) in Stuttgart. His commanding officers included the brilliant early armoured corps officer, Freiherr von Weichs, and the gifted trainer of soldiers, Geyr von Schweppenburg. Rather too tall for steeplechasing, he turned instead to showjumping, taking part in countless competitions with his own well-schooled horses and bringing more than the occasional trophy home. As Regimental Adjutant (equivalent to Brigade Major) of 3rd Cavalry Regiment (KR3), he moved to the country outside Hanover, the regiment's garrison. Since the Army's School of Equitation was in the city, it is hardly surprising that he took such an interest in competition riding, but it was not horsemanship alone that claimed his attention during this period. He was deeply involved with the debate, then at its fiercest, on high-level tactical doctrine. He was never a member of the General Staff. Though he had passed the Staff College entrance examination in the 1920s, he was too old to join the Staff course by then. He was involved, for example, in the seminal manoeuvres of 1934 under General von Witzleben (later to be executed for his part in the 20 July 1944 plot against Hitler), in which the role of the mechanized Cavalry Division was first defined.

The Nazi assumption of power was scarcely noticeable in day-to-day life at first. True, the hopes for democracy had been shattered, but there seemed some germ of hope that the worst effects of extreme polarization might have been overcome.

But it was not long before his religious sensitivities and his unusually world-aware outlook began to be troubled by the first alarm signals. In the *Oberkommando des Heeres* (OKH) in Berlin as Chief of Staff of the Cavalry Inspectorate, he experienced at close quarters the murders of Generals von Schleicher and von Bredow. The cruel arrogance of the régime was revealed and was even vaunted as 'rightful opposition to dilettantism'.[6] The Röhm affair provided some comfort that the worst of the Nazis were at least equally prepared to murder each other.[7]

Nevertheless, hope that all would end well continued to evaporate. In career terms, however, there were two quite different activities that demanded much of his attention. The first was the Army Manual of Horsemanship. It remains the basis of much of what is taught today. In direct contrast, the other activity concerned the modernization of the Cavalry Arm, that is to say, mechanization.

Senger entered the debate against the proponents of the new view that the tank, in its various forms, would cope with all phases of war – a view that had its strongest adherents among the British 'All Tank' theorists. His wartime experience led him to maintain a belief that eventually success in battle depended on the infantryman. He supported, therefore, the formation of four so-called 'Light' Divisions of Cavalry, each with five strong motorized battalions. These motor battalions were to fulfil the roles previously assigned to the Cavalry Corps (*Heereskavallerie*) and were largely formed from cavalry regiments. Thus the Panzergrenadier or mechanized infantry in the German service derived from the cavalry, not, as in Britain, from the infantry.

In 1938 Hitler formed an all-new branch of service or arm and placed it under the control of Guderian. It was to be known as *Schnelle Truppen* (fast troops). It was to consist of three former elements of the Armoured Branch; tanks, anti-tank and armoured reconnaissance units with an infantry element drawn from the motor battalions of the Panzer (Armoured) Divisions and from the old *Heereskavallerie* regiments forming the dismounted element of the Light Divisions. It even contained some horsed cavalry units. He later wrote:

> Sadly, the *Schnelle Truppen* is far too large and diverse ever to become a new arm of service alongside the old branches. Mechanization does not automatically produce a new arm of service; the infantry stay infantry whether motorized or not. Only tanks are completely new; and they are not the successors of the old cavalry. The fact is that the entire Army will eventually be mechanized and it is bad luck on the Infantry and Cavalry that no one has yet included them in the experimental formula for motorization.

And on the usage of the infantry and armoured elements in the organization of an armoured division, he wrote:

> The reorganization followed exactly the line suggested in the papers on *Schnelle Truppen* presented by KR3 in 1937/38. We said at the time that the armoured division should contain:
>
> - two infantry regiments, each of two battalions (despite the tactical disadvantages of only two manoeuvre elements, three would have been too cumbersome).
>
> - a second tank battalion but with its light armoured company under command of the infantry regiment.
>
> - disband the motorized cavalry element in favour of a lighter more mobile unit equipped with motor-cycle combinations and light armoured reconnaissance vehicles.
>
> - many more automatic weapons in the rifle companies.
>
> - development of lightly armoured infantry fighting vehicles mounting support weapons and used for reconnaissance and in the offence.[8]

Even at this early stage the regiment's (KR3) papers foresaw the development of the half-tracked armoured infantry fighting vehicle, some mounting a 75 mm cannon.

Life in the bustling Berlin of the years between 1934 and 1938 reached a pitch that the post-war era of want and drab necessity cannot begin to recall: at least an hour's early-morning exercise on a thoroughbred in the Grünewald, then home to a spacious well staffed house. Perhaps conversation at the dinner tables concentrated less on political subjects in the aftermath of the Blomberg and Fritsch crises. There vanished just a little more of the reserve of hope. No thought of fear . . . yet. One concentrated a little more on Cardinal Prägnitz' sermons on a Sunday. Weekend visits to the country seats of relations – Jewish relations as well – were a source of intellectual and cultural delight. So long as they were obtainable, foreign newspapers were the only press to be found in the Sengers' house.

In 1938 the long-awaited posting arrived – regimental commander of KR3 in Göttingen, then a peacetime unit of 60th Corps. It was a regiment that traced its ancestry back to the Zieten Hussars of Frederick the Great's Army whose silver kettledrums were still in regular use. Its mobilization role would be to provide seven divisional recce battalions for the infantry divisions of the Corps.

Among the officers of the regiment, whose general development and instruction he viewed as his principal task,[9] there was not a single Nazi. From his notebook of September 1938[10] the following list of points were to be tackled at a routine conference with all eleven squadron commanders of the regiment:

1. Training programme for two-year men.
2. Training programmes for candidates for reserve commissions.
3. Correct form on parade.
4. Theft in the lines.
5. Church attendance.
6. 1st *Abteilung* [cavalry equivalent of Battalion] saddles.
7. Staff directives.
8. Congratulations to the 2nd *Abteilung* for vehicle driving.
9. Training of machine-gun teams in indirect fire.
10. Officers' training in mortar-fire control.
11. Marksmanship.
12. Remounts.
13. Weapon maintenance.
14. Winter warfare exercises.
15. Promotion of officer candidates to *Fahnenjunker* (Ensigns).
16. Welfare work, for unmarried men as well.
17. VD.

Such were the ageless and, to regimental officers in any army, familiar thoughts and concerns of a regimental commanding officer at the time that Neville Chamberlain talked of 'Peace in our time'. At least it kindled new hope.

A schooling in the classics made it an easy matter for him to master Italian and to qualify as an interpreter in the language. The qualification was a means to acquire foreign currency and so to indulge a passion. For next to showjumping came a deep appreciation for the art of Italy. With the soul of a born aesthete, he had an equal passion for harmony in the beauty of nature and in the works of man. A personality rooted in the concept of duty, Christian morality, with the world-wide outlook of a convinced liberal democrat, he remained utterly unblemished by Nazism or any of its influences. His ever-broadening knowledge of *beaux arts* in all their forms, his charm, backed by an uncomplicated Christian faith, made him a great many friends and admirers, among them many who quickly realized that they dealt here with a man who allowed no compromise of his principles. Thus he made the significant and delicate appointment of the untainted non-Nazi cavalry reserve officer, Baron von Cramm, as his NFSO (National-Socialist political officer).[11] Later, he took on to his staff the son of General Oster who bore the disgrace, awarded under Nazi law to an entire family, of his father's guilt as an anti-Nazi resister.

He valued nothing more highly than the trust and friendship of his sub-ordinates and among them none more than of Ernst-Günther Baade, at that time a squadron commander in KR3 and later GOC of 90th Panzergrenadier Division in Senger's Corps. Baade was an avowed anti-Nazi, a renowned individualist and a superbly able leader of soldiers. He actually had his own NFSO shot for treachery near the end of the war and had to go underground as a consequence. Baade did not survive the war. On virtually its last day he was killed by a roving Allied fighter-bomber close to his own estate in Schleswig-Holstein.

At the outbreak of war Frido von Senger had not the slightest idea that Stalin would occupy half Poland and the Baltic states and place 23 millions under Soviet rule. He had no notion of Stalin's pact with Hitler on the division of these East European spoils when Zhukov announced the defeat of the bulk of the Japanese mechanized forces at Kalchem-Jol in Mongolia (Jap.: Nomonhan). But, unwittingly, he had played a part in these events by passing information to the Japanese on Soviet troop movements gained on his trans-Siberian journey to Tokyo on a diplomatic mission.

He took no part in the Polish campaign, deeply regretting his inactivity since it seemed to signal the end of his career. He learned from officers of his own regiment returning from Poland of the terrible excesses of SS units against the civilian population. He confided his disgust in a letter[12] to a lady friend:

> Oh the loneliness when one hears of such things on which one must be silent. The talk among the officers in the Mess this evening was of the civil administration in Poland. There seemed to be a refrain: 'I'm ashamed to be a German.' What can one do but stay silent. I do. Do they know what I am trying to say with my silence? Sometimes it seems to me that the boys feel my deep pain in my silence.

Once more a fading of hope for a happy ending: his advice to his friends was at all costs to try to keep the Army out of it and to do their duty honourably. The campaign in the west seemed to pass like a live-firing exercise. He took part as commander of the cavalry brigade operating in northern Holland and later between the Somme and the Atlantic in command of a motorized brigade-group. The long years of theoretical training of officers in command several levels higher than those applicable to their rank bore fruit. The unexpected pace of the advance gave scope for initiative and flexibility never since achieved. He wrote later:

> In quiet moments of reflection after the terrific pace of the campaign our whole tragic dilemma struck me. It was the tragic dilemma of so many officers at the time: as dutiful and brave soldiers they fought for victory; yet for love of the Fatherland they only wanted defeat.[13]

In his view, the defeat of France had two consequences. The uncommitted German became more trusting and less critical of the régime, and secondly, it became clear to the régime's opponents that only military defeat would get rid of it.[14]

In the period following the campaign he took part in the Franco–Italian armistice conference in Turin where he was able to gain a clearer picture of the capabilities of Germany's allies. One glance at the situation in North Africa showed the dire position of the Axis powers, and from his semi-diplomatic post in Turin he wrote on 2 October 1940:

> I believe that the war in Africa will be decided soon. The papers here take the view that Africa and Europe together will become a sort of German-Italian bloc. Such decisions are not going to be made simply between the states of Europe, but between the four great world powers; Europe (to which Africa belongs) the USSR, USA and Japan. The British Empire will stay a loose organization of states with no political power as Britain is as closely tied to Europe-Africa as is Canada to USA. The big issue will be control over the Philippines, India and Australia. For Australia the Philippines, the South Pacific and Singapore will be disputed between Japan and the USA and may even be so in the course of this war, just as India will be later disputed between Japan and the USSR. It would all be simple for us, were it not for our need to control the Eastern Mediterranean in competition with the USSR – a much more awesome prospect of conflict with the '250 million bloc'. These are my private thoughts.[15]

He had no idea that Hitler had decided by July 1940 to push the USSR out of eastern Europe and equally no notion that Molotov had claimed the Dardanelles. From that moment on, the Mediterranean campaigns became a sideshow. To Senger, the east remained somehow outside his western-oriented outlook. In the summer of 1941 there was indeed some hope, or perhaps more accurately, speculation that further fighting in western Europe might even be avoided. Thus he wrote in a letter dated 2 June 1941 that he saw no prospect of serious battles on any of the fronts. He foresaw, rather, an extension of Axis power without conflict in southeast Europe and the Near East.[16] In this, perhaps, he was a victim of the disinformation and propaganda put about among the troops that transports were ready to take German troops into the Levant while the Soviet Union stood idly on the sidelines.

His job in Turin allowed him to observe over a period of two years the collapse of fascist imperialism in Italy, to notice the failure of the two dictators to co-ordinate their war objectives, to watch the ebb and flow of the North African campaign, and above all to witness the shadowy fate of France so wracked by contradiction that she found herself at war with both Germany and Great Britain at once.[17] His judgment of the tragedy in Italy was that its constitutional weaknesses silenced any effective direction or leadership. It hurt him all the more that he had to appear as a broker in what was clearly for the Italians an ill-fated alliance with Hitler.[18]

His reaction to the attack on Russia is not recorded in his memoirs. However it is highly probable that in common with most Germans, he shared the Nazi-inspired fear that Stalin would have tried to break German hegemony in Europe sooner or later in order to steal a march on the western powers.

Bitterly disappointed to be away from service in the field, he took careful note, none the less, of the operational peculiarities of the campaign of 1941. On 4 August 1941 he wrote:

It is essential to fill the gap between attacking armour and the slower infantry. But how? More mechanization? More mechanized infantry and artillery within the armoured divisions? More concentration of armour with reserves held in rear to sustain their breakthrough? Perhaps, on the other hand, a shorter rein on the armoured divisions to keep them close to the infantry divisions. The same old problems are turning up for the new mechanized cavalry that their horsed forebears had.[19]

In October 1941 he returned to the Inspectorate of Cavalry, his chief concern being the further development of the *Schnelle Truppen.*

The real trouble is that both tanks and motorized infantry have a limited value in the attack as they offer too good a target to the defence. But the difference between the two is that when the armour gets enmeshed in the enemy's anti-tank defence, the infantry can dismount and maintain the momentum by pressing on on foot as in a normal infantry attack. And a second important point: each main arm must be equally capable of defence and offence and to be able to change from one to the other as is so often demanded in warfare, at a moment's notice. On this argument the mechanized infantry is the main arm and armour (tanks) a supporting arm.[20]

The initial successes of Operation *Barbarossa* did not deflect him from the view that the end of the war was not in sight. Watching the winter disaster before Moscow of 1812 being repeated in 1941–42, he expected the follow-up campaign in 1942 to turn on the south Russian oilfields because of their strategic importance.[21] It was at this stage of the war that his long-standing doubts on the improbability of military victory solidified into a calculated conviction that defeat was certain. It was an outcome that privately he knew would be for the best. The actual date can be pinpointed to 7 December 1941, the day when Hitler declared war on the USA and the German offensive against Moscow ground to an icy halt.[22] The Army of the Reich had simply overreached itself in the Russian wastes. The new strategies in the air and at sea offered no relief to the prospect of eventual doom.[23]

In the autumn of 1942 he took over command of the largely Swabian and Bavarian 17th Panzer Division on the Eastern Front. For him it meant the start of the real war.

As a front-line commander he took part in battles in both major theatres which saw the best and most successful feats of arms by German troops in all the phases of war; offence, defence, delay and withdrawal. In each his own formation provided brilliant examples on at least two occasions and with telling strategic consequences.

In the offensive his division was the spearpoint of the 4th Panzer Army operation to relieve the 6th Army surrounded in Stalingrad. Later, in February 1943, his division was a major element in von Manstein's counter-strokes between the Dnieper and the Donetz which stabilized the southern sector of the Eastern Front. Between these two offensives took place the first of the great delaying operations of January 1943 between the Kalmuck steppe and Stalingrad which allowed the 1st Panzer Army to withdraw from the Caucasus. Of his withdrawals, the first took place in the circumstances of the collapse of the 6th Italian Army in Sicily, and involved the extraction of 14th Panzer Corps from Sicily over the straits of Messina in July 1943. The second withdrawal was the operation to pass two divisions to the Italian mainland from Sardinia and Corsica in September 1943. This must be counted an exceptional achievement in view of the Allied sea and air superiority and the very few casualties suffered on the German side.

The first defensive battle on the Cassino front between January and May 1944 as commander of 14th Panzer Corps, and opposed by the 5th US army, is the cornerstone of his renown as a leader of troops. These successes were the fruits of the enormous capability of the German Army, then after four years of war at the pinnacle of tactical skill and pitted against a still inexperienced opponent. Less well known but of equal brilliance in execution was the second of his delaying operations from Cassino to the Gothic Line between 17 May and 15 August 1944. His leadership of the defensive operations of the 14th Army in the area of Bologna once again brought the Allies to a standstill. At the time these operations appeared to give a breathing space desperately needed to allow an orderly withdrawal from the Balkans and to check Soviet advances in southern Austria. In the event it was a mistaken strategy, as Churchill had agreed as early as May 1944 to Stalin switching his main effort towards Poland, while leaving Romania and the Balkans for later.

At the heart of Senger's system of command and control was his concern with standards of training and leadership at all levels. Unlike many Allied commanders, he sought daily contact with those two or three levels below his own immediate subordinates. He made personal reconnaissance of the enemy from forward positions. Above all he made absolutely sure that he understood the capabilities and condition of his own troops. He insisted that his subordinates at all levels knew the main points of his appreciation and plan. Because of this, orders consisted only of a minimum of co-ordinating detail. Execution of the minutiae of battle could be left to the German Army's disciplined application of drills. His relations with his subordinates were extraordinarily close and he never tired of concern for the smallest details of their welfare. There is an example of this style in the letter of February 1941 already quoted:

> From earliest times when troubadours sang chivalrous ballads in Provence, to the time when Prussia perfected the ideal of the 'perfect professional officer', and our enemy of today that of the 'perfect gentleman officer', the one guiding principle was that the feudal lord or the officer, the man set in authority, should devote himself to the protection of the weak. Your subordinates are placed there by the authority that the state has entrusted in you. They are placed there in your protection and they are totally dependent on your judgment, your care and your decisions. They are the weak – just as are they who inhabit the lands on which you now stand as conqueror.[24]

His innermost thoughts are revealed again in the same letter[25] (it was to officers of his old regiment):

> Lucky is he who with a laugh and a joke can set his subordinates at ease. But if this wonderful gift is denied, if you are simply not that kind of man, there is none the less some kind of magic which the good officer possesses. It is revealed in some fleeting glance at the right moment and which carries the soldier through some small crisis of morale.

And what effect, it may be asked, did his fundamental anti-Nazism have on his troops and on his style of command? A few examples may suffice for answer.

In attack and in the pursuit, he committed his divisions decisively and often accepting high risks and, if need be, without waiting for orders from above. But even the troops who served him longest never had the feeling that he called for super-human efforts. In situations where the opposing forces had overwhelming superiority, he would draw back. Obstinate clinging to defensive lines, dependence on well built fortifications, the characteristics of officers most trusted by Hitler, were entirely contrary to his own methods which, even in defence, were based on quick reactions and flexibility.[26]

In September 1943, while the withdrawal of the division from Corsica to the mainland was in progress, he received orders to execute all Italian officers on the island who had not continued to co-operate with the Germans after 10 September – the day on which Badoglio's régime had signed the armistice with the Allies. In the circumstances it was, as he later wrote,

> perfectly clear that the moment had come to disobey a direct order. I spoke at once to Field-Marshal Kesselring on the radio link to his HQ and told him that I refused to carry out the order. The Field-Marshal listened to my news without comment and then said he would say exactly the same to OKW in Berlin. I arranged for the officers concerned to be shipped to the mainland where they were at least safe from the gallows. I owe a debt of gratitude to Kesselring that he entirely accepted my refusal to obey orders and let the matter rest.[27]

With the front now back in the area of Bologna in January 1945, the predicament of the German forces worsened. The Italian population longed for capitulation there and then. Partisan groups dealt savagely with those German soldiers and collaborators whom they could lay hands on. The fascist Blackshirts on their part took equally bloody toll on the partisans, but they succeeded chiefly in terrorizing the war-weary population. The German occupying forces had to co-operate with the fascist Republican authorities just in order to maintain a supply of necessities for civilians. It required a high degree of diplomatic skill and Senger became the *de facto* Commandant of Bologna. He declared the city out-of-bounds to Germans and expelled the chief Blackshirt (a lecturer at the university). German repressive measures against villages suspected of partisan sympathies were stopped. The overall effect was to bring some measure of calm. With Field-Marshal Kesselring there was a tacit understanding that the Italian cities of Bologna, Pisa, Lucca and Florence with their irreplaceable treasures would not be included in the defensive plan. The Allies also bypassed them in their advance.

One of the recurrent themes of modern histories of the period is the accusation that it was the generals who carry the blame for the failure to topple Hitler from power. On 22 June 1943 Senger found himself face to face with the Führer to receive at his hands the orders for the defence of Sicily. He wrote later about this moment: 'Of Hitler's renowned personal magnetism I felt not the slightest sign. I thought only with disgust and horror of all the misfortunes which this man had brought upon my country.'[28]

It appeared to him that open opposition to the totalitarian régime was not effective. Generals Beck, von Fritsch and von Hammerstein had resigned in protest without the slightest effect on Hitler's conduct of strategy and policies of genocide. The general population were, in his view, too deeply subject to the Nazi system to give general and widespread support to resistance. Opposition, on the other hand, to senseless or immoral orders by individuals in their own posts was achievable. He viewed the right to disobey when circumstances justified such action as entirely consistent with Prussian military tradition.[29]

He learned of plans which lead to the 20 July 1944 plot through younger officers of his own staff. He knew Colonel Count Stauffenberg well from his service in OKH. He was a friend of Fabian von Schlabrendorff. But he was sceptical about the possible success of such actions. He expressed his reasons after a second encounter with Hitler in late April 1944:

What was one to do? Possibly Hitler can be assassinated. But what about the rest of the gang, all holding the reins of power, all inured to criminality? Many of my young friends convinced themselves that the Western Powers would negotiate with a new régime headed by a group of generals after a successful putsch. They had no conception of the deeply held belief, even among the Westerners (fewer now than in the First World War) with a good understanding of Germany and the Germans – a belief that it was militarism that had been responsible for the existence of the Hitler régime despite the fact that his strongest opponent had been the Army (as opposed to the other Services).[30]

Just as he had reacted to his discovery of the SS atrocities in Poland, his reaction as a senior commander at the front when he learned of the attempt on Hitler's life was to carry on as if nothing special had happened. Contrary to the express wishes of the political leadership that all functionaries should show publicly their jubilation that the Führer had survived and voice frenzied castigation of the culprits, Senger actually ignored the whole event in front of his troops, hoping that the more alert of his soldiers would draw their own conclusions from his silence. All higher commanders who took this attitude were now threatened and more closely watched. For him it was a period in limbo: the end seemed no nearer, yet its inevitability remained unaltered. There was just a hope perhaps that this single example of violent opposition from the establishment would earn some self-respect for German society of the future.[31]

How could a very senior officer, aware as he must have been of the criminality and fecklessness of the Nazi régime, conscientiously and deliberately continue to conduct a war for that same régime? What was it that took him to the front, led him on to military endeavour that could only delay the final capitulation that he himself recognized as a necessity? As a soldier he felt a calling – professionally – to do the best that the operational situation, the supply of *matériel* and the morale of his soldiers allowed. From the first moment of the war he had longed only to join his brother officers at the front. He trusted himself to be a better and a more responsible leader to his troops than many others.

Anyone who knows he has a talent for leadership at a high level will find exactly its challenge fascinating. To be denied it is to feel like the left-behind hunter who paws at the loose-box door as his stable-mates are led out for the day. I do not believe that these sorts of feelings have anything to do with militarism. War provides the challenge. Despite its senselessness and the hopelessness of the strategy in which it is conceived and the inescapability of the fateful outcome, one is bound by its challenge to be an exponent of battle.[32]

Soldiering was his calling.[33]

At the end of the war he passed through several British camps in Italy, eventually reaching the generals' camp at Bridgend where he was a prisoner of war for three years. The camp's inmates, from Field-Marshal to Nazi Civil Worker official with general's rank, he found to be divided into three groups: one consisting of those who accepted defeat, who wished to break deliberately from the past, who accepted the consequences and recognized their culpable responsibility. A second group consisted of those who for years had put their faith in the régime, professed themselves ignorant of the 'unmentionable horrors' but now accepted the critical judgment made on them. The third were the stubborn, who refused to acknowledge their crimes and considered the acceptance of blame as undignified pandering to the wishes of their gaolers. He counted himself among the first group. The second formed the majority among the inmates.

Looking back on the war, there were two causes of particular grief to him. The first was a consequence of his own direct action in the Italian campaign. The desperate defence of the strategically vital valley beneath the monastery of Monte Cassino by his own 14th Panzer Corps had led to the tactically mistaken bombing of the old Benedictine Abbey by the Allies. Was he to blame?

Such was the fate of leaders on the German side. Could they have disobeyed simply because they knew that the war was lost? Could they withdraw from a line, where fate seemed to favour them temporarily, where the bravery of their troops and maybe of their leadership scored victories in defence, which at least kept enemy air bases further away from home? With this background the destruction of the Abbey seems but a minor detail. For many, however, the fact that the Abbey was destroyed a third time in history through violence in spite of an initial silent agreement on both sides to refrain from this useless act remains a '*rammarico anzi a dolore*': to be deplored rather, with great pain.[34]

The second event is more of a general and historical nature: the unhappy experience of Germany in its central position in the European balance of power. After the war Senger developed his own theory on the cause and spread of both world wars, expressed in this short passage:

The Second World War is astonishingly similar to the First in its course, development and result. In both instances, the German governments sought to control their smaller eastern neighbours as a buffer against the Russian colossus. In both instances it was a conflict with the Euro-Asian great power that was telling. In both instances, Germany considered itself as acting as a 'western' power and reckoned on at the least neutrality from the other western powers. In both instances the German leadership was wrong in its presumptions; the western powers joined Russia's side to crush Germany. In both instances the German leadership hoped that the USA would stay out of the conflict. In both instances it was wrong.[35]

In contrast nevertheless to the situation in the First World War when the political leaders had played puppet to the General Staff's strings, the Second World War saw a disastrous combination of Commander-in-Chief and political leader. It permitted the primacy of a senseless and criminal political system and at the same time ensured the loss of military strategic skill.[36]

Senger was released from British captivity in May 1948. Through his friend Kurt Hahn's influence, he was appointed a housemaster at Salem, the public school near Lake Constance and the sister school of Hahn's foundation of his emigré years at Gordonstoun. In the 1950s he became increasingly involved in journalism as military correspondent of the Südwestfunk Broadcasting Service and of the *Deutsche Zeitung*. He covered German rearmament within NATO, not without trenchant criticism. From 1952 onwards he served on a secret committee under Adenauer concerned with setting the guidelines for the new *Bundeswehr* and resulting in the important document now known as the *Himmeroder Denkschrift* (Himmeroder Report). As a member of the official screening committee he was responsible for preventing a good many officers too tainted by Hitler's influence from joining the *Bundeswehr*. His judgment was by the standards he himself had set.[37]

He had indeed served Hitler's state loyally. Within the sphere of his own commands he had permitted not one deviation from the accepted code of Christian morality. It was the state, not its Führer, that he had served; he was never one of Hitler's generals.

NOTES

1 Frido von Senger und Etterlin, *Krieg in Europa*, Cologne: Kiepenheuer & Witsch, 1960.

2 Letter as former CO to officers of KR3, Turin, 23 February 1941. Archiv Senger (hereafter cited as AS).

3 Due to the author's death before this memoir was finished, not all the passages quoted can be found in the papers. Where this is so, as here, only the general source can be shown; AS.

4 Letter to his son, Turin, 18 October 1941. AS. Cf. 'Fragebogen Cecil Rhodes Stipendium', Happach/Haeg, 10 March 1959. AS.
5 *Krieg in Europa*, pp. 19–20.
6 Letter to the publisher of *Magnum*, Happach, 30 June 1961. AS.
7 *Krieg in Europa*, p. 47.
8 AS.
9 Letter to KR3 Turin 23 November 1940. Cf. letter to Cecile von Keudell, Hannover, 27 November 1939.
10 The notebook is in the AS.
11 The NSDAP implanted a Party adherent into each *Wehrmacht* unit down to regimental level in order to control the ideological cast of the Armed Forces. Frido von Senger chose Baron von Cramm as NSFO while in command of 14th Corps at Cassino. Von Cramm qualified as he had been a member of the 'Stahlhelm' in the 1920s. The 'Stahlhelm' had been integrated into the SA in 1933. Cramm never joined the NSDAP and had never been confirmed in his appointment as NFSO by the party as was the rule. See *Krieg in Europa*, p. 375.
12 Letter to Cecile von Keudell, Hannover, 18 December 1939. AS.
13 *Krieg in Europa*, p. 39.
14 Letter to his son, Turin, 2 October 1940. AS.
15 Letter to his son, Turin, 2 June 1941. AS.
16 Letter to his son, Turin, 2 October 1940. AS.
17 *Krieg in Europa*, p. 67.
18 Letter to his son, Turin, 4 August 1941. AS.
19 Letter to his son, Turin, 7 October 1941. AS.
20 Letter to his son, Turin, 9 October 1941; Cf. *Krieg in Europa*, p. 432. On the other hand in his letters to KR3 in 1941 he frequently refers to forthcoming demobilization and the responsibility of officers to ensure a decent deal for their soldiers transferring to civilian life. Did he still at that time expect a German victory?
21 *Krieg in Europa*, p. 64; Südwestfunk broadcast: 'Die Gründe des militaerischen Zusammenbruchs' (The causes of the military collapse), 5 May 1955.
22 Unpublished lecture to the USAF Staff College: 'The Interval Between the Wars'. No date. AS.
23 Letter to officers of KR3, Turin, 23 February 1941. AS.
24 Alhard Freiherr von der Borch recounted a striking example of Senger's leadership style in a letter to Hilda von Senger of 19 January 1963. Von der Borch had been Commanding Officer of 15th Panzer Grenadier Division's Armoured Recce Regiment on the Cassino front.

> When Cassino had fallen and we were withdrawing, I encountered the General [Senger] on two occasions which completely endorsed my respect and love for him. Out of my 1500-odd men at the start only 3 officers and 30 or so soldiers were left. We were in a defensive position in a valley position in a valley near Pontecorvo. It was infantry work. [This was a light armoured unit. Tr.] I was summoned to Corps Headquarters. The General listened to my situation report and then, contrary to his own orders from Army HQ, ordered my unit to be withdrawn. On leaving the General, I bumped into the Chief of Staff [Oster's successor], who was furious and made out that I had given the General a false report. In any event he gave us counter-orders that we were to stay put. Knowing that we were just too weak to do any

good where we were and that it would have been dotty to try to hold on, I knocked once more on the General's door. But on going in didn't have the gumption to say what I thought and mumbled about having left something behind at the briefing, but obviously in a bit of a stew. I was conscious of the General's quizzical glance. He saw straight through me and then repeated his orders leaving me in no doubt as to what he wanted. We withdrew that night. (AS.)

25 *Krieg in Europa*, p. 123.
26 *Krieg in Europa*, p. 204.
27 *Krieg in Europa*, p. 153.
28 This tradition was epitomized for him in the words of one of the most famous instructors in the Prussian service who said: 'The King has made you a Staff officer so that you know when to comply with an order and when not to.' Cf. Südwestfunk transcript of broadcast on 15 July 1955. AS.
29 *Krieg in Europa*, p. 308.
30 *Krieg in Europa*, p. 346. Cf. 'Die Wiederstandsbewegung im deutschen Heer'. Unpublished MS. No date. AS.
31 *Krieg in Europa*, p. 352.
32 Letter from Philipp Freiherr von Boeselager to Hilda von Senger, Kreuzberg/Ahr 18 January 1963. Boeselager was also a member of the Screening Committee from 1955 to 1957. In this letter he added; 'His [Senger's] name is a byword for resistance to terror and wrongdoing. He seems to epitomize the ideal of a soldier, the very essence of soldierhood.' Freiherr von der Borch, in the letter cited in note 24 expresses the contradiction of being an honourable soldier for a criminal régime very well:

> I found it difficult then, and still do, to describe the wonderful atmosphere under his leadership: it was quite simply, I suppose, a spirit of freedom. Perhaps he made it clear to all his officers (just as with Baade though in a different way) without making a fuss, that he was a real opponent of the régime. He managed to separate the business of soldiering and of doing our duty from the rest of the doubts and worries.

33 *Krieg in Europa*, pp. 448–9.
34 AS.
35 *Krieg in Europa*, pp. 419–20.
36 Südwestfunk Broadcast: 'Die Gründe des militärischen Zusammenbruchs'. AS.
37 Letter from Freiherr von Boeselager to Hilda von Senger. 18 January 1963: 'He was the very man who influenced the Screening Committee's work in a decisive way for the good. . . . He was never reticent about his opinions and gave them to the committee unembellished . . . it was one of the reasons why he was not exactly adored by everybody on the Board.'

CHRONOLOGY: FRIDO VON SENGER UND ETTERLIN

1891, September 4	Born in Waldshut on Swiss-German border
1910	Service in 76th (5th Baden) Field Artillery Regiment
1910–11	Student, Freiburg University
1912–14	Rhodes scholar, St John's College Oxford
1914–18	Artillery officer, Western Front
1918	Lieutenant, Staff of 14th Reserve Corps
1919	Officer in *Land-Jäger* Corps in anti-bolshevik campaign Saxony

1919	Married Hilda von Kracht
1920	Joined *Reichswehr* Cavalry School
1920–32	Regimental officer in 18th Horse (Reiter Regiment 18) and extra-regimental appointments on Cavalry staff
1927	*Rittmeister* (Captain of Cavalry)
1934	Major
1934–38	Chief of Staff Cavalry Inspectorate
1936	Lieutenant-Colonel, Commanding Officer 3rd Cavalry Regiment (KR3)
1938	Colonel
1939	Commanding Officer 22nd Cavalry Regiment
1940	Commander 1st Cavalry Brigade Groningen (Netherlands)
1940	Commander *ad hoc* motorized brigade, breakthrough Weygand Line, capture of Le Havre and Cherbourg
1940–42	Head German delegation Franco-Italian armistice commission Turin
1942, July	Commander 10th Panzer Grenadier Brigade in occupied France
1942, Autumn	Major-General, GOC 17th Panzer Division Eastern Front
1942, December	Relief offensive Stalingrad
1943, February	Operation *Citadel* (battle of Kursk)
1943, June	Lieutenant-General, Commander 14th Panzer Corps and Commander German Forces Sicily
1943	Command of withdrawal from Sardinia and Corsica
1944, Jan.–May	Commander 14th Panzer Corps, Cassino front
1944–45	Withdrawal to Gothic Line and defence of Bologna sector
1944, January 1	*General der Panzertruppe*
1945, May	Chief negotiator at surrender of German forces in Italy
1946–48	Prisoner-of-war, Bridgend, Glamorgan
1948	Appointed headmaster of Spetzgart – a branch of Salem school
1952	Military correspondent, South West German Radio
1952	Co-author of 'Himmeroder Denkschrift' – Adenauer's plan for rearmament
1955–56	Member of screening committee for selection of *Bundeswehr* officers from former members of *Wehrmacht*
1963, January 4	Died in Freiburg

KLUGE

17

KLUGE

Field-Marshal Gunther von Kluge

RICHARD LAMB

Gunther von Kluge came of an aristocratic Prussian military family in Posen, the Prussian province transferred to Poland in 1919. His father Max had long service with the Prussian Army; typical of his generation, he was proud of Bismarck's victories over the Austrians in 1866 and the French in 1870. Gunther Hans von Kluge (1882–1944) was born on 30 October 1882 at Poznan (then part of Prussia). His father Max (1856–1934) was ennobled in 1913. Gunther began his army career (with Wilhelm Keitel) in the Lower Saxony Field Regiment of Artillery. After attending the Military Academy he was on the General Staff from 1910 to 1918, reaching the rank of Captain on the Western Front. During the build-up of the *Reichswehr* into the *Wehrmacht* between the wars he became Colonel in 1930, Major-General in 1933, and Lieutenant-General in 1934. On 1 April 1934 he took command of 6th Division at Münster.

When Hitler began openly to expand the German Army in 1935, Kluge was an obvious candidate for promotion. After commanding a division he became commander of the 6th Corps in 1936, and soon after was appointed to command the 6th Army Group (Hanover), which was to become the 4th Army at the start of the Second World War.

On 30 June 1938, during the crisis over the Sudetenland, he received, in common with other German commanders, a directive from Hitler that he intended if necessary to smash Czechoslovakia in the near future. Kluge, like most of the generals, feared Hitler's crude militarism would lead to disaster.

He also disliked the underhand and dishonest methods the Nazis used to disgrace General von Fritsch, while the pogrom against the Jews and the concentration camps were anathema to him with his Prussian tradition of gentlemanly conduct.

During the summer of 1938, when General Ludwig Beck, Chief of the General Staff, organized a plot with the right-wing politician Carl Gördeler and Ernst von Weizsacker, head of the Foreign Office, to arrest Hitler and set up a democratic anti-Nazi government, Kluge, with his friends General von Hammerstein and von Witzleben (both commanding divisions), were accomplices. It came to nothing because the British government rejected the overtures from the conspirators, and just when the plotters were about to act, Chamberlain at Munich persuaded the French leaders that Hitler should be given the Sudeten part of Czechoslovakia.[1]

From then on Kluge's attitude was ambivalent. Much as he disliked the Nazis he was delighted that Hitler had recovered *Lebensraum* for the Reich as every German wanted during the inter-war years. He was proud of the efficiency of the new German armoured and motorized divisions and, full of professional zeal, took great pleasure in his command.

With the outbreak of war in September 1939 Kluge's 4th Army invaded Poland. Again Kluge was torn. At the beginning of the campaign he considered the invasion justified because he believed fabricated Nazi propaganda that the Poles were committing atrocities against Germans in Danzig and the Polish corridor. He felt that parts of Poland should belong to Germany and he was pleased by the performance of his troops. But he was appalled at the brutality with which the Nazis treated the Polish Jews, and in particular at the indiscriminate slaughter of innocent Polish civilians.

The 1939 German campaign in Poland saw the first display of mobile warfare by modern armour and air forces in combination. Kluge, with a flair for innovation, was an ideal general for this. By 3 September when belatedly Britain and France entered the war, Kluge's 4th Army had already reached the lower Vistula, so that the bulk of the Polish Army was trapped and Poland was doomed. Soon after, Kluge was slightly injured in an air crash. But his conduct of the initial advance convinced Hitler that Kluge was his most brilliant general, and it marked the beginning of the Führer's admiration for him.

Hitler's decision in October 1939 to attack France and the Low Countries that autumn came as a shock to Kluge who, like Brauchitsch, the Commander-in-Chief, and Halder, Chief of the General Staff, feared that the numerical inferiority of the German Army would lead to defeat. Kluge and his fellow generals were so disturbed that they contemplated such desperate measures as sending a picked force to occupy Berlin and overthrow Hitler, but they abandoned this plan because the Polish victory, coming on top of the occupation of Austria and Czechoslovakia, had raised Hitler to such a peak of popularity that it was thought the soldiers would not obey if they were ordered to turn against their beloved Führer.

Hitler first fixed the date for the attack in the west as 12 November, but bad weather was later forecast for that day and the attack was postponed; on 23 November Kluge was present at the meeting where Hitler harangued his generals and convinced them that he would win. From then on Kluge co-operated loyally, and was enthusiastic for Hitler's plan of open warfare with armoured formations operating in front of the main body of troops.

When the campaign finally opened on 10 May 1940, Kluge's 4th Army attacked through the Ardennes Forest to the Meuse at the point where French troops linked up with Belgians. The Germans were inferior in overall numbers to the Allies; their advantage lay in air power and superior technique in handling their tanks and air support. At this Kluge was a master.

Kluge's aim was to cross the Meuse between Givet and Namur, and he entrusted this to 5th and 7th Panzer Divisions. Rommel commanded 7th Panzer. Little resistance was encountered in the approach to the Meuse which was reached by Kluge's advanced troops on 17 May.

On the French side of the Meuse stood the French 9th Army under General Corap. This was fortunate for Kluge because they were the weakest link in the entire French front. Corap's sole claim to fame at the age of sixty-two was that he had received the surrender of the rebel Riff Chieftain at the end of the Riff War in Morocco in 1926. A newspaper article described him as 'a timid man, unmilitary in appearance and running to fat around the middle' who had 'trouble getting into a car', and with his staff and senior commanders forming 'a group of amiable old men'. His troop consisted of B–category divisions of 'fat and flabby men who needed to be retrained'.

Corap's cavalry of light tanks and horsed units had moved into the glades and thickets of the Ardennes Forest on the outbreak of war with orders to hold up Kluge's forces for at least five days, only to be annihilated by the German panzers by the second day. That evening Corap received a signal from aerial reconnaissance: 'Two large armoured masses moving west.' Corap took it calmly, feeling safe in the knowledge that he was behind the fast-flowing Meuse, nowhere less than 60 yards wide, unfordable, and with steep banks on his side, and in his belief that it would take several days before the Germans could mount an offensive. He could not have been more wrong.

By nightfall of the 12th the survivors of the French horse and tank units had recrossed the Meuse in defiance of orders, and 5th and 7th Panzer Divisions were being allowed to form up along the Meuse without significant opposition, although shelling from the French artillery was heavy. Kluge's orders were that Rommel's 7th Panzer Division should rush a crossing of the Meuse as they followed on the heels of Corap's defeated cavalry. Just as the leading tanks approached the bridges at Dinant and Houx they were blown up by the French on the afternoon of 12 May.

After visiting all his front and narrowly escaping death from near misses, Rommel drove back to his divisional headquarters for a conference with Hoth, the corps commander, and Kluge. Kluge wanted to stop and plan a set-piece crossing after reinforcements and more artillery had arrived on the east bank of the Meuse. Rommel argued that he could effect an immediate crossing with infantry in rubber boats, provided heavy casualties were acceptable, and that once over the river he could exploit the situation by a lightning drive with his armour. Kluge agreed, attracted by the chance of open warfare on which his heart was set. Little did he realize how this decision was to establish his reputation as one of the most brilliant of German army commanders.

When the attack across the river faltered, Rommel himself took command of the 7th Rifle Regiment of his division and crossed the Meuse in one of the first boats. Then rapid progress was made, and a cable ferry was established to bring over the advancing riflemen and transport back the numerous wounded. The German attackers had been badly shaken by the intensity of the French fire, and Rommel's personal intervention was crucial.

Soon a 16-ton pontoon bridge was in position and tanks, anti-tank guns and armoured cars rolled into the bridgehead. Rommel in a tank led the advance, and by night had created a gaping breach in the French line. French counter-attacks with tanks made with gallantry but little skill in command had small success.

On 15 May Kluge asked for the bulk of the Luftwaffe dive-bomber support to be allocated to Rommel. A potentially dangerous counter-attack towards Dinant by the French 1st Armoured and 4th North African Division failed to develop owing to incompetent Staff work and command, and by nightfall Rommel had penetrated to near Philippeville, 7 miles beyond the Meuse.

On the morning of 16 May Kluge visited Rommel's headquarters and was surprised to find that the Division had not already moved off; he told Rommel to sweep forward at top speed, pushing his armour through the French frontier defences (less heavily fortified than the Maginot Line) and forward to Avesnes, with the infantry following as fast as possible in trucks. Avesnes was reached at 0400 on 17 May. Here the German panzers after a sharp struggle overcame French tanks, and Rommel brought his divisional headquarters into the town and deployed all his infantry units in the territory he had occupied.

The 7th Panzer Division losses on 16–17 May were only 35 killed and 59 wounded, but they had taken 10,000 POWs and captured 100 tanks. Their official history states: 'The Division had not time to collect large numbers of prisoners and equipment.'

At midnight on 17 May Kluge ordered Rommel to continue the advance on 18 May towards Cambrai. All went well for Rommel on 18 May and he reached Le Cateau, but now French opposition was fiercer and he paused for a day. As Rommel was holding a battle conference he received a message that Kluge wanted a postponement of the attack because the troops must be exhausted. Rommel replied: 'A night attack in moonlight will result in fewer losses.' Kluge let him have his way.

On 20 May Rommel's tank spearhead reached Beaurains, two and a half miles west of Arras, at 0600. However his infantry could not keep up, and the French infiltrated into his lines of communication. Suddenly Rommel was in a tight corner.

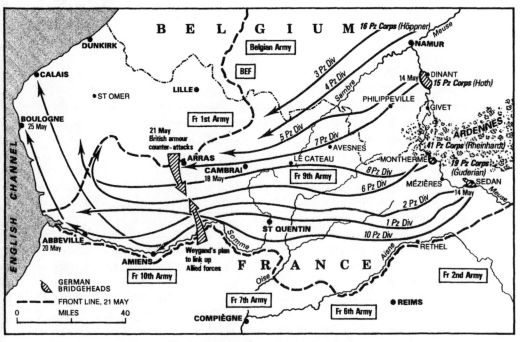

The invasion of France, May 1940

On the outbreak of Hitler's attack the nine divisions of the British Expeditionary Force had been sent forward into Belgium to the line of the Dyle river, but had been quickly withdrawn because of the German breakthrough. Each day the French and British thought the German armoured attack must exhaust itself so that they could launch well-prepared attacks against the spearheads, but as the German tanks kept moving forward unpredictably the Allies were unable to deploy their reserves to attack them. However, on 21 May the British 5th and 50th Divisions were hastily assembled at Arras together with the 1st Army Tank Brigade (infantry tanks) while the French promised to co-operate with two mechanized divisions and two infantry divisions to the south. Their plan was to punch out Kluge's salient with a tank attack simultaneously from the south and the north. The attack took longer to mount than expected, and when on 24 May came the dire news that Guderian's Panzer Corps had raced through Amiens and reached the sea near

Abbeville, so cutting the Allied armies in two, the British decided to attack without waiting for the French, although 70 French tanks did co-operate on the right flank.

Just when the British attack looked like being a success, 14 out of 16 Matildas broke down or caught fire and the scales were turned in the Germans' favour. Out of 62 British tanks 46 were lost in a nine-hour battle. With little infantry and artillery support and no help from the RAF, the tank attack ground to a halt in the face of Rommel's swiftly established defensive line and heavy Stuka attack. Rommel described Arras as 'a very heavy battle against hundreds of enemy tanks and following infantry' – a vast exaggeration.

This British tank attack was the only serious counter-stroke made by the Allies and it gave Kluge a shock. The British armour inflicted losses on 7th Panzers of 89 killed, 116 wounded and 173 missing, four times the loss suffered during the breakthrough to date, and Kluge was now worried that if his panzers advanced again, they might be cut off before the infantry divisions could arrive to support them. After a conference between Hitler and Kluge, a Führer order was given on 24 May to Kluge's army to halt –when German forward troops were only 10 miles from Dunkirk – by then the only possible escape route for the entrapped British Army. The halt order was lifted on 26 May, but the British and French used the 48 hours' respite to build a shield around Dunkirk, greatly helped by widespread inundations. As a result the BEF was saved, and 338,000 British and French troops were evacuated to Britain from Dunkirk. Nevertheless Hitler sent personal congratulations to Kluge and Rommel, and visited Kluge's troops in the sunniest of moods.

On 20 May General Weygand, who had succeeded General Gamelin as Supreme French Commander, made frenzied efforts to organize a defence of the line of the Somme, but the enemy had already established bridgeheads on the south bank at Amiens and Abbeville. The British could give the French little help. The British 1st Armoured Division disembarked at Cherbourg on 21 May. It was incomplete and consisted only of two armoured brigades; its two motorized infantry battalions and one armoured brigade had been sent on Churchill's express orders to help in the hopeless defence of Calais, and had been captured. Still one armoured regiment went into the line on the south bank of the Somme west of Amiens. The only other British formation available was the 51st Highland Division under General Fortune which had been doing duty on the Maginot Line. They detrained at Rouen on 27 May after considerable delays due to bombing.

General Marshall-Cornwall arrived in France on 31 May to take charge of the remnants of the British forces in France. He was to be followed by a new BEF comprising 52nd Lowland and 1st Canadian Division under General Sir Alan Brooke. Marshall-Cornwall formed a very low opinion of General Altmayer's Staff at 10th French Army under whose orders he was placed, and also of one of the British Commanders.

In Marshall-Cornwall's words,

> On the following morning [5 June] Colonel-General Hans Gunther von Kluge's
> 4th Army opened a violent attack on the whole front of the 10th Army from
> Amiens to the sea. This drove a wedge between Altmayer's 10th Corps on the
> right and his 9th Corps on the left; he completely lost touch with 10th Corps.[2]

Kluge brilliantly exploited this gap with 5th and 7th Panzer Divisions. It was
the final nail in the coffin of the Allies, and the ultimate victory which set
Kluge apart as the most successful German general of the 1940 campaign.

On 7 June British tanks of 1st Armoured Division held up Kluge's motorized
units which were penetrating towards Rouen and the Seine valley, but it was
a hopeless struggle. Marshall-Cornwall telephoned to the War Office asking
for permission to withdraw 51st Highland Division who were now in deadly
danger of being cut off by Kluge. Permission was refused because the British
believed the French would continue the struggle from Brittany. Instead on 12
June part of the 52nd Lowland Division disembarked at Cherbourg and
immediately went into the line, but there was a wide gap between them and
the nearest French troops.

By the morning of 10 June, Rommel's 7th Panzer had reached the Seine.
Kluge immediately ordered Rommel to swing northwest towards the sea. On
11 June Rommel wrote to his wife: 'Over 60 miles in pursuit yesterday; reached
the sea west of Dieppe and cut off several divisions (French and British).'

Rommel had driven 51st Highland Division on to the beach at St Valéry
en Caux, and set the seal on Kluge's triumph. Cut off from their supplies of
food and ammunition, they surrendered at midday on 13 June after putting
up a disappointing resistance. Rommel courteously asked Fortune and his
senior Staff officers to lunch, but they refused because they had 'plenty of
food of their own'. In the afternoon Rommel was surprised to see Fortune
and other British officers laughing as they walked round the house in which
they were confined.

On the same afternoon General Sir Alan Brooke arrived and set up his
Corps HQ at Le Mans, confident that the French were preparing a redoubt in
Brittany. Marshall-Cornwall made a 77-mile dash to meet him, and insisted
on evacuation; Brooke telephoned to the War Office who by now no longer
believed in the Brittany redoubt, and agreed the only possible course was
immediate re-embarkation of all the British troops. Marshall-Cornwall then
went to 10th Army HQ where the French still talked of the *Reduit Breton*. But
the news from the front was so bad that Marshall-Cornwall told Altmayer that
he must cut 'the Gordian Knot', having already ordered all British troops back
to Cherbourg. From Cherbourg Marshall-Cornwall embarked 30,500 men and
26 tanks, but left behind hundreds of lorries, many in perfect condition.
Meanwhile Kluge had sent Rommel's 'Ghost Division', as it had become

known, in hot pursuit; after racing 150 miles in one day it was only 3 miles from Cherbourg when the last British ship left. It was the 125th anniversary of Waterloo, but Marshall-Cornwall remarked it was more like Corunna.

After the fighting was over, staff at Hoth's Corps criticized Rommel for his unorthodox method of commanding from the front, and for disobeying orders by signposting his communications roads with the sign 'DG 7' to enable units following behind to close up quickly. There were also complaints that contact had been lost between Rommel and his divisional staff. Kluge took Rommel's side in this controversy, as well he might, because Rommel's spirited generalship had done so much to establish Kluge's own reputation. Both Kluge and Rommel basked in Hitler's favour, and were applauded to the hilt by German radio and press. It was to be four years before Kluge and Rommel were to work in harness again, and then in very different circumstances.

When on 26 June 1941 Hitler sent his armies into Russia, Kluge, promoted Field-Marshal, still commanded 4th Army. It was placed in Army Group Centre under Bock. The first aim was to trap as many Russian troops as possible around Minsk. Kluge insisted that the jaws of the pincer must be closed early because his infantry were not fully motorized and could not arrive in time for a deeper encirclement. He was right, and Hitler appreciated his good judgment.

Smolensk was soon taken. But the jaws of another pincer movement beyond failed by 10 miles to close, and although 300,000 Russian POWs were taken by 5 August, 200,000 Russians escaped. Kluge found that bad roads prevented him from bringing up reinforcements quickly enough, and chafed at the delay before the offensive towards Moscow could be resumed. Meanwhile in August Hitler caused further delays by detaching part of Bock's armour and sending it southward in a victorious offensive to encircle Kiev, and closing another trap in which 600,000 Russian troops were encircled. A further encirclement on 30 September around Vyasma on the road to Moscow produced great numbers of Russian POWs, and for a short period Kluge believed he had a clear road to Moscow. However, at the end of October the weather broke and the roads became morasses just as massive numbers of fresh Russian troops appeared in front of Moscow.

Bock wanted to push on to Moscow with his mechanized units, leaving slow-moving infantry to mop up the pockets of resistance in the rear, and some of his armoured detachments actually reached the outskirts of Moscow on 2 December although the main advance was held up in the forests around the capital. Immediately a massive Russian counter-offensive under Zhukov pushed back the tired Germans, outflanked them, and produced a critical situation.

The more intelligent Kluge had been opposed to an unsupported armoured advance on Moscow, realizing better than Hitler and his superiors the inherent dangers, and perhaps mindful of the critical moments the year before around Arras when Rommel's tanks had advanced too far without infantry support. By 4 December Kluge was reporting to Hitler that his infantry was at a standstill because of impassable roads frozen at night and quagmires by day.

On 22 December Kluge complained to Hitler that the General Staff were flying half-frozen troops to Smolensk without weapons or winter gear, and on New Year's Eve asked Hitler for permission to make minor withdrawals because of the incessant Russian attacks. Hitler replied that in the First World War he and his comrades had stood fifteen days of ceaseless bombardment and had held the line. Kluge rejoined that they had not been fighting in 25 degrees of frost, and that one of his corps commanders had told him one division would not obey an order to stand fast because the troops were so exhausted. Hitler said angrily: 'If that is so, then it is the end of the German Army.' However, Hitler gave permission for Kluge to withdraw certain formations of his Army Group – a tribute to his trust in his Field-Marshal. But Hitler was adamant that he would not allow any large-scale strategic withdrawal, and after lengthy long-distance telephone calls refused Kluge's repeated requests to withdraw a 90-mile sector of his front 20 miles. Kluge was not timid in expressing his views to Hitler, but he knew when to stop before Hitler got too angry.

Not until May 1942 did Hitler's armies regain the initiative, and during the winter partisan activity in the rear of Kluge's Army devastated railway bridges and foodstores. A barbaric struggle against the partisans ensued. Thousands were killed, whether combatants or not, in large-scale sweeps, and brutal methods were used to force hundreds of thousands of Russians in rear areas to work as slave labourers.

Kluge was sickened by the lack of humanity of his compatriots and now believed that Hitler's Russian campaign would bring disaster to Germany. He appreciated the menace implicit in Hitler's declaration of war on the USA in December 1941, and his faith in Hitler faltered.

On 13 July 1942 Hitler again showed his trust in Kluge by promoting him to command Army Group Centre when Bock was stricken by a sudden temporary illness. At Bock's headquarters Kluge became a close friend of Baron Henning von Tresckow, a high-up Staff officer deep in the resistance movement. Tresckow belonged to the younger generation of aristoctrats in the *Wehrmacht* and was a hard-working soldier with a good brain and blessed with good looks and charisma. Kluge soon became very much under his influence.

At Army Group Centre headquarters there was a clique of younger staff officers who, disgusted by the brutality with which the German occupation of Russia was being enforced, and the impossibility of bringing the war to a successful conclusion, had become dedicated to overthrowing Hitler and making peace with the Allies in the west.

Kluge was sympathetic to the machinations of the Tresckow clique. They persuaded Kluge that in the interests of the German nation an attempt must be made to kill Hitler. Tresckow even got Kluge to agree to see the influential German anti-Nazi politician Gördeler at Smolensk. After making a long and dangerous journey Gördeler was convinced that he had won Kluge over to his cause, but he had not reckoned with Kluge's ambivalence and indecision. Not for nothing was he known as 'der Kluge Hans' ('Clever Hans'). A close friend of Tresckow and Kluge's, von Schlabrendorff, who miraculously escaped Hitler's hangmen, summed it up after the war, writing: 'Time and time again he [Tresckow] thought he had brought Kluge to the brink of action, only to find that the next day he had relapsed into uncertainty.'[3] Kluge stayed outwardly subservient to Hitler. Whether Hitler suspected Kluge's disloyalty at this stage is not known, but in October 1942 the Führer surprisingly sent Kluge a cheque for a quarter of a million marks for the benefit of his country estate as a tax-free testimonial for his conduct of the war. Kluge, after considerable doubts, accepted. To have refused would have betrayed his disloyalty to the Führer. Tresckow told Kluge that posterity would only understand his acceptance of the gift if Kluge made it appear he accepted it to avoid dismissal so that he could preserve a position from which he might eventually overthrow Hitler.

In March 1943 Hitler decided to visit Kluge. The conspirators at Kluge's headquarters thought the time had come to kill Hitler. They proposed to Kluge that a firing-squad should arrest Hitler and execute him. Kluge toyed with the idea; then he dilly-dallied and finally rejected it. Disappointed, Tresckow instead placed a time bomb on Hitler's plane as he flew home. Unfortunately the detonator cap did not work, and Hitler never again visited Kluge.

Kluge co-operated loyally with Hitler during the final desperate offensive on 5 July 1943 against the Kursk salient (see map on page 238), but he angered Hitler by withdrawing his Panzer Divisions from a dangerous position when the ferocious Russian counter-attack developed. However, he later cleverly slipped most of his troops out of the Russian trap east of the Dnieper. Then on 12 October 1943 his car overturned on the Minsk-Smolensk road, and he was *hors de combat* for many months.

On 30 June 1944 Kluge, fully recovered from his motor accident, was summoned by Hitler to Berchtesgaden. He looked well and was fresh and confident.

On 29 June Field-Marshal Rundstedt and Field-Marshal Rommel, the Commanders-in-Chief in the west, had been ordered to report to Hitler on their progress in repulsing the Allied invasion. They were pessimistic about the chances of success of a German counter-attack; this displeased Hitler who dismissed them without inviting them to dinner. The next day on the telephone Keitel, Hitler's Chief of Staff, asked Rundstedt: 'What shall we do now?' The exasperated Rundstedt is reported to have replied, 'Make peace, you fools.' Keitel reported this to Hitler who immediately sacked Rundstedt and appointed Kluge in his place.

Thus Kluge assumed a key appointment in which, if he had thrown his lot in with the Stauffenberg-Beck-Gördeler conspirators, he could have ended the war in the west and halted Russia's advance into central Europe. Unfortunately he vacillated. So important was his role in the tragedy that several contemporary German historians have analysed his character in depth. On the Eastern Front, Kluge had been tenacious and an expert on improvisation as German equipment failed to stand up to the rigours of the Russian winter. He loved the Army and his troops. He always demanded the utmost from his subordinates. Under an impassive exterior he was very emotional. He loved talking about the countryside and adored his woods and river in East Prussia. Although he disliked the Nazis, he was susceptible to the hypnotism of Hitler's personality, and when he came to Berchtesgaden, away from Tresckow's influence, in June 1944, he appeared to be under a keen sense of obligation to Hitler for the gift of money.[4]

Hitler took great pains with Kluge during their few days together; he made him sit in on the War Conference at the Berghof where Hitler showed much irresponsible optimism, and the Führer persuaded his Field-Marshal that the success of the Allies in their invasion of Normandy was mainly due to the mistakes and poor leadership of Rundstedt and Rommel. Hitler emphasized that Rommel was over-conscious of the 'alleged overpowering effect of the Allies' air power and artillery', and that this made him pessimistic, and in addition Rommel was too 'self-willed' so that he did not always carry out the Führer's orders implicitly. Hitler explained to Kluge that he no longer had full confidence in Rommel. Hitler also convinced Kluge that once the invasion was halted, V-1 flying bombs and even more potent secret weapons would annihilate Britain within a few months.

Kluge's former sympathies with the resistance had vanished. Like a chameleon he now was the Führer's 'man', convinced that Hitler alone would save Germany from the dreadful fate of being defeated by the Allies, who now offered only unconditional surrender and a wretched future for all Germans under the Morgenthau Plan.

This mood did not last long. As soon as Kluge, full of Hitler's optimism, arrived at Rommel's headquarters at La Roche Guyon there was a row. Kluge summarily warned Rommel that he must always obey orders unconditionally. Rommel replied with a raised voice that he had interpreted the military situation correctly to Hitler, and made it crystal clear that it would be impossible to hold the Normandy front much longer. So heated was the argument that Kluge had to ask the staff officers present to withdraw. Afterwards Rommel made a written request to Kluge to withdraw his accusations.[5]

In an effort to patch up the quarrel Kluge agreed to tour the front and discuss the situation with the formation commanders. There, with his quick brain and professional competence, Kluge was convinced that what Hitler had told him was false and neurotic, and that Rommel was right. Saul became Paul. Kluge decided that Hitler lived by wishful thinking and, when his dream faded, searched for scapegoats, which he had done in Russia. Quick to change his mind, and with his strong streak of ambivalence, Kluge turned against Hitler again.

On 12 July Kluge returned to Rommel's headquarters. Now the two Field-Marshals were agreed that the war was lost and, as Hitler would not bring it to an end by political action, he must be liquidated. If the resistance could kill Hitler, both Kluge and Rommel would support a new Beck-Gördeler government, and call on Montgomery to negotiate surrender terms under which the Germans would leave their heavy equipment in France, and withdraw their troops behind the Rhine to help their eastern armies to keep the Russians out of Germany.

Rommel had already opened a radio link with the Americans, and on 2 July and 9 July medical personnel and severely wounded had been passed through the lines.[6] Hitler was furious when he heard of this. On 16 July, after discussions with Kluge, Rommel prepared what he called a 'Blitz' message to Hitler stating that his troops 'were fighting heroically', but the German front would crumble inevitably 'within fourteen days to three weeks', and: 'It is my duty to state this clearly.'

The conspirators in Berlin, through their accomplice General Karl Stülpnagel, Military Governor of Paris, sent a message to Rommel that Stauffenberg would try to kill Hitler at his War Conference on 20 July, and a Beck-Gördeler government would be proclaimed to replace the Nazis.[7] Kluge agreed to cooperate if Hitler was killed; Rommel on 17 July told Stülpnagel he would act 'openly and unconditionally' as soon as Hitler was liquidated whether Kluge went along with him or not. But that evening Rommel's car was attacked by Spitfires and he was taken to hospital severely wounded.

Now the conspirators' hopes in the west rested on Kluge. He was to prove spineless and vacillating. On 19 July, according to Walter Bargatzky (post-war head of the German Red Cross), Kluge came to Paris for a conference with Stülpnagel; Kluge was told the assassination was planned for the next day, and he agreed to honour Rommel's commitment.[8]

On 20 July Stauffenberg's bomb exploded during Hitler's conference at Rastenburg. Unfortunately the Führer was only wounded and not killed, and the revolt in Berlin was quickly snuffed out, with the immediate execution of Beck and Stauffenberg.

In Paris Stülpnagel and his fellow conspirators received a telephone call that the coup was 'on' and Hitler dead. Later they received a message that 'all was lost'. As planned, Stülpnagel had ordered the arrest of over 1,000 Gestapo and SD leaders in Paris; they were put in prison without violence. When the news came that the plot had failed in Berlin, Stülpnagel drove to Kluge's headquarters in a last desperate attempt to persuade him to surrender the Western Front and continue the uprising from France. According to General Blumentritt, one of Kluge's senior Staff officers, when Kluge first heard the news that Hitler was dead he had said: 'If the Führer is dead we ought to get in touch with the other side at once.' Unfortunately soon afterwards a message came from Keitel at Rastenburg that Hitler was only wounded. Kluge's nerve failed, and by the time Stülpnagel arrived at La Roche Guyon, he had decided irrevocably to turn his back on the conspirators.

Stülpnagel argued desperately, but Kluge remained adamant that he had only agreed to co-operate once Hitler was dead. It is conceivable that his personal oath of loyalty to Hitler weighed with him. Kluge even threatened Stülpnagel with arrest. In return Stülpnagel considered blackmailing Kluge by threatening to expose his promise to join the plot, but eventually decided to return to Paris and release the Gestapo personnel. Stülpnagel's part in the plot had become clear to the Gestapo and the next day he was summoned back to Berlin and arrested after a failed attempt at suicide.

The Normandy campaign went atrociously for Kluge, as it was bound to. A counter-offensive against the advancing Americans, when Rommel's line of defence had been shattered, was ordered by Hitler against Kluge's advice. Faithfully, Kluge, who had suggested a retreat to behind the Seine, executed the Führer's orders, but his remaining panzer divisions were sacrificed uselessly. Thereupon Kluge changed his mind again and tried to surrender.

On 15 August with his troops in dire straits, Kluge was out of contact with his Staff all day. At Hitler's headquarters an Allied radio signal was monitored asking where Kluge was. Immediately Hitler suspected that Kluge was trying to negotiate an armistice and said it was 'the worst day' of his life. Kluge's son-in-law, Dr Udo Esche, who later gave Kluge cyanide with which to commit suicide, told Allied interrogators after the war that Kluge had discussed with him surrendering and 'went to the front lines but was unable to get in touch with the Allied commanders'. George Pfann, secretary to General Patton's 3rd US Army, stated that Patton vanished for an entire day in mid-August and, when he returned, said he had tried to make contact with a German emissary who had not turned up at the appointed place. Brigadier Sir Edgar Williams, Montgomery's Chief of Intelligence, told the author he could recall the day when Kluge was reported missing and he had warned Montgomery they might get something from Kluge at any moment.[9]

Late that night Kluge reappeared at his headquarters and said his radio van had been damaged by enemy aircraft in the morning, so he could not stay in touch as he visited his forward units. This did not satisfy Hitler who immediately sacked Kluge and replaced him with a fanatical Nazi, Field-Marshal

Model. Kluge wrote to Hitler: 'My Führer, make up your mind to end the war. The German people have undergone such untold suffering that it is time to put an end to this frightfulness.'

Too late, Kluge, who had such difficulty in making up his mind, had tried to end the war and failed. He committed suicide on his way back to Germany, knowing that his part in the plot had been revealed to Hitler. The most able of Hitler's generals, he was tortured by the conflict between his desire to see a victorious Germany, and his hatred both of Nazi methods and the pro-longation of a war which could only bring further useless horrors to the German people.

NOTES

1 Gerhard Ritter, *German Resistance*, pp. 83–112.
2 Letters to author, 1981, from General Sir James Marshall-Cornwall. *War Monthly*, Issue 45. *Normandy 1940* by James Marshall-Cornwall, pp. 65–66.
3 Fabian von Schlabrendorff, *Revolt Against Hitler*.
4 *Ibid.*
5 *The Rommel Papers*, ed. B. H. Liddell Hart, pp. 481–485.
6 *Hansard*, House of Commons, 18 July, 1944. The German signals are at Stanford University, California.
7 P. Hoffman, *History of the German Resistance 1933–1945*, pp. 470–478. Stauffenberg, an aristocrat, was a high Staff Officer in the German War Office.
8 Bargatzky Memorandum, Stanford University.
9 David Irving, *Hitler's War*, p. 696; Richard Lamb, *The Ghosts of Peace*, p. 305.

CHRONOLOGY: GUNTHER HANS VON KLUGE

1882, October 30	Born
1901	Joined Lower Saxony Artillery Regiment
1908	Military Academy
1910–18	General Staff officer; rose to Captain on Western Front
1918	Joined *Reichswehr*
1930	Colonel
1933	Major-General
1934, April 1	Command of 6th Division at Munster
1937	General of Artillery and command of 6th Army Corps
1938, December 1	Command of 6th Army (Hanover), which became, on outbreak of Second World War, 4th Army (Hanover)
1939–40	Commanded 4th Army in Poland, France and Russia
1940, July	Promoted, Field-Marshal
1941, July 19	Succeeded Field-Marshal Bock as Commander of Army Group Centre in Russia
1943, October 12	After a serious car accident, went on prolonged sick leave

1944, July 7	Became Commander-in-Chief West in France in place of Field-Marshal von Rundstedt, and on 17 July assumed, after Rommel was wounded, command of Army Group B in Normandy
1944, August 17	Dismissed by Hitler; two days later he committed suicide at Valmy, France

MANTEUFFEL

DIETRICH

18

DIETRICH AND MANTEUFFEL

SS Colonel-General Josef 'Sepp' Dietrich
General of Panzer Troops Hasso von Manteuffel

FRANZ KUROWSKI

Sepp Dietrich was one of the first German tank soldiers of the First World War. Moreover, as one of Hitler's first followers he accompanied him on his engagements so it was inevitable that he should play an important role, being directly responsible to Hitler and responsible for Hitler's safety. Hitler trusted this fighter and fellow veteran of the war implicitly. He had good reason since Sepp Dietrich was a person of high integrity. Dietrich, prototype of a valiant fighter, a model of loyalty and reliability, always spoke his mind to Hitler – in an open though inoffensive manner. If 'Papa' Paul Hausser was considered to be the creator of the Waffen-SS, then Sepp Dietrich was the soldier of the First and Second World Wars who implanted that fighting spirit into the Waffen SS which, according to the words of Otto Skorzeny, 'equalled that of Napoleon's Imperial Guard'.

Although the professionally trained leaders of the *Reichswehr* made their papers and books available to him and gave him every possible support, and although, in addition, he gained practical experience from commanding a regiment or a division, all this could not outweigh the shortcomings in his military knowledge compared to those officers who had gone through the long process of traditional training, first in the Cadet Corps and then in the General Staff. None the less, Sepp Dietrich was a leader of panzer units of high capability.

Joseph 'Sepp' Dietrich was born on 28 May 1892 in the Hawangen district of Memmingen in the Allgäu. He went to primary school in Kempten and after that started an apprenticeship in the hotel business, which he concluded successfully in Zürich.

In 1911 he joined the 4th Bavarian field artillery regiment 'König' in Augsburg as a volunteer. In 1912 he was seconded by his unit to a corporal college, after which he served for two years as a corporal training mounted troops.

On 1 August 1914 he went into front-line service with the 6th reserve field artillery regiment and in 1915 he was transferred to the 7th HM Bavarian field artillery regiment, 'Prinz Luitpold'. From there he moved to the 10th infantry rifle unit which had earned itself a special reputation as first 'panzer killer'. Finally, after another assignment with the 8th infantry regiment, he served in the 2nd assault battalion.

After the introduction of the first German panzer combat vehicles, Sergeant Dietrich applied to join the 13th motorized assault panzer unit, where he underwent a specialized training. On 21 March 1918 he drove the first panzer near St Quentin and in July in the tank battle of Villers-Cotterets, in which the enemy went into action with over 400 tanks. It was Dietrich who fired the first shots. After four years' fighting on the Western Front and in Italy as a front-line non-commissioned officer, he had received the Iron Crosses Second and First Class, the Panzer Medal in silver, the Bavarian Cross for Distinguished Service, Third Class, the Austrian Medal for Bravery, and in 1921, after service in Upper Silesia, the new German Republic awarded him the Silesian Order of the Eagle, First and Second Class.

As troop leader and Lance-Sergeant he had been involved in launching this totally new weapon, the tank. From this moment on up to his crowning appointment as commander of a panzer army, a career unfolded which today is a legehd. In this essay an attempt is made to draw an outline of the man and his achievement from the myth of fiction and fact.

After Sepp Dietrich was discharged from the Bavarian Army in March 1919, he joined the *Freikorps* 1st Defence Regiment, Munich, as a Sergeant. As member of this *Freikorps* unit he took part in the forcible overthrow of the ruling Red (communist) régime in Munich.

In 1920 he joined the Bavarian National Police as Sergeant-Major and became a troop leader. From 1920 to 1926 he was at the same time member of the *Freikorps* 'Oberland'. During this time, in May 1921, he went into action in Upper Silesia as volunteer against similarly unofficial Polish 'volunteers', and distinguished himself during the storming of the Annaberg on the 21st. From 1927 he worked for three years as manager of a petrol station as well as a forwarding agent for a large south German publishing concern.

In May 1928 he was accepted into the *Schutzstaffel* of the Nazi Party, membership number 1177, and on 1 August Hitler appointed him *Sturmbannführer* of the *Schutzstaffel*. From then on Dietrich positively stormed up the ladder of success. He accompanied Hitler on all his engagements, discussed all kinds of matters with him, and showed himself in all ways a man to Hitler's taste. So it was inevitable that on 18 September 1929 he became *Standartenführer* and commander of the SS Bavarian Brigade. With his appointment to SS *Oberführer* on 11 July 1930 he became, at the same time, leader of the SS Group South. Only 18 months later he became SS *Gruppenführer*, on 18 December 1931. In between, in 1930, he was elected a member of the German Reichstag. On 1 October 1932 he was promoted leader of SS Group North. In this capacity Dietrich on Hitler's behalf successfully and without bloodshed ousted Walter Stennes from his post as SA leader in eastern Germany.

After the National-Socialists came to power on 30 January 1933 Sepp Dietrich became one of Hitler's closest and most constant associates. He often joined Hitler for lunch and dinner. After 30 January he was assigned by Hitler to create an SS unit which would be armed and quartered in barracks. This unit was initially called 'SS-Watch-Battalion Berlin'. When the unit had increased from 120 volunteers to 800 in September 1933 it was renamed the *Leibstandarte* (Life Guard) SS Adolf Hitler.

In October 1933 Sepp Dietrich took over the SS Upper Sector East of the general (unarmed) SS and became an honorary judge at the Supreme and Disciplinary Court of Honour of the German Labour Front. In the same year he was appointed Prussian Privy and Civic Councillor in Berlin. Together with his namesake, the Reich press chief Dr Otto Dietrich, Sepp Dietrich belonged to the closest team of advisors who, in the side wing of the Führer's apartment in the Chancellery, had to be on call day and night. He therefore moved into a room of his own in the Führer's suite. Moreover, he was not only commander of the continually expanding *Leibstandarte* but also chief of Hitler's escort and as such responsible for Hitler's safety. Nicolaus von Below, Hitler's adjutant, said of him: 'Unpretentious, not erudite but equipped with common sense, he commanded everyone's respect because of his honest character.'[1]

Sepp Dietrich's participation in the liquidation of the SA leadership on 30 June 1934, for which he was put on trial before a German court after the Second World War (see below, p. 421), has been reported incorrectly in various publications. As Sepp Dietrich told Paul Hausser after the Second World War, one battalion of the *Leibstandarte* was sent from Berlin to south Germany on 29 June. The transfer permit was issued by General von Reichenau from the Defence Ministry. When this battalion arrived by train in Augsburg it was met by a transport team of the *Reichswehr* and taken to Munich. During its stay in Munich the battalion was provided with board and lodging by the *Reichswehr*. The battalion had absolutely no idea what the game was, but everyone knew that the *Reichswehr* was on its side. The criticism, if indeed one can use this word, that the SS in these Munich days protected Hitler, is simply unfounded. Sepp Dietrich described the situation exactly as follows:

'Hitler and his entourage were staying in the *'Braunes Haus'* [Brown House] in Munich not under the protection of the *Leibstandarte* or the 'political stand-by teams' but under that of a company of the *Reichswehr* Pioneer Battalion No. 7.' Although Dietrich did not take part personally, the *Leibstandarte* provided a shooting-party of seven at the Stadelheim prison in Munich, where Röhm, the SA Chief of Staff, and five other senior SA leaders were shot. A post-war Munich court was to sentence Dietrich to 18 months' imprisonment for 'being an accomplice to manslaughter' in regard to the Röhm shootings.

On 1 July 1934 Dietrich was promoted to SS *Obergruppenführer*, the equivalent to an Army full general. General Baron von Fritsch, who liked Dietrich very much, lent Dietrich his war-college notes and essays for further study and also personally instructed him, thus laying the foundation stone for his development into a commander of troops. The Defence Minister von Blomberg, on his frequent inspections of the *Leibstandarte*, was full of praise for the way it was trained. At the invitation of the Army, Dietrich participated in many planning exercises, such as in 1936 in Zossen and in 1938 at the panzer-troop school at Wunsdorf. So on the barrack squares of Berlin Lichterfelde and on the drill fields, the *Leibstandarte* developed into a combat unit which later proved its worth in vigorous action.

On 1 September 1939 the *Leibstandarte*, placed under command of the 17th Infantry Division, marched from Silesia via Kreuzberg-Pitchen to the Polish border. At 0445 an assault party of the unit blew up the frontier post, occupied the Posna bridge and advanced to, and captured, Boleslawiec. In the evening of this first day of battle a Polish cavalry division was successfully beaten back. The breakthrough to a position on the Warthe, the successful encirclement of Kutno and the battle on the Bzura were highlights of Dietrich's operations. On 18 September the attack on Warsaw and the siege of the fortress of Modlin followed. After the capture of Warsaw on 27 September, and of Modlin on the following day, Dietrich was awarded the bars to both Iron Crosses.

In February 1940 the *Leibstandarte* was incorporated into the 227th Infantry Division at Rheine as a fast unit. At the beginning of the German offensive in the west in May 1940, the *Leibstandarte* took the bridge of De Poppe in Holland by a surprise attack and after rapidly advancing 50 miles it occupied Swolle. With the capture of Geertruideberg the *Leibstandarte* was able to support Student's 1st Parachute Regiment which had taken over the Maas-Waal, the Moerdijk bridge, in a surprise landing – alas not without heavy fighting – and go on to take the Hague and Scheveningen.

From 24 May 1940, the *Leibstandarte* served as part of the 1st Panzer Division in Guderian's 19th Panzer Corps in the advance towards Dunkirk. In an assault on his own initiative during the High Command's temporary halting of the panzer divisions, Dietrich crossed the Flanders-Aa canal and took the 230-foot high Mount Wattenberg, a tactically commanding height. General Guderian, on arrival, approved Dietrich's initiative and – while both were sheltering from surprise enemy fire – he gave Dietrich the order for a further attack on Wormhout. The 2nd Battalion, the Royal Warwickshire regiment defending Wormhout, eventually had to surrender to Dietrich's troops with all its 17 officers and 750 men. Approximately 50 yards away from the enemy position just outside Esquelbecq, Dietrich's assault vehicle was destroyed. He and his adjutant, Max Wünsche, had to shelter in a water conduit for four hours before an assault party, led by *Oberscharführer* Oberschelp, rescued them.

During the second phase of the French campaign the *Leibstandarte* was allocated to the 3rd Panzer Division and together they crossed the Oise and the Aisne. Eventually they reached the area of Villers-Cotterets where Dietrich had fought as a tank commander twenty-two years earlier. Château Thierry was taken from the enemy and, spearheading the 3rd Panzer Division in its rapid pursuit, Dietrich's troops reached St Etienne 300 miles further south. On 5 July 1940 Sepp Dietrich received the Knight's Cross of the Iron Cross from Hitler personally.

In the Balkans campaign of spring 1941 *Leibstandarte* was equipped to brigade status and provided with an assault-gun detachment and additional anti-aircraft and artillery weapons. On 6 April 1941, it advanced from Bulgarian territory into Yugoslavia and, together with the 9th Panzer Division, advanced to Skopje via Kyustendil and Kumanovo. At Skopje the *Leibstandarte* turned south and along narrow mountain roads drove towards Monastir (Bitola). They reached Prilep but their advance towards Monastir was halted at the Zrna because the enemy had blown up the bridge over the river. But the advanced guard managed to cross the river within a few hours by means of a temporary bridge. By 12 April they had taken the Klidi pass, defended by Anzac troops of the British Expeditionary Force sent by Churchill to defend Greece. This opened the way into Greece. The next target of the bodyguard was Lake Kastoria. On 19 April they reached Koritsa across the stubbornly defended Klusara pass, where they easily took the staff quarters of the 3rd Greek Army Corps in a surprise attack. The leader of the unit carrying out this attack was *Sturmbannführer* Kurt Meyer, later nicknamed 'Panzermeyer'; 12,000 Greek soldiers surrendered to him. When on 20 April the Metsovon pass in the Pindos mountains was taken, the Greek Epirus-Macedonia Army capitulated. Sepp Dietrich personally drove to the Greek headquarters near Joannina and negotiated with the Commander-in-Chief of these troops, General Tsolakoglu. On the same day Dietrich and the Greek general signed the capitulation document. Sepp Dietrich consented to General Tsolakoglu's request that all the Greek officers should be allowed to continue carrying their pistols. After the signing of the document, resulting in a total Greek capitulation a few days later, Sepp Dietrich was the guest of the Archbishop.

In the pursuit battles, starting on 24 April 1941, the *Leibstandarte* brigade reached the Gulf of Patras and made contact with the parachute regiment under Colonel Sturm, which had dropped on the Corinth canal on 26 April. The *Leibstandarte* completed its action in Greece with an advance via Pirgos and Tripolis, overcoming the last enemy resistance in the port of Kalamai. Sepp Dietrich thanked his men in the Olympic stadium of Athens for their bravery and devotion, remembering those who had fallen or been wounded during the campaign. After a brief respite in Athens the brigade was re-deployed to a position east of Prague, in Czechoslovakia, in readiness for Operation *Barbarossa*.

On 27 June 1941, almost one week after the start of the Russian campaign, the *Leibstandarte*, now equipped as a motorized infantry division, marched to Beuten, crossed the Vistula near Annapol on 30 June and shortly afterwards reached the Russian border near Sokal. Incorporated into Army Group South, the division followed the advanced panzer units and, after catching up with them, fought against the Red Army for the first time on Russian soil near Dubno and Ulika. Near Novo-Mariupol they broke through the Stalin Line, and thereafter kept open the supply line to the 3rd Panzer Corps. Near Novo Arkhangel'sk on 31 July 1941 the encirclement of Uman was completed.

Sepp Dietrich's division, fighting in the 1st Panzer Group, now crossed the Ingul near Kiryanovska, engaged in battle in the area around Novo Gdansk, and advanced with a reconnaissance unit to the town of Kherson, 37 miles further south, which they captured. Thanks to Sepp Dietrich's daring leadership the thrust forward to Perekop, the battle at the Tatar valley and the advance into the Crimean peninsula via the Sivash dam were all successful. This was the sort of warfare in which the soldier and fighter Sepp Dietrich excelled. On 8 October a special military communiqué announced the advance of the *Leibstandarte* towards Mariupol. In a battle on the Sea of Asov, Sepp Dietrich proved his competence in leading a fast unit. The Asov steelworks and the shipyards of Mariupol were taken intact by the Germans.

From 10 October 1941, the *Leibstandarte* began its onslaught towards the River Mius, formed the first bridgehead across it and took the port of Taganrog in a surprise attack. The next objective was Rostov. As part of the 3rd Panzer Corps under General von Mackensen and shoulder-to-shoulder with the 13th and 14th Panzer Divisions of the Army, Sepp Dietrich's division advanced on the city of Rostov, and attacked it in a temperature of minus 30 degrees centigrade. On 20 November the *Leibstandarte*, reinforced by the tanks of 13th Panzers, took possession of this important town too. The vital railway bridges across the Don south of Rostov were also taken, thus forestalling their planned demolition. However, Russian counter-attacks across the frozen Don forced the Germans to relinquish Rostov. Sepp Dietrich managed to withdraw his entire command and its heavy weaponry, and post them in defensive positions along the River Mius. From there the division managed to hold on during the winter of 1941-2. On 31 December 1941 Sepp Dietrich became the forty-first

German soldier to be awarded the Oakleaf for the Knight's Cross of the Iron Cross for the successful leadership of his division during the battle on the Sea of Azov.

In the icy Russian winter of 1941–2 Sepp Dietrich acted not only as a commander but also as a father to his young soldiers. He knew every man by name. As a one-time front-line NCO, his relationship with his men was closer than that of any other commander. Nevertheless, he expected the highest performance from his soldiers. He himself augmented his knowledge between battles by taking courses.

At the end of May 1942, relieved from their winter positions, the survivors of the *Leibstandarte* marched towards Stalino. At the beginning of June they were transferred from there across Europe to the Paris area for reorganization. Here in the following months Dietrich's command was expanded into the 1st SS Panzer Division *Leibstandarte* Adolf Hitler. At the end of 1942 the division comprised 20,000 men of all ranks. In January 1943 this enlarged division, now incorporating two panzer regiments, was thrown into the bitter defensive battle between the Donetz and the Dnieper with the assignment to halt the attacking 6th Soviet Army and to cover the retreat of the 298th Infantry Division positioned east of Kupyansk. Although the Russian attack on the Donetz bridgeheads was repulsed, the enemy broke through in the south and outflanked the defence positions of the *Leibstandarte*. *Obergruppenführer* Dietrich therefore withdrew his troops from 9 February onwards in order to form an attacking wing of the SS Panzer Corps. At Alexeyevka he successfully crushed the attack of the 6th Soviet Cavalry Corps. But the general commanding the SS Panzer Corps, *Obergruppenführer* Hausser, caught in a critical situation near Kharkov, ordered the evacuation of the town. Dietrich's units fought on to the south of Kharkov. Thanks to the leadership of Dietrich, the *Leibstandarte* escaped at least seven times from annihilation. A natural front-line soldier, he knew how to extricate his troops even in the worst of battle situations and redeploy them swiftly for a deadly counter-attack.

When in March 1943 Hausser's divisions launched a counter-attack on Kharkov, the *Leibstandarte* was the first one to move forward on the 4th. Two days later, it successfully broke through the very strong defence line between Moskalsova-Gavrikovka, crossed the Misha River and on the 8th took up a position west of Kharkov. By 11 March panzer-grenadiers and panzers of the *Leibstandarte* had broken into the town from the north and northeast and reached the Red Square in the centre. By 15 March the tractor factory, the centre of the last Soviet resistance, was taken. Thrusting northeastwards the Tiger heavy tank company of the division and the half-track battalion under Jochen Peiper took Belgorod on 18 March. For the re-capture of Kharkov, Sepp Dietrich was the twenty-sixth German soldier to be awarded the Swords to the Knight's Cross with Oakleaf.

During the last major German offensive in the east, codenamed *Citadel*, against the Kursk salient, the *Leibstandarte* was in the thick of the fighting and involved in the heaviest tank battle of the Second World War, on the ridge between Prokhorovka and Teterovino. The 5th Soviet Guards Tank Army under General Rotmistrov, trying to take the HKL of the division by surprise, lost 90 of the 150 tanks engaged in this sector in a panzer-to-panzer confrontation whilst the panzer-grenadiers destroyed a further 30 enemy tanks in close combat, thus dealing the 5th Soviet Guards Tank Army a final blow. After Hitler had broken off the battle, Dietrich's division was relieved and sent to northern Italy for regrouping.

On 27 July 1943 *Obergruppenführer* Dietrich was instructed to form the 1st SS Panzer Corps, *Leibstandarte* Adolf Hitler with its associated troops. Sepp Dietrich, tackling this assignment with great enthusiasm, informed Hitler of the completion of this task by the end of the year 1943. On 20 April 1944 he was promoted to SS *Oberstgruppenführer*, equivalent to a Colonel-General in the German Army.

From 8 June 1944, the 1st SS Panzer Corps was engaged in Normandy in the battle to fend off the Allied invasion forces. Together with the 12th SS Panzer Division *Hitlerjugend*, they halted the advance of British troops on Caen and, despite air attacks, managed to hold the town against greatly superior forces. On 12 June Sepp Dietrich had to take over command of the Panzer Group West and a little later also command of the 5th Panzer Army (as Panzer Group West had then been renamed) after members of its officer corps had been wounded or killed in an air raid that day. On 6 August Sepp Dietrich became the sixteenth German soldier to receive the Diamonds to the Knight's Cross with Oakleaf and Swords from the hands of Hitler in person.

Although Sepp Dietrich quietly began to dissociate himself from his Führer because, in his opinion, many things were not handled properly, so influencing the fate of his troops adversely, he was none the less outraged when he heard about the assassination attempt on Hitler on 20 July 1944. He was absolutely disgusted by the 'cowardly act of the plotters' and on 22 July he explained to Admiral Ruge that it was those responsible for this act of sabotage who 'had got the German war machine into a mess'. On 17 July Sepp Dietrich received General Field-Marshal Rommel at his command post and had a long and serious talk with him. At the end of their meeting Rommel asked Dietrich whether he would carry out orders given him by Rommel even if they were in contradiction to those of the Führer? Sepp Dietrich is alleged to have replied: 'You, Field-Marshal, are my Commander-in-Chief and I shall obey only you, whatever the order!'[2]

On his return to his own command post Rommel told his adjutant Lang that 'Dietrich is now on our side'.[3] Later that day Rommel's car came under heavy fire from a low-flying enemy aircraft, and Rommel was hurled out, gravely injured. Whatever Rommel's intentions may have been, now the enemy had put him out of action they became of no significance for the further development of the war.

Dietrich's greatest disappointment came during the battles in Normandy when his requests for reinforcements were totally ignored by the Führer's Headquarters. He commented on this after the war, when in prison in Schwäbisch-Hall:

> After 64 days of fierce fighting the invasion front collapsed. It had not been possible for the army on its own to stem the invasion. Requests for help were ignored by the Führer's Headquarters. When they finally responded it was already too late. The success of our Western opponents, reinforced by fresh troops, could not be reversed.[4]

After Sepp Dietrich had handed over command of the 5th Panzer Army to Hasso von Manteuffel, Hitler appointed him General Officer commanding the 6th Panzer Army, with the instruction to assemble this army as swiftly as possible and turn it into a powerful battle force. The panzer army for which Dietrich became responsible to the Commander-in-Chief West from 10 November 1944 consisted of the 1st and 2nd SS Panzer Corps (with four SS divisions) and the 67th Army Corps. As well as the four SS panzer divisions the Army comprised in addition four Volks-Grenadier divisions and the 3rd Parachute Division. Moreover it was reinforced by strong artillery corps and mortar brigades. Dietrich himself had not requested the leadership of this panzer army. But Hitler, as Supreme Commander of the *Wehrmacht*, was particularly fond of Dietrich who had worked his way up from ordinary soldier to general and who had, by a series of acts of bravery, proved that he was able to command and to fight. Hitler from the first saw in Sepp Dietrich a kindred spirit, a comrade-in-arms, whose loyalty to him was unshakeable. He therefore overlooked Dietrich's self-evident weaknesses and some of his shortcomings as a soldier. In an order of the day to his troops (which later gained special significance) before the launching of the Ardennes offensive in December 1944 (Operation *Herbstebel* – 'Autumn Smoke'), Dietrich said: 'The Führer has placed us in a decisive position. We will break through the enemy front and advance across the Meuse. I expect every one of my soldiers to do his duty, sparing no effort. Our first target is the Meuse!'[5]

With a total force of 120,000 men, a third of whom were soldiers of the Waffen SS, the offensive began early in the morning of 16 December 1944.

In the Battle of the Ardennes the 6th Panzer Army was to suffer a total loss of 23,451 men. Since Dietrich had been allocated the main task, he had also been provided with the strongest reserve units. No fewer than five divisions at full fighting strength stood ready to take advantage of the initial breakthrough by advancing towards the Meuse from either side of Liège, cross the Albert canal and finally capture Antwerp. When Hasso von Manteuffel, commanding the 5th Panzer Army, on Dietrich's left, sent out his first request for support, the command of the 6th Panzer Army ignored it, since it contradicted Hitler's original orders. Sepp Dietrich could have earned himself eternal fame had he set the reserve divisions in motion on 17 December 1944 in support of the 5th Panzer Army (which was making good progress), instead of waiting for Hitler's permission. But Dietrich was still under the illusion that he himself would achieve the breakthrough according to the plan and then, after carrying out the final thrust with the reserves, emerge as the victorious commander of the Ardennes offensive. In fact, his leading unit, Battle Group Peiper, advanced as far as Stoumont, but was cut off there, forced to destroy their last tanks at La Gleize due to fuel shortage and then start to retreat on foot.

At the end of January 1945, after the German withdrawal, the 6th Panzer Army was officially renamed 6th ss Panzer Army. Hitler despatched it to Hungary with the impossible task of smashing the Russian bridgeheads over the River Gran. Dietrich's attacks in February and March foundered in mud and blizzard. Redeployed to the front southeast of Vienna, the 6th ss Panzer Army fended off a Russian attack west of Stuhlweissenburg between Papa and Plattensee, postponing the Russian advance to the eastern edge of the Alps and Vienna. But its strength was no longer sufficient, and Dietrich had to fall back into Vienna. It was Dietrich's last battle.

His reward was to have his corps accused by his Führer of want of fighting spirit. On 22 April 1945, Hitler ordered the entire 6th ss Panzer Army to remove its distinctive sleeve-bands and at the same time announced a 'freeze' on promotion 'because it had not fulfilled its Hungarian mission, had abandoned its position for the protection of the Reich southeast of Vienna and also exposed the capital of the Ostmark.'[6] Dietrich did not pass on Hitler's instructions to his divisions. Colonel-General Guderian, who was to bring the Führer's order to the 6th ss Panzer Army personally, refused to do so. He saw in Sepp Dietrich a friend who had stood by him in a critical moment in December 1941, when Hitler had relieved him of his command. At that time it was Sepp Dietrich who not only openly stood by the disgraced Colonel-General by paying him a personal visit but also resolutely defended to Hitler Guderian's stand about the futility of trying to advance further. According to Guderian, Dietrich 'never disguised from Hitler his view that my dismissal was a mistake.'[7] This influenced Hitler in later re-installing Guderian.

On 8 May 1945, the units of the 6th ss Panzer Army laid down their arms in the Krems area, when Sepp Dietrich surrendered his army in total to the us General George S. Patton. He was taken initially as a prisoner of war to Kufstein. After stays in the prison camps for generals at Augsburg and the camps at Wiesbaden, Oberursel, Nuremberg and Dachau, he was finally taken to the prison at Schwäbisch Hall. As the superior officer of Jochen Peiper, accused of massacres of us soldiers near Malmédy, during the Ardennes offensive, Dietrich was accused likewise and on July 1946 the US General Military Government Court at Dachau sentenced him to life imprisonment on a charge of 'offence against customs and ethics of war'. Dietrich's sentence by the victorious Allies was unfounded. The charge that Dietrich in an order of the day to the 6th Panzer Army had incited his men to acts of terror during the Ardennes offensive lacked any factual foundation. Still in existence, this order contains not a single word that could have been interpreted in this manner. Senior commanders like Field-Marshal von Rundstedt, Colonel-General Guderian, Generals Speidel and Westphal, as well as numerous officers and soldiers of the army, pleaded for *Oberstgruppenführer* Dietrich in vain.

On 10 August 1951 the sentence against Sepp Dietrich was commuted to 25 years' imprisonment, and on 22 October 1955 he was released from US imprisonment in Landsberg on the Lech on 'parole'. With this release on 'parole' Dietrich and all other soldiers freed under similar conditions were silenced for all time, for no sooner did they try to clear their names than they were once more taken into custody.

On 14 May 1957 a German court – the court of assizes at the Landgericht Munich (Regional Court) – sentenced Sepp Dietrich to 18 months' imprisonment on a charge of 'being an accomplice to manslaughter' (i.e. the massacre of the SA leaders in 1934) although Dietrich had not been directly involved in this horrifying event.

Sepp Dietrich had to serve this sentence at the penal institution in Landsberg on the Lech. When in February 1958 Sepp Dietrich was released from Landsberg custody, all his old friends, headed by his fellow SS General Paul Hausser, welcomed him back. Not only soldiers of the former Waffen SS units he had commanded, but also Army officers converged on Landsberg to greet this honest soldier in his newly gained freedom.

Sepp Dietrich died on 21 April 1966, aged seventy-four, in Ludwigsburg from a heart attack. Seven thousand wartime comrades of the former Waffen SS and the former German forces, as well as soldiers and officers of the former enemy, accompanied 'Sepp' to his last resting-place and sang the German anthem at his grave.

Sepp Dietrich exemplified the self-taught non-commissioned officer, rough-hewn in personality and manners, in contrast to the aristocrats who dominated the German Army, but a great natural fighter and front-line leader of men. These characteristics, coupled with his early close association with Hitler, made him very much a 'National-Socialist' soldier. Yet he was far from sharing the extreme views usually associated with the name 'SS'. His loyalty to his soldiers came first; and he protected them against snooping by Himmler – the 'Reichsheini', as he called him. He also personally protested twice to Hitler about the shooting of Jews about which he had received information.

Dietrich's lack of a traditional staff training and his consequent want of strategic grasp were displayed during the Ardennes offensive in December 1944, when he continued to try to fight his way forward against stiff opposition instead of switching the main German effort behind Manteuffel's successful advance.

Otto Skorzeny, a soldier not lacking in boldness, paid tribute to Dietrich's prowess as a leader of men in battle: 'He gave to the Waffen SS a style and an *esprit de corps* which may possibly be compared only with Napoleon's Imperial Guard.'[8]

Whereas Sepp Dietrich joined the tank arm from its beginnings and was actively engaged in tank battles in the First World War, and whereas he owed his phenomenal rise from sergeant in the Bavarian Army to an SS *Oberstgruppenführer* and Colonel-General of the Waffen SS to his Nazi Party membership, Hasso von Manteuffel, in contrast, progressed via the élite Cadet Corps and the cavalry to the panzer troops.

At a cursory glance we can see already that the careers of these two commanders of panzer armies ran along totally different paths, although leading, ultimately, to the same position. We will see later that their qualities of leadership was different too.

Hasso von Manteuffel was born on 14 January 1897 in Potsdam near Berlin, son of Captain Eccard von Manteuffel. In Berlin where for centuries German history had been made, the young Manteuffel encountered those ideals on which he tried to model himself. The highlights of his Potsdam childhood were the parades on the Kaiser's birthday, when the soldiers of the local garrison, accompanied by a clanging band, marched through the city.

The Manteuffels were an old military family which had already supplied German history with numerous generals. Their aristocratic origins were recorded in Pomerania as early as 1287. Hasso's model was Edwin Baron von Manteuffel, erstwhile Prussian Field-Marshal and ADC to Kaiser Friedrich Wilhelm IV and Kaiser Wilhelm I.

After finishing primary school in 1908 he entered the preparatory Cadet Corps at Naumburg. In 1911 he transferred to the Cadet Academy in Berlin-Lichterfelde. In the 7th Company von Manteuffel, only 4 feet 8 inches tall, was placed on the left wing. At the Cadet Academy, teaching comprised the same syllabus as that of the gymnasium as well as pre-military training. In addition flexibility, subordination, good behaviour, comradeship and obedience had to be learned.

At the beginning of the First World War von Manteuffel was not selected for front-line service. In 1916 he passed his Abitur examination at the Cadet Academy and successfully joined the 3rd Brandenburg Hussar Regiment von Ziethen where, a fortnight later, he was promoted to Second Lieutenant. Shortly afterwards he was despatched to France for active service in the 6th

(Prussian) Infantry Division, which deployed the 5th Squadron of the 3rd Hussars on mounted messenger and reconnaissance patrol duties. In the offensive against Verdun von Manteuffel was in action in the front line with the task of observing the frequently changing combat situations and reporting them to the divisional staff.

On 10 October 1916, having been transferred to the Battle of the Somme, he received a shrapnel injury in his right thigh and was taken to the military hospital in Münster in Westphalia. He discharged himself and without identity papers absconded to the front, an act which earned him three days' detention. At the beginning of the armistice in November 1918 the 6th Infantry Division received the order to protect the Rhine bridges near Cologne in order to safeguard the retreat of the field army, a task Manteuffel carried out. When the young second lieutenant returned to his squadron at Rathenow he found revolutionary red flags and banners flying. The 'Soldiers Council' was in session in the regiment's mess. But there was no question of removing epaulettes. The Ziethen Hussars were part of Rathenow.

After demobilization, Hasso von Manteuffel wanted to pursue a career in industry. He had his employment contract already in his pocket when his uncle, the Commercial Privy Councillor in Berlin, succeeded in changing his nephew's mind. 'You must remain a soldier, for you were born one!' was his uncle's response to Hasso's 'strange idea'. So Hasso did not end up in industry but in the *Freikorps* 'von Oven', stationed in Berlin. This is the first similarity with the career of the panzer leader Sepp Dietrich, who had fought with the *Freikorps* 'Oberland' in Silesia. The committee which shortly afterwards selected the officers for transfer to the provisional *Reichswehr* also recommended Second Lieutenant von Manteuffel. With this obstacle removed, von Manteuffel was to progress along a continuous path to become a general, however not before hard study and numerous command appointments related to the development of the panzer units were completed. Sepp Dietrich, in contrast, passed all the stages of such a long-drawn-out maturing process in a flash, becoming *Obergruppenführer* at an early age.

Initially the young Manteuffel served in the combined Cavalry Regiment 25A at Rathenow. Subsequent to the formation of the 100,000-man Versailles Treaty Army he became squadron-leader in the 3rd Horse Regiment, as part of Cavalry Regiment 25A was re-titled. After that he remained an adjutant for seven years. On 1 February 1930 Lieutenant von Manteuffel became chief of the technical squadron of his regiment. These newly formed squadrons were the disguised forerunners of the first tank units. Manteuffel assisted his commander, Colonel Brandt, later Inspector of Cavalry, to set up these squadrons. A little while before that Manteuffel, a keen rider, had acquired a small stable and had won many tournaments. On 2 January 1931 he was awarded the Golden Equestrian Medal, highest accolade for equestrian events.

On 1 October 1932, von Manteuffel was appointed a squadron leader in the 17th Horse Regiment at Bamberg.

While serving in the 17th Horse Regiment he saw the National-Socialists come to power. On 1 February 1933 Manteuffel was riding with his squadron through Bamberg back to the barracks after exercise. When his squadron passed the town hall many residents were gathered staring at the newly hoisted swastika flag of the Third Reich. On passing it he raised his arm in salute. Next morning the papers reported that the *Reichswehr* too had acknowledged the new flag.

Whereas Sepp Dietrich as SS leader had 'longed for' the day when the Nazis seized power with a 'burning desire' (as he once had emphasized), Manteuffel had become a subject of this new régime automatically; however, Hitler's assumption of authority alarmed neither him nor his colleagues. Manteuffel once remarked to the present author:

> The change of leadership in Germany did not impress us adversely, rather favourably. As far as we could judge, we believed that life in Germany would improve. The defamation of the *Reichswehr* and of the police, the contempt for and the abuse of the officer rank ceased immediately. Unemployment disappeared. My friend Stauffenberg agreed with me. Overnight order returned to the streets where, during the previous months, gunshots had echoed. The serious loss of authority of the government and other state bodies was recovered. The state and its new government regained reputation at home and abroad.[9]

And if Paul von Hindenburg, the 'protector of national stability' accepted Hitler, then the soldiers of the *Reichswehr* could accept him too.

The new régime – not least on the advice of the army leaders – won Hindenburg's support and could also hope for the support of the Army and the entire *Reichswehr*. Hitler's favourable attitude towards the armed forces, the proclaiming of German national sovereignty in matters of defence, seemed to fulfil all the *Reichswehr* and later the *Wehrmacht* hoped for. In his funeral address for Field-Marshal von Hindenburg who died on 2 August 1934 Hitler declared that the *Wehrmacht* was to be the sole weapon-bearer of the nation. With this statement a fundamental change in Germany's defence policies seemed to have been initiated. As Hasso von Manteuffel explained:

> So it came about that the majority of officers of our regiment, including me, did not reject National-Socialism. However, there was no cause for us to be politically active since the Army and also the *Wehrmacht* possessed neither a passive nor an active vote. We had the deep belief that the Army had to be a politically reliable tool for any government of the Reich. This belief has been imprinted in us by Colonel-General von Seeckt, the Commander-in-Chief for many years: the Army must serve *any* government that is in power, because *the government is the pillar that supports the state*.[10]

It cannot be denied that all the great powers of the world acknowledged Hitler; perhaps even feared, but none the less respected, him. Why should the *Wehrmacht*, which he had newly created, not also respect him?

By December 1933 von Manteuffel had been squadron leader for three years. One evening in the mess General von Schwedler took him aside and told him that a new panzer force was being formed and that officers were needed to introduce some of the spirit of the cavalry into the panzer troops. The duties would be similar to those of the cavalry. Schwedler said: 'You will be provided merely with a new mount; instead of a horse you will have an iron vehicle.'[11] Hasso von Manteuffel accepted and on 1 October 1934 he became a squadron leader in 2nd Motor-Cycle Rifle Battalion in Eisenach. Here von Manteuffel again met Colonel Guderian who had become Commander of the 2nd Panzer Division, stationed in Würzburg. Guderian was *the* architect of the new German panzer troops and this novel army strongly reflected his extraordinary personality. Initially von Manteuffel served as a staff-major. One day 'Fast Heinz' – as Guderian was nicknamed – told him: 'Manteuffel, you will have to take over the training of all cadets and cadet officers of the division.'[12] This provided von Manteuffel with a position which stretched him fully. No fewer than 5,000 aspiring officers went through his teaching in the Panzer Training School at Wünsdorff, near Berlin. At the end of February 1937 Colonel Radlmaier, the commander of the training school, called von Manteuffel into his office and informed him that he was to join the Inspectorate of Panzer Troops asked for by Major-General Guderian, Chief of the Inspectorate, himself. On 1 March 1937 von Manteuffel started in this new post. It became his responsibility to deal with the motorization of four infantry divisions. It was mainly the cavalry officers who wrote the regulations for the 'fast troops', and it was to Guderian's advantage to avail himself of these men, since the methods of operational leadership of the new panzer arm corresponded in detail with those of the cavalry. Foreign senior officers, still convinced that the tank could only be an auxiliary to the infantry and not operate independently, were amazed when they came to Berlin to watch military manoeuvres which employed the totally different German conception of deploying panzer units. On 1 February 1939 Hasso von Manteuffel joined the Panzer-Troops Training School II in Berlin-Krampnitz as head of the directing staff. His direct superior was Colonel Friessner, later Colonel-General and Army-Group commander.

The Polish campaign of 1939 and the second *Blitzkrieg* campaign against France in 1940 convinced even the sceptics that the panzers had proved their worth. Guderian's motto 'Not penny-packets but mass' had proved right. At the end of the offensive against France in 1940 Lieutenant Hasso von Manteuffel had an assignment as commander of the 2nd Battalion 7th Rifle Regiment of the 7th Panzer Division which, under Major-General Rommel, had earned itself the nickname 'Ghost Division'. At the start of Operation

Barbarossa, the 7th Panzer Division began to roll within the 39th Panzer Corps under General Schmidt. The Corps in turn belonged to Panzer Group 3 under Colonel-General Hoth, itself part of Army Group Centre under the command of Field-Marshal von Bock. In the attack across the Beresina River, von Manteuffel found a bridge still intact south of Lepel. At night he started out on his own initiative, crossed the river and secured the crossing for the division. During the advance via Vitebsk to Yartsevo, northeast of Smolensk, his battalion was always in the front line. Colonel von Lungershausen, Manteuffel's regimental commander, described this as follows: 'Once again Manteuffel thrust forward and cleared the way.'[13] The battle for the Stalin Line in July took Manteuffel's soldiers as far as the road to Vitebsk and on 15 July Battle Group Boineburg, to which Manteuffel's battalion belonged, reached the Minsk-Smolensk-Vyazma highway. After the death on the battlefield of Colonel von Unger, Lieutenant von Manteuffel took over the command of the 6th Rifle Regiment of the division. Using this regiment as a spearhead force Manteuffel, on 2 October 1941, advanced via the Kokosch sector towards the River Dnieper. The Battle Group crossed the river and formed a 50-yard-deep bridgehead on the opposite bank, ready for the division to occupy. Vyazma was the next target, where a large pocket was closed. The onslaught on Moscow was now halted, in order to concentrate offensive strength in the south from Kiev to the Crimea, to interrupt the Russian oil supply from the Caucasus, and to secure the coal region of the Donetz basin for Germany.

In the first week of October, three weeks after the great battle of entrapment round Kiev had been concluded, the double envelopment of Vyazma and Briansk was completed and the divisions of Army Group Centre now received their orders for the 'final assault' on Moscow. Towards the end of October the units, including the 7th Panzer Division, reached their start-lines for the attack against the Soviet metropolis. But on 25 October the rainy season began and the German formations had to flounder through knee-deep mud. The 7th Panzer Division began its attack towards Moscow and the Moscow-Volga canal on 16 November 1941. On the 23rd, Manteuffel's rifle regiment took Klin. By 27 November the area $2\frac{1}{2}$ miles northwest of the bridge at Jakhroma over the Moscow-Volga canal was occupied. Early on 28 November Manteuffel's battle group began its attack on the bridge, with the further aim of crossing the canal. They achieved both objectives. One of Manteuffel's sergeants later recalled: 'I was participating in the assault across the Moscow-Volga canal near Jakhroma and witnessed our little one (as the Colonel was then nicknamed) switch off the Muscovites' power in the power station of Jakhroma. He was the first in the attack and the last to retreat.'[14]

Moscow lay within a hand's grasp of the 7th Panzer Division, less than 22 miles distant. Manteuffel requested reinforcements for the final thrust towards Moscow. His divisional commander, General Baron von Funck, asked Corps HQ to send up motorized troops and tanks, but the general commanding the

56th Panzer Corps, General Schaal, had not a single man to spare. The Corps had reached its present position literally at its last gasp. General Schaal therefore had to order Manteuffel to withdraw from the bridgehead.

As a result of the Red Army's winter offensive on 5 December 1941 (it having been reinforced by fresh Siberian divisions), the 7th Panzer Division was now forced to retreat, halting when Hitler issued his strict 'hold-fast' order to the German armies on the Eastern Front. On 31 December 1941 Colonel Hasso von Manteuffel was awarded the Knight's Cross of the Iron Cross for his assault on the bridge of Jakhroma.

On 6 May 1942 the division was transferred to France for reorganization. On 15 July Colonel von Manteuffel took over 7th Rifle Brigade and was posted to take command in a division in North Africa. When from 8 November onwards, after Anglo-American troops under General Eisenhower landed near Casablanca, Oran and Algiers, it became necessary for the German High Command to assemble a joint force there as swiftly as possible. General Walther Nehring had received orders from Field-Marshal Kesselring, Commander-in-Chief South, to concentrate the 90th Army Corps and to defend the Tunisian area. Colonel von Manteuffel's first task in North Africa was to go to Bizerta together with General Gause and submit to Admiral Dérien, the local French Commander, the German request for his capitulation! All French garrisons and positions as far as Gabes were disarmed in a similar fashion. Following this, Manteuffel, at the request of Colonel-General von Arnim, the new Commander-in-Chief in North Africa, created the 'Manteuffel' Division from a mixture of units, including a *Bersaglieri* brigade. Manteuffel managed to turn this mixed bag into a battle-worthy division which was able to defeat much superior enemy forces in actions at Cap Serrat, at Djebel Abiod and in St Temara. Towards the end of the fighting in Africa the 'Manteuffel' Division was pushed out of Jefna and Mateur, although it managed to hold on to the fortress of Bizerta for several days. On 30 April 1943 Hasso von Manteuffel collapsed on the battlefield. Both his doctor and Colonel-General von Arnim urged that he be transferred to a military hospital back home. General von Arnim told the present writer after the war: 'Hasso von Manteuffel was one of the best combat leaders and divisional commanders I had in Tunisia. He sacrificed himself to the extent that he collapsed on the battlefield. It was only on my strict order that he left the African theatre of war on the next hospital ship. In that way he was saved for the German Armed Forces.'[15] He went back via Rome to Berlin, where his family lived.

After a long period in hospital following his collapse in Africa, von Manteuffel was transferred to the Führer-reserve. However, a few days later he received instructions to report to the Führer's headquarters, as the Führer wished to speak to him personally. Back in February 1943 Hasso von Manteuffel had already been summoned back from Africa to the Führer's headquarters. At the Wolfschanze ('Wolf's Lair') in Rastenburg he stood, a small, wiry equestrian figure, face-to-face with Hitler, delivering a two-hour report about the Tunisian situation without being interrupted by Hitler. Now, much to Manteuffel's amazement, Hitler asked him what was the purpose of his coming to Rastenburg? Von Manteuffel replied that the Führer himself had summoned him there and that he, Manteuffel, now 100 per cent fit, was hoping to be re-employed. When Hitler asked him what he had in mind, Manteuffel replied with the utmost honesty: 'I want the 7th Panzer Division. General von Funck has led it for a long time and will probably soon be given command of a corps.' 'So be it,' replied Hitler, 'You will get the 7th Panzer Division.'[16] Thus, on 16 June 1943, Hasso von Manteuffel, now a Major-General, took over 7th Panzer, which was then engaged in heavy defensive fighting in the area of Akhtyrka on the Eastern Front. It was in Akhtyrka that Lieutenant Adalbert Schultz, commander of the 25th Panzer Regiment, on 23 August 1943, won the Swords for the Knight's Cross with Oakleaf.

Three days after taking command of his division von Manteuffel, driving to the front line, was hit by shrapnel from a grenade. With seventeen splinters in his back he was taken to the nearest field first-aid station, returning to his division in plaster. The 7th Panzer managed to fight its way back safely to the other side of the Dnieper by September 1943. During this time the defensive achievements of the division under von Manteuffel were frequently reported in military communiqués.

In the battle for Kiev the 7th Panzer Division was eventually forced by superior numbers to give way, but Manstein's counter-offensive on Zhitomir, which began on 14 November, brought Manteuffel's division total success. Until the 19th, Zhitomir remained firmly in the hands of the division. On 23 November 1943 von Manteuffel became the 332nd German soldier to receive the Oakleaf for the Knight's Cross. Once again he was summoned to the Führer's headquarters, since Hitler wished to present this decoration personally, but Manteuffel could not spare the time. It was not until Christmas, when the situation became less critical, that he made the trip to Rastenburg. After he had made the award, Hitler said: 'You will leave the 7th Panzer Division and take over the command of the *Grossdeutschland* Panzer-Grenadier Division.' Noticing the little general's disappointment, Hitler added: 'You, Manteuffel, will turn this division into the strongest task battle formation of the Army.' Strangely enough, Hitler added: 'Ask Sepp Dietrich how to do it!'[17]

On 12 February 1944 General von Manteuffel ordered his new division into its first major attack, but the Russians beat them back at Blagodatnoye. At the beginning of March the Red Army launched its great offensive aimed at breaking through to the Romanian oilfields. After the fall of Oymino on 9 March 1944, the *Grossdeutschland* found itself encircled. By means of flexible manoeuvring von Manteuffel managed to free his division from this menacing trap without losing a single weapon. In a military communiqué on 14 March

1944 the achievement of the division and Lieutenant-General von Manteuffel were highly praised. The *Grossdeutschland* returned to the Cornesti region eastwards of Jasy and, in the course of April 1944, held off attacks by hugely superior Russian forces, and also launched successful counter-strokes of its own.

On 22 February 1944 Hasso von Manteuffel, who had already been the fiftieth soldier to be awarded the Oakleaf for earlier battles, had been awarded the Swords to the Knight's Cross. Subsequently he was asked again and again when he would be able to go to headquarters to receive this decoration. However, the time was still not opportune, because on 2 May 1944, twenty Russian divisions launched a fresh major offensive in an attempt to break through to the oilfields of Ploesti. On the first day of this battle the tanks and assault-guns of Manteuffel's division, together with the Army FLAK Detachment with the *Grossdeutschland*, destroyed about 250 enemy tanks and brought the Russian avalanche to a halt. On 8 May 1944 a military communiqué announced this success too.

Meanwhile strong enemy forces in the northern sector of the Eastern Front were preparing for a thrust into East Prussia, and consequently the *Grossdeutschland* was transferred from Romania to East Prussia. They took up positions in the stud town of Trakehnen. Manteuffel, having been summoned to the Führer's headquarters, had confirmation from the Führer personally that the division should only be deployed as a unity. Unfortunately, on 9 August 1944, an order from the Führer arrived telling Manteuffel to carry out an attack on Wilkowischken where the Russians were launching a major offensive. Although the panzer battle-groups were not yet fully concentrated and before proper reconnaissance could be carried out, the division had to deploy for attack. It succeeded in taking Wilkowischken but lost 82 tanks in this battle. Hitler, furious, again summoned the divisional commander. When Manteuffel stood face-to-face with Hitler, the latter scolded him for suffering such losses. After Hitler had calmed down, Manteuffel managed to say a word: 'My Führer, I have your order here.' 'Then read it,' Hitler requested. Hasso von Manteuffel read out the order – which instructed his division to go into attack before being fully assembled and before having had the chance to carry out reconnaissance. Hitler was puzzled and remained silent. Then he rang for his adjutant and asked him to call Field-Marshal Keitel. When Keitel appeared, Manteuffel had to read the order a second time, after which a second storm from the Führer unleashed itself upon Keitel. It transpired that Hitler had never issued this order. During a briefing Hitler had merely mentioned that the *Grossdeutschland* could be deployed against Wilkowischken, but made no reference that Manteuffel's division should attack before it was fully assembled and had reconnoitred the ground. Without proper authorization Keitel had in haste fabricated an order out of this remark.[18]

On 1 September 1944 von Manteuffel received another order to appear at the Führer's headquarters. On his arrival, Manteuffel was straight away taken to the Führer. Hitler told him: 'My general, you will take over command of the 5th Panzer Army and be promoted to General of the Panzer Troops.' In Manteuffel's words: 'So I was entrusted with the army that had been led first by General Geyr von Schweppenburg and later by Sepp Dietrich during the Normandy campaign.' Hasso von Manteuffel was now one of the youngest of the panzer generals and also one of the youngest army commanders. Von Manteuffel told the present author later: 'I entered the Führer's headquarters as a divisional commander; I was leaving it as an army commander.'[19]

With his new army, part of Army Group G on the Western Front, he was to conduct a counter-stroke against the southern flank of the 3rd US Army under General George Patton, which was advancing towards Metz.

On 17 September 1944 General Patton began the assault on Metz which Manteuffel's 5th Panzer Army managed to stem. Lunéville, already taken by the 3rd US Army, was recaptured. At the same time, however, the first German town, Aachen, of symbolic importance as Charlemagne's 'Imperial City', was attacked by the Americans, and Lunéville had to be given up again while the 5th Panzer Army was forced to abandon its own counter-offensive. It was then transferred to strengthen Army Group B, west of the River Roer, in the battle for Aachen.

On 3 November 1944 General von Manteuffel was summoned to the headquarters of Army Group B. Field-Marshal von Rundstedt, the Commander in Chief West, Field-Marshal Model (Army Group B), and Generals Krebs and von Manteuffel had been assembled in order to meet Colonel-General Jodl who was expected to bring an important order from the Führer. Jodl appeared that morning to announce that Hitler had decided to launch a new crucial offensive to take Antwerp and cut the Allied armies in two. This plan, later known as the Battle of the Ardennes, was to be the last major offensive of the German *Wehrmacht*. Jodl explained that, if successful, 25 to 30 enemy divisions would be wiped out. The offensive was to start in the middle of November and the plan had been worked out in complete detail. What surprised everybody was the fact that Sepp Dietrich, who was to command the 6th Panzer Army, the second of the two panzer armies to be deployed in the Ardennes and the one charged with making the main thrust, had not been called to the meeting. Field-Marshal Model made the impromptu suggestion – a 'small' plan, that of pinching off the Allied salient round Aachen, which he thought offered the optimum chance of success. This plan was sent to the Führer's headquarters next morning after it had been vetted once again by all. Hasso von Manteuffel had been actively involved in working out this new plan, which gave the earliest date for an attack as 10 December. But Hitler overruled this 'small' plan. The preparations for the *Wacht am Rhein* (code name for the offensive, later changed to *Herbstnebel* – 'Autumn Smoke') were in progress. The divisions of the 5th Panzer Army were already in a state of readiness in the Trier-Krefeld area. Rumours were being spread that this mobilization was taking place in order to repel an American attack on Cologne.

On 2 December 1944 the Commanders of the planned offensive met in Berlin. This time *Oberstgruppenführer* Dietrich was also present. Once more Manteuffel and Model pleaded for their 'small' plan, pointing out the weaknesses in the Antwerp project, but Hitler remained adamantly in favour. He was absolutely determined to go ahead with it. Later Hasso von Manteuffel told the present writer: 'It was incomprehensible to me that not one of the eighty senior officers present dared speak out in order to clarify obvious discrepancies or ask questions, not to mention supporting us in this matter of life and death.'[20] However, Sepp Dietrich, for his part, voiced his doubts about certain matters which in fact presented grave obstacles later in the Battle of the Ardennes. Von Manteuffel was once more summoned to Hitler. But despite a long discussion, the basic concept of the offensive remained unchanged.

Operation *Herbstnebel* began on 16 December 1944. The troops of the 5th Panzer Army were on full alert from 0530 onwards. On their right flank the Waffen SS units of the 6th SS Panzer Army under Sepp Dietrich were in position. It was to the latter that the task had been allocated of achieving a swift breakthrough and dealing the decisive blow. Although Battle-Group Peiper achieved a spectacular initial breakthrough of the American front, the remainder of the 6th Panzer Army came to a halt on 17 December, and dissipated itself in small local actions. Immediately after going into action hopeless confusion resulted along the 15-mile-wide front of this army and, in Manteuffel's words, 'Sepp Dietrich, totally disregarding his assignment – i.e. to thrust forward and aim for one mighty breakthrough, irrespective of what was happening to the right or the left of the penetrating units – allowed himself to get bogged down in heavy fighting in the Elsenborn-Krinkelt area.'[21] For this reason Dietrich failed in his task, so rendering the pursuit formations, waiting behind the front of his panzer army to pour through the breach, totally useless.

By the evening of 17 December 1944 the goal of the 6th Panzer Army – to occupy the crossings over the Meuse and to penetrate to Antwerp via Liège – was already unachievable. Although Manteuffel's 5th Panzer Army had been delayed in fulfilling its operational plan, at least it was still on the move. Its 2nd Panzer Division as well as its *Panzer Lehr* Division were gaining further ground which, given proper support, could be utilized for the breakthrough. At this moment when von Manteuffel was requesting help, Sepp Dietrich should have kept in mind the overall pattern of success of the army in the Ardennes and, ignoring Hitler's order that he (Dietrich) was to make the breakthrough, he should have supported von Manteuffel by re-deploying the motorized reserves from behind his own 6th Panzer Army front to the 5th Panzer Army sector. Instead, this old soldier referred to the Führer's order, i.e. that he (Hitler) alone could decide how and when to employ the reserves.

The *Panzer Lehr* Division reached St Margaret and advanced up to $1\frac{1}{2}$ miles beyond Bastogne, where they were stopped by US reinforcements. Hasso von Manteuffel went to Bastogne and ordered Lieutenant-General Bayerlein, commander of the *Panzer Lehr*, to leave one regiment positioned there to surround the American garrison, and move on with the remainder of the division south of Bastogne to capture St Hubert. By this decision von Manteuffel avoided abandoning the entire plan on which the Ardennes offensive was based. Meanwhile the 116th Panzer Division of his army was still engaged in an attack on Houffalize. It was here that Manteuffel had wanted to deploy two of the panzer divisions lying in reserve in the rear of the 6th Panzer Army. But the two SS divisions and the three German Army panzer divisions behind the front of the 6th Panzer Army remained where they were. By the time Hitler had given the instructions for their transfer, it was too late.

On 21 December, against all promises, the fuel supply ran out. The 2nd Panzer Division came to a halt at Tenneville, Battle Group Peiper at La Gleize, where (as has been narrated) they had to destroy their panzers and retreat on foot. The *Panzer Lehr* Division which had reached Morhet and was advancing towards Rochefort also experienced similar difficulties. The garrison of Bastogne was relieved by the enemy on 26 December 1944. Now even the 'little plan' was no longer feasible. The only remaining option was to retreat, and on 3 January 1945 the counter-offensive by the Americans and the English finally closed down the battle.

The decisive error of the Ardennes offensive lay in the failure to transfer the centre of gravity from the stuck-fast 6th Panzer Army to the advancing 5th in time. Sepp Dietrich took no action to initiate this transfer which, as regards his reputation as commander, was a disaster. Field-Marshal von Rundstedt makes the following comment:

> It was a fundamental mistake to deploy the panzer reserves behind the front of the 6th Panzer Army and to keep them there only for the purpose of giving Colonel-General Dietrich the chance of a magnificent victory. It unbalanced the entire offensive and jeopardized a potential victory.

On 10 January 1945 Hitler announced that the 6th Panzer Army would be withdrawn from the front and sent to Hungary. The departure of this army, still fighting-fit, made a bad impression on the soldiers left on the Western Front, particularly those of the 5th Panzer Army. These divisions felt betrayed by their SS comrades.

The tying-up of the German reserves in the Ardennes offensive proved a godsend for the Red Army, which opened its great winter offensive on the Eastern Front on 12 January 1945, eventually enabling it to reach its desired destination, Berlin, first. On 28 February 1945 Hasso von Manteuffel was summoned to the Führer's headquarters yet again. He was awarded the Diamonds to the Knight's Cross of the Iron Cross with Oakleaves and Swords, but declined the endowment of 200,000 marks which Hitler instructed his adjutant to hand over to him.

On 2 March 1945 Hasso von Manteuffel took over command of the 3rd Panzer Army on the Eastern Front, where he held the position on the Oder until 26 April 1945 when he was forced to retreat. By 3 May 1945 he reached the demarcation line of the British occupation zone, so managing to lead his entire army into British captivity, thereby safeguarding his soldiers' survival.

Manteuffel later recorded his own impressions of Hitler as supreme commander:

> In retrospect, one must admit, Hitler had a magnetic, a simply hypnotising personality. I myself had analysed the Führer of the Third Reich during my first encounter and had determined how to deal with him rationally and consequently how to put forward my arguments. I did not feel intimidated by him. However, I knew at once: Hitler baffled people through his extraordinary memory, particularly for figures, as well as through his factual knowledge of technical and military data. His astonishing farsightedness enabled him to become the creator of an army equipped with modern weapons.
>
> He lacked the disciplined approach and the definitive individual judgment which distinguished our General-Staff officers. He lacked the sound assessment of all possibilities and premises; though he understood operational concepts. I might cite as examples here von Manstein's plan for the French campaign and his own conception of the Ardennes offensive in December 1944. Hitler, in his dealings with me, always kept to military protocol and never was abusive.[22]

In drawing up a final balance sheet of his combat experience in the Second World War, Hasso von Manteuffel commented:

> The lesson that neither of the world wars has relieved global tension, coupled with the theoretical possibility of a nuclear war annihilating the whole of mankind, makes it quite clear that a future war will claim such sacrifices that there will never be a victor. As a constructive peace has been denied us after these two world wars, so no advantage will be gained by a third one.[23]

The diminutive von Manteuffel, a bantam of a fighting commander, impressed his contemporaries alike for his professional zeal and energy, and for his qualities as a traditional officer and gentleman. Guderian commented: 'He is a leader excelling in every respect. He combines superb military skills with a pronounced sense of the essential.' General of the Panzer Troops Balck thought him 'the embodiment of everything that was good in German military tradition on every front he served.' And a subordinate told the present writer: 'Hasso von Manteuffel was my commander and fatherly friend. I have never before or since experienced so sovereign a panzer leader as him, who, on account of his humanity and self-evident courage, became a model to all soldiers of the 'Grossdeutschland' Panzer-grenadier Division.'[24]

NOTES

1 Below, Nicolaus von: *Als Hitlers Adjutant 1937–1945* (As Hitler's A.D.C. 1937–1945), p. 30, von Hase & Koehler-Verlag Mainz, 1980.
2. Krätschmer, E. G., *Die Ritterkreuzträger der Waffen-SS* (The Bearers of the Knight's Cross of the Waffen ss), Preussisch Oldendorf, 1982, 3rd edition.
3. *Ibid.*
4. *Ibid.*
5. *Ibid.*, p. 46.
6. Weidinger, Otto: *Kameraden bis zum Ende* (Comrades till the End), Preussisch Oldendorf, 1962, pp. 369–70.
7. *Ibid.*
8. Skorzeny, Otto: *Meine Kommandounternehmen*, Limes-Verlag, Wiesbaden-Munich, 1976.
9. Interview with present author, 1970.
10. *Ibid.*
11. Schaulen, Joachim von: *Hasso von Manteuffel – Panzerkampf im Zweiten Weltkrieg* (Hasso von Manteuffel – Panzer Combat in the Second World War) by Vowinckel-Verlag, Berg/Starnberger See, pp. 30 and 33.
12. *Ibid.*
13. *Die 7. Panzer-Division im Zweiten Weltkrieg – Einsatz und Kampf der Gespenster-Division 1939–1945* (The 7th Panzer Division in the Second World War – Deployment and Combat of the Phantom Division 1939–1945). Prepared by Hasso von Manteuffel, General (retd.) of the Panzer Troop. Editor: Traditionsverband of the former 7th P.D.
14. Interview of Sergeant Walther Lenfers by the author.
15. Interview with the author.
16. Schaulen, p. 121.
17. 'Der Krieg in 40 Fragen' (The War in 40 Questions) Kurowski manuscript: von Manteuffel, for publisher La Table Ronde (not published) and: von Schaulen. Kurowski interview of von Manteuffel in his house in Diessen/Ammersee, 1970 and 1971.
18. *Ibid.*
19. Interview with the author, 1971.
20. *Ibid.*
21. H. Saunders: *Die Wacht am Rhein* (The Watch on the Rhine), p. 259.
22. Interview with the author, 1971.
23. *Ibid.*
24. Interview by the author of General Horst Niemack.

CHRONOLOGY: JOSEF 'SEPP' DIETRICH

1892, May 28	Born in Hawangen, district of Memmingen
until 1907	Primary School in Kempten/Allgäu
1908–10	Apprenticeship in hotel business
1911	Volunteer of 4th Bavarian Field-Artillery Regiment 'König'
1912	Attended NCO School
1914, August 1	Front-line service with 6th Reserve Field Artillery Regiment
1916–17	Corporal in 10th Infantry Artillery Battery
1917, from autumn	1st Battalion 8th Infantry Regiment and 2nd Assault Battalion
1918, from January	13th Assault Tank Detachment
1918, March 21	First tank deployment near St Quentin
1918, July 18	Tank deployment at Villers-Cotterets
1919, from April	Sergeant in 1st Defence Regiment, Munich (*Freikorps*)
1920	Sergeant-Major in 1st Bavarian National Police Force
1921	*Freikorps* 'Oberland', engaged in the liberation of Upper Silesia from Polish invaders (storming of the Annaberg on 21 May 1921)
1923	Joined NSDAP
1927–9	Petrol station manager, forwarding agent for publisher
1928, May	Accepted into *Schutzstaffel* (SS), membership number 1177
1928, August 1	Appointed to SS-*Sturmbannführer*
1929, September 18	Appointed to SS-*Standartenführer* and Commander of SS-Brigade Bavaria
1930, July 11	SS *Oberführer* and appointment to Commander of SS-Group South
1930	Elected NSDAP delegate to the Reichstag
1931, December 18	SS *Gruppenführer*
1933, October	Leader of SS-Upper Sector East: nominated member of Prussian Privy Council and Civic Councillor of Berlin
1933, January 30	Dietrich forms SS *Wachtbataillon Berlin*
1933, September 1	Renamed unit *Leibstandarte* SS Adolf Hitler
1934, July 1	Appointed to SS *Obergruppenführer*
1939, from September 1	With *Leibstandarte* Adolf Hitler in Poland campaign
1940, from May 10	Deployment in western campaign
1940, July 5	Awarded the Knight's Cross for the Iron Cross
1941, from April 6	Active service in the Balkans campaign
1941, April 20	Sepp Dietrich signs the capitulation document of the Greek Epirus Army
1941, from June 30	Participates in Russian campaign. Battle of the Sea of Asov. Capture of Rostov
1941, December 31	Awarded Oakleaf for the Knight's Cross of the Iron Cross
Summer 1942	Reorganization of the *Leibstandarte* and renaming as 1st SS-Panzer Division *Leibstandarte*, Adolf Hitler

1943, end of January	Active service in Russia – Battle of Kharkov
1943, March 11	Recapture of Kharkov by 1st ss Panzer
1943, March 16	Awarded Swords for the Knight's Cross with Oakleaf
1944, from June 12	Command of Panzer Group West and of 5th Panzer Army (to which Panzer Group West was subsequently renamed)
1943, from July 5	Deployment in Operation *Citadel* – panzer Battle of Prokhorovka
1943, July	Relief and recovery in North Italy
1944, June 6	Deployment of 1st ss-Panzer Corps, formed by Sepp Dietrich, in Normandy
1944, August 6	Awarded Diamonds for the Knight's Cross with Oakleaf and Swords
1944, August 6	Promoted to ss *Oberstgruppenführer* and Colonel-General of Waffen ss
1944, November	Commander-in-Chief of 6th Panzer Army
1944, from December 16	Deployment in the Ardennes offensive
1945, from February 18	Deployment of 6th ss-Panzer Army in Hungary
1945, May 8	Surrender of 6th ss-Panzer Army to General Patton and prisoner of war
1946, July 16	Sentenced to life imprisonment
1955, October 22	Release on 'parole'
1957, May 14	Charged by court of assizes in Munich I for 'being an accomplice to manslaughter (in the Röhm coup)' and subsequently sentenced to 18 months' imprisonment
1958, February 2	Released from prison
1966, April 21	Died in Ludwigsburg

CHRONOLOGY: HASSO VON MANTEUFFEL

1897, January 14	Born in Potsdam
1908	Joined the 9th cadet preparatory corps, Cadet School, Naumburg
1911	Cadet Academy Berlin-Lichterfelde
1916, May	Joined 3rd Brandenburg Hussar Regiment 'von Ziethen' as 2nd Lieutenant, served in France
1916, October	Transferred with the 5th Squadron to the 6th (Prussian) Infantry Division
1916, October 14	Wounded in the Battle of the Somme
1918, November	Protected the Rhine bridges to safeguard the retreat of the field army
1919	Served in *Freikorps* 'von Oven' in Berlin
1920	Squadron leader in 3rd Cavalry Regiment in the 100,000-man *Reichswehr*, followed by seven years as adjutant in the cavalry regiment

1930, February 1	Lieutenant and Chief of the technical squadron of his regiment
1931, January 2	Equestrian medal in gold
1932, October 1	Squadron leader of 17th Cavalry Regiment, Bamberg
1934, April 1	Cavalry captain
1934, October 10	Transfer (with two squadrons of 17th Cavalry Regiment) to 2nd Motorcycle Rifle Battalion (under the disguise of Cavalry Regiment Erfurt)
1935, December	Transfer to 2nd Panzer Division as squadron leader of 2nd Motorcycle Rifle Battalion (under divisional commander, Colonel and later Major-General Guderian)
1936–7	Staff Major and training-officer of all cadets and cadet officers of 2nd Panzer Division
1937, February 25	Official adviser to the Inspectorate of Panzer Troops under Guderian at Army Headquarters (OKH)
1939, February 1	Head of directing staff at Panzer Troops School II in Berlin-Krampnitz
1941, July	As Lieutenant-Commander of the 2nd Rifle Regiment of 7th Panzer Division
1941, August 21	Takes over 6th Rifle Regiment
1941, October 1	Promotion to Colonel
1941, October 2	'Final assault' on Moscow. Crossing of the Moscow-Volga canal at Jakhroma
1941, December 31	Knight's Cross of the Iron Cross
1942, July 15	Command of a division in North Africa. Until 30 April 1943, commander of 'Manteuffel' Division
1943, May 1	Promotion to Major-General
1943, August 1	Commander of 7th Panzer Division at Akhtyrka
1943, November 19	Recaptured Zhitomir
1943, November 23	Awarded Oakleaf for the Knight's Cross of the Iron Cross
1943, December 27	Commander of Panzer Grenadier Division *Grossdeutschland*
1944, February 1	Promoted to Lieutenant-General
1944, February 22	Awarded the Swords for the Knight's Cross with Oakleaf
1944, August 9	Deployment of PGD *Grossdeutschland* in northern section of Eastern Front
1944, September 1	Appointed Commander-in-Chief of 5th Panzer Army
1944, September 1	Promoted to General of the Panzer Troop
1944, December 16	Deployment in the Ardennes offensive
1945, February 18	Awarded the Diamonds for the Knight's Cross with Oakleaf and Swords
1945, March 2	Commander-in-Chief of 3rd Panzer Army in the east
1945, May 3	Conducted the withdrawal of the 3rd Panzer Army to British-occupied territory and captivity
1978	Died in Diessen on the Ammersee

PART V

The Innovators

GUDERIAN

19

GUDERIAN

Colonel-General Heinz Guderian

KENNETH MACKSEY

On 28 March 1945 Heinz Wilhelm Guderian, the last Chief of the German General Staff, confronted Adolf Hitler in the final of many angry and forthright disagreements and, for the second time in four years, was dismissed – albeit this time on sick leave – by a Supreme Commander at the end of his tether. It was a fitting climax to a tumultuous career in which Guderian had won an almost unique reputation as a brilliantly imaginative officer who had survived to reach the top of his profession despite repeated outbursts with those superior officers whose bungling tried his patience beyond limits. Yet it was also typical of Guderian that, after fifteen years' involvement with Hitler, he had managed by extraordinary self-control to remain loyal to a Führer who had all too obviously been ruining the beloved Fatherland.

The first meeting between the two had taken place at Kummersdorf in January 1934 when, as Chief of Staff to the Inspectorate of Motorized Troops, Guderian had demonstrated the elements of what grew into panzer divisions. Apart from a few motor-cycle combinations, trucks and tracked vehicles, everything was in embryo. There was not even a proper tank to show, only the chassis of a tracked machine called an Agricultural Tractor. But, according to Guderian, Hitler was enthused: although whether he understood the military significance of panzer divisions then (or at any other time) is another matter.

Guderian was a Prussian – in mentality, on many matters, more Prussian than the Prussians – who was born at Kulm on the Vistula on 17 June 1888, the son of a lieutenant in the élite, fast-marching 9th *Jäger Battalion*. The

Army was a life-long obsession from the moment he joined the Principal Cadet School at Gross-Lichterfelde. He passed out high in 1907 to join the unit commanded by his father, the 10th Hanoverian *Jäger Battalion*, where soldiers were not only taught to think and move swiftly, but also encouraged to innovate. So when Heinz seemed bent on marriage in 1911, a little too soon for his career prospects, the cooling-off process insisted upon by his father took the form of a long course on wireless – a subject so vital to his future.

Henceforth, apart from two short spells at regimental duty, his career was to diverge from the infantry. By the time he married Margarete Görne in 1913 he was a qualified Signals Officer in command of the Wireless Detachment with 5th Cavalry Division, and less than a year later he was the youngest officer attending the course at the Potsdam War Academy, with his future as a member of the Great General Staff seemingly assured. But when the war broke out, the course was closed and he was riding with his radio detachment in 5th Cavalry Division towards defeat on the River Marne. And there, not for the last time, his rage exploded at a general (the commander of the division) whose incompetence all but landed him in enemy hands, making it prudent for his own good to post him elsewhere. So it was as Assistant Signals Officer at HQ 4th Army that he became involved in the First Battle of Ypres, where, in October 1914, he witnessed the demise of the mobility without which, in his ingrained opinion, victory was impossible. At Ypres he saw the brave soldiers being pounded by artillery, scythed by machine-guns, caught on barbed wire and compelled to dig trenches for their very lives. Like nearly all his generation, though perhaps not in the mind of a certain infantry battalion runner called Hitler who was very nearby in that holocaust, it was a stalemate which could not be allowed to continue – though how, at that moment, to change it he had not the faintest idea.

As a Signals Officer, Guderian had many opportunities to visit the front and become closely involved with Staff work. Sometimes he flew as observer in an aeroplane. Always he was dynamic and a most valuable member of whichever unit he was attached to for specific tasks. And so long as he survived and managed to avoid open criticism of his commander with quite the same force as GOC 5th Cavalry Division had received, his chances of wearing the carmine stripe of the General Staff improved. At last in 1917 the call came to complete the course which war had terminated in 1914 by attending a special practical war course. It consisted of short attachments for experience with infantry and artillery formations at the front, followed by a two-months' course at Sedan and then appointment to the General Staff Corps as 'the proudest moment of my life' on 28 February 1918.

Throughout the great German offensives on the Western Front in 1918, and for a large part of the subsequent Allied counter-offensives which broke the spirit of the German Army, Guderian was engaged in logistic Staff work at Corps level. It provided invaluable experience in the problems of supply in attack, defence and pursuit as, at last, the trench stalemate began to dissolve under the impact of the tank; and also of the improved artillery and infantry tactics which restored the factor of surprise to operations. But when sent as an Operations Staff officer to the German forces in Italy in October 1918, he arrived just in time to witness the collapse of discipline among the troops as the war abruptly drew to its close. In person he experienced the degradation of threats and insults by soldiers who had thrown away their weapons and were pouring home to a Fatherland Guderian loved, but which had been replaced by factions. He saw the rabid Bolshevik mobs in Munich and Berlin and, like any loyal Monarchist who suffered from that treatment, was marked for life and liable to go to extremes to restore German prestige and power to its traditional place. It was therefore with considerable relief that, in January 1919, he was posted to the newly formed 'Eastern Frontier Force' set up under General Hans von Seeckt, as a bulwark against incursions by Russians and Poles into the ancient Prussian territory which was also Guderian's homeland.

For nearly a year he was immersed in the violent and devious politico-military imbroglio of *Freikorps* affairs with the celebrated Iron Division of the *Freikorps* under Major General Rüdiger von der Goltz in the Baltic States. After the Division had seized Riga in May, von Seeckt and his Chief of Operations, Major Werner von Fritsch (both of whom in due course would become Army Commanders-in-Chief with enormous influence on Guderian), sent Guderian to join this volatile division's staff in order to impose General Staff control. With them he not only saw action but also became emotionally involved in their nationalist politics to the extent that, once more, he was insubordinate. And this time, to no less than von Seeckt when it was announced that, under the Versailles Treaty, Germany would forfeit the Baltic States. Yet once more, however, an understanding General Staff posted him to safety – somewhere free of temptingly extremist politics where a valued future could be ensured.

As a matter of sheer necessity the 100,000-man Army imposed on Germany at Versailles had need of Guderian's dynamic qualities as a member of the select group which, in absence of the proscribed General Staff, would secretly substitute for that organization. Modernization was the theme. In 1922 he was charged with the vital task of investigating motorization in an Army forbidden tanks, and took up the challenge with typical enthusiasm. Making as much use as possible of the hopelessly inadequate supply vehicles at his disposal in the 7th (Bavarian) Motorized Transport Battalion, he read everything on the subject he could find and began lecturing until he became an authority on mechanized warfare and on tanks in particular. Mostly it was theoretical, although he inspected a few tanks which with German expertise were being secretly worked on in Sweden, Russia and in German factories. He could read about the experiments under way in Britain with the concept of massed armoured formations controlled by radio. And in 1929 he could carry out a few experiments of his own in war-games and with mock-up vehicles to confirm the lessons he had learnt from the latest British manuals. But it was through his own intellect that he arrived at a philosophy and doctrine which was in advance of others, basing conclusions upon the theme of 'dynamic punch' (*Stosskraft*) in which, he said, the dynamic punch of future battle formations would be provided by the tank and not, as in days gone by, by the bayonet, the machine-gun or artillery. It was clear to him that 'tanks working on their own or in conjunction with infantry could never achieve decisive importance'. But he was convinced that formations of all arms supported by airpower and with adequate logistic support would be capable of striking long-range strategic blows to paralyse whole nations. And at the head of that kind of all-arms team he envisaged highly aggressive commanders who 'led from the front and not from behind', and did so by radio which reached out to every combat vehicle. Indeed it was in the world of signal communications, capitalizing upon his considerable experience and knowledge of radio, that he made his greatest technical contribution to the tank forces, keen though he also was on automotive matters, on armour and on guns.

But his most important contribution, apart from recognizing the deep, underlying power of the tank-dominated formations which became known as panzer divisions, was in his brilliant exposition of any case and in his perfect sense of timing in knowing when to seize an opportunity to advance a cause. Resistance to tanks by the horse-minded within the German Army was quite as stubborn as within the British, French and American armies. It took much persuasion at the highest level to obtain approval and funding for new and unproven equipment. Undeniably it was largely due to Guderian's verve and determination that Germany did steal a lead in that particular race when European rearmament began in earnest after Hitler came to power.

There has never been the slightest suggestion that Guderian was a Nazi sympathizer or, indeed, that he had any pronounced political leanings, other than as a Royalist who abhorred Communism. After the Iron Division fiasco and in accordance with von Seeckt's requirements as Commander-in-Chief of the new *Reichswehr* he steered clear of party-political involvements. He supported the government in power – always longing, however, for the day when Germany's Saviour would come. He was therefore conditioned to follow the lead of such Nazi-oriented senior officers as General Werner von Blomberg and Walter von Reichenau when as, respectively, Minister of War and Head of the *Ministeramt* (later the *Wehrmachtamt*) they supported Hitler in power. And like so many another who fell under the new Chancellor's almost hypnotic spell, he pledged his loyalty to a Head of State who not only was intent upon rearmament but seemed also to give priority to the fast, motorized panzer division idea.

Guderian probably assumed too much when, at sight of the motorized troops at Kummersdorf in January 1934, Hitler said, 'That's what I need!

That's what I want to have!' The ex-infantryman Führer did not really comprehend the importance of tanks and other armoured fighting vehicles until after they had been effectively demonstrated in Poland in 1939. In 1934 he was much more intent upon creating armed forces which would bluff and terrify people into thinking Germany was far stronger than she actually was. That was why the Luftwaffe, under the well-favoured old Party comrade Hermann Göring, received much higher priority and larger funding than the Navy, and the Army with its *Panzerwaffe*. The Luftwaffe, it was underlined, could strike at centres of population and rapidly make nations grovel. The older arms would take so much longer and might fail as they had failed before.

Indeed, Guderian's task as the main driving force behind fast motorized troops was all the more difficult because Hitler actually sided with generals who wished to create infantry, cavalry and artillery formations not so very dissimilar to those which had lost the war in 1918. Guderian had to struggle continuously and enormously in the corridors of power to win over colleagues who were by no means entirely sympathetic to his aims of making the *Panzerwaffe* an élite main striking force within the Army. He made enemies when he mounted a carefully reasoned propaganda campaign to educate the Army and the nation to his opinion that 'tanks would be able to play their full part within the framework of a modern army when they were treated as that army's principal weapon and were supplied with fully motorized supporting arms ... permanently attached'. In a 1933 newsletter he envisaged panzer divisions in 'the wide-spread attack against enemy flank and rear – separated from the other slower units; but it can achieve also considerable success in a breakthrough on the front. When used in pursuit it can throw a fleeing enemy into confusion.... The manner of its engagement is not in prolonged battles but short well timed operations launched by brief orders. The principle of surprise in order to avoid or avert enemy defensive action.'[1]

Within this statement, amplified in many lectures and discussions and in his 1937 propaganda book *Achtung! Panzer!* Guderian not only encapsulated the basic doctrine of modern fast armoured troops, but moved ahead of the British and French whose experimental armoured divisions resembled the panzer division but whose strategic and tactical concepts fell short of the German ideal. It was the greatest compliment to Guderian's charismatic advocacy that he managed in 1935 to win approval for the formation of three panzer divisions – albeit without tanks since so few, as yet, had been built – nor without opposition from the traditionalists who persisted in regarding the first panzer brigade as a prime instrument of infantry support only.

Demonstration of what the panzer troops could do was, of course, hampered by lack of tanks and other equipment while the rearmament programme was in its infancy. Not until sufficient tanks were available could their potential in mass be understood by the die-hards. Many junior officers, including cavalrymen, were enthused by Guderian, but even they were frustrated until machines were in their hands. And the first light training tanks were distinctly unimpressive from a combat point of view, as several crews found to their cost when committed in them prematurely to battle in Spain in 1937.

It was simply another of Guderian's significant contributions to eventual acceptance that he not only managed, in principle, to win acceptance of allocating all the available tanks to the panzer divisions, thus avoiding their wasteful misuse by the infantry, but that he was also able, for the most part, to reach agreement on the building of tanks which were reasonably combat-worthy and reliable. Much as he would have liked to have heavy tanks capable of withstanding all known anti-tank guns, he had to accept that they were, for the time being, beyond budget and manufacturing capability. Sensibly he settled upon three types – a light one for reconnaissance, and two mediums, one for tank-versus-tank combat and the other for close support when the artillery could not easily contribute. At the same time a proposal to have the artillery adopt self-propelled armoured pieces, which could operate in the forefront of the tank battle, was resisted by Gunners who occupied most top appointments and who, as Guderian sardonically remarked, 'accustomed for five hundred years to draw their guns with muzzle pointing backwards, they successfully opposed this proposal (for a vehicle with gun pointing forwards)'.[2]

As Hitler's relationships with his generals worsened and the outbreak of hostilities drew closer, Guderian's contacts with his Führer and Supreme Commander became much more frequent. In July 1934, after Hitler had purged the SA and demanded that the *Reichswehr* should swear personal loyalty to him (instead of the Constitution), Guderian expressed in a letter to his wife: 'Pray God that both sides may abide by it equally for the welfare of Germany. The Army is accustomed to keeping its oaths. May the Army, in honour, be able to do so this time.'[3] Already he was seeing Hitler as something apart from the Nazi Party, much of which he disliked. The von Blomberg scandal and the charges against his old chief, von Fritsch, in 1938 caught him in several minds: distaste for von Blomberg for having married a prostitute; anger with the new Commander-in-Chief, General Walter von Brauchitsch, for deserting his predecessor, von Fritsch, when falsely accused of homosexuality; disapproval of senior party members (including Göring and Himmler) for their role in the affairs; and naive praise for the Führer 'who has acted, as usual, with the finest human decency'. The Führer's complicity simply did not occur to him. But, as he also now realized, 'I will have to provide myself with a thick hide'.[4]

When Guderian took command of 16th Corps with its panzer divisions in February 1938, unavoidably he became more deeply involved in politics than perhaps he liked. His frequent appearances at Hitler's side when his troops marched into Austria in March and into the Sudetenland in October bred jealously in those who feared and disapproved the rise of the *Panzerwaffe*. No less than Generals von Brauchitsch and his Chief of Staff (General Ludwig

Beck) (both Gunners) plotted the deflection of Guderian away from the main stream of promotion to the highest appointments. It was guilefully proposed to Hitler that he appoint Guderian as Chief of Mobile Troops to control all the panzers and motorized infantry and cavalry – a worthless appointment, in many ways, because it lacked power to implement changes. Thus the traditionalists would have their way, the panzer divisions would be confirmed to orthodoxy and, to make quite sure it remained that way in war, Guderian's mobilization role would be as a Reserve Infantry Corps commander.

Unfortunately for the Poles and those other nations which Hitler chose to attack, von Brauchitsch and his new Chief of Staff, General Franz Halder (another Gunner) failed to deprive Guderian of a panzer command when war broke out in September 1939. Nor did the obdurate resistance of the traditionalists do more than hinder the development of the *Panzerwaffe* in the last few months of peace while Guderian endeavoured, without much success, to impose an up-dated doctrine upon it. When the invasion of Poland began on 1 September, the ten panzer or light divisions were much more than a match for an ill-equipped, immobile Polish Army, even though only 225 of the 3,195 German tanks were of the latest medium kind. And nobody employed those panzer divisions with greater verve than did Guderian, whose 19th Panzer Corps (with one panzer and two motorized infantry divisions) struck hard across the base of the well defended Polish Corridor in the direction of his own birthplace of Kulm.

In stiff fighting in difficult country he was, by sheer force of personality and drive, to overcome not only a brave enemy but also the doubters in his own side who were far too cautious for their Corps commander's liking. Officers who did not command from the front were shown the error of their ways. Men who planned badly and then failed to take risks were castigated. He reached all his objectives within schedule, in time to show Hitler and his entourage triumphantly, in the immediate aftermath of the battle, what the tank was capable of, then to declaim with pride, when Hitler asked, as of inevitability, if some enemy guns had been destroyed by the Luftwaffe's dive-bombers, 'No! By our panzers!' Thus the Führer was converted to panzer power, an education which was taken a stage further as the days went by and his maps blossomed with rapidly lengthening arrows to show how rapidly the unstoppable élite fast troops were tearing the enemy to shreds.

Guderian's triumph was complete when those of the High Command who had tried to sidetrack him came round to appreciate the potential of the weapon system his genius had placed in their hands. No longer was it safe for them (even had they so wished) to block a man who in battle had won the Supreme Commander's praise. As professional soldiers they themselves naturally and ambitiously grasped at something which won battles as never before. It was exhilarating to see how operationally flexible were radio-controlled units, and how sustained their progress despite a few logistic breakdowns which improvisation soon overcame. It was therefore an act of conciliation when Guderian was ordered to move his Corps into East Prussia, immediately after crossing the Corridor, to raid the enemy rear by a southwards strategic thrust such as he had always claimed to be decisive. It was indeed the epitome of what Hitler dramatically called *Blitzkrieg*.

How proud Guderian was on 17 September, after an advance of 100 miles in 8 days, to reach the historically symbolic city of Brest-Litovsk. But how shaken were many officers to come face-to-face with their Corps Commander who arrived in the midst of a hot battle to point out their errors of inertia and communication failures and then blow life into attacks which had been permitted to fizzle out. As Guderian realized, of course, many hesitations were the result of sheer inexperience when confronted by very tough enemy resistance. But the lessons they all learnt together not only laid the foundations of innumerable victories of the future, but also emphasized how right he had always been to teach that command from the front by senior officers equipped with voice radio was the real key to success. Hitler had much to thank him for and from now on understood rather better what panzer divisions could do for him.

No sooner had the fighting ended in Poland and it had become plain that Britain and France had no intention of condoning the German aggression by calling off the war, than Hitler was impatiently instructing OKW to launch an attack in the west within a matter of weeks. Beyond doubt he was strengthened in his conviction of such an operation's feasibility by the remarkable success of combined air and tank operations – and he demonstrated it in public on 27 October 1939 by bestowing on Guderian the Knight's Cross of the Iron Cross and having him sit on his right hand at dinner, indulging in animated conversation about the Polish campaign and the evolution of the fast troops. It was a timely discussion, bearing in mind that, already, von Brauchitsch and Halder at OKH were expressing doubts about launching the Army in a 1914–Schlieffen-Plan-like sweep through Holland and Belgium into northern France. Correctly they feared the effect of waterlogged ground on tanks and trucks.

A few days later Guderian was brought into the debate by General Wilhelm Keitel, Chief of OKW, whose attention had been drawn on 10 November to separate suggestions from General Gerd von Rundstedt, the Commander of Army Group A, to OKH and by Hitler himself to General Alfred Jodl, Chief of OKW Operations Staff, for a reversal of the existing 'Plan Yellow'. Instead of aiming the main punch by Army Group B through Holland and Belgium, with a subsidiary blow by Army Group A through the Ardennes, why not, it was suggested, pass the mass of fast divisions through the Ardennes and make Army Group B's role subsidiary? OKH's reaction to this had been less than enthusiastic. But at OKW, Jodl had mentioned the idea to Keitel who took the opportunity a few days later to call in Guderian, his relative by marriage, for an expert opinion on the feasibility of moving a mass of mechanized troops through such difficult terrain as the Ardennes. Guderian's response was predictably favourable. He knew the Ardennes, was a keen advocate of employing mechanized formations in difficult country where they would be least expected, and was confident that the traffic-control problems could be overcome. Moreover, when told that his own 19th Corps would spearhead Army Group A in the existing subsidiary role, he at once insisted that its two panzer divisions must be increased to three.

For over two months OKH resisted the revised plan (which was really the brain-child of General Erich von Manstein) while Plan Yellow hung fire in a series of postponements until it was finally killed off when vital documents fell into Allied hands in January 1940. Again Guderian found himself the centre of controversy when OKH was compelled to take the von Manstein plan seriously after Hitler also threw his weight behind it. There were several occasionally bitter debates in which Guderian, against the majority, argued not only the feasibility of penetrating the Ardennes with no fewer than seven out of the ten panzer divisions, along with motorized infantry formations, but also of reaching and crossing the River Meuse between Sedan and Dinant in five days without calling upon a mass of heavy artillery to crack the Maginot Line, or waiting for marching infantry divisions to catch up. At a celebrated final presentation before Hitler in February, the Führer, who had already told von Brauchitsch that he insisted upon full implementation of the Manstein Plan, asked Guderian what he intended to do after he had crossed the Meuse at Sedan. Guderian replied, without contradiction, 'I intend to advance westwards. . . . In my opinion the correct course is to drive past Amiens to the English Channel.'[5]

So it came to pass on 14 May 1940 when, having seized bridgeheads across the Meuse at Sedan the previous evening, the mass of von Rundstedt's motorized forces plunged westwards on a wide front, only briefly hindered by static French infantry formations and fortifications and overwhelming those armoured formations which, piecemeal, sought to bar the way. The decisive moment for Guderian had occurred at the village of Cheméry on the 14th when he visited a panzer division commander to seek his opinion about whether, despite fierce enemy counter-attacks from the south, it was prudent to start the westward thrust. He had been told in forcible terms by officers indoctrinated with Guderian's military ideas that it was!

From that moment, as the thrust increased in momentum and masses of prisoners and equipment were garnered from a rapidly expanding battlefield, Guderian never doubted that he would reach the Channel and win the campaign. Unfortunately for him there were those who lacked his insight, notably von Rundstedt and Hitler who, no sooner than the fast formations had shot off ahead of the much slower marching infantry, began to fret. Despite intelligence reports which made clear that the enemy was in complete disarray, with the bulk of his strong armoured divisions already destroyed, they feared for the southern flank and the danger of a counter-stroke cutting off the panzer divisions. Von Rundstedt, filled with respect for the French High Command, did not comprehend that the sheer speed of the German advance had paralysed the Allied defence. Nor could he envisage how the high mobility of motorized troops could enable them to react swiftly and powerfully against threats to their flank and rear. So in the days to come, Guderian and the other panzer leaders were subjected to a series of halt orders – one of which, by his senior at Panzer Group, Kleist, drove Guderian to resign on the spot until ordered to carry on with what was airily called 'a reconnaissance in force'.

Little did he realize at the time, however, from whom the ultimate halt order came when he stood poised to destroy the French and British Northern Army Group by cutting it off from the sea at Dunkirk. For the worried von Rundstedt was abetted by Hitler, who still did not grasp the true meaning of Guderian's style. Thus it came about that when, on the evening of 23 May, von Rundstedt again took counsel of his fears that the marching infantry were too far behind for safety (and was supported in that fear by General Günther von Kluge, the commander of 4th Army, an infantry formation), he ordered a halt on the 24th – which was confirmed within a few hours by Hitler when, once more, he visited Army Group A to express his concern. No matter what excuses were later made for this decision, which gave the Allies just sufficient time to bring their troops back safely to hold a perimeter, round Dunkirk, a golden opportunity to inflict a deadly, war-winning blow upon the enemy had been thrown away by men who had lost their nerve. For no such doubts inhabited the minds of von Brauchitsch, Halder or Guderian – or a great many other officers and men at the front who could recognize a beaten enemy when they saw one.

Of far less account than the throwing away of total victory, but highly important for Guderian in the years to come, was that for the second time he had found himself at cross-purposes with von Kluge (yet another Gunner). They had disagreed mildly in Poland over von Kluge's attempt to disperse 19th Panzer Corps among the infantry. Now they had disagreed again, with Guderian holding the belief that von Kluge had been largely instrumental in stoking von Rundstedt's fears. Henceforward they would be like cat and dog in professional mistrust – the more senior von Kluge (on the eve of being promoted Field-Marshal) condemning Guderian for taking unwarranted risks; the hot-headed but more brilliant Guderian enraged at being thwarted by an over-cautious mediocrity. Strangely enough, however, Guderian did not condemn Hitler for his part in the matter, though he was soon aware of it. Typically, in his Prussian way, he adopted the stance that once the Head of State (or King) had made a decision, it had to be obeyed unswervingly. It was a strict code that was to cause him much anguish in the years to come.

Meanwhile he dutifully tried to take Dunkirk when the halt order was rescinded and duly failed before 19th Panzer Corps was pulled out of the line to ready itself for the final engulfment of France. And now he was assuaged by proof of Hitler's favour, on being appointed Commander of Panzer Group Guderian with two corps, each of two panzer divisions and a motorized division under command. It gave him enormous pride to see the big G painted on his vehicles and to bask in the knowledge that his theories had been proved right in one of the swiftest complete victories over a major military power in history. For the time being he could cast aside concern about the opportunities which, with fatal consequences, had been lost. He might also minimize his disappointment at obvious signs of vacillation in the High Command as Hitler took an increasingly damaging part in decision-making. Partly in jest he would tell his wife of the confusion caused by repeated switching of objectives, 'The battle against one's own superiors sometimes makes more work than against the French.'[6] And he went on compassionately to mourn the horrors of war inflicted on the enemy: 'The country is in a catastrophic condition ... there is indescribable refugee misery and all the cattle are dying.... The Middle Ages were humane compared with the present.'

Far worse was to come, of course, the following year. But in the aftermath of his greatest achievement he could modestly enjoy unstinted praise along with promotion to Colonel-General and a prominent place in the victory celebrations in Berlin. Overnight he became one of Göbbels's propaganda idols – and did not relish that as much as some. Reflectively he knew that Britain must at once be knocked out of the war, and he indirectly conveyed a plan to Hitler. But Hitler had his mind on Russia and within a few months was to shock Guderian, as well as the world, by his gamble of invading her.

Guderian did more in protest than most senior commanders when word reached him that Russia was to be the next victim. He expressed his disappointment and disgust at a war on two fronts and sent his Chief of Staff to protest upon his behalf against a project which was all too obviously extremely risky and difficult to justify. But von Brauchitsch, long ago cowed by Hitler, was unmoved. So, filled with trepidation, Guderian set about doing all in his power to produce the essential quick victory by means of the one force which could make it possible – the fast troops. In addition to training his own panzer divisions with reinforced vigour, he went beyond his responsibilities (almost as if he was still Inspector of Mobile Troops) by having Hitler press upon Dr Fritz Todt, the Minister for Armaments, the vital necessity of expanding tank production from the present totally inadequate 125 per month to something between 800 and 1,000. They might have saved their breath. To do so, it was pointed out, would cost a vast sum, require factories and workers which were unavailable, and cripple such other important programmes as U-Boat construction. In the upshot, the German Army was to enter Russia on 22 June 1941, embarked upon a war which the High Command deluded itself could be over in six weeks, with logistic support and war maintenance reserves barely sufficient to see the troops through a summer campaign, let alone a winter one, for which no significant preparations were made.

To Guderian's Panzer Group 2 with its three Panzer Corps consisting of 5 panzer, $3\frac{1}{2}$ motorized infantry divisions and a horsed cavalry division went the leading role, along with General Hoth's Panzer Group 3, as the spearhead of Field-Marshal Fedor von Bock's Army Group Centre aimed at Smolensk on the road to Moscow (see map on page 88). His relationship with von Bock was excellent and he owed the Field-Marshal some gratitude for saving him the sight of Hitler's notorious 'Commissar Order', which von Bock refused to transmit to his subordinates. But clearly Guderian knew what was going on in the conquered territories, and he showed strong disapproval. He also frequently found his Panzer Group working alongside von Kluge's 4th Army and sometimes subordinated to it. Disagree though they frequently did about the conduct of operations, to begin with they collaborated well in the battles at the frontier near Brest-Litovsk and during the approach to Smolensk. He strenuously and successfully resisted von Kluge's natural desire to tie the fast troops to the slow infantry, and brushed aside von Kluge's fears that Guderian's operations depended too much on a shoe-string.

Von Bock's steadfast encouragement of the Panzer Groups to race far ahead and net hordes of prisoners with masses of equipment was entirely justified, even though it was extremely difficult to secure so much booty with meagre resources until the infantry caught up. Far more worrying was the problem of maintaining momentum when logistic shortages began to apply a brake. And even more disturbing was the unexpectedly sustained Russian resistance. Although, by mid-July, the High Command and Hitler were beginning to believe they had won the campaign, so immense were Russian losses, so relatively few their own, they were wide of the mark because their Intelligence departments had served them ill. Though scores of divisions and thousands of tanks and guns were annihilated as Army Group Centre alone succeeded in doing on its way to Smolensk, more Russian formations yet would appear and attack. Of a sudden an unexpected crisis of decision confronted Hitler who, all along, had declined to say what next he might do if the enemy was not crushed within the first six weeks.

Everybody waited while the Supreme Commander and his Generals debated. Progressively they grew more heated in their deliberations. The main bone of contention lay in whether to make for Moscow (as all the principals at OKH and in Army Group Centre wished) or diverge from the political objective towards Leningrad or into Ukraine, as Hitler preferred. Inevitably Guderian became involved in the wrangling. As was his way, Hitler sometimes consulted Guderian about the tank situation, and did so now when both von Brauchitsch and Halder were out of favour and Guderian was even under consideration as the next Commander-in-Chief. Meanwhile, at the front early in August, he fought a fierce little limited campaign against the Russians to the south of Smolensk while he prepared for the assumed renewed advance to Moscow, only to be told to side-step southwards (which he called 'a crime') as a preliminary to attacking into Ukraine.

In some confusion, along with von Bock and Hoth, Guderian was called to a conference with von Brauchitsch and Halder at OKH on 23 August. Halder, Bock, Hoth and Guderian intended to make one final effort to convince Hitler that Moscow was the only objective likely to bring the Russians down. It was a turning point in Guderian's career. To begin with, von Brauchitsch informed him that the Ukraine decision had been made and further debate was forbidden. Halder, however, relied upon Guderian (who might any moment be the new Commander-in-Chief) to stick to his guns and win Hitler round to going for Moscow. But faced on his own by Hitler and his entourage, Guderian fell into line – using as pretext the orthodox Prussian explanation that he '... could not debate a resolved matter with the Head of State in the presence of company'.[7] He may also have considered that a headlong row with Hitler at this crucial moment would have denied him the appointment of Commander-in-Chief, and with it the opportunity to save Germany from the mess into which he knew she was being led. As a result he for ever forfeited Halder's goodwill. The OKH Chief of the General Staff collapsed in anguish and rage when told by Guderian that, in view of Hitler's direct order, he now felt it 'his duty to make the impossible possible'.[8] But Halder himself had been astonishingly insincere in withholding from Guderian that detailed orders had already been issued to attack southwards in the Ukraine. Either he had been deviously naive in hoping Guderian would succeed with Hitler when everybody else had failed, or he hoped Guderian would overstep the mark and put paid to his promotion prospects.

Panzer Group 2 now plunged deep into the Ukraine to net further hordes of Russians, though still without a conclusive result as the German Army got weaker and a winter war drew closer. In mid September, far too late, came at last the order to seize Moscow. It found Panzer Group 2 (about to be renamed 2nd Panzer Army) at 50 per cent of tank strength, far to the south and to the east of Kiev, and thus unable to partake as a major element with Army Group Centre in a concentrated thrust against the enemy's capital. It would also find an angry Guderian, who had been denied support in the Ukraine by Halder and von Bock, the former of whom had quite openly intrigued against him with Hitler in accusations of disobeying orders. Thus a distraught OKH Chief of the General Staff was taking revenge by blackening a rival's name before a Supreme Commander whose mistrust of all generals was chronic.

On 28 September 1941, after a truly brilliant switch of axis and deployment, 2nd Panzer Army struck again, its centre line projected towards Orel, Tula and Moscow. All went well until, on 6 October, Nemesis intervened at Mzensk. Here the leading panzer division was thrown back by a well concentrated blow from several score heavy KVI and medium T34 Russian tanks, none of which could be penetrated by the German tanks' guns.

For the first time Guderian was thrown on the defensive as, that night, it began to snow. Thereafter, the enemy was given the opportunity to repair his defences, as chaos built up along the German lines of communication, and as the underclad soldiers began to suffer appallingly from the bitter cold. Momentum was lost. Dominated by the weather and the enemy, the advance could proceed only by fits and starts as Guderian despairingly called to his superiors for a help which was simply not available. Not only was the entire logistic system foundering, but also dire shortages of material and manufacturing resources on the home front made it impossible to produce enough munitions for the *Wehrmacht*. It was only by the mightiest triumph of will and by sheer professional ability that Army Group Centre came within sight of Moscow and 2nd Panzer Army reached Tula on 1 December. At this point the latter could struggle forward no more.

Guderian's pleas for his men's welfare and for a withdrawal from this lunacy make heart-rending reading. But neither from OKH, OKW nor Hitler did he receive sympathy. Von Rundstedt (Army Group South, in the Ukraine) was a sick man; Halder, desperately worried as he stared defeat in the face. From a warm headquarters Halder could not imagine what it was like to fight in 30 degrees of frost in summer clothing. Bit by bit, however, withdrawals took place everywhere, despite a peremptory order from Hitler forbidding them. Regardless of Hitler's blandishments, Guderian was among those who withdrew as he thought fit, whenever his Army's security was imperilled. A personal interview with Hitler in an attempt to show him the error of German strategy proved fruitless. When von Kluge was placed over him and persisted in denying the freedom of action against Russian attacks that Guderian demanded in order to prevent catastrophe, the latter deliberately disobeyed. A furious row broke out between the two men, with personal recriminations thrown in, making inevitable Guderian's dismissal – on Christmas Day 1941.

As he marched into retirement, exhausted and suffering from a mild heart attack, he carried with him a lasting mistrust and dislike of von Kluge and an irreparable breach with Halder. But about Hitler he remained tactfully ambivalent, as he contemplated a bleak future.

For the next fourteen months he rusticated, slowly recovering his strength while, with mounting anxiety, he observed the erosion of Germany's position. He was shaken when America was brought into the war in December 1941, but rejoiced when the Army in Russia resolutely checked the Russian winter offensives and rebounded to invade the Caucasus in the summer of 1942. News of American and British defeats in the Far East were celebrated, but when old friends and comrades came to tell him how run-down German industry now was, how short the *Wehrmacht* of vital equipment and how illogical was Hitler's interference in military affairs, he feared the worst. But when contacted by a group of civilians and disaffected Army officers who wished him to join a plot to remove Hitler, Guderian was sceptical – especially when he heard that General Beck was involved. And, in the words of his son to the present writer, he 'exploded angrily in his bed' when it was let slip that von Kluge was also in the business. That, for the time being, ended the matter. Guderian now clung to a belief that his best contribution to the salvation of Germany lay in his being appointed to a senior post at Hitler's side guiding the Führer's steps.

Not until February 1943, in the aftermath of the disaster at Stalingrad and when the *Panzerwaffe* had declined to an all-time low, did the call come. It was a strange business, brought about by officers in Hitler's entourage in desperation against the Führer's whims. Very few senior officers were ever recalled by Hitler once they had forfeited his trust. It is certainly arguable that Guderian and von Rundstedt were now chosen for re-appointment because both were rigidly patriotic as well as prepared, up to clearly defined sticking points, to bend to the Führer's circumlocution if they felt it might advance their patriotic aims by keeping them in office. Ambitious though Guderian was, he could never justly be accused of self-seeking.

It took a great deal of persuasion on the part of those OKW officers to have Guderian brought back to take over the new appointment of Inspector-General of Armoured Troops, for which Guderian wrote the Charter. In Hitler's preamble it was stated that Guderian 'is responsible to me for the future development of armoured troops along the lines that will make that arm of the Service into a decisive weapon for winning the war. The Inspector General is immediately responsible to me, has the status of a Commander-in-Chief of an Army, and is the Senior Officer of the Panzer Command.'[9] He thus had direct access to Hitler and needed it, for although Brauchitsch and Halder had been replaced, there remained powerful opponents who were instinctively his enemies. His task was to organize and train not only the *Panzerwaffe*, but also certain field units of the Luftwaffe and Waffen SS; to collaborate closely with the Minister for Armaments, Albert Speer, in the development and production of weapons; and to create new formations while up-dating tactical doctrine.

The task would have been Herculean even if the *Panzerwaffe* had not been so neglected as it had by OKH, with Hitler's inept connivance. Battle losses had been exacerbated by a collapse of the repair and maintenance system which was desperately short of spares. New production fell well short of replacing battle losses, let alone of expanding the force. The up-gunning and up-armouring of existing tanks had been laggardly and the new medium (Panther) and heavy (Tiger) tanks, built to compete with the KVIs and T34s, were slow coming into service and, like all new machinery, plagued by teething troubles.

With the aid of a dedicated Staff, who worked with frenetic loyalty for a man in whom they had unbounded faith and affection, the organization, training and doctrinal matters were tackled with marked success. Undeniably the benefits from this ensured the superiority of the panzer divisions against

most opponents right through to the end of the war. Of course Guderian suffered a few failures which made him very angry, such as his inability to persuade Hitler to incorporate the armoured assault-gun units of the Artillery into the *Panzerwaffe*. And occasionally he had to fight desperately hard in combination with Speer to steer the design, development and production of tanks on rational lines when Hitler, or one of his sycophants, tried to introduce wild-cat schemes for operationally dubious machines. But technically he largely succeeded in his aims.

Where he largely failed was in curbing Hitler's operational misuse of the *Panzerwaffe* and therefore, by implication, of the Army. His efforts to dissuade Hitler from committing the folly of attacking without benefit of surprise such an obvious objective as Kursk in July 1943, and his inability to guide the Führer into something better than a poor compromise in positioning armour for the defence of Normandy, are only the two best-known examples of an unending and often unrewarding struggle for strategic sense. The trouble was that Guderian, like every other commander, could always be overruled by this ungovernable megalomaniac, and therefore could never get the Führer's measure. Hitler was all too adept at deflecting Guderian's reasoned arguments with bland excuses – such as 'my Generals do not understand politics'; or 'If I had known about the Russian tanks' strength in 1941 I would not have attacked'; or 'You see they are all against you and so I can do nothing to help'; or simply some long-winded, rambling explanation designed to fob off a frustrated and bored listener who had something better to do.

As Germany's condition regressed in 1943 and 1944 throughout a train of defeats in Russia, North Africa, the Atlantic, in the air over Europe, in Sicily, Italy and Normandy, the sheer impossibility of controlling Hitler was forced upon Guderian at the same time as the anti-Hitler plotters had drawn the conclusion that his assassination followed by a coup d'état were unavoidably essential. After their rebuff in 1942 no further approach to Guderian was made by the plotters prior to July 1944, although it was well known that he was seriously disenchanted, frequently at odds with Hitler and often fighting hard to curb the Führer's witch-hunts against officers who, struggling in impossible circumstances, were accused of treachery.

At the beginning of July, when the plotters decided to strike, they had chosen as their figurehead the propaganda hero, Field-Marshal Rommel. But when he was wounded on 17 July, on the eve of the assassination attempt, it was felt vital to find a substitute. On the periphery of the plot was the colourless von Kluge, but his line was that he would only join them if they pulled it off. So General von Barsewisch, an old Luftwaffe comrade, was sent to enlist Guderian's aid. After four hours' discussion, however, in which he admitted the need to remove Hitler, Guderian declined to take part on the grounds that he could not break his oath to Hitler and must do his duty as an officer. Yet his attitude was not so very different to that of 'my special friend' von Kluge.

Although it was Guderian's duty to report the plot, which he knew was set for 20 July, he did not. Instead he took a long walk in the woods, hunting roebuck on his estate and making sure, in a totally uncharacteristic manner, that he was out of communication with everybody at the critical moment, in the manner in which he recalled von der Golz once doing for prudence's sake in 1919.

By the time he had been found, the bomb had exploded at Rastenburg, and news came that a putsch was in progress, but that Hitler and most of his closest entourage had survived. For a while there were several in authority who thought it likely that Guderian was behind the affair, particularly when a tank brigade, sent to Berlin to crush the revolt, refused to obey anybody other than General Guderian! But fortunately for him, as the plotters were being rounded up, shot or kept for trial, his innocence was proven long enough for him to obey an order from Hitler to come to Lötzen at once and take over as Chief of Army Staff. Halder's successor, General Kurt Zeitzler, had been sacked for opposing Hitler, and his successor had been seriously wounded in the explosion at Rastenburg. There would be those who spread the rumour that Guderian had given the plot away, but that was baseless; and also those who sneered at the way he had 'reached the summit of his ambitions'. In fact he was placing himself in deadly peril by working with, and standing up to, a man who was capable of murdering generals at the slightest hint of disloyalty. He took the risk because he felt it was his duty 'to attempt to save the eastern armies and my homeland'.[10] It was a task he and his wife had foreseen and often discussed. This staunch woman wrote to him of this 'dreaded development. . . . I get panic-stricken sometimes when I think of all that is piling upon you. May God maintain for you his [the Führer's] close confidence. That is the foundation of all. If that is lost so is everything else.'[11]

Working for a man of nihilist bent who would not admit to the inevitability of defeat, and for whom peace overtures were unthinkable even when the enemy entered Poland, drew closer in the Balkans and Italy, and would soon reach the western frontier of the Reich, was of course a hopeless task. Yet Guderian persisted in seeking a solution by which conditions for making peace could be obtained without breaking his oath – a ridiculous goal in a mad environment, but all that remained for him. In effect, all he could perhaps save was something from that wreck of the Army which Hitler had progressively and deliberately achieved by subordinating it to OKW and, far worse, Heinrich Himmler's criminal SS. In the latter aim he was to succeed, though more as the outcome of Himmler's complete military incompetence, when tested, than through any diplomatic skill on his part.

For the rest of his time as the last Chief of the once great German General Staff, Guderian is to be seen as a rather lonely and abrasive figure among the frightened sycophants; standing up whenever he could against some monstrous mistake or misjudgment on Hitler's part; endeavouring to shield innocent

457

comrades from threatening injustices: managing to evade, except on one brief occasion, sitting on the Court of Honour set up to deliver military plotters into the hands of the pitiless civil authority for torture and execution; keeping his temper with incredible patience while under the most dreadful provocation by people who had lost sight of reality in a cloud of lies and disaster.

By some miracle, abetted by a collapse of Russian logistics, he was able to halt the Soviet summer offensive of 1944 at Warsaw. Then he began a final attempt to assemble a central reserve after Army Group Centre in the East and the Army in Normandy had both been virtually destroyed owing to Hitler's refusal to give ground in time. Yet he was to lose the argument against committing that reserve to a quite senseless offensive in the west, through the Ardennes, in December 1944, knowing it had not the slightest chance of repeating the knock-out blow he himself had spearheaded in 1940. Unavailing, too, (as Hitler clung to a last ridiculous hope that victory might be found in the Ardennes, even after defeat was assured) were his attempts to transfer troops to meet the next Russian offensive aimed at Berlin. Faced by such obduracy, Guderian systematically employed methods which so often had landed him in hot water in the past – ignoring some bad orders, circumventing others – but never getting away with it for long enough or over major issues. Gradually his hard-enforced self-control began to give way until, as Speer reported with deep respect, furious open quarrels broke out in conferences. Never before, said Speer, had anybody stood up to Hitler before his entourage as Guderian now did when he refused to obey an order and Hitler failed to overcome the resistance. Guderian's final triumph (if such it was in so petty a situation) came when, for two hours, he stood up to Hitler in insisting that a senior member of the Army Staff be attached to Himmler's ss staff – an argument he won not only because he got his way, but because, in keeping his own temper, he managed at last to make Hitler lose his!

Throughout February and on into March 1945, as Germany's defensive front contracted and Guderian won just a little more time at the front by judicious counter-attacks (also attempting to persuade von Ribbentrop to try peace overtures again), he continued to dominate the daily Führer conference by his brave resistance. Everybody knew he was taking his life in his hands, yet for some unexplained reason, Hitler respected him; indeed forbade Guderian to resign. One asks what might have happened if previous Chiefs and Commanders-in-Chief had been equally courageous?

On 27 March 1945, in defence of a colleague against Hitler's accusations of incompetence, Guderian flatly contradicted Hitler to his face. Whereupon Hitler adjourned the meeting to tell Guderian, in the presence of Keitel alone, that he must take sick leave to recover his health. At the end of the conference, Hitler asked Guderian to return in six weeks when the situation would be very critical: 'Then I shall need you urgently.' It was a final act of face-saving, but also a tribute by this deranged dictator to a man who had stood up to him as none before. But in six weeks Hitler would have no need of anybody, for he would lie dead amid the ruins of Berlin, while his last Chief of Staff was entering American captivity along with the Staff of the Panzer Command, command of which he had retained while Chief of Staff and never relinquished.

Try though the Poles would to arraign him for war crimes alleged to have been committed during the defence of Warsaw in 1944, they were denied by the Americans. It was to history's benefit that Guderian was taken under the American wing after the war and given the opportunity, along with several other distinguished officers (including Halder), to put on paper his story of the war and, subsequently, write his invaluable Memoirs. They remain a fitting memorial to a man whose code was bound by honour and who, when faced by unpalatable facts, would deftly omit the whole truth. As history tells us, there are few great men who reach high places with entirely clean consciences, and none at all among Hitler's top commanders, all of whom were compelled to live a lie.

NOTES

1 Kenneth Macksey, *Guderian: Panzer General*, London, Macdonald & Jane's, 1975, p. 69.
2 *Ibid.*, pp. 62–3.
3 *Ibid.*, p. 60.
4 *Ibid.*, p. 70.
5 Heinz Guderian, *Panzer Leader*, London, Michael Joseph, 1953, p. 92.
6 Macksey, p. 122–3.
7 Guderian, pp. 200–2; Macksey, pp. 147–8.
8 Macksey, p. 148.
9 Guderian, p. 289.
10 Macksey, p. 187.
11 *Ibid.*

BIBLIOGRAPHY

Heinz Guderian, *Panzer Leader* (London, Michael Joseph, 1953).
Kenneth Macksey, *Guderian: Panzer General* (London, Macdonald and Jane's, 1975), which contains many letters and personal details lacking in *Panzer Leader*.

CHRONOLOGY: HEINZ GUDERIAN

1888, June 17	Born
1908, January 27	Commissioned
1918, February 28	Transferred to General Staff

1930, February 1	Commander 3rd (Prussian) Motor Transport Battalion
1934, July 1	Chief of Panzer Troops Command
1935, October 15	Commander 2nd Panzer Division
1938, February 4	Commander 16th Army Corps
1938, November 20	Chief of Mobile Troops
1939, August	Commander 19th Panzer Corps
1940, November 16	Commander 2nd Panzer Group (later Army)
1941, December 26	Dismissed
1943, March 1	Inspector General of Panzer Troops
1944, July 21	Chief of Army General Staff
1945, March 28	Sent on leave
1954, May 14	Died

STUDENT

20

STUDENT

Colonel-General Kurt Student

GENERAL SIR JOHN HACKETT

Of all the German generals who came to prominence in the Second World War, Kurt Student is certainly one of the most interesting. His own personality and career exemplify some of the best characteristics of German professional soldiers, while the attitude of some around him to his imaginative ideas might be thought typical of German military conservatism. He was chiefly responsible for that innovation which more than any other (except for the nuclear attack on Japan) sets the Second World War apart from other wars, that is, the use of airborne forces. He was fated to exercise command in the field in only two major airborne operations, the highly successful advance into Holland of *Flieger Division 7* (backed up by the air-landed 22nd, also under his command) in May 1940 and the capture of Crete a year later. There had been earlier uses of the German airborne forces he had himself largely created, in operations planned and prepared under his authority but carried out under subordinate command. They were used in Norway and Denmark, for example, and in the brilliantly successful coup-de-main at Fort Eben Emael in Belgium, in May 1940, the airborne action which outshines all others. After the taking of Crete, however, in May 1941, no large-scale airborne operation would be undertaken by the Germans during the remaining four years of war, though much use would be made of airborne forces by their British and American enemies. German airborne troops would still be extensively employed in many and varied engagements and would give, as a result of their special training and high morale, a generally outstanding account of themselves, but they would almost never go into action airborne again. Their value would lie, not in their performance in the specific mode for which they were raised and trained, but in the skills and toughness and cohesion which made them formidable opponents in the land battle.

German airborne forces were almost the unique creation of this one man and were largely sustained by his continuing determination and drive, through a daunting succession of frustrations and disappointments. The refusal of Kurt Student to allow discouragement to turn him from his chosen course and the vigour with which he followed it, through great difficulties, throw an important light upon the man himself, who embodied so much of what he sought to instill into others. The zest with which he applied himself to each new task, the dedication he brought to it and the depth of military professionalism upon which he was able to draw in carrying it out make up a picture of the German High Command and, even more, of the German General Staff, which demands respect. That the system could produce military operators like Kurt Student, and the men upon whom he could rely to do what he saw had to be done, goes far to explain why the German Army, after a war which ended in total and crushing defeat, had to be recognized as the superior of any other army engaged in it.

Kurt Student, like so many who would rise to distinction in the German Army, came of Prussian stock, born into a family of minor landed gentry in Brandenburg. They were not well enough off to launch all four sons into careers of their own choice. The eldest elected military service and joined a military preparatory school, for which there were no fees. Kurt, the third son, would have liked to be a doctor, but since the family could not afford that, he too, like his eldest brother, went into a military school, admitted at eleven years of age into the Royal Prussian Military Cadet School at Potsdam. In 1905, at fifteen years of age, he was transferred to the chief cadet school at Lichterfelde and five years later, on 3 March 1910, accepted as a *Fähnrich* (ensign) in the Royal Prussian 1st Battalion of the Regiment Graf Yorck von Wartenburg, in which, on 20 March 1911, he was promoted lieutenant. He was happy to find himself in a regiment whose station in East Prussia was near his home, the pursuits of whose officers were those which he, as a country boy, most enjoyed. It was almost absent-mindedly that, with little skill in mathematics and a dislike of heights, he found himself on a pilots' training course and came back from it to his regiment with his whole life changed. He spent the First World War as an aviator, commanding a fighter squadron (*Jagdstaffel*, or *Jasta*, 9) from October 1916 onwards and receiving in 1917 a severe wound in aerial combat. At the war's end he returned, dispirited, to his Prussian home. 'I had served an apprenticeship,' he said, 'only to discover that I had no sphere in which to practise my profession.'

In the confusion of the post-war years one of the very few important German institutions to retain some degree of continuous stability was the

General Staff, though now disguised as the *Truppenamt*. The Treaty of Versailles, today seen as the perfect seedbed for another war, in addition to crippling reparations and the seizure of overseas colonies, laid severe restrictions upon the German armed forces. The Army was to be restricted to 100,000 volunteers, with light weapons only; the Navy would be limited to coastal defence and there would be no air force at all. The Great General Staff was to be abolished. It was the general body of opinion among senior members of the old General Staff, however, that the acceptance of the Treaty was the only way of avoiding a long Allied occupation which would put a military resurgence out of the question. Under von Seeckt the former General Staff officers quietly got to work, setting up the cadres and bringing in the officer material and specialists who would form the skeleton of a revived German Army. Military aviation was forbidden, but there was always gliding. Student, wondering what to do with his life, found himself posted to the *Fliegerzentrale*, where a group of aviators was busy planning a military air force whose nursery would be the gliding clubs.

The German-Soviet Treaty of Rapallo in 1922 contained secret provision for Soviet support of German rearmament. This included assistance in the preparation of an air force, for which airfields were made available in the Soviet Union, notably at Lupetsk. The scope of the *Fliegerzentrale* was growing, though there was not yet a squadron in service. Student was before long compelled to return to his parent infantry regiment to qualify for appropriate promotion. The five years he now spent as an infantry officer brought him to command of a battalion and also saw Adolf Hitler installed, on 30 January 1933, as Chancellor of the Reich. From now on German plans for rearmament could go ahead more in the open. In fact, although the Allied Control Commission had been withdrawn from the Reich in 1927, after a weak final report which gave ample evidence of breaches of disarmament provisions in the Versailles Treaty, Germany was still formally bound by the Treaty, and was a member of the International Disarmament Conference.

In the years between the signature of the Versailles Treaty in January 1919 and Hitler's succession as Chancellor, considerable progress had been made, in spite of many political and economic uncertainties, in the formation and development of the 100,000-strong army permitted under the Treaty. Soviet Russia had been of some further help in the testing of equipment and the training of tank personnel and aircrew. Hitler at once stepped up the process, tripling the strength of the Army immediately, with the addition to it of the armour and artillery forbidden under the Treaty, laying down warships and preparing for an air force of a thousand aircraft to be under the control of Hermann Göring.

Student had now completed his tour of command of an infantry battalion and was selected to be Director of Technical Training Schools for the air arm, which had been detached from the War Ministry and put under a new Ministry of Aviation headed by Göring. He now faced a demanding task. The creation of an air force almost from scratch, the gathering and training of an air staff, the creation of embryo squadrons, the organization of aircraft manufacture, these and other aspects of the birth of the Luftwaffe were accompanied by a huge and growing demand for technicians, which Student's schools were there to produce. He himself, of Prussian *junker* origin, had little sympathy for National-Socialism and regarded his chances of an air command as slim. His dedication to whatever task he had in hand, however, which was a characteristic of his whole life, and his capacity for sustained hard work carried him forward under a heavy load, into the year when Hitler publicly renounced the Versailles Treaty, in March of 1935, reimposed conscription and brought the Luftwaffe out from such concealment as it still retained into the full light of day. In August of 1935 Student was promoted Colonel as Commander of the Test Centre for Flying Equipment (the *Erprobungsstelle für Fluggerät*) in Rechlin. Among other important work, the aircraft types Me 109, Me 110, He 111, Do 17, Ju 86, Ju 87 and Ju 80 were all being brought in this time to the point of serial production. Early in 1938 he was overjoyed to be given what he coveted most, an air command, that of the *Fliegerdivision 7* (7th Air Division), then forming at Münster. There was no general agreement as to how parachute troops would be used but Student recalled seeing 1,500 Russian parachutists dropped in 1937 and he and his able and enthusiastic subordinate Heinrich Trettner worked on the concept of the use of airborne troops, not in the small sabotage operations some expected, but in mass. The Ju 52 aircraft was being replaced in its role as a bomber and was now available as a transport, silk parachutes were in plentiful supply, and a parachute school had opened in 1937 in Stendal.

Though Student now had the materials to work on to create a light airborne division he was preoccupied from very early on with the need in airborne operations for supporting weapons and motor transport. Against doubts and criticisms around him he turned his attention to gliders, but had made little progress in developing appropriate aircraft, weapons and vehicles when he was ordered to prepare *Fliegerdivision 7* for an operation in September 1938 in the Sudetenland. There was in the event no fighting. The Czechs, abandoned by their friends, gave way at the Munich conference and the Sudetenland was peacefully annexed on 30 September. Student's *Fliegerdivision 7* was flown in by a fleet of 242 Ju 52s as part of the occupation force.

The German High Command now decided to form two airborne divisions, *Fliegerdivision 7* as a parachute formation and the 22nd Division to be airlanded. Student kept command of *Fliegerdivision 7* but was made Inspector of Airborne Forces with control over both. He could now pursue the question of gliders, using the experimental station at Darmstadt to produce, under pressure, the design of the DFS 230. This, carrying 9 fully equipped troops in addition to the pilot, was the largest glider that could be towed by the Ju 52/3.

Fifty had come into service with the Luftwaffe by the outbreak of the Second World War.

Student had to work hard and put all possible pressure on his superiors to improve the slow rate of progress in his divisions, which were short both of men and equipment. The first mass drop of the 1st Parachute Regiment took place in Niedersachsen in the summer of 1939. By the time of the invasion of Poland on 1 September (for which Student's command, to his chagrin, was to be held in reserve) he had the 1st Parachute Regiment complete and two battalions of the 2nd, with the third forming, together with 16th Infantry Regiment complete and one battery each of 75 mm pack howitzers and 20 mm anti-tank guns, as well as engineers, signals and medical support. In the event the force saw no action in the Polish campaign. German armoured tactics with Stuka dive-bomber support were wholly effective and by 17 September, when the Russians came in on the German side, the campaign was over. Nothing had happened to establish that airborne forces were necessary. Neither the Army nor the Luftwaffe greatly liked them, partly because, though they were to remain under Luftwaffe command, it was never really clear to whom they actually belonged. Student's headquarters was in Berlin from which a temporary advanced command post was put forward to Wiedenbrück to handle the coming operation in Holland. He remained as determined as ever to try out his concept of the true airborne assault on the first possible occasion.

Though the time for action on a grand scale lay nearly two years ahead, there was still much to demand urgent attention. Hitler's plan for the defeat of the forces of France and Britain in the west demanded the outflanking of the Maginot Line by a move through neutral Holland and Belgium, for which the Führer sought to ensure complete surprise by volunteering a declaration of friendship to both on 6 October 1939, shortly before orders were issued for the invasion of each. Hitler was now an enthusiast for airborne operations and Student was offered nine options to choose from, of which a further close study was to be made of two. These were the capture of the fortresses of the Belgian 'National Redoubt' near Ghent, and the seizure of bridges over the Meuse south of Namur. A third task was soon given to Student, replacing both the others, now compromised by accidental disclosure. The new task included the airborne capture of the world-famous Belgian fortress of Eben Emael, north of Liège. Completed only in 1935, this was a heavily fortified and completely self-contained complex housed in steel and concrete emplacements burrowed into a cliff a hundred sheer feet above the Albert Canal. It commanded in most formidable fashion the entry across the canal from Maastricht in the Netherlands into Belgium. Eben Emael was proof against attack by armour and infantry, and air bombing and artillery could do it little harm. It has been said that Hitler inspired the concept of a glider-borne coup-de-main himself. Student and his Chief of Operations Staff, Major Heinrich Trettner, took the idea up enthusiastically and went into the planning of the whole highly complicated operation with their customary vigour and in the utmost secrecy. A *Sturmgruppe* (Assault Group) of 11 officers and 427 men, formed in November at Hildesheim from Hauptmann Koch's company in the 1st Parachute Regiment, was to be prepared for a crash-landing, in 42 DFS 230 gliders, with the best glider pilots in the country, towed by Ju 52s, on four objectives – three bridges over the Albert Canal and, the hardest nut to crack of all, the newest and most formidable fortress to be found in Europe. Eben Emael was to be attacked by a party of 2 officers and 83 men, all pioneers or engineers with training in explosives, under *Oberleutnant* Witzig, carried in 11 gliders to be landed squarely on top of the target. Student argued forcibly that this operation still used far too little of his airborne assault capability and urged that his own *Fliegerdivision 7* and the 22nd Infantry should be used as well in central Holland north of the Maas. There was reluctance in the German High Command to place so much reliance on untested methods but in the end Student had his way, though irritated by orders to have, in addition, limited operations carried out by a parachute battalion in the earlier invasion of Denmark and Norway. He feared that this would prejudice surprise, but the French and the British (who mopped up what eventually came in of this little force with some ease) paid scant attention to this, their first experience of airborne assault.

Early on 10 May 1940 the gliders bearing *Sturmgruppe Koch* took off. With almost complete surprise but against fierce Belgian opposition the three river crossings were all secured before midnight on 10 May, though one bridge had been blown. Three of the gliders making for Fort Eben Emael itself landed right on top of it, or very near, and the men in them raced for bunkers, casemates and steel cupolas, to thrust in explosive charges and devastate the defenders with grenades and automatic weapons fired through embrasures and the breaches they had themselves blasted. The glider carrying the officer in charge, Lieutenant Witzig, had force-landed on the German side of the Rhine, with a parted tow-rope. Another Ju 52 was flown up and landed in the same field. It then towed Witzig's glider out and off again and he was put down on the fort, to resume command in the suppression of a Belgian garrison which was still, in part of the fortress, fighting hard under very heavy Stuka attack. By the late afternoon of 11 May German troops following up had made contact. The Belgian garrison, about a thousand strong, now capitulated. Of Witzig's 85 soldiers, 6 had been killed and 20 wounded. General Student was to say of the assault on Eben Emael after the war, with complete justification: 'It was a deed of exemplary daring and decisive significance.' His study, he said, of all the battles of the Second World War, with a host of brilliant actions on both sides, produced nothing to compare with it. It is difficult to disagree.

In Holland Student was now commanding two divisions, his own 7th Air Division and the 22nd, but without a Corps Staff so that command was exercised through the HQ of 7th Air Division. Student himself with his

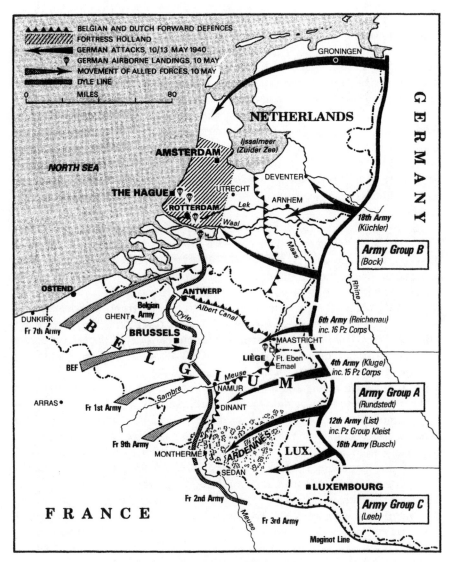

The invasion of Holland and Belgium, May 1940

divisional staff (where Trettner, not yet a Lieutenant-Colonel, was already a key figure) laid down all plans for the preparation for action of both divisions, with firm orders for dropping and landing zones and other essential detail. The 22nd Division, with which Student and Trettner both flew in on 10 May, played a decisive role in securing what was known as 'Fortress Holland' (the vital corner containing Amsterdam, Rotterdam, Utrecht and Dordrecht), operating in depth ahead of oncoming German armour. The seizure of three important pairs of bridges, at Moerdyk, Dordrecht and Rotterdam and key airfields (notably Waalhaven) was crucial. Shrinkage of the operational area deprived the 22nd Division of further opportunity for airborne action and it could now be fairly described almost as an independent division. This, Trettner has written to me, was an emergency arrangement: '*alles war sehr unkonventionell*'. It does illustrate, however, the German Army's ability to make bold adaptations of accepted practice when necessary. On 14 May 1940, the day the Dutch laid down their arms in Rotterdam, Student was severely wounded in the head by a sniper's bullet. He was to be out of action till September of that year, when he was promoted *Generalleutnant*. Trettner too was promoted, to *Oberstleutnant* on 1 October 1941, and the partnership continued.

Meanwhile airborne troops had become widely recognized as a corps d'élite. They were not, however, fully accepted by the more conservative officers of the General Staff and Göring was unable to persuade the *Wehrmacht* to raise, as a matter of urgency, four more airborne divisions. Göring was to say, in 1945, that with these he would have urged Hitler to mount a swift invasion of England, before there had been a chance to recover from the evacuation of the BEF, most of which had been brought back to Britain in generally low spirits and poorly equipped and armed. Student considered the establishment of an airborne beachhead in England in the Folkestone area, with only one airborne division, whether on an initiative of his own or as a part of OKW's planned invasion of England in Operation *Sealion*, but it seems to have been thought rather too audacious by the Staff. In any event Hitler, anxious for a negotiated peace with Britain before invading Russia, delayed his invasion long enough to enable Britain to recover balance and in part re-arm. He was then to be prevented by the RAF from establishing that mastery of the air without which no invasion could succeed. In Britain the brilliant success of German airborne troops in the Low Countries had not gone unnoticed. Churchill demanded parachute troops. Five thousand volunteers were soon forthcoming, a parachute school was opened at Ringway and development work on Horsa and Hamilcar gliders was put in hand.

Student's attention was now turned southwards to the Mediterranean. Göring caused him to study the possibility of attacking Gibraltar, Malta, Crete and Cyprus. German troops had already enforced the capitulation of Yugoslavia and invaded Greece, where the British had deployed a force of two divisions and a tank brigade. The Greek army laid down its arms on 21 April 1941, in a document signed at Larissa by General Papagos, and a British withdrawal to Egypt was begun, first from ports in Attica and then from the Peloponnese. On 20 April Student and Trettner flew to see Hitler at his headquarters on the Semmering and next day there was discussion of airborne action to exploit German successes in the Mediterranean area. Crete and Malta offered the most interesting opportunities. Most of those present at the conference expected Hitler to choose Malta but in the event his choice was for Crete. Student appears to have persuaded him that the capture of Crete was essential and that it could be carried out by airborne assault. Before this could happen, however, a successful airborne action was mounted in Greece to hamper the British withdrawal from southern Greece, by the seizure on 28 April of the bridge over the Corinth Canal. This operation, though carried out by the 7th Air Division, was curiously enough the only German airborne operation ever mounted without Student's knowledge.

Of the various courses discussed at the Semmering, a plan was settled on to stage four airborne attacks on Crete. First of all, the key to the whole operation, Maleme airfield and Canea, adjacent to the important harbour of Suda Bay, would be taken. In a second lift in the afternoon Rethymnon, with a useful airstrip, and Heraklion, with a good airfield, would be secured by troops coming in on return flights of Ju 52s.

Wavell, British Commander-in-Chief in the Middle East, was not only keenly aware of the critical importance of Crete but knew that airborne assault was probable. Much was done to improve the island's defences against it, while on the German side the strength and morale of the Commonwealth (British, Australian and New Zealand) and Greek forces were considerably underestimated. Neither Student, who had set up the HQ of *Fliegerkorps 11* in the Grande Bretagne Hotel in Athens, nor *Oberstleutnant* Trettner, now his Chief of Operations at 11th Corps headquarters, underestimated the difficulties before them. This was to be a totally airborne battle, without armour coming up the road to help. A seaborne convoy of light and somewhat primitive craft was expected to bring over some heavier weapons. *Generalmajor* Ringl, commanding the war-hardened and tough 5th Mountain Division, which was put under *Fliegerkorps 11* for the operation, and much of whose heavy equipment was expected to come in by sea, described the ferrying operation as crazy. Little was expected to get past the Royal Navy and in the event almost none did. It is clear now that had this little makeshift fleet tried the crossing in daylight instead of at night it would have done better. The Luftwaffe had established virtually complete domination of the air by day while by night the Royal Navy could still be effective, especially since night navigation for this motley collection of shipping was particularly difficult. The impossibility of surface action in daylight by the Royal Navy in those waters was not at the time fully appreciated.

The first wave of airborne troops took off for Crete from a complex of airfields in Greece early on 20 May 1941, following a powerful bombing attack along the north coast of the island. Things did not go well. The enemy was stronger and better prepared than expected. Incoming parachute troops were met by a storm of well-directed fire from the ground and many were hit in the air.* The attempt to capture Maleme airfield, of critical importance to the second lift and all subsequent operations, failed. The question arose in Athens whether the operation should now be cancelled. Student would have none of it. All-out efforts were to be made to capture and open Maleme airfield. There is little doubt that if those great fighting men from New Zealand had been led into early and determined counter-attack against the insecure German footing on Maleme airfield during the morning of 20 May the whole operation for the

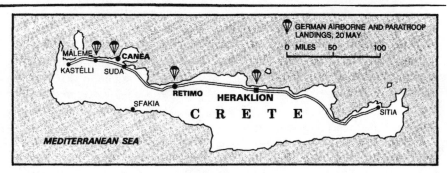

Crete, May 1941

capture of Crete would have been a disastrous failure. A counter-attack which, at 1000 hours on 20 May, would have caught the Germans off-balance, did not come in until seven hours later, when they had greatly improved their position. It was repulsed. During the night of 20 May the New Zealanders, to the surprise of the Germans, were pulled back. From the morning of 21 May, Maleme airfield was in German hands and the airborne build-up, with a constant stream of Ju 52s, could continue. The taking of Canea, Rethymnon and Heraklion was now only a matter of time. A British War Office communiqué of 1 June finally made it known that Crete had been lost. The Royal Navy managed to take off 16,500 men from the south of the island, leaving behind 13,000 killed, wounded or captured. The Germans lost about 6,000 of all ranks, 3,674 being airborne officers and men.

It was an audacious operation and a costly one, and could easily have ended in disaster. It was also to be the last airborne operation on any but a minor scale to be undertaken by the nation which had made of airborne forces a novel and important weapon of war. When the Führer on 19 July met the men who had been awarded *Ritterkreuze* (Knight's Cross) for this action, he

---

* Particularly effective fire came from the 1st Argyll and Sutherland Highlanders, whose rifles accounted for some scores of descending parachutists. In late 1942 this writer was putting a parachute brigade together at Kabrit, in the Suez Canal Zone of Egypt. He was not very imaginatively offered the same Highland Battalion to convert to airborne. He thought not and was given the First Sussex instead, who became a splendid parachute battalion to be known as the 10th. They were to be virtually obliterated at Arnhem.

said to Student: 'Crete has shown that the day of the paratroops is over.' The Russian campaign, then hardly a month old, would hold the centre of the stage for the next three years. German parachute troops would fight on many fronts, in Africa, in Russia, in Sicily, in Italy, in France, in Holland and finally in Germany, and always give a good account of themselves as infantry of very high quality. When, for example, the port of Taranto in southern Italy was taken in a seaborne assault by the British 4th Parachute Brigade, under this writer's command, on 9 September 1943, it was against rearguards of German parachute troops from the 1st Parachute Regiment under the redoubtable *Oberstleutnant* Schulz that we fought our way up country, in an early instance of parachute troops opposing each other in battle, where neither side had brought theirs in by air. Among many forceful and effective officers trained in the forces Student raised, far too many to mention individually, Karl-Lother Schulz is worth singling out. A parachutist since 1937, by the time his paratroops and mine clashed in Italy he had already fought with much distinction in Holland (notably at Waalhaven), in Crete and Sicily. He was to be in the thick of it at Cassino and was soon to become a Major-General commanding the 1st Parachute Division, with further service in Russia and in northwest Europe. He was an outstanding fighting soldier and in German airborne forces there were many like him.

Student's grandest dreams could never be realized. Hitler planned an airborne attack launched from the Crimea on the Black Sea port of Batum near the Soviet oilfields, to hold it until the German land offensive came down into the Caucasus. Fortunately for *Fliegerdivision 7* a breakthrough on the Eastern Front required its diversion there as a stop-gap, saving it from certain annihilation in the Caucasus. The airborne occupations of a part of the Kola peninsula in the north of Russia was proposed by OKW, but did not survive closer study. Student was variously credited with schemes which could certainly never have been supported with the means available, but the fact that these were rumoured throws an interesting light on his reputation for boldness. He was said to have ideas of an airborne panzer division of 126 tanks, with two paratroop regiments and an airborne panzer-grenadier division, to attack armaments factories in the USSR, using 150 Gigante gliders and 300 smaller ones. Another theory was that he put forward a plan for an airborne panzer division to cut the British 8th Army's supply routes in the Nile Valley. The German High Command would certainly have turned all such ideas down as requiring the uneconomic use of resources badly needed elsewhere, but Trettner tells me he cannot believe that his old chief ever had notions that would have looked exaggerated even to a Jules Verne.

None the less, under Student's driving vigour, with Göring's support (for airborne troops were still under Luftwaffe command) much was done after Crete to develop and improve Germany's airborne capability. Hitler, though his earlier interest in airborne troops had now declined, had not cancelled previous orders to meet their requirements, and he was now too preoccupied with the Eastern Front to pay much attention to what Student, with Göring's support, was doing. In late 1941 the 4th and 5th Parachute Regiments, of three battalions each, were quietly formed and also a battalion of engineers. Improvement in glider and parachute design and in tug-aircraft followed. In the winter of 1941 thoughts turned again to the capture of Malta. Student was inevitably brought in, as the commander of a *Fliegerkorps*, now comprising *Fliegerdivision 7* (his own command), the Italian *Folgore* division and a light air-landed division. This initiative petered out in April 1942, but Hitler now had a renewed interest in airborne troops. Student's next airborne operation was to be the rescue of Mussolini, in hiding after dismissal by his sovereign on 25 July 1943. The snatch of Mussolini from the Gran Sasso, publicized not entirely correctly as a triumph for *Sturmbannführer* Otto Skorzeny, was Student's last airborne success.

Kurt Student was a German professional soldier, typical of the best of his kind, totally devoted to his calling and to his country, though by no means in full sympathy with Nazi leadership. It was Student who put airborne forces on the world's military map. It is he who must be recognized as chiefly responsible for the outstanding performance of German airborne troops in the Second World War. I myself, a British parachutist who fought against German parachutists in more than one theatre in the Second World War, can personally testify wholeheartedly to their high quality as soldiers and as men.

Student had been one of those devoted officers who did much to help rebuild German military strength after the First World War. It is of interest that his trusted subordinate and friend Heinrich Trettner, an airborne soldier from 1938 onwards, was to discharge a by no means dissimilar function after the Second World War. As a General he was to be Inspector-General of the *Bundeswehr* from 1964 to 1966, during the early building up of the Federal Republic's newly reborn armed forces. It was in that capacity that this writer, serving in Germany at the time as Commander-in-Chief, British Army of the Rhine, got to know General Trettner and to value his acquaintance. He told me on one occasion of a Staff study carried out in Crete after the German invasion when he was acting as Student's *Erster Generalstabsoffizier* (Ia), which is worth exploring as throwing light on the savagery of partisan warfare and the ruthlessness of the Reich, as well as on Student's own measured and rational approach. Broadcasts from Cairo by the King of Greece, evacuated to Egypt by the Royal Navy on 24 May 1941, had urged Cretans to use every possible means, not excluding assassination, to carry on unrestrained partisan warfare against the German occupation. Cretans, men of mountain and shore, can be very tough and also very cruel. Their action, often against unarmed parachutists, included mutilation and nailing up on barn doors and had enraged and disgusted not only the troops but the High Command. In spite of having signed the Hague Convention condemning partisan warfare the

Greek government, it was claimed, had now deprived the civilian male inhabitants of Crete of any claim to non-combatant status. Göring ordered the severest counter-measures and consideration to be given to the execution or deportation of all male Cretans. Student wanted time and the means to undertake proper criminal investigation. The Staff study carried out under Major-General Schlemm, Student's Chief of Staff, with the assistance of Trettner, so the latter told me, clearly indicated that difficulties of collection, concentration, transportation, guarding, maintenance and eventual disposal were all so great as to put any such ideas out of the question. Student knew it would be useless to put up political objections, let alone any consideration of morality. He accordingly conducted a covert delaying action, largely on logistical lines, and Göring's intentions were thwarted.

Student's performance in the Second World War, while commanding respect for the organizational skills to be found in abundance in the German General Staff, is an object lesson in constancy and resilience. He pressed hard from the outset for the fullest use of *Fliegerdivision 7*, and any other available troops which were capable of air transportation into battle, against more conservative opinions which mistrusted reliance on an untried arm. The success of airborne action in the Low Countries, in north Holland and Belgium, and particularly the brilliant achievement at Eben Emael, changed all that. Student as a *Generalleutnant* and *Fliegerkorps* Commander thereafter faced huge demands in organization and administration, in development and training, without any clear and consistent concept in the German High Command of how and where the formidable weapon he was forging would be used. Crete saw its full employment for the first and last time. Airborne units and formations were now all too often taken for the Russian front. The invasion of Malta in 1942 was planned and then cancelled, though the use by the Allies of airborne forces in Africa gave Hitler some renewed interest in his own. Student's Corps HQ was then in Brittany, training formations to resist airborne attack. He was taken from that for the rescue of Mussolini, while his Corps was being broken up and used piecemeal, largely in Russia. A new 4th Parachute Division was formed, to be commanded by Trettner, whom Student reluctantly saw leaving him after their five hard-working and fruitful years together. Other new formations were raised and the airborne training machine was overloaded to produce high-grade soldiers who would never go into battle by air. In six months Student created three new divisions, together with a Corps HQ, Corps troops and two more training regiments.

By the time of the Allied invasion of Continental Europe in June 1944 German airborne troops numbered more than 160,000. Göring intended to form a Parachute Army with Student in command, but for what purpose other than to do *ad hoc* jobs and furnish well trained troops for others to use was not clear. Student's HQ was from July 1944 in Berlin, where the formation, on paper at least, of the 1st Parachute Army was being set up. He was now put to organizing, with whatever forces could be found, a defensive screen across Holland against the advancing Allies coming up out of France through Belgium.

The Anglo-American airborne assault in Holland, Operation *Market Garden*, began on 17 September 1944. Student's task was a difficult one, rendered no happier by having now deployed against him the sort of resources for which he had always craved in vain. 'If', he said to a staff officer, Major Berlin, as he watched from his headquarters house in Holland the Allied airborne armada moving in on 17 September, 'if only I had ever had such resources at my disposal....' The Ardennes adventure was to follow, with Student promoted into command of Army Group H, to be replaced soon, in typical Führer fashion, by Blaskowitz, to whom, in fact, Student himself was later to be sent back as deputy. In all this time, since Crete in fact, he had been put to task after task, always disappointed and never doing less than his whole-hearted best. It was ironic that his ground-borne Parachute Army should have to defend as infantry against the airborne assault of an enemy disposing of means beyond his own wildest hopes, in a mode of warfare he can be said very largely to have invented. It was even more ironic that he should now, in 1944, be defending, with airborne troops on the ground, water obstacles he had triumphantly overcome, in true airborne action, in 1940.

His brief and far from fulfilling command of Army Group H (after that of the 1st Parachute Army) was in effect to be his last. The end of the war was now near. In April 1945 *Generaloberst* Student was ordered to Mecklenburg to stabilize the area's defence. In the same month, in Schleswig-Holstein, he was made a prisoner by the British. He was charged in Lüneburg with having condoned war crimes in Crete, and convicted, but the sentence of five years' imprisonment was never confirmed. A striking feature of his trial was the powerful evidence in his favour given by the New Zealand Brigadier Inglis. This made a deep impression on the court and greatly helped to bring about a strong connection between New Zealand veterans of Crete and German parachutists. He lived after that quietly in Westphalia, in the Federal Republic of Germany. His happy marriage, from October 1917, to his beloved wife Gertrud, ended when she pre-deceased him. His son, the third member of a closely knit family, had been killed flying in the Luftwaffe in 1944. He himself died in Lemgo, at the age of 88, on 1 July 1978.

STUDENT – A PERSONAL MEMOIR BY GENERAL HEINZ TRETTNER

Note by Sir John Hackett: In writing about General Kurt Student, General Sir John Hackett has been much assisted by communication from General Heinrich Trettner, now living in retirement in the Federal Republic. Few people could have known General Student as well as his long-term and deeply trusted subordinate, Heinz Trettner. In response to a request for some more direct personal information about Student, General Trettner has written a piece which is worth adding in its entirety.

The personality of General Kurt Student is difficult to describe. It was of a very complicated nature and not without apparent contradictions.

From the point of view of outward appearance it is impossible to say that General Student was ever an imposing figure, like a Kesselring or a von Richthofen. His high voice and – after his head wound in Holland – his hesitant manner of speech were a disadvantage to him in discussion with more accomplished speakers and his modest bearing could give the impression of mediocrity.

Nothing could be less correct than that. Student had a sort of 'sixth sense', with which he foresaw developments which did not rest on rational proof. I have often had the experience that faced with more brilliant interlocutors he would be justified in a matter of a few weeks. His logic was of a different sort from that of others.

General Student was industrious. He worked slowly, but with the utmost precision, and even in apparently simple decisions thought through not only the immediate results, but also long-term consequences and indirect side effects. He had a truly phenomenal memory for people and names. Even after years he was able to reproduce the exact words of what had been said in some connection or another.

An inclination to the new, the unconventional, even to the adventurous, marked him out in high measure and illuminated the structure of a working method which would otherwise have seemed pedantic. It was a rare mixture. Coupled with firm persistence and toughness, this inclination enabled him to build up a new arm of the Service, whose characteristics and objectives still lay in the mists of uncertainty.

Student's manner of working was for those who worked with him pleasant in the highest degree. Everything went calmly and in a businesslike way. His patience in listening to others was inexhaustible. Often after month-long study of the map – it was his rule to learn the map off by heart – he set out the critical figures of his orders in his own handwriting. For example, in the operation against Holland he prescribed the landing places and attack objectives down to individual companies. Then he handed over his notes to his Staff, who only had to add in the frills, like the enemy situation, the operative framework, flanking formations, supply and so on. When the whole 'opus' was ready, Student offered thanks for it as though he had not himself done most of the work.

Student had absolutely no fear of danger. In an almost irresponsible manner he found his way into impossible situations, driving with a very noticeable vehicle in areas held by partisans, in cities occupied by the enemy or in terrain dominated by enemy bombing – never with any security precautions. He paid no attention to random shots that flew around and seemed to be surprised when those who were with him threw themselves under cover. He wanted to give a visible example.

This naturally made an impression on parachutists, who from the outset comprised only selected and sternly tested volunteers, brought up to unconditional combat readiness and unlimited fighting spirit.

The creation of this 'Parachutists' Spirit' was without doubt Student's greatest achievement. This could only happen through a personality which displayed not only conviction over the practicability and necessity of the new arm and would make almost superhuman demands upon his troops, but had also a warm heart for every subordinate and could generously overlook small mistakes and human weaknesses. He cared only about essentials.

His personal modesty – in his lifestyle there was no luxury and he refused all favours, such as for example the building of a new house through the state – was as an outstanding example, as was his courage.

I have never known him to take any step which would secure him personal prestige and recognition from above. The realistic needs of his country and his troops completely determined what he did. There were no party-political influences and he sometimes even went too far in his putting behind him family concerns and needs. Harmonious though his family life was, in following his duty he paid it no regard.

Completely honest, severe on himself and full of human warmth towards his soldiers, with unlimited dedication to his own mission and his country, he was able to build out of nothing a tradition in the best soldierly manner which still persists in German parachute troops today.

CHRONOLOGY: KURT STUDENT

1890	Born in Neumark, Brandenburg
1911	Commissioned 1st Battalion *Yorkschen Jäger* at Ortelsburg
1913	Flying School Course at Johannisthal
1916, September	Command of *Jagdstaffel* 9 in France
1917, October	Married
1917, October	Wounded in aerial combat
1918, June	Captain
1920	Posted to *Fliegerzentrale*
1922–33	Service with own regiment up to command of a battalion
1933, March	Director of Technical Training Schools for the air arm
1933, November	Lieutenant-Colonel
1935, August	Colonel

1938	Command of *Fliegerdivision 7* (7th Air Division) at Münster
	Generalmajor
	Inspector of Airborne Forces
1940, May 10	Attack on Belgian Reduit National (including Fort Eben Emael) and Rotterdam
1940, May 14	Serious head wound
1940, September	*Generalleutnant*
1941, April 26	Corinth Canal Operation
1941, May 20	Assault on Crete
1943, September 12	Rescue of Mussolini
1944, March	HQ of Parachute High Command set up at Nancy
1944, July	Student's HQ of the 1st Parachute Army in Berlin
1944, September	Promoted *Generaloberst* in command of Army Group H, to be replaced by Blaskowitz to whom he was then sent as deputy
1945, April	Captured by British in Schleswig-Holstein
1948	Freed
1978	Died in Lemgo, West Germany

GERMAN ARMY RANK STRUCTURE

German Rank	English Equivalent
Leutnant	Second lieutenant
Oberleutnant	Lieutenant
Rittmeister (cavalry)	Captain
Hauptmann	Captain
Major	Major
Oberstleutnant	Lieutenant-Colonel
Oberst	Colonel
Generalmajor	Major-General
Generalleutnant	Lieutenant-General

General der
  Infanterie
  Kavallerie
  Artillerie
  Pioniere
  Panzertruppen
  Nachrichtentruppen
	General

Generaloberst (Colonel-General)	(No equivalent)
Generalfeldmarschall	Field-Marshal

INDEX

489